MBE DECODED—MULTISTATE BAR EXAM

MBE DECODED— MULTISTATE BAR EXAM

*MARY BASICK * TINA SCHINDLER*

To contact Customer Service, e-mail customer.service@aspenpublishing.com,
call 1-800-950-5259, or mail correspondence to:

Aspen Publishing
Attn: Order Department
PO Box 990
Frederick, MD 21705

Printed in the United States of America.

4 5 6 7 8 9 0

ISBN 978-1-5438-3090-3

Library of Congress Cataloging-in-Publication Data application is in process.

SUSTAINABLE FORESTRY INITIATIVE Certified Chain of Custody
At Least 10% Certified Forest Content
www.sfiprogram.org
SFI-01028

ABOUT ASPEN PUBLISHING

Aspen Publishing is a leading provider of educational content and digital learning solutions to law schools in the U.S. and around the world. Aspen provides best-in-class solutions for legal education through authoritative textbooks, written by renowned authors, and breakthrough products such as Connected eBooks, Connected Quizzing, and PracticePerfect.

The Aspen Casebook Series (famously known among law faculty and students as the "red and black" casebooks) encompasses hundreds of highly regarded textbooks in more than eighty disciplines, from large enrollment courses, such as Torts and Contracts to emerging electives such as Sustainability and the Law of Policing. Study aids such as the *Examples & Explanations* and the *Emanuel Law Outlines* series, both highly popular collections, help law students master complex subject matter.

Major products, programs, and initiatives include:

- **Connected eBooks** are enhanced digital textbooks and study aids that come with a suite of online content and learning tools designed to maximize student success. Designed in collaboration with hundreds of faculty and students, the Connected eBook is a significant leap forward in the legal education learning tools available to students.
- **Connected Quizzing** is an easy-to-use formative assessment tool that tests law students' understanding and provides timely feedback to improve learning outcomes. Delivered through CasebookConnect.com, the learning platform already used by students to access their Aspen casebooks, Connected Quizzing is simple to implement and integrates seamlessly with law school course curricula.
- **PracticePerfect** is a visually engaging, interactive study aid to explain commonly encountered legal doctrines through easy-to-understand animated videos, illustrative examples, and numerous practice questions. Developed by a team of experts, PracticePerfect is the ideal study companion for today's law students.
- The **Aspen Learning Library** enables law schools to provide their students with access to the most popular study aids on the market across all of their courses. Available through an annual subscription, the online library consists of study aids in e-book, audio, and video formats with full text search, note-taking, and highlighting capabilities.
- Aspen's **Digital Bookshelf** is an institutional-level online education bookshelf, consolidating everything students and professors need to ensure success. This program ensures that every student has access to affordable course materials from day one.
- **Leading Edge** is a community centered on thinking differently about legal education and putting those thoughts into actionable strategies. At the core of the program is the Leading Edge Conference, an annual gathering of legal education thought leaders looking to pool ideas and identify promising directions of exploration.

SUMMARY OF CONTENTS

CONTENTS

PART 4 CRIMINAL LAW 259

PART 5 EVIDENCE 349

PART 6 REAL PROPERTY 417

PART 7 TORTS 521

PART 8 GLOSSARY OF ABBREVIATIONS 595

PREFACE

Dear Bar Taker,

Thank you for buying this book and we hope you find it helpful. We wrote it because we wanted a similar book to use with our students and there was no such book readily available that included thorough coverage of the MBE tested rules in a condensed format. Preparing to pass the bar exam is a lot of work, and with this book we are trying to do our part to make the preparation more manageable and bar passage more attainable.

This book is a handy reference that can be used during law school, for early bar study (which we highly recommend) and during the traditional post-graduation bar prep study period. We included examples from MBE fact patterns to illustrate the concepts to aid rule understanding and short-cut pattern recognition. Having spent a lot of time analyzing MBE questions, we noticed patterns in the way the bar examiners attempted to entice bar takers into selecting the wrong answer (which we call decoys), and we have shared those insights with you. Through working with bar takers, we have discovered an effective way to attack MBE questions and study for success on the MBE. We hope this information assists you as you study to pass the bar exam. Remember that you will need to use an additional source to actually practice MBE questions.

We wish you all the best on the bar exam and in all your future endeavors.

Mary Basick & Tina Schindler

ACKNOWLEDGEMENTS

We could not write this book without the motivation provided by our students and the support of many. We owe a debt of gratitude to our research assistants, and most especially Carlos Soriano, Liliana Sanchez and Blake Ribisi. We are lucky to be inspired every day by our students and our many outstanding colleagues working in bar preparation. We are grateful for the support of Southwestern Law School and want to especially thank Jonathan Miller and Ronald Aronovsky for their assistance with this project. We are thankful and delighted to work with Noah Gordon, Stacie Goosman and the rest of the Aspen Publishing team. We must however, extend our deepest appreciation to our long suffering families for putting up with us even though we foolishly thought it made sense to write a book during a pandemic.

INTRODUCTION

MBE AT A GLANCE

The multistate bar exam (MBE) is developed by the National Conference of Bar Examiners (NCBE) and is administered in 49 U.S. states and 5 U.S. territories.

SUBJECTS

- Civil Procedure
- Constitutional Law
- Contracts
- Criminal Law and Criminal Procedure
- Evidence
- Real Property
- Torts

* For a listing of topics, see the NCBE Subject Matter Outlines at www.ncbex.org

EXAM FORMAT

- Multiple choice
- Random subject order
- Administration twice a year, in February and July
- 200 Questions in 6 hours. This averages to 1.8 minutes per question (this is an average and some questions take longer to solve than others.)
  - 100 Question set in a 3-hour morning (a.m.) session
  - 100 Question set in a 3-hour afternoon (p.m.) session
- Several versions of the test are utilized to inhibit cheating. The a.m. and p.m. sets may not be of equivalent difficulty and which set is more difficult may vary between students answering different versions of the question sets.

EXAM SCORING

- 175 Questions of the 200 Questions are scored (25 Q per each subject).
- 25 Questions of the 200 Questions are unscored pretest questions, which the NCBE uses to vet future questions. (You can't tell which questions are the pretest questions, but as a result, you may notice some subjects seem more heavily tested than others. You may even be surprised to encounter questions in a non-tested subject that may be added to the test in the future.)
- The NCBE releases "scaled scores" for each administration. This is done to ensure that each administration of the exam has an equivalent difficulty level. The passing "cut score" based on that scaled score is determined individually by each jurisdiction that administers the MBE exam (and is typically combined with the scores from the written portion of the bar exam to determine bar passage). Jurisdictional information is available at www.ncbex.org.
- Most bar takers want to know what "raw" score (percentile correct) they need to score to pass the exam in their jurisdiction, but frustratingly, the NCBE does not release this information. Nonetheless, we can make an estimate. To hit the passing cut score, you would need approximately 58% correct for jurisdictions with the lowest cut scores (129); approximately 62% for jurisdictions with the national average cut score (135); and approximately 68% correct for the jurisdictions with the highest cut scores (145). Your goal should be to score a few points over these estimates to fall comfortably in the passing zone. The book *Strategies and Tactics for the MBE* has a very good and understandable explanation of MBE scoring if you are interested in more detail.

TWO KEY COMPONENTS FOR SUCCESS ON THE MBE

There are two equally important components for MBE success:

1) **Skill** at solving MBE style questions; and
2) **Rule knowledge** and memorization.

SKILL: HOW TO SOLVE MBE QUESTIONS

Using good technique to solve MBE questions can increase your score by 10-15%, which can be the difference maker in achieving a passing MBE score. MBE questions are hard. They test a huge volume of rules from memory in excruciating detail. In addition, the bar examiners have designed the answer choices to *hide the correct answer* and entice you into selecting the wrong answer. Many bar takers are not intuitively good at this testing style, but the good news is, MBE test taking is a skill, and like any other skill, you can learn good techniques and improve your outcome. Using a good proactive problem solving strategy allows you to avoid the bar examiners' traps and achieve a passing score.

SOLVING MBE QUESTIONS DECODED

Read the call of the question first:

- Since the subjects are in random order, reading the call first will sometimes identify the **subject** (i.e. torts) and **issue** (i.e. strict liability) being tested so you can read the fact pattern with the appropriate rules in mind. If you can't identify the subject or issue by reading the call of the question, usually a glance at the sentence *before* the call of the question will provide the subject information.
- This "starting at the bottom" approach might take some getting used to, but in the end it will save you time and increase your accuracy.

Solve the problem *before* looking at the answer choices (when possible):

MBE questions are nothing more than a hypothetical problem posed by a pretend client. Your job is to solve the problem.

- **Read the fact pattern** carefully looking for *legally significant* facts. Every fact is included for a reason. A fact is either included to satisfy a rule element, or as a decoy fact to distract you from the issue being tested and provide material for a wrong answer choice. (See below for more on MBE Decoys.)
- **Issue/Rule:** What rule is going to solve the problem? Identify the general rule, including all elements and/or any sub-rule being tested (if you were not already able to do so from reading the call of the question/preceding sentence).
- **Analyze:** Solve the problem by applying facts to the rule/elements. Try to pinpoint the precise element/sub-element/exception/defense being tested by the facts.

- **Conclude**:
  - ◇ If possible, answer the call of the question with a "because" statement that identifies the precise element on which the question turns. Be specific. Precision here will help you to tease through the answer choices, especially when choosing between two seemingly viable options.

    Example: P's defamation action will not prevail *because* no special damages are shown as required for regular slander (the pinpoint issue raised by the facts.)

  - ◇ For some questions, you will not be able to conclude without first looking at the answer choices. For example, if the call asks what is the most serious crime for which defendant can be convicted, you will first need to see the options available. Then, using a process of elimination analyze each choice and conclude accordingly.
  - ◇ For questions that ask for the "most helpful" or "strongest argument," try to role play and come up with good arguments a lawyer would make *prior* to looking at the answer choices so you have some options in mind to compare against the choices provided.

Solving first puts you in charge and prevents the bar examiners from clouding the issue to distract you by introducing other tangentially related concepts into your thought process. It is much harder to entice you into selecting a wrong answer when you have already solved the problem by focusing on the question call and the facts, decided what the right answer should be, and identified why.

Decode the available options to select the best answer:

- After solving first (when possible), look for the answer choice that best comports with your analysis.
- Use the process of elimination to eliminate all poor options.
- Consider every option and identify *why* each is right or wrong. Doing so will help you gain extra rule review, provide pattern recognition on the decoy answers and identify your own patterns when selecting wrong answers.

  Example: Answer "A" is wrong *because* it overstates the applicable standard; intent is not required in negligence.

- If an answer choice raises a rule you didn't consider, analyze it now, but trust your gut on the rule you identified as being at issue. A rule that didn't jump out at you in the first place is likely a decoy.
- Look out for decoy answers (see below).
- Pick the best answer.

For each subject we have provided step-by-step guided analysis of select practice MBE questions so you can familiarize yourself with using this proactive approach. It may feel uncomfortable at first to try something new, but stick with it. Like any skill, you will improve and get faster with practice.

Most bar takers approach MBE questions using the same old school approach they have always used with multiple choice questions (e.g., read the question, read the answers, and if you know the content of the question the correct answer will "pop out" and be obvious.) If you have tried to answer any MBE questions, you already know the old school multiple choice approach won't be sufficient. This is because the bar examiners typically try every trick in the book to get you to pick the *wrong* answer.

MBE DECOYS

One of the ways the bar examiners get you to select a wrong answer is by using a decoy, which is the use of particular phrasing or another tool of distraction to purposely lead you away from the correct answer. This is how you can get a question wrong even when you know the law being tested. Some decoys are universal and employed across all subjects, but many are subject/rule specific and those are included in each subject's chapter. We identify these throughout this book with a decoy duck.

Hide the ball: The most frequently used decoy is to hide the correct answer in plain sight. These are some of the bar examiner's favorite tactics:

Decoy facts are added to the question to distract. All facts are included in the question to either lead you to the correct answer or provide a decoy answer.

Example: The facts may include recording act language when it is irrelevant to solving the problem posed. There will be a *wrong* answer choice provided that relates to that irrelevant recording act rule/facts.

Layman's language substituted for a legal concept in the *right* answer. You are looking for key legal terminology, so the correct answer choice seems too casual or fact focused or vague to be correct. You may need to interpret the answer choice to link it to the legal meaning of the plain language utilized in the answer choice.

Example: In a res ipsa loquitur call of the question, the correct answer is that the defendant was *not* negligent because the defendant did not have exclusive control over the canned tuna that caused the plaintiff's injury (boxes of canned tuna fell on the plaintiff). The analysis is that since another party could be responsible for the canned tuna mishap, res ipsa loquitur can't be used to establish defendant's liability. The correct answer identified that the defendant was not negligent, but merely recited the fact that "...the case of tuna had been knocked over by the workmen." From this you had to interpret the language to mean a third-party other than the defendant, (here, the workmen) caused the damage, consequently the tuna was not in the exclusive control of the defendant as required for res ipsa loquitur. Had the answer included the correct legal terminology you were likely looking for, instead it would have stated that the canned tuna was "not in the *exclusive control* of the defendant."

Buzz word that relates to the applicable rule is placed in *wrong* answer.

Example: In the example above, after analyzing the question, the key words that you are looking for of "not in the exclusive control of defendant," would be placed in the *wrong* answer choice so if you read quickly you might not notice that the rest of the wording in that choice makes that answer incorrect.

Boo! They like to scare you and play on your fears that you haven't prepared well enough to pass the exam. Wrong answer choices will include:

Made up rules: Be wary of selecting any answer choice implicating a "rule" you have never heard of; it is likely a decoy. Ask yourself, "If this was a real rule, wouldn't I have learned it?" It is unlikely you have graduated from law school and prepared for the bar exam and yet there is still some magic rule that is a correct answer and yet you have never stumbled across it before. Be confident, trust your preparation, and believe in yourself!

Obscure rules: The bar examiners also use more obscure rules as decoys. These can be real rules that are not tested outright much but sound intimidating (e.g. attornment of a lease,) or are old rules that are obsolete (e.g. res gestae).

Decoys based on rule knowledge: These are the more typical type of decoys you would expect on a multiple choice exam. These rule based decoys are often used in combination with some of the sneakier decoys identified above.

- **General rule** is a choice when the **rule exception** is satisfied, and visa versa.
- **General rule** is a choice when a **defense** is satisfied, and visa versa.
- **Wrong rule** or **inapplicable standard** is a choice.

  <u>Example</u>: In a question on equal protection for a quasi-suspect class, there will be *wrong* answer choices reciting the language of rational basis (a standard too low) and/or strict scrutiny (a standard too high) and/or pairing the appropriate intermediate scrutiny language with an incorrect statement that the plaintiff bears the burden of proof (when the government bears the burden of proof).

- **Rule surrogates:** A correct answer choice may use a sub rule or other identifiable rule language as a surrogate for the rule.

  <u>Example</u>: In an impeachment by bias evidence question, the correct answer choice may use language that the evidence is "admissible extrinsic evidence," as a surrogate for the impeachment by bias rule, which allows extrinsic evidence (in contrast to the rule for impeachment by character for truthfulness, which does not allow extrinsic evidence.)

- **Inapplicable rules:** The bar examiners will use rules with similar elements as decoys for each other.

  <u>Example</u>: If the question is testing the hearsay exception of Past Recorded Recollection, you can bet Present Recollection Refreshed will be included as a wrong answer choice.

Author's note: A word about the examples and rules in this book.
There are a lot of examples throughout this book which are used to illustrate rules and concepts. Almost every example in this book is derived from actual NCBE questions. We have purposely not rephrased the questions for greater clarity in an effort to expose you to the type of (at times) obtuse and confusing language facing you on the exam. All parentheticals in the examples are author commentary included to aid understanding. Further, you will find the *examples* are not always written in a gender neutral way, as they derive from drafted NCBE questions, though the remainder of the book uses current practices of gender neutrality (with the exception of some traditional rules, such as in estates in land.) Lastly, the NCBE does not provide specific guidance regarding the rules eligible for testing on the MBE, beyond an unhelpful broad listing of topics in the NCBE Subject Matter Outlines. We have purposely included all rules previously released as NCBE tested. It is possible they could test on a rule nuance not included here, and questions drafted by bar prep companies may include some unusual topics not included. However, we purposely opted to cover the known most testable rules, rather than every imaginable possibility, to keep the length as short as possible, while still enabling you to succeed on the exam. Finally, while there are images of children and animals (they are our real life children and pets), rest assured that no children or animals were injured during the making of this book.

HOW TO STUDY TO SUCCEED ON THE MBE

The MBE tests a vast amount of law, which you must understand and memorize in a compressed time period. Simultaneously, you need to familiarize yourself with MBE testing styles and patterns by doing a lot of MBE practice questions (approximately 2500 MBE practice questions results in a passing score for most bar takers, even in high cut-score jurisdictions, though this number varies based on an individual's MBE aptitude and cut score required). The key to managing all of this successfully is to learn the law by *doing* practice MBE questions and start doing practice MBE questions early (get started during your final year of law school). It is not realistic to wait and practice *after* you've learned the law because you will run out of time.

It is helpful to think of preparing for the MBE in two stages. How you study for this exam will evolve as you get closer to the bar exam testing date.

1) **Phase one:** Study each subject in turn and refresh your memory on the law and/or learn some of the law from scratch. Practice single subject MBE questions, mostly, without timing yourself. Circle back to the subjects you've already completed as you tackle new subjects.
2) **Phase two**: After the law is refreshed, practice MBE with the subjects mixed together, and start timing yourself.

MBE STUDY- PHASE ONE

(Depending on your bar study plan, this phase takes 4-5 weeks.)

RULES

Your goal is to learn as many rules as you can during phase one of review. Some subjects and topics will come back more easily than others.

- **Focus on the most heavily tested rules first.**
- **Learn and review rules** with an emphasis on **understanding** the rules. Understand the rule, rule elements, sub-rules, sub-definitions, nuances, exceptions, and defenses. Your goal is to understand what each word in a rule means, such that you could give a lecture on the rule or explain the rule to a pretend client including an example of facts that *would* satisfy each element and facts that *would not* satisfy each element of each rule. If you can't think of factual examples, you probably don't understand the rule well enough to pass the bar.
- **You will not have full rule mastery:** Through the process of frequent review and working with a subject by doing practice MBE questions (and essays,) most students will recall around 60-70% (give or take depending on the subject) by the time they move on to focus on the next subject. You will memorize the rest of the rules by continuing to review and practice with them over time. It isn't realistic to learn 100% of the rules in each subject during phase one of study (the first pass through of a subject) and you shouldn't try to do so because it is not possible and you will fall behind in bar prep and not get to all the subjects.

PRACTICE

Your goal with completing practice MBE questions is to gain **rule mastery** by *using* rules to solve hypothetical problems, increase important MBE **pattern recognition,** and improve **MBE test taking skills** all at the same time.

> **Study tip:** You will need a practice bank of MBE questions. Retired NCBE questions are the best to practice with because they are most similar to what you will encounter on exam day. Many bar companies, license the NCBE questions. Additionally, the book *Strategies and Tactics for the MBE* includes licensed NCBE questions, has excellent answer explanations, and is very economical.

- **Practice for rule understanding and comprehension at first.** For the first day or two on a subject, you can complete questions one at a time (e.g., answer question one, review the answer explanation for question one, then answer question two, etc.). After the first few days, work in sets of at least 5-10 questions at a time before looking up answer explanations. After working with a subject for a few days, work practice questions in sets of 17 and work up to sets of 33 questions.
- **Practice without timed conditions at first.** Your goal here is quality of review, not speed. At first it may be slow going, especially if you are solving the questions before answering and working **open book**. As you gain rule recall and competence with MBE testing style, your speed will increase.
- **Practice MBE questions to increase pattern recognition:** There are only so many ways to ask a hypothetical question testing a concept. Completing many MBE questions increases pattern recognition, which improves issue spotting and accuracy.
- **Practice MBE questions to improve MBE test taking skills:** Most students can score around 55% after studying for the MBE, but that is an insufficient score to pass in most jurisdictions. Using the "solve first" technique described above increases scores

by 10-15% for most students, which gets you right in the passing zone. You need to practice a lot of MBE questions to get good at the skill of solving MBE questions. With increased practice you will more easily see the decoys and become adept at avoiding them.

- **Review all missed rules regularly.** Depending on your study preferences, there are a lot of ways to incorporate regular review. If you use flashcards, you can employ a color coded system to identify the frequency of review needed. For example, cards in the red pile need daily review until you get the rule down. Once you do, that card moves to the yellow pile. Cards in the yellow pile are reviewed two times a week. Cards in the green pile are rules you now feel comfortable with; review them once a week to keep them fresh.

Completing practice questions:

- **Work on one subject at a time initially,** but plan to circle back to the subjects you've already completed as you tackle new subjects.
- **Review the subject** before doing questions to help your brain to recall the rules. The cheat sheets in this book are perfect for this review.
- **Use the "solve first" technique** to answer MBE questions.
- ***Try* to answer the questions from memory first**. Identify the rule that applies to solve the problem, including all sub-rules and sub definitions. Read the question and try to solve the problem from memory by identifying the specific rule (or rule element or exception upon which the facts turn) that will solve the problem.
- **Use an open book *if needed*:** Look up the rule, element, or exception if needed in this book, and then solve the problem. You will remember the rule better by *using* it to solve a question, rather than purely guessing. Don't worry about timing yet; you are practicing the skill, gaining pattern recognition and learning rules all at the same time.

Reviewing practice questions answers:

- **Review all answer explanations**. At first, reviewing the answer explanations may take longer than answering the questions. Quality is more important than quantity (but both are important). As you learn more rules, the review of answers will take less time.
- **Do something to learn missed rules:** For rules you **got wrong** *or* **needed to do open book**, *do something* extra to identify and learn that rule. What you do depends on your study preferences, but you need to memorialize that rule on a flashcard, handwritten on paper (a 7-subject notebook works well,) add it to an outline or word document, or you can annotate directly in this rule book.
- **Add the facts** from the questions to your flashcard (or other study tool) to illustrate the rule. Doing so gives your brain **two ways** to retrieve a rule;
  1) By recalling the black letter law, and
  2) By recalling a similar fact pattern, which you can use to reverse engineer to determine the rule.
- **Do a quick IRAC for missed questions/rules:** A great technique to learn missed rules is to *write* a quick 1-2 sentence IRAC (like you would for an essay) that applies the facts from the question to the rule/element to cement the rule in your memory with an attached example so you can *learn* and *memorize* the missed rule. Add the IRAC to a flashcard, handwritten list of missed rules, or your outline.

> <u>Example IRAC</u>:
> **I: Contract modification**
> **Common law- consideration required**
>
> **R:** Additional consideration is required to modify a contract under the common law. The UCC does not require additional consideration, but only good faith.
>
> **A:** When Builder and Painter agreed Painter would also paint an additional outbuilding, this was not a valid contract modification *because* while there was mutual assent, there was no additional consideration, as required under common law.
>
> **C:** Therefore, the modification was not valid.

- **Mind-meld examples:** Sometimes you may know a rule, but get the answer to a question wrong anyways because you don't analyze the facts in the same way as the bar examiners when required to make a judgment call. On the MBE there is no mechanism to explain your answer, so you want to mind-meld and analyze the facts similarly to the bar examiners. It is helpful to make a master flashcard (or a log or spreadsheet) for these rules where you can track the analysis of multiple fact patterns on a particular topic in one place, identifying facts that satisfy the rule/element (examples) and facts that do not (non-examples). Reviewing these cards will improve pattern recognition, deepen rule mastery and most importantly, enable you to mind-meld and match your analysis to that of the bar examiners.

> <u>Mind-meld example</u>:
> **Rule: Prescriptive easement/Adverse possession**:
> Actual use,
> Continuous use for the statutory period,
> Open, notorious, visible use; and
> **<u>Hostile use</u> (without permission)**

Hostile	Not hostile
◆ Use *unknown* to owner ◆ Unsure of boundary, plant trees and erect fence on 10 foot strip of neighbor's land	◆ With permission of one co-T

- **Track why are you getting questions wrong:** If you are struggling with low MBE scores, slow down and track a few sets of questions to determine **why** you are missing each question. Identify if the problem is insufficient rule knowledge, or poor MBE technique, or both. If you can narrow the answer down to two good options, but have a hard time picking between the two, analyze the answer explanations to determine why one answer is better. See the "Troubleshooting Tips" for more ideas on making improvements.

Question tracking example

Possible reasons why answer was wrong:

Rule:

- Rule knowledge poor (didn't know rule/element/nuance well enough)
- Tricked by a non-rule/inapplicable rule

Analysis:

- Analysis incorrect (knew correct rule, but misapplied the facts)

MBE technique:

- Reading comprehension
- Decoy facts/rule

Set facts: June 1	76%	17Q	Adaptibar-mixed set	
Q	**Subject**	**Rule**	**Element @ issue**	**Why I got it wrong...**
5	Torts	IIED	Bystander liability	Rule nuance: P must *know* D present for IIED to a bystander
8	Property	Life estate	Vested remainder	Decoy: RAP n/a to vested remainders, tricked by RAP in Q
10	Evidence	Settlement offer	Applies to disputed claims only	Rule nuance: Claim must be in dispute, here blurted offer @ scene so no dispute
14	Property	Foreclosure	Junior interest can't bind senior interest, so foreclosure buyer took "subject to" mortgage.	Read too fast. Got confused. Lots of decoy facts, too. Total guess.

SCORES

Scores are typically low on the first few days working with a subject. As you continue to work with the subject over subsequent days, your scores should improve as you retain more rules and practice. With each new subject you tackle, expect the pattern to repeat.

MBE STUDY- PHASE TWO

(This phase usually takes 4-6 weeks, which varies by jurisdiction.)

RULES

- Continue to review all rules frequently.

- Work on learning the most heavily tested rules first and try to learn as many of the less frequently tested rules as you can.
- The final 2-3 weeks of bar study is the time to work on active short-term memorization (similar to what you did to prepare for final exams.) See the "Memorization Tips" below.

PRACTICE

- **Answer questions closed book primarily:** Once you have your rules mostly memorized, **work from memory.** Use an open book as a crutch to look up the part of the rule you can't remember only when necessary.
- **Do mixed subject sets:** Work mostly on mixed subject sets.
- **Do targeted topic specific question sets** for special practice in subjects or topics of difficulty.
- **Do questions under timed conditions.** Timing becomes more important as you get closer to the exam. Work on completing sets under timed conditions. Pay attention to your timing and **don't go too fast or too slow.** If you go too fast you are missing questions for poor reading comprehension. (Do not go faster than 5 minutes fast per hour, which is 33 questions in 55 minutes). If you go too slow you risk not finishing enough questions to pass the exam. (If you are slow, the goal is to finish at least 90 questions with good accuracy in 3 hours.)

PRACTICE PACING CHART	
# Questions	**Target Time**
17	30 minutes
33	1 hour
50	1.5 hour
100	3 hours

MBE timing goals: If you are going faster than 1.6 minutes per question, or 33 questions in 55 minutes, you are leaving reading comprehension points on the table. Slow down and watch your scores increase, usually by 10-15%. If you are not able to finish more than 90 questions in 3 hours, you need to speed up.

- **Increase the number of questions in each set:** Practice MBE questions in increasingly larger sets of questions to build exam day stamina. Do questions mostly in a set of 33 questions and work your way up to 50 questions (particularly in the last few weeks of bar study.) Once you have completed all MBE subjects in bar review, aim to do a set of 100 questions each week (to build up the stamina needed on exam day). If stamina is an issue, work on a larger set of questions every 2nd or 3rd day of bar study, instead of a completing smaller sets of questions daily.
- **Complete an MBE simulation:** Exam simulations (full day 200-question MBE exams) are essential in helping you build your stamina and allow you to get much needed practice working in 3-hour blocks of time. Do the questions open book if you still need a crutch, but do the simulation. An MBE simulation also helps you to identify weaknesses. Afterwards, pay attention to your own focus and attention issues over the course of the long day so you can adjust your final study plan to remedy any issues.

SCORES

- Expect your scores to go down when you move into doing all questions in full mixed subject review. It is much harder on your brain to retrieve a rule from a much larger pool of rules (seven subjects) and scores typically decrease for a few days (to as long as 7-10 days) as your brain adjusts to the increased cognitive load.
- Once your brain adjusts to mixed subject review, you can expect your scores to jump back to approximately where they were as you *ended* working on each subject.
- Scores should continue to increase as you gain rule mastery and get closer to the exam date.

EFFECTIVE MBE STUDY DECODED

Effective MBE study is flexible and evolves over the typical 8-11 weeks of bar study. The goal in the beginning is rule understanding and acquisition. As the exam date nears the focus shifts to competence under timed exam conditions.

	PHASE ONE One subject at a time: first 4-5 weeks	**PHASE TWO** All subjects mixed: final 4-6 weeks
Memory	◆ Doing Q open book at first. ◆ As recall increases, work towards closed book from memory.	◆ O.k. to peek at rules occasionally ◆ Work towards totally closed book from memory. ◆ See memorization tips.
Q Sets	◆ Doing one Q at a time o.k. at first. ◆ Move towards completing sets of 17 Q and 33 Q.	◆ Always work in sets, mostly of 33 (sets of 50 in last few weeks) ◆ Aim to do a set of 100 Q each week (for stamina). ◆ Do a simulated MBE exam.
Timing	◆ At first, work at your own pace. ◆ Doing Q open book to learn rules as you go takes more time.	◆ Work under timed conditions. ◆ Troubleshoot any timing problems.
Scores	◆ In each subject expect scores to start low and climb as you gain competence in that subject. ◆ Scores will fall and repeat the pattern as each new subject is introduced.	◆ Scores will drop when you move to all mixed review (it takes time for your brain to adjust to working with all subjects simultaneously). ◆ Scores should continue to climb as you gain rule mastery and get closer to the exam date.
Review	◆ Review all previously studied subjects weekly. ◆ Continue to complete MBE Qs in previously studied subjects.	◆ Review all subjects regularly. ◆ Do MBE Qs in all subjects mixed. ◆ Identify any problem areas and do targeted review and MBE sets on that topic.

MBE PRACTICE TIPS

- **Practice how you will be tested on exam day:**
  - ◇ **Online exam:** If only digital scratch paper will be available on exam day, plan to use as little scratch paper as possible. Reading line by line and solving the questions as you go will help minimize the need for scratch paper and is a strategy that will work for most questions. The virtual scratch paper provided on exam day will likely be similar to a word document, so practice MBEs using a word document for any notes, but only use notes for the questions that truly require scratch paper to solve (typically questions with multiple parties/events in contracts, real property, and/or civil procedure).
  - ◇ **Paper exam:** Do at least 1/3 of your MBE practice on paper since that is what you will be doing on exam day. It feels different than doing questions online for both the process and timing (bar takers tend to go too fast online). Making notes on the questions themselves is most efficient and helpful.
- **Always fill in a bubble (answer each question).** Flag the ones you need to come back to (if you have time), but always fill in an answer choice before moving on to the next question so you don't accidentally mark your answers off by a number.
- **Try to use more than one source for MBE practice questions.** Using different sources ensures you are not simply familiarizing yourself with the language cues of the question author(s). The NCBE released questions are the most similar to what you will see on exam day. You can purchase questions directly from the NCBE website or through a bar prep company that licenses the questions.
- **Watch your speed practicing online:** Students tend to go too fast doing practice MBE questions in online formats.
- **Don't worry if you do a set of Qs and score poorly**. It happens. You could be tired or randomly got a disproportionate set of questions on rules you don't know well. More importantly, pay attention to your scoring pattern over time since you want to base your study plan on the overall pattern, not an aberration.
- **Self-assessment is key to improving MBE scores.** Determine <u>why</u> you are getting questions wrong to identify skill and substance deficiencies, so they can be fixed.

RULE MEMORIZATION TIPS

Many bar takers are rightly concerned about having enough time to memorize all the material. Think of the task as a huge pile of rules you need to know. Bit by bit you refresh your memory and learn rules and move them from the big pile of rules you need to know into the pile of rules that you do know.

Rule understanding is the goal:

- <u>**Preview**</u>: This is where you familiarize yourself with a subject *before* doing a deep review of a subject. You can start with the subject **cheat sheet** or chapter in this book, or review your own notes, outlines, or flashcards. The idea with a preview is to **refresh your memory** on the subject before the deep dive review. The cheat sheets in this book work well.
- <u>**Deep review**</u>: Study the subjects deeply with a **focus on rule understanding**. You must understand all the rule elements and key terms to spot issues and apply rules correctly. If you understand how a rule works, it is much easier to recall. Be strategic and **focus on the heavily tested rules first**. Most bar takers do a deep subject review through a commercial bar prep program utilizing videos or some lecture method of substantive review.

- **Active Review**: This is the process of working with the rules after you've done a deep review. Your goal is to **understand** the rules, including all elements, sub-elements, and sub-definitions, not just rote memorization. Use the following techniques to ensure you have sufficient depth of rule understanding:
  - **Build a subject outline from memory:** Start with a checklist (the big topics macro structure of the subject), then working in small chunks pick one section at a time and build by adding all rules, elements, and sub-elements. Each time you review a subject, start with the same checklist, but alternate the section(s) where you start the detailed rule build out so that you allot equal time to all sections/topics (otherwise you will know the first half of the subject better than the back half). Keep a running list of the topics that need more review. This technique is versatile depending on your study preference, and can be done verbally, by hand on paper, using a whiteboard, on a computer document, using flashcards, etc.
  - **Pretend you are explaining the rules to a client:** For each rule, identify the elements, and all sub-rules and sub-definitions. For each element and sub-element or sub-definition give an example of a fact that would *satisfy* the element, and a fact that would *not satisfy* the element. You can enlist the help of family and friends or even your dog to do this.
  - **Do Practice MBE** (and essay) questions. ***Using* the rules** to solve problems aids memorization and depth of rule understanding.
- **Memorize**: Once you understand, start committing rules to memory.

Regular weekly review: Frequent review is key to memorization. As you move from subject to subject, review all of the subjects you have already covered weekly to pick up a few more rules and ensure you don't forget the rules you already know. You can review a different subject for 20 minutes each day, or designate one day a week to spend reviewing all the subjects you've already studied.

Short-term memory, which is the type of memory we use when we "cram" for a test, only lasts for a short time so it isn't possible to cram and memorize the many rules you need for the bar exam. The final 2-3 weeks before the bar exam is when you will actively use short-term memory to try to memorize the rules that haven't managed to stick in your memory yet. If you have prioritized studying the heavily tested rules first, do the best you can here, but it is fine (and normal) if you go into the bar not knowing every single rule that is potentially tested.

MBE TROUBLESHOOTING TIPS

If your MBE scores are lower than desired, first identify the problem. MBE scores can be low for a lot of reasons. Before you despair, consider the following:

SYMPTOM	DIAGNOSIS	HOW TO FIX
Frequently can't pick between two tempting answer choices	Weak rule knowledge	◆ **Increase rule mastery**. You need to understand what all the words in each rule mean. ◆ Rote memorization is not sufficient. ◆ **Rule recall**: If you can't remember a rule use an open book as a crutch. Afterwards, do something to actively memorize that rule. ◆ **Target problem areas**: Do some targeted MBE questions in highly tested areas where you are weak. ◆ See the sections on "Study Phase 1" and "Rule Memorization Tips" for strategies on increasing rule understanding.
	Poor MBE technique	◆ Slow down ◆ Solve the Q all the way through before looking at the answer choices ◆ Try to pinpoint the element being tested/at issue before looking at the answer choices ◆ Answer the call of the question with "because" explaining what the answer should be and why (if possible) ◆ Mechanically apply law to fact ◆ Do not peek at the answer choices to "help" solve the problem. ◆ See the section on "Skill: How to Solve MBE Questions"
◆ Mind wanders ◆ Get confused reading answer choices & have to reread facts	Reading comprehension	◆ Slow down (read carefully once) ◆ Make notes/draw a diagram ◆ Outline/identify key terms/dates
	Fatigue	◆ Don't practice MBE when you are tired ◆ Take a break
	Stamina	◆ Complete a set of 100 Qs weekly in phase 2 of study ◆ Take a simulated MBE exam ◆ **Slow to warm up:** If you do poorly on the first 5-10 questions in a set, do 5 warm up questions first. ◆ **Sluggish in the a.m. p.m.:** Practice MBE questions during the time of day that is difficult for you. You can also vary your meals to see what gives your brain staying power for the morning or afternoon session. ◆ **Hitting the wall after X number of questions:** Aim to do practice sets 10-15 questions longer than your hit-the-wall number to build stamina. ◆ **Plan for a brain break:** If you have maxed out your attention and can't complete 100 questions straight, build in a break to regain focus (e.g., get up to stretch, take a seated meditation break, etc.)

Have a bad set (or a few bad sets)	Fatigue	◆ MBEs require the full attention of a well-rested brain. If you are ending your day with MBE practice, you are probably losing points simply because of fatigue. Try moving your MBE practice to the afternoon or morning to get a more realistic view of your scores.
Picking the answer that makes sense or feels right	Getting tripped up by the facts and/or decoys	◆ Don't use your own "real world" knowledge to solve Qs ◆ Have no sympathy for the "MBE people" (they are not real and the good guy often loses) ◆ Mechanically apply law to fact
Your timing is off and you are going: ◆ Too fast (with poor accuracy), or ◆ Too slow (and risk not finishing in the allotted time).	Timing problem	◆ **Too fast**: Slow down and annotate the question itself. IRACing the question will also force you to slow down. ◆ **Too slow**: This is often a **disguised technique problem**. Read more deliberately on the first read, use good technique to increase accuracy and annotate the question as you read it. Being methodical will save time in the long run. ◆ **Too slow- a slow reader**: Your goal is to finish at least 90 questions in 3 hours (guess on the last 10). Accuracy is most important. You may opt to skip long fact patterns, which will enable you to answer more questions (but bubble skipped answers so you don't mess up the numbering). ◆ **Too slow- a very slow reader**: Try speed reading drills.
All of the above		**Practice, practice, practice**: More practice is what leads to bar passage. When in doubt, do actual practice problems over reviewing the rules one more time to feel "ready." You will never feel ready enough, so do the practice.

TAKING THE BAR EXAM ONLINE

TAKING THE BAR EXAM ONLINE

Traditionally, students took the MBE exam on paper. Using paper enabled students to directly mark-up questions on a hard copy as they solved the questions, which is a useful method to both track significant facts and help maintain focus. Modernly, many jurisdictions (and the NCBE) are providing online bar exams. While the thought of taking an online MBE exam might cause you to panic, don't! Keep in mind that the rules will still be the same and you know those. Also, the manner in which you approach an MBE question will remain the same. What will be different is how you annotate or mark-up the actual question when online. Like anything, you can learn a new skill with some practice!

The NCBE online software provides online tools to enable you to annotate, highlight, and cross off incorrect options when taking the MBE exam online. The NCBE (usually through each jurisdiction) offers a mock bar exam to help students familiarize themselves with the tools available and the experience of taking the bar exam remotely. We strongly encourage you to make use of any and all mock bar exams that are offered in your jurisdiction. To find more information about mock bar exams as they relate to the MBE portion, computer requirements, etc. visit the NCBE website at https://www.ncbex.org.

On a positive note, most bar exam companies now offer their MBE questions online as well. We recommend that you practice doing these questions online rather than printing them out and doing them on paper. In contrast, if your bar will be administered on paper, be sure to practice using questions printed on paper to better replicate the experience. Most bar companies also offer some type of highlighting and/or strike through feature so practice using those when doing practice questions.

Below is a review of some important tools that may be valuable to you when taking an online exam. While the tools that are available on any particular online exam administration (or online practice bank of questions) may be slightly different, this guide should give you an idea of how they can be used to efficiently work through the questions without annotating the questions themselves or using paper scratch paper.

ONLINE MBE EXAM TOOLS:

- ✓ **Digital scratch paper (essentially a notes box):** You should use this to type up rule elements and/or key facts after you spot the issue (using shorthand as you would on paper). For issues with simple rules, you will likely be able to answer those without using the scratch paper. For other questions you will likely need to jot down some of the rule or try to summarize the key facts and/or parties (particularly for more complicated fact patterns in real property, civil procedure and contracts.) See the example below.
- ✓ **Flag questions:** You will be able to "flag" questions that you want to come back to later (but note, you can only return within the same exam session time period). WARNING: Be sure to fill in your best guess correct answer for the time being in case you run out of time and can't come back.

- ✓ **Strike through:** You have the ability to strike through incorrect answer options once you determine that an answer is not correct. WARNING: Remember you must still select the correct answer and not just strike through the incorrect ones to get credit for the question.
- ✓ **Highlighting:** You can highlight words or sentences within the question. WARNING: Be careful to figure out what the issue is before you highlight any facts so you only focus in on applicable facts. Otherwise, you risk highlighting everything including the decoy facts.
- ✓ **Timer:** You can set up a timer once you start the exam. The timer will then automatically count down the allocated time for the session. Pay attention to your timing as you go through the questions.

Exam integrity reminders: Since the exam is online, there is software that the examiners use to record your session. Your session will be recorded and monitored by artificial intelligence. Make sure you review the rules in your jurisdiction as most jurisdictions do not allow applicants to leave their seats or view of the webcam. In addition, you cannot have prohibited items in your exam room (which includes books, electronic devices, and other people and animals). Make sure you use the restroom before the exam session and do not bring any food or drinks into the exam room.

EXAMPLE of using online tools to take an MBE question online

A builder borrowed $10,000 from a lender to finance a small construction job under a contract with a homeowner. The builder gave the lender a writing that stated, "Any money I receive from the homeowner will be paid immediately to the lender, regardless of any demands from other creditors." The builder died after completing the job but before the homeowner paid. The lender demanded that the homeowner pay the $10,000 due to the builder directly to the lender. The homeowner refused, saying that he would pay directly to the builder's estate everything that he owed the builder.

Is the lender likely to succeed in an action against the homeowner for $10,000?

A. No, because the builder's death terminated the lender's right to receive payment directly from the homeowner.
B. No, because the writing the builder gave to the lender did not transfer to the lender the right to receive payment from the homeowner.
C. Yes, because the builder had manifested an intent that the homeowner pay the $10,000 directly to the lender.
D. Yes, because the lender is an intended beneficiary of the builder-homeowner contract.

Approach

1. Read the call — action against the homeowner for $10,000 — probably real property.
2. Issue? Not clear so read facts first to see if you can determine the issue. The facts that you might have highlighted are highlighted above. In the first sentence, you can see that there are three parties involved (builder, lender, homeowner) so the issue likely revolves around third parties as it relates to the lender v. homeowner call (builder clearly involved but need to see how the parties play out so jotting down their relationship might be helpful).
3. What you might write down on your virtual scratch paper:

B ------$10k from L

B has K w/ H

B-----writing to L – give $ from H to L

B died before H paid

L -------wants $ from H
Assign.? – *rights given to another? no b/c no writing says H gives to L NOT to B (which would be an assignment) -K between B and H for $$ NOT B and L* (the part in italics would mostly be figured out without actually writing it down to save time, but it is included here to demonstrate the thought process that supplement the notes.)

4. After jotting down some notes, I can see that H has no duty to pay B because there was not an assignment. I could next look at the answer choices and use the strike through function if I wanted to (but sometimes you won't need to do this). So I could just select the correct answer choice, which is B and move on to the next question.
5. Characters that might be helpful:
   - Use the first letter only for names or parties to save time: B for builder
   - Dashes to connect parties horizontally or to connect facts: ---------
   - V or I letters if you want to make a connection vertically (by hitting return or enter between each letter to bring you to the next row):

   (B) Builder--------------(H) homeowner
   v
   v
   v
   (L)Lender

   OR

   (B)Builder--------------(H) homeowner
   I
   I
   I
   (H)Homeowner

STUDENT FEEDBACK (IT'S A MIXED BAG!)

Online MBE exams are brand new in 2020. Below is feedback and advice from students who sat for the first MBE online exam. Their advice is inconsistent, but since everyone is different, this may provide some ideas that you find useful to try. The most important thing is to find an approach that works for you.

- I did not use the online tools. I took the MBE the way I practiced, which did not include any annotations. For property questions, where it is usually helpful to draw a diagram, I simply tried to slow down for these questions and envision the diagram in my head.
- The online tools were similar to functions I was used to from my [bar company's] layout. The bar's highlighting feature definitely lagged but I used it mainly to highlight the question stem before answering the question. I only annotated in the virtual scratch paper if the question needed it (e.g., a recording statutes question).
- I highlighted and sometimes used the strike out function. On more detailed questions, I used [digital] scratch paper to write rules or order of people (like on property).
- I did not use the tools. I became comfortable with the online format, preparing for the worst case of no highlights/no notes, and continued to use that. I flagged a couple of answers and came back to them at the end.
- I used the highlighter function on the exam to highlight important words/details, but also simultaneously used the virtual scratch paper to document important issues for each question. I used the virtual scratch paper to document the parties in the question, the timing of issues in the fact pattern for questions involving contracts, civ pro, and property, and wrote my short answer to the question before looking at the MBE provided answers. It was a bit frustrating to have to click to open the virtual scratch paper on each question since it did not remain open when moving from one question to the other. But I found it helpful nonetheless, especially since I practiced taking online MBEs before with a small Word doc open next to [my bar company] online practice questions. Plus, [my bar companies] have a highlighting function on their MBEs to practice using highlighters during the test.
- I used the highlighting tool for the MBEs and I found it very helpful. I would read the question/facts then go back and highlight it quickly and this helped me get organized and stay focused on the call of the question. I didn't use the highlighter for every question because I realized I was wasting time highlighting so towards the ends of the exam I stopped using it. I did not annotate anything.

MBE DECODED—
MULTISTATE BAR EXAM

PART 1 CIVIL PROCEDURE

CIVIL PROCEDURE TABLE OF CONTENTS

★ Favorite Testing Area

CIVIL PROCEDURE MBE OUTLINE

MBE CIVIL PROCEDURE AT A GLANCE

Applicable law: The Federal Rules of Civil Procedure (FRCP) and sections of Title 28 of the U.S. Code pertaining to trial and appellate jurisdiction, venue and transfer apply on the MBE. Federal common law (case law) is also tested.

17 Questions (approx.)	**8 Questions** (approx.)
Subject matter jurisdiction Supplemental/removal jurisdiction Personal jurisdiction Service of process/notice Venue/transfer/forum non conveniens Inunctions/temporary restraining orders Pleadings (amended/supplemental) Rule 11 Joinder parties/claims/class actions Discovery (disclosure/sanctions) Adjudication without trial Pretrial conference and orders Pretrial motions: pleadings, dismiss, MSJ Motions: JMOL Post-trial motions: relief from judgment, new trial	State law in federal court Federal common law Right to a jury trial Jury selection/composition Jury instructions Defaults and dismissals Jury verdicts: types/challenges Judicial findings & conclusions Issue and claim preclusion Appeals—interlocutory review Final judgment rule Scope of review—judge and jury

MBE tip: Civil Procedure was added as eligible for MBE testing in 2015. As of the printing of this book, the NCBE (creators of the MBE) has provided little guidance on the specifics of the rules eligible for testing and has only released 40 total practice questions (in comparison to hundreds that have been released for the other subjects). For this reason, there are fewer examples in this chapter.

Civ. Pro. MBE testing tips:

- Know the details of numerous Federal Rules of Civil Procedure (FRCP).
- Know when rights are waived if not asserted.
- The typical two-sided civil procedure issues (where the result is ambiguous) that law professors like to test, will be tested in a more superficial way on the MBE. This is because in MBE testing format, there has to be a correct answer, so many MBE questions will ask specific questions or "best argument" type questions.

Common Civ. Pro. testing call: Many released civil procedure questions test your strategizing problem skills by asking, "What is the *best* argument" or "*best* response" for one of the parties involved? Look for an option that accomplishes the most for the party. For example, it is important to know which method is best to have a case dismissed (e.g., it is better to find an answer choice that dismisses a case rather than an opportunity for the other party to amend). Even though 2-3 of the answer choices might be a viable option for the party in question, only one will be the *best* answer.

I. PROPER COURT—PRELIMINARY ISSUES

The first inquiry in civil procedure always centers on whether it is proper for the court selected to resolve the case at hand. To hear a case, the court must have jurisdiction over the **persons** involved, the **subject matter** of the suit, the case must be held in the proper **venue,** the defendant must have **notice** of the suit, and the **proper law** must be used to resolve the issues.

A. **Personal jurisdiction** means the court must have proper **jurisdiction over the parties** to an action, and it is established through a traditional basis or using the minimum contacts standard.

1. **Traditional basis for personal jurisdiction** exists where the defendant:

a. **Consents (express or implied)** to jurisdiction in the forum state. One can expressly consent by contract, or one can impliedly consent by failing to make a timely objection to a lack of personal jurisdiction.

b. Is **domiciled** in the forum state. A person's domicile is the state in which they have **physical presence** (physical element) and the **subjective intent to remain** (mental element).

c. Is **present** in the forum state **when served** with process (tag jurisdiction).

1. **Except: Presence by force or fraud is invalid**. A defendant's presence in the forum when served will not be valid when the presence in forum is secured by **force** or **fraud** ***of the opposing party.***

2. **Except: "Involuntary" presence is invalid.** Most states consider a defendant's presence in the forum is considered involuntary and not the basis for service while present if the presence is to take part in another **judicial proceeding** or to make a **special appearance to contest jurisdiction,** or for **military transfer.**

2. **Modernly,** the **minimum contacts standard** allows personal jurisdiction over nonresidents of the forum state provided there is a **long-arm statute,** **and** the exercise of jurisdiction is in keeping with the constitutional due process requirements of the **minimum contacts standard** (due process), meaning an analysis is required on the **nature of the defendant's contacts** with the forum state **and** the **fairness** factors (reasonableness based on contacts).

a. A **long arm statute** is the mechanism that gives a state the power to reach beyond its own borders and assert jurisdiction over a nonresident.

1. **Co-extensive long arm statutes:** Some jurisdictions give their state courts power over any person or property **to the extent allowed by the Constitution,** meaning the minimum contacts standard is applied.

2. **Limited long arm statutes** (enumerated act): Some jurisdictions have specific long arm statutes that give its courts power over nonresidents **only for enumerated acts**—e.g., the commission of a tort while in the state. Where a specific long arm statute applies, the exercise of jurisdiction must satisfy that statute and also meet the constitutional requirements of the minimum contacts standard.

b. **Nature of the defendant's contacts:** A defendant must have sufficient **minimum contacts** with the forum state such that asserting jurisdiction over the defendant does not offend **traditional notions of fair play and substantial justice**.

1. **Minimum contacts:** When the defendant has **purposefully availed** themselves of the **benefits and protections of the state** such that it is reasonably **foreseeable that they could be haled into court** (in the forum), the defendant has minimum contacts with the forum state.

Example: Activities that show purposeful availment of the benefits and protections of a state include driving on a road in the forum state (availing themselves of use of the road maintenance and emergency responders) or conducting business in the forum state (availing themselves of use of the forum state laws to make money).

2. **Relatedness of claim to forum state:**

   a. **Specific Jurisdiction:** A claim arising from **activity in the state provides specific jurisdiction** over the defendant for **that claim only**.

   Example: Driving in a state is sufficient activity in the state to find specific jurisdiction over the driver for suits arising from the driving.

   Example: Franchisor, from State A, and Franchisee, from Canada, entered into a franchise contract. The contract was negotiated in State A and Franchisee understood that much of Franchisor's work to support Franchisee and oversee Franchisee's conduct pursuant to the contract would occur by Franchisor in State A. The contract specified State A law applied. For a suit regarding the franchise agreement, Franchisee's contacts are sufficient to find specific jurisdiction.

   b. **General Jurisdiction:** Where a defendant is **"essentially at home"** in the forum state, **general jurisdiction** will be found and the forum state may exercise jurisdiction over the defendant for **any cause of action.**

   > **MBE tip:** The NCBE may still use the old terminology of "continuous and systematic contacts" for the general jurisdiction standard instead of the newer "essentially at home" language. Consider them synonymous.

      i. **Corporation:** A corporation is always essentially at home in the **state of incorporation *or*** the state of their **principal place of business.** A corporation is unlikely to be found essentially at home for general jurisdiction in any other forum, except in extraordinary cases.

      Example (not essentially at home): An out-of-state corporation has a large amount of economic activity derived from the forum state, and 60% of their sales are *delivered* to buyers in the forum state. This is insufficient to determine the corporation is "essentially at home" in the forum.

      ii. **Subsidiary corporation:** A subsidiary corporation is one that has a parent company owner. The "essentially at home" **status of the subsidiary controls,** not the parent company.

      Example: Plaintiff (of State A) sued a parent corporation (of State B) and one if its foreign subsidiaries, a tire manufacturer, in State A federal court for wrongful death stemming from a car accident that killed his wife in Europe. The parent company does significant business throughout the U.S., including in State A. The foreign subsidiary manufactures tires for the European market, with 2% of its tires distributed in State A through the parent corporation. There is no personal jurisdiction for the subsidiary company because the claim does not arise from activity in State A (specific jurisdiction), and they do not have sufficient minimum contacts in State A to be "essentially at home." The contacts of the parent company are decoy ducks and irrelevant to determine the personal jurisdiction of the subsidiary (but it is unlikely the parent company is essentially at home in the forum either).

iii. **Foreign (non U.S.) corporations operating abroad cannot be essentially at home.** In-state contacts, such as through the use of independent contractors, are not imputed to a foreign parent corporation for purposes of jurisdiction.

iv. **Internet websites:** The law is unsettled in this area and there is **no clear test or standard.**

a. **Passive websites** are websites where information is made available, but business is not transacted (e.g., no e-commerce takes place). These **generally do not meet** the rules for minimum contacts, as they simply make some postings available to the public.

b. **Targeted interactive websites,** where there is communication between a user and operator, **may meet** the rules for minimum contacts as they are designed to conduct direct business transactions and are integral to the defendant's business.

Example: State A hotel targeted State B consumers by providing rate information, and accepting reservations on its website. They also advertised their proximity to State B and provided driving directions from State B. This targeted website subjects the State A hotel to personal jurisdiction in State B.

v. **Stream of commerce cases:** There is not a clear standard and decisions are case-by-case.

a. **Stream of commerce alone is insufficient.** Simply knowing a product may end up in a state through the stream of commerce without more is an insufficient basis for general jurisdiction. Other than that, there is not a case law consensus on stream of commerce cases.

b. **Intentionally targeting the forum, intentionally serving the needs in a state** (e.g., modifying a product to comply with state regulations and having a local presence), or a **sufficiently regular flow of business** in the forum **may** be sufficient minimum contacts.

3. **Fairness factors** (reasonableness based on contacts): The exercise of jurisdiction must be **fair** and **not offend traditional notions of fair play and substantial justice.** To analyze fairness, assess:

a. The **burden to the defendant.** Consider the location of witnesses and evidence, and the burden on the defendant to travel to the forum state.

b. The **forum state's interest** in adjudicating in the forum and in regulating activity within its borders and protecting its citizens.

c. **Plaintiff's interest** in litigating in the forum state and obtaining convenient and effective relief.

d. The **legal system's interest in efficient adjudication.**

e. Any shared **interest of the states in furthering substantive social policies** (e.g., the state's interest in promoting family harmony).

MINIMUM CONTACTS EXAMPLES	
Yes Minimum Contacts	**No Minimum Contacts**
◆ Franchisee in State A is in a 20-year contract with Franchisor from State B. The franchise contract directs most aspects of the business and calls the Franchisor to receive a percentage of the Franchisee's profits. The Franchisor sues in State B. Franchisee has purposely availed of State B and has sufficient minimum contacts.	◆ A financial services company in State B has locations only in State A and B. Unknown to the financial services company, one customer moved to State C and wants to sue the company in State C. The financial services company does no other business in State C. The financial services company has insufficient minimum contacts to support personal jurisdiction. ◆ A State B corporation has no business dealings in State A, except for the one-time hiring of an independent contractor who got in a car accident while driving in State A. The other driver sues the corporation in State A, but there are no minimum contacts in State A for the State B corporation.

3. **Other forms of personal jurisdiction:**

   a. **Federal statutes can provide personal jurisdiction:** A federal statute (e.g., an antitrust statute) can contain provisions for "nationwide service of process" to attain personal jurisdiction, however such provisions are not automatic and must be specifically included in a statute. FRCP 4(k)(1)(C).

   b. **In rem jurisdiction:** Jurisdiction is exercised **over property located in the forum state.** The property can be real property, personal property, (e.g., a car) or intangible property (e.g., a bank account). When jurisdiction cannot be exercised over the defendant personally, the court makes a disposition regarding the property rights and it is binding on all (meaning everyone, including those not party to the suit). In rem cases are rare.

   Examples: Distribution of real property from an estate; a condemnation proceeding on a piece of property.

   c. **Quasi-in rem jurisdiction:** It is similar to in rem jurisdiction, however the court will render a judgment on property ownership **binding the plaintiff and defendant *only***, as opposed to a ruling binding on all.

   d. **100 mile "bulge" provision:** A federal court has personal jurisdiction **over a defendant (joined through impleader or required joinder)** who is **served** (or waived service) within a judicial district of the U.S. **not more than 100 miles** from where the **summons was issued.** FRCP 4(k)(1)(B).

4. **Federal courts *may* hear a case without proper personal jurisdiction.**

   a. **Waived if not raised timely.** Failure to raise a defense of personal jurisdiction in the ***first* Rule 12 response** to the complaint (e.g., in a pre-answer motion or answer) constitutes consent to jurisdiction by waiver.

★ B. **Subject matter jurisdiction** (SMJ) means the court must have proper **jurisdiction over the subject matter** of an action. Federal courts have limited subject matter jurisdiction and may hear cases involving **federal questions** or **diversity of citizenship** between the parties.

> **<u>MBE tip</u>:** Federal question and diversity subject matter jurisdiction are primarily tested on the MBE, though federal courts also have exclusive jurisdiction over certain types of cases, such as admiralty, etc.

1. **Federal question jurisdiction:** Federal district courts have subject matter jurisdiction over civil actions **arising under federal law** (e.g., U.S. Constitution, federal statutes, treaties, etc.). 28 U.S.C. §1331.

   <u>Examples</u>: Suits arising under federal law would include claims under a federal employment discrimination statute, copyright, patent infringement, federal truth in lending statute, free speech (1st Am.), violation of Federal National Labor Relations Act, etc.

   a. **Concurrent jurisdiction: State and federal** courts have concurrent jurisdiction over federal question claims (meaning plaintiffs can sue in *either* state or federal court) unless Congress has specifically stated that federal courts have exclusive jurisdiction over the subject matter.

      1. **Exclusive jurisdiction cases:** Cases where federal courts have exclusive jurisdiction include cases involving bankruptcy, patent, copyright, trademark, securities cases, antitrust, maritime, suits between states, etc.

   b. **Well-pleaded complaint:** For federal question cases, plaintiff's federal claim must appear **on the face of plaintiff's complaint** itself (not in the defenses, anticipated rebuttal, counterclaims, answers, etc.).

      <u>Example</u>: Starlet, from State A, sues Tabloid, from State A, for defamation and asserts in her claim the First Amendment does not protect the defamatory statement. Since Starlet is anticipating a possible defense by asserting there is *not* a violation of the First Amendment, there is no federal question jurisdiction.

   c. **Arising under federal law:** The plaintiff must be **seeking to enforce a federal right** for the case to "arise under" federal law. This includes:

      1. Cases that involve a **real and substantial issue** of federal law and its determination must necessarily depend on resolution of the federal issue.

      2. If the federal issue is **substantially important** to the resolution of a **state law claim.**

      > **<u>MBE tip</u>:** If you're in doubt as to whether the plaintiff is seeking to enforce a federal right, ask yourself if the federal law implicated provides a **right** (benefit) that the plaintiff is attempting to *enforce* (to receive the benefit).

      <u>Example (arising under federal law)</u>: Entrepreneur, from State A, sells hot sauce. Company, incorporated in State B and headquartered in State C, sues Entrepreneur for $50,000 for infringing on their federal trademark. The court has federal question jurisdiction because the trademark infringement claim arises under **federal law**. (The facts about citizenship and the amount in controversy are irrelevant decoy ducks.)

      <u>Example (not arising under federal law)</u>: Railroad gave a married couple lifetime passes for free train rides in settlement of a claim. Subsequently, Congress passes a law forbidding railroads from providing free passes, so Railroad refuses to honor the couple's passes. The couple sues in federal court based on breach of contract, that the new federal law does not apply to them, and if it does, it is unconstitutional. Despite a federal law being involved in the dispute, the claim does **not arise under** federal law because the law does **not provide a right** that the plaintiffs are attempting to enforce.

Quite the opposite, the federal law *voids* their right to free train rides. Thus, the plaintiffs do not have a federal question basis for jurisdiction.

Decoy tip: Be alert for questions with elaborate decoy duck facts about party citizenship and/or the amount in controversy, or an answer choice that seems appealing because it correctly points out that there is insufficient diversity or amount in controversy. If **federal question is the basis for SMJ**, those facts are included to distract you and are irrelevant, as in the first example above.

2. **Diversity of citizenship jurisdiction:** Federal district courts have subject matter jurisdiction over actions (1) where the parties are **diverse** (**between citizens of different states**), **and** (2) where the **amount in controversy *exceeds* $75,000.** 28 U.S.C. §1332.

MBE tip: Diverse parties will most often be citizens from different states [Citizen (State X) v. Citizen (State Y)], but diverse parties also include:
- Citizen (State X) v. Foreigner (except if Foreigner is a permanent resident domiciled in same state)
- Citizen (State X) v. Citizen (State Y) + Foreign additional party
- Foreign state/agency v. Citizen(s) (from any state)

a. **Complete diversity of citizenship is required** at the time the action is commenced. No plaintiff may be a citizen of the same state as any defendant.

1. **Citizenship determination:**

a. **Person:** A natural person's citizenship is determined by their **domicile.**

i. **Person's domicile:** A person's domicile is the **state** where they are **physically present** (physical component) **and** have the **subjective intent** (mental component) to make their permanent home (intent to remain indefinitely). Each person can only have **one domicile** at a time.

Decoy tip: Both elements used to determine domicile (physical presence *and* a mental subjective intent) must be satisfied. In changing domicile, from one state to another state, a person retains their previous domicile until *both* elements are met. Look for facts of a person intending a permanent move who is not yet physically present in the new state; they retain their old domicile.

MBE tip: A U.S. citizen domiciled abroad is a U.S. citizen, but is not considered a citizen of any particular state for determining diversity citizenship if they intend to remain abroad.

ii. **Child's** (minor's) **domicile** is the same as their **parent's domicile** (e.g., a child away at boarding school has the domicile of their parent).

iii. **Legal representatives:** The citizenship of **minors, decedents, and incompetent** parties is determined by their **own citizenship,** *not* the citizenship of their legal representative (subject to the rule above for minors). 28 U.S.C. §1332(c)(2).

Example: An adult son (domiciled in state A) is killed in a car accident. His personal representative (one who can sue on behalf of an estate) is his mother (domiciled in state B.) If his mother brings a wrongful death action on behalf of her son against the driver of the other car (domiciled in state A) there will *not* be complete diversity of citizenship because the citizenship of the son at the moment of his death controls.

b. **Corporation:** A corporation may be the citizen of **more than one** state. 28 U.S.C. §1332 (c)(1). A corporation is a citizen of both:

i. **Every state of incorporation** (though often there is only one state); **and**

ii. The ***one*** **state** where the corporation has its **principal place of business** (PPB).

1. **Nerve center test:** The **principal place of business** is determined by the **"nerve center" test** and refers to the place where a corporation's **officers direct, control, and coordinate the corporation's activities.** Typically, this is where the corporation maintains its headquarters. This is not necessarily where the bulk of the physical operations are located.

> **Decoy tip:** Questions often include decoy duck facts identifying the state where most of the physical corporate operations occur, or where most employees work, or where they conduct a substantial amount of business. These facts are irrelevant to determining the citizenship of a corporation for *diversity purposes* and are included to provide decoy answers.

c. **Unincorporated associations** are citizens of **every state** in which ***each*** **partner/member is a citizen**, including limited and general partners. 28 U.S.C. §1332 (c). These are business entities that are not incorporated (e.g., partnerships, associations, LLCs, etc.). Diversity is defeated if *any* one partner shares citizenship with an opposing party.

d. **Alienage** (foreign) **citizenship included:** The "citizens of different states" requirement includes disputes **between a U.S. citizen *and* an alien** (foreign citizen), unless that alien is also a U.S. permanent resident sharing a domicile state with the opposing party. 28 U.S.C. §1332 (a)(2).

i. **Alienage restriction:** There is no federal jurisdiction for an action by an **alien against another alien**, unless there are also **U.S. citizens on both sides** of the controversy.

ii. **U.S. citizens domiciled abroad** may not use "alienage" jurisdiction for purposes of establishing diversity if they intend to remain abroad but are still citizens of the U.S. They are also not considered domiciled in any particular U.S. state if they intend to remain abroad.

e. **Class action:** Citizenship is determined by the citizenship of the **named class representative**(s).

2. **Time of** (lawsuit) **filing determines citizenship.** The citizenship of the parties at the time the cause of action arose is irrelevant, as is a change of citizenship after filing the suit.

a. **Except where the party "line-up" changes:** Where an actual **party is *replaced*** (e.g., because the wrong party was sued) through joinder or dismissal, subject matter jurisdiction will be **reassessed immediately** after the joinder or dismissal.

Example: There are two Ps; P1 from State A and P2 from State B. The D is from State A. If P1 voluntarily dismisses herself from the action, the citizenship will immediately be reassessed and now complete diversity will be met and the case can proceed in federal court.

> **MBE tip:** Diversity is determined at the time of filing, but if the parties change through joinder or dismissal, the claim is reassessed.

3. **One diverse claim is required:** Diversity is required as to one claim (the main claim), but it may be possible to add additional claims without complete diversity if "supplemental jurisdiction" extends. (See sec. I.B.4.)

4. **No collusive assignments allowed to create diversity:** A party may not assign their interest in a case improperly or collusively to create diversity to invoke subject matter jurisdiction. 28 U.S.C. §1359. Where one party has a claim, and they assign that claim to another and that assignee essentially functions as a debt collection agent, the assignment will be found to have been made collusively to invoke jurisdiction and is not allowed.

   Example: Foreign Company A and foreign Company B have a contract dispute. Since they are both foreign citizens, they cannot sue each other in federal court. Foreign Company A assigned the contract cause of action (debt collection suit) to a U.S. lawyer in exchange for $1 and the lawyer promised to pay 95% of the recovery back to foreign Company A. This is an improper assignment made collusively to obtain diversity jurisdiction and is not allowed.

b. **The amount in controversy must *exceed* $75,000,** not including attorney fees (unless recoverable by statute or contract), interest, and costs.

> **Decoy tip:** The amount in controversy must *exceed* $75,000 (e.g., $75,000.01); not *equal* $75,000.

1. **Aggregation:** Claims can be aggregated (add multiple claims together) to meet the $75,000 amount in controversy requirement if there is **one plaintiff and one defendant,** or where there are multiple **joint tortfeasor** defendants and the claims are **common and undivided.**

   a. **One plaintiff v. one defendant:** P **may aggregate** all claims **against a single D,** even if the claims are unrelated.

      Example: P (of State A) sues D (of State B) for $10,000 for breach of contract, $30,000 for negligence from a slip and fall accident, and $40,000 for fraud. These three claims by one plaintiff against one defendant may be aggregated to meet the amount in controversy requirement even though the claims are unrelated.

   b. **No aggregation of claims asserted by or against multiple parties** (multiple Ps and/or multiple Ds), **except:**

      i. **Joint claims/liability cases *only* may aggregate.** Joint claims or joint liability are those claims with a **common undivided interest,** such as with joint tortfeasors where any one of the defendants could be responsible for the *entire* loss. In joint claims/liability cases, several Ps may aggregate against one D, or one P may aggregate against several Ds.

         For the examples below, assume the parties are diverse:

         Example (aggregate—several Ps and one D): Four joint owners of a single piece of real property worth $100,000 file an action against a defendant seeking to quiet title. The plaintiffs may aggregate their claims because they share a common undivided interest in the piece of property.

Example (not aggregate—several Ps and one D): Four pedestrian plaintiffs suffer $25,000 each in damages when hit by a defendant in a single car accident. The plaintiffs cannot aggregate their claims against the defendant since each plaintiff has individual suits for injuries. Though the *cause* of their injuries is the same, and they coincidentally have claims in the same amount, their claims/interests are not common and undivided. Each plaintiff has their own individual unique claim (e.g., one pedestrian may have a broken leg and another a broken wrist).

Example (aggregate—one P several Ds): One plaintiff has a car accident with two other drivers and suffers $100,000 in damages. The plaintiff can aggregate claims against the two defendants since the plaintiff has *one total damages claim*, which is common and undivided because each defendant may be liable for the totality of the single claim.

Example (not aggregate—one P several Ds): One plaintiff bought a home in disrepair from Seller and contracted with Builder to remodel the home. Plaintiff sues Seller for fraud for non-disclosure of electrical problems ($50,000) and sues Builder for breach of contract ($50,000.) The plaintiff cannot aggregate the claims because these are two separate claims.

c. **Counterclaims do not aggregate:** The value of any counterclaim cannot be aggregated with the original claim to meet the exceeding $75,000 requirement.

Example: If a plaintiff has a breach of contract claim for $50,000 and the defendant has a counterclaim for $40,000, the claims cannot be aggregated to meet the $75,000 threshold and the amount in controversy will not be satisfied for diversity SMJ.

2. **"Legal certainty" test:** A plaintiff's **good faith** claim for the amount in controversy will be sufficient unless it appears to a **legal certainty at the time of filing** that the plaintiff cannot recover over $75,000.

Decoy tip: If the ultimate award in a case ends up being $75,000 or less, it has no effect on the legitimacy of jurisdiction (since it is assessed at the time of filing), but this often provides the basis for a decoy answer.

3. **Valuation of equitable relief claims:** Courts will evaluate equitable claims, such as an injunction, based on the **value of the harm** caused. Jurisdictions are split, but the court can assess this from the point of view of the plaintiff or defendant, and either test can be utilized to satisfy the amount in controversy requirement.

a. **Harm to plaintiff:** The act causing the need for injunctive relief must **harm** the plaintiff more than $75,000.

Example: Plaintiff (of State A) sues Neighbor (an absentee owner domiciled in State B) to enjoin him from building a home that will block Plaintiff's view, in violation of a covenant. If the blocked view will reduce Plaintiff's property value by $100,000, the amount in controversy is satisfied since that is the valuation of the harm.

b. **Cost to defendant:** The **cost** to the defendant to comply with the injunction is more than $75,000.

Example: Using the same example as above, assume Neighbor has already started building in violation of the covenant and it will cost him $80,000 to tear down the building to comply with an injunction, the amount in controversy is satisfied since that is the cost of compliance for the defendant.

3. **Federal courts cannot hear a claim without proper subject matter jurisdiction** because federal courts do not have the authority to hear claims outside their jurisdiction.

   a. **No waiver:** A party cannot waive subject matter jurisdiction. A case without subject matter jurisdiction will be dismissed. FRCP 12(h)(3).

   b. **Improper SMJ can be raised at any time in the proceedings,** even on appeal. If subject matter jurisdiction was lacking on a case that endured years of litigation and went to trial, the judgment will still be set aside.

   c. **Court *must* raise SMJ sua sponte** (on its own initiative) **if improper,** even if a party does not raise the issue.

   d. **Exceptions to federal subject matter jurisdiction:** Federal courts will not hear actions involving **family law or probate** matters, such as issuance of divorce, alimony or child support, or to probate an estate.

<u>MBE tip</u>: Always affirmatively look for SMJ. It is always required and may arise in questions about other matters (e.g., intervention, removal and remand, issue or claim preclusion, etc.), but the question may hide the ball by not mentioning the words "diversity" or "subject matter jurisdiction" at all to tip you off.

<u>Decoy tip</u>: A decoy answer may state an objection to subject matter jurisdiction was not timely. Since subject matter jurisdiction can be **raised at any time,** this will never be the correct answer.

4. **Supplemental jurisdiction** allows the extension of subject matter jurisdiction for an additional claim(s) that has been joined, that **does not itself invoke federal subject matter jurisdiction** (federal question or diversity), but **where the additional claim shares a common nucleus of operative fact** with a claim that *does* properly invoke federal subject matter jurisdiction, such that they should reasonably be tried together as part of the same **case or controversy**. This includes claims involving **joinder** or **intervention** of **additional parties.** 28 U.S.C. §1367(a).

   a. **Common nucleus of operative fact (CNOF):** This includes claims that arise from the **same transaction or occurrence** as the underlying (anchor) claim and extends even more broadly to claims with a "loose factual connection."

      1. **Federal question case:** Supplemental jurisdiction is allowed so long as there is a common nucleus of operative fact between the federal question claim and the state law claim.

      2. **Diversity only case limitation:** There are limits to supplemental jurisdiction in diversity cases. The **plaintiff** may not use supplemental jurisdiction to overcome a lack of diversity **(but the defendant can!)** U.S.C .28 §1367(b). **Supplemental jurisdiction is not allowed** over claims:

         a. By a ***plaintiff* <u>against</u> persons made parties** under:

            i. **FRCP 14** (third-party claims/impleader, meaning one who may be liable to a defending party in the original action);

            ii. **FRCP 19** (required joinder/indispensable party);

            iii. **FRCP 20** (permissive joinder); or

            iv. **FRCP 24** (intervention by absentee party), or

         b. By a proposed ***plaintiff* to be <u>joined</u>** under FRCP 19 (compulsory joinder/ **indispensable party**), and

   c. By a proposed **plaintiff absentee person** (not a party) **seeking to intervene** under FRCP 24 (intervention).

3. **Plaintiff only limitation:** The plaintiff-only limitations noted only apply to plaintiffs. A defendant or third-party defendant does not become a "plaintiff" for purposes of 28 USC §1367(b) by also asserting a claim.

b. Court has discretion to deny supplemental jurisdiction in certain situations. 28 U.S.C. §1367(c). The court may deny supplemental jurisdiction where:

1. **State law claim is novel** or complex;
2. **State law** claim is likely to **predominate** over the federal claim;
3. **Federal claim has been dismissed;** or
4. **Exceptional circumstances** (i.e., an ongoing state proceeding).

   Example: Where the original claim has been dismissed for failure to state a claim fairly early in the proceedings, the court would likely dismiss an additional claim that only had supplemental jurisdiction.

SUPPLEMENTAL JURISDICTION DECODED

Solving MBE questions with more than one claim: All claims must have SMJ. Either on its own merit (original SMJ) or through supplemental jurisdiction (jx).
To solve these questions, use the following approach:

STEP # 1: Does the additional claim have **original SMJ** (diversity or federal question)?

YES ——————▶ Additional claim has SMJ.

NO ——————▶ Go to step 2.

STEP # 2: Does the additional claim share a **common nucleus of operative fact** with the original claim?

YES ——————▶ Go to step 3.

NO ——————▶ Supplemental jx does NOT apply to the additional claim.

STEP # 3: Is the original claim based on **federal question or diversity** jurisdiction?

Federal Q ——————▶ Supplemental jx applies to the additional claim.

Diversity ——————▶ Go to step 4.

STEP # 4:

- Is the ***plaintiff*** the one **adding a claim <u>against</u>** a person made a party under third-party claim, adding an indispensable party, permissive joinder of Ps or Ds, or intervention; **<u>or</u>**
- Has a ***plaintiff*** **joined as an indispensable party** added a claim; **<u>or</u>**
- Is an absentee party trying to **intervene** as a ***plaintiff***?

YES ——————▶ Supplemental jx does NOT apply to the additional claim.

NO ——————▶ Supplemental jx DOES apply to the additional claim.

STEP # 5: The court still has discretion if the state claim is novel, the state law claim predominates, the federal claim has been dismissed, or exceptional circumstances exist.

Supplemental Jurisdiction Allowed	Supplemental Jurisdiction NOT allowed (Diversity only cases)
◆ Compulsory counterclaims ◆ Compulsory counterclaims w/ addl. parties ◆ Cross claims	◆ Permissive counterclaims (no CNOF)
◆ TPP v. TPD ◆ TPD v. TPP ◆ D impleads TPD	◆ Original P v. TPD ◆ Co-P and/or co-D joined by P to solve lack of *diversity* (FRCP 20) ◆ Original P v. intervening P or D ◆ P joined as indispensable P ◆ Intervening P v. original P or D
◆ Multiple Ps joined to jointly satisfy *amount in controversy* requirement (FRCP 20)	◆ Multiple Ps joined to jointly satisfy *amount in controversy* requirement (FRCP 20) but end up defeating diversity

<u>MBE tip</u>: These concepts are difficult to conceptualize. The best way to understand how they apply on the MBE is to do practice questions.

5. **Removal from state to federal court:** A **defendant may remove** a case to federal court that was originally filed in state court where the case could have properly been brought in federal court in the first place. 28 U.S.C. §1441. A removal is "of right," meaning the court simply accepts the case. (This process is similar to a case transfer, but transfers apply *within* the same court system, and since the movement here is from state court to federal court, the correct term is "remove.")

   a. **Only defendants are eligible to remove** cases, and **all defendants must agree** to the removal.

      Example: A plaintiff (from State A) sues a defendant (from State B) in State B court for federal copyright infringement in the amount of $100,000. The defendant may remove to federal court because this is a federal question claim (federal copyright) that should have originally been brought in federal court. (The same removal rule would apply if the claim were based in diversity jurisdiction.)

      1. **Plaintiffs may not remove** to federal court even if plaintiff's circumstances change or the defendant files a counterclaim in state court that the original plaintiff would prefer to be heard in federal court.

      2. **Waiver by litigating in state court:** A defendant who opts to litigate in state court (e.g., file a permissive counterclaim, or engage in discovery) *before* removal may waive the right to remove to federal court.

   b. **Time limit of 30 days:** The defendant must remove no later than 30 days after **service of the first "removable" document**, which means the document from which the grounds for removal become apparent. Typically this is service of process of the initial pleading, but not always. Each defendant gets their own 30-day window and previously served defendants can join. (See example below under the one-year time limit section.)

   c. **Limitations on removal for diversity cases *only*.** The limitations below only apply to cases where the basis for federal subject matter jurisdiction is **diversity** and do not apply if the basis is federal question jurisdiction.

      1. **In-state defendants excluded:** The defendant may not remove to federal court if **any defendant** is a citizen of the forum state in which the original state action is pending.

         Example: A plaintiff (from State A) sues two defendants (from State B and State C) in State C court for defamation for $100,000. Since the basis of federal subject matter jurisdiction is diversity and one defendant resides in forum State C, the case cannot be removed to federal court.

      2. **One-year time limit:** A defendant cannot remove a case more than one year after it was filed in state court. The time limit will not apply if the plaintiff has acted in bad faith. The general time limit for removal is 30 days from the first "removable" document, which is usually the service of process and typically happens much earlier than the one-year limit. However, sometimes the first "removable" document is filed later.

         Example: A plaintiff (from State A) sues two defendants (from State B and C) in State C court for defamation for $100,000. Since one defendant resides in forum State C, the case cannot be removed to federal court. If the plaintiff later voluntarily dismisses the State C defendant from the case, that *dismissal* becomes the "removable" document. The remaining State B defendant would have 30 days to remove, but only if that is not later than one year from the original filing in state court (because this is a diversity case and the one-year time limit applies.)

   d. **Removal venue—special rule:** The case must be removed to the federal district court embracing the place where such state action is pending (i.e. the federal district where the defendant should file the notice for removal). This venue rule (not the normal venue rule) controls for a removal action. Thus, venue will be proper in the federal district embracing the pending state action, even if venue would not have been proper there in the first place.

6. **Remand to state court:** When a defendant removes a case to federal court and the **removal is improper,** if the plaintiff's motion for remand is timely, the federal court will **remand the case back to state court.** Since the defendant does not need permission to remove a case, removals are sometimes improperly done and need to be remanded back to state court. U.S.C. §1447(c).

   a. **Time limit:** The plaintiff must move to remand the case within **30 days** of the removal, or remand is deemed waived. U.S.C. 28 §1446 (b).

      1. **Except: Right to remand for lack of SMJ is never waived,** so no time limit applies. If the federal court lacks subject matter jurisdiction over the case, a request for remand can be made at any time before final judgment. U.S.C. 28 §1447 (c).

   b. A remand order is generally **not appealable.**

   Example: Plaintiff sues Employer in state court for sex discrimination under both state and federal law. Plaintiff's attorney did not like the assigned judge, so Plaintiff's attorney promptly removed to federal court. Employer's attorney moves for remand. The remand will be granted since the removal was improper because only defendants are eligible to remove cases to federal court.

> **MBE tip:** Take your time solving a removal and remand question. The rules are specific and technical, and the concepts are intertwined since if the removal was improper, the plaintiff will move for remand back to state court.
>
> **MBE tip:** Removal and remand is also a mechanism used to test if there was subject matter jurisdiction in the first place since only a case that could have properly been brought in federal court is eligible for removal.

C. **Venue** concerns which **geographic district is the proper place** for a particular case to be heard. (In addition to proper venue, there still must be jurisdiction over the subject matter of the claim (SMJ) and personal jurisdiction (PJ) over the parties. 28 U.S.C. §1391(b).

> **MBE tip:** If you are curious, there are 94 federal districts. Many states have only one, but some states have two, three, and the most populous states have four. The districts have geographic names (e.g., Southern district of State A). If a question includes information about the **district courts,** it is likely testing venue.

1. **Proper venue: Venue is proper** where the **defendant resides** *or* the **claim arose:**

   a. The district where **any defendant resides,** *if* **<u>all</u> defendants are residents of the state** in which the district is located (also called residential venue); **<u>or</u>**

   b. The district in which a **substantial part of the events** or omissions giving rise to the **claim occurred** (also called transactional venue); **<u>or</u>**

   c. ***If no U.S. district satisfies a or b*** *above,* then in a judicial district in which **any defendant** is subject to the court's **personal jurisdiction** for the action (also called fallback venue).

2. **Residential venue:** Where any **defendant resides** if all defendants reside in the same state. 28 U.S.C. §1391(c)(1)(2)(d).

a. **Definition of "reside" for venue purposes:**

1. **Natural persons reside** in the district of their **domicile.** Aliens who are lawful permanent residents are treated the same as citizens for venue.

2. **Corporations, business entities, and unincorporated associations:**

   a. **Plaintiffs** are deemed to reside **only in the judicial district** in which they maintain their **principal place of business** (PPB).

   b. **Defendants** are deemed to reside in **any judicial district** in which they are **subject to personal jurisdiction** if the district were a state, meaning all districts in which they would be subject to personal jurisdiction in the suit at hand. If no such district exists, the corporation will be deemed to reside in the district in which the corporation has the most significant contacts.

> MBE tip: A corporation's "residence" for venue purposes is not defined the same way as a corporation's "citizenship" for diversity purposes. The venue definition is slightly broader since it includes any district satisfying the personal jurisdiction minimum contacts standard and is not limited to only the principal place of business and incorporation state(s).

3. **Transactional venue:** Where the **claim occurred** (e.g., where the injury occurred; contract was entered into; defective product purchased, etc.) or where a **substantial part of the property** at issue is located. 28 U.S.C. §1391(b)(2).

   a. **Advertising may be sufficient:** Targeting a district with advertising and marketing may constitute a substantial part of events giving rise to the claim for that product.

   b. **More than one district may qualify** as a location where a substantial part of the events or omissions that gave rise to the claim occurred.

   Example: A manufacturer designs a defective product in District A, then ships and sells that product in District B. Both District A and B are proper venue locations because a substantial part of events occurred in both districts.

4. **Fallback venue:** Applies ***only*** if there is **no district** where all defendants reside, or where a substantial part of the claim arose. Then jurisdiction is proper in a district in which **any defendant** is subject to the court's **personal jurisdiction.** 28 U.S.C. §1391(b)(3). This will most often come up when no substantial amount of the claim arose in the U.S. and no district satisfies residential venue.

5. **Federal courts *may* hear a case without proper venue.**

   a. **Waiver if not raised timely:** A **venue objection must be raised in the *first* Rule 12 response** to the complaint (e.g., a pre-answer motion or answer) or the defense is **waived**. The parties may agree to waive improper venue (unlike subject matter jurisdiction, which is not waivable).

   b. **Courts may raise improper venue *sua sponte*** (on its own motion) but have no duty to do so, (unlike subject matter jurisdiction where the court must raise improper subject matter jurisdiction.)

6. **Transfer of venue** allows a case to be transferred from one venue to another within the same system (federal court). The case goes from the transferor district to the transferee district.

   a. **Transferor district:** Venue may be transferred when **another venue may be more convenient**, though the **original venue is technically proper, or when the original venue was improper.**

1. **Proper original venue—convenience of parties and witnesses:** Where a case was originally brought in a venue that is proper, venue may still be transferred to another federal district for the **convenience of the parties/witnesses**, in the interests of justice. The case can transfer to a venue where the case **"might have been brought"** (meaning where it could have been originally brought with proper SMJ, PJ, and venue) *or* where **all parties consent**. 28 U.S.C. §1404(a). The court has **enormous discretion** to determine if a transfer of venue is warranted and will consider the following factors to determine "the center of gravity" for the case in the **interests of justice**, including:

   a. **Public factors** include the **local interest** in the controversy and the extent to which there is an interest in having trial in a forum familiar with the **law that applies in the case.**

   b. **Private factors** include the convenience of the parties, location of witnesses and evidence, access to relevant documents and things, etc.

   Example: A small airplane crashes in State A, killing all aboard. The passengers and pilot were citizens of State B. The airline that owned and operated the plane is incorporated and has its principal place of business in State C. The estates of the pilot and passengers file a wrongful death action against the airline in federal court in State A. If the airline wants to prevent litigating in State A federal court, they should move for a transfer of venue to federal court in State C because though venue in State A is proper (claim occurred there) the case "might have been brought" in State C (case has SMJ and venue and airline is subject to PJ in State C) and the convenience of the parties and witnesses may be better served in State C, though the judge has wide discretion to grant the transfer or not.

2. **Improper original venue:** Where a case is originally filed in an improper venue, the court **may transfer** to a venue in which the case could have been originally brought, **or dismiss** the case. 28 U.S.C. §1406(a). Transfer of venue is preferred over dismissal.

b. **Transferee district requirements:** (Applies whether the original venue was proper or improper.)

   1. The transferee district must be a place where the case **could have *originally* been brought**, meaning the transferee district must have **proper venue**, **subject matter jurisdiction**, and **personal jurisdiction over the defendant**; *or*

   2. To any district to which **all parties consent.**

      a. **Venue forum selection clauses deemed consent:** Valid forum selection clauses in contracts are **binding** and will be deemed a district to which all parties have **consented**, thus parties waive the right to challenge the selected forum based on inconvenience.

      Example: A bakery (of State A) had a dispute with their flour supplier (of State B). The bakery sued the supplier in federal court in State A for breach of contract for $100,000. The contract contained a clause designating State B courts as the venue for contract disputes. The precedent in state court A is that forum selection clauses are against public policy, though they are enforceable under U.S. Supreme Court precedent. The supplier moves to transfer the case to federal court in State B citing the forum-selection clause and the convenience of the parties. The court will likely grant this motion because the court will find the forum-selection clause is binding and pre-determines the convenience of the parties. (State A's precedent on forum selection clauses is a decoy because 28 U.S.C. §1404(a) applies and the U.S. Supreme Court has interpreted it to apply to forum selection clauses.

c. **Choice of law requirements:** In diversity cases, the transferee federal district court must apply the "choice of law" rules **of the original transferor federal district court, except** in cases where the original venue was **improper** or there was a valid forum selection clause.

7. **Forum non conveniens:** When **another court is substantially more appropriate** for the litigation than the current court (e.g., a court in another judicial system, such as another state or country), a court may **dismiss** or **stay** the case to compel the plaintiff to bring the case in the more appropriate forum. (Stay means to hold the case in abeyance without litigation taking place.) The moving party has a heavy burden of proof. In making the decision, the court will consider the following factors (similar to the factors used to determine venue transfer) to determine "the center of gravity" for the case including:

   a. **Public factors** include the **local interest** in the controversy and the extent there is an interest in having trial in a forum familiar with the **law that applies in the case.**

   b. **Private factors** include the convenience of the parties, location of witnesses and evidence, access to relevant documents and things, etc.

   c. **The other forum is available and adequate.** While many foreign courts use different standards than U.S. courts (e.g., tort recovery rules that disallow pain and suffering recovery or the right to a jury trial), they will be found **adequate, unless they provide essentially no remedy** at all.

   Example: A French company manufactures skis and has all operations in France. The company purchases resin from a State A corporation, but they fail to deliver the resin. The contract provides that French law will govern any dispute between the parties. If the French company sues in State A, the resin manufacturer can move to dismiss under forum non conveniens, and the motion will likely be granted since France is a more appropriate forum given the location of the witnesses, evidence, and the contract provision.

Decoy tip: Forum non conveniens or motion to dismiss is a frequent decoy answer to a question about venue. Venue questions usually apply to motions to *transfer*, not dismiss.

PROPERLY FILED CASE DECODED				
PJ	The "WHO"	**Person's Domicile**	**Corporations**	**Partnership/Assoc.**
		◆ Physical presence ◆ Subjective intent to remain	Must meet: ◆ Specific jurisdiction (jx) or ◆ General jx (minimum contacts std.)	
SMJ	The "WHAT"	◆ Physical presence ◆ Subjective intent to remain	**Domicile of:** ◆ Inc. (every state) & ◆ PPB	**Domicile of:** ◆ *Every* partner/ member
Venue	The "WHICH" Fed. Dist. Ct.	◆ Physical presence ◆ Subjective intent to remain (**Reside** = domicile)	◆ Plaintiffs: **Reside** only in the PPB judicial district ◆ Defendants: **Reside** in any district in which they are subject to PJ	

D. **Notice:** A defendant must be **properly notified** of a pending action by a reasonable method and must be given an opportunity to be heard. FRCP 4.

> **MBE tip:** See the Civil Procedure cheat sheet for "Dates Decoded," which includes all important deadlines in federal litigation.

1. **Service of process** means to provide a defendant with notice of a pending action by **delivery to defendant** of a **summons** (formal court notice of suit and time for response) and a copy of the **complaint.** Process must be served within **90 days** of the filing of the case.

   a. **Summons:** The court issues the **summons** and it informs a defendant they have been **sued,** advises they must **respond within 21 days** and provides information about the **court and the case.**

      1. **Waiver of service process:** Response time may be extended to 60 days or 90 days with a waiver of personal service. See sec. I.D.4.

      2. **Service on U.S. agency or employee:** Response must be filed within 60 days.

   b. **Complaint:** The complaint is the **pleading filed by the plaintiff** that recites their claims against the defendant.

   c. **Subsequent filings** (e.g., discovery requests, motions, etc.) may be mailed to a party, or if a party agrees subsequent filings can be emailed, rather than formally served in person and no summons is required. FRCP 5 (b)(2).

2. **Method of service:** Service or process can be made by anyone who is at least **18 years old** and **not a party** to the action. The method used must be reasonably calculated under the circumstances to provide notice.

> **Decoy tip:** A party may not personally serve the opposing party.

   a. **Following state law** for service of process in the **state in which the federal action is pending** or the **state in which service takes place** is allowed. FRCP 4 (e)(1). Following state service of process laws is allowed even when the federal suit is based on a federal question.

      1. **Out of state service:** If the **forum state law permits** out of state service (e.g., through a long-arm statute) it is allowed.

      2. **Service by mail is frequently allowed by state law,** though it is not **typically permitted by the federal rules.**

   b. **Service on a person:** There are three **formal "federally authorized" methods** of service. FRCP 4(e)(2). Service may also be made in accordance with the rules of the ***state law* of the forum state** (see immediately above) and a defendant may **waive formal service** (and accept mail service.) See waiver of service in sec. I.D.4 below.

      1. **Personal service** is always adequate and occurs when the notice is personally **hand delivered** to a defendant.

         a. **Exception immunity for a civil case appearance:** Personal in-state service cannot be executed where one is **in the state solely** as a party or witness **in another civil case.**

      2. **Defendant's abode:** Service may be **left at defendant's dwelling or usual abode** and served (in person) upon someone of **suitable age and discretion who *resides* there.**

a. **Usual abode** is the dwelling one is **living in at the time of service.** For someone with multiple homes, it is the home they currently reside in. This does not include someone's workplace.

b. A person of **suitable age and discretion who *resides* there** can potentially include a responsible teenager.

> **Decoy tip:** Watch out for service questions where the notice is improperly left at the defendant's *workplace* or with a neighbor or babysitter who does not *reside* at the defendant's abode.

3. **Service to an authorized agent:** This is permissible where the defendant has *authorized* an agent to accept service of process on their behalf. This provision is interpreted narrowly and a general mandate that an assistant or colleague can act on one's behalf is insufficient absent explicit permission that the assistant or colleague may accept service of process.

Example (authorized): An authorized agent is a registered agent for a corporation; a managing agent; an agent appointed by contract, etc.

Example (not authorized): A summons and complaint were served on a defendant by handing the documents to the defendant's administrative assistant at the defendant's office. This is insufficient service of process because it was neither served at defendant's home (abode) or on an *authorized* agent.

c. Service on a **corporation, partnership, or association:** Service can be effected by following state law or by delivering the summons and complaint to an **officer**, a **managing or general agent**, or **another agent** authorized by appointment or by law **and** also **mailing a copy to each defendant.** FRCP 4(h).

> **Decoy tip:** Don't assume that any person working at a corporation, or an officer's administrative assistant is an authorized agent for the purpose of accepting service of process unless the facts make that clear.
>
> **Decoy tip:** Service by email is not allowed.

d. **Service in foreign countries:** Unless federal law provides otherwise, service can be by any internationally agreed means, or absent an agreement, by an internationally agreed upon means that is **reasonably calculated to give notice** (e.g., the method proscribed by the Hague convention).

3. **Timing:** A defendant, not in a foreign country, must be served within **90 days** after plaintiff files the complaint unless the plaintiff can show good cause for the delay. Failure to serve timely will result in a dismissal without prejudice (without any loss of rights or privileges).

4. **Waiver of (formal) service:** The **Federal Rules prefer that a defendant waive the right to formal service** of process and **accept service by mail** since a defendant has a duty to avoid unnecessary expenses.

a. **Plaintiff requests a waiver of formal service:** Plaintiff **serves** defendant **by first-class mail** (or other reliable means such as overnight/certified type delivery) along with a **request** that **defendant waive formal service of process.** The plaintiff serves the summons and complaint, two copies of the request for waiver of service, and a prepaid envelope. **If** the defendant opts to **sign and return** the waiver, the requirement of **formal service is waived.** Once the plaintiff **files the returned waiver,** the summons and complaint is deemed **served.** FRCP 4(d).

b. **Failure to waive: If defendant does not return the waiver,** thus failing to waive service, the **plaintiff must still formally serve the defendant** through an appropriate method (following state law or one of the federally authorized methods).

   1. **Failure to waive without a good faith reason:** The **defendant is liable for expenses** incurred in making the service of process and any reasonable expenses, including attorney fees, or any motion required to collect the service expenses. This provision creates a strong incentive for a defendant to waive formal service of process.

c. **Time to return the waiver:** A defendant must be allowed a reasonable time of at least **30 days** (60 days if foreign country) to return the waiver.

d. **Time to file answer after waiver:** After returning a waiver, a defendant has **60 days** from the time the request was sent to answer the complaint as opposed to the original 21 days (**90 days** permitted if in a foreign country).

e. **Defendant can still object** to venue or jurisdiction, even if they waive formal service of process.

5. **Waiver—service of process objection is waived if not raised timely:** A service of process objection **must be raised in the *first* Rule 12 response** to the complaint (e.g., a pre-answer motion or answer) or the defense is **waived.**

6. **Notice requirements for interlocutory injunctions:** An interlocutory injunction is an equitable remedy where the court orders one to perform an act (affirmative or mandatory injunction), or refrain from performing an act (negative injunction), during the pendency of a cause of action. The purpose is to maintain the status quo while the suit is pending.

   a. **Temporary restraining order (TRO)** is designed to **preserve the status quo** and **avoid irreparable injury** that would occur during the waiting time for a preliminary injunction hearing on the same matter.

      1. **Notice is required** (though it may be less formal and be done orally), **but a TRO can be obtained ex parte** (without notice) at the judge's *discretion* in exceptional circumstances, FRCP 65(b), such as where the moving party does the following:

         a. **Immediate irreparable injury:** Identifies specific facts demonstrating the immediate and irreparable injury that will result before the opposing party can be heard.

         b. **Notice efforts and reasons why notice not required:** Moving party's attorney certifies the efforts made to give notice to the opposing party that have been unsuccessful, and the reasons why notice should not be required (e.g., when notice would result in the very harm one is trying to avoid, such as the opposing party concealing the property in dispute).

         c. **Security:** Provides security (bond) for potential damages in the event the court finds the TRO was issued in error.

      2. **Short duration:** A TRO is typically granted for 14 days, unless the court allows an extension for 14 more days.

   b. **Preliminary injunction** is designed to **preserve the status quo** and **avoid irreparable harm** that would occur pending a full trial on the merits. FRCP 65(a).

1. **Notice to the opposing party is required,** and the opposing party must be given an opportunity to be heard.
2. **Requirements** (the elements listed here are discussed in detail in the contracts chapter):
   a. **Irreparable harm** during the waiting time pending resolution at trial.
   b. **Likelihood of success on the merits.**
   c. **Inadequate legal remedy.**
   d. **Balancing of hardships** favors moving party.
   e. **No valid defenses** available to defendant such as laches, unclean hands, sale to a bona fide purchaser, etc.

FEDERAL COURT SERVICE OF PROCESS

Service may be effectuated in accordance with the federally authorized method **or** by any method permitted in the state in which the federal action is pending or the state in which service takes place **or** formal service may be waived.

Federally Authorized Method	OR	Forum State Law Method
Individual ◆ Personal service ◆ Left at D's abode w/ one of suitable age & discretion who resides there ◆ Authorized Agent Corporation/Business ◆ Officer ◆ Agent: Managing/general/another Waiver (and accepting mail service) is encouraged		◆ Service by mail is often allowed ◆ Service out of state is often allowed ◆ Will vary by state

MBE tip: Should a case go to judgment, but there was never proper service of process, the judgment is void.

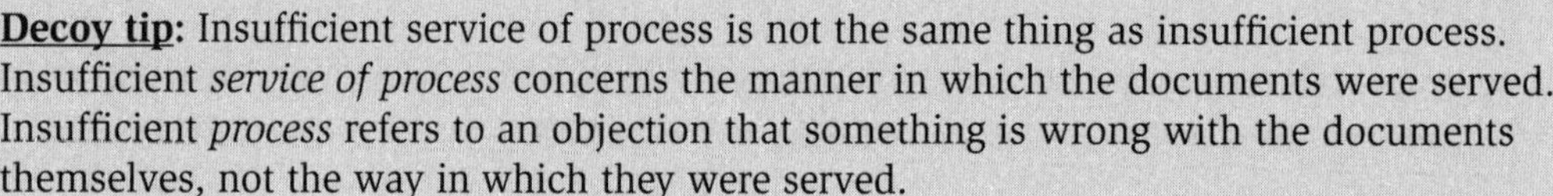

Decoy tip: Insufficient service of process is not the same thing as insufficient process. Insufficient *service of process* concerns the manner in which the documents were served. Insufficient *process* refers to an objection that something is wrong with the documents themselves, not the way in which they were served.

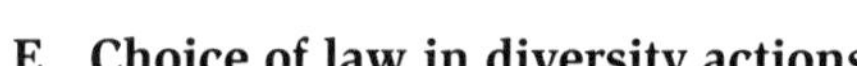

E. Choice of law in diversity actions

1. **State law in federal court** (*Erie* doctrine): A federal court sitting in **diversity** must apply **substantive law of the state** in which it is sitting **and federal procedural law.**
   a. **Federal statutes and rules on point are applied** (e.g., a FRCP, or federal statute).

      Examples (federal procedural law): Proper court issues (i.e., venue), pleadings issues, service of process, right to a jury trial, assessment of attorney fees, equitable versus legal issues, etc.

   b. **If no federal law is on point,** determine if the law is **procedural or substantive.** Where a rule seems to reflect a strong state policy interest, the law is substantive.

1. **Statutes of limitations** are substantive law. The federal court will follow the statute of limitations rule from the state in which the federal court sits.

2. **Conflicts/choice of laws rules** are substantive law. Where several states are involved in the controversy, the federal court will follow the conflicts of law rules from the state in which the federal court sits.

Example: Motorcyclist (of State A) and Driver (of State B) had an accident in State B that injured Motorcyclist. Motorcyclist filed a federal diversity case for negligence in State B for $100,000. The federal court in State B should determine which state's negligence law a state court in State B would apply and then apply that law to the case.

Examples (state substantive law): Statute of limitations, choice of law rules, notice of claim requirements, elements of a claim or defense, burden of proof, remittitur and additur rules (to grant a new trial for verdicts that are too high or too low), issue and claim preclusion rules, etc.

3. **Other rules:** If it is unclear whether a law is substantive or procedural, then the court will employ one of the following tests: [Since the law is unclear here, it is unlikely to be MBE tested.]

a. **Outcome determinative test:** A law is substantive if it substantially affects the outcome of the case.

b. **Balance of interests:** The federal interest in having the federal law applied is balanced against the state interest in having the state law applied. If the state has a greater interest, the law is substantive.

c. **Forum shopping avoidance:** If not applying the state law would lead litigants to flock to federal court, the law is substantive.

2. **Federal common law** (case law) applies when a federal court relies on federal case precedent. The courts create federal substantive (common) law through case precedent when interpreting statutes, or the U.S. Constitution, or filling in gaps in regulatory schemes.

II. PRETRIAL PROCEDURES

A. **Rule 11 requirements: Rule 11** requires all attorneys or a party representing themself to **sign** all pleadings, written motions and papers, certifying that: (FRCP 11.)

1. The paper is filed in **good faith** with no improper purpose,

2. The legal contentions are **warranted by existing law,** or by a nonfrivolous argument for modifying or reversing existing law, or establishing new law,

3. The **factual contentions have evidentiary support,** or will after a **reasonable opportunity to investigate,**

4. The **denials of factual contentions** are warranted on the evidence or are **reasonably based** on belief or a lack of information.

5. **Sanctions** (used as deterrence) may be imposed on any attorney, firm or party, for violations of this rule, even on the court's own initiative, but subject to a:

a. **21-day safe harbor:** A party filing for sanctions **must first serve** the motions for sanctions on the other party, who then has **21 days** to withdraw or correct the pleadings giving rise to the sanctions (cannot file with court until after this period). FRCP 11(c).

6. **Exception:** Rule 11 **does not apply to** discovery documents.

B. **Pleadings** are the documents that set forth the claims and defenses to a case. FRCP 7.

1. **Purpose of pleadings:** The purpose of pleadings is for the parties to communicate their claims and defenses with the opposing party and the court.

   a. **Notice pleading** is used to provide the opposing party with reasonable notice of the nature and scope of the claims being asserted and **facts showing a plausible claim.** This standard applies to all pleadings.

2. **Types of pleadings**

   a. **Complaint:** A complaint is used by a plaintiff to state claims and must include: (FRCP 8.)

      1. **Identification of the parties.**

      2. A statement of proper **subject matter jurisdiction.**

      3. A statement of the claim showing the **factual basis on which plaintiff is entitled to relief.**

         a. **Notice pleading** typically only requires stating **enough facts to support a plausible claim.**

         b. **Exceptions — must plead specific facts for the following:** (FRCP 9.)

            i. Capacity or authority to sue, *if* necessary to show jurisdiction,

            ii. Fraud or mistake,

            iii. Conditions precedent, *if* denying the condition occurred,

            iv. Time and place, when testing the sufficiency of a pleading, and

            v. Special damages.

      4. A **demand for judgment.**

      5. The **signature** of the plaintiff, or their attorney.

   b. **Response: Rule 12** requires a defendant to **respond** by either filing **(1) a pre-answer motion or (2) an answer** within **21 days** after service of process (or within 60 or 90 days if service is waived). See sec. I.D.4. above. FRCP 12.

      1. **Pre-answer motions.** If a pre-answer motion is denied, the party has **14 days** to file an answer to the complaint.

         a. **Motion for a more definite statement** is used where the complaint is so vague or ambiguous that the defendant cannot reasonably prepare a response. FRCP 12(e).

         b. **Motion to strike** aimed at pleadings containing an insufficient defense, scandalous, immaterial, or redundant issues (e.g., demand for a jury trial when there is no right to one). The court may act on its own or by a motion made by a party. FRCP 12(f).

         Example: P, a purchaser, filed a breach of contract action against D, a seller. D answered the complaint and included as a separate defense an allegation that P had brought and lost a similar claim against a different seller earlier to show a pattern of frivolous lawsuits. P believes the earlier suit was completely different and irrelevant. If asked what P's "best" response is, P should move to strike the separate defense as irrelevant since the prior suit was completely different (note this response would be better than denying the separate defense, moving for sanctions, or moving to amend the complaint to explain the differences because the motion to strike immediately eliminates the issue unlike the other options).

> **MBE tip:** If asked about a party's "best response" to avoid an issue, the best answer is often a motion to strike or a motion to dismiss because this eliminates the issue as opposed to filing an answer or amending a complaint, etc. which does not eliminate the problem.

c. **Motion to dismiss** stating the reasons for the dismissal and including supporting evidence. See Rule 12(b) defenses below for specific motions that can be raised in a pre-answer. A motion to dismiss does not seek to resolve factual allegations but instead seeks to determine, whether, if taken as true, the factual allegations are sufficient to state a claim for relief as a matter of law.

 2. **Rule 12(b) defenses** (these can be raised by filing a pre-answer motion or in the answer).

a. **Must raise in first response or are deemed waived:** (FRCP 12(h)(1).)

i. **Lack of personal jurisdiction.**

ii. **Improper venue:**

a. **By court order:** Even *if* waived, the court still may order a change in venue, *if* justice so requires, *if* the original venue was improper.

iii. **Insufficient process** (something is wrong with the papers).

iv. **Insufficient service of process** (papers not served properly).

b. **May raise *after* first response:** (FRCP 12(h)(2).)

i. **Lack of subject matter jurisdiction:** This can be raised **any time before all appeals are exhausted.**

ii. **Failure to state a claim** on which relief can be granted (including the failure to assert facts that establish that claim): This can be raised **anytime until the trial is concluded.** Courts resolve all doubts and reasonable inferences in the pleader's favor. If the court considers materials **outside the pleadings,** it must treat the motion as a **summary judgment motion.**

iii. **Failure to join an indispensable party:** This can be raised **anytime until the trial is concluded.**

 3. **Answer:** An answer is the defendant's response to the complaint. A defendant must respond within **21 days** after service of process (or if service is waived within 60 days in the U.S. or 90 days for foreign countries). This assumes the defendant did not file a pre-answer motion. If a defendant's **pre-answer motion is denied then their answer must be served within 14 days** after notice of the court's action. FRCP 4.

a. **The defendant must respond to the allegations** by denying them, admitting them, or stating they lack sufficient information to do either (failure to deny can operate as an admission). FRCP 8.

b. **The defendant must also assert any affirmative defenses** in the answer or they will be deemed waived, except: (FRCP 12.)

i. **Lack of subject matter jurisdiction.**

ii. **Failure to state a claim** upon which relief can be granted.

iii. **Failure to join an indispensable party.**

c. **The defendant must also raise any compulsory counterclaims** in the answer (or an amended answer) or they will be deemed waived. FRCP 13.

Example: P, a pedestrian who was domiciled in State A, was crossing the street in State B when he was hit by a car driven by D, a citizen of a foreign country. Both P and D suffered injuries. P filed a negligence claim against D in State B seeking $100,000. D believes P was crossing the street illegally. State B is a contributory negligence state. If D seeks advice from an attorney, the attorney's "best" advice would be to have D file an answer raising an **affirmative defense** of contributory negligence AND assert a **counterclaim** for negligence (this would be a better answer than suggesting D move for judgment on the pleadings, or file a motion to dismiss based on personal or subject matter jurisdiction, which were the other options).

Decoy tip: Answers to questions that are testing pleadings often include decoy facts that go to jurisdiction. The wrong answer choices will focus on these decoy facts and raise the wrong issues.

d. **Failure to answer:** If defendant fails to answer a complaint, plaintiff can **request the court clerk to enter a default** and then the court can enter a default judgment after plaintiff's request. FRCP 55.

c. Amended pleadings:

1. **As a matter of course:** A party has a **right to amend** its pleading **once** as a matter of course within **21 days** after serving it, or

2. **Responsive pleading or pre-answer motion:** If the pleading requires a response, a party can **amend once** within **21 days** of service of the responsive pleading, or the pre-answer motion, whichever is *earlier*. FRCP 15.

- **Pleadings:** Documents that set forth claims and defenses to a case (e.g., the complaint). Some pleadings are responsive pleadings.
- **Responsive pleadings:** When the answers respond to the factual assertions of an opponent's prior pleading (e.g., denying factual assertions, an answer to a complaint, etc.).

Example (responsive pleading): P files a complaint (pleading that requires a response) against D for negligence. D's answer (a responsive pleading) responds to factual allegations asserted by P by denying them. This denial is an example of a responsive pleading because it responds to P's allegations. However, if D did not respond to the allegations and filed a motion to dismiss based on other grounds (i.e., lack or jurisdiction), then it would not be a "responsive" pleading.

Example (amendment deadlines): P files a complaint against D on June 1. P as a matter of course can amend their complaint for 21 days (up to June 22). A complaint is a pleading that requires a response, so D responds on June 20 with an answer denying the allegations in P's complaint. D has 21 days to amend their answer (which is their responsive pleading) and for P, the clock essentially resets and P now has 21 days to amend their complaint since they had not yet amended (both have until July 11). In contrast, if D never filed an answer, but instead filed a motion to dismiss for lack of subject matter jurisdiction on June 10, then P would only have 21 days from June 10 (so up until July 1) to amend their complaint.

3. **Amendment by consent/leave of court:** To amend after the time allotted or more than once, a party may amend with **written consent** of opposing party, or must seek **leave of court** to amend, which the court will freely grant **if justice so requires.**

   Example: A State A citizen filed an antitrust action against a State B corporation in federal district court. 14 days after filing the complaint and before any response, the citizen sought to amend their complaint to add a breach of contract claim. The claim was unrelated to the antitrust claim. The citizen may amend their complaint without leave of the court because it is within 21 days (the fact that the new claim is unrelated to the first claim is irrelevant and a decoy).

4. **Relation back doctrine:** Amends back to the **date of the original filing.** FRCP 15(c).

   a. **Amended claims "relate back"** (after the statute of limitations has run) if they concern the same **conduct, transaction, or occurrence** as the original pleading.

   > **MBE tip:** If the statute of limitations is mentioned in the question, consider if the relation back doctrine is at issue.

   b. **Amended defendants** (new parties) **"relate back"** if:

   i. They concern the **same conduct, transaction, or occurrence** as the original complaint;

   ii. The **new party** had **notice** (see sec. I.D. above) of the original action within **90 days** of its filing so it will **not be prejudiced** in defending on the merits; and

   iii. The new party also **knew,** or should have known that, **but for a mistake,** they **would have been named** as a defendant in the original complaint.

d. Pleadings limitation under common law: Election of remedies doctrine was a pleading limitation at common law that prevented a plaintiff from presenting alternative or inconsistent claims when the plaintiff had a choice among inconsistent remedies. The federal rules reject this doctrine.

> **Decoy tip:** The pleadings limitation doctrine (election of remedies) is a frequent decoy answer choice, since the federal rules have rejected this doctrine.

e. Computing time: When **calculating the number of days** a party has to file a pleading, respond, etc. that has a time limit (i.e., 21 days), a party should:

1. **Exclude the day of the event that triggers** the period;
2. **Count every day,** including ***intermediate*** **weekends and legal holidays;**
3. **Include the *last* day** of the period, ***but if*** the last day is on a Saturday, Sunday or legal holiday, the period **continues to run until the end of the next day** that is not a Saturday, Sunday, or legal holiday.

PLEADINGS CHEAT SHEET		
Type	**Purpose for pleading**	**Timing**
Complaint	Raise claims against D	Marks the beginning of the case
Pre-answer Motion for a more definite statement.	Complaint too vague or ambiguous	◆ 21 days after service ◆ If service waived: ◇ 60 days (U.S.) ◇ 90 days (foreign)
Pre-answer Motion to strike	◆ Insufficient defense ◆ Scandalous ◆ Immaterial ◆ Redundant issues, etc.	◆ Same as above (21/60/90 days)
Pre-answer Motion to dismiss	◆ No personal jx* ◆ Improper venue* ◆ Insufficient process* ◆ Insufficient service of process* ◆ No SMJ** ◆ Failure to state a claim*** ◆ Failure to join an indispensable party***	◆ Same as above (21/60/90 days) *Must raise in 1st response or deemed waived **Raise before all appeals exhausted ***Raise any time until trial concluded
Answer	◆ D's response to the complaint IF D did not file a pre-answer motion or their motion was denied ◇ Must raise affirmative defenses ◇ Must raise compulsory counterclaim ◆ All of the above defenses in motion to dismiss can also be raised in an answer	◆ Same as above (21/60/90 days) ◆ If D's pre-answer motion is denied, D must file an answer within 14 days ◆ If D fails to answer, P can request clerk to enter default & court can enter default judgment at P's request
Amended	◆ May amend once (matter of course), or ◆ May amend once after responsive pleading or pre-answer motion (earliest) ◆ Can amend again with written consent of opposing party or leave of court	◆ 21 days after serving pleading, or ◆ 21 days after receiving responsive pleading, or pre-answer motion, whichever is earlier

C. Joinder of parties and claims

1. Joinder of parties:

a. **Permissive joinder:** Plaintiffs and/or defendants may be joined if the claims arise from the **same transaction or occurrence (T/O)** and raise at least **one common question.** FRCP 20.

1. **SMJ required:** There still must be **subject matter jurisdiction** if the original claim is based solely on diversity jurisdiction (joinder cannot destroy diversity).

b. **Required joinder:** Joinder of a **necessary party.** FRCP 19.

1. **Definition:** A party is a **necessary party if:**

a. The court **cannot provide complete relief** without the necessary party; or *b.* The absent party's **interest will be harmed** if they are not joined; or

c. The existing party would be **subject to multiple inconsistent obligations.**

2. **Join: A necessary party must be joined if:**

a. The court has **personal jurisdiction** over them;

b. Joining them **doesn't destroy diversity,** where diversity is the basis of federal subject matter jurisdiction; and

c. **Venue** is proper.

3. **Unable to join:** If a **necessary party** cannot be joined because of one of the reasons noted above, the court will consider if there is an **alternative forum** available, assess the **likelihood and extent of prejudice to the parties and the absent party,** and whether the court can **shape relief** to avoid the prejudice. The **court may either:**

a. **Dismiss** the case because the party is **indispensable;** or

b. **Proceed** with the case without the **necessary party.**

c. Indispensable party/joinder not feasible: A party is indispensable *if* they are **necessary** and they are **unable to be joined.** When a party is indispensable the **case must be dismissed. The court will consider:**

1. Extent of **prejudice to existing/absentee party,**

2. Extent to which **prejudice can be lessened or avoided,**

3. **Adequacy of judgment** in person's absence, and

4. Adequacy of **plaintiff's remedy if dismissed.**

> **MBE tip**: The term indispensable does not appear in Rule 19 (the rule uses the term "required joinder"), but cases and lawyers use the term regularly and Rule 12(b)(7) is often referred to as a motion to dismiss for failure to join an indispensable party.
>
> **MBE tip**: While the terms "necessary" and "indispensable" are often used interchangeably and can be confusing (even in case law), necessary indicates a party that should be joined and when that party cannot be joined and the case must be dismissed, that party is labeled indispensable.

 **d. Impleader** is a mechanism a **defending party** can use to **add a third-party defendant** in order to seek indemnity, subrogation, or contribution. A defendant may serve a third-party claim only on a nonparty **who is or may be liable to them for all or part of the claim against them.** FRCP 14.

1. **Permissive:** Impleader is permissive and not required.

2. **Supplemental jurisdiction will apply** because the claim will meet the "common nucleus of operative fact" requirement and no independent basis for subject matter jurisdiction is required.

3. **Venue:** Venue **need not be proper** for the third-party defendant.

Example: A consumer from State A filed a $100,000 products liability action against manufacturer, M, located in State B. In its answer, M asserted a third-party complaint against the product designer, also in State B. M believes the consumer sued the wrong defendant and claimed that the product designer was solely responsible for the flaw. The designer is aware that M did not follow all of the designer's specifications when making the product. In moving to dismiss the third-party complaint, the designer should argue that M's complaint failed to state a proper third-party claim (this is because M thought the consumer sued the wrong D, which does not meet the definition of a third-party claim that the third-party is liable for all or part of the claim against the third-party plaintiff; the basis for the claim must be derivative liability not that the consumer sued the wrong defendant). Note: the fact about M not following the proper specifications would not be grounds to dismiss because it is a factual allegation which a motion to dismiss does not resolve.

Decoy tip: Decoy answers might focus on an act that the third-party did wrong that contributed to plaintiff's injury, but these are wrong answer choices because a motion to dismiss does not resolve factual allegations. If there is an answer that goes to which party is more to blame, that will not be the best answer. Other decoy answers will focus on a lack of SMJ but supplemental jurisdiction applies to third-party impleader claims, so that is also a decoy wrong answer.

e. **Intervention** (often called intervene as a matter of right) applies when **a nonparty claims an interest** in the property or transaction that is the subject of the pending lawsuit and disposition in their **absence will impair or impede their ability** to protect their interest, **unless existing parties adequately represent** that interest. FRCP 24.

   1. **Permissive intervention** applies when a party cannot intervene as a matter of right, but the court may permit intervention if the party has a claim or defense that shares with the main action a **common question of law or fact.**

   2. **SMJ required:** The court must have **SMJ over the intervenor's claim** if the original claim is based solely on diversity jurisdiction (joinder cannot destroy diversity). This is required for intervention as a matter of right and permissive intervention.

Decoy tip: If the nonparty seeking to intervene can still protect their interest in another forum/case and there is no preclusive effect (claim or issue preclusion does not apply) then an answer choice permitting the nonparty to intervene would be a wrong answer choice (or not the "best" option for the nonparty). This is because their rights would not be impaired by not intervening.

Example: A and B were walking down the street when they were struck by C who ran a red light. A and B are both from State X. C is from State Y. A sued C for injuries totaling $100,000 in State X. B seeks to intervene but only had limited injuries so his damages are $40,000. Since B does not meet the SMJ requirements, he cannot intervene (his intervention would not be necessary because he could protect his interest by filing a separate claim against C in state court in State X where the accident occurred so an answer choice that said he should be able to intervene would be wrong).

f. **Interpleader** is an action where the **one holding property** (the stakeholder) forces all potential claimants (people who claim the property) into a **single lawsuit** to avoid multiple and inconsistent litigation. There are two types of interpleader:

   1. **Statutory:** Requires only that **one claimant must be diverse** (same as subject matter jurisdiction diversity rules) from one other claimant and the amount in controversy must be **$500** or more. 28 U.S.C. §1335. The stakeholder must be willing to either **deposit the property** at issue with the court **or post a bond** in an appropriate amount.

      a. **Service:** Statutory interpleader allows nationwide service of process (rule 22 interpleader below does not).

2. **Rule 22 interpleader:** Requires that the stakeholder must be **diverse from every claimant** and the amount in controversy must **exceed $75,000.** FRCP 22. (SMJ is the same as normal here whereas statutory interpleader is more relaxed.)

MBE tip: For interpleader, if there is not complete diversity with the stakeholder, then statutory interpleader should be used. Determine which parties are diverse and the amount in controversy to determine which option is viable.

Example: A man dies with $1 million in his bank account. His wife, brother, two kids, and butler all claim the money in the account is theirs. The bank is the stakeholder as it is the one holding the property. If the bank was in State A, the wife and butler were also in State A, and the kids were in State B, then the bank would need to bring the action under statutory interpleader and not Rule 22 because there is not diversity as required for Rule 22 (because the bank and wife and butler are all from the same state). *However*, if the bank is in State A and all claimants are in State B, then Rule 22 would need to be used and statutory interpleader would not work because all claimants are from the same state.

JOINDER OF PARTIES DECODED

Type	When to use	Separate SMJ needed	IF no Fed. Q or diversity
Permissive	◆ Claims arise from same T/O ◆ Claims raise a common question	Yes	Party can't join
Required - Necessary party	◆ Court cannot provide complete relief without absent party ◆ Absent party's interest will be harmed, or ◆ Existing party is subject to multiple inconsistent obligations ◇ Indispensable if can't provide relief w/o party but they are unable to join	Yes *Need PJ too (can be through bulge provision)	◆ Dismiss (if indispensable) or ◆ Proceed w/o party (if not indispensable)
Impleader	Defending party adds third-party defendant (indemnity, subrogation, contribution) who is liable for all or part of claim	No (b/c supplemental jurisdiction ok)	Supplemental jurisdiction applies
Intervention	A nonparty claims an interest in the property/transaction (rights impaired)	Yes	Party can't join
Interpleader	One holding property forces all potential claimants into a single lawsuit to avoid multiple and inconsistent litigation	**Statutory:** ◆ 1 claimant diverse from 1 other claimant ◆ $500 or more **Rule 22:** ◆ Stakeholder diverse from all claimants ◆ Over $75,000	Can't join if requirements not met

2. **Joinder of claims:** A party may bring as many claims as it has against an opposing party. FRCP 18(a).

   a. **Counterclaim** is an offensive claim against an opposing party.

      1. **There are two types:**

         a. **Compulsory counterclaims** arise from the **same transaction or occurrence** as the plaintiff's claim, *and* **must be raised** in the pending case or the claim is deemed **waived.** FRCP 13(a).

            i. **Supplemental jurisdiction applies:** An **independent basis** for subject matter jurisdiction is **not required** since supplemental jurisdiction will extend to a compulsory counterclaim.

         b. **Permissive counterclaims** do not arise from the same transaction or occurrence and **may be raised** in the pending case or in a separate case. FRCP 13(b).

            i. **No supplemental jurisdiction:** A permissive counterclaim **must have an independent source of subject matter jurisdiction.**

   b. **Cross claim** is an offensive claim against a **co-party** (one on the same side of the v. – P v. P or D v. D) and **must arise from the same transaction or occurrence.** Cross claims are **never compulsory.** FRCP 13(g).

      1. **Supplemental jurisdiction applies:** An **independent basis** for subject matter jurisdiction is **not required** since supplemental jurisdiction will extend to a cross claim.

JOINDER OF CLAIMS DECODED

Type	Parties	When to use	Waived if not raised	Supplemental Jx applies
Compulsory Counterclaim	Any opposing party	◆ Claims arise from same T/O as P's claim	Yes	Yes
Permissive Counterclaim	Any opposing party	◆ Claims do *not* arise from same T/O	No	No (need separate SMJ)
Cross claim (permissive)	Any co-party	◆ Claims arise from same T/O	No	Yes

D. **Class action** is a case where a representative sues on behalf of a group. FRCP 23.

1. **Requirements:** A federal class action is proper if the class meets the following requirements:

   a. **Numerosity:** There are too many class members for joinder to be practical;

   b. **Commonality:** The questions of law or fact are common to the class;

   c. **Typicality:** The representative's claims or defenses are typical of those in the class;

   d. **Adequacy** of representation such that it will fairly represent the class; and

   e. **Type of class:** The class must also fit within one of the following types of classes:

1. **Prejudice:** Class treatment is necessary to avoid inconsistent results or persons participating in a fund as individuals from depleting the fund; or
2. **Injunctive or declaratory relief is sought;** or
3. **Questions of law/fact common to the class predominate** over questions affecting individuals, and a class action is a **superior method** to resolve the issues (e.g., damages for a mass tort).

f. **Court approval required:** The court must approve a class action settlement.

2. **Class action citizenship issues**

a. **Diversity action:** To determine citizenship for class actions based on diversity, **only the citizenship of the named representative** is taken into account, and the $75,000 **amount in controversy requirement can be satisfied by *any named* class representative.**

b. **Class Action Fairness Act** (2005) relaxes the federal jurisdictional requirements for some class actions. It applies where there isn't complete diversity and allows a federal court to hear a class action if the following requirements are met:

1. **Diversity:** Any class member is diverse from any defendant; and
2. **Aggregation:** The class claims aggregate to exceed **$5 million;** and
3. **100 members:** There are at least 100 class members.

E. **Discovery**

1. **Discovery Conference**: Rule 26(f) **requires parties to confer,** unless exempted, as soon as practicable to consider the **possibilities for settling** or alternatively **prepare a discovery plan** to submit to the court within **14 days** of their conference.

a. **Discovery plans can include** the timing, form, or requirements for disclosures, issues regarding privileges or protection of materials, and other things related to the discovery period. The court will issue further orders (e.g., scheduling) on discovery matters. See sec. II.F. for pre-trial conferences.

2. **Mandatory disclosure requirements:**

a. **Rule 26 requires the mandatory disclosure** of information about the pending case to the opposing party (even if the opposing party doesn't request the information). There are three types of mandatory disclosures:

1. **Mandatory initial disclosures** are to be submitted within **14 days** after the parties' discovery conference and supply information about disputed facts, including: (FRCP 26(a)(1)(A and C).)

a. **Identifying those likely to have discoverable information** that support the party's claim or defense, **including contact information;**

b. Copies or description of all **documents, electronically stored information, and tangible evidence** in its possession that may be used to support the claim or defense;

c. A **damages computation** and supporting documentation; and

d. Copies of applicable **insurance documents.**

e. **Proceedings exempt from initial disclosure:** (FRCP 26(a)(1)(B).)

i. Actions for review on an **administration record** or to quash or enforce an administrative summons or subpoena;

ii. **Forfeiture action in rem** arising from a federal statute;

iii. **Petition for habeas corpus** or challenges to criminal convictions or sentences;

iv. **Actions brought without an attorney** by a person in the custody of the U.S., state, or subdivision;

v. **Action by the U.S. to recover benefit payments** or collect on student loans;

vi. A proceeding ancillary to a **proceeding in another court;** and

vii. An action to enforce an **arbitration award.**

2. **Expert testimony** information to be submitted at least **90 days** before trial, including: (FRCP 26(a)(2).)

a. **Identity** and **contact information** of the expert,

b. The expert's **qualifications,** and

c. The expert's **final (not draft) written report** that includes opinions the witness will express and the basis for them, facts the witness considered, exhibits, the witness expert's compensation, and cases the witness has testified as an expert in during the last four years. (For exceptions see sec. 4.b.*1.* below).

3. **Pretrial disclosures,** including a list of all non-expert **witnesses** intended to be called, **witness testimony** presented through deposition or transcript, and a list of **documents, physical evidence,** or **exhibits** to be submitted within **30 days** before trial. FRCP 26(a)(3).

DISCOVERY DISCLOSURES CHEAT SHEET

	Mandatory initial disclosures	Expert witness disclosures	Pretrial disclosures
Must disclose	◆ Identity and contact info for those likely to have supporting information ◆ Copies of documents, electronically stored data, and tangible evidence ◆ Damages computations ◆ Copies of insurance documents	◆ Identity and contact information of expert ◆ Expert's qualifications ◆ Expert's written final report	◆ List of all non-expert witnesses intended to be called ◆ Witness testimony presented through deposition or transcript ◆ List of documents, physical evidence, or exhibits
Timing	Within 14 days of Rule 26 discovery conference	90 days before trial	30 days before trial
Do not need to voluntarily disclose	◆ Actions for review of administrative records ◆ Forfeiture action in rem ◆ Petition for habeas corpus ◆ Actions brought without an attorney by person in custody ◆ Action by the U.S. to recover benefit payments ◆ Proceeding ancillary to a proceeding in another court ◆ Action to enforce an arbitration award	◆ Expert draft reports	◆ Privileged material ◆ Attorney work product generally ◆ Electronically stored data not reasonably accessible

3. **Discovery tools** cannot be requested until ***after* the parties have conferred** to arrange for initial disclosures and prepared a discovery plan at the Rule 26(f) discovery conference.

   a. **Depositions:** An examination of a witness that occurs **under oath** and is recorded by sound, video, and/or stenography. Questions can be **oral or written** but the **answers are oral.** FRCP 30, 31.

      1. **Parties** can be deposed and **nonparties,** including corporations, can be deposed by means of a subpoena.

      2. **Once only:** A person may not be deposed twice without court approval.

      3. **Limits:** Only **10 depositions** are permitted by each **side,** (not per party, but by each side of the v.) and oral depositions **cannot exceed one 7-hour day** unless the court orders otherwise.

      4. **Failure to appear:** When a party who received notice, fails to appear, the opposing party may recover **reasonable expenses** incurred in attending, including attorney fees.

      5. **To perpetuate testimony:** A person may be permitted to conduct a deposition ***before* any suit has been filed** by seeking a court order to perpetuate **testimony if the petitioner expects to be a party but cannot presently bring the action.** The court will **grant the request if** the testimony may **prevent a failure or delay of justice.** FRCP 27.

         a. **Additional requirements:** The petition must also show the subject matter of the expected action, the facts the petitioner wants to establish and the reasons to perpetuate it, the names or descriptions of adverse persons, and the name, contact information, and expected substance of the testimony of each deponent.

   b. **Interrogatories:** Questions propounded in writing **to another party,** which must be answered **in writing under oath** and the responding party must respond within **30 days.** An attorney who objects must sign those objections. Interrogatories **may not be asked of nonparties**. FRCP 33.

      1. **Limits:** No more than **25 questions,** including subparts, unless the court orders otherwise.

      Example: An attorney for P served D with the summons, complaint, and 25 interrogatories asking questions about D's contentions in the case. D is likely to obtain a protective order if they can show that the parties have not yet conferred to arrange for initial disclosures and prepare a discovery plan (because this is required *before* interrogatories can be sent).

> **Decoy tip:** Pay attention to the timeline/sequence of events in the facts. If there are interrogatories or depositions sent before a pretrial conference, they are not proper. If improper, D can refuse to answer them or seek a protective order since the timing is not proper under the Federal Rules.
>
> **MBE tip:** Don't get tricked by a call asking about a protective order. Although protective orders often involve protecting embarrassing or annoying information (see sec. E.5 below), arguably one can also seek protection from being required to disclose information that is not yet discoverable due to a lack of proper procedures, such as attendance at the pretrial conference required under Rule 26.

   c. **Requests for admissions** request another **party** to admit the truth of any discoverable matter (documents asked about must be included with the request if not already made available). The purpose is to identify areas that are not in controversy. Requests for admission **may not be asked of nonparties.** FRCP 36.

      1. **Time to respond:** A matter will be **deemed admitted** unless the party to whom the request is made fails to object or deny (in their answer) within **30 days** after being served and signed by the party or attorney.

d. **Requests for production of documents and other items:** Any party may request another **party** to make available for review and copying **documents, electronic copies or other tangible items, or permit entry onto property.** FRCP 34.

1. **Nonparties:** A nonparty may be compelled to produce documents or other tangible things, or allow entry onto property **only if subpoenaed** to do so.
2. **Time to respond:** The party to whom the request is made must respond within **30 days** after being served or within 30 days of the pretrial conference if the request was made *prior* to that conference.
   a. **Failure to respond:** If a party fails to respond, the requesting party can **move to compel production.**
3. **Electronically stored data:** If such data is **not reasonably accessible** because of burden and cost, the court may still order production and impose **cost-sharing measures.** See below sec. II.E.4.d.

e. **Physical or mental examination** of a **party** may be sought by an opposing party. A party requesting such an exam must obtain a **court order** upon a showing of **good cause** that the examination will provide information about the physical or mental condition of the party **where it is at issue.** FRCP 35.

DISCOVERY TOOLS CHEAT SHEET

	Depositions	Interrogatories	Requests for admissions
When	After pretrial conference (unless to perpetuate testimony)	After pretrial conference	After pretrial conference
Number allowed	◆ 10 per side (not party) ◆ Can only do more with court's permission	◆ 25 questions (including subparts) ◆ Can only do more with court's permission	N/A
Time limits	One 7-hour day	30 days to respond	30 days to respond
Manner asked	Oral or written	Written	Written (with copies of documents asked about)
Manner answered	Oral under oath	Written answer under oath and objection signed by attorney	Written answer or objection signed by party or attorney
Recipients	◆ Parties ◆ Nonparties, including corporations, if subpoenaed	◆ Parties ◆ NO nonparties	◆ Parties ◆ NO nonparties
Failure to comply	◆ Attorney fees and expenses for failure to show for deposition ◆ Motion to compel ◆ Sanctions	◆ Motion to compel ◆ Sanctions	◆ Matter deemed admitted ◆ Motion to compel ◆ Sanctions

4. **Scope of discovery**

   a. **Relevant discoverable material:** Material **relevant to a party's claim or defense** (includes documentary evidence and individuals with knowledge) that is **proportional** to the needs of a case, **can be discovered even if not admissible.** Courts consider a variety factors in making this determination (e.g., parties' relative access to materials). FRCP 26(b).

      1. **Limitation on relevant material:** Evidence may not be discovered if it is **unreasonably cumulative or burdensome.**

   b. **Privileged and protected trial preparation material is not discoverable.** FRCP 26(b).

      1. **Expert *draft* reports and communications: Draft reports** from experts and **communications between an expert witness** and a party's attorney **are protected** trial preparation materials and are not discoverable. FRCP 26(b)(4)(B).

      2. **Exceptions for communications that:** (FRCP 26(b)(4)(C).)

         a. Relate to the **expert's compensation,**

         b. Identify **facts or data that the party's attorney provided** and the **expert considered** in forming opinions,

         c. Identify **assumptions that the party's attorney provided** and the **expert relied on** in forming opinions.

      3. **For more privileges** see the Evidence chapter, sec. VII (attorney-client, marital, self-incrimination, physician-patient, etc.).

      4. **Disclosure of privileged material:** If a party inadvertently discloses privileged material to an opposing party, it may still invoke the privilege by **notifying the opposing party** of the disclosure and the **basis for the claim.** Once notified, the opposing party must **promptly return, sequester, or destroy** the information and take reasonable steps to retrieve it if disclosed to others. FRCP 26(b)(5)(B).

   c. **Trial preparation material** (attorney work product) **is not generally discoverable.** FRCP 26(b)(3).

      1. **General rule:** Work product is material **prepared in anticipation of litigation** or for trial and is **generally not discoverable.**

      2. **Exceptions:** The court **may order** the following materials discoverable. *However*, if discovery is permitted, it must protect against disclosure of the **mental impressions, opinions, conclusions, and legal theories** of a party's **attorney** or **representative.**

         a. **Substantial need shown:** Materials may be discovered if there is a **substantial need** and without undue hardship, an **inability to obtain** the information through other means.

         b. **Previous statement:** Any party or other person **may obtain the person's own previous statement** about the action or its subject matter. **A previous statement is either:**

            i. A **written statement** that the person has **signed** or otherwise **adopted or approved,** or

            ii. A **contemporaneous** stenographic, mechanical, electrical, or other **recording or transcription** of the person's **oral statement.**

d. **Electronically stored information:** A party need not provide discovery of electronically stored information from sources **not reasonably accessible** because of **burden or undue cost.** The court can still order discovery with good cause. FRCP 37(e).

   1. **Preservation:** Parties must take **reasonable steps to preserve** evidence, including electronically stored data when litigation is reasonably foreseeable, or **sanctions may apply.**

      a. **Except—good faith destruction or deletion:** When electronically stored information is destroyed or deleted, **sanctions may not be imposed if** the destruction or deletion is a **routine, good faith operation** of an electronic information system.

5. **Protective orders:** Any person may move for a protective order **to prevent disclosure** of evidence if made in good faith. FRCP 26(c).

   a. **Court order:** The court may, for **good cause,** issue an order to protect a party or person from annoyance, embarrassment, oppression, or undue burden or expense (e.g., by specifying the time and place for disclosure, identifying persons who may be present, sealing a deposition, etc.).

6. **Discovery disputes:** Where there are disputes, the parties must first **meet and confer** *before* seeking a **motion to compel or protective order.** Noncompliance can result in sanctions. FRCP 37.

7. **Sanctions:** For violations of discovery, sanctions may be imposed including holding a noncomplying party in **contempt, prohibiting the disobeying party from supporting or opposing claims, directing matters or facts to be established, striking pleadings, staying proceedings, imposing fees, dismissing an action, and ordering a default judgment.** FRCP 37.

F. **Pretrial Conference:** The court may order attorneys to appear at one or more pretrial conferences **to expedite disposition of the action, facilitate settlement, improve the quality of the trial,** etc. FRCP 16(a).

1. **Timing:** *After* receiving the parties' **discovery plan report** under Rule 26(f) (see above), or after consulting with the parties, the court **must issue a scheduling order** (within 90 days after D has been served the complaint or 60 days after D has appeared, whichever is earlier).

2. **Scheduling order** (to manage the case): The **scheduling order must** limit the time to join other parties, amend any pleadings, complete discovery, and file motions. In addition, the court may issue orders on other appropriate matters (e.g., the court may modify the timing for disclosure).

3. **Final pretrial conference:** The court may hold a **final pretrial conference** to formulate a trial plan, including a plan to facilitate the admission of evidence. The court can **modify the order** *after* a final pretrial conference, even *after* the jury has been selected, but **only to prevent manifest injustice.**

III. DISPOSITION OF A CASE WITHOUT A TRIAL

Sometimes a case will be resolved prior to the end of the trial.

A. **Dismissal** FRCP 41.

1. **Voluntary dismissal:** A plaintiff may obtain **one** voluntary dismissal **without prejudice** (so it may be relitigated) before the defendant serves its answer or files a motion for summary

judgment (MSJ). The trial court also has discretion to grant a dismissal **after an answer** or motion for summary judgment is filed, **unless substantial prejudice** to the defendant would occur. FRCP 41(a).

a. **Adjudication on the merits:** After one voluntary dismissal **the next dismissal** will be viewed as **adjudication on the merits** (meaning the party can't bring subsequent claims on the same issue).

   Example: P filed an action against D. D filed a motion to dismiss for failure to state a claim. Instead of opposing the motion, P voluntarily dismissed the action and filed a new action, alleging the same claims but also addressing pleading defects outlined in D's motion to dismiss. D then moved to dismiss the second action, and P voluntarily dismissed the second action instead of filing opposition papers. P then filed a third action, alleging the same claims including allegations responsive to D's second motion to dismiss. D moved to dismiss the third action and P opposed it. The court will grant D's motion to dismiss because P's previously dismissed actions operate as an adjudication on the merits.

2. **Involuntary dismissal:** The court may do this at the defendant's request, or on the court's own motion. Such a dismissal is an adjudication on the merits (dismissal with prejudice), so it may not be relitigated. FRCP 41(b).

   a. **Exceptions:** Dismissals based on **jurisdiction, venue, and required joinder** are **not adjudication on the merits** so it is a dismissal **without prejudice** and they may be relitigated.

      Examples for basis of dismissal: Lack of jurisdiction, improper venue, insufficient process or service or process, failure to state a claim, failure to join an indispensable party, discovery sanction.

> MBE tip: Certain involuntary dismissals such as those based on lack of jurisdiction or venue are not viewed as an adjudication on the merits (so not all dismissals bar subsequent claims from being brought). See cheat sheet below for examples.

B. **Default judgment:** A **default judgment** is entered against one who fails to oppose a case. This occurs if the defendant fails to respond within **21 days** after service (or 60 days in the U.S. or 90 days outside the U.S. if service is waived). FRCP 55.

1. **Process:** The plaintiff must ***first*** **request the court clerk to enter a default,** which is a notation in the court file that there has been no response. ***Second,*** the court then **notifies all parties** of the default, which can be set aside by the court. FRCP 55(b)(2).

   a. **Exception—entry by clerk allowed:** *If and only if* plaintiff's **claim is for a sum certain or a sum that can be made certain** by showing computation, the **clerk can enter the default judgment** based on plaintiff's affidavit showing the amount due. FRCP 55(b)(1).

      Example (clerk can enter default judgment): P sues D for breach of contract. D owes P $10,000 for construction P completed on D's house. P can show the original contract signed by both parties as to the amount owed as well as a supporting affidavit that the work was completed, and the costs were equivalent to the amount claimed in the contract for $10,000. D failed to appear in the action and is competent (e.g., not a minor). P can request entry of the default judgment by the clerk.

      Example (court must enter default judgment): If the claim was for injunctive relief or an uncertain amount or punitive damages then this exception would not apply and P would need to seek default judgment through the court.

2. **Notice of hearing:** A party, who has appeared personally or by a representative, must be provided **written notice** of the **application for a default judgment** at least **7 days** before the **hearing.**

   Example: A company in State A sued a plumber in State B for negligent installation of pipes resulting in $250,000 in damages. The plumber filed a motion to dismiss for lack of personal jurisdiction. The court denied the motion. Thereafter, the plumber did not answer the company's action. 60 days after the court's order denying the motion to dismiss, the company asked the clerk to enter default and the clerk did so. The company applied to the court for entry of a default judgment and notified the plumber 3 days before the default judgment hearing. After an ex parte hearing, the court entered a default judgment. 10 days later the plumber filed a motion to set aside the default judgment. The court will grant the plumber's motion because the plumber was not given adequate notice of the hearing (7 days required).

3. **Set aside default judgment:** The court may set aside an entry of default judgment **for good cause,** or for grounds discussed in sec. V.C. below. FRCP 55(c).

C. **Motion for judgment on the pleadings:** After the **pleadings are closed,** but early enough not to delay trial, a party may move for judgment on the pleadings (for matters outside the pleadings, a party must file a motion for summary judgment). FRCP 12(c).

   1. **Court findings:** In reviewing the motion, the court **accepts all facts alleged in all the pleadings as true,** and a **failure to deny** any allegations in the complaint constitutes **an admission.**

D. **Motion for summary judgment** (MSJ) will be ordered where the moving party can establish there is **no genuine dispute of material fact** and that the movant is **entitled to judgment as a matter of law** (once established, the court *must* grant). FRCP 56.

   Example: A patient filed a medical malpractice action against a hospital alleging the hospital failed to diagnose the patient's cancer based on an X-ray taken at the hospital. The patient's cancer was diagnosed 6 months later, based on the same X-ray, when the patient sought a second opinion. In the interim, the cancer had spread. Discovery had been completed and the hospital moved for summary judgment and submitted a memorandum of facts not in dispute including a report from the hospital's radiologist who found no signs of cancer on the X-ray. If asked *how* the patient can raise a genuine dispute of material fact, on these facts, a proper answer could be for the patient to submit an affidavit from the patient's expert radiologist with findings that contradict the report of the hospital's radiologist (because this shows a genuine dispute of material fact).

   > **MBE tip:** When a party files a MSJ, look for facts that show a dispute, such as conflicting reports, statements, affidavits, etc. If there are any genuine disputes of material fact, then the court should *not* grant the MSJ.

   1. Evidence viewed in **light most favorable to the non-moving party.**

   2. Evidence must be comprised of **firsthand knowledge,** from an affiant (person who swears an affidavit) or declarant who is **competent to testify,** and set out facts that would be **admissible evidence.**

      a. **Credibility is not weighed** here, but allegations about credibility often create genuine factual disputes about a material fact. MSJ is almost never granted when credibility is a central issue.

         Example: A woman was fired and sued her former employer alleging sex discrimination. The woman's complaint contained a lengthy description of what her supervisor had said and done over the years, quoting calls and emails. The employer moved for summary judgment alleging the woman was a pathological liar who filed the action fictitiously. The woman's attorney was at a lengthy out-of-state trial and failed to respond to the motion. The court granted the motion and entered final judgment. The woman appealed. The appellate court will not uphold the trial court's ruling on the summary judgment motion because the employer's basis for the MSJ was that the woman was not credible, which creates a factual dispute based on the woman's facts and evidence.

Decoy tip: Slow down here and consider if the *quality* of the evidence presented is sufficient to establish the fact. A witness affidavit of what they saw is firsthand knowledge, whereas a witness affidavit of what another person would say as a witness, is not the *declarant's* firsthand knowledge, and is insufficient evidence to establish that fact. Similarly, reference to facts asserted in the pleadings is insufficient to establish a fact.

a. **Burden of persuasion:** Once the **moving party** has presented evidence to support their contention, the burden of persuasion **shifts to the non-moving party to provide evidence** to counter the showing that there is no genuine dispute of material fact.

   1. **Request for more time:** In **response to a MSJ**, the non-moving party may request more time **for additional discovery** attaching a declaration describing the desired discovery.

3. **Timing:** A MSJ may be filed any time up until **30 days** *after* the **close of all discovery.** FRCP 56(b).

4. The court has **broad discretion** and can grant: (FRCP 56(f and g).)

   a. **Partial** summary judgment as to one of several causes of action,

   b. *Sua sponte* (based on a ground the court comes up with on its own),

   c. On **grounds other than those sought,** and/or

   d. In **favor of the non-moving party.**

Decoy tip: Don't get tricked by facts in a question that are directed toward opinions or the witness's credibility as these types of facts are never relevant to determine whether there is no genuine dispute of "material fact" for a MSJ. These decoy facts will lead you to the wrong conclusion.

DISPOSITION WITHOUT A TRIAL CHEAT SHEET

Type	Reasons	Adjudication on the merits? (Yes = res judicata applies)
Voluntary Dismissal	P sues D and dismisses the case on their own volition (often instead of opposing D's motion).	1st dismissal - No 2nd dismissal - Yes
Involuntary Dismissal	◆ Failure to state a claim for relief ◇ Insufficient facts ◇ Allegation negates one or more elements ◆ Discovery misconduct	Yes
	◆ Lack of PJx and SMJx ◆ Improper venue ◆ Failure to join a party ◆ Insufficient process ◆ Insufficient service of process	No
Default judgment	D fails to respond within 21 days of service, or if service waived - 60 days (U.S.) or 90 days (foreign).	Yes
Judgment on the pleadings	After the pleadings are closed, a party may move for judgment on the pleadings.	Yes
MSJ	Moving party can establish that there is no genuine dispute of material fact *and* is entitled to judgment as a matter of law.	Yes

IV. TRIAL

A. Right to a jury trial

1. **Seventh Amendment:** In federal court, the Seventh Amendment preserves the **right to a jury** in **civil actions at law;** however, a **judge decides issues of equity.** FRCP 38.

   a. **Legal issues first, then equitable:** If a case has both legal and equitable claims, the **jury decides the factual legal issues** first, and then the **judge determines the equity claim.**

   Example: A football team entered into a 10-year lease with a city for use of a stadium. 5 years into the lease, the team threatened to leave the stadium and move to another city. The city sued the team seeking a permanent injunction to prevent the team from leaving. The team counterclaimed seeking $10 million in damages for losses caused by city's failure to maintain the stadium as required by the lease. The team demanded a jury trial on the counterclaim. The court should first hold a jury trial for the team's counterclaim (legal issue of damages) and then a nonjury trial for the city's claim (equitable relief: permanent injunction).

b. **Demand for jury:** Plaintiff must demand **in writing** no later than **14 days** after service of the **last pleading** that they are raising a jury triable issue and demand a jury trial **or it is waived.** FRCP 38(b, c, d).

  1. **Demand in complaint:** Plaintiff can include a demand for a jury trial in their complaint as well. If plaintiff files an **amended complaint** within the required **21-day period** then they can add the demand for a jury trial in their amended complaint.

  2. **Other claims:** A demand for jury trial applies to **counterclaims** and **cross claims** as well.

  Example: A retailer sued an architect for fraudulent misrepresentation in the architect's design of the store. The complaint did not include a jury demand. The architect timely moved to dismiss the action for failure to state a claim but did not file an answer. 20 days after being served with the motion, the retailer moved to amend his complaint to add a defamation claim. In the amended claim, the retailer demanded a jury on both claims. This is proper because the architect never filed an answer and it is within the 21 days allowed for retailer to amend his complaint (P can amend his pleading once within 21 days of the responsive pleading or pre-answer motion and here D filed a pre-answer motion and it has only been 20 days). And since D did not file an answer, P is also properly demanding the jury within 14 days of the last pleading (answer not filed yet so not yet the last pleading).

> **MBE tip:** The timing of requesting a jury trial is tied to the conclusion of the pleadings stage so demanding a jury trial at the end of discovery will likely be too late to satisfy this rule.

c. **Jury composition**

  1. **Each side** has **unlimited** challenges on *voir dire* for **cause** and **three peremptory** (without a reason) challenges (though they still must be used in a gender and race-neutral way). FRCP 47; 28 U.S.C. §1870.

  Examples (for cause): Bias, prejudice, juror is related to a party or worked for a party, juror has stock in a corporation that is a party, a financial relationship between a juror and party, juror has a relationship with a trial participant, juror says they will not decide the case on the facts.

  2. A jury may contain **6-12 jurors** with no alternates (a case must **begin with** at least **6 jurors**); and a **unanimous vote** is required, unless the parties agree otherwise. A jury of at least 6 members must return the verdict, unless the parties stipulate otherwise. FRCP 48.

  Example: A man sued a bus company seeking damages sustained in an accident. The man demanded a jury trial. Six jurors and two alternate jurors were chosen. During the trial, two jurors became ill and were replaced by the alternate jurors. At the conclusion of the trial, a third juror also became ill and the court excused that juror. The parties' attorneys stipulated to the return of a verdict from a five-person jury. The jury returned a verdict for the company. The man filed a motion for a new trial arguing the five-person jury was not large enough. The court will not grant the man's motion because the jury started with six jurors as required and the parties stipulated to the five-person verdict so the verdict is valid.

d. **Jury polling:** After a verdict is returned, but before the jury is discharged, the court ***must* on a party's request,** or may on its own, poll the jurors individually. FRCP 48(c).

1. **Juror unanimity and assent:** If the poll finds the jury lacks unanimity or assent, the court can order the jury to **deliberate further** or order a **new trial.**

e. **Special verdict:** The court **may require the jury** to return only a special verdict in the form of a **special written finding** on each issue of fact by: (FRCP 49.)

1. Submitting written questions susceptible of categorical or brief answers;

2. Submitting written forms of the special findings from pleadings and evidence; or

3. Using any other method the court considers appropriate.

2. **Jury instructions:** A judge must instruct the jury on the law that governs the verdict, but a **party may propose specific jury instructions.** FRCP 51.

a. **General verdict instructions:** The court **may submit** to the jury forms for a general verdict, together with **written questions** on one or more issues of fact that the jury must decide. The court **must then give the instructions and explanations** necessary to enable the jury to render the general verdict and answer the questions in writing, and **must direct the jury to do both.** FRCP 49(b).

b. **Special verdict instructions:** For a special verdict, the court **must** give the **instructions and explanations** necessary to enable the jury to make its findings on each submitted issue. FRCP 49(a).

c. **Waiver:** A party **must object** to the jury instructions before they go to the jury or **they waive** the ability to raise the issue on appeal. FRCP 51.

Example: Before the close of evidence, D submitted a proposed jury instruction on contributory negligence. Before instructing the jury, the judge informed the parties of the instructions she would give, which did not include D's requested instructions or any instructions on contributory negligence. Neither party objected at any time. The jury returned a verdict for P and the judge entered judgment. D cannot appeal the verdict on the ground the judge should have instructed the jury on contributory negligence because D failed to object to the instructions the judge indicated she would give.

B. **Judgment as a matter of law (JMOL)** (formerly called a directed verdict) occurs when one party files a motion after the other side has been heard at trial (so a defendant can usually move twice, after the case in chief and after any rebuttal), contending that **a reasonable jury would not have a legally sufficient evidentiary basis** to find for the party on that issue, and asks for a judgment as a matter of law. FRCP 50(a).

Example: A man sued his insurance company alleging it breached its duty under his policy by refusing to pay for his medical expenses from a biking accident. At the jury trial, the man presented evidence that he paid all premiums and that the policy covered medical expenses arising from accidents. After he rested his case, the company presented evidence that a provision excluded payment for injuries from accidents caused by "unduly risky" behavior. A witness testified that the accident had occurred in an area where posted signs warned bikers not to enter. The company moved for judgment as a matter of law. The court should deny the company's motion because whether the man's behavior was unduly risky is a question of fact for the jury to resolve.

1. **Weight of evidence:** Evidence is viewed in the light **most favorable to the non-moving party.**

2. **Timing:** This request must occur ***before*** **the court submits the case to the jury, but *after* the non-movant has been fully heard** on the issue. Essentially this serves to take the case away from the jury.

Example: A retailer sued a wholesaler for breach of contract and fraudulent misrepresentation. After the parties presented their evidence, the court instructed the jury on the law. Neither party filed a motion for judgment as a matter of law before the case went to the jury. The jury found for the retailer on both claims. After the court entered judgment on the verdict, the wholesaler moved for a new trial and for judgment as a matter of law arguing the evidence was insufficient to support the jury verdict. The court denied the motions. The wholesaler appealed, challenging the sufficiency of the evidence. The appellate court should not consider the wholesaler's challenge because it did not raise the issue before the case went to the jury. (Note the sufficiency standard is the JMOL standard and has nothing to do with the new trial. The facts about the new trial were decoys.)

> **MBE tip:** Many MBE questions in all subjects will use Civil Procedure motions as a mechanism to frame the call of the question (e.g., can plaintiff get a directed verdict for a negligence issue). Note that some older questions use the term "directed verdict" but modernly it is called a JMOL.

C. **Bench trial:** the court is required to make **findings of fact and conclusions of law** when entering judgment. FRCP 52.

1. **Manner:** The findings of fact and conclusions of law **must be stated separately** but **may be stated on the record** after the close of evidence **or in an opinion or decision** filed by the court.

   Example: A manufacturer sued a buyer for breach of contract. The case was tried solely on documentary evidence. Immediately after the close of evidence, the judge announced that judgment was for the manufacturer and entered judgment. The buyer has appealed. One argument the buyer could use to appeal the judgment would be that the judge erred by not providing findings and conclusions.

   a. **Partial findings:** The court is **still required to enter findings** of fact and conclusions of law when it enters judgment on partial findings.

> **Decoy tip:** A written opinion is not required and can be a decoy answer. If a judge states the findings of fact and conclusions of law on the record this is sufficient, even if the judge never issued a written opinion.

2. **Exceptions:** The court **does not need to make findings of fact or conclusions** of law when ruling on a **Rule 12 motion** (against the complaint) or a **Rule 56 motion** (summary judgment).

V. POST-TRIAL ISSUES

A. **Renewed judgment as a matter of law (RJMOL)** (formerly called a judgment notwithstanding the verdict—JNOV) occurs after the jury has reached a verdict, contending that **a reasonable jury would not have a legally sufficient evidentiary basis** to find for the party on that issue, and asks for a judgment as a matter of law. FRCP 52(b).

1. **Prerequisite: The losing party must have originally filed a JMOL** or they cannot later file a RJMOL since it is a *renewal* of the earlier motion.

2. **Timing:** The motion must be made **after the jury has reached a verdict** and within **28 days** after entry of judgment.

3. **Standard to evaluate:** The court will determine whether there is **substantial evidence** in the record to support the verdict, resolving all disputed issues **in the non-moving party's favor.**

B. **Motion for a new trial:** After judgment has been entered, the losing party requests a new trial **based on errors** made at trial. FRCP 59.

1. **Timing:** The motion must be made within **28 days** after entry of judgment.
2. **Grounds for a new trial include the following:**
   a. **Prejudicial/plain error** at trial that makes the judgment unfair;
   b. **New evidence** that could not have been obtained for the original trial through due diligence;
   c. **Prejudicial misconduct** of a party, attorney, third-party, or juror (including where a jury poll reveals a lack of unanimity or lack of assent), judicial error (e.g., improper instructions);
   d. Judgment is **against the great weight of the evidence; and**
   e. **Excessive damages or inadequate damages.**

   Example: After the jury returned a verdict for D in a negligence case, one of the jurors told P that she researched a confusing issue during a recess and reported the results to the rest of the jury, which favored D. P then filed a motion for a new trial based on jury misconduct. The court will likely grant P's motion because a juror conducting independent research during the trial is misconduct.
3. **New trial on damages only: Remittitur and Additur**
   a. **Remittitur** occurs when a judge orders that a new trial for the defendant will take place unless the **plaintiff agrees to a reduced award** of damages because the judge finds that the damages awarded by the jury were **so excessive as to shock the conscience.**
   b. **Additur** occurs when a judge orders that the plaintiff will get a new trial unless the **defendant agrees to an increased award** of damages because the judge finds that the damages awarded by the jury were insufficient. **Additur is not permitted in federal court.**

   > **MBE tip:** Although additur does not apply in federal court, it could apply in a question that requires an application of the *Erie* doctrine where the federal court is required to follow the substantive law of a particular state and that state follows the law of additur.
4. **Exception—harmless error:** Errors that **do not affect a party's substantive rights** are considered harmless errors and a **new trial will not be granted** unless justice requires it. FRCP 61.

   > **MBE tip:** If asked about the "best" argument a party can make for a new trial, pick an answer that uses the language of one of the grounds for a new trial.

C. **Motion to seek relief from a judgment** can be based on: (FRCP 60.)

1. **Clerical errors;**
2. **Neglectful mistakes;**
3. **Newly discovered evidence** that could not reasonably be discovered for the original trial; or
4. **Fraud, misrepresentation,** or other **misconduct** of a party;
5. **Judgment is void for lack of due process; or**
6. Any other **reason that justifies relief.**

7. **Timing:** A motion to set aside a judgment based on fraud, neglectful mistakes, or newly discovered evidence may **not be brought more than one year after the judgment.**

   Example: P sued D for injuries arising out of an accident. P presented evidence that her injuries left her legs permanently paralyzed. The jury found in favor of P and awarded her $5 million. Two months after the court entered judgment, D was given a videotape made that day showing P jogging with her doctor. The "best" way for D to seek relief is to move for relief from the judgment on the ground P committed a fraud in obtaining damages for permanent injuries.

   MBE tip: If you are asked about the "best way" to seek relief from a judgment, it is always better to select an answer choice resulting in the judgment being reversed or set aside without the possibility of a new trial because the party could still lose at a new trial.

VI. APPEAL

A. **Final judgment rule:** Only final judgments may be appealed. A final judgment is an ultimate decision made by the trial court on the merits of an entire case such that there is a final judgment as to all parties and all causes of action. The rule is triggered when the court issues its last order that leaves nothing else for the court to do except to enforce the judgment. 28 U.S.C. §1291; FRCP 54.

   Example (appealable): A motorcyclist was involved in a collision with a truck. The motorcyclist sued the truck driver for damages. The jury returned a verdict for the truck driver and the court entered judgment. This is a final judgment.

   Example (not appealable): A denial of a motion for summary judgment is not appealable as it is not a final judgment.

B. **Exceptions to the final judgment rule:** Despite the rule, the following orders may be appealed before a final judgment:

   1. **Injunctions and some interlocutory orders** (orders made during the pendency of the legal action). 28 U.S.C. §1292.

      a. **Temporary restraining orders** can be appealed if the court extends the time period from the typical short time period to a time more consistent with the timing for a preliminary injunction.

      Example: Two days before his home was to be sold at a foreclosure sale, a homeowner obtained a temporary restraining order (TRO) preventing his lender from proceeding with the sale for 14 days or until a preliminary hearing could take place. When the hearing could not be scheduled within 14 days, the court extended the TRO for another 30 days. The lender appealed the court's order extending the TRO. The owner moved to dismiss the appeal. The appellate court is not likely to dismiss the appeal because the 30-day extension makes the TRO equivalent to a preliminary injunction and therefore appealable.

   2. **Trial court certifies an interlocutory order for appeal:** When a judge believes that an order (that is otherwise not appealable) involves a controlling question of law as to which there is a substantial ground for difference of opinion and that an immediate appeal from the order may materially advance the ultimate termination of litigation, the judge can certify an order for an interlocutory appeal. Essentially, the judge has discretion to certify an interlocutory (case is still pending) order for an appeal. 28 U.S.C. §1292(b).

3. **Collateral orders** that involve a serious and unsettled legal question, and would be effectively unreviewable if the court waited until final judgment to hear the claim or issue.
4. **Multiple claims or parties** are involved in the case and some issues are pending, but the issue is resolved as to one claim or party (but not all) and the judge expressly determines that there is no just reason for delay. FRCP 54.
5. **Extraordinary writ:** If an order is not otherwise appealable and the circumstances are exceptional, the aggrieved party may seek a writ of mandate to compel the lower court to act, or refrain from acting. 28 U.S.C. §1651.
6. **Certification of class actions.** FRCP 23(f).

C. **Time limits for appeals:** Must file notice of appeal within **30 days** after entry of final judgment. Federal Rules of Appellate Procedure 4.

VII. CLAIM AND ISSUE PRECLUSION

Where a claim or issue has already been resolved by litigation it may be barred from being relitigated.

A. **Claim preclusion (res judicata) precludes relitigation** of a **claim** that has **already been decided in prior litigation** between the same parties. A subsequent suit based on the **same claim will be barred** where the first claim meets the following requirements:

1. There is a **valid final judgment on the merits** (when judgment is rendered).
2. The **same plaintiff and same defendant** were parties (or privies) in the prior case and subsequent case.

   a. A **privy** is a successor in interest to the property or claim, or is a representative (e.g., trustee) of the party.

   b. **"Strangers"** to the prior litigation **cannot be bound** under res judicata.

3. The **same claim** (cause of action) is asserted or could have been asserted in both the prior case and the subsequent case (meaning the claim derives from the **same transaction or occurrence**).

   Example (claim preclusion bars relitigation): A motorcyclist was involved in a collision with a truck. The motorcyclist sued the truck driver for damages. The jury returned a verdict for the truck driver and entered judgment. The motorcyclist then sued the company that employed the driver and owned the truck. The company moved to dismiss based on the prior judgment against the truck driver. A court can grant the company's motion based on claim preclusion (the truck driver, who was the company employee, has already been absolved from negligence).

   c. **Applicable law:** The law of the court that renders a judgment determines what preclusive effect that judgment should have in another court.

   Example: A car manufacturer produced a car that was sold nationwide. Problems with the car's brakes caused several accidents. Two individual buyers each filed a class action, in different states against the manufacturer for products liability claims on behalf of all buyers nationwide. One action was filed in federal court and one in state court. The parties in the federal action reached a settlement and the court entered judgment dismissing the action with prejudice. The manufacturer's attorney moved to dismiss the state court action on the basis of res judicata. The state court should look to federal law because the judgment was entered in federal court.

> **MBE tip:** If the facts indicate the court dismissed the action with prejudice then this is a valid final judgment on the merits and res judicata (claim preclusion) applies.

B. **Issue preclusion (collateral estoppel) precludes relitigation** of a particular **issue** that has **already been decided in prior litigation.** A subsequent suit based on the same issue will be barred where the first claim meets the following requirements:

1. There is a **valid final judgment on the merits** (when judgment is rendered).
2. The same issue was **actually litigated.**
3. The **issue was necessarily determined (essential to the judgment)** in the first case.
4. **Collateral estoppel can be used only *against*** someone who was a **party (or in privity with a party) in the prior suit** in the interest of fairness (so they have an opportunity to defend the action).
5. **Collateral estoppel can only be used *by*:**
   a. **Traditionally the rule of mutuality applied** and a party asserting collateral estoppel had to be a party (or a privy) in the prior case to assert collateral estoppel in the subsequent case. Thus, a **"stranger" to the first case could *not* use a prior judgment.**
   b. **Nonmutual issue preclusion** jurisdictions (where the mutuality rule is not employed) **allow a "stranger" to the prior case to rely** on a prior judgment if doing so is **"fair."**
      1. **Defensive use** of prior litigation to *avoid liability* on a subsequent suit will be allowed where the party against whom collateral estoppel is being asserted had a **fair opportunity to be heard on the critical issue** in the prior case.
      2. **Offensive use** of the prior litigation to *establish an issue* in a subsequent suit is disfavored and will be allowed only when it is **fair and equitable employing a balancing test,** and the **defendant could not have easily joined** in the first case.

C. **Full faith and credit:** State court judgments shall have the **same full faith and credit in every federal court** as they have in the courts of such state from which they are taken (e.g., if the state that rendered the prior judgment does not require mutuality then the federal court in a later action can apply the same issue preclusion rules the first state court used).

Example: An individual investor purchased stock through a company's stock offering. When the price of the stock plummeted, the investor sued the company in State A state court claiming fraud. A university that had purchased the company's stock through the same offering sued the company in State B federal court claiming violations of securities laws. The individual's suit went to trial. The state court ruled that the company's materials contained false information and awarded damages. The university moved for partial summary judgment arguing collateral estoppel on the issue of whether the company's stock offering materials contained false information. Neither State A nor State B permits nonmutual issue preclusion. The court should not grant the university's motion because State A does not permit nonmutual issue preclusion so under the full faith and credit clause, the federal court can't give greater issue preclusive effect to a state court judgment than the state's own courts would give to that judgment.

USE OF FINAL JUDGMENT CHEAT SHEET

Claim Preclusion (Res Judicata)	Issue Preclusion (Collateral Estoppel)
◆ Valid final judgment on the merits	◆ Valid final judgment on the merits
◆ Same *claim* (same transaction or occurrence)	◆ Same *issue* actually litigated ◆ Same *issue* necessarily determined (essential to the judgment)
◆ Same P and D were parties or privies in both cases ◆ Strangers cannot be bound	◆ Only use **against** a party or privy in prior suit ◆ Only use **by**: ◇ Traditional rule (mutuality) - Same P and D or privies (no strangers) ◇ Nonmutuality rule - Can be used by strangers to: ❖ **Avoid liability** if party against whom CE being asserted had opportunity to be heard, or ❖ **Establish an issue** if fair and equitable

MBE tip: Questions use the terms res judicata and collateral estoppel, claim and issue preclusion, preclusion, and preclusive effect interchangeably.

VIII. STANDARD OF REVIEW

A. **Questions of fact determined by judge:** A trial court's **findings of fact** may not be set aside unless **"clearly erroneous,"** which occurs when the appellate court, based on the entirety of the evidence, is left with the definite and firm conviction that a mistake has been committed.

Example: A trial judge's report of his required findings of fact on the record after the close of evidence, (whether the findings were based on oral or documentary evidence) as to the amount of damages to be awarded to plaintiff, would be reviewed under a clearly erroneous standard.

B. **Questions of fact determined by a jury:** A factual finding by a jury is reviewed using an even more deferential standard than that applied to a trial judge's findings because the appellate court will view the jury's factual findings **in a light most favorable to affirming the jury's verdict,** and determining whether a **reasonable jury** could have reached the **same conclusion.**

C. **Matters of law:** Review of legal rulings is **de novo,** which means the appellate court will use the trial court's record, but it reviews the evidence and law without deference to the trial court's ruling and can substitute its own judgment for that of the trial judge.

Example: An appeal based on a trial court's grant of motion for summary judgment.

D. **Mixed questions of fact and law** are reviewed **de novo,** which means the appellate court can substitute its own judgment for that of the trial judge.

E. **Matters discretionary to the judge** (e.g., admissibility of evidence, a court's determination of whether evidence is highly prejudicial or irrelevant) are reviewed under the **abuse of discretion** standard.

Example: A student sued a university for negligence after he fell from scaffolding in a university-owned theater. At trial, the court permitted the jury to hear testimony that there have been several prior accidents in the same building. The jury found for the student and the university appealed. The university argued on appeal that the previous accidents should have been excluded as irrelevant and highly prejudicial. The proper standard of review for this argument is using an abuse of discretion standard (because the trial court has broad discretion to determine whether evidence is relevant or prejudicial and should be admitted).

F. **Exception: Harmless error standard** will be found when the court's erroneous admission of evidence did not affect any party's substantial rights (there is no ground for a new trial, setting aside a verdict, etc. for harmless error).

CIVIL PROCEDURE CHEAT SHEET

PERSONAL JURISDICTION

Traditional Basis

- Consent: express or implied
- Domiciled in forum state
- Present and served

Other Forms of Personal Jurisdiction

- Federal statutes
- In rem jurisdiction
- Quasi-in rem jurisdiction
- Personal jx waived

Federal courts **can hear** case without proper personal jurisdiction

Long-arm statute ⟶ Minimum Contacts

Nature of contacts
- Minimum contacts w/ forum
- Not offend traditional notions of
- Fair play & substantial justice

Minimum contacts
- Purposeful availment
- Foreseeable to be haled into court

Relatedness between claim and contacts
- *Specific jx*: claim arose from activity in state
- *General jx*: essentially at home if forum st. has jx over D
  - ◇ Corp: state of inc. & principal place of business
  - ◇ Subsidiary: subsidiary controls not parent company
  - ◇ Foreign corp.: not at home
  - ◇ Websites & stream of commerce: no clear standards

Fairness factors
- Burden on D
- Forum state interest
- Legal system efficiency
- P's interest
- Shared states interests

SUBJECT MATTER JURISDICTION

Federal Question, *or*

Diversity of Citizenship

(1) No P from same state as any D (at time of filing not when cause of action arose), **&**
- Person: domicile
  - ◇ Physically present & intent to make permanent home
- Child: domicile of parents
- Legal representative: represented person's citizenship controls
- Corp.: every state of incorporation & principal place of business
- Unincorporated association: every state each partner/member is a citizen
- Alienage: foreign citizen & U.S. citizen ok for diversity
- Class action: citizenship of named class representative

(2) Amt. in controversy exceeds $75,000
- No attorney fees, interest, and costs
- Can aggregate claims if:
  - ◇ One P v. one D, or
  - ◇ Joint tortfeasors w/common & undivided interest
- No aggregation for counterclaims
- Amt. good faith claim at time of filing
- Equitable = harm to P or cost to D

SUPPLEMENTAL JURISDICTION

Extends SMJ to an additional claim if:
- Additional claim shares a common nucleus of operative fact
  - ◇ Same transaction/occurrence
- Original claim does have proper SMJ

Diversity case limitations

P can't use supplemental jx to defeat diversity so NOT allowed for:

Claim by **P against parties** brought as:
- Third-party claims/impleader
- Compulsory/indispensable party
- Permissive joinder
- Intervention by absentee party

Claim by **P who is joined** as an indispensable party

Court has discretion to deny supp. jx if

- State law claim novel or complex
- State law claim predominates fed. claim
- Federal claim dismissed, or
- Exceptional circumstances

- Federal courts **can NOT hear** a case w/out proper SMJ (must raise *sua sponte*)
- No waiver of SMJ is allowed
- Lack of SMJ can be raised at any time (even on appeal)
- Fed. court can't hear family law/probate

REMOVAL: STATE CT. ⇨ FED CT.

- D (not P) can remove case from state to fed. court if either ct. proper
- D's right to remove waived if D files a permissive counterclaim
- D has **30 days** after service of 1st removable document to remove
- Except in diversity cases:
  - ◇ D may not remove if any D is a citizen of the forum state
  - ◇ D can't remove after 1 year from filing

REMAND

- If removal was improper
- P has **30 days** from removal or waived

VENUE

Proper district where:
- In any district in which any D resides if all Ds residents of the state, or
- Where claim occurred
- *If neither of above,* then where any D is subject to PJ (fallback venue)

Reside for venue:
- Person: domicile
- Corp/Part./Assn:
  - ◇ Ps- PPB jud. dist.
  - ◇ Ds- any PJ district

- Waived if not raised in first Rule 12 response
- Court may raise *sua sponte*

TRANSFER OF VENUE

- Fed. to fed. court (different district)

Proper original venue:
- Transfer to where originally could have brought case, or
- All parties consent
- Court has discretion: look at
  - ◇ Public factors: local interests
  - ◇ Private factors: convenience of parties, location of witnesses, access to info., etc.

Improper original venue:
- May transfer where could have originally been brought, or
- Dismiss case

Transferee district must have:
- Proper venue, SMJ, PJ, or
- All parties consent
  - ◇ Valid forum selection clauses deemed consent = binding

VENUE LAW

Diversity cases:
Apply law of the original transferor court (if original court was proper)

FORUM NON CONVENIENS

- Court can dismiss or stay case if another court is substantially more appropriate
- Available/adequate
- Same public/private factors as transfer

Federal courts **can hear** a case without proper venue (can be waived or consent)

NOTICE

Process of Service

- D must be served with notice of action
- Summons & complaint
- W/in **90 days** of filing
- By a nonparty at least 18 years old

Waiver of Service

- P can request that D waive service
- D liable for expenses if no waiver w/o good cause
- D has **30 days** to waive

Method of Service

- Personal service
- D's abode left w/ one of suitable age who resides there
- Authorized agent
- Corp./partn./assn.: follow state law or serve to officer or agent authorized
- Foreign countries: int'l agreed means or reasonable way

Interlocutory Injunctions

- TRO: can be done ex parte (w/o notice) in exceptional circumstances
- Need immediate irreparable injury
- P posts security bond in case error

- Preliminary inj.:
- Notice required
- Preserves status quo until trial
- Irreparable harm
- Likely to succeed on the merits
- Inadequate legal remedy
- Balance hardships
- No valid defenses

CHOICE OF LAW (DIVERSITY CASES)

- **State law in fed. ct. (*Erie*)**: apply state substantive law; federal procedural law
- Statute of limitations/conflicts/choice of law rules are substantive
- If unclear: Outcome determinative test—substantive law if it substantially affects outcome; Court balances federal and state interests; Avoid forum shopping

PRETRIAL PROCEDURES

Pleadings

Notice pleading: Facts
Rule 11: atty./party sign:
- Filed in good faith
- Not frivolous
- Facts to support
- Denials reasonable
- Sanctions if violated
  - **21-day** safe harbor

Complaint

P must raise issues &:
- Identify parties
- State proper SMJ
- Facts for relief (notice pleading usually ok)
- Demand for judgment
- P/attorney signature

Must plead specifically:
- Capacity if to show jx
- Fraud/mistake
- Conditions precedent if denying condition
- Time/place if testing sufficiency of the pleadings
- Special damages

Pre-answer Motions

- More definite statement
- To strike (scandalous, immaterial, redundant, etc.)
- To dismiss (no claim for relief stated)

Answer

- Respond within **21 days**
- If service waived: **60 days** U.S.; **90** foreign
- If pre-answer denied, answer w/in **14 days**
- Must assert affirmative defenses & compulsory counterclaims

Rule 12(b) Defenses

D can raise in either pre-answer motion *or* answer

Defense	
Lack of PJ →	Raise in 1st response or waived
Improper venue →	Raise in 1st response or waived
Insufficient process →	Raise in 1st response or waived
Insufficient service of process →	Raise in 1st response or waived
Lack of SMJ →	Raise anytime until appeals exhausted
Failure to state a claim to grant relief →	Raise anytime until trial is concluded
Failure to join an indispensable party →	Raise anytime until trial is concluded

Failure to answer = P can seek default judgment

Amended Pleadings

- P can amend **once** before D responds w/in **21 days**
- D can amend once after answer w/in **21 days**
- More than 1 or late need court permission or consent

Relation Back Doctrine

Amended claims relate back to the original filing date if same transaction/occurrence
Amended Ds relate back if:
- Same conduct/transaction/occurrence
- New party had notice within **90 days**, and
- Knew/should have would be named but for mistake

JOINDER OF PARTIES

Permissive: same transaction/occurrence
- SMJ required

Necessary party if:
- Court can't provide relief w/o
- Absent party's interest harmed
- Existing party subject to multiple inconsistent obligations
- Must be joined if PJ & diversity ok

If necesssary party can't join:
- Proceed w/o necessary party, or
- Dismiss if indispensable (necessary & can't provide relief in their absence)

Impleader

D adds a third-party D
- Supplemental jx applies

Intervention

Nonparty claims an interest (2 types)
- Need SMJ

Interpleader

Property holder forces all claimants into one action: avoids multiple/inconsistent litigation

Statutory:
- 1 claimant diverse from 1 other claimant
- $500 or more

Rule 22:
- Stakeholder diverse from all claimants
- Over $75,000

JOINDER OF CLAIMS

Compulsory counterclaim	Permissive counterclaim	Cross claim
◆ Same transaction/occurrence ◆ Must raise or waived ◆ Supplemental jx applies	◆ Not same transaction/occurrence ◆ No supplemental jx ◆ Need independent SMJ	◆ Offensive claim against co-party ◆ Same trans./ occur. ◆ Supple. jx applies

Class action

Requirements: ◆ Numerosity ◆ Commonality ◆ Typicality ◆ Adequacy	Type: ◆ Need ct. approval ◆ Prejudice ◆ Injunctive/declaratory relief ◆ Questions common to class predominate individual questions	◆ Diversity: citizenship of repres. & $75,000 by any named representative Class Action Fairness Act ◆ Any member diverse from any D ◆ $5 million & 100 members

DISCOVERY

Discovery Conference	Initial Disclosures	Expert testimony
◆ Mandatory to confer ◆ Prepare discovery plan ◆ Submit w/in **14 days** ◆ Court can modify pretrial order if injustice	◆ People w/discoverable info ◆ Documents/tangible evidence ◆ Damages computation ◆ Insurance documents ◆ Except exempt proceedings	◆ **90 days** before trial ◆ Expert ID/contact info ◆ Qualifications ◆ Final written report ◆ NOT draft report
Pretrial Disclosures	**Depositions**	**Interrogatories**
◆ **30 days** before trial ◆ Non-expert witnesses ◆ List of documents, physical evid., exhibits	◆ Oral or written (under oath) ◆ 10 by each side (not party) ◆ Only once; one 7-hour day ◆ Parties & nonparties	◆ Written (under oath) ◆ 25 Qs (incl. subparts) ◆ Respond within 30 days ◆ Parties only
Request for admissions	**Requests for documents**	**Physical or mental exam**
◆ Written (w/documents) ◆ 30 days to respond ◆ Parties only	◆ Includes other tangible items ◆ 30 days to respond ◆ Party; nonparty if subpoena	◆ By court order ◆ Show good cause ◆ Of party if at issue

Discovery limits	Protective order/disputes
◆ Ok if not admiss. - Ok if reas. calculated to lead to evidence ◆ No privileged materials – if disclosed notify and return ◆ No atty. work product – except substantial need, mental impressions, opinions, etc. or own statement ◆ Electronic. stored data not reas. accessible/undue cost	◆ Can seek protective order to prevent disclosure for good cause ◆ Dispute: meet to confer ◆ Mtn. to compel/sanctions

ADJUDICATION WITHOUT A TRIAL

Dismissal	Default Jdg.	Jdg. on pleadings	MSJ
◆ Voluntary: 1 time only w/ out prejudice ◆ Invol.: w/prejudice ◆ Failure to state claim	1. Request clerk 2. Ct. notifies all ◆ If sum only, ok clerk w/o court	◆ Post pleadings ◆ Ct. accepts all facts as true in pleadings	◆ No genuine dispute of material fact ◆ Jdg. matter of law ◆ **30 days** after disc.

TRIAL ISSUES

Right to jury trial
- Legal issues 1st then eq.
- Demand in writing
- **14 days** after last plead.
- Applies to counter & cross claims

Jury Composition
- Unlimited challenges for cause
- 3 peremptory challenges (gender/race neutral)
- 6-12 jurors (start w/at least 6)
- Unanimous vote unless agree

Poll/jury instructions
- Can poll jury
- Require special verdict (written Qs/findings)
- Jury instructions – object or waive

Judgment as a Matter of Law (JMOL)
- After other side heard at trial
- No reas. jury would find for other side
- Viewed in favor of non-moving party
- Request before case goes to the jury

Bench Trial (no jury)
- Court must make findings of fact & conclusions of law
- Stated separately on record or decision
- Does not apply to Rule 12 or MSJ

POST-TRIAL ISSUES

Renewed JMOL
- Must have filed JMOL
- Within **28 days** of entry of judgment
- No reas. jury would find for other side

Motion to seek relief from judgment
- Clerical errors
- Lack of due process
- Newly discovered evidence
- Fraud, misrepresentation, misconduct
- Neglectful mistakes
- Justifiable reason

Motion for new trial
- Based on errors at trial:
  - Prejudicial/plain error
  - New evidence
  - Prejudicial misconduct
  - Against weight of evidence
  - Excessive/inadequate damages
- Within **28 days** after entry of judgment
- Except ok if harmless error

Conditional new trial on damages only
- <u>Remittitur</u>: b/c damages too high
- <u>Additur</u>: b/c damages too low (not in fed. ct.)

APPEAL

Final Judgment Rule
- Decision on the merits of an entire case
- Only final judgments can be appealed
- Appeal w/in **30 days** after final judgment

Exceptions (can appeal)
- Injunctions & some TROs (extended)
- Court certifies & collateral orders
- Extraordinary writs & class actions

USE OF FINAL JUDGMENT

Res Judicata (claim preclusion)
- Valid final judgment on the merits
- Same claim asserted or could have been
- Same P and D (or privies)
- Law of ct. that rendered the judgment determines preclusive effect

Full Faith and Credit
State court judgments have same full faith and credit in federal courts

Collateral Estoppel (issue preclusion)
- Valid final judgment on the merits
- Same issue litigated or could have been
- Issue essential to judgment
- Used *against* prior party or privy
- (Traditional) used *by* prior party or privy
- (Nonmutual) used *by* stranger ok if fair
  - Avoid liability for defensive use
  - Establish an issue for offensive use

STANDARDS OF REVIEW

◆ Questions of fact determined by judge →	Clearly erroneous
◆ Questions of fact determined by jury →	In light most favorable to affirming jury (if reas. jury could reach same conclusion)
◆ Matters of law →	De novo (can substitute its own judgment)
◆ Mixed questions of fact and law →	De novo (can substitute its own judgment)
◆ Matters discretionary to judge →	Abuse of discretion
◆ Exception: →	Harmless error used when erroneous admission of evidence didn't affect any party's substantive rights

DEADLINES DECODED
7 Days
◆ Notice of default hearing
14 Days
◆ TRO ◆ Answer if pre-answer motion denied ◆ Discovery plan & mandatory initial disclosures after discovery conference ◆ Demand jury trial (after last pleading served, but if pleading amended within 21 days, can add jury demand to amended pleading)
21 Days
◆ Pre-answer motion *or* answer after service of complaint, counterclaim or crossclaim* ◆ Default judgment (entered for failure to respond)* ◆ Amend pleadings (after pleading was served) ◆ Rule 11 safe harbor for sanctions (to withdraw/amend pleadings) *If service waived, D has extra time to respond: 60 days (U.S.); 90 days (foreign)
28 Days (most posttrial filings)
◆ RJMOL (after entry of judgment) ◆ Motion for new trial (after entry of judgment)
30 Days (most discovery deadlines)
◆ Notice of removal (after receipt of initial pleading *or* first removable document) ◆ Motion to remand (after notice of removal filed) ◆ Pretrial disclosures ◆ Respond to interrogatories, requests for admissions, and production of documents ◆ MSJ (after close of all discovery) ◆ Notice of appeal (after entry of judgment) ◆ Time to return waiver (for service of process in the U.S.)
60 Days
◆ Answer *or* pre-answer motion after waiver of service of process (from U.S.) ◆ Serve answer after service of process on U.S. agency or employee ◆ Time to return waiver (for service of process in foreign country)
90 Days
◆ Service of process after complaint filed ◆ Answer *or* pre-answer motion after waiver of service of process (from foreign) ◆ Disclose expert testimony information before trial ◆ Relation back to amend and add new defendant (who had original notice)
One Year
◆ Notice of removal based on diversity (within 30 days of receipt of removable document, but no later than one year) ◆ Motion to seek relief from judgment
No time limit
◆ Motion to remand for lack of SMJ (any time before final appeal)

CIVIL PROCEDURE MBE PRACTICE QUESTIONS

These questions are designed to reinforce the skill in how to approach MBE questions. While they will also test your knowledge in the limited areas addressed, you will not master your knowledge by only practicing these questions. To fully master the rules, you need to do practice questions outside of these from your bar company and/or the NCBE.

QUESTION 1

An entrepreneur from State A decided to sell hot sauce to the public, labeling it "Best Hot Sauce." A company incorporated in State B and headquartered in State C sued the entrepreneur in federal court in State C. The complaint sought $50,000 in damages and alleged that the entrepreneur's use of the name "Best Hot Sauce" infringed the company's federal trademark. The entrepreneur filed an answer denying the allegations, and the parties began discovery. Six months later, the entrepreneur moved to dismiss for lack of subject-matter jurisdiction.

Should the court grant the entrepreneur's motion?

A. No, because the company's claim arises under federal law.
B. No, because the entrepreneur waived the right to challenge subject-matter jurisdiction by not raising the issue initially by motion or in the answer.
C. Yes, because although the claim arises under federal law, the amount in controversy is not satisfied.
D. Yes, because although there is diversity, the amount in controversy is not satisfied.

QUESTION 2

A shop owner domiciled in State A sued a distributor in a federal district court in State A for breach of a contract. The shop owner sought $100,000 in damages for allegedly defective goods that the distributor had provided under the contract. The distributor is incorporated in State B, with its principal place of business in State C. The distributor brought in as a third-party defendant the wholesaler that had provided the goods to the distributor, alleging the wholesaler had a duty to indemnify the distributor for any damages recovered by the shop owner. The wholesaler is incorporated in State B, with its principal place of business in State A.

The wholesaler has asserted a $60,000 counterclaim against the distributor for payment for the goods at issue, and the distributor has moved to dismiss the counterclaim for lack of subject-matter jurisdiction.

Should the motion to dismiss be granted?

A. No, because the wholesaler's and the distributor's principal place of business are diverse.
B. No, because there is supplemental jurisdiction over the wholesaler's counterclaim.
C. Yes, because there is no diversity of citizenship between the distributor and the wholesaler.
D. Yes, because there is no diversity of citizenship between the shop owner and the wholesaler.

QUESTION 3

A plaintiff domiciled in State A brought a wrongful death action in federal court in State A against a State B parent corporation and one of its foreign subsidiaries. The plaintiff alleged that a tire manufactured by the subsidiary in Europe had caused his wife's death in an automobile accident in Europe.

The parent corporation does significant business throughout the United States, including in State A. The subsidiary conducts no business and has no employees or bank accounts in State A. The subsidiary manufactures its tires for the European market, but 2% of its tires are distributed in State A by the parent corporation. The subsidiary has moved to dismiss for lack of personal jurisdiction.

Should the court grant the subsidiary's motion?

A. No, because 2% of the subsidiary's tires entered State A through the stream of commerce.
B. No, because of the general personal jurisdiction established over the parent corporation.
C. Yes, because the accident did not occur in the United States.
D. Yes, because the subsidiary lacks continuous, systematic, and substantial contacts with State A.

QUESTION 4

A bakery incorporated and headquartered in State A had a dispute with a mill incorporated and headquartered in State B over the quality of the flour the mill had delivered to the bakery. The bakery sued the mill in a federal court in State A for breach of contract, seeking $100,000 in damages.

The contract between the bakery and the mill contained a clause designating State B courts as the sole venue for litigating disputes arising under the contract. Under precedent of the highest court in State A, forum-selection clauses are unenforceable as against public policy; under U.S. Supreme Court precedent, such clauses are enforceable.

The mill has moved to transfer the case to a federal court in State B, citing the forum-selection clause in the parties' contract and asserting the facts that the flour was produced in State B and that the majority of likely witnesses are in State B.

Is the court likely to grant the mill's motion?

A. No, because State A law treats forum-selection clauses as unenforceable.
B. No, because the mill should have instead filed a motion to dismiss for improper venue.
C. Yes, because federal common law makes the forum-selection clause controlling.
D. Yes, because federal law governs transfers of venue, and it would be more convenient for the witnesses and parties to litigate the claim in State B.

QUESTION 5

A mail clerk domiciled in State A slipped and fell on ice that had formed near the loading dock of the building in State B where the clerk's State B employer leased space for its headquarters. The building was owned and operated by a State C corporation. As a result of the fall, the clerk was injured and the employer's expensive computer he was carrying was badly damaged.

The clerk sued the building owner for negligence in a federal district court in State B, seeking $100,000 in personal-injury damages. The employer has filed a timely motion to intervene asserting an $80,000 negligence claim against the building owner for the damage to its computer.

Is the court likely to grant the employer's motion to intervene?

A. No, because although the employer has an interest in the clerk's action, that interest is not likely to be impaired in the employer's absence.
B. No, because the clerk chose not to join the employer as a co-plaintiff in his action.
C. Yes, because the employer is an indispensable party.
D. Yes, because the employer's claim shares common questions of law and fact with the clerk's action.

QUESTION 6

A retailer brought a federal diversity action against an architect, alleging fraudulent misrepresentations in the architect's design of the retailer's store. The complaint did not include a jury demand.

The architect timely moved to dismiss the action for failure to state a claim; he did not file an answer. Twenty days after being served with the motion, the retailer amended the complaint to add a defamation claim based on the architect's recent statements about the retailer in a local newspaper. In the amended complaint, the retailer demanded a jury trial on both claims.

Has the retailer properly demanded a jury trial?

A. No, because the retailer filed the demand more than 14 days after service of the motion to dismiss.
B. No, because the retailer filed the demand more than 14 days after service of the original complaint.
C. Yes, but on the defamation claim only, because the original complaint did not contain a jury demand.
D. Yes, on both claims, because the architect had not answered the original complaint when the retailer filed the amended complaint with the jury demand.

QUESTION 7

A construction worker sued an insulation manufacturer in federal court, claiming that he had developed a chronic health condition as a result of 20 years of exposure to the manufacturer's insulation at his work sites. The manufacturer answered, denying all liability and stating that it had never supplied its insulation to the worker's employer.

The worker's attorney deposed the manufacturer's president, and the manufacturer's attorney deposed the worker. Immediately thereafter, the manufacturer moved for summary judgment on the ground that the worker had no evidence showing that the insulation had ever been used by the worker's employer.

What would be the worker's best response to the motion for summary judgment?

A. Argue that more time is needed for additional discovery to show the manufacturer's liability, and attach a declaration describing the desired discovery.
B. Argue that the motion should be denied, because a central issue in the case will be the manufacturer's credibility on the question of its distribution of the insulation, and only a jury can decide questions of credibility.
C. Argue that the motion should be denied, because the manufacturer failed to attach any evidence to its motion to show that the insulation was not used by the worker's employer.
D. Make a cross-motion for summary judgment arguing that the manufacturer has introduced no evidence to show that its insulation did not harm the worker.

QUESTION 8

A plaintiff sued a defendant in federal court for injuries arising out of an accident involving the parties. The plaintiff alleged and presented evidence at trial demonstrating that her injuries had left her legs permanently paralyzed. The jury found in favor of the plaintiff and awarded her $5 million in damages. Two months after the court entered judgment, the defendant was given a videotape made that day showing the plaintiff jogging with her doctor.

What is the best way for the defendant to seek relief from the judgment?

A. Move for a new trial or in the alternative for remittitur to reduce the award in light of the shortened duration of the plaintiff's injuries.
B. Move for relief from judgment on the ground that the judgment was based on the jury's mistaken belief that the plaintiff's injuries would be permanent.
C. Move for relief from judgment on the ground that the plaintiff committed a fraud in obtaining damages for permanent injuries.
D. Move for relief from the judgment on the ground that there is newly discovered evidence that the plaintiff's injuries were not permanent.

QUESTION 9

An individual investor purchased stock through a company's stock offering. When the price of the stock plummeted, the investor sued the company in a state court in State A, claiming that the company's offering materials had fraudulently induced him to purchase the stock and seeking $25,000 in damages.

A university that had purchased the company's stock through the same offering sued the company in federal court in State B, claiming that the offering materials violated federal securities laws and seeking $1 million in damages.

The individual investor's suit proceeded to trial. The state court ruled that the company's offering materials contained false information and awarded the investor a $25,000 judgment. The university immediately moved for partial summary judgment in its federal action against the company, arguing that the state court judgment bound the federal court on the issue of whether the company's offering materials contained false information. Neither State A nor State B permits nonmutual issue preclusion.

Should the court grant the university's motion?

A. No, because State A does not permit nonmutual issue preclusion.
B. No, because the federal court sits in a state that does not permit nonmutual issue preclusion.
C. Yes, because federal law permits nonmutual issue preclusion.
D. Yes, because the issue of whether the materials contained false information was actually litigated and necessarily decided.

QUESTION 10

A student at a private university sued the university in federal court for negligence after he fell from scaffolding in a university-owned theater building. At trial, after briefing from both parties, the court permitted the jury to hear testimony that there had been several previous accidents in the same building. The jury found for the student, and the university appealed. One of the university's arguments on appeal is that the testimony about the previous accidents should have been excluded as irrelevant and highly prejudicial.

Which standard of review applies to this argument?

A. Abuse of discretion.
B. Clearly erroneous.
C. De novo.
D. Harmless error.

CIVIL PROCEDURE ANSWER KEY	
Question	**Answer**
1	A
2	B
3	D
4	D
5	D
6	D
7	A
8	C
9	A
10	A

Use this quick answer key to get a general idea of how you did on this set of questions. The answer explanations that follow provide a step-by-step deconstruction of each question.

CIVIL PROCEDURE MBE ANSWER EXPLANATIONS

START HERE **FACTS**

Q1

An entrepreneur **from State A** decided to sell hot sauce to the public, labeling it "Best Hot Sauce."

A company **incorporated in State B** and **headquartered in State C** sued the entrepreneur in federal court in State C. The complaint sought **$50,000 in damages** and alleged that the entrepreneur's use of the name "Best Hot Sauce" ***infringed the company's federal trademark.*** The entrepreneur filed an answer denying the allegations, and the parties began discovery. **Six months later**, the entrepreneur moved to dismiss **for lack of subject-matter jurisdiction.**

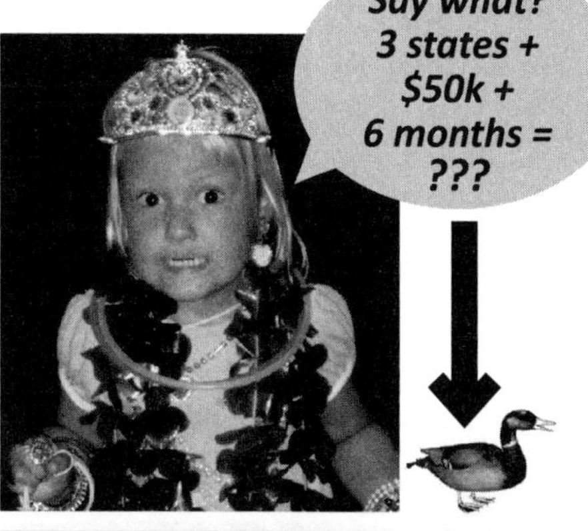

CALL Should the court grant the entrepreneur's motion?

Issue ← *If the issue is not stated in the call, you need to see what the motion is about to find your issue (SMJ, so Civ. Pro.)*

SOLVE

Q **Should the court grant the entrepreneur's motion** (to dismiss for lack of SMJ)?

MBE TIP: ***Fed. Q duck decoy:***
Multiple states & $$ facts & dates/timing

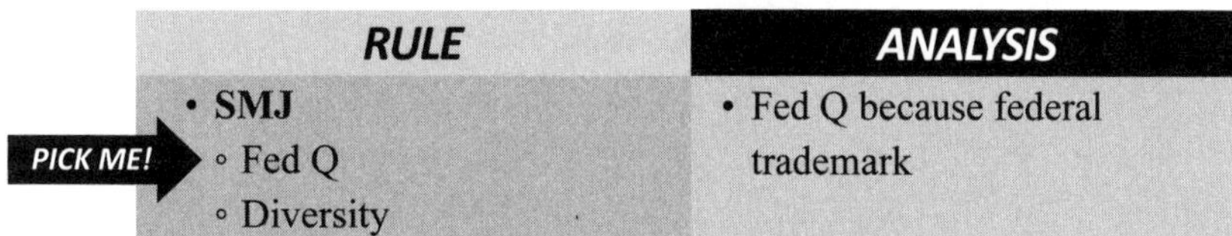

RULE	ANALYSIS
• **SMJ** PICK ME! → ◦ Fed Q ◦ Diversity	• Fed Q because federal trademark

TIP: If you went down the path of diversity jx, stop following the ducks!

......................CLIFF AHEAD!!!

A The court should not grant the motion **because** federal question provides subject matter jurisdiction.

DECODE

→ Now look for an answer choice that comports with your analysis.

A. No, because the company's claim arises under federal law.

Correct, because the claim arises under federal law which provides SMJ.

~~B.~~ No, because the entrepreneur waived the right to challenge subject-matter jurisdiction by not raising the issue initially by motion or in the answer.

Not a correct rule statement. SMJ cannot be waived. The facts about a 6-month delay are duck decoys.

~~C.~~ Yes, because although the claim arises under federal law, the amount in controversy is not satisfied.

Wrong analysis. Federal question SMJ does not require an amount in controversy.

~~D.~~ Yes, because although there is diversity, the amount in controversy is not satisfied.

Wrong rule analyzed. SMJ diversity requirements are irrelevant when there is a federal question.

FACTS **Q2**

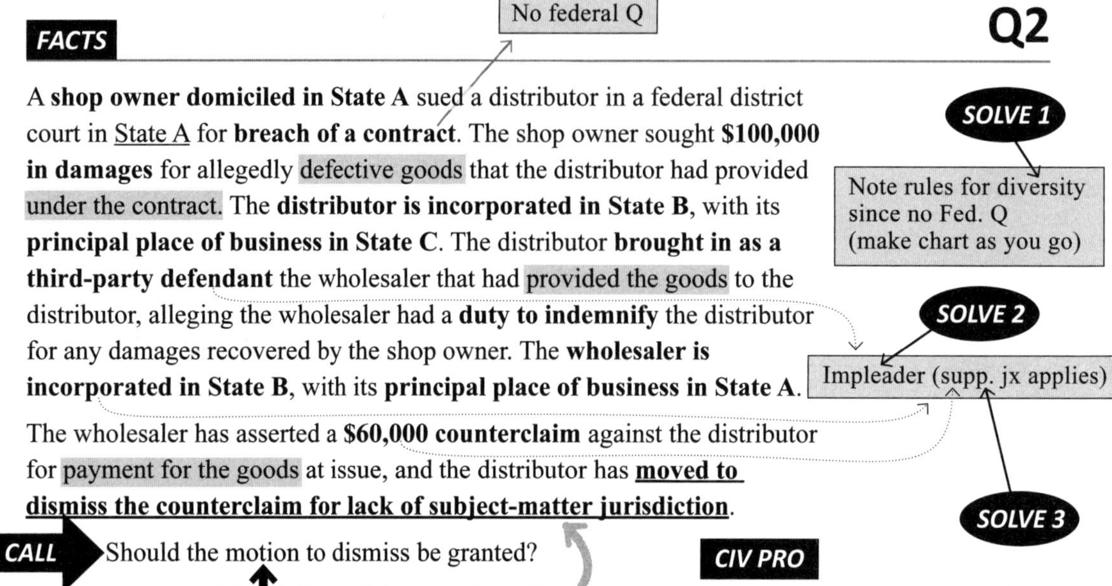

A **shop owner domiciled in State A** sued a distributor in a federal district court in State A for **breach of a contract**. The shop owner sought **$100,000 in damages** for allegedly defective goods that the distributor had provided under the contract. The **distributor is incorporated in State B**, with its **principal place of business in State C**. The distributor **brought in as a third-party defendant** the wholesaler that had provided the goods to the distributor, alleging the wholesaler had a **duty to indemnify** the distributor for any damages recovered by the shop owner. The **wholesaler is incorporated in State B**, with its **principal place of business in State A**. The wholesaler has asserted a **$60,000 counterclaim** against the distributor for payment for the goods at issue, and the distributor has **moved to dismiss the counterclaim for lack of subject-matter jurisdiction**.

CALL Should the motion to dismiss be granted?

SOLVE

Q **Should the motion to dismiss be granted** (lack of SMJ)?

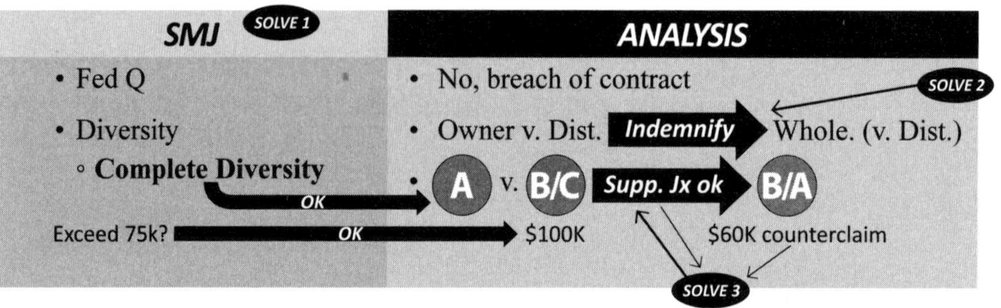

A The motion should not be granted **because** the original parties have **SMJ** (solve 1) and Dist. can bring in Wholesaler under **impleader** (solve 2) with supp. jx (so no diversity ok for impleader). Wholesaler counterclaim = same transaction/occurrence **so supp. jx applies** (solve 3).

Now look for an answer choice that comports with your analysis.

DECODE

A. No, because the wholesaler's and the distributor's principal place of business are diverse.

Wrong analysis. Even though their PPBs are diverse, both corporations have the same state of incorporation so they are not diverse as a corporation is a citizen of both PPB and state of incorporation. This is why supplemental jx must apply to allow the claim to come in.

B. No, because there is supplemental jurisdiction over the wholesaler's counterclaim.

Correct. The counterclaim is based on the same T/O as the original claim (diversity jx exists for original claim), so wholesaler can come in under supplemental jx (impleader) and his claim can also come in (same T/O).

C. Yes, because there is no diversity of citizenship between the distributor and the wholesaler.

Wrong analysis. The absence of diversity citizenship does not matter since supplemental jx applies.

D. Yes, because there is no diversity of citizenship between the shop owner and the wholesaler.

Wrong analysis. The counterclaim is between the wholesaler and the distributor (not the shop owner).

Q3

FACTS

A plaintiff **domiciled in State A** brought a **wrongful death** action in federal court in State A against a State B parent corporation and **one of its foreign subsidiaries**. The plaintiff alleged that a **tire manufactured by the subsidiary in Europe** had caused his wife's death in an automobile **accident in Europe**. **= No specific jx in State A**

So far subsidiary actions all in Europe (not State A)

The parent corporation does significant business throughout the United States, including in State A. **The subsidiary** conducts **no business** and has **no employees or bank accounts in State A**. The subsidiary **manufactures its tires for the European market**, but 2% of its tires are distributed in State A by the parent corporation. The subsidiary has **moved to dismiss for lack of personal jurisdiction**.

Several facts lean toward no contacts for the subsidiary in State A.

Facts about the parent corporation (shaded) are irrelevant to PJ of the subsidiary corporation. These are duck decoys. STOP following the ducks!

Should the court grant the subsidiary's motion?

Figure out what the motion is

SOLVE **CIV PRO**

Q **Should the court grant the subsidiary's motion** (for lack of PJ)?

RULE	ANALYSIS
Traditional basis	
• Consent	• No consent by subsidiary to suit in State A
• Domiciled	• Subsidiary domiciled in Europe
• Present when served	• Subsidiary not served in State A
• Minimum Contacts	
◦ Long arm statute	• Presume LAS
◦ Min. Contacts	
» Purposeful Availment	• No benefits or protections received by Subsidiary from State A
» Relatedness (general jx needed)	• No specific jx because accident in Europe & not essentially at home in State A as located in Europe
» Fairness Factors	• Stream of commerce alone not enough; and only parent company distributes 2% (not direct); subsidiary has no employees, no bank accounts, does no business in State A so would not be fair to bring to court to defend an action in State A

A Yes, **because** there are no traditional basis or minimum contacts that would justify the court haling the subsidiary into court in State A. → Now look for an answer choice that comports with your analysis.

DECODE

~~A.~~ No, because 2% of the subsidiary's tires entered State A through the stream of commerce.

Wrong analysis. Stream of commerce alone is insufficient to establish general jx and the subsidiary does not have sufficient contacts with State A to justify PJ.

~~B.~~ No, because of the general personal jurisdiction established over the parent corporation.

Wrong rule. The PJ over the parent corporation does not affect the jx over a subsidiary corporation (it stands on its own).

~~C.~~ Yes, because the accident did not occur in the United States.

Wrong analysis. The court can have PJ through general jx (minimum contacts) and this answer implies that specific jx is the only way to have PJ.

D. Yes, because the subsidiary lacks continuous, systematic, and substantial contacts with State A.

Bingo!! The facts all lean toward the subsidiary having no contacts with State A resulting in the court not being able to assert PJ over it. (Note the answer does not use the terms general jx or minimum contacts or essentially at home, but rather is using the terms "continuous, systematic and substantial contacts" as a surrogate.)

FACTS

Q4

A bakery incorporated and headquartered in **State A** had a dispute with a mill incorporated and headquartered in **State B** over the quality of the flour the mill had delivered to the bakery. The bakery sued the mill in a federal court in State A for breach of contract, seeking **$100,000** in damages.

Facts establish SMJ ok

The **contract** between the bakery and the mill **contained a clause designating State B courts as the sole venue** for litigating **disputes** arising under the contract. *Under precedent of the highest court in State A, forum-selection clauses are unenforceable as against public policy; under U.S. Supreme Court precedent, such clauses are enforceable.*

Forum-selection clause for **venue (important– the transfer is due to venue)**

Facts about State A precedent are duck decoys because Federal Rules (FRCP) govern venue and transfer.

The mill has moved to transfer the case to a federal court **in State B**, citing the **forum-selection clause** in the parties' contract and asserting the facts **that the flour was produced in State B** and that the majority of likely **witnesses are in State B**.

Facts that go to reasons to transfer the case

CALL Is the court likely to grant the mill's motion?

Figure out what the motion is

CIV PRO

SOLVE

Q **Is the court likely to grant the mill's motion** (to transfer)?

State A	State B
• Bakery • Case filed	• Mill • Forum-select. clause

RULE 1: First analyze whether the original venue was proper.

RULES	ANALYSIS
(1) The district where any D resides, if all Ds are residents of the state in which the district is located; OR	(1) Not met- D (Mill) in State B
(2) The district in which a substantial part of the events or omissions giving rise to the claim occurred; OR	(2) Over quality of flour (made in State B); unclear where K signed but forum clause says State B; facts don't show sub. part of events in State A
(3) If no U.S. district satisfies (1) or (2) above, then in a judicial district in which any D is subject to the court's PJ for the action.	(3) Court likely has PJ over mill in State A because signed K with bakery there and delivered flour

Original venue proper

SOLVE *(continued)*

Transfer of Venue

Standard: Interests of justice considering public & private factors

RULE 2: Next analyze whether transfer of venue is proper.

ORIGINAL VENUE PROPER	ANALYSIS
A case may be transferred to another district court where the action "might have been brought" or "to which all parties have consented." (SMJ, PJ, Venue ok) Courts may balance the relative convenience of the parties and witnesses offered by the alternative forums.	By signing a contract with a forum-selection clause both parties consented to venue in State B as the clause was part of the contract. So the bakery **waived the right to challenge venue** in State B by signing the contract and agreeing to the forum-selection clause. Also witnesses in State B and flour/mill there as well so convenient there too.

 Yes, **because** the bakery consented to venue in State B and State B would be convenient.

 Now look for an answer choice that comports with your analysis.

DECODE

(A) No, because State A law treats forum-selection clauses as unenforceable.

Inapplicable rule. Venue is controlled by federal law since there is a federal statute on point (FRCP) so state law is not relevant or applicable as to transferring venue.

(B) No, because the mill should have instead filed a motion to dismiss for improper venue.

Wrong analysis. Venue was not improper in State A originally.

(C) Yes, because federal common law makes the forum-selection clause controlling.

Inapplicable rule. Federal common law is not applicable when there is a federal statute on point that controls (FRCP as indicated above controls the transfer of venue). 

D. Yes, because federal law governs transfers of venue, and it would be more convenient for the witnesses and parties to litigate the claim in State B.

Correct because FRCP allow a transfer of venue and it would be more convenient for parties and witnesses since most in State B (note how it did not mention the forum-selection clause or consent – hiding the ball on the obvious part of the answer).

FACTS **Q5**

A **mail clerk domiciled in State A** slipped and fell on ice that had formed near the loading dock of the building in **State B where the clerk's State B employer leased space** for its headquarters. The **building was owned and operated by a State C corporation**. As a result of the fall, the **clerk was injured** *and* the **employer's expensive computer** he was carrying was badly **damaged**.

The **clerk sued** the building owner for **negligence** in a federal district court in State B, seeking **$100,000** in personal-injury damages. The employer has filed a timely motion to intervene asserting an **$80,000 negligence** claim against the building owner for the damage to its computer.

Facts establish SMJ ok for clerk since State A v. State C & $100K

Important as it triggers intervention rules for intervenor's SMJ since original claim based on diversity jx

Intervenor also has SMJ since State B v. State C & $80,000K

CALL Is the court likely to grant the employer's motion to **intervene**?

SOLVE ***CIV PRO and issue clear in call! YAY!***

***MBE tip:** When a rule is discretionary such as the court "may" permit something, the question will often also be discretionary (as this one is) by asking if the court is "likely" to do something.*

INTERVENTION RULES	ANALYSIS
• Nonparty claims an interest in the transaction.	• Employer is a nonparty as the suit is between mail clerk and the building owner.
• Court may permit if the party has a claim or defense that shares with the main action a common question of law or fact.	• The employer has a claim (negligence) that shares with the main action (mail clerk's negligence claim) because both claims are based on the building owner not maintaining the loading dock as it was iced over.
• Separate SMJ is required over the intervenor's claim if original claim based solely on diversity jx.	• Employer has separate SMJ since he is from State B and the building owner from State C and the amount is $80,000.

A Yes, **because** the employer's action shares a common question of law and fact with the main claim and the employer has separate SMJ.

DECODE Now look for an answer choice that comports with your analysis.

A. No, because although the employer has an interest in the clerk's action, that interest is not likely to be impaired in the employer's absence.

Wrong rule. This states the requirement for intervention as a matter of right rather than permissive intervention which is at issue here.

B. No, because the clerk chose not to join the employer as a co-plaintiff in his action.

Wrong analysis. The clerk joining as a co-plaintiff is irrelevant to permissive intervention as a party might be able to intervene even if they could have originally been a co-plaintiff.

C. Yes, because the employer is an indispensable party.

Wrong analysis. An indispensable party is one that is required or the court cannot proceed without them and here the court could proceed without employer and employer could seek damages in a separate suit if needed.

D. Yes, because the employer's claim shares common questions of law and fact with the clerk's action.

Correct, because this states the rule and reason under permissive intervention that the court is likely to permit the employer to intervene as it is the same negligence action (ice near dock).

FACTS **Q6**

A retailer brought a federal diversity action against an architect, alleging **fraudulent misrepresentations** in the architect's design of the retailer's store. The **complaint did not include a jury demand.**

> Good to note since only allowed a jury trial for civil actions at law.

The architect **timely moved to dismiss the action for failure to state a claim; he did not file an answer.** Twenty days after being served with the motion, the retailer **amended the complaint** to **add a defamation claim** based on the architect's recent statements about the retailer in a local newspaper. **In the amended complaint**, the **retailer demanded a jury trial on both claims.**

> Since the call is about a demand for jury trial and the complaint didn't have one, there must be further facts about demanding a jury trial. Usually a party amends the complaint to include a jury demand. When this occurs, timing matters so look for days/dates.

CALL Has the retailer **properly demanded a jury trial**?

CIV PRO. Issue clear in call! YAY!

ISSUES TO ADDRESS:
(1) If amended complaint allowed &
(2) If demand for jury trial timely

SOLVE

Rule: A jury demand needs to be (1) in writing and (2) no later than 14 days after service of the last pleading or it is waived.

WRITING	AMENDED COMPLAINT	JURY DEMAND TIMING	
FACTS	VALID?	RULE	ANALYSIS
• Not in original complaint • In amended complaint **Next step**	• Can amend once w/in 21 days of pre-answer motion • Here 20 days and first time so amended complaint ok **Next step**	• W/in 14 days after service of last pleading • If P amends complaint w/ in 21-day period allowed, then they can add a demand for jury trial in their amended complaint	• The last pleading would be an answer and D has not yet filed one so it is within 14 days of the last pleading (not yet filed). • Note the motion to dismiss is not the last pleading (it is a decoy to make you think 20 days is too late since it is beyond 14 days from that motion).

A Yes, **because** the retailer properly demanded a jury and since he properly and timely amended his complaint, both claims would be included in his demand for a jury trial.

DECODE

Now look for an answer choice that is similar to any of the reasons here.

~~A.~~ No, because the retailer filed the demand more than 14 days after service of the motion to dismiss.

Wrong analysis. The 14 days is from the last pleading which would be the answer and not the motion to dismiss here (the motion to dismiss was a decoy).

~~B.~~ No, because the retailer filed the demand more than 14 days after service of the original complaint.

Wrong rule applied here because the rule is 14 days from the "last" pleading not the first one.

~~C.~~ Yes, but on the defamation claim only, because the original complaint did not contain a jury demand.

Wrong analysis. An amended complaint can contain a demand for a jury trial so long as the amended complaint was within the 21-day period allowed.

D. Yes, on both claims, because the architect had not answered the original complaint when the retailer filed the amended complaint with the jury demand.

Correct because the complaint was timely and properly amended to include the demand for a jury trial and the demand was made within 14 days of the last pleading since the architect has not yet answered the complaint (which would be the last pleading).

FACTS **Q7**

A construction **worker sued an insulation manufacturer** in federal court, claiming that he had developed a **chronic health condition** as a result of **20 years of exposure to the manufacturer's insulation** at his work sites. The **manufacturer answered, denying all liability** and stating that it had **never supplied its insulation** to the worker's employer.

Parties & COA (note so you can follow which party filed a MSJ)

The worker's attorney deposed the manufacturer's president, and the manufacturer's attorney deposed the worker. Immediately thereafter, the **manufacturer moved for summary judgment** on the ground that the **worker had no evidence** showing that the insulation had ever been used by the worker's employer.

Looking for facts that would possibly show a "genuine dispute of material fact" to respond to a MSJ (these facts don't show anything so far).

D filed MSJ so P will need to respond (and show there is some dispute).

CALL What would be the worker's **best response** to the **motion for summary judgment**?

CIV PRO

Note this type of call – "best" response usually implies more than 1 response is correct but only 1 is the "best."

Since the issue involves responding to a MSJ, you need to know what a MSJ requires so you can argue against it.

SOLVE

MSJ RULES	FACTS	ANALYSIS
• No genuine dispute of material fact • Entitled to judgment as a matter of law • Evidence -first hand knowledge • Credibility not weighed • Evidence viewed in light most favorable to non-moving party • BOP on moving party to show no genuine dispute of material fact • If BOP met, then BOP switches to non-moving party • In response, non-moving party may request more time for add'l discovery w/declaration	• Both sides had depositions – no facts as to what occurred or was questioned in those • D denied all liability – said never supplied insulation • D moved for SJ due to no evidence (infer - no evidence came from depositions).	• P needs first-hand knowledge evidence. • Credibility won't matter for any witnesses. • Evidence will be viewed in favor to P (so need to find evidence). • If D met BOP (no evidence from depositions), then P will need to be able to prove that there is some genuine dispute of material fact. • P may need add'l time for discovery to find evidence to rebut D (if D met BOP). • P could argue that D didn't meet BOP since both sides claim opposite arguments (evidence not clear from facts so need to see answer choices).

Need to find some arguments to fight the MSJ now (for P). Think of what P would need to prove.

SOLVE *(continued)*

A It is unclear what P's best response would be until we read all answer choices, but going into the answer choices, we know the various arguments P could use (based on comments in analysis). Hopefully, one of the answer choices will be similar to one of the arguments we came up with.

→ Now let's look at the choices.

> ***"Best" answer tip:* It is always better to have an idea of what arguments are available to P as possible answers/options, before looking at the choices so the second-best answer choice doesn't jump out at you as you will have considered all options.**

DECODE

A. Argue that more time is needed for additional discovery to show the manufacturer's liability, and attach a declaration describing the desired discovery.

Yes, this is one of the options based on our rules that is available to P and it is better than all of the other answer choices!! This is a tough question since there is no one correct answer but this is the best of the options provided.

~~B.~~ Argue that the motion should be denied, because a central issue in the case will be the manufacturer's credibility on the question of its distribution of the insulation, and only a jury can decide questions of credibility.

Wrong analysis. Credibility is not weighed so the credibility of the manufacturer is irrelevant.

~~C.~~ Argue that the motion should be denied, because the manufacturer failed to attach any evidence to its motion to show that the insulation was not used by the worker's employer.

Not the best argument because the manufacturer would not have to attach evidence if the original party never presented any evidence at all to support its original claim. While the BOP for MSJ is on the moving party, if the original party never presented evidence, then there would be no need to present counter evidence for the MSJ. This would have been your second-best answer (which is why it is still wrong!).

~~D.~~ Make a cross-motion for summary judgment arguing that the manufacturer has introduced no evidence to show that its insulation did not harm the worker.

This would not help the worker as he would still need to have evidence to show on his cross-motion and the problem now is he doesn't appear to have sufficient evidence so he would not meet his BOP for the MSJ.

FACTS **Q8**

A plaintiff sued a defendant in federal court for injuries arising out of an accident involving the parties. The **plaintiff alleged and presented evidence** at trial demonstrating that her **injuries had left her legs permanently paralyzed**. The **jury found in favor of the plaintiff and awarded her $5 million in damages**. Two months after the court entered judgment, the defendant was given a **videotape made that day** showing the **plaintiff jogging with her doctor**.

YES!!! Another Q with the issue in the call! I've got this! Now.....what are all the ways to seek relief from judgment.......I just need to list them and pick the best one!

CALL What is the **best way** for the defendant **to seek relief from the judgment**?

CIV PRO

Noting that it seems odd that someone who is "permanently" paralyzed and awarded $5 million for her injuries would be able to jog two months later......something seems off.......

SOLVE

OPTIONS AVAILABLE	FACTS/ANALYSIS
Motion to seek relief from a judgment can be based on: • Clerical errors • Neglectful mistakes • Newly discovered evidence that could not reasonably be discovered for the original trial • Fraud, misrepresentation, or other misconduct of a party • Judgment is void for lack of due process; or • Any other reason that justifies relief. • **Timing**: A motion to set aside a judgment based on fraud, neglectful mistakes, or newly discovered evidence may not be brought more than one year after the judgment.	• P permanently paralyzed – presented evidence of such • Jury awards $5 million for her injuries • Was miraculously able to jog two months later • WITH her doctor???

Do our facts appear to align with any of these?

Best options?
If you could pick 1 what would it be?

Best way to seek relief seems to be fraud or misrepresentation or misconduct. Perhaps the jury was mistaken (but that is less likely since evidence was presented and injuries were "permanent.") Timing ok as well since 2 months (w/in 1 year).

Now look for an answer choice that comports with your analysis.

DECODE

(A.) Move for a new trial or in the alternative for remittitur to reduce the award in light of the shortened duration of the plaintiff's injuries.

Not the best answer. First note that a new trial was not one of our options so now we have to consider it and it is not the best option. The best option would be an answer that would provide relief without needing to go through another trial (where the same result is possible). And the timing is too late as a motion for a new trial must be filed within 28 days after judgment and it is now two months later.

(B.) Move for relief from judgment on the ground that the judgment was based on the jury's mistaken belief that the plaintiff's injuries would be permanent.

Not the best answer because as noted above, the best would be based on fraud. It is unlikely the jury mistook what "permanent" meant since there was evidence to corroborate that. Fraud would be a better answer.

C. Move for relief from judgment on the ground that the plaintiff committed a fraud in obtaining damages for permanent injuries.

Yes!!! This is what we found above to be the best answer as it would essentially void the judgment without the need for a new trial.

(D.) Move for relief from the judgment on the ground that there is newly discovered evidence that the plaintiff's injuries were not permanent.

This is not the best answer because new evidence would not provide relief from the judgment. Rather, it would enable P to seek a new trial based on the new evidence, which would not be as good of an option since again D could lose at a new trial and would have to go through another trial.

FACTS

Q9

An individual investor purchased stock through a company's stock offering. When the price of the **stock plummeted**, the investor **sued the company** in a state court in State A, claiming that the company's offering materials had **fraudulently induced him** to purchase the stock and seeking **$25,000 in damages**.

After knowing you are looking for issue preclusion – look to see what the issue is (false info). University wants to use it in State B fed. ct. (from investor's case in State A state ct.)

A **university that had purchased the company's stock** through the same offering **sued the company in** federal court in State B, claiming that the offering materials **violated federal securities laws** and seeking **$1 million in damages**.

The **individual investor's suit proceeded to trial**. The **state court ruled** that the company's offering **materials contained false information** and **awarded the investor a $25,000 judgment**. The university immediately **moved for partial summary judgment** in its federal action against the company, **arguing that the state court judgment bound the federal court on the issue of** whether the company's offering materials contained false information.

Motion for partial SJ, but need to see what its about – based on issue preclusion – THAT is your issue.

RED FLAG RAISED HERE

Neither **State A nor State B** permits **nonmutual issue preclusion.**

CALL Should the court grant the university's motion?

Figure out what the motion is

SOLVE

Q Should the court grant the university's motion (for issue preclusion to apply)?

ISSUE PRECLUSION (COLLATERAL ESTOPPEL)	FACTS/ANALYSIS
A **subsequent suit** based on the **same issue** will preclude relitigation of that **particular issue** if:	Suit 2 (in State B fed. ct) trying to use Suit 1 (in State A state ct.) to preclude issue on providing false materials.
• **Valid final judgment on the merits**	• Suit 1 had final judgment as case went to trial and judgment entered.
• Same issue **actually litigated**	• Issue of false information actually litigated in suit 1 as ct. found materials contained false info.
• Same issue **necessarily determined**	• Issue necessarily determined since COA about fraud which includes the element of falsity/inducing.
• Can only **use *against*** a party or privy in prior suit	

(chart continued on the next page)

SOLVE *(continued)*

ISSUE PRECLUSION (COLLATERAL ESTOPPEL)	FACTS/ANALYSIS
• Can only **use by**: ◦ **Mutuality**: traditional rule (strangers cannot use) ◦ **Nonmutuality** (permitted in some jx): » **Defensive use:** stranger can use (to avoid liability) if fair & party against whom CE asserted had opport. to be heard. » **Offensive use:** stranger can use (to establish an issue) if fair and D could not have easily been joined in first case. • **Full faith & credit**: State ct. judgments have same full faith and credit in fed. ct. (fed. ct. gives no more preclusive effect than the state ct. itself would do).	• CE being asserted BY university (offensively) to establish the issue of false info • BUT problem here is State A does not permit nonmutual issue preclusion. Since in state court a stranger could not use the earlier judgment, the full faith & credit clause will not allow its use in federal court here (because doing so would give the state court judgment more preclusive effect in federal court than in state court).

A No, the court should not grant the motion **because** university was not a party in the suit by the investor (and State A does not permit issue preclusion so the traditional rule must be followed).

→ Now look for an answer choice that comports with your analysis.

DECODE

A. No, because State A does not permit nonmutual issue preclusion.

Correct because State A does not permit nonmutual issue preclusion so the federal court cannot give greater preclusive effect to a state-court judgment than the state court itself would do under full faith and credit. So the traditional rule must be followed and the university was a stranger to the first case with the investor so the state court's finding on the issue is not binding on the federal court.

~~B.~~ No, because the federal court sits in a state that does not permit nonmutual issue preclusion.

Wrong analysis. The court at issue is the state court in State A and its judgment not a judgment from a court in State B where the federal court is located. The State B court is not relevant and is a decoy (and since the university's suit is about federal securities laws, State B law would not apply anyway).

~~C.~~ Yes, because federal law permits nonmutual issue preclusion.

Wrong analysis. Under CE, the court would apply the state, not federal law, on whether nonmutual issue preclusion applies. (Note it would apply federal law to the actual COA – federal securities laws).

~~D.~~ Yes, because the issue of whether the materials contained false information was actually litigated and necessarily decided.

Wrong analysis as it does not analyze all of the rule. This answer correctly states part of the rule (two elements) but ignores the other elements such as mutuality.

FACTS

Q10

A **student at a private university sued** the **university** in federal court for **negligence** after he fell from scaffolding in a university-owned theater building. At trial, after briefing from both parties, the **court permitted the jury to hear testimony** that there had been several **previous accidents** in the same building. The **jury found for the student**, and the **university appealed**. One of the university's arguments on appeal is that the testimony about the previous accidents should have been excluded as irrelevant and highly prejudicial.

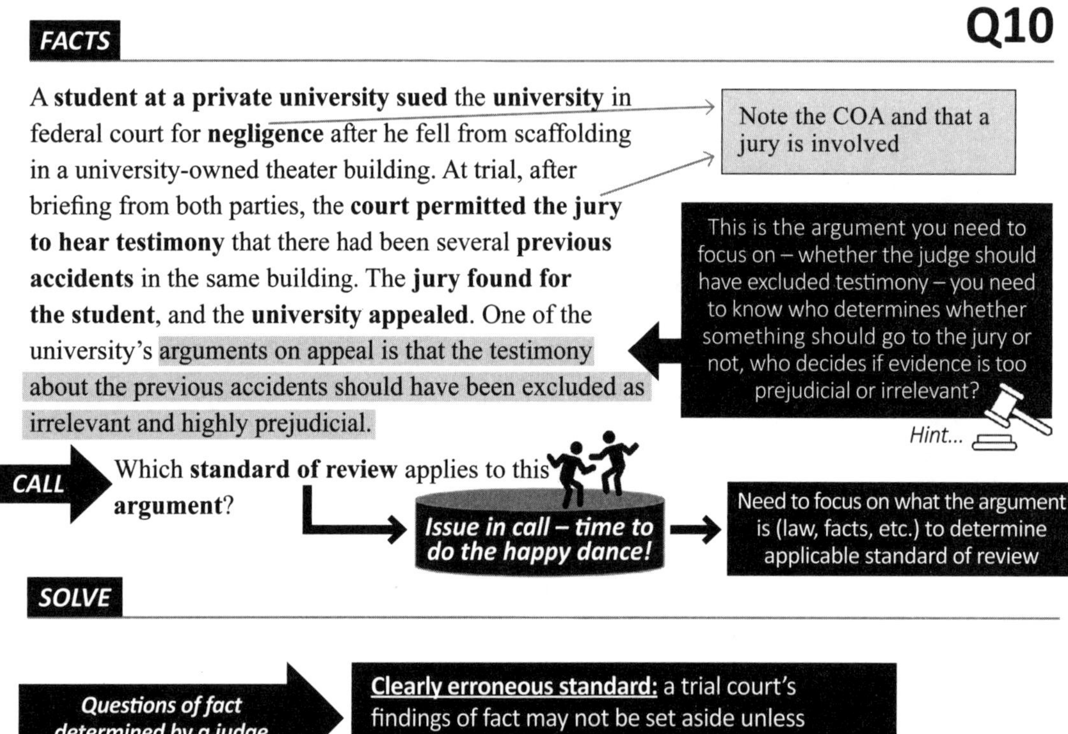

CALL Which **standard of review** applies to this **argument**?

SOLVE

Questions of fact determined by a judge	**Clearly erroneous standard:** a trial court's findings of fact may not be set aside unless clearly erroneous.
Questions of fact determined by a jury	**Reasonable jury determination:** juries are given more deference than a judge so look at whether a reasonable jury could reach the same conclusion.
Matters of law	**De novo:** the appellate court will use the trial court's record, but reviews the evidence and law without deference to the trial court's ruling.
Mixed questions of fact and law	**De novo:** same as above (so as is the case with the above, the court can substitute its own judgment for that of the trial judge).
Matters discretionary To the judge	**Abuse of discretion:** appellate court will look to see if the judge abused its discretion in admitting the evidence (usually a judgment call).

Here, the judge had discretion as to whether the previous accidents were relevant and/or too prejudicial so abuse of discretion standard would apply.

Exception: *Harmless error standard will be found when the court's erroneous admission of evidence did not affect any party's substantial rights.*

A Abuse of discretion **because** the argument was based on discretionary matters (since a judge has discretion to determine whether testimony/evidence is too prejudicial or irrelevant).

→ Now look for an answer choice that comports with your analysis.

DECODE

A. Abuse of discretion.

Correct because the judge had discretion as to whether the previous accidents were relevant and/or too prejudicial.

(B.) Clearly erroneous.

Wrong standard. This is used for matters of fact determined by a judge. Whether something is admissible or not is not a matter of fact, but rather a discretionary matter.

(C.) De novo.

Wrong standard. This standard is used for matters of law of mixed questions of fact and law. Here, the judge had discretion as to whether to allow the testimony of previous accidents as it was not a matter of law or mixed fact/law.

(D.) Harmless error.

Wrong rule. This is an exception that did not apply here. This exception is used when the judge erroneously admitted evidence not when a judge had discretion to admit evidence.

PART 2 CONSTITUTIONAL LAW

CONSTITUTIONAL LAW TABLE OF CONTENTS

★ Favorite Testing Area

CONSTITUTIONAL LAW MBE RULE OUTLINE

MBE CON LAW AT A GLANCE

12-13 Questions (approx.)	**12-13 Questions** (approx.)

State Action
Privileges & Immunities Clause
Contracts Clause
Religion
Speech
Association
Press
Due Process
Equal Protection
Takings
Ex Post Facto laws
Bill of Attainder
	Justiciability/standing
	Source of Power
	   Congress powers
	   Executive powers
	   Judiciary powers
	Federalism (Fed. and state powers)
	Federal preemption
	Dormant Commerce Clause

COMMON CON LAW DECOY ANSWERS

- The wrong standard: A standard that is too high or too low (i.e. strict scrutiny language instead of rational basis).
- Often, more than one answer will work (e.g., as a method to challenge a law) but one answer will be a "stronger" argument or defense since that rule will provide a more heightened standard of review for the issue than the other choices do.
- Sometimes, none of the answers will work, but one will provide a colorable argument, and that will be the "strongest" answer choice available.
- "Hit list" rules from the list below.

CON LAW DECOY HIT LIST

Though **the rules below may be tested**, they are more **frequently used as wrong decoy answer choices**. Be sure to know the rules on the list below very well.

- Privileges & Immunities (14th Am.) — travel, vote
- Privileges & Immunities (Article 4) — commerce rights
- Bill of attainder — punish without trial
- Ex Post Facto laws — laws with retroactive punitive effect
- Contracts Clause — laws impairing obligation of contract
- No federal police power exists (with limited exception for federal lands)
- Tax and spend for the general welfare *only*. (Can't legislate, regulate or provide for...)
- "_________(fill in the blank) is a privilege not a right." This is never the right answer.

CON LAW MBE QUESTION APPROACH

MBE tip: It helps to have a methodical approach to solving Con. Law MBE questions because otherwise it is easy to overlook a key rule and pick the wrong answer.

1. Any threshold issues? (Consider first because if implicated it is dispositive).

◆ Justiciability ◇ Advisory opinions ◇ Political questions ◇ Standing ◇ Ripeness ◇ Mootness ◇ 11th Amendment	◆ Authority to enact law ◇ State Powers ◇ Congressional Powers ◇ Executive Powers ◇ Judiciary Powers ◇ Allocation of power between federal and state governments

2. Is there state action?

3. Is the State or Federal government acting?

State Only Government Issues	State and/or Federal Government Issues	
◆ Preemption ◆ Dormant Commerce Clause ◆ Privileges & Immunities ◆ Contracts Clause ◆ Full Faith and Credit	◆ Religion ◆ Speech ◆ Association ◆ Press ◆ Due Process	◆ Involuntary Servitude ◆ Equal Protection ◆ Takings ◆ Ex post facto ◆ Bill of attainder

4. Apply the correct rule or standard of review.

I. JUSTICIABILITY IN FEDERAL COURT

A. **Case or controversy:** There must be an actual case or controversy in dispute.

1. **Declaratory judgments** are permitted. Declaratory judgments are those that state the legal effect of a regulation or the conduct of parties in regard to a controversy.

2. **Advisory opinions** are not permitted. An advisory opinion would be a formal opinion given by a judge on a matter of law that has no binding effect.

   Example: Congress enacts a law that disagreements between the U.S. and a state over specific funds shall be settled in federal district court, but once the court makes a determination, that judgment is transmitted to the agency dispensing such funds. However, if the agency is given the discretion to execute the judgment or not, then the court is only issuing an advisory opinion rather than deciding an actual case or controversy and this is not permitted.

MBE tip: It is difficult for the examiners to ask an advisory opinion question without a convoluted fact pattern. They do this so the issue isn't as easy to spot. This is a common testing pattern in constitutional law questions.

B. **Political questions** may not be heard by federal courts. If an issue is **committed to another branch** of the federal government (President or Congress), or if there are **no manageable standards** by which the court can resolve the issue, it is a political question and the federal court won't hear the issue (e.g., the courts would likely refuse to review impeachments for this reason). [This issue is rarely MBE tested.]

> **MBE tip: Spot the issue**—MBE questions on political questions can be hard to spot and may look like questions regarding standing, ripeness, or mootness. Political question MBE questions usually have facts where the *President is acting* (or Congress) on some power that the Constitution recognizes, whereas standing and ripe/moot questions usually involve private parties or the conduct of local governments/organizations.

C. **Standing**

1. **Individual standing** requires a plaintiff to prove **injury, causation,** and **redressability.**
   a. **Injury:** An **"injury in fact"** which is an actual or imminent injury that is **concrete and particularized.**
      1. **Concrete and particularized** means the injury is **measurable** and **individual to the person bringing the suit** (it need not be economic).
      2. **No "general" taxpayer standing:** Status as a taxpayer does not provide a concrete injury from which to challenge a general statute **unrelated to** a tax the taxpayer is subject to paying. However, there is federal taxpayer standing in limited circumstances, as discussed below.
      3. **No third-party standing absent injury:** There is no third-party standing for alleged injuries to other parties unless the third-party has a concrete injury of their own. In other words, a person must assert a violation of *their own rights*. See third-party standing rule below.
   b. **Causation:** The action challenged is the **cause in fact** of the injury such that the connection to the injury is not too attenuated.
   c. **Redressability:** A **favorable decision** must **redress the injury.** This means a ruling in the plaintiff's favor will solve their problem. (Ask yourself: If the plaintiff wins, will it solve their problem? If not, the injury is not redressed by the suit, and there is no standing.)

> **MBE tip:** Declaratory actions, such as a request for an injunction to invalidate an ordinance, are particularly prone to lack standing because they often do not seek to establish a more concrete injury. For example, asking for a statute or ordinance to be deemed invalid on behalf of others it affects will not provide standing, rather those directly affected are the ones who actually need to bring the action.

2. **Third-party standing** requires the plaintiff to prove they have:
   a. **Individual standing, and**
   b. A **special relationship** between the plaintiff and the third party, **or**
   c. That it is **difficult for the third party** to assert their own rights.
3. **Organizational standing** requires:
   a. The **members have standing** in their own right,
   b. The interests asserted are **related to the organization's purpose,** and
   c. The case **does not require participation** of individual members.

> **MBE tip:** Unless third-party or organizational standing requirements are satisfied, a person may not assert a violation of *another*'s constitutional rights. Watch out for this in MBE questions since these requirements are rarely satisfied.

4. **Federal taxpayer standing:** A federal taxpayer only **has standing** to sue when the taxpayer can establish the challenged measure:
   a. Was enacted by Congress under the **power to tax and spend,** and
   b. It **exceeds some limitation on that power.**
      1. The **Establishment Clause** is the only court-recognized limitation. Consequently, federal taxpayer standing is very limited.

STANDING CHEAT SHEET

MBE tip: A correct answer choice might be worded in a confusing way. For example, "Plaintiff does not have an interest as there is no Article III controversy" actually means that the plaintiff does not have standing and thus there is no case.

STANDING	NO STANDING
◆ Person intending to make a speech on Capitol steps during prohibited times has an injury (the rule prohibited all speech during particular times). ◆ Contractors have an injury when awarded contracts to build highways but a statute prevents funding for the highway work unless the state sets a lower speed limit (contractors cannot get paid for the contracted work).	◆ Legislator who voted against a statute being enforced (legislator has suffered no concrete injury). ◆ Third parties seeking redress for another person, such as a landlord, friend, governor acting on behalf of residents, etc. (Third parties cannot show injury for someone else.) ◆ Wrong defendant is named (if plaintiff names the wrong defendant, then plaintiff is not injured by that defendant so plaintiff has no standing in that case). ◆ Car owner who lives in a state and uses a highway does not have an injury when a statute prevents highway improvement funding in the absence of a set lower speed limit (the car owner's injury is not particularized enough, *but* compare to the contractors who do have standing for a similar situation). ◆ A candidate does not have an injury to seek declaratory relief from a statute requiring mayors to have a 5-year residency when he has not yet won the election (any injury is abstract and not yet concrete since he might not win so there is no standing; note this is also not ripe for the same reason).

Decoy tip: The answers below are frequent decoy (wrong) answers seen in MBE questions on standing:

- Taxpayer standing (almost every time they test individual standing there is a wrong answer choice that refers to taxpayer standing when it does not apply). Make sure all elements to taxpayer standing are met prior to selecting it as a correct choice because most standing questions test individual standing.
- Organization/association/members who are seeking an injunction or desire a law to be deemed unconstitutional or invalid when the question is only testing individual standing.
- Federal question or federal statute (not relevant to standing).
- Nonjusticiable political question.
- 11th Amendment.

D. Timeliness:

1. **Ripeness:** A case will not be heard if there is **not yet a live controversy** or immediate threat of harm. A future wrong will not be ripe for adjudication.
2. **Mootness:** A case will not be heard if a live controversy existed at the time the complaint was filed but **events occurring after** the filing have deprived the litigant of an ongoing stake in the controversy.
   a. **Except** the case will not be found moot (and can be heard) if:
      1. The controversy is **capable of repetition, regarding the same plaintiff, yet evading review** (e.g., abortion litigation); or
      2. **Voluntary cessation** of the activity by the defendant (since the defendant could opt to resume the activity); or
      3. **Collateral consequences** remain that are adverse.

      Example: A criminal defendant who has served his full sentence for a crime can still appeal because there are negative collateral consequences to a felony conviction, such as losing the right to vote and reputational damage.

MBE tip: If a case is moot or not ripe (i.e., injunction requested for possible future regulations or standards that have not yet been adopted), the correct answer will be for the court to **dismiss** the case and not to issue a stay since the court shouldn't entertain a case that is not ripe. MOST of the time when tested in MBE questions the case is not ripe or is moot.

Decoy tip: Common decoys for ripeness/mootness (wrong answers):

- Nonjusticiable political question
- Federal question
- 11th Amendment

E. The **Eleventh Amendment** provides **immunity to states** from any federal suit brought by private parties against a state.

1. **Actions that have been barred** include suits for damages by citizens (this includes Native American tribes) of the same state.
2. **Actions that are not barred** include suits by states or the federal government against other states, suits against subdivisions of the state (such as cities or counties), and suits seeking injunctions against state officials.
3. **States have sovereign immunity** from private damage suits brought under federal law against the state in the state's own courts, though states can waive their sovereign immunity.
4. **Abrogation of immunity:** Congress has the power to abrogate state immunity from liability if it is acting to enforce rights created by the 13th, 14th, and 15th Amendments, and does so expressly.

II. STATE ACTION

A. **State action requirement:** For an action to violate the Constitution, there must be **government involvement** with the challenged action.

1. **Private actor:** The action of a **private actor can qualify** as state action if:

   a. **Public function:** The private actor performs functions that are **traditionally and exclusively public functions** which are governmental in nature (e.g., private groups running elections, company towns, parks, prisons, municipal districts, etc.); <u>or</u>

   b. **Heavy involvement:** Where the **state is heavily involved** in the activity, such as by **commanding, encouraging,** or being **entangled** with the activity. The following are examples that the courts have found ***do not rise to the level of heavy involvement:***

      1. **Accreditation, regulation, and private funding** of a university by the state does not render the university's conduct state action.

      2. **Granting of money** by itself is not sufficient to show state action.

      3. **Inviting the public** to an activity or by **renting out a government facility** by a private actor is insufficient (mere acquiescence by a state to the action of a private actor is insufficient to show state action).

> **<u>MBE tip</u>:** It is rare to find heavy government involvement constituting state action when a private party is the actor (as indicated in the above court examples as well as the below MBE tested examples).

STATE ACTION EXAMPLES

State action is mostly tested two ways:

1. Most state action questions conclude there is **no state action** because private companies or individuals are acting rather than a government actor.
2. After a convoluted fact pattern, other questions will ask, "Which of the following is plaintiff's **strongest argument**?" What they are asking is what answer choice gives plaintiff the best ability to pursue their claim **compared to the other options.** For example, if plaintiff is suing based on equal protection, you want to find an answer that best attributes state action to the state so plaintiff can pursue their claim.

<u>MBE tip</u>: Some questions will not use the words "state action" or "state actor" when that is exactly what they are testing (see "strongest argument" question examples below).

1. NO STATE ACTION	2. "STRONGEST ARGUMENT"
◆ Private insurance company charging different rates to residents based on crime rates in areas—no state action even though the state insurance commissioner inspects insurance companies. ◆ State grant of $10 million to a baseball team not sufficient to show state action when the baseball team, a private franchise, hires all white male contractors. ◆ A city-owned auditorium can be rented out to organizations that publicize their events and restrict their highest offices to men. In a suit against the organization, there is no state action because the organization is private and merely renting out a city auditorium does not make the organization a state actor. ◆ Private university is accredited by the state and receives 25% funding from the state—no state action for a professor who was fired. ◆ Private company hired a less qualified woman over a man because he was known to have radical political views. If the man sues the company based on freedom of expression, there is no state action because the company is private. ◆ Private mall open to the public prevented protestors in front of a store from protesting animal fur products. In a suit against the mall based on freedom of speech, there is no state action because the mall is a private company, even if it is open to the public.	◆ State provides textbooks to schools, licenses their teachers, and accredits them (all actions combined together could show a **stronger argument** for state action **compared to the other choices** which only had one fact in support). ◆ State bar association requires all lawyers to become members of the state bar; the state bar board also pays staff members' dues for a *private* club with discriminatory practices. The **strongest argument** for a member (plaintiff) to pursue an equal protection action is that the state bar association is an agency of the state (this is how they test state action without using the more obvious words "state action" or "state actor"). This is plaintiff's **best argument** over the other answer choices such as answers that involve "private rights" as the basis for the suit, or the "failure of the State to act," neither of which allow plaintiff to pursue equal protection because they fail to show state action.

III. POWERS RESERVED TO THE STATES

A. **Federalism** is the concept that the federal government and state governments coexist.

1. **Federal law generally cannot be applied to state legislators** acting in the course of their official duties.

2. **Voting:** States are free to set their own rules for providing for representation of their citizens for voting as long as they retain a republican form of government as required by Article IV, section 4.

   Example: States can authorize a 5-member state reapportionment board to redraw state legislative districts every 10 years.

3. **Congress cannot require the states to enact particular laws.** The 10th Amendment and the principles of Federalism embedded in the Constitution prevent Congress from requiring states to enact laws or administer federal law.

<u>**Example**</u>: National statistics showed an increase in drug use in school-aged children. Congress responded by enacting a statute *requiring each state legislature* to enact a state law making it a crime to sell drugs within 1000 feet of any schools. Congress has no authority to require a state legislature to enact any specific legislation, so the statute is unconstitutional.

4. **States have police power** to provide for the health, safety, and welfare of its citizenry.

   a. **Limitation on regulation: States may not regulate the federal government** and cannot make the federal government obey even generally applicable regulations.

   b. **Limitation on takings:** States cannot take property without just compensation. See sec. VI. G.

> <u>MBE tip</u>: While states have police power, in contrast, there is no "general" federal police power (with a limited exception for federal lands), though this is such a commonly used decoy answer it is on the "hit list."

B. The **Tenth Amendment** provides that the **powers not delegated to the federal** government or prohibited by the Constitution are **reserved to the states.** Therefore, Congress can't compel a city or state to pass a law.

1. **Federal government cannot commandeer the states:** The federal government cannot commandeer the states by demanding the states pass particular laws or imposing targeted or coercive duties on state legislators or officials.

   <u>**Example**</u>: The federal government **cannot order the states to enact a law** requiring background checks before issuing gun permits because that would be commandeering. However, it **can impose regulatory statutes of generally applicable laws,** which require background checks that apply to both private and state actors, to obtain the same result.

2. **Federal government cannot tax the states:** The federal government can't tax property used in, or income from, a state's performance of its basic governmental function.

   <u>**Example**</u>: The federal government can't place a federal property tax on a state's capital building that the state uses to perform its functions.

3. **States can lay and collect taxes:** States have the authority to structure their **tax system** in any manner that does not violate the Constitution.

   <u>**Examples**</u>: **Proper taxes include** gross receipts tax on business conducted within a state; tax on the manufacture of widgets; tax on the income of residents of the state; tax on the rental value of any automobile provided by the taxpayer's employer for personal use; tax on purchases by antique collectors even if the purchaser agrees to sell the antique to a National Park Service (a federal entity).

   a. **State cannot directly tax the federal government:** A state may not impose a tax *directly* on the federal government or any of its agencies or instrumentalities **if the "legal incidence" of the tax falls on the federal government,** and not just the economic burden, unless Congress consents. However, states can tax products and sales to purchasers even if the purchaser has a contract with a federal agency.

      <u>**Example (state tax not permitted)**</u>: A state cannot levy a tax on receipts from a federal national lottery permitted by a federal statute for the tickets sold in state.

      <u>**Example (state tax permitted)**</u>: A vendor under a cost-plus contract to the federal government (e.g., if a contractor billed the government at 10% over their costs for a building project) is not immune from state taxes, even though the "cost" of the tax (the economic burden) is passed directly on to the customer, who is the federal government.

IV. FEDERAL POWERS

There are three branches comprising the federal government: the **legislative** branch (Congress), the **judicial** branch (courts), and the **executive** branch (President).

A. **Legislative: Congress** has **limited, enumerated powers** granted by the Constitution. Consequently, there must be a **source of power** for any congressional action. Congress has the following enumerated powers:

> **MBE tip:** When a question asks whether Congress has properly enacted a federal statute, the correct answer will focus on a **power given to Congress**, most commonly it is power under the Commerce Clause or to tax and spend.
>
> 
>
> **Decoy tip:** Eliminate all answer choices that (1) correspond to **state powers** (such as the Privilege and Immunities Clause of Article IV), or (2) state an answer that is **not an enumerated power** (such as the enforcement clause of the 14th Amendment).

1. **Regulate commerce** (Article 1, section 8): **This is the broadest and most important source of federal power.** This includes interstate commerce (between states), intrastate commerce (within one state), commerce with foreign nations, and commerce with the Indian tribes. This **very broad source of power** encompasses many activities, even regulation of some purely private conduct.

   a. **Interstate activity regulations:** Congress may regulate activities **between states**, including the:

      1. **Channels** of interstate commerce (e.g., roads, air travel, rivers, etc.);

      2. **Instrumentalities** of interstate commerce (e.g., things needed to carry out commerce such as cars, trucks, boats, wires, internet, etc.);

      3. **Persons and articles** (any item that can be sold, bought, or transported across state lines) moving in interstate commerce (e.g., driver, kidnap victim, tires, groundwater, etc.); and

      4. **Affectation Doctrine:** Congress may regulate **activities that substantially affect** interstate commerce.

         a. This includes collective commercial activity and activities that are purely local and **intrastate** (within one state) as well as **foreign** activities.

         b. **Even purely private conduct can be regulated,** but it still must pertain to commercial activity. [This is rarely MBE tested.]

         Example (Congress can regulate): A private restaurant refusing to serve people based on color or race (the restaurant had interstate connections as it bought meat from other states).

         c. **Commercial or economic activity** may be regulated if there is a **rational basis** to believe that the activity in **"inseverable aggregates"** will cause a **substantial economic effect** on **interstate commerce,** or if there is a **substantial cumulative economic effect on interstate commerce.** [This is frequently MBE tested.]

         Examples (Congress can regulate): growing wheat or marijuana, renting out homes, or requiring only organic dry cleaning materials. The cumulative activities of all (farmers, renters, dry cleaners) have a substantial effect on interstate commerce by creating demand or sales that will cross state lines).

d. **Noncommercial or noneconomic activity** potentially may be regulated if the activity has a **direct and substantial economic effect** on **interstate** (between states) **commerce**. However, these are usually outside of Congress' power and are rarely permitted (e.g., possession of guns in school zones and violence against women regulatory acts were **not** permitted). [This is rarely MBE tested.]

FEDERAL COMMERCE POWER CHEAT SHEET

MBE tip: Congress' power to regulate commerce has been interpreted so **broadly** that it encompasses almost any economic act that could conceivably have some kind of impact, even secondarily, on the stream of commerce.

- Regulation of oil, natural gas, and electric power
- Regulation of the sale and resale of products for human consumption
- Licenses for computers
- Legislation affecting rent or purchase of housing
- Regulation of marijuana grown for one's own use
- Regulation on labeling of imported produce
- Requiring all owners of bicycles in the U.S. to register their bicycles with a federal registry because bicycle theft impacts interstate commerce
- Wages paid to dry cleaner employees because they impact the national economy and the flow of goods and services on interstate commerce

MBE tip: When a question asks about the source of power to enact legislation, the correct answer is almost always some variation of the "Commerce Clause."

MBE tip: The language "in inseverable aggregates" is commonly used to refer to the cumulative economic effect of the commercial activity being regulated (e.g., an answer choice might state, "Congress could determine that in inseverable aggregates bicycle thefts affect interstate commerce.").

Common commerce power answer decoys: The **source of power** to enact the legislation in question comes from:

- Congress' power to *provide* for the general welfare. (There is no such power so that will never be the right answer. Congress can only *tax and spend* for the general welfare.)
- Tax and spending power. (If the regulation is related to commerce, commerce power is the better answer.)
- Enforcement power of the 14th Amendment. (If the regulation is related to commerce, commerce power is the better answer.)

MBE tip: Congress has plenary (absolute) authority over commerce, so Congress can enact a federal statute based on its commerce power that serves to overrule a prior U.S. Supreme Court case on point.

2. The **Taxing and Spending Clause** (Article I, section 8) gives Congress the broad right to **tax and spend for the general welfare** of the United States. The allocation of conditional funding may be done so long as it is unambiguous, in a related area, and not excessively coercive.

   Example: The federal government could deny highway funding to states who refused to raise the legal drinking age to 21.

   a. **Direct taxes:** Congress can adopt direct taxes provided they are in proportion to the national census. There is no requirement that what is spent or how it is spent be related to what is taxed.

      Example: Congress can impose an excise tax on new computers sold in the U.S.

   b. The **President cannot unilaterally suspend** the effect of a valid federal statute imposing a duty to spend monies appropriated by Congress.

   c. **Conditional grant of federal funds:** Congress can condition the grant of federal funds to public bodies **on compliance with measures related to the public welfare** as long as the public body is free to accept or reject the grants.

FEDERAL TAX AND SPEND POWER EXAMPLES

- Federal statute requiring colleges receiving federal funds to offer students aid solely on the basis of need (spend)
- Federal statute denying federal highway funding to states with speed limits over 55 mph (spend)
- Appropriations act by Congress over the President's veto that $1 billion shall be spent on a new military weapons system (spend)
- Federal statute to provide $100 million in funding to dental education—even though the President ordered programs to be cut, Congress has authority to spend and can still spend the $100 million without cutting money already appropriated by statute (spend)
- Federal statute providing grants of federal funds for the restoration and preservation of courthouses built before 1900 that are still in use provided they add in ramps for handicapped people (spend)
- Federal tax of $25 on airline tickets issued in the U.S. to provide funds for a system of new major airports near the 10 largest cities in the U.S. (tax)
- Federal statute authorizing the construction of a monument—President cannot cancel the monument's construction due to a trade dispute because Congress has the power to spend (spend)

Decoy tip: Congress does not have the power to *regulate* or *legislate* or *provide* for the general welfare; Congress **only** has the **power to tax and spend for the general welfare.** Watch out for decoy answers that incorrectly state Congress has the authority to enact a statute because Congress can regulate or legislate or provide for the general welfare.

MBE tip: Spot the issue—Be sure the question is dealing with a **federal tax** and **not a local state tax** (which would be raising an issue regarding state power and not Congress' power to tax and spend).

3. **Pass laws** (legislate) pursuant to the enumerated powers.

   a. **District of Columbia:** Congress has the power to make all the laws for the District of Columbia under the Constitution.

b. **Limitation:** Article I, section 7 provides that every bill that passes through the House and Senate by majority vote must be **presented to the President for signature or veto** before it can have effect. Congress can **override a presidential veto** by 2/3 vote of each house.

c. **Legislative veto power:** Congress may overturn the action of an executive agency only by enacting a statute. However, a *congressional committee* or just one house cannot do so since that would be an unconstitutional legislative veto.

4. The **war powers grant** Congress the power to **declare war** and to raise and support the armed forces.

   a. Congress has the implied **power to preserve the federal monopoly over foreign affairs.** However, the President alone has the authority to **represent the U.S.** in foreign affairs.

   Example: Congress can make it a crime for any U.S. citizen not authorized by the President to negotiate with a foreign government for the purpose of influencing a dispute resolution.

5. **Naturalization and bankruptcy:** Congress has the power to establish uniform laws of naturalization and bankruptcy.

   Example: A federal statute providing that a person who files federal bankruptcy receives an automatic stay of all proceedings against him will override a state law that provides unpaid employees must have cases decided in 10 days—the federal law is valid both under the Supremacy Clause and Congress' power to establish uniform rules for bankruptcy.

6. **Post-Civil War Amendments:** Congress has the power to enforce the post-Civil War Amendments (13th, 14th, and 15th Amendments). [This is not heavily MBE tested. The 14th Amendment is heavily MBE tested, but not in the context of Congress' power, but rather in the rights afforded by the 14th Amendment, which are referenced throughout this chapter.]

   a. The **13th Amendment prohibits slavery** and the badges of involuntary servitude.

   Example: Congress can enact a statute punishing conspiracies entered into for the purpose of denying black persons employment, education, etc. based on race.

   1. This amendment is unique in that it **applies to both private and government action.**

   b. The **14th Amendment**, section 5, gives Congress the power to enforce the provisions of the 14th Amendment by appropriate legislation if the legislation (1) seeks to remedy actions by state or local governments that violate provisions of the 14th Amendment, and (2) requirements are **congruent with and proportional to** the 14th Amendment violations it addresses.

   1. Congress may **change federal civil statutes** and direct federal courts to apply those changes in all actions in which a final judgment has not been rendered.

   2. Congress **cannot regulate wholly private conduct** under this Amendment.

   c. The **15th Amendment** prohibits both the state and federal governments from **denying any citizen the right to vote on the basis of color or race.**

   d. Congress can **override the 11th Amendment immunity** of states under these Amendments.

   Example: A federal statute that allows an employee to sue an unconsenting state in federal court, when the employee is forced to retire by a certain age, is permitted as Congress may enact remedial legislation under the 14th Amendment as it did here.

7. The **Necessary and Proper Clause** grants Congress broad authority to enact laws that shall be **necessary and proper to execute** any of **their enumerated powers.** The law need only be **rationally related** to the implementation of a constitutionally enumerated power and not specifically forbidden.

> **Decoy tip:** Congress only has the power to execute any of their **enumerated powers** so an answer choice that only refers to the Necessary and Proper Clause without reference to one of their enumerated powers is a decoy answer.

8. **Federal Property (Article IV, section 3):** Congress has the power to exercise exclusive legislation over federal property (i.e., federal public lands, D.C., reservations, military grounds including military ships and airplanes, Native American reservations, post offices, hospitals and hotels located within federal national parks, grasslands, etc.).

   a. This includes the power to regulate wild animals and the hunting of such animals on federal property.

   b. Congress may **delegate rule-making** authority over federal property to federal agencies (so long as the below delegation standards are followed).

> **Decoy tip:** With the limited exception for federal lands (as noted above), Congress does not have a **general police power** to *regulate, legislate,* or *provide* for the health, safety, or welfare of the citizenry. Only states have this power. This is a frequent decoy answer.

9. **Limit the appellate jurisdiction of the U.S. Supreme Court** to hear particular types of cases.

   a. Congress has the **power to create special courts under Article I**, and the judges for those courts do not have the protections of Article III, such as life tenure and the guarantee to no reduction in salary. Congress also has the power to create and/or eliminate lower federal courts and limit the cases they may hear.

   b. **Congress cannot frustrate the establishment of a supreme and uniform body of federal law.**

   Example: Congress cannot remove an entire subject of constitutional cases from the appellate jurisdiction of the Supreme Court if removal would frustrate the establishment of a supreme and uniform body of law, such as abortion.

10. The **Speech and Debate Clause (Article I, section 6)** provides **immunity** to **members of Congress** (and their assistants if performing acts that would be covered if done by a member) from **criminal** or **civil** suits and **grand jury investigations** relating to their legislative actions. (**Limitation:** This protection only applies to legislative actions, so giving an interview to a reporter would not be covered, while giving a speech on the floor of Congress would.)

> **MBE tip:** The above powers are the most commonly tested powers. However, this list is not exhaustive. Congress also has other powers that have yet to be tested on the bar exam (from the NCBE's released representative questions), such as the power to coin and print money, establish post offices, issue patents and copyrights, etc. It is possible that one of these other powers could arise on a bar company MBE question. Each time you are tested on a new power, you can add it to your list of Congress' powers.

11. **Delegation/Committees:** Congress may delegate some of its power to the President or executive branch so long as Congress provides **intelligible standards,** though this is interpreted very leniently and the delegation of power will be valid unless there is a total lack of standards.

    Example: The Federal Automobile Safety Act created a five-member Commission to investigate automobile safety, to make recommendations to Congress for new laws, to make further rules establishing safety and performance standards, and to prosecute violations of the act. The chairman is appointed by the President, two members are selected by the President pro tempore of the Senate, and two members are selected by the Speaker of the House of Representatives. This newly created Commission would be allowed to continue investigating automobile safety and making recommendations to Congress as those are two legislative functions. But the Commission cannot prosecute violations since that would be an executive and judicial function.

a. **Standards deemed intelligible examples:** Specific standards the President must use in setting percentages that energy users must reduce consumption by; criteria for conducting essay contests and awarding prize money to help stop drug use with judges appointed by the President, with advice and consent from the Senate.

b. **Limitations**:

1. **Voting/Approval:** Congress cannot permit a **standing committee,** that it created with its delegation power, to affect legal rights and obligations of others without a **majority vote by Congress and without the President's approval** (the Constitution requires Congress to vote, not the standing committee, to enact law).

2. **Legislative authority:** Congress **cannot delegate** its legislative authority to make law.

3. **Improper Legislative Veto:** A congressional committee, or the House or Senate acting alone, cannot overturn an executive agency's decision. However, Congress may overturn the action of an executive agency by enacting a statute that is signed by the President or enacted over the President's veto.

4. **Appointments:** The Constitution allows Congress to **vest appointments in inferior officers only** in the President, the courts, or the heads of departments (Congress cannot appoint its own members).

Decoy tip: Be careful when there are questions with facts that give rise to Congress' power to delegate AND facts regarding committees that Congress delegated power to. Often the correct answer will be about the proper delegation and the decoy answers will involve actions the committee took (e.g., a committee trying to overturn an executive decision or change law, which is not permitted without Congress' vote). Just because the *delegation* was proper it does not mean that *what the committee is actually doing* is proper.

MBE tip: Some MBE answer choices will have answers that refer to the Section number and Amendment number (such as Section 5 of the Fourteenth Amendment or Article I, section 8), so make sure you know the Article, Amendment, and Section numbers along with the rules themselves involving the Constitution. If you don't, start noting them each time you get a question that addresses them.

B. **Executive branch:** Powers of the **President under Article II:**

1. **Execution of laws** made by Congress **("take care"** that the laws be faithfully executed).

a. **Prosecution:** The decision to prosecute is reserved solely to the executive branch under Article II, section 3 (i.e., if a former U.S. Ambassador is cited for contempt after refusing to answer questions and a grand jury later indicts them, the Attorney General can refuse to sign the indictment as the decision to prosecute is at the discretion of the executive branch).

b. **Limitation:** The President has **no power to decline to spend funds** specifically appropriated by Congress when Congress has expressly mandated they be spent.

2. **Supervise the executive branch**, including federal agencies, by issuing an executive order.
   a. **Executive orders** are valid unless they are inconsistent with a congressional statute or some specific provision of the Constitution itself.

      Example: The President cannot override a congressional act that was passed over a presidential veto by issuing a subsequent executive order.

   b. The President **does not have the power to direct the actions of persons outside** the executive branch unless Congress authorizes such direction.

      Example: The President can issue an executive order requiring the U.S. Weather Bureau to use the metric system but cannot order privately owned radio and television stations to do so, even if they are federally licensed.

3. **Make treaties** with **foreign nations,** subject to two-thirds Senate approval, and recognize foreign governments.
   a. **Self-executing v. non self-executing treaties:** A **self-executing** treaty is effective without implementation from Congress, whereas a **non self-executing** treaty requires Congress' approval so the President cannot implement it in ways that create rights or obligations.

      Example: A valid treaty between the U.S. and a foreign country provides for the elimination of all tariff barriers between the two countries. It authorizes the president of either country to issue a proclamation nullifying any state law that impedes imports from the other country. The foreign country uses the metric system (liters, etc.) and a law in a state of the U.S. requires all goods sold in its state to use the American system for measurement (quarts, etc.). Because the law impedes imports from the foreign country, the President is allowed (under the treaty) to issue a proclamation nullifying the state law.

   b. **Executive agreements** with other governments are usually within the President's broad power over foreign relations and will supersede conflicting state laws.

4. **Speak for the U.S. in foreign policy** and negotiate executive agreements with foreign countries.

   Example: The President can agree to release a prisoner when negotiating with a foreign country to secure the release of a U.S. Ambassador that was kidnapped in that country.

   a. The **President alone has the authority** to represent the U.S. in foreign affairs.

      Example: The President can direct ambassadors not to comply with a statute that Congress enacted directing them to send formal letters to other countries to protest.

5. **Commander in chief** of the armed forces, including state militia, when called into the actual service of the U.S., but Congress retains the power to declare war.

6. **Appoint ambassadors,** with the advice and consent of the Senate, and receive foreign ambassadors.

7. **Appoint top-level federal officers** subject to 50% Senate approval (e.g., federal judges, cabinet members, panel/commission members with significant executive power, and ambassadors). Congress has the authority to determine *who* appoints inferior federal officers, but does not make the appointments.
   a. **Removal of officers:** The Constitution is silent as to removal, but the President can remove top-level federal officers unless Congress provides limitations on removal.

8. **Issue pardons** for federal (not state) criminal (not civil) offenses, except cases of impeachment (Congress does not have authority to qualify or limit this power).

9. **Veto a bill passed by Congress** in its *entirety* by sending it back to Congress unsigned with a message stating the reasons for rejection. A line-item veto is unconstitutional.

10. **Executive privilege:** Under executive privilege, Presidents have a **qualified right** to refuse to disclose **confidential information** relating to their performance of their duties. It is qualified to the extent that other compelling governmental interests may outweigh a President's right to refuse to disclose information.

11. **Antiquities Act:** Under the Antiquities Act, the President, by presidential proclamation, has the power to **create national monuments** on federal lands to protect significant natural, cultural, or scientific features.

    Example: A statute passed by Congress and signed by the President authorized a federal agency to select a site and construct a monument honoring veterans. The statute appropriated the necessary funds, but limited expenditure of the funds until Congress approved of the agency's plans for the location of the monument, without presenting it to the President. This would be an improper legislative interference with an executive function because Congress already appropriated the funds and cannot later limit use of the funds since the site choice is an executive function.

SOURCE OF POWER-SEPARATION OF POWERS CHEAT SHEET

The judicial branch is not included here since it is less frequently tested and judicial branch issues are distinct and not easily confused with the other two branches.

CONGRESS	PRESIDENT
◆ Pass laws	◆ Execute/prosecute laws ◆ Veto a bill passed by Congress
◆ Raise/support armed forces ◆ Declare war	◆ Commander in chief of armed forces
◆ Delegation/committees	◆ Appoint ambassadors ◆ Appoint top-level federal officers
◆ Preserve federal monopoly over foreign affairs	◆ Make treaties with foreign nations ◆ Speak for the U.S. in foreign policy
◆ Federal lands/animals on the land	◆ Create national monuments
◆ Speech & Debate (immunity)	◆ Executive privilege
◆ Limit appellate jurisdiction of S. Ct.	◆ Supervise (executive orders)
◆ Post-Civil War Am. (13th, 14th, 15th)	◆ Issue pardons for federal criminal offenses
◆ Tax and Spend	
◆ Commerce Clause	
◆ Naturalization/Bankruptcy	

CONGRESS (LEGISLATIVE) v. THE PRESIDENT (EXECUTIVE) BATTLE OF THE BRANCHES EXAMPLES

FACTS	ANALYSIS
Former U.S. Ambassador is cited for contempt and refuses to answer certain questions. She is later indicted but the Attorney General (AG) refuses to sign the indictment. The House wants the AG to prosecute her. Who wins?	The AG because the **decision to prosecute** is reserved solely to the **executive** branch.
Federal Auto Safety Act creates a 5-member Commission to investigate auto safety, make recommendations to Congress, and prosecute violations; one member is appointed by the President, and two by the Senate and House. Will the Commission's rules be enforced?	No, because even if the delegation was ok, the **President** has the power to **appoint top-level federal officers and execute the laws.**
Congress passed a bill prohibiting the President from granting a pardon to any person who had not served at least 1/3 of their sentence. Can Congress do this?	No, because the **President** has the power to grant **pardons** (except impeachment).
Congress enacted a statute authorizing the construction of a monument and another statute appropriating $3 million for the construction. The President announced he was canceling the monument's construction and would not spend the funds. Who wins?	**Congress**, because the appropriation is a valid exercise of Congress's **spending power** and the President must abide by this spending.
A statute authorizes a federal agency to issue rules to grant funds for research. The statute also provides that rules issued by the agency may be set aside by a majority vote of a standing committee of Congress. Is this allowed?	No, because **Congress cannot** allow a **standing committee** to **enact law** without Congress' vote and the President's approval.

C. Judiciary

1. **Federal judicial power** allows federal courts to review cases:

   a. **Arising under the Constitution** or the laws of the United States,

   Example: A federal question is one such as the denial of a property right or the right to travel for a barber who cannot get a barber license in a state unless they have resided there for two years and are a U.S. citizen.

   > MBE tip: Most questions involving the power of a court to hear a case are due to a federal question being involved so this is a common correct answer choice.

   b. **Admiralty**,

   c. Between **two or more states**,

   d. Between **citizens of different states**, and

   e. Between a state or its citizens and a **foreign country or foreign citizen**.

2. **Review of a state court decision** by the Supreme Court is only allowed to the extent the decision is based on federal law.

3. **Independent and adequate state grounds:** The Supreme Court will not review a case where there are independent and adequate state law grounds for the state court's decision, even if there is a federal question involved.

   Example: A state law restricted abortion. The state's highest court ruled that the law violated the Due Process Clause of both the U.S. and the state's constitutions. Thus, the U.S. Supreme Court would not have jurisdiction to review the state court decision because the state court's decision is based on law independent from federal law (its own state constitution) and is adequate to sustain the result.

   Example: A state law provides for damages against anyone who publishes the name of a rape victim. A woman sued for her name being published. The state supreme court found the state law likely violates the 1st Amendment but they did not decide that issue because its own state constitution provided even greater protection to the right of the press to report the news. So the U.S. Supreme Court would not hear the case as the state supreme court's decision rested on adequate and independent state law grounds.

   > **MBE tip:** As indicated in the examples above, the bar examiners will have to give the issue away in the question by providing a (usually convoluted) fact pattern where the underlying decision is based both on state and federal law. Be aware of questions where state and federal laws are similar and the court's decision was based on state law (and not federal). This implicates the independent and adequate state grounds exception and the judiciary will not review the case.

4. **Exceptions Clause of Article III:** Congress has the power to strip the U.S. Supreme Court of its appellate jurisdiction to hear particular types of cases (and the Supreme Court's own decisions support this view). However, such limitations must be based on a **broad and neutral basis**, not a narrow basis.

   Example: Congress may not limit the Supreme Court's power to hear abortion cases just because they are controversial since that would not be based on a broad and neutral basis for such a limitation.

5. **Concurrent jurisdiction:** State and federal courts have concurrent jurisdiction over cases arising under federal law.

6. **Supreme Court has original (not appellate) jurisdiction** when the **state is a party** or for **cases affecting ambassadors.**

V. LIMITATIONS ON STATE POWER (NOT THE FEDERAL GOVERNMENT)

A. The **Supremacy Clause** states that the Constitution is the supreme law of the land. Any state law that **directly conflicts** with federal law, **impedes the objectives** of federal law, or regulates an **area traditionally occupied** by Congress, will be **preempted** by federal law (including valid treaties).

   1. **Conflict preemption:** Where a state law is inconsistent with a valid federal law covering the same subject matter, the state law is invalid.

2. **Field preemption:** Where the federal government intends to **"occupy the entire field"** the states cannot regulate in that field.

   Example: The regulation of buses or tires in a state is preempted by the Commerce Clause even if the fact pattern does not tell you that the Commerce Clause is the federal law because buses and tires are instrumentalities of commerce so Congress has the power to regulate those.

3. **Different purposes:** When there is a federal law and a state law that do not conflict because they have different purposes, even if they touch on the same topic, preemption is not an issue.

   Example: Federal law that regulates the design of hunting traps to protect human safety does not conflict with a state law that prohibits using traps to hunt due to near extinction of a particular animal—the purposes of the regulations are different and the federal law does not preempt the state law even though they both mention hunting traps.

4. **Consent:** A state cannot regulate the federal government without the federal government's consent.

   Example: A state cannot prosecute operators of a federally operated building for using an old, pollution-generating heating system that exceeds the state's pollution standards without the federal government's consent.

> **MBE tip:** Supremacy Clause questions don't always have a clear federal statute specifically stated in the fact pattern; sometimes you will need to make an inference from Congress' source of powers, such as when the Commerce Clause applies.

B. The **Dormant Commerce Clause** (DCC) (also called the Negative Implications of the Commerce Clause) **restricts the states** and local governments from regulating activity that **affects interstate commerce** if the regulation is (1) **discriminatory,** or (2) **unduly burdensome.**

> **MBE tip:** Bar examiners use the language "commerce" interchangeably with "Dormant Commerce Clause." But remember that the Commerce Clause applies to actions by the *federal* government and the Dormant Commerce Clause applies to actions by *states or local* governments.
>
> **Issue spotting tip:** Dormant Commerce Clause fact patterns frequently involve protectionistic type rules favoring locals and regulations near state borders (e.g., a rule requiring that doctors at the local hospital must be in-state residents).

1. **Discriminatory:** A regulation that is **discriminatory** against out-of-towners (protectionist to local interests) will be permitted *only if* it is **necessary** to achieve an **legitimate noneconomic governmental interest** such that there are **no reasonable alternatives.** Facially discriminatory regulations are virtually **per se violations** of the DCC.

   a. The term **"out-of-towners"** refers to favoring **local interests** over nonlocal interests and need not apply literally to favoring one state over another, but can apply to favoring towns and localities as well.

      Example: State A requires out of state businesses to perform certain functions, such as vitamin bottle labeling, in state. This is discriminatory to out-of-towners and favors local vitamin bottlers.

2. **Undue burden:** A regulation that **unduly burdens** interstate commerce will be permitted if it is:

   a. **Rationally related** to a

   b. **Legitimate government interest,** and

   c. The **burden imposed on interstate commerce must be outweighed by the legitimate benefits** to the state.

   [This is essentially a rational basis test plus balancing.]

      1. **Various state laws in conflict:** Regulations leading to a lack of uniformity among various states regulations may constitute an **undue burden.**

         Example: State A requires all semi-trailer trucks to have 20-inch mud flaps, when all other states require 15-inch mud flaps. This is an undue burden.

      2. **Requiring out of state businesses to perform certain operations in state** will constitute an undue burden.

         Example: It would be unduly burdensome if State A required all citrus grown out of state, but sold in state, to be packaged for sale in State A.

> **MBE tip:** Many laws will be found unduly burdensome under the DCC. The undue burden prong is tested much more than the discriminatory prong.

3. **Exceptions**

   a. **Market participant:** When the state is not acting as a regulator, but rather **owns or operates a business and therefore participates in the economic marketplace,** it may favor local interests over nonlocal interests.

   Example: State A owns a lumber mill and gives a discount on any lumber sold to any buyer willing to process the lumber to produce products that will remain in State A. This is allowed since State A is a market participant.

   b. **Congressional consent** to the regulation.

   Example: A state tax imposed only on out-of-state insurance companies is allowed because Congress had enacted a law permitting states to regulate insurance in any manner they wished.

> **MBE tip:** Look for questions where Congress enacts a federal statute that permits states to require an act that might otherwise be discriminatory or burdensome for this exception to apply. Again, the statute at issue will of course be a state statute for the DCC to apply.

   c. **State or city promoting public operations** that are traditional state functions.

   Example: A rule requiring all consumers to use the city-run waste disposal service is allowed.

DORMANT COMMERCE CLAUSE EXAMPLES

<u>**MBE tip:**</u> Dormant Commerce Clause (DCC) is primarily MBE tested two ways:

1. Analyze if a law imposes an undue burden (usually it will).
2. Identify the "best argument" to challenge a law that impacts interstate commerce (which will be DCC instead of Equal Protection Clause (EPC) or Due Process Clause (DPC) or a "hit list" rule.)
   Sometimes the answer choice will simply say "Commerce Clause" rather than specify that it is the Dormant Commerce Clause. Most of the time the answer choice will specifically use the words "undue burden."

<table>
<tr><th>UNDUE BURDEN</th><th>NO UNDUE BURDEN</th></tr>
<tr><td>◆ State requires licenses for barbers and only gives licenses to those who graduated from an in-state barber school and have been state residents for 2 years.</td><td rowspan="7">◆ State statute requires a fee of 2 cents per bird on all poultry farming to pay for a state inspection system to ensure no poultry raised in the state is infected with a fatal virus that transfers from poultry to humans (burden is outweighed by the public health benefit).</td></tr>
<tr><td>◆ State requires every business with annual sales in the state over $1 million to purchase goods and/or services in the state equal to ½ of its annual sales in the state.</td></tr>
<tr><td>◆ All buses that drive on the highways in the state must be equipped with seat belts for all passengers (buses cross state lines often).</td></tr>
<tr><td>◆ State requires all manufacturers and wholesalers who sell goods to retailers in State to do so at prices no higher than the lowest prices at which they sell them to bordering states.</td></tr>
<tr><td>◆ State requires all manufacturers that use fabric to have the fabric tested for flame retardancy at a private in-state company and by no other companies.</td></tr>
<tr><td>◆ Ordinance of a particular County only allows taxicabs registered in that County to pick up or discharge passengers. And only residents of that County can register taxicabs.</td></tr>
<tr><td>◆ A state passes a statute that requires the sale of all toys that purport to represent extraterrestrial objects to satisfy specified scientific criteria. Some out-of-state toy manufacturers created extraterrestrial toy sets that do not meet the criteria, unlike the in-state manufacturers, but the toys are still safe and durable. Barring the sale of toys from these out-of-state manufacturers has a substantial effect on interstate commerce.</td></tr>
</table>

Decoy tip: DCC overlaps with EPC because protectionist legislation also creates a classification scheme where similarly situated persons are treated differently because in-staters are being treated better than out-of-staters. DCC will provide the **best argument** to defeat the rule (instead of EPC or DP or a "hit list" rule) because the DCC test will be harder to meet since there is a balancing component, while under EPC or DP it will usually be subject to mere rational basis.

Common DCC decoys (wrong answers):

- Privileges and Immunities Clause (either one).
- Due Process Clause (even if implicated, the right at issue is usually not a fundamental right so rational basis would apply).
- Equal Protection Clause (usually there is no classification because burden is tested most of the time and not discrimination; but even if discriminatory usually rational basis applies and is easily met).

C. The **Privileges and Immunities (P & I) Clause of Article IV** prevents a **state or city from discriminating** against **nonresidents** regarding rights **fundamental to national unity** when the laws were enacted for the **protectionist purpose** of burdening out-of-staters.

Reminder: this limitation does not apply to the federal government.

MBE tip: While the P & I Clause of Art. IV is a frequent decoy answer, it also gets tested outright. When it is tested, make sure the state statute is discriminating against *nonresidents* and not its *own residents*, because if the statute discriminates against its own residents, this rule is not applicable.

1. **Rights fundamental to national unity** are limited to **commercial** activities, such as one's **ability to work,** the right to support oneself, the right to engage in business, practice one's profession, or pursue a common calling.
2. **Corporations and aliens are not considered citizens** for this rule so they will not be afforded protection, though they may raise an equal protection claim.
3. **Discrimination against nonresident citizens will only be allowed if** the nonresident citizens are:
   a. A **peculiar source of the evil** the state is trying to regulate (i.e., the nonresident citizens are the cause or a part of the problem), and
   b. The discrimination is **substantially related** to this evil, and
   c. There are **no less discriminatory (i.e., restrictive) alternative** means available.

   [This test is a hard standard to meet.]

PRIVILEGES & IMMUNITIES (P & I) CLAUSE (ART. IV) EXAMPLES

(Where P & I Clause, Art. IV, actually applies and is **not a decoy answer**)

Example: A doctor who resides in the state of Green is licensed in the states of Green and Red and often treats patients in Red. A new state statute requires all doctors treating patients in Red to reside in Red. Since the state cannot show that the doctor's out-of-state residence is a peculiar source of evil, the statute violated the P & I Clause (Art. IV).

Example: A commercial fisherman frequently fishes in a neighboring state. The state enacted a statute to protect the fishing industry that requires all in-state fisherman to pay a license fee and establish that they had been commercial fishing in that state for 8 years. This statute violates the P & I Clause (Art. IV) because other options can be used to protect the industry without discriminating against out-of-state fisherman.

Decoy tip: P & I Clause (Art. IV) is a frequent decoy answer. The rule is very narrow so carefully review the examples above to understand when it does actually apply. Remember that for P & I Clause (Art. IV), the state statute is usually limiting one's ability to practice their profession (such as commercial fishing above, NOT fishing for sport). IF this is not the case, then DCC is likely the correct answer choice and not P & I Clause.

D. **The Privileges and Immunities Clause of the 14th Amendment** prohibits **states** from depriving **citizens** of the privileges or immunities of U.S. citizenship, which are the **rights of "national" citizenship.** The U.S. Supreme Court has never applied this clause to actions of the federal government.

1. The most important rights of national citizenship are the right to:
   a. **Travel from state to state.** This right is implicated when **newly arrived residents are treated less favorably** than those who have resided in the state for a long time.
      1. Note: The right to freely travel from state to state is also a fundamental right subject to strict scrutiny under equal protection and substantive due process analysis.
   b. **Vote in national elections.**
   c. **Enter public lands.**
2. **Corporations and aliens are not considered citizens** for this rule so they will not be afforded protection, though they may raise an equal protection claim.
3. **Strict Scrutiny** applies. Any such regulation must be:
   a. **Narrowly tailored** to achieve a
   b. **Compelling** government interest.

PRIVILEGES & IMMUNITIES CLAUSE (14TH AM.) EXAMPLE

(Where P & I Clause, 14th Am. actually applies and is **not a decoy answer)**

Example: A state statute providing that persons moving into a community to attend college may not vote in any elections for state officials violates the P & I Clause (14th Am.) because the statute could be more narrowly tailored to ensure only residents of a community vote.

Decoy tip: This is a frequent decoy answer. The actual rule is very narrow so carefully review the example above when it does actually apply.

THE TWO PRIVILEGES & IMMUNITIES CLAUSES DECODED

	P & I (Article IV)	**P & I (14th Am.)**
Rule Source:	Article IV of the U.S. Constitution	14th Am. to the U.S. Constitution
Rule Purpose:	To facilitate unification of states into one nation (allowing people to travel between states and work and receive the same treatment).	To provide equality on a national level.
Applies to:	Citizens only (NOT corporations and aliens)	Citizens only (NOT corporations and aliens)
Protects:	Rights **fundamental to national unity** such as: ◆ Right to **pursue a livelihood** ◆ **Commercial** not recreational activities ◆ Right to **courts**	Rights of **national citizenship** such as: ◆ Right to **travel** ◆ Right to **vote** for federal officeholders ◆ Right to enter **public lands**
Standard if applicable:	**Scrutiny test**: ◆ Peculiar source of the evil the state is trying to regulate (cause of problem), and ◆ Discrimination is substantially related to this evil, and ◆ No less discriminatory alternative/ restrictive means available.	**Strict scrutiny**: ◆ Narrowly tailored to achieve a ◆ Compelling government interest.
Issue spotting/ fact triggers	◆ State statute (not federal) ◆ One's **livelihood or profession** is being affected ◆ Statute treating residents and nonresidents differently	◆ State statute (not federal) ◆ One's ability to **travel/move or vote** is being affected ◆ Statute treating people differently

E. The **Contracts Clause** (Article I, section 10) prevents **state governments** from passing laws that **retroactively** and **substantially** impair **existing contracts. Note:** a similar rule applies to federal legislation under the 5th Amendment (but Article I, section 10 is limited to states and the multistate bar exam has only tested state legislation in regard to the Contracts Clause).

1. **Private contracts:** If the state is **substantially impairing** private contracts, the law must be:

   a. **Reasonable and appropriate** (for social and economic regulations it must also be **necessary**) to serve

   b. An **important and legitimate public purpose.**

2. **Public contracts:** Similar to the test above but the court will interpret it more strictly, focusing on the law being:

   a. **Necessary** to serve

   b. An **important public purpose.**

   Example: A state entered into a contract with a construction company to build a turnpike. Prior to construction, the state legislature repealed the statute authorizing the turnpike in order to provide funds for parks. Funding for parks was not an important enough public purpose and the repeal was not necessary so the legislation violated the Contracts Clause.

   MBE tip: The Contracts Clause does not apply to employer's rightfully altering employment contracts (e.g., police stations are permitted to amend existing employee benefits over time, even though these benefits might vary from a police officer's original employment contract because most jobs are at will).

F. The **Full Faith and Credit Clause** (Article IV, section 1) prohibits state courts from re-litigating cases in which the court of another state, with proper jurisdiction, rendered final judgment on the merits, so each state must give the judgment of any other state the same effect the judgment would have in the state that rendered the judgment.

1. This clause applies when courts of **two different states' courts** are involved in the same controversy.

   Example: State B must enforce a money judgment issued in State A; State B can't opt to ignore the State A judgment.

2. Even if the **first state made an error of law** (i.e., applied the wrong law under conflict-of-law), the **second state must still honor** the first state's decision, with a **narrow exception** that they need not if the first court did not have **proper jurisdiction.**

G. The **right to abortion** is a right protected by the Substantive Due Process Clause, but states do not have the right to ban all pre-viability abortions. See Substantive Due Process in sec. VI.D.1. for specific rules.

VI. LIMITATIONS ON FEDERAL AND STATE POWER: INDIVIDUAL RIGHTS AND OTHER CONSTITUTIONAL LIMITATIONS

MBE tip: The following constitutional protections provide for individual rights for the people and apply to all federal and state governmental actions. Questions on individual rights comprise approximately half of the Con. Law MBE questions.

A. **Freedom of religion** is a First Amendment limitation on Congress's actions and is also applicable to the states through the Fourteenth Amendment. There are two clauses.

1. The **Free Exercise Clause** bars any law that prohibits or seriously **burdens the free exercise** of religion, unless it is:

a. **Necessary** to achieve

b. A **compelling government interest.**

To violate the Free Exercise clause, the government must coerce a person to do something, or not do something, against the dictates of their religion.

Example: A public official can't be forced to take an oath stating a belief in God.

1. **Except:** A **law of general applicability** (a law that regulates the conduct of all persons) is allowable if it does **not intentionally burden religious beliefs** and is:

a. **Rationally related to**

b. A **legitimate government interest.**

Example: The government can prevent the use of illegal drugs, such as peyote, even if taking those drugs is a sincerely held tenet of a religious faith.

i. **"Religious belief" is construed very broadly.** The belief must be **bona fide**, but need not be theistic (based on the existence of a supreme being) or widely held or even reasonable, so long as the belief is **genuine or sincerely held.**

ii. **Time, place, and manner regulation:** The government may regulate the **time, place, and manner of religiously motivated conduct** as long as the regulation is:

a. **Neutral** and serves

b. An **important public interest.**

Example: A religious group likes to take an annual mountain trip and dance around a large campfire as part of a religious ritual. An ordinance prohibiting lighting fires in the area is valid because it is a neutral law (not religious) and the interest of public safety regarding fire danger is important.

2. **Except:** The **Religious Freedom Restoration Act** allows a person to challenge a **federal law of general applicability** if there is a **substantial burdening** of religious free exercise and then the government must meet **strict scrutiny** and the law must be:

a. **Narrowly tailored** to achieve

b. A **compelling government interest.**

Example: A small closely held company cannot be required to provide contraceptive coverage to employees since it violates the company owner's religious beliefs. While the U.S. Supreme Court found protecting one's interest in contraceptive methods is a compelling interest, mandating that all companies provide free contraceptives is not the least restrictive means of providing such care as the government could provide alternate means for women to obtain contraceptives (so the law is not narrowly tailored).

2. The **Establishment Clause** prohibits laws respecting the establishment of religion. The government **can't endorse or favor** specific religious groups.

   a. **Incidentally favoring** one religion over another in an attempt to benefit a wide variety of people is allowable.

   b. **Sect preference:** A sect preference would be favoring one distinct religious group over another (e.g., favoring Christians over other religious groups). If the government action contains a sect preference, **strict scrutiny** applies and the action must be:

      1. **Narrowly tailored** to achieve

      2. A **compelling government interest.**

   c. **No sect preference:** If the government action contains no sect preference, it must satisfy the ***Lemon*** **test** and the action must:

      1. Have a **secular legislative purpose,**

      2. Have a **primary secular effect,** which neither advances nor inhibits religion, and

      3. Not foster **excessive government entanglement** with religion.

FREEDOM OF RELIGION CHEAT SHEET		
	Free Exercise	**Establishment Clause**
General rule	Cannot **burden** religion	Cannot **endorse or favor** religion
Standard of review	**Strict Scrutiny** ◆ Necessary to ◆ A compelling gov. interest	Sect preference = **Strict Scrutiny** ◆ Necessary to ◆ A compelling government interest No Sect preference = ***Lemon*** **test** ◆ Secular purpose, ◆ Primary secular effect, ◆ No excessive govt. entanglement
Exception	Law of general applicability = **Rational Basis** ◆ Rationally related to ◆ A legitimate gov. interest	◆ Incidental favoring allowed
MBE tip:	◆ Not tested that often ◆ When tested, not usually violated	◆ Tested often ◆ When tested, it is often violated

Free Exercise Example (violated)
◆ Statute makes committing fraud for personal gain a crime. D solicited cash donations to support his efforts to spread the word about his new religion. Donors claimed D defrauded them because his beliefs were false and thus he received donations for personal gain (**strongest defense** for D is that his free exercise of religion rights are violated).

Free Exercise Examples (not violated)
◆ A religious group likes to take an annual mountain trip and dance around a large campfire as part of its rituals. An ordinance prohibits them from lighting fires and is valid because it is a **law of general applicability.** ◆ A law requires an autopsy for all deaths not obviously caused of natural causes, but a family's religion maintains bodies must be buried immediately. The law is valid because it is a **law of general applicability.**

Establishment Clause Examples (violated)
◆ General sales tax on books and magazines with an exemption for religious books violates the Establishment Clause because it is essentially a subsidy of recognized religious faiths and **excessive entanglement** with govt. ◆ Nativity scene placed in City's capital would be deemed to have a religious effect and **not a secular purpose** under *Lemon*. ◆ Prayer and bible readings in public schools, whether voluntary or not. ◆ State law requires vacant public school buildings to be sold at auction to the highest bidder. A church wanted to acquire the building at a price lower than its fair market value so the school board proposed a new law that would authorize this. This is not permitted as it would constitute an **establishment of religion.**

Establishment Clause Examples (not violated)
◆ Free distribution of textbooks to a religious school—secular purpose and no govt. entanglement (would be the **strongest argument** for why distribution of books is okay). ◆ Grants offered to all private and public colleges including colleges with operating churches. This is not supporting religion and is incidental favoring at most, so it is okay. ◆ City operates a cemetery and a city ordinance requires tax funds be spent to maintain the flowers, mow grass, and plow snow if the funds raised from selling burial plots is not enough. Secular purpose and no excessive govt. involvement, so the ordinance is okay.

B. **Freedom of Speech:** The First Amendment protects an individual's right to free speech and is applicable to the states through the Fourteenth Amendment.

1. **Two classes of speech:** Speech prohibitions can be content based or content neutral, and the rules vary depending on this distinction.

★ a. **Content-based** speech regulations are those that forbid speech based on either its **subject matter** or **viewpoint.**

1. **Strict scrutiny** applies to content-based restrictions, with the courts showing the least tolerance for viewpoint-based regulations. Content-based restrictions are rarely allowed. The **government has the burden of proof** to show that the regulation is:

a. **Necessary** (narrowly tailored) to achieve

b. A **compelling governmental interest.**

Example: A statute assesses an excise tax of 10% on the price of admission to public movie theaters when they show films that contain actual scenes of human sexual intercourse. Thus, the statute is content-based and subject to strict scrutiny.

> **MBE tip:** Where a regulation renders an entire topic or category of speech off limits but is viewpoint neutral, such as a regulation prohibiting picketing in front of abortion clinics (both pro-life and pro-choice), the regulation is still considered content-based and subject to strict scrutiny. Similarly, a regulation will also be deemed content-based if it limits the time, place, or manner of speech based on the content of the speech (e.g., special rules or time limits on political speech).

2. **Unprotected categories** of speech must still be **regulated in a content-neutral way** (see sec. IV.B.1.b).

a. **Obscenity:** Speech that describes or depicts sexual conduct that, taken as a whole, by the average person:

i. Appeals to the **prurient interest** in sex (under a community standard);

ii. Is **patently offensive** (under a community standard); and

iii. **Lacks serious Literary, Artistic, Political, or Scientific** value (under a national reasonable person standard).

> **Memorization tip:** Think **LAPS** since obscenity is a lapse in judgment.

> **MBE tip:** Nudity alone does not make speech/videos obscene (i.e., selling pictures of nude sunbathers on a beach where nude sunbathing is common is protected speech). Be sure that the facts prove each element above to prove obscenity; it is hard to prove and rarely met on the multistate bar exam.

b. **Misrepresentation and defamation** are torts and are covered in detail in the Torts Rules Outline. Both are unprotected speech.

c. **Inciting imminent lawless action:** The government can ban speech advocating imminent lawless action if it is **intended to incite** or produce imminent lawless action and is **likely to produce** such action (speech presenting a clear and present danger).

d. **Fighting words/threats of violence** are words that are **likely to cause** the listener to commit an **act of violence** or **true threats** used to intimidate another individual. However, causing another to be angry alone is insufficient.

Example: A man disliked his neighbors and intended to frighten them one night so he spray painted threats that he was going to shoot them on their house. The man claimed free speech as his defense and that he did not actually intend to shoot them but only to scare them. The man's free speech defense is not valid because free speech does not protect threats of violence.

b. Time, place, and manner restrictions seek to regulate speech (or communicative conduct) based on **something other than the subject matter** of the expression, such as the external factors of the time, place, and manner (e.g., maximum volume requirements or limits on the size of signs) in which the speech may be communicated. The rules differ depending on the **type of forum** in which the speech or conduct occurs, but the government cannot regulate in purely private forums, such as homes, clubs, or private office buildings. All regulations **must be viewpoint neutral** (or they are deemed content-based and subject to strict scrutiny).

1. **Public and designated public forums: Public forums** are forums that are **traditionally open to the public** for free speech purposes (e.g., streets, sidewalks, parks). **Designated public forums** (also called unlimited public forums) are forums that are not traditionally open to the public, but are **opened up to the public at large broadly for expressive activities** (e.g., government meeting places, public classrooms, or auditoriums that could be opened, for example, as a voting center) but designated forums can be un-designated. Speech restrictions in public and designated public forums must:

a. Be **content neutral** (content neutral means neutrality as to both the **subject matter** and the **viewpoint** expressed by the speaker),

Example: Subject matter (topic) = abortion; viewpoint (for or against the topic) = pro-life or pro-choice regarding abortion.

b. Serve a **substantial/important government interest,**

c. Be **narrowly tailored** to serve that interest, and

d. Leave open **alternative channels** of communication.

Example: The owner of a milk manufacturer wanted a new law repealed so he went to the Capitol steps on a weekday at noon to express his views on the law. A statute prohibits all speech making and public gatherings on the Capitol steps on weekdays between 11am and 1pm. This is a public forum (the question merely required students to *identify the applicable test*, which required identifying the proper forum).

> **MBE tip:** When a fact pattern has a two-sided argument or is ambiguous, the correct answer will simply require you to identify the proper forum and/or applicable test that applies rather than analyze whether the test is satisfied under the facts.
>
> **MBE tip:** The Supreme Court has used the words "significant," "substantial," and "important" interchangeably when discussing the government's interest. The NCBE released answers have also used the words "substantial" and "important" to describe public and designated public forum standards, so make sure you know that these words are interchangeable when analyzing these forums.

2. **Limited and nonpublic forums: Limited public forums** are forums that are opened for **limited use by certain groups** or discussion of a certain subject (e.g., a school room opened up to the girl scouts for a meeting). **Nonpublic forums** are forums that are **closed to the public** for speech purposes, such as the reception area at the local jail. Speech restrictions in limited and nonpublic public forums must:

a. Be **viewpoint neutral** (not required to be subject matter neutral),

b. Serve a **legitimate government interest,** and

c. Be **reasonably related** to serve that interest.

> **MBE tip**: Note that while nonpublic and limited public forums must be viewpoint neutral, they do not need to be subject matter neutral too like public and designated public forums (e.g., some limited public forums are opened up for a particular discussion or a certain subject, such as abortion, so it wouldn't be subject matter neutral but it must be viewpoint neutral so that groups with different viewpoints on the subject, such as pro-life and pro-choice, are both able to use the forum).

3. **Zoning powers—secondary effects:** Even if a city is using its **zoning powers** to limit or prohibit a **speech-related activity,** the regulation is acceptable if the city is **reasonably targeting** the **secondary effects** of that speech rather than targeting the expressive content so time, place, and manner standards would apply.

   Example: A city may prohibit the location of adult theaters and bookstores in residential areas to protect exposure to children so the regulation is not based on content but rather time, place, and manner so those standards would apply.

2. **Commercial Speech:** Commercial speech must be truthful. **False or misleading** commercial speech is **not constitutionally protected** speech. The government **may restrict commercial speech** (advertising) *only if* the regulation:

   a. Serves a **substantial government** interest,

   b. **Directly advances that interest,** and

   c. Is **narrowly tailored** such that there is a **reasonable fit** (but need not be the least restrictive means) to serve that interest.

   Example: A city banned machines selling commercial advertisement publications from all public sidewalks. The statute was enacted to prevent litter on the sidewalks. However, the city still allows machines selling newspaper publications. This regulation will not be permitted since there is not a reasonable fit between litter and this ban targeting advertisements because other publications could also litter the sidewalks.

3. **Symbolic Speech** is the freedom to **communicate an idea by use of a symbol or communicative conduct,** and includes the freedom **not to speak.** The government **may restrict symbolic speech** if the regulation:

   a. Furthers an **important governmental interest** unrelated to the suppression of speech (content neutral), and

   b. **Prohibits no more speech** than necessary (least restrictive means).

   Example: A protester entered an IRS building during office hours to denounce the income tax and set fire to the pages of his tax return. He was arrested for violating a law against starting a fire in a building. Because there is an important government interest in not having fires inside buildings, which is unrelated to suppressing speech, free speech will not provide a defense.

4. **Limitations on free speech regulations:**

a. **Vagueness:** A speech regulation is unconstitutionally vague if it is so unclearly defined that a **reasonable person would have to guess** at its meaning.

Example: A statute banning all retailers from selling products that would be "harmful to minors because of violent content," would be too vague since a retailer would have to guess at what violent content would be harmful to minors in violation of the statute.

b. **Overbreadth:** A speech regulation is unconstitutionally overbroad if it bans **both protected speech and unprotected speech.**

Example: An airline falsely claimed in an ad that a competitor had an inferior safety record. The claim was based on erroneous information found on an advocacy website. A state law imposes penalties for "any public statement containing false or misleading information about a service or product." The airline was charged under state law for the statement. If asked about the airlines *best defense* based on the First Amendment, a good answer would be that the law is overbroad because it bans more speech than necessary as it applies to "any" public statement, and "misleading" and "service or product" are also very broad so this could ban protected speech too. Overbroad would be a better defense (and hence the correct answer) in this question over other answer choices such as protected noncommercial speech, prior restraint, or acting with malice.

c. **Permit schemes with unfettered discretion:** A speech related regulation, licensing scheme, or permit regulation must be **content neutral** and is unconstitutional if it leaves unfettered discretion to the decision maker by not setting forth **narrow and specific grounds** for denying a permit, **or** where the permit mechanism is **not closely tailored to the regulation's objective.** Further, the regulation must be a **reasonable means** of maintaining public order.

Example: A public park permit scheme would be struck down where a permit is granted for charities to conduct recruiting drives, but did not allow a religious group to hold a recruiting drive.

> **MBE tip: Public employees** have rights to **speak freely** on issues of public concern and the employer cannot discharge the employee unless the statements impair that employee's ability to do their job.

5. **Prior restraints** prevent speech from being heard **before it even occurs.** These are rarely allowed and carry a heavy presumption of unconstitutionality. A prior restraint is only allowed where the government can show that some **irreparable or serious harm** to the public will occur and then there must be **narrowly drawn standards** and a **final determination** of the validity of the restraint (restraining body must seek an injunction to prevent dissemination).

a. **Collateral bar rule:** Under the collateral bar rule, if a prior restraint is issued by a court, one cannot violate it and then defend oneself by asserting that the action is unconstitutional, even if this is correct.

> **MBE tip:** For prior restraint to be triggered look for facts that require permission from a government official before something can be done (such as putting up a sign or having a parade or reporting on a war).

FREE SPEECH CHEAT SHEET

MBE tip: Use the following approach to answer free speech MBE questions:

1.) Is there a threshold issue (standing/state action/etc.)?
2.) Is the regulation content-based? (Look for symbolic, commercial, unprotected, etc.)
3.) If time, place, or manner (T,P,M), identify the forum.
4.) Apply the rule, but watch out for the limitations such as overbroad, prior restraint, etc.

TYPE	STANDARD OF REVIEW	
Content-based *Govt. almost always loses	◆ **Strict scrutiny (**most heavily tested**)** ◆ Necessary to achieve ◆ A compelling government interest	
Less or unprotected	**Obscenity** ◆ Appeals to prurient int. ◆ Patently offensive and ◆ Lacks serious LAPS	**Defamation** **Misrepresentation** **Fighting Words/ Threats**
Time, Place, Manner (TPM)—public & designated public forum	◆ Content neutral and viewpoint neutral ◆ Substantial/important government interest ◆ Narrowly tailored ◆ Open alternative channels of communication	
TPM—limited & nonpublic forum *Govt. almost always wins	◆ Viewpoint neutral ◆ Legitimate government interest ◆ Reasonably related	
Commercial (advertising)	◆ Substantial government interest ◆ Directly advances that interest ◆ Narrowly tailored such that there is a reasonable fit	
Symbolic (communicative)	◆ Important governmental interest unrelated to speech ◆ Prohibits no more speech than necessary	
Reasonableness Factors	◆ Vague (reasonable person needs to guess at meaning) ◆ Overbroad (bans protected speech too) ◆ Unfettered discretion (no standards for licenses/ permits)	
Prior Restraint *Govt. almost always loses	◆ Irreparable or serious harm to the public will occur ◆ Narrowly drawn standards ◆ Final determination of the validity	

Common decoys answers: Often the wrong answers identify the **wrong standard** (i.e., the language of rational basis when the rule is strict scrutiny) OR the **wrong burden of proof** (i.e., the decoy will state the challenger bears the Burden of Proof (BOP) in reference to a heightened standard of review (e.g., strict scrutiny) when the government actually has the BOP for strict scrutiny).

Common call of the question style for free speech: The call of the question often asks what is the "strongest" argument or defense regarding the rule in question (you are simply identifying the applicable standard, but you are not typically required to apply the standard to the facts).

C. **Freedom of association:** First Amendment case law recognizes an individual's **right to freely associate** with other individuals in groups. A group has the same right to engage in legal, non-violent, expressive activity as a group that an individual would have.

Example: Groups can get together to bring lawsuits or conduct non-violent economic boycotts.

1. The **government can only prevent freedom of association** or require individuals to associate in regard to First Amendment freedoms if there is a:

    a. **Compelling governmental interest** that

    b. Cannot be achieved by **less restrictive means (narrowly tailored).**

    Example: A state adopted a rule denying admission to its state bar association to anyone who is or was a member of a subversive group. Although the state bar had a compelling government interest in determining the character and professional competence of bar applicants, it had other means to make these determinations that were less restrictive, so the rule violated the freedom of association.

2. **Not for social purposes:** Freedom of association applies only to freedoms protected by the **First Amendment** and is not for social association purposes.

> MBE tip: Keep in mind freedom of association will not permit activities that are otherwise not protected pursuant to the First Amendment such as fighting, illegal activities, etc.

3. **Public job or benefit:** Freedom of association also prevents the government from denying a public benefit or job based on a person's association.

    a. **Government job protected:** The Supreme Court has held that the government may not fire an employee because of their **political views or affiliations** unless certain views or affiliations are required for the effective performance of the employee's job.

    Example: A clerical employee of a city water department was responsible for sending bills to customers. The employee's sister was running for mayor and he was supporting her. After the sister lost the mayoral race, the new mayor fired the employee for supporting his sister. This violated the employee's right to freely associate (and his right to free speech) so the firing was not constitutional.

    b. **Loyalty Oaths:** Public employees may be required to take loyalty oaths promising they will support the Constitution and oppose the violent or illegal overthrow of the government.

4. **No forced inclusion:** The Supreme Court has held that **forced inclusion** of an unwanted person in a group **violates the group's freedom of association** if including that person would **significantly affect** the group's ability to express its viewpoints.

    Example: An environmental organization's mission is to support environmental causes. Its bylaws state it is open to the public but it can refuse to admit anyone who does not adhere to its mission. The organization was opposing a local plan to begin mining. Residents in favor of mining tried to join the organization and were denied admission. This is allowed since an organization's right to freedom of association allows it to refuse membership to those who do not adhere to its mission. Note that there is also no state action here, but the answer choices focused on freedom of association and not state action as possible answers.

5. **Membership in a group alone cannot be illegal,** but it can be part of an offense/crime where the group is actively engaged in unlawful activity, and the individual knows and intends to further the group's illegal goals.

Example: It isn't illegal to be a member of the Communist party, but if the group is planning to overthrow the government and a member is aware of this, the membership could be part of the illegal offense.

D. **Freedom of the Press**

1. **Matters of public concern:** The press has the right to **publish matters of public concern** and the public has a right to receive the information (the press is not afforded any more protection than all citizens).

   a. **Limitation:** The press does not have the right to access internal records kept by the **executive branch,** records prepared for **law enforcement purposes,** and records that **violate one's privacy rights.**

   Example: A state enacted a statute to close the official records of all arrests and prosecutions of persons acquitted to protect them from further publicity or embarrassment, but the statute does not prohibit publication if private parties have access to the information. A prominent businessman was acquitted for rape and a news reporter wanted access to his official records. The news reporter does not have the right to access the records from the state/courts. However, if the news reporter gained access from a private party who had the records somehow then she could report on his case.

2. **Trials:** The public and the press have the right to attend criminal trials unless the judge finds an overriding interest.

3. **No immunity:** The Press does not have immunity for free speech activities (unlike legislators who do have immunity under the Speech and Debate Clause).

   Example: A professional motorcycle rider put on a show in a private stadium and charged $5 per spectator. A local television station filmed the whole event without permission and broadcast the entire performance on the news. The rider successfully sued the reporter because he had a property right in the commercial value of his performance and the television station does not have immunity against this tort.

E. **Due Process** binds the **states through the Fourteenth Amendment**, and the **federal government through the Fifth Amendment**. There are two types: substantive due process and procedural due process.

1. **Substantive Due Process (SDP)** limits the **government's** ability to regulate certain areas of human life, such as the **substantive interests in life, liberty, or property.** (Primarily regulating one's **personal autonomy and privacy.**)

   a. **Rights subject to SDP** are categorized either as fundamental, nonfundamental, or relating to abortion, and different rules apply to each.

   1. **Fundamental rights:** Under SDP this refers to rights relating to marriage, living with one's family, child bearing, child rearing, sex in marriage, right to travel from state to state, right to vote (access to the ballot), right to privacy (including use of contraceptives), and First Amendment rights.

   a. **Strict scrutiny** applies to fundamental rights under SDP. The government action must be:

   i. **Necessary** to achieve a

   ii. **Compelling** government objective.

   The **government** has the burden of proof.

Example: To counteract an increase in juvenile crime, a state enacted a law terminating the parental rights of any resident whose child under 16 years of age is convicted of a violent crime. This law fails strict scrutiny analysis because it is not necessary to serve a compelling government interest.

Most frequently MBE tested SDP fundamental rights: Use of contraceptives, raising children, right to vote, right to marry, and right to travel.

Decoy tip: Questions often disguise the actual fundamental right being tested so carefully read all of the facts. For example, a state has a statute that provides free medical procedures for residents unable to pay, but requires the resident to have lived in the state for one year. A woman moved to the state 6 months ago for a new job and is in need of surgery. She could successfully challenge the statute under SDP since it places an undue burden on her **fundamental right to travel.** However, the facts might lead you think the issue is about healthcare or a job, which are not fundamental rights (but will provide great decoy wrong answers).

2. **Nonfundamental rights:** Under SDP this analysis applies to everything else that is not a fundamental right or abortion related. Typically this will be social and economic regulations (e.g., regulations for housing rentals, business and labor regulations, etc.).

   a. **Rational basis** applies to non-fundamental rights under SDP. The government action need only be:

      i. **Rationally related** to achieve a

      ii. **Legitimate** government objective.

      The **challenger** of the government action has the burden of proof.

      Example: A regulation requiring paroled felons to live one mile from schools is a social regulation subject to the rational basis test.

   b. **Adult sex outside of marriage:** The right to adult sex outside of marriage is not a fundamental right, but the Supreme Court found that the government does not have a legitimate interest to intrude into the private relations of adults and their sexual relations (so even though rational basis applies this is one of the rare areas the government would likely lose under the rational basis/balancing test).

3. **Abortion:** The right to abortion is not a fundamental right, but is protected by the Substantive Due Process Clause. States do not have the right **to ban** or place an **undue burden** on access to **pre-viability abortions.**

MBE tip: Abortion laws are developed through case law, so the rules have evolved in the Supreme Court over the years. The rules can be unclear so examples of how this issue is tested are noted below for clarification. Note: while each state has its own rules, which can differ, the rules on the MBE are limited to those from the Supreme Court that all states must follow.

   a. **Pre-viability definition:** States can regulate abortion *only if* it **does not place an undue burden** or **substantial obstacle** on the woman's right to choose a **pre-viability abortion.** Pre-viability is not clearly defined but at a minimum, it extends longer than the first trimester.

Example: A statute permits a woman to have an abortion on demand during the first trimester of pregnancy, but prohibits an abortion after the first trimester unless necessary to save her life. The state tried to balance its interest in preserving human life and a women's right to reproductive choice. The statute is unconstitutional because it places an undue burden on a woman's fundamental right to reproductive choice prior to fetal viability.

b. **Public facilities:** States are not required to provide **public facilities** or **publicly-employed staff** to perform abortions.

c. **Funding:** States are not required to fund abortions.

Example: A statute prohibits the use of state-owned facilities to perform abortions that are not necessary to save the life of the mother. A woman sought an abortion in a state hospital in her second trimester that was not necessary to save her life. The hospital refused to perform the abortion. The statute was deemed constitutional because it does not impose an undue burden on the women since she can seek an abortion elsewhere and states are not required to fund abortions.

d. **Waiting periods** of short duration and **informed consent** rules are permitted and do not constitute an undue burden.

e. **Significant residency requirements:** Rules requiring residency periods are subject to **strict scrutiny** and must be:

i. **Necessary** to achieve

ii. A **compelling** government interest.

f. **Parental notification requirements** violate a minor's right to an abortion unless there is a satisfactory **judicial bypass** procedure and an exception when an emergency abortion is required to protect the minor's life or health.

i. **Judicial bypass** must allow a court to approve an abortion for a minor without parental notification if the court finds: (1) the **minor is sufficiently mature and informed** to make an independent decision to obtain an abortion; **or** (2) the abortion would be in the **minor's best interest.**

Example: A statute requires, without exception, that a woman under 18 years of age notify her parents at least 48 hours before having an abortion. The statute is unconstitutional because there is no bypass procedure for certain circumstances.

4. **Other SDP liberty interests:**

a. **Personal autonomy** interests include the right to die and decline unwanted medical procedures. (It is unclear if this is a fundamental right or the standard of review, so on the MBE you would merely be asked to identify it as a concept eligible for some protection.) There is no right to die or right to assisted suicide but there is a right to refuse life-saving treatment.

b. **Freedom of bodily movement:** Restraints of a person cannot be **grossly disproportionate** to the offense. This most often arises in the context of physical restraints used in prisons, mental institutions, or schools. (If tested, you would likely be required to identify that this raises a SDP issue.)

> **MBE tip**: Use the following approach to answer SDP questions:
>
> (1) Is there **state action**?
>
> (2) Is there a **personal privacy** (life, liberty, or property) interest at stake?
>
> (3) Is the right **fundamental, nonfundamental,** or related to **abortion**?
>
> (4) **Apply** the rule to the facts.

2. **Procedural Due Process (PDP)** requires the **government** to use **fair process** before **intentionally** depriving a person of **life, liberty, or property.**

   a. **Life, liberty, or property interests:** The harm shown here must be **individuated** to the person suing. A person cannot assert a violation to another person's rights.

      1. **Liberty interest:** Includes **physical liberty** as well as intangible liberties, such as the right to drive, raise a family, etc. (but does not include entitlement to loans for occupational purposes as there is no liberty to enjoy a particular occupation).

      2. **Property interest:** Includes real property, personal property, public education, welfare benefits, disability benefits, government **employment** with a **"legitimate claim of entitlement,"** etc.

      Examples: A public employer has a handbook, or publicized custom of only firing for cause with explanation, or promises made and relied on (but there is no property interest in a job application), government **licenses** (e.g., barber, lawyer), and government **benefits that one is already receiving** (but one does not have a property interest in benefits not yet received unless provided for by statute).

      a. **Burden of proof is on the challenger** to establish their property interest.

PROCEDURAL DUE PROCESS EXAMPLES

MBE tip: For PDP the main inquiry will typically require determining if there *is* a property right, rather than assessing the adequacy of the process provided.

PROPERTY INTEREST	NO PROPERTY INTEREST
A person receiving food stamps has a property interest in benefits they are already receiving and the food stamps could not be properly discontinued without fair procedures and process.	A professor is hired to teach at a public college. She is in her third consecutive one-year contract, and cannot obtain tenure until after 5 years. After her third year she was informed she was not being rehired. She has no property interest in her job under PDP because she did not have a "legitimate claim of entitlement" until *after* she reached the 5-year mark for employment.

   b. **Process due:** This includes the fair process and procedures (e.g., notice and an opportunity to be heard) that must be used before government deprivation of a life, liberty, or property interest.

      1. **For judicial proceedings** this includes the right to a hearing, counsel, to call witnesses, a fair trial, and appeal.

2. **For nonjudicial proceedings,** courts use a **balancing test** to weigh:
   a. The **individual's interest** in the right that will be affected by the government action,
   b. The added value of the **procedural safeguards** used and the possibility of substitute procedural safeguards, and
   c. The **government's interest** in fiscal and administrative efficiency.
   d. **Fair process usually requires notice** of the government action and an **opportunity to be heard *before* termination** of the interest.

PROCEDURAL DUE PROCESS EXAMPLES	
MBE tip: **Look for hidden standing issues.** If the result would be the same if hearing/process were provided, then there may be no redressable injury, thus the claimant lacks standing.	
SUFFICIENT PROCESS	**INSUFFICIENT PROCESS**
A doctor licensed to practice medicine was convicted for abusing his prescription writing and thus his license was revoked by the medical board (per state statute that any abuse of prescription writing requires revocation of license) without an opportunity for a hearing with the medical board. No PDP violation because the facts were determined in a criminal trial and thus any further trial was not necessary to show the doctor abused his prescription writing privileges.	A licensed barber works in a state that has a licensing statute that allows a Board to revoke a license if it finds the licensee has used his business premises for an illegal purpose. The barber was arrested for selling cocaine in his barber shop. Charges were later dropped but the Board still had a hearing to review his license and affidavits were offered by informants, but the informants were not present or able to be cross-examined. PDP violated because process didn't allow the barber to cross-examine accusers.

MBE tip: Use the following approach to answer PDP questions:

(1) Is there a **standing** issue?
(2) Is there **state action**?
(3) Is there **individuated harm**? (If the harm is directed at a group, think EPC.)
(4) Has life, liberty, or property been taken?
(5) Was process "due" before the taking and if so, what process?

F. **Involuntary Servitude** under the 13th Thirteenth Amendment is applicable to **both governmental and private action.**

   1. The 13th Amendment provides that neither **slavery nor involuntary servitude** (forcing someone to perform work by threatening physical injury or restraint or legal sanction) shall exist within the United States.

G. The **Equal Protection Clause (EPC)** of the 14th Amendment applies to the states (and is also applicable to the federal government through the 5th Amendment DPC) and prohibits the **government** from **treating similarly situated persons differently,** which is commonly called discrimination. No state shall deny to any person within its jurisdiction the equal protection of the laws.

> **MBE tip:** There must be **state action** for an EPC violation, and pay attention to **who is the state actor** (state, local, or federal). EPC applies to **the federal government through the 5th Amendment, and states/local governments through the 14th Amendment**. You may see this referenced in MBE questions and answers (e.g., answer choices on the MBE might vaguely describe the Equal Protection Clause as "the Due Process Clause of the 5th Amendment," or simply "due process" to hide the ball when the federal government is acting).

1. **Intentional** different treatment for similarly situated people is required for **heightened review to apply** (which is strict scrutiny and intermediate scrutiny) under EPC, and not just that a regulation has a disparate impact or an incidental burdening effect. **Intent** can be established by facial discrimination, discriminatory impact as applied, or discriminatory motive.
   a. **Discriminatory on its face:** The government treats people differently in a statute or regulation.

      Example: All women must present identification to apply for government housing.

   b. **Discriminatory impact and motive:** The government treats people differently through the administration of a statute. The government statute or regulation will appear neutral on its face but it will have a disproportionate impact on a particular class of persons (such as racial minorities). A court must find that the statute was enacted for a **discriminatory motive.**

      Example: A test used for a government job promotion has the unintended effect that particular minorities pass at a much lower rate than Caucasians. This will *not be subject to strict scrutiny* analysis because the differential *effect is not intentional* because there was no governmental discriminatory motive to impact minorities.

      > **MBE tip:** Don't assume that heightened scrutiny (strict scrutiny or intermediate scrutiny) applies simply because an outcome affects people differently. There must be a *discriminatory intent.*

      Example (yes intent): An all-male military institute may not exclude women because of concerns that only men are strong enough to handle the school's harsh militaristic methods because this would show an intent to discriminate against women.

      Example (no intent): A law giving preference to veterans in civil service jobs which had a disparate impact on women because more veterans were men (no intent to discriminate against women because the intent was to help veterans).

2. **Three levels of review can apply to EPC**
   a. **Strict scrutiny** requires the **government to prove** that the classification is:
      1. **Necessary** to achieve
      2. A **compelling** government interest.
         a. The **burden of proof is on the government.**
         b. Strict scrutiny is hard to satisfy, so the classification will often fail.

b. Intermediate (mid-level) **scrutiny** requires the **government to prove** that the classification is:

1. **Substantially related** to achieving

2. An **important** government interest.

a. The **burden of proof is on the government.**

c. Rational basis (low-level scrutiny) requires the classification be:

1. **Rationally/reasonably related** to

2. A **legitimate** government interest.

a. The **burden of proof is on the challenger** of the classification.

b. Rational basis is easy to satisfy, so the classification will often be allowed.

3. Classification scheme: EPC is at issue when people are treated differently based on classifications. It is concerned with the scheme itself, not that a particular person might argue they belong in one classification or another.

 **a. Suspect classifications** include only those based on **race**, **national origin** (ethnic heritage), and state **alienage** (not a U.S. citizen) and are subject to **strict scrutiny.**

Examples: Race conscious affirmative action, race preferential admissions to state schools, minority set asides, citizens versus lawful resident aliens, or drawing election districts around racial divides are all suspect classifications subject to strict scrutiny.

1. **Alienage exception:** When **alienage** classifications restrict the right to participate in **functions that are central to self-government** and involve the formulation, execution or review of public policy such as voting, running for office, holding certain government jobs or serving on a jury, **rational basis is applied** and not strict scrutiny.

> **MBE tip:** Discrimination based on national origin pertains to the heritage of a person, or their status as a naturalized citizen who originally came from another country. Alienage discrimination concerns whether a person is a U.S. citizen or not.
>
> **Examples:** A rule preventing naturalized citizens who originally came from Cuba from being state police officers is an example of a national origin classification. A rule preventing non-U.S. citizens from practicing law is an example of an alienage classification. Both would fail strict scrutiny.

b. Quasi-suspect (also called semi-suspect) **classifications** include only those based on **gender** and **illegitimacy** and are subject to **intermediate** (mid-level) **scrutiny.**

1. **Most gender classification will be struck down,** especially those reinforcing gender stereotypes.

2. **Gender classifications can be attacked by either gender.**

a. Gender classifications based on race-conscious affirmative action to remedy past discrimination against women will often be upheld.

Example: The Supreme Court has permitted social security and tax exemptions that entitle women to greater benefits to make up for past workplace discrimination.

GENDER CLASSIFICATION EXAMPLES

VALID	INVALID
◆ All male draft. ◆ Statutory rape laws. ◆ Requiring men but not women to prove parentage to children born abroad for citizenship purposes.	◆ Attorney eliminated all female arbitrators for an arbitration panel of a woman claiming sexual harassment. ◆ Law permitting the sale of beer to women at 18 but men had to be 21. ◆ Gender-based death benefits (social security death benefits cannot be permitted for women only when the husband dies but not for men when the wife dies). ◆ Tax exemptions for full-time female college students but not male full-time college students. ◆ Alimony for women only.

MBE tip: It is very unlikely gender-based classifications that reinforce stereotypes would pass intermediate scrutiny (e.g., women aren't strong enough to be prison guards).

Be alert! Some fact patterns might appear to be gender related, but are not (usually because there is no discriminatory intent).

Example: A city passed an ordinance requiring individuals to obtain a license to care for children under the age of 12 for pay. The ordinance affects women disproportionately to men because there are more female babysitters—rational basis only because disparate impact on women without more is not sex discrimination.

c. **Nonsuspect classifications** include everything else, including those based on nonsuspect and nonfundamental rights, such as economic and social welfare, are subject to **rational basis** review.

Examples: Housing, healthcare, age, wealth, public school education, etc.

d. **EPC fundamental rights:** The fundamental rights under the EPC are subject to **strict scrutiny.** The most common rights at issue on the MBE involve:

1. **Voting** in state and local elections.

   a. **Except special purpose districts are permitted.**

   Example: A special-purpose water district rule that restricts voting on the district board members to landowners within the district would be permitted and not subject to strict scrutiny.

2. **Political candidate:** Being a political candidate can be a fundamental right. Restrictions based on **wealth** (e.g., a $700 filing fee with no waiver provision for indigent candidates) or those that substantially **limit the ballot access of minor parties** or independent candidates are impermissible.

   Example: A requirement that a party on the ballot have the signature of 15% of voters, or an elaborate party structure, or that a final primary must be held are impermissible. *In contrast,* minimum age or reasonable residency requirements are permissible.

3. Having **access to the courts** (e.g., indigent defendants have the right to defense counsel).

4. **Migrating from state to state (travel):** This concerns one's right to change one's state for the **purpose of residence or employment.**

   Example: A state regulation that imposes a lengthy waiting period before a new resident is eligible to receive welfare benefits would be subject to strict scrutiny.

5. **First Amendment rights** (freedom of speech, religion, association, and press). Note: while some of these rights have their own standards and tests (i.e., symbolic speech), if the fundamental right is invoking the EPC then you would apply strict scrutiny whereas if you are analyzing the validity of the statute under a free speech violation you would apply the free speech rules pertinent to the particular issue being tested.

6. **Privacy interests under substantive due process** where there is a classification scheme (i.e., right to marry, procreate, child-rearing, abortion).

> **Decoy tip:** There is no fundamental right to necessities of life, such as food, shelter, or education. These would be subject to the rational basis test.

4. **Level of review required**

   a. **Suspect classifications and EPC fundamental rights receive strict scrutiny. Strict scrutiny** requires the **government to prove** that the classification is:

      1. **Necessary** to achieve
      2. A **compelling** government interest.

   b. **Quasi-suspect** classifications receive **intermediate scrutiny** and require **intent** on the part of the government to treat individuals differently. **Intermediate scrutiny** requires the **government to prove** that the classification is:

      1. **Substantially related** to achieve
      2. An **important** government interest.

   c. **Nonsuspect** classifications receive **rational basis review.** The **burden of proof is on the challenger** of the classification. **Rational basis (low-level scrutiny)** requires the classification to be:

      1. **Rationally related** to
      2. A **legitimate** government interest.

WHAT RIGHT IS IMPLICATED? DUE PROCESS OR EQUAL PROTECTION?

When a right is violated, but the law affects everyone *equally*, substantive due process is implicated. When a right is violated, but only certain *classes* of people are affected, equal protection is implicated (look for a classification scheme).

Example (SDP): A law that prohibits **all people** from using contraceptives implicates substantive due process analysis because it affects all people equally.

Example (EPC): A law that **prohibits unmarried people (not all people)** from using contraceptives creates a classification and treats unmarried people differently from married people and thus implicates equal protection. Even though the classification scheme is not a suspect class, since the fundamental right to privacy/child bearing (use of contraceptives) is implicated, strict scrutiny will apply.

MBE tip: On questions when both legal theories are implicated, the answer choices will usually ask about the standard of review/burden of persuasion (this is because the standard of review in these questions will be the same regardless of which theory is applied). For example, in both equal protection and substantive due process, a law that affects a fundamental right would be evaluated under strict scrutiny (regardless of which theory is applied).

EQUAL PROTECTION CLAUSE (EPC) DECODED

Approach: To answer EPC questions use this approach.
(1) Is there **state action**?
(2) Is there a **classification** scheme? (Who is being treated differently and why?)
(3) What **standard of review** applies? (Consider if the government had an *intent* to discriminate if strict or intermediate scrutiny applies; if not use rational basis.)
(4) **Apply** the standard of review to the facts.

Testing style: Many EPC questions will ask what standard of review applies to the facts and/or which answer choice best states the burden of persuasion. Since many of the fact patterns have two-sided arguments, it is less common that you are asked to actually apply the appropriate standard to the facts to solve the problem.

Classification	Standard of Review	BOP	Analysis
Suspect Class ◆ Race ◆ Alienage Fundamental Rights	**Strict Scrutiny** ◆ Necessary to achieve/narrowly tailored (no less restrictive means) ◆ Compelling govt. interest	Govt.	Hard to satisfy so often fails
Quasi-suspect ◆ Gender ◆ Legitimacy	**Intermediate (mid-level) Review** ◆ Substantially related to ◆ Important govt. interest	Govt.	
Nonsuspect ◆ Economic ◆ Everything else	**Rational Basis** ◆ Rationally (reasonably related) to ◆ Legitimate govt. interest	Challenger	Easy to satisfy so often allowede

H. **The Takings Clause** of the 5th Amendment (applicable to the states through the 14th Amendment) provides that **private property** may not be **taken for public use** without **just compensation.** This is also called eminent domain.

1. **Taking for public use** is liberally construed and satisfied if the state's use of the property is **rationally related** to a **conceivable public purpose** and this can include economic development or public benefit rather than actual public usage.

   Example: A taking was proper when 15 unblighted waterfront homes were condemned and turned over to private developers as part of a neighborhood economic development plan (but the owners are entitled to just compensation).

   a. **Burden of proof is on the government** to establish public use.

2. **Just compensation** is intended to be "fair" and is typically measured by the **market value of the property** at the time of the taking.

   a. **Compensation is owed to all with an interest** in the land, including those holding leases, future interests, easements, profits, etc. The condemnation award is shared **proportionately to all with an interest** in the land.

3. **Taking or mere regulation:**

   a. **Total taking: Regulatory actions** are total ("per se") takings if there is a:

      1. Permanent **physical invasion or confiscation** (no matter how minor) **of property** will be deemed a taking of that portion, or

      Example: A state requirement that landlords allow cable TV companies to install cable lines on the landlord's building is considered a taking.

      2. **Use restriction** that denies ***all*** **economically beneficial use** of property.

      Example (no taking): A company owned a large tract of land that contained coal deposits that the company intended to mine. The company acquired the mining equipment and planned its mining operations. Congress then enacted a statute that imposed environmental regulations on all mining operations. The statute made the company's mining plans economically infeasible. The sale price of the land allowed the company to recover its original investment, but not the cost of the mining equipment or expected mining profits. There is no taking here because the use restriction did not deny ***all*** economically beneficial use.

   b. **Temporary taking:** To determine if a regulation, which denies all economic use temporarily, is a taking requiring just compensation the court will consider all relevant circumstances including the **economic impact** on the owner, the **length of the delay,** the **reasonable expectation** of the owners, and the **good faith** of the government planners.

   c. **Regulatory taking:** Land use regulations, such as zoning ordinances, that **decrease the economic value** of the property by prohibiting the most beneficial use are not considered takings if there is still an **economically viable use** for the property.

      1. **Zoning:** Land use regulations typically not considered takings include those related to zoning, environmental protections, and landmark preservation laws.

      2. **Balancing test:** To make a determination, the court will employ a **balancing test** and consider:

         a. The **character** of the invasion (value to the community of the social goal being advanced), *b.* The **economic impact** (diminution in value) on the owner, and

c. The extent of interference with the **investment backed expectation** of the owner.

Example: A man purchased land in the mountains to build a resort. Soon thereafter, the county adopted a regulation that prohibited all development in the mountains to conserve the natural habitat and wildlife. The purchaser has been unable to sell or lease the property. Realtors have told the man the property is worthless. Since the county did not pay him for his loss and the regulation eliminated his investment backed expectation to build a resort, and eliminated or substantially decreased his economic value, it is likely a taking even though there is some value to preserving wildlife.

4. **Building and development permits:**

   a. **To justify a condition on a building or development permit,** the government must show that there is:

      1. A **nexus** between a **legitimate government interest,** and

      2. The **adverse impact** of the proposed building or development on the area is **roughly proportional** to the loss caused to the property owner.

      Example: A company wanted to expand the size of its building, which already housed a supermarket, to include a coffeeshop on land it owned. City officials refused to grant a required building permit unless the company agreed to establish a childcare center in 20% of the building. Without the government showing a legitimate state interest for a childcare center and the proportionality to the loss, this is a taking.

5. **Profits:** A profit is the **right of one person to go onto the land of another** and take from it part of the land or a product of the land.

   a. **Profit holder:** A holder of a profit is entitled to **share in a condemnation award** when a profit is **extinguished by eminent domain** if the profit holder has a profit for an indefinite time or for life.

   Example: A landowner's land contained large quantities of special mud. He gave his neighbor the right to use as much mud as he wanted during his lifetime. The neighbor sold the mud to contractors regularly. The state government informed the landowner that they were taking the property by eminent domain. Both the landowner and the neighbor are entitled to just compensation at the condemnation hearing.

> **Decoy tip:** Adding a tax to the sale of a product does not constitute a taking so don't get confused by this on a question that is testing the Tax and Spending Clause rather than takings. The takings answer is often the decoy answer.

I. **Ex Post Facto Laws are prohibited:** Under Article I, section 10, both the state and federal governments are **prohibited** from passing any **"ex post facto" law,** which is a law that has **a retroactive punitive effect.** This prevents the government from imposing a punishment on conduct that was not punishable at the time it occurred.

Example: A state makes it illegal to use a cell phone while driving effective Jan. 1. One could not be punished for using a cell phone while driving on Dec. 31 since it was not yet illegal to do so.

1. **Punish is construed narrowly** and is limited to **criminal or penal** consequences, not civil consequences. This is in contrast to the definition of "punish" for a bill of attainder.

__Example__: A person can be disbarred based on retroactive law since that penalty is not criminal or penal.

2. **Includes increased punishment:** The government **cannot increase the punishment** for a crime more than what was permissible at the time the crime was committed.
3. Congress may change federal civil statutes and may direct federal courts to apply those changes in all actions in which a **final judgment has not been rendered.**

J. **Bills of Attainder:** Under Article I, section 10, both the state and federal governments are prohibited from passing any **"bill of attainder,"** which is a law that **punishes named or easily identifiable individuals** or groups, **without a judicial trial.**

__Example__: A federal statute named three individuals identified in a report about terrorist activities and further provided that these individuals could not hold any federal government employment when all three were federal park rangers. This is an impermissible bill of attainder.

1. **Punish is construed broadly** and includes the loss of a government job, in contrast to the narrow definition of "punish" for an ex post facto law.
2. Measures that involve **pure regulation** (i.e., company policies change) are **not bills of attainder.**

__Decoy tip__: Statutes that prohibit conduct or regulate others, but apply to *everyone* are not bills of attainder. Watch for a call that asks about certain individuals that are carrying out that regulation or conduct. If the statute applies to everyone, it will not be a bill of attainder.

CONSTITUTIONAL LAW CHEAT SHEET

JUSTICIABILITY

Case/Controversy	Political Questions	Ripe
◆ No advisory opinions ◆ Declaratory judgments ok, but often lack standing	◆ Not allowed by federal court ◆ Issue committed to other branch, or ◆ No standards	◆ Live controv. or ◆ Immediate threat of harm
Individual Standing	**Organization Standing**	**Moot**
◆ Injury ◆ Causation ◆ Redressability	◆ Members have standing ◆ Interests related to organization's purpose ◆ No participation needed	◆ Controversy over, unless ◇ Capable of repetition ◇ Voluntary cessation, or ◇ Collateral consequences
3rd Party Standing	**Fed. Taxpayer Standing**	**11th Amendment**
◆ Individual stand. & ◆ Special relationship, or ◆ Difficult for 3rd party to assert	◆ Source is Congress' power to tax & spend ◆ Measure exceeds power ◆ Establishment clause is the only recognized limit	◆ Can't sue state in fed. ct. except: ◇ States v. states/fed. gov., ◇ Subdivisions of states, or ◇ Injunction v. state official

STATE ACTION

◆ Gov. acting, or ◆ Private actor but public function ◆ Private actor but gov. entanglement

❖Federalism	STATE POWERS	❖10th Amendment
Federal gov. cannot: ◆ Apply federal law to state legislators in their duties ◆ Commandeer the states ◆ Tax property used in a state's performance of its functions ◆ Make states enact laws	**States cannot:** ◆ Tax the federal government ◆ Regulate the federal government	**States can:** ◆ Set their own voting rules ◆ Set their own tax structure ◆ Use police power to provide for health, safety, and welfare of citizens

CONGRESSIONAL POWERS

Commerce Clause		Tax and Spend
◆ Instrumentalities ◆ Persons and articles ◆ Activities that substantially affect ◆ Includes intrastate regulations	◆ Commercial/economic: ◇ Rational basis ◇ Inseverable aggregates cause substantial cumulative effect ◆ Noncommercial/noneconomic: ◇ Direct & substantial effect	◆ Direct taxes ok ◆ Conditional grant of funds **Federal Property** ◆ Includes animals/hunting ◆ Delegate rule-making over fed. property to fed. agency
Post-Civil War Amend.	**Pass Laws**	**Limit S. Ct. jurisdiction**
◆ Enforce 13th,14th,15th Am. ◆ 13th – prohibit slavery ◆ 14th – legislate & change federal civil statutes ◆ 15th – can't deny rt. to vote on basis of color/race	◆ Make all D.C. laws ◆ Present bills to the President ◆ Legislative veto power **Naturalize/Bankruptcy** ◆ Establish uniform laws	◆ Create special courts ◆ Cannot frustrate supreme and uniform law **Necessary and Proper** ◆ Execute enumerated power ◆ Rationally related
Speech and Debate	**War Powers**	**Delegation/Committees**
◆ Immunity to Congress members ◆ Relating to their legislative actions	Preserve fed. monopoly over foreign affairs	◆ Ok if intelligible standards ◆ Vest appointments in inferior officers only ◆ Standing committees can't make law alone, or ◆ Overturn an executive agency decision

EXECUTIVE POWERS

◆ Execution of laws (take care) ◆ Supervise executive branch ◇ Executive orders ◇ No outside direction ◆ Issue fed. crim. pardons	◆ Make treaties with foreign nations (+2/3 Senate) ◆ Speak on behalf of U.S. in foreign policy ◆ Commander in chief	◆ Appoint top-level federal officers/ambassadors ◆ Veto a bill ◆ Executive privilege ◆ Create national monuments

JUDICIARY POWERS

Fed. courts can review cases: ◆ Arising under U.S. Constitution or U.S. laws ◆ Admiralty ◆ Two or more states ◆ Citizens of different states ◆ Suit with a foreign country	Can review state court decision if: ◆ Based on federal law Can't review case if: ◆ Independent and adequate state grounds	◆ Exceptions Clause: Congress can limit appellate jx ◆ Concurrent jx with state and federal courts for federal law ◆ Supreme Ct. original jx: when a state is a party or cases affecting ambassadors

LIMITS ON STATE POWER (NOT THE FEDERAL GOVERNMENT)

Dormant Commerce Clause	**Privileges & Immunities: *Art. IV***	**Privileges & Immunities: *14th Am.***
◆ Discriminatory, or ◆ Undue burden ◆ If discriminatory: ◇ Necessary to ◇ Legitimate noneconomic government interest with ◇ No reas. alternatives ◆ If undue burden, must be: ◇ Rationally related to a ◇ Legitimate gov. interest & ◇ Burden imposed outweighed by benefit to state ◆ Exceptions: ◇ Market participant ◇ Consent/Public operations	◆ Can't discriminate against nonresidents unless: ◇ Peculiar source of evil ◇ Substantially related ◇ No less discriminatory alternative ◆ Applies to rights fundamental to national unity (right to work) ◆ No protectionist purpose ◆ Corp./aliens not citizens	◆ Can't deprive rights of nat'l citizenship unless: ◇ Narrowly tailored to ◇ Compelling gov. interest ◆ Rights include: ◇ Interstate travel ◇ Vote in nat'l elections ◇ Enter public lands ◆ Corp./aliens not citizens

Supremacy Clause	**Abortion**
Federal law preempts state law if they conflict	States can't ban all pre-viability abortions

Full Faith and Credit

State courts can't relitigate other states final judgments

Contracts Clause

- ◆ States can't pass laws that retroactively/substantially impair existing contracts unless:
- ◆ Reasonable and appropriate
- ◆ Serves an important & legitimate purpose
- ◆ Necessary if social or economic regulation
- ◆ Private contracts strictly interpreted

LIMITS ON FEDERAL AND STATE POWER

Religion: Free Exercise Clause	**Religion: Establishment Clause**
◆ Can't burden religion unless: ◇ Necessary to achieve a ◇ Compelling government interest ◆ Except: Law of general applicability ◇ Rationally related to ◇ Legitimate government interest ◆ Religious Freedom Restoration Act: if substantial burden—need strict scrutiny	◆ Can't endorse/favor religion ◆ Incidental favoring ok ◆ If sect preference, gov. must show: ◇ Narrowly tailored to ◇ Compelling government interest ◆ If no sect preference, satisfy the *Lemon* test: ◇ Secular purpose ◇ Primary secular effect ◇ No excessive government entanglement

Speech

Content-based Speech

- Necessary to a
- Compelling gov. interest
- Rarely allowed

Unprotected Speech

- Obscenity
  - ◇ Prurient interest
  - ◇ Patently offensive
  - ◇ Lacks L.A.P.S
- Misrepresentation
- Defamation
- Inciting lawless action
- Fighting words/violence

Prior Restraint

- Prevents speech before it occurs
- Not allowed unless:
  - ◇ Irreparable/serious harm
  - ◇ Narrowly drawn standards
  - ◇ Final determination

Time, Place, Manner

Public/designated public forums

- Content neutral (Subject & viewpoint neutral)
- Substantial & important gov. interest
- Narrowly tailored
- Open alternative channels

Limited/nonpublic forums

- Viewpoint neutral (Not subject matter neutral)
- Legitimate government interest
- Reasonably related
- Gov. usually wins

Zoning

Can affect speech if:

- Reasonably targeting
- Secondary effects

Commercial Speech

- Must be truthful
- May restrict if:
  - ◇ Substantial gov. interest
  - ◇ Directly advances gov. interest
  - ◇ Narrowly tailored so reasonable fit

Symbolic Speech

- Communicate an idea or symbol
- May restrict if:
  - ◇ Important gov. interest
  - ◇ Unrelated to suppression of the speech
  - ◇ Prohibits no more speech than necessary (least restrictive means)

Vagueness

Reasonable person has to guess meaning

Overbreadth

Bans protected speech too

Unfettered Discretion

No standards for decisions

Freedom of Association

- Gov. can prevent if:
  - ◇ Compelling gov. int.
  - ◇ Narrowly tailored
- Applies to 1st Am. freedoms
- Gov. can't fire for political views or affiliations
- Loyalty oaths allowed
- No forced inclusion
- No illegal activity

Freedom of Press

- Publish matters of public concern
- Except no executive branch records
- No immunity

Substantive Due Process

- Deprive life, liberty, or property
- Fundamental rights
  - ◇ Necessary to
  - ◇ Compelling gov. int.
  - ◇ Gov. has BOP

Examples: marriage, child bearing/rearing, travel, 1st Am. rts, etc.

- Nonfundamental rights
  - ◇ Rationally related
  - ◇ Legitimate gov. int.
  - ◇ Challenger has BOP

Abortion

- No pre-viability bans
- No undue burden on pre-viability
- States not required to fund or provide facilities
- Waiting periods & informed consent ok
- Residency requirement gets strict scrutiny
- Parental notification requires judicial bypass

No right to die

- Restraints can't be grossly disproportionate

Procedural Due Process

Fair process required if:

- Deprive life, liberty, property
- BOP on challenger to establish property interest

Process due for:

- Judicial proceedings
  - ◇ Hearing/Counsel
  - ◇ Call witnesses
  - ◇ Fair trial/Appeal
- Nonjudicial proceedings
  - ◇ Balance individual interest
  - ◇ Procedural safeguards &
  - ◇ Gov. fiscal interest

Equal Protection			
Classification	Suspect Class ◆ Race ◆ National origin ◆ State alienage Fundamental rights	Quasi-suspect ◆ Gender ◆ Legitimacy	Non-suspect ◆ Social welfare ◆ Economic (age, health, education, etc.)
Standard of Review	Strict scrutiny ◆ Necessary to ◆ Compelling gov. interest	Intermediate scrutiny ◆ Substantially related to ◆ Important gov. interest	Rational basis ◆ Rationally related ◆ Legitimate gov. interest
Burden of proof	Government	Government	Challenger
Intent Required	Yes — on face, or in impact and motive	Yes — on face, or in impact and motive	No

5th Am. Takings	
Gov. can take private property for public use if: ◆ Rationally related to a ◆ Conceivable public purpose	◆ Just compensation owed ◆ Proportional award ◆ Burden of proof on gov.

Total taking (per se)	Temporary Taking	Regulatory Taking
◆ Physical invasion or ◆ Confiscation, or ◆ Use restriction that denies all economical beneficial use	◆ Denies all use temporarily ◆ Court considers: ◇ Economic impact ◇ Length of delay ◇ Reasonable expectation of owner ◇ Good faith of gov. planner	◆ Decrease in value but still economical use ◆ Court will balance ◇ Character of invasion ◇ Economic impact ◇ Investment backed expectation of owner

Building and Development Permits	Profits
To justify condition on building, gov. shows: ◆ Nexus between legitimate gov. interest, ◆ Adverse impact of proposed building, & ◆ Roughly proportional to loss	◆ Right of person to go on land of another ◆ Profit extinguished by eminent domain ◆ Profit holder gets share in condemnation award

Ex Post Facto Laws	Bills of Attainder
◆ Bans laws that have a retroactive punitive effect ◆ Includes increased punishment ◆ Congress can change statutes if final judgment not rendered ◆ Punish = criminal or penal consequences	◆ Bans laws that punish named or easily identifiable individuals ◆ Without a judicial trial ◆ Pure regulations not bills of attainder ◆ Punish viewed broadly (i.e., loss of job)

CONSTITUTIONAL LAW MBE PRACTICE QUESTIONS

These questions are designed to reinforce the skill in how to approach MBE questions. While they will also test your knowledge in the limited areas addressed, you will not master your knowledge by only practicing these questions. To fully master the rules, you need to do practice questions outside of these from your bar company and/or the NCBE.

QUESTION 1

A nightclub owner applied for a required zoning permit to open a nude-dancing nightclub in the theater district of a city. An organization of influential city residents began an intensive lobbying effort to persuade the city council to deny the owner a permit to operate any type of nude-dancing facility at any time or in any place in the city.

The owner has sued the city in an appropriate federal court, seeking an injunction that would prohibit the city council from considering the organization's views, on the ground that if the organization is successful in its lobbying efforts, the owner's First and Fourteenth Amendment rights would be violated. The city has moved to dismiss the action.

Should the court dismiss the owner's action?

A. No, because nude dancing is symbolic speech and is therefore protected by the First and Fourteenth Amendments.
B. No, because the organization does not seek a reasonable time, place, and manner regulation of nude dancing, but instead seeks a total ban on the owner's opening any type of nude-dancing facility at any time or in any place in the city.
C. Yes, because the action is not ripe.
D. Yes, because the First and Fourteenth Amendments do not protect obscenity, and nude dancing is obscene.

QUESTION 2

A state law imposed substantial regulations on insurance companies operating within the state with respect to their rates, cash reserves, and financial practices.

A privately owned insurance company operating within the state advertised that it wanted to hire a new data processor. After reviewing applications for that position, the company hired a woman who appeared to be well qualified. The company refused to consider the application of a man who was better qualified than the woman, because he was known to have radical political views.

The man sued the company, alleging only a violation of his federal constitutional right to freedom of expression. Is the man likely to prevail?

A. No, because hiring decisions are wholly discretionary and thus are not governed by the First Amendment.
B. No, because the company is not subject to the provisions of the First and Fourteenth Amendments.
C. Yes, because the company is affected with a public interest.
D. Yes, because the company is substantially regulated by the state, and thus its employment decisions may fairly be attributed to the state.

QUESTION 3

A federal statute extends federal minimum wage requirements to all dry cleaning stores. The statute contains express findings that, when combined, the wages received by dry cleaning workers have a substantial impact on the national economy and on the flow of goods and services in interstate commerce. These findings are supported by information presented to Congress during committee hearings on the legislation.

A small dry cleaning store operates exclusively within a community in the center of a geographically large state. It has no customers from outside the state. It employs three workers, each of whom is paid less than the federal minimum wage.

Must this dry cleaning store comply with the statute imposing the federal minimum wage requirements on all dry cleaning stores?

A. No, because the store does no business in interstate commerce.
B. No, because the wages of the store's three workers do not have a substantial impact on interstate commerce.
C. Yes, because the commerce clause vests Congress with plenary legislative authority over labor relations.
D. Yes, because the wages paid by dry cleaning stores have a substantial impact on interstate commerce.

QUESTION 4

A state law provides for an award of damages against anyone who publishes the name of a rape victim. Pursuant to that law, a woman sued a local newspaper in state court after the newspaper identified her as a rape victim.

The state trial and appellate courts rejected the claim, holding that the state law was invalid under both the state constitution and the First Amendment of the U.S. Constitution. The state supreme court affirmed, holding specifically: "We think that this well-intentioned law very likely violates the First Amendment of the federal Constitution. We need not, however, decide that issue, because the law assuredly violates our state constitution, which provides even greater protection to the right of the press to report the news." The woman petitioned for review in the U.S. Supreme Court.

Is the U.S. Supreme Court likely to review the state supreme court judgment?

A. No, because the First Amendment prohibits the imposition of liability for the publication of truthful information.
B. No, because the judgment of the state supreme court rests upon an adequate and independent state-law ground.
C. Yes, because the supremacy clause does not permit a state to create rights greater than those conferred by the federal Constitution.
D. Yes, because the U.S. Supreme Court's appellate jurisdiction extends to cases arising under federal law.

QUESTION 5

A state owned and operated an electric power system, which included a nuclear power plant. In order to ensure the availability of sites for the disposal of spent fuel from the nuclear power plant, the state refused to supply electric power to out-of-state purchasers residing in states that would not accept spent fuel from the plant for storage or disposal.

Assume that no federal statute applies.

Which of the following is the strongest argument that the state's action is constitutional?

A. A state may condition the sale to out-of-state purchasers of any products produced in that state on the willingness of those purchasers to bear the fair share of the environmental costs of producing those products.
B. The generation of electricity is intrastate by nature and therefore subject to plenary state control.
C. The state itself owns and operates the power system, and therefore its refusal to supply power to out-of-state purchasers is not subject to the negative implications of the commerce clause.
D. The state's action is rationally related to the health, safety, and welfare of state citizens.

QUESTION 6

A police officer was employed on a city's police force for 10 years. When the officer accepted the job, the city's employee benefit plan provided a death benefit to the spouse of any employee who died as a result of any job-related injury. Last year, the city amended its employee benefit plan to deny its death benefit in cases where the death "was caused by the employee's refusal to accept, for any reason other than its excessive risk to life or health, reasonably available medical care prescribed by a physician."

After this amendment took effect, the officer was shot while on duty. Because of a sincerely held religious belief, the officer refused to allow a prescribed blood transfusion and, as a result, died from loss of blood. When the officer's spouse applied for the death benefit, the city denied the application on the basis of the amendment to the employee benefit plan. The officer's spouse has challenged the amendment, claiming that, as applied to the officer, it violated the officer's constitutional right to the free exercise of religion.

Is the court likely to find the amendment to the employee benefit plan constitutional as applied to the officer?

A. No, because it effectively discriminates against a religious practice.
B. No, because it violates the vested contractual rights of city employees who were hired before the amendment took effect.
C. Yes, because it does not single out religious reasons for the denial of benefits and is a reasonable limitation on the award of such benefits.
D. Yes, because it imposes a condition only on the award of a government benefit and does not impose a penalty on an individual's conduct.

QUESTION 7

To preserve the appearance and accessibility of its capitol building, a state enacted a law prohibiting "the display of any sign on any portion of the public sidewalk surrounding" the building.

A group of five demonstrators who wanted to protest inadequate state funding for children's services applied for a permit to march single file on the sidewalk surrounding the capitol building. Each demonstrator planned to carry a two-foot-square sign that would read, "Our lawmakers do not care about our children."

The group's permit application was denied pursuant to the state law, and the group has filed an action challenging the law's constitutionality.

Should the court uphold the law's constitutionality?

A. No, because even though the sidewalk at issue is not a public forum, the prohibition against the display of signs is more restrictive than needed to serve a legitimate government interest.
B. No, because the sidewalk at issue is a public forum, and the prohibition against the display of signs is not narrowly tailored to serve a substantial government interest.
C. Yes, because even though the sidewalk at issue is a public forum, the prohibition against the display of signs is necessary to serve a compelling public interest.
D. Yes, because the sidewalk at issue is not a public forum, and the prohibition against the display of signs is reasonable.

QUESTION 8

To improve the quality of rental housing within its boundaries, a city proposed an ordinance requiring all new and existing rental housing units to provide at least one full bathroom for each bedroom, plumbing and electrical hookups for a washer and dryer, and a covered parking space.

A majority of the owners of existing rental housing in the city opposed the ordinance. They argued that it would dramatically decrease the number of low-income rental housing units because owners would be unable to raise rents enough to recoup the investment required to comply. Without denying these contentions, the city enacted the ordinance. A plaintiff who owns low-income rental housing has sued the city, claiming only that the ordinance is unconstitutional on its face.

Which of the following best states the burden of persuasion in this action?

A. The city must demonstrate that the ordinance is necessary to serve a compelling state interest, because it adversely affects the fundamental right of rental housing owners to use their property in the manner they deem most economically efficient.
B. The city must demonstrate that the ordinance is necessary to serve a compelling state interest, because it will have a substantial and disproportionate negative impact on low-income persons.
C. The plaintiff must demonstrate that the ordinance is not substantially related to an important state interest, because it requires some owners of rental housing to invest money that they will not be able to recoup from increased rents.
D. The plaintiff must demonstrate that there is no rational relationship between the ordinance and any legitimate state interest, because the ordinance regulates economic activity of a type normally presumed to be within state regulatory authority.

QUESTION 9

A state generally provides funding for the medical care of its residents who cannot afford such care. State law, however, prohibits use of this state funding for surgery for any person who has resided in the state for less than one year, except in emergency situations.

A woman moved to the state two months ago seeking permanent employment. Her physician recommends non-emergency surgery to treat a medical condition. The surgery would qualify for state funding if the woman had resided in the state for a year. The woman has sued to invalidate the state law that prohibits state funding of her surgery.

Should the woman prevail in her action?

A. No, because the law reasonably conserves the state's limited resources.
B. No, because the law reasonably prevents the expenditure of state funds on transient nonresidents.
C. Yes, because the law burdens the woman's fundamental right to health care.
D. Yes, because the law burdens the woman's fundamental right to travel.

QUESTION 10

A company owned a large tract of land that contained coal deposits that the company intended to mine. The company acquired mining equipment and began to plan its mining operations. Just as the company was about to begin mining, Congress enacted a statute that imposed a number of new environmental regulations and land-reclamation requirements on all mining operations within the United States. The statute made the company's planned mining operations economically infeasible. As a result, the company sold the tract of land to a farmer. While the sale price allowed the company to recover its original investment in the land, it did not cover the additional cost of the mining equipment the company had purchased or the profits it had expected to earn from its mining operations on the land.

In an action filed against the appropriate federal official, the company claims that the statute effected a taking of its property for which it is entitled to just compensation in an amount equal to the cost of the mining equipment it purchased and the profits it expected to earn from its mining operations on the land.

Which of the following is the most appropriate result in the action?

A. The company should prevail on its claims for the cost of the mining equipment and for its lost profits.
B. The company should prevail on its claim for the cost of the mining equipment, but not for its lost profits.
C. The company should prevail on its claim for lost profits, but not for the cost of the mining equipment.
D. The company should not prevail on its claim for the cost of the mining equipment or for its lost profits.

CONSTITUTIONAL LAW ANSWER KEY	
Question	**Answer**
1	C
2	B
3	D
4	B
5	C
6	C
7	B
8	D
9	D
10	D

Use this quick answer key to get a general idea of how you did on this set of questions. The answer explanations that follow provide a step-by-step deconstruction of each question.

CONSTITUTIONAL LAW MBE ANSWER EXPLANATIONS

START HERE **FACTS** **Q1**

A **nightclub owner applied for a required zoning permit** to **open a nude-dancing nightclub** in the theater district of a city. An organization of influential city residents began an intensive **lobbying effort** to persuade the city council **to deny the owner a permit** to operate any type of nude-dancing facility **at any time or in any place** in the city.

The **owner has sued the city** in an appropriate federal court, **seeking an injunction** that would prohibit the city council **from considering the organization's views**, on the ground that if the organization is successful in its lobbying efforts, the **owner's First and Fourteenth Amendment rights** would be violated. The **city has moved to dismiss** the action.

Zoning, see time/place discussion/possible speech or conduct related = likely in the land of Con Law

Action = injunction but city wants to dismiss

CALL Should the court **dismiss the owner's action**?

Need to figure out what "action" the owner is seeking (at this point we don't even know what subject we are in). Read the facts.

MENTAL NOTE: Anticipating future concerns may raise ripeness issues.

It could mean no injury yet. Slow down and double check. You may need to stop here!

SOLVE

Should the court **dismiss the owner's action** (seeking injunctive relief to stop the city council from considering an organization's views)?

STEP 1 Look to see that all preliminary matters are satisfied before looking into bigger issues – if these are not satisfied then there is no moving on to other issues.

RULES	ANALYSIS		
☑ Not a political Q	• Political Q, moot, 11th Am.	☑	= MOVE TO NEXT STEP
• P has **standing** ◦ Injury ◦ Causation ◦ Redressability	• P arguably not yet injured since city has not yet heard the organization's views (and may not) and even if they do hear them, that does not mean that his permit will be denied. **So P likely does not have standing.**	☒	UH OH. = GAME OVER! Come back when you actually have an injury.
• **Ripe** (immediate threat of harm/live)	• Ripe (same reason as above – the threat is not immediate and may not even happen). **Case not ripe yet.**	☒	= GAME OVER! Come back when the threat is immediate/actual.
☑ Not moot (event no longer exists)			
☑ No 11th Am. restriction			

Run through each quickly

MBE TIP: *If you initially freaked out because you didn't know what the issue was, start with justiciability – the process usually ends there when you aren't sure what is being asked.*

SOLVE (continued)

Yes, **because** he does not yet have an injury and there lacks standing. His issue is also not ripe since he might not be harmed at all. So his case is not justiciable.

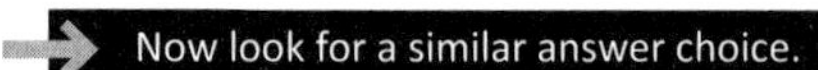

Now look for a similar answer choice.

DECODE

~~A.~~ No, because nude dancing is symbolic speech and is therefore protected by the First and Fourteenth Amendments.

Wrong analysis. Your analysis should have never exceeded justiciability. Since the case is not ripe and plaintiff does not have standing, you never get to the substantive issues involving the First and Fourteenth Amendments.

~~B.~~ No, because the organization does not seek a reasonable time, place, and manner regulation of nude dancing, but instead seeks a total ban on the owner's opening any type of nude-dancing facility at any time or in any place in the city.

Wrong analysis. Your analysis should have never exceeded justiciability. Since the case is not ripe and plaintiff does not have standing, you never get to the free speech issues mentioned.

C. Yes, because the action is not ripe.

Yes! Notice the answer only mentions ripeness. It could have also stated that plaintiff doesn't have standing or that there is no case/controversy. Any of these preliminary issues would have been a correct answer so you never get to the underlying substantive issues.

~~D.~~ Yes, because the First and Fourteenth Amendments do not protect obscenity, and nude dancing is obscene.

Wrong analysis. As stated above, you never get to the substantive issues of the First and Fourteenth Amendments since the case is not ripe (and plaintiff doesn't have standing).

FACTS

Q2

A state law imposed substantial regulations on insurance companies operating within the state with respect to their rates, cash reserves, and financial practices. **Key Word**

1st paragraph all ducks!! Trying to make you think the state is doing something when the action doesn't involve the state at all.

A **privately owned** insurance company **operating within the state** advertised that it **wanted to hire a new data processor**. After reviewing applications for that position, the **company hired a woman** who appeared to be **well qualified**. The company **refused to consider the application of a man** who was **better qualified** than the woman, **because he was known to have radical political views.** **Key Word**

Even though there are other issues that could be raised, this is the only one the man brought.

The man sued the company, alleging ***only*** a violation of his federal constitutional right to **freedom of expression**.

CALL Is the man **likely to prevail**?

Seems like this is the issue, BUT you can't just dive headfirst blindly.

(1) Make sure there is water (translation = justiciability)...and

(2) That it is deep enough (translation = state action). If both, then

(3) Dive (translation = tackle the substantive issue).

CHECK FIRST
If ok, then dive like a crazy person

SOLVE

Q Is the man likely to prevail (on violation of freedom of expression)?

STEP 1: JUSTICIABILITY

- **Political Q** – N/A
- **Ripe** – ok (injury occurred – not hired & better qualified)
- **Standing** – injured (no job), caused by company not hiring him/ redressability if company didn't hire the woman
- **Moot** – live controversy (not hired & better qualified)
- **11th Am.** – N/A

SOLVE *(continued)*

STEP 2: STATE ACTION

- For an action to **violate the Constitution**, there must be **government involvement**. (Here, private company acting).
- Private actor qualifies *if*:
  - Function performed is traditionally and exclusively a public function (hiring employees not public function), or
  - The state is heavily involved in the activity. (Just because the state imposed regulations on insurance companies does not mean they are involved in the actions of a private insurance company.)

STEP 3: SUBSTANTIVE ISSUE

Freedom of expression – never made it to STEP 3 because no state action (you can't dive into the water because it is not deep enough..........if you dove first without checking then you are in trouble = you likely picked the wrong answer choice.

A No, the man is not likely to prevail **<u>because</u>** there is no state action to seek a violation of the Constitution. The company is a private company and was not involved in a government public function.

→ Now look for a similar answer choice.

DECODE

~~A.~~ No, because hiring decisions are wholly discretionary and thus are not governed by the First Amendment.

Wrong analysis. The hiring decisions would be governed by the First Amendment if they were made by government officials or actions by the government, but here they are made by a private company so the private company's hiring decisions are not governed by the First Amendment.

B. No, because the company is not subject to the provisions of the First and Fourteenth Amendments.

Yes!! The company is a private company and there is not government involvement (state action). Note the answer choice hides the ball by not using key words like state action or government involved.

~~C.~~ Yes, because the company is affected with a public interest.

There is no such rule. A public interest is not relevant to whether freedom of expression applies to a private actor. State action does not involve an assessment of the public interest.

~~D.~~ Yes, because the company is substantially regulated by the state, and thus its employment decisions may fairly be attributed to the state.

Wrong analysis. This is the decoy answer. The facts about the state regulations have nothing to do with the private company's hiring practices. The regulations are separate from the hiring decisions and the state is not involved in the company's hiring practices.

FACTS

Q3

Gov. Acting

A **federal statute** extends **federal minimum wage requirements to all dry cleaning stores**. The statute contains express findings that, when combined, the **wages** received by dry cleaning workers **have a substantial impact on the national economy** and on **the flow of goods and services in interstate commerce**. These **findings are supported** by information presented to Congress during committee hearings on the legislation.

WHO/WHAT is being regulated

Findings as to what the statute impacts

Key words here – it matches our initial thoughts about Congress and its ability to regulate – nice that they spell it out for us (we'll take it!)

A **small** dry cleaning store **operates exclusively within a community** in the center of a geographically **large state**. It has **no customers from outside the state**. It **employs three workers**, each of whom is **paid less** than the federal minimum wage.

CALL Must this dry cleaning store comply with the **statute imposing** the **federal minimum wage requirements** on all dry cleaning stores?

Do you really want to follow the duck parade off the cliff?

DECOY FACTS

Issue not clear from the call – but it has something to do with compliance with a statute (federal minimum wage). A statute w/ FEDERAL implications leans itself toward Congress and its ability to regulate. Read facts to verify.

SOLVE

There are three branches of government. First, determine which branch is acting.

(1) The **legislative** branch (Congress),

(2) The **judicial** branch (Courts), or

(3) The **executive** branch (President)

Next, run through a list of powers the acting branch has, to determine if they have the power to do the challenged action.

(continued on next page)

SOLVE *(continued)*

CONGRESS POWERS

- **Regulate commerce**
- Taxing and spending
- Pass laws
- Declare war/support armed forces
- Naturalization and bankruptcy
- Post-Civil War Amendments
- Necessary and proper clause
- Federal property
- Limit appellate jx
- Delegation/ committees

AT ISSUE HERE

- This question tips you off by telling you that the wages affect interstate commerce.
- If it didn't tell you that, you would go through the list to see which power applies.

FEDERAL COMMERCE POWERS

- Broadest power – can regulate activities between states
  - □ Channels, instrumentalities, persons & articles (anything that can be sold, bought, or transported across state lines)
- **Intrastate activities** if rational basis to believe that the activity in inseverable aggregates will have a substantial economic effect on interstate commerce, or if there is a substantial cumulative economic effect.

ANALYSIS

- Dry cleaner wages affect the flow of goods and services in interstate commerce
- Also they have a substantial impact on the national economy
- Small company w/ only 3 employees & no customers outside the state – all irrelevant if the activity (dry cleaning) as a whole affects interstate commerce

Yes, <u>**because**</u> the statute is within Congress' broad commerce powers and the dry cleaning activity affects interstate commerce.

→ Now look for an answer choice that is similar.

DECODE

~~A.~~ No, because the store does no business in interstate commerce.

Wrong analysis of the commerce clause. The focus is not on whether the store "does no business" in interstate commerce, but rather whether the wages affect interstate commerce, which they do because employees spend money they earn, which affects interstate commerce; and fair wages for all employees also helps facilitate a smooth functioning interstate commerce.

~~B.~~ No, because the wages of the store's three workers do not have a substantial impact on interstate commerce.

Wrong analysis of the commerce clause. It doesn't matter how many employees there are; the wages of employees affects interstate commerce not the number of employees.

~~C.~~ Yes, because the commerce clause vests Congress with plenary legislative authority over labor relations.

Wrong reasoning. The reason the statute is constitutional comes from Congress' commerce power not its ability to pass laws and legislate. While Congress does have the power to legislate, the President can veto legislation, and the Supreme Court has found legislation over labor relations unconstitutional at times. The better answer involves Congress' broad commerce power.

D. Yes, because the wages paid by dry cleaning stores have a substantial impact on interstate commerce.

Correct! Congress has broad authority to regulate articles and activities that affects interstate commerce. Since employees spend their wages, those wages affect both the economy and interstate commerce; also fair wages for all employees helps facilitate a smooth functioning interstate commerce.

FACTS

Note state not federal law

Q4

A **state law provides** for an award of damages against anyone who publishes the name of a rape victim. Pursuant to that law, **a woman sued** a local newspaper **in state court** after the newspaper identified her as a rape victim.

Case filed in state court

The **state trial and appellate courts rejected** the claim, holding that the state law was **invalid under both** the ***state constitution* and *the First Amendment of the U.S. Constitution***. The **state supreme court affirmed**, holding specifically: "We think that this well-intentioned law very likely violates the First Amendment of the federal Constitution. We **need not, however, decide that issue**, because the law assuredly **violates our state constitution**, which provides even greater protection to the right of the press to report the news." The woman petitioned for review in the U.S. Supreme Court.

To test adequate and independent state grounds, the facts must provide 2 reasons for the decision: (1) based on state law and (2) based on federal law.

Decoy & irrelevant because

CALL Is the U.S. **Supreme Court likely to review the state supreme court judgment**?

Issue about judicial powers – can the Supreme Court review.... AND when it is talking about reviewing a state supreme court decision, the issue is usually adequate and independent state grounds.

SOLVE

FEDERAL JUDICIAL POWERS

- Federal courts can hear cases:
  - Arising under the U.S. Constitution
  - Admiralty
  - Between 2 or more states
  - Between citizens of different states
  - Between a state or its citizens and a foreign country/citizen
- Review a state court decision only to the extent it is based on federal law
- **Except**: The Supreme Court will not review a case where there are independent and adequate state law grounds for the state court's decision, even if there is a federal question involved.
- **Except**: Congress can strip the Supreme Court of its appellate jx to hear certain cases.
- Concurrent jx w/state courts over cases arising under federal law
- Original jx (not appellate) when state is a party or cases affecting ambassadors

Did NOT know the issue from the call?

IF you were not sure what the issue was after reading the call (since the call didn't mention it by name), you could just go through a list of all of the judicial powers and stop at the ones that involve the Court's ability to review state supreme court case

SOLVE *(continued)*

ANALYSIS

Since the state court decision made it clear that it didn't need to analyze the issue of whether the law was valid under the U.S. Constitution because they were able to decide the issue on the state constitution, the Supreme Court will not review the case even if it did involve the U.S. Constitution.

No, **because** the state supreme court decision rests upon an adequate and independent state ground since the law violates the state's state constitution.

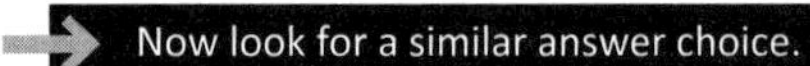

DECODE

~~A.~~ No, because the First Amendment prohibits the imposition of liability for the publication of truthful information.

Wrong issue and analysis. The First Amendment is not relevant since the state court based its decision on the state constitution. The Supreme Court will not review a state supreme court case based on its own state laws, even if a federal question is involved.

B. No, because the judgment of the state supreme court rests upon an adequate and independent state-law ground.

BINGO! Because the state supreme court did not base its decision under federal law, but rather on its own state constitution, the Supreme Court will not review the decision.

~~C.~~ Yes, because the supremacy clause does not permit a state to create rights greater than those conferred by the federal Constitution.

Incorrect rule statement. A state can grant more protections under its own constitution than those afforded to its citizens under the U.S. Constitution. The supremacy clause limits states on conduct that directly conflict with federal law.

~~D.~~ Yes, because the U.S. Supreme Court's appellate jurisdiction extends to cases arising under federal law.

Wrong reasoning because the adequate and independent state ground exception prevents this case from being one arising under federal law since the decision was based on the state constitution.

Q5

FACTS

State acting (not fed. gov.)

A **state owned and operated** an electric power system, which included a nuclear power plant. In order **to ensure the availability of sites for the disposal of spent fuel from the nuclear power plant**, the **state refused to supply electric power to out-of-state purchasers** residing in states that would not accept spent fuel from the plant for storage or disposal.

State's reason for the restriction

Restriction against out-of-staters (even if you haven't looked at the answer choices yet, this screams out DCC or P & I Clause b/c of the discrimination against out-of-staters)

Assume that **no federal statute applies.**

Tells you that preemption is not the issue.

CALL Which of the following is the **strongest argument** that the state's **action is constitutional**?

You need to evaluate each answer choice to pick the "strongest argument," rather than trying to solve the question first.

But you know you are looking to see if the state's action is constitutional, so you at least know the subject.

SOLVE

A	B	C	D
A state may condition the sale to out-of-state purchasers of any products produced in that state on the willingness of those purchasers to bear the fair share of the environmental costs of producing those products.	The generation of electricity is intrastate by nature and therefore subject to plenary state control.	The state itself owns and operates the power system, and therefore its refusal to supply power to out-of-state purchasers is not subject to the negative implications of the commerce clause.	The state's action is rationally related to the health, safety, and welfare of state citizens.
WEAK. Unclear what issue is being argued to show the action is constitutional. The language matches no rule or test.	**WEAKEST.** Plenary state control is not a valid legal theory to find an action by a state constitutional.	**STRONGEST.** Identifies an exception to DCC since state market participant; so the action is constitutional.	**GOOD.** True statement but that doesn't make the action constitutional because it is not a defense or exception to a DCC violation.

SOLVE (continued)

Rule: *The Dormant Commerce Clause (DCC) – also called the Negative Implications of the Commerce Clause – restricts the states and local governments from regulating activity that affects interstate commerce if the regulation is* ***(1) discriminatory,*** *or* ***(2) unduly burdensome****.*

DISCRIMINATORY
(against out-of-towners)

- Permitted only if necessary to achieve an legitimate noneconomic gov. interest &
- No reasonable alternatives

UNDUE BURDEN
(on interstate commerce)

- Permitted if rationally related to a
- Legitimate gov. interest, &
- Burden imposed on interstate commerce outweighed by benefits to the state

EXCEPTIONS:

- Market participant (state not acting as a regulator, but owns or operates a business/participates in the marketplace)
- Congressional consent
- State or city promoting public operations

ANALYSIS

- The state is discriminating against out-of-staters by refusing to supply electric power
- But the state is acting as a market participant because it owns and operates an electric power system

A Answer choice C is the strongest argument **because** it is the only exception that applies to the DCC making the state's action constitutional.

Now look for a similar answer choice.

DECODE

(A.) A state may condition the sale to out-of-state purchasers of any products produced in that state on the willingness of those purchasers to bear the fair share of the environmental costs of producing those products.

Made up rule. There is no such rule or exception that exists to the negative implications of the commerce clause (DCC).

(B.) The generation of electricity is intrastate by nature and therefore subject to plenary state control.

Made up rule. There is no such rule on plenary state control to allow a state to discriminate against out-of-staters.

C. The state itself owns and operates the power system, and therefore its refusal to supply power to out-of-state purchasers is not subject to the negative implications of the commerce clause.

Yes!!! The issue raised here is that the state's action violates the negative implications of the commerce clause (DCC) unless an exception applies. The market participant is a valid exception (but note how they don't use the words market participant in the answer choice to hide the ball).

(D.) The state's action is rationally related to the health, safety, and welfare of state citizens.

Wrong reasoning. While it is true that the state's action is rationally related to the health, safety, etc. of citizens, that is not a valid excuse to shield the state from a DCC violation.

FACTS

Q6

A **police officer** was employed on a **city's police force for 10 years**. When the officer accepted the job, the city's employee benefit plan provided a **death benefit** to the spouse of any employee who died as a result of any **job-related injury**. Last year, the **city amended its employee benefit plan** to **deny its death benefit in cases** where the death "was caused by the **employee's refusal to accept**, for any reason other than its excessive risk to life or health, **reasonably available medical care** prescribed by a physician."

State action needed for 1st Am. action – city acting so ok

Reason death benefit can be denied (amendment)

After this amendment took effect, the **officer was shot while on duty**. Because of a sincerely held religious belief, the officer refused to allow a prescribed blood transfusion and, as a result, died from loss of blood. When the officer's **spouse applied for the death benefit**, the **city denied** the application on the **basis of the amendment** to the employee benefit plan.

Issue we need to evaluate as it relates to religious beliefs

The officer's **spouse has challenged the amendment**, claiming that, as applied to the officer, it **violated the officer's constitutional right** to the **free exercise of religion**.

Arguing officer's rt., but spouse still has standing b/c injured – can't get benefit

CALL Is the court likely to find the **amendment** to the employee benefit plan **constitutional as applied** to the officer?

Call about the constitutionality of an amendment and a quick read of the sentence before tells you it is about the free exercise of religion (nice!).

SOLVE

FREE EXERCISE CLAUSE
• Bars any law that prohibits or seriously burdens the free exercise of religion, unless • Necessary to achieve a • Compelling gov. interest

SOLVE (continued)

EXCEPTIONS	ANALYSIS
• A law of general applicability (regulates the conduct of all persons) is ok if: ◦ No intentional burden on religious beliefs & ◦ Rationally related to a ◦ Legitimate gov. interest ◦ Time, Place, Manner of religiously motivated conduct ok if neutral & important public purpose • Religious Freedom Restoration Act (RFRA) – can challenge a federal law of general applicability if: □ Substantial burden of free exercise & □ Narrowly tailored to □ Compelling gov. interest	• Law prohibited the police officer from having spouse receive death benefit if he refused medical treatment (and died) based on his religious beliefs • BUT law was one that regulated the conduct of all officers/ employees and did not intentionally burden any religious belief • Legitimate gov. interest to have employees protect their own health and seek reasonable help • Rationally related b/c if get medical help less likely to die (here died as a result of not getting the transfusion) • RFRA – N/A b/c no fed. law here

Yes, the court is likely to find the amendment constitutional under the free exercise clause **because** it is a law of general applicability and does not intentionally burden the officer's religious belief.

Now look for a similar answer choice!

DECODE

Ⓐ No, because it effectively discriminates against a religious practice.

Wrong analysis. The amendment does not intentionally discriminate against a religious practice, but rather applies to all persons regardless of religious practice.

Ⓑ No, because it violates the vested contractual rights of city employees who were hired before the amendment took effect.

Wrong issue. The challenge is based on the free exercise of religion not the contracts clause. Carefully read the call and determine what the issue is prior to looking at the answer choices.

C. Yes, because it does not single out religious reasons for the denial of benefits and is a reasonable limitation on the award of such benefits.

Correct! It is a law of general applicability and not intentionally burdensome. Also, it is rationally related to a legitimate gov. interest ("reasonable limitation" language used rather than the actual rational basis scrutiny test language to hide the ball a bit).

Ⓓ Yes, because it imposes a condition only on the award of a government benefit and does not impose a penalty on an individual's conduct.

Wrong reasoning. The free exercise clause is not limited to conduct only, but rather applies to any law that burdens the free exercise of religious beliefs, even if it is through the award of benefits.

FACTS — State action

Q7

To **preserve the appearance and accessibility of its capitol building**, a **state enacted a law** prohibiting "the display of any sign on any portion of the public sidewalk surrounding" the building.

Reason for law – goes to the gov. interest (varies depending on level of scrutiny/test at issue)

Law - public sidewalk so public forum test; note words like "any" which tend to indicate too broad or not narrowly tailored

A group of five demonstrators who **wanted to protest** inadequate state funding for children's services **applied for a permit** to **march single file** on the **sidewalk** surrounding the capitol building. Each demonstrator planned to **carry a two-foot-square sign** that would read, "Our lawmakers do not care about our children."

Action at issue – protest w/ single file march w/ 2 ft sign (sign prohibited by law above)

The **group's permit application was denied** pursuant to the state law, and the group has filed an action challenging the law's constitutionality.

So they have standing

CALL Should the court uphold the **law's constitutionality**?

Subject matter clear, but issue not. BUT the prior sentence about a group's application being denied – usually that is a Time, Place, Manner issue.

MBE tip: Usually when the issue isn't in the call, it is listed in the sentence before the call. Take a quick glance there if not in the call. Then read the facts.

SOLVE

STATE ACTION & STANDING OK

CONTENT BASED V. CONTENT NEUTRAL

CONTENT BASED

Strict scrutiny
- Narrowly tailored
- Compelling gov. int.

Unprotected?
- Obscenity
- Misrepresentation
- Defamation
- Lawless/fighting

Other issues?
- Commercial speech
- Symbolic speech
- Overbroad, vague, unfettered discretion
- Prior restraint

CONTENT NEUTRAL

Time, place, manner
- Forum type?

Public/designated public

or

Limited/nonpublic

AT ISSUE HERE (See next page)

SOLVE *(continued)*

PUBLIC/DESIGNATED PUBLIC	ANALYSIS
• Content neutral (subject matter & viewpoint neutral) • Substantial/important gov. interest • Narrowly tailored • Alternative channels open	• Content neutral b/c prohibits any sign • T, P, M restriction b/c on any public sidewalk surrounding the capital building • Public sidewalk = public forum • Any sign is subject matter & viewpoint neutral • Appearance/accessibility to capital building arguably an important gov. interest (people need access) • Not narrowly tailored because could have certain areas or paths where protests/signs allowed to provide access and limit the numbers for appearance (here only 5 people single file – would not cause an appearance or accessibility issue) • No alternative open channels available
LIMITED/NONPUBLIC	
• Viewpoint neutral • Legitimate gov. interest • Reasonably related	

 No, **because** the law is not narrowly tailored and there are no open alternatives.

Now look for a similar answer choice.

DECODE

~~A.~~ No, because even though the sidewalk at issue is not a public forum, the prohibition against the display of signs is more restrictive than needed to serve a legitimate government interest.

Wrong categorization and wrong level of scrutiny/test evaluated. The public sidewalk is a public forum and legitimate interest goes to limited or nonpublic forums.

B. No, because the sidewalk at issue is a public forum, and the prohibition against the display of signs is not narrowly tailored to serve a substantial government interest.

YES!! Proper forum analyzed and proper test. Note the correct rule language with narrowly tailored and substantial government interest. The key to con law questions is to evaluate the proper standard and apply the correct level of scrutiny/test.

~~C.~~ Yes, because even though the sidewalk at issue is a public forum, the prohibition against the display of signs is necessary to serve a compelling public interest.

Wrong level of scrutiny/test evaluated. Even though it is a public form (correct forum), a compelling government interest is too high of a standard and the wrong level of scrutiny.

~~D.~~ Yes, because the sidewalk at issue is not a public forum, and the prohibition against the display of signs is reasonable.

Wrong categorization and wrong level of scrutiny/test evaluated. The public sidewalk is a public forum, and the reasonable standard goes to limited and nonpublic forums.

Q8

FACTS

State action | Gov. interest

To **improve the quality of rental housing** within its boundaries, a **city proposed** an ordinance **requiring all new and existing rental housing units** to provide at least one full bathroom for each bedroom, plumbing and electrical hookups for a washer and dryer, and a covered parking space.

Applies to ALL rental housing units (affects ability to rent/contract) so likely substantive due process, BUT you could argue equal protection because rentals v. owned housing units (classification)

A majority of the owners of existing rental housing in the city opposed the ordinance. They argued that it would **dramatically decrease the number of low-income rental housing units** because owners would be **unable to raise rents enough to recoup the investment required to comply. Without denying these contentions**, the city enacted the ordinance. A **plaintiff who owns low-income rental housing has sued the city**, claiming only that the **ordinance is unconstitutional on its face.**

Argument against ordinance (city didn't deny existed) – will need to analyze test/scrutiny to see if this matters

= standing to sue

CALL Which of the following best states the **burden of persuasion** in this action?

Subject/issue not clear. But the previous sentence indicates the constitutionality of an ordinance is at issue. Con law Qs that ask about burden of persuasion are asking you which level of scrutiny/ test should apply (and which party has the BOP) so you need to read the facts to see which legal theory (issue) is being tested.

NOTE: This Q arguably implicates both SDP and EP, but since the BOP is the issue, the scrutiny level will be the same regardless of which theory you applied.

SOLVE

SUBSTANTIVE DUE PROCESS	***ANALYSIS*** (state action & standing ok)	Did you analyze ***EQUAL PROTECTION*** instead?

• Limits gov. ability to regulate certain areas of human life - **life, liberty, or property**
• **<u>Fundamental rights</u>** (child rearing, travel, vote, etc.):
  ◦ Necessary to
  ◦ Compelling gov. interest
  ◦ **BOP on gov.**
• **<u>Nonfundamental rights</u>** (social, economic, etc.):
  ◦ Rationally related to
  ◦ Legitimate gov. interest
  ◦ **BOP on challenger**
• Abortion (hybrid)
	• Ordinance interferes with property owners and their ability to rent (contract) with renters depending on the condition of their properties
	• Regulation concerning housing units not a fundamental right
	• Rational basis applies – burden on challenger (owner)
	• Gov. interest to improve quality of housing is legitimate &
	• Having a bathroom, place to park car, washer/dryer rationally related to improve housing quality
		• Same test would apply because classification not based on fundamental right or suspect or quasi-suspect class
		• Housing regulations would be a non-suspect class and get rational basis

SOLVE *(continued)*

The owner of the rental unit would have the burden to show that the ordinance is not rationally related to the government's interest to improve the quality of rental housing (they could also try to argue that the government's interest is not legitimate). This is a very difficult burden to meet for a challenger.

→ Now look for an answer choice that is similar to your answer.

DECODE

~~A.~~ The city must demonstrate that the ordinance is necessary to serve a compelling state interest, because it adversely affects the fundamental right of rental housing owners to use their property in the manner they deem most economically efficient.

Wrong on all accounts. The burden is on the challenger not the city. The use of property is not a fundamental right. And the level of scrutiny is rational basis, not strict scrutiny.

~~B.~~ The city must demonstrate that the ordinance is necessary to serve a compelling state interest, because it will have a substantial and disproportionate negative impact on low-income persons.

Wrong on all accounts. The burden is on the challenger not the city. The level of scrutiny is rational basis, not strict scrutiny because low-income is economic and not a fundamental right.

~~C.~~ The plaintiff must demonstrate that the ordinance is not substantially related to an important state interest, because it requires some owners of rental housing to invest money that they will not be able to recoup from increased rents.

Wrong level of scrutiny. Rational basis should be applied, not intermediate scrutiny which goes to quasi-suspect classifications for equal protection.

D. The plaintiff must demonstrate that there is no rational relationship between the ordinance and any legitimate state interest, because the ordinance regulates economic activity of a type normally presumed to be within state regulatory authority.

BINGO! The burden is on the challenger (plaintiff-owner) and rational basis is the proper standard/ level of scrutiny because the ordinance regulates economic activity which is not a fundamental right.

FACTS — Q9

A **state generally provides funding** for the **medical care** of its **residents who cannot afford** such care. **State law**, however, **prohibits** use of this state **funding for surgery** for **any person who has resided in the state for less than one year**, except in emergency situations.

A **woman moved to the state** two months ago seeking **permanent employment**. Her physician recommends **non-emergency surgery** to treat a medical condition. The surgery **would qualify** for state funding **if the woman had resided** in the state **for a year**. The woman has **sued to invalidate the state law** that prohibits state funding of her surgery.

State action

Law affects the ability to receive funding for surgery based on residency – may be thinking equal protection (citizens > 1 yr. v. citizens < 1 yr.)

BUT

Not just about timing (1 yr.), but also affects right to move/travel between states (fundamental right)

= no funding for her since only 2 months (gives her standing to sue)

CALL Should the woman **prevail in her action**?

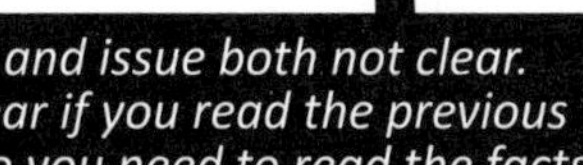

***MBE tip:* Due process & equal protection can overlap, but if there is a classification scheme, (here residents for > 1 year v. residents < 1 year) equal protection is at issue.**

SOLVE

__Rule:__ Equal protection prohibits the government (state and federal) from treating similarly situated persons differently.

SUSPECT CLASS/ FUNDAMENTAL RIGHTS	QUASI-SUSPECT CLASS	NONSUSPECT CLASS
• Race/ National original • State alienage • Rt. to travel, vote, access courts, 1st Am., etc. (Must show INTENT)	• Gender • Illegitimacy (Must show INTENT)	• Economic rights • Social welfare • Public school education • Age, wealth, etc.
Strict scrutiny • Narrowly tailored • Compelling gov. int. • BOP on gov.	Intermediate scrutiny • Substantially related • Important gov. int. • BOP on gov.	Rational basis • Rationally related • Legitimate gov. int. • BOP on challenger

SOLVE *(continued)*

ANALYSIS
(state action & standing ok)

- Right to travel state to state for the purpose of residence or employment affected here since the woman moved to seek permanent employment (fundamental right)
- Intent to treat people differently on the face of the law
- Gov. int. likely to save money (not likely compelling); maybe to prevent others from temporarily moving to receive free health care
- Not narrowly tailored – other ways to ensure people moved there legitimately and not just for healthcare (like permanent job)

Yes, **because** the law burdens her fundamental right to travel and it is not narrowly tailored to a compelling government interest.

Now look for a similar answer choice.

DECODE

A. No, because the law reasonably conserves the state's limited resources.

Wrong scrutiny level applied. The law must meet strict scrutiny, not just be reasonable.

B. No, because the law reasonably prevents the expenditure of state funds on transient nonresidents.

Wrong scrutiny level applied. The law must meet strict scrutiny, not just be reasonable.

C. Yes, because the law burdens the woman's fundamental right to health care.

Wrong rule and analysis. It correctly identifies that it burdens a fundamental right but there is no fundamental right to health care.

D. Yes, because the law burdens the woman's fundamental right to travel.

Correct!! The proper fundamental right and reason is identified. Note how none of the answer choices made you analyze the actual level of scrutiny, but rather just identify the classification.

Q10

FACTS

A company **owned a large tract of land** that contained **coal deposits** that the company **intended to mine.** The company **acquired mining equipment** and **began to plan its mining** operations. Just as the company was **about to begin mining, Congress enacted a statute** that imposed a number of new **environmental regulations** and **land-reclamation requirements on all mining operations** within the United States. The **statute made** the company's planned mining **operations economically infeasible.** As a result, the **company sold the tract of land to a farmer.** While the sale price allowed the company to **recover its original investment** in the land, it **did not cover the additional cost of the mining equipment** the company had purchased **or the profits it had expected** to earn from its mining operations on the land.

Gov. action

Statute affects mining requirements

Impact on company

Not a total loss, but did lose $ (= standing)

In an action filed against the appropriate federal official, the company claims that the statute **effected a taking of its property** for which it is **entitled to just compensation** in an amount equal to the **cost of the mining equipment** it purchased **and the profits it expected to earn** from its mining operations on the land.

Company wants costs for equipment & lost profits

CALL Which of the following is the **most appropriate result** in the action?

Subject/issue unclear in call, but can see taking is the issue above

SOLVE

Q Which of the following is the **most appropriate result** in the action (takings claim)?

Rule: *The Takings Clause provides that private property may not be taken for public use without just compensation.*

PRIVATE PROPERTY TAKEN?	***TOTAL TAKING*** (per se)	***TEMPORARY TAKING***	***REGULATORY TAKING***
For **public use** (Rationally related to any conceivable purpose) ↓ **Just compensation** (market value)	Physical invasion or confiscation of land **OR** ↓ Use restriction that denies ALL economically beneficial use	Denies all economic use temporarily **Consider:** ↓ • Economic impact on owner • Length of delay • Reasonable expectation of owner • Good faith of gov. planners	**Zoning, etc.** • No taking if still economically viable use • Decrease economical value ↓ Balance: • Character of invasion • Economic impact • Interference w/ investment backed expectation

SOLVE *(continued)*

ANALYSIS

- No physical invasion/actual taking of prop.
- All economic use not denied since able to sell land
- Regulatory taking at issue since statute restricts use w/ mining regulations
- Still economically viable use (able to sell it and use land for farming) = no taking

The plaintiff will not likely recover for the costs of equipment and lost profits under the takings clause **because** there was still economically viable use as the company was able to the sell the land and it can be used for farming.

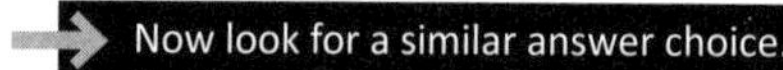

Now look for a similar answer choice.

DECODE

A. The company should prevail on its claims for the cost of the mining equipment and for its lost profits.

Wrong analysis. There was no taking since the statute did not deny all economically viable use of the land since the company was still able to sell the land and it can used for farming.

B. The company should prevail on its claim for the cost of the mining equipment, but not for its lost profits.

Wrong analysis. There was no taking since the statute did not deny all economically viable use of the land since the company was still able to sell the land and it can used for farming. Since there was no taking, the company cannot recover any money for anything under the takings clause.

C. The company should prevail on its claim for lost profits, but not for the cost of the mining equipment.

Wrong analysis. There was no taking since the statute did not deny all economically viable use of the land since the company was still able to sell the land and it can used for farming. Since there was no taking, the company cannot recover any money for anything under the takings clause.

D. The company should not prevail on its claim for the cost of the mining equipment or for its lost profits.

Correct. Since there was no taking, the company will not prevail. Note that it is possible they could recover under other theories for its lost expectation and profits, but not under the takings theory and the company limited its action to the takings clause. Don't get caught up in what seems fair – just focus on the law at issue.

PART 3 CONTRACTS

CONTRACTS MBE TABLE OF CONTENTS

Page

 Favorite Testing Area

CONTRACTS MBE OUTLINE

MBE CONTRACTS AT A GLANCE

Applicable law: Approximately 25% of all questions will be based on Articles 1 and 2 of the UCC; 75% of the questions will be based on common law.

12-13 Questions (approx.)	**12-13 Questions** (approx.)

Formation
  Offer
  Acceptance
  Consideration
  Promissory estoppel/reliance
Conditions/Waiver/Excuse
Modifications
Breach
  Anticipatory Repudiation
  Material breach
  Risk of loss
  Warranties
Discharge of duties
  Impossibility
  Impracticability
  Frustration of purpose
  Accord and satisfaction
  Novation
	Parol evidence rule/terms
	Third-party beneficiaries
	Assignment/Delegation
	Defenses
	  Statute of frauds
	  Misrepresentation/Fraud
	  Unconscionability
	  Mistake
	  Duress/undue influence
	  Capacity
	  Illegality/Public policy
	Remedies
	  Damages and limitations
	  Restitution/Replevin
	  Reformation/Rescission
	  Specific performance

CONTRACTS MBE APPROACH

1. Read the call of the question first to determine the issue being tested (if possible).
2. If the call is not specific, read the preceding sentence to see if the issue is there; if not, then read the facts to spot the issue.
3. Determine the applicable law—common law or UCC.
4. Use the appropriate common law or UCC rule and apply it to the facts.
5. Reach a conclusion and then look at the answer choices to find the correct answer.

Common law and UCC rule distintctions: Where the common law and UCC rules differ they are so labeled. Where not so noted, the rules essentially are the same.

COMMON DECOY ANSWER

Answer choices that have rule language for the UCC when the common law applies (and vice versa).

Testing style: Contracts MBE questions test a lot of small nuanced rules. Contracts (like Real Property) has many unrelated issues/rules that a MBE fact pattern can raise when they are only testing one of those issues. A contracts MBE question may also test several rules in combination with each other as many rules relate to each other. However, unlike essay questions, it is not helpful to issue spot MBEs using the life cycle of a contract as a framework. You may notice that contracts "tests" differently on MBE and essay questions. But for both it is important to pay attention to timelines so make a note of dates.

I. APPLICABLE LAW TO GOVERN THE CONTRACT

A. **Applicable law:** The applicable law governing a contract depends upon the subject matter of the contract.

1. **UCC:** The Uniform Commercial Code (UCC), Article 2, governs contracts for the **sale of goods.** Special UCC provisions apply when one or more parties are merchants.

   a. **Goods** are defined as movable, **tangible property**.

   b. **Merchant:** A merchant is one who **deals in goods of the kind**, or one holding oneself out as having **special knowledge or skills** regarding the practices or goods involved in the contract. Merchant is construed broadly.

> **Decoy tip:** Watch out for questions where the party is identified as a "merchant," but not in the goods of the kind of the bargain at hand; therefore, that party will not qualify as a merchant under the UCC rules.
>
> **MBE tip:** As a general principle, the UCC interprets more liberally than common law and endeavors to find that a contract exists wherever possible.

2. **Common law:** The common law governs all other contracts, except those for the sale of goods. Typically, this involves contracts for the provision of **services,** or contracts relating to **real property.**

B. **Predominance test:** Where a contract includes **both goods and the provision of services,** the predominance test determines if the UCC or common law governs the contract. Determine the **predominant purpose** for the contract as a whole and the law governing that area **provides the applicable law for the entire contract.** Some jurisdictions will divide the contract if possible and apply the UCC to the goods portion and the common law to the services portion.

C. **Objective theory of contracts applies:** A party's intent is deemed what an objective reasonable person in the opposing position would think the party's intent was.

> **MBE tip:** While the applicable law rules are not MBE tested outright, you must know these rules well to identify the body of law applicable to any particular question (e.g., contract modification rules differ between the common law and the UCC, so you first must determine the applicable law to properly analyze a contract modification MBE question).

II. CONTRACT FORMATION

A valid contract requires **mutual assent, which consists of an offer and acceptance, and consideration.**

A. **Offer (common law):** An offer is a **manifestation of willingness to enter into a bargain,** which is made in such a way that **the offeree is justified in thinking their assent will conclude a bargain.** An offer requires a demonstration of **intent** to enter into a contract, **definite and certain terms,** and **communication to the offeree.**

> **Offeror:** Person making the offer.
>
> **Offeree:** Person who may accept the offer.

1. **Intent:** The words or conduct of the offeror (the person making the offer) must demonstrate a present intent to enter into a contract.
   a. **Language:** The language used by the offeror can help establish the offeror's intent. While precise language, such as "I offer," clearly establishes an offer, it is not required. The **objective standard** of how **a reasonable person** would interpret the language is used to determine intent.
   b. **Context:** The context in which an offer is made can help establish intent.
      1. **Offers in jest:** An offer made in jest is not a valid offer.
      2. **Preliminary negotiations:** A party's language may invite preliminary negotiations but lack present willingness to contract (e.g., "I'm thinking of selling my car," or "I'd consider taking $5000 for my car.").
         a. **Solicitation of bids** is likely preliminary negotiations.
         b. **Advertisements** are typically invitations to deal and not offers to sell.
            i. **Exception:** Ads containing **words of commitment** where the **offeree can be identified** with specificity can be sufficiently definite to be an offer. An advertisement stating the sale of a particular number of units at a particular price, available at a specific time and place named, would likely be sufficiently specific to be deemed an offer.

            Example: Faculty, seeking to encourage legal research, posted an advertisement on the school bulletin board stating: "Any student at this school who wins the current National Constitutional Law Competition will receive an additional $500. All competing papers must be submitted to the Dean's office by March 1." This is an offer because it identifies the offeree (a student at that school), the amount ($500), and it is limited to the one student who wins (an identifiable offeree).
         c. **Catalogs** with specified goods and prices are typically an invitation to deal, not an offer.
      3. **Rewards and auction bids** can be offers if a reasonable interpretation of its words and the circumstances surrounding the reward or bid make it clear who can accept the reward or win the bid.

      Example: A series of arsons occurred in a city. The City Council adopted a resolution to pay $10,000 for the arrest and conviction of anyone guilty of any of the arsons. The foregoing was telecast by television. This reward would be an offer because it is reasonable to interpret the words and circumstances as inviting anyone to provide the information necessary to arrest and convict the suspects.
2. **Definite and certain terms:** The offer must contain definite and certain terms such that the **content of the bargain can be determined** and enforced. The parties can communicate back and forth, which as a whole provides the essential terms, and the **court may supply some missing terms** under an objective standard.
   a. **Quantity:** The quantity term must be stated or be ascertainable.
      1. **Requirements contracts** are permissible. A requirements contract is a contract wherein **a buyer promises to order all of the goods** the buyer requires from the seller. It is implied that the seller is the exclusive supplier. There is an **implied duty of good faith.**
      2. **Outputs contracts** are permissible. An outputs contract is where **a seller promises to provide their entire output of a product** to a particular buyer. It is implied that the buyer is exclusive. There is an **implied duty of good faith.**

b. Time of performance can be a missing term supplied by the court as a "reasonable" time.

c. Identity of the parties: The parties must be identified.

d. Price: Price must be stated for real estate contracts. However, the common law will use a "reasonable" price if one is missing.

e. Subject matter must be identified clearly. For land sale contracts there must be a clear property description, though it need not be in any particular format.

> **Memorization tip:** Use **QTIPS** to memorize the essential terms of a valid contract: **Q**uantity, **T**ime of performance, **I**dentity of the parties, **P**rice, and **S**ubject matter.

f. Meeting of the minds required: A significant misunderstanding of terms prevents contract formation. A contract **will not be formed where:**

1. The parties have a **different subjective belief** regarding a contract term;

2. The term is **material;** and

3. **Neither party knows** of the misunderstanding.

a. **Exception:** Where **one party knows,** or should know of the differing understandings, **the innocent party's understanding prevails.**

Example (yes meeting of the minds): A farmer who wanted to sell her land received a letter from a developer offering to pay $1100 an acre for the land. The farmer's reply letter accepted the offer. Unbeknownst to the farmer, the developer intended to offer $1000 but mistakenly typed $1100. Both parties knew that comparable land had been selling between $1000 and $1200. Here, there is a valid contract because $1100 was reasonable objectively based on comparable land and the farmer as the innocent party had no reason to know of the typo so his innocent understanding would prevail.

Example (no meeting of the minds): A farmer offers to sell a developer Blackacre. The farmer owns two properties named Blackacre. The farmer intended to sell Blackacre 1 and the developer intended to buy Blackacre 2. Neither party had reason to know they meant different properties so there is no mutual assent due to the misunderstanding of the material term, Blackacre.

> **Decoy tip:** For questions involving mutual assent, focus only on the parties' objective manifestations of assent. Wrong answers often focus on the subjective intent of the parties, which is irrelevant.

3. Communicated to the offeree: An offer must be communicated to the offeree, such that the **offeree has knowledge** of the offer.

4. Types of offers: The type of offer can impact the appropriate method of acceptance.

a. Bilateral: A promise in exchange for a **return promise.**

Example: A promises to pay B $50,000 in exchange for B's promise to give A title to Blackacre.

b. Unilateral: A promise made in exchange for an **act/performance.**

Example: A promises to pay B $5000 in exchange for B to paint A's house.

c. **Implied-in-fact:** A contract that is **inferred** from the parties' **conduct** or from the surrounding circumstances. It is based on a tacit, rather than an express promise.

Decoy tip: Do not confuse implied-in-fact contracts (real contracts inferred from conduct) with implied-in-law contracts (which are quasi-contracts where no real contract exists).

B. **Offer (UCC):** Inviting acceptance **in any manner** and **by any medium reasonable** in the circumstances.

1. **Intent:** The UCC allows for a more liberal interpretation and finds offers easily (e.g., a purchase order is typically an offer under the UCC because the order is construed as inviting acceptance by a shipment of goods).
2. **Definite and certain terms:** The UCC will use gap fillers for missing terms except for **subject matter** and **quantity.**
   a. **Price:** The UCC provides **"reasonable price at the time of delivery"** if the price is missing.

OFFER EXAMPLES

NO OFFER	YES OFFER
After a few meetings, a well driller sent a proposal to a developer that he would drill for $5000 and that the proposal would not become a contract until after the developer signed it and returned it back to the driller ***and the driller signed it.*** (NOT an offer because it does not manifest an intent to conclude a contract upon mere signing by the developer since the driller also has to sign it.)	After a few meetings, a well driller sent a proposal to a developer that he would drill for $5000 and that the proposal would not become a contract until after the developer signed it and returned it back to the driller. (Yes, this is an offer because it manifests an intent to conclude a contract upon mere signing by the developer.)
An uncle mailed a letter to his adult nephew that stated: "I am thinking of selling my pickup truck. I would consider taking $7000 for it." (NOT an offer because merely stating a possible interest and suggestion is not a manifestation of intent to be bound.)	After an uncle wrote his adult nephew a letter suggesting he *might* be willing to sell his truck for $7000, the nephew mailed a response to his uncle stating, "I will buy your truck for $7000 cash." (The nephew's statement is an offer because the nephew manifested an intent to bound to buying the truck.) Note: the uncle's letter was not an offer.

Decoy tip: Don't assume the first interaction is the offer. It might be an offer made in jest or a preliminary negotiation, and if so, then the next communication may be the offer (see the truck examples above).

C. **Termination of the offer:** For an acceptance to be valid, the offer must still be open.

1. **Rejection:** A rejection terminates the offer.

   a. **Express:** An outright rejection of the offer by the offeree, except where there has been a right to accept reserved by either party.

   b. **Implied:** Accepting part of an offer will imply a rejection to the rest of an offer.

   Example: Owner offered to sell Buyer any or all lots of a subdivision numbered 101 to 150. Buyer accepted the offer with respect to lot 101. Thus, Buyer impliedly rejected lots 102 through 150 by only accepting to buy lot 101.

   c. **Revival:** After an offer has been rejected, the offeror can revive the offer.

   Example: Seller offered to sell Buyer magnets for $5 each. Buyer rejected the offer. Seller told Buyer to reconsider and let him know the next day. This was a revival of the original offer.

2. **Counteroffer:** A counteroffer is an offer made by the offeree to the offeror regarding the same subject matter as the original offer but containing different terms. It is a **rejection** and a **new offer.**

   a. **Distinguish counteroffer from inquiry:** Inquiring about the possibility of another deal will not serve as a counteroffer and rejection. Analyze the language used.

   Example (counteroffer): Painter offered to paint Homeowner's house for $5000, and said he would prepare all walls and prime them first. In response, Homeowner said he would not pay more than $4000 and wanted premium paint used. This is a counteroffer (rejection and new offer) since it is the same subject matter but contains different terms.

   Example (inquiry): Painter offered to paint Homeowner's house for $5000, and said he would prepare all walls and prime them first. Homeowner asked if the price would be different if painter didn't have to prime the walls first. This is not a counteroffer (not a rejection or new offer) since Homeowner is merely inquiring about the price as it relates to the services provided.

3. **Revocation:** An offeror can revoke an ordinary offer (not irrevocable offers) at **any time before acceptance,** which terminates the power of acceptance. **Revocations are effective upon receipt;** thus, a lost revocation never becomes effective. A revocation can be:

   a. **Direct or indirect** (information learned from third parties who are reliable).

      1. **Public offers** can be revoked by publication of the revocation if the revocation is publicized equal to the offer and no better means of notification is reasonably available.

   b. **Unambiguous words or conduct** inconsistent with the intent to contract (e.g., selling the good that is the subject matter of the contract to another party).

      1. **Offeree is aware:** The offeree must be aware of the offeror's words or conduct indicating the offer was revoked.

      Example (no revocation): A wealthy widow wanted to make a substantial gift to her beloved adult stepson. She established with a bank a passbook savings account for him with $10,000. The bank issued the passbook to the widow solely in her name. That same day, with disinterested witnesses being present, she handed the passbook to her stepson and said, "As a token of my love for you, I give you this $10,000 savings account." Shortly thereafter, she changed her mind and wrote her stepson a letter revoking the $10,000 savings account and asked him to return the passbook immediately. The widow died a few days later. This was not a valid revocation because her completed gift was already accepted and no longer revocable. (Note: you might be thinking about consideration here as this was a gift, but this was a valid assignment, so the gift was effective and once accepted it becomes irrevocable.)

<u>**Example (yes revocation)**</u>**:** On May 5, B wrote his friend S a letter stating he would buy his motorcycle for $1000 if S delivered it to B's house by May 25. S responded by mail that he accepted the offer. S's response was misdirected by the postal service accidently and did not get to B until May 23. B told S that he bought another motorcycle the day before. This was a direct revocation as B told S that he purchased another motorcycle. (Note: to understand the timing, you needed to notice how the acceptance of mailing the letter was not a valid acceptance since the offer was for performance of delivering the motorcycle to B's house, so the revocation was before the valid acceptance.)

c. **No actual knowledge: Receipt of revocation does not require actual knowledge** of the revocation **but merely possession** (including people authorized to receive it), meaning the revocation **need not be read** by the recipient to be effective.

<u>**MBE tip**</u>**:** Contracts MBE questions often require analysis of multiple issues in one question. In the example above, although they were testing revocation, you also had to understand how acceptance of a unilateral contract works to reach the correct conclusion. You need to understand how all of the issues involving a contract relate to each other to properly analyze many MBE questions.

<u>**Decoy tip**</u>**:** Ordinary offers can be revoked even if the offer itself states that it is irrevocable. Thus, the offer itself can lie about its own revocability. Most offers are revocable (exceptions below).

d. **Exceptions: Some offers are irrevocable, including:**

1. **UCC "firm offers"** are **irrevocable even without consideration.** "Firm offers" require the following:

   a. **Made by a merchant** (one dealing in goods of the kind).

   b. **Signed writing:** In writing and signed (electronic signatures are acceptable) by a merchant holding the offer open.

   c. **Gives assurance it will be held open** for a specified time, during which time it's irrevocable.

   <u>**Example**</u>**:** Manufacturer gives Retailer a writing stating, "I agree to supply you with as many toys in the enclosed catalog that you need at the listed prices. This offer will remain open for 90 days." This is a firm offer that is not revocable for 90 days.

   d. **Three-month limit on irrevocability without consideration:** No offer can be irrevocable for longer than three months without consideration. Even if a "firm offer" states it will remain open for longer than three months, it will only be irrevocable for three months. But, the offer is *not automatically revoked after three months*. For the first three months the offeror cannot revoke the offer, but after three months the offeror *can* revoke the offer. If the offeror *does not revoke* their offer *it will remain open* and can still be accepted.

   <u>**Example**</u>**:** Manufacturer gives Retailer a writing stating, "I agree to supply you with as many toys in the enclosed catalog that you need at the listed prices. This offer will remain open for 120 days." After three months, Manufacturer is allowed to revoke the offer, despite the promise that it will remain open for 120 days. However, if Manufacturer doesn't specifically revoke the offer, it will remain open and subject to acceptance for a "reasonable time."

> **Decoy tip:** Watch out for non-firm offers that are revocable, but are not revoked and therefore still valid, and open offers.
>
> **MBE tip:** When firm offer is tested, the MBE answer choices usually do not use the term "firm offer." Rather, answers will refer to a party not being a merchant (when it isn't a firm offer) or if the offer is a firm offer, the correct answer will often involve a merchant being involved, a signed assurance, or some part of the rule language.

2. **Option contract:** An option contract is one where the offeror grants the offeree an "option" to enter into a contract for a specified period of time and promises the offer will be held open during that time.

   a. **Consideration is required** for an option contract. Modernly (the MBE rule unless told otherwise), the consideration need only be stated, though at common law it was required that the consideration be actually paid.

   b. The offer will be **irrevocable for the stated option period.** If no time is stated, then the offer will remain open for a reasonable time.

   Example: Owner and Buyer signed a writing in which Owner, in consideration of $100 to be paid to Owner by Buyer, offered Buyer the right to purchase Blackacre for $100,000 and he promised that this offer would remain open for 30 days. This is an option contract and Owner cannot revoke it for the stated 30 days.

3. **Detrimental reliance and partial performance:** An offer will be irrevocable if the offeree has made preparations to perform in **reasonable detrimental reliance** on the offer, or offeree has **performed in part**.

   a. **Unilateral contract:** Once performance has begun, an option contract is created making the offer irrevocable.

   b. **Bilateral contract:** Making **preparations to perform** may make the offer irrevocable **if justice requires** (e.g., subcontractor bids).

   Example: A wallpaper hanger sent a general contractor a letter stating he would do all paperhanging on a new building for $14,000 if the contractor accepted within a reasonable time after being awarded the main contract. Three other competing wallpaper hangers submitted bids for higher amounts. The general contractor used the wallpaper hanger's $14,000 figure in preparing and submitting the bid for the job. The general contractor had to submit a bid bond and could not withdraw the bid without forfeiting the bond. The general contractor won the main contract. The wallpaper hanger realized he made a $4000 computation error and wrote to the contractor that his offer was revoked. The contractor relied on the first computation to make his own bid. He was awarded the main contract and cannot change it without forfeiting the bond. Thus, the wallpaper hanger's offer for $14,000 should not be revocable due to the contractor's detrimental reliance.

4. **Lapse of time:** The offeror can set a **time limit** for acceptance, **or** if none is stated, it remains open only for a **"reasonable" time.** Once the time has passed, the offer lapses and may not be accepted.

   a. **Oral offers:** An oral offer typically lapses at the end of the conversation.

5. **Death or incapacity of either party:** If either the offeror or offeree dies or loses the legal capacity to enter into a contract, the power to accept an outstanding offer is **terminated automatically,** regardless of notice to the other party.

a. **Except—option contracts:** The offer will not terminate if it was an **option** with **paid consideration.**

b. **Minors:** Minors (those under the age of 18 in most states) may form contracts, but their **obligations are voidable by the minor only (not the other party)** due to incapacity.

   1. **Disaffirming the contract:** The minor can disaffirm a contract by **words or deeds** that **objectively** signify the election to **avoid liability.**

      a. **Exception—necessaries:** Minors can be held liable for contracts **for necessaries** (e.g., food, medicine, shelter, etc.).

   2. **Affirming the contract:** The minor can affirm their contract after reaching the age of majority thereby binding their performance.

      Example: A 17-year-old teenager agreed in writing to pay an electronics dealer $400 for a television set on July 1, when he turned 18 and expected to receive the proceeds of a trust. On July 1, the teenager sent a letter stating he would only pay $300. The dealer would not be able to enforce the original offer because the teenager had voidable rights under the contract due to his lack of capacity to contract (age).

c. **Insanity:** Individuals with mental defects who **cannot understand the nature and consequences** of the contract lack capacity to contract and their **obligations are voidable.**

> **MBE tip:** Know the difference between void and voidable for contracts as the different terminology can be in the answer choices.
>
> **Void** means that a contract cannot be enforced by either party and is treated as if no contract was ever formed (e.g., a contract to sell cocaine would be void as it is illegal).
>
> **Voidable** means a contract is valid but only one party is bound by the contract and the unbound party can cancel the contract (e.g., a minor who entered a contract to buy a car can cancel the contract due to lack of capacity).

TERMINATION OF OFFER CHEAT SHEET

Offer terminated	Offer NOT revocable/terminated
Rejection (express or implied)	UCC Firm offer (merchant signed offer with assurance to hold it open; 3 months max.)
Counteroffer (not an inquiry)	
Revocation (before acceptance)	Option contract (consideration to hold open)
Lapse of time (reasonable time)	Detrimental reliance (reasonable reliance)
Death (power to accept terminates)	Part performance (preparation ok if justice requires)
Incapacity (minors and insane persons)	

Memorization tip (in order listed): Really Cute Rabbits Like Dandelions & Ivy NOT Ugli Fruit Or Dead Plants. (Ugli fruit is a real fruit.......google it!)

D. Acceptance: An acceptance is the **manifestation of assent to the terms of the offer.** This can be by **words** (oral or written) creating an express contract, or by **conduct** creating an **implied-in-fact contract.** The offeror is the master of the offer and can prescribe the method and manner of acceptance.

1. **Methods of acceptance:** The offeror is the master of the offer and thus proscribes the method by which the offer can be accepted.

   a. **Bilateral:** A bilateral contract is where **both parties make promises** to perform. See example above in types of offers.

      1. **Silence:** Silence will operate as acceptance **only if the *offeree* intends for their silence to manifest acceptance.**

      Example: After several days of negotiations, Owner wrote to Plumber: "Will pay you $3000 if you will install new plumbing in my new office building. I must have your reply by May 30." (*offer*) Plumber replied by a letter that Owner received on May 15: "Will not do it for less than $3500." (*counteroffer and rejection of first offer*) On May 20, Plumber wrote to Owner: "I changed my mind and will do it for $3000. Unless I hear from you to the contrary, I will begin work on June 5." (*new offer*) Owner received this letter on May 23, but did not reply to it. Plumber, without Owner's knowledge, began the work on June 5. There was no acceptance because Owner's (offeree) silence did not intend to manifest acceptance.

      a. **Exception:** Where **prior dealings** between the parties, or **trade practices** known to both, create a commercially **reasonable expectation** by the offeror that **silence represents an acceptance.**

   b. **Unilateral:** A unilateral contract exchanges the **offeror's promise** for the **offeree's actual performance** of the requested act.

   Example: A unilateral offer exists where a store owner offers to pay a private investigator to investigate a recent robbery in an effort to catch the perpetrator. The acceptance is made by the act of investigating the robbery, not the promise to do so.

      1. **Notice:** A unilateral contract typically requires **reasonably prompt notice of acceptance** after performance, but **not before** performance has begun.

      Example: Borrower asked Lender to lend her $1000. Lender replied that he would do so only if Borrower's father would guarantee the loan. At Borrower's request, her father mailed a signed letter to Lender: "If you will lend $1000 to my daughter, I will repay it if she doesn't." After receiving the father's letter, Lender lent $1000 to Borrower. The father died the next day. Unaware of the father's death, Lender mailed the father a letter confirming that he made the loan to his daughter. Borrower stopped making payments and Lender brought an action against the father's estate. The father's estate will be bound by the contract because the father's letter was a unilateral contract offer and was accepted when Lender performed by lending his daughter the $1000. The father did not have prior notice of the performance, but it was not required and thus did not affect the acceptance.

   c. **Acceptance by conduct (implied-in-fact contract):** Where both parties engage in conduct which recognizes the existence of a contract.

   Example: An attorney received a document at his office with an attached note from a client for whom he just finished drafting a will. The note read, "Do you think this contract of sale for my boat complies with state law? I would have talked to you in person but I had to leave town and will be back next week." The client's conduct creates an offer that reasonably invites the attorney to accept by reviewing the contract considering their past relationship and recent transaction.

d. **Ambiguous:** If the manner of acceptance is unclear, **either a promise** to perform **or actual performance** is acceptable.

Example: A toy collector purchased 10 antique toys over the last several years and had them restored by a toy restoration expert. On June 1, the collector sent the expert his 11th toy with a signed note: "Here is another toy for you to restore. As with all prior jobs, I will pay no more than $500." On June 4, the expert began restoring the toy. On June 6, the collector died. On June 7, unaware of the collector's death, the expert sent the collector a note that he had begun restoration. The offer was accepted before the collector died because the method of acceptance was ambiguous so the expert was allowed to accept by either promise or performance. Once the expert began performance the offer was accepted so the collector's death did not affect the acceptance. The June 7 notice of acceptance was reasonably prompt notice as required for a unilateral contract.

Decoy tip: Most questions testing acceptance will use an improper method of acceptance in the wrong answer choices (e.g., if they are testing a unilateral contract, the wrong answer choices will often contain bilateral and/or implied-in-fact contract acceptance language, and vice versa). It is important to understand the differences, so you know what type of contract is at issue.

2. **Power of acceptance:** The power of acceptance is subject to some limitations:

a. **Timing:** Acceptance must be within a **"reasonable time."**

b. **Only by offeree:** Only a person at **whom the offer is directed** may accept.

c. **Knowledge of the offer:** The offeree **must know of the offer** before accepting.

Example: Where a reward has been offered to provide the police information on a recent crime, a person performing the requested act without knowing about the reward cannot "accept" by performance.

1. **Cross offers:** When **both parties make an offer with identical terms,** but the other party **does not know** about the other's offer, there is **no acceptance** and no contract because neither party has expressed a willingness to be bound by the other's terms.

Example: Seller mails a letter to Buyer to sell 200 widgets for $5 each. The same day, Buyer mails a letter to Seller to purchase 200 widgets for $5 each. Both letters were mailed at the same time. Before either party received the other's letter, there is no contract despite the crossing offers because neither party expressed a willingness to be bound as both made offers.

d. **Manner of acceptance:** An offer must be accepted in the **manner required by the offer.** But, if no method is specified, acceptance can be by **any "reasonable" means.**

e. **Objective standard:** Acceptance by performance is judged by an objective standard.

3. **When an acceptance is effective:**

a. **Mailbox rule:** The mailbox rule provides an **acceptance is effective** upon **proper dispatch.**

Example: On May 3, Nephew mailed a letter to his uncle that he would buy Uncle's truck for $7000. On May 6, Uncle mailed Nephew a letter that he accepted his offer. On May 7, Nephew called Uncle to say he no longer wanted the truck and he had not yet received the letter of acceptance. Under the mailbox rule, Uncle's acceptance was effective on May 6 regardless of whether Nephew received it yet because it was effective on proper dispatch.

1. **Proper dispatch** requires that the offeree **no longer has control or possession** of the acceptance, such as with a properly mailed letter.

   Example (properly dispatched): An acceptance letter that is given to the mailman or picked up by the mailman, or dropped off at the post office is properly dispatched (the offeree no longer has possession and cannot change their mind so the dispatch is effective as an acceptance).

   Example (not properly dispatched): An acceptance letter left on one's doorstep for the mailman to pick up, or in one's mailbox is not properly dispatched (since the offeree could access the letter and change their mind, they still have control and possession).

2. **Lost or delayed in transmission:**

   a. **Properly addressed/dispatched:** Mailbox rule applies, even if never received.

   b. **Not properly addressed/dispatched:** Mailbox rule applies **only if the acceptance is actually received** within the same time frame as if it had been properly addressed/dispatched.

b. **Mailbox rule exceptions:**

1. Where the **offer itself provides otherwise,** the terms of the offer control, thus, the offeror can suspend the mailbox rule.

   Example: An apartment complex received an offer from a retailer offering to sell the complex 1200 window air conditioners. The offer stated it would remain open until May 20, but that the acceptance must be received on or before that date. On May 16, the complex posted a letter of acceptance. On May 17, the retailer telegraphed the complex that it was revoking the offer. The telegram reached the complex on May 17, but the complex's letter didn't reach the retailer until May 21. The offer was effectively revoked because the acceptance was received late (even though it was dispatched under the mail box rule, the language of the offer specified that acceptance had to be *received* by a set date and since it was not, the acceptance was not valid).

2. **Option contract is effective upon receipt.**

3. **If both an acceptance and a rejection are sent,** the rule depends on which was dispatched first.

   a. **Rejection dispatched first,** the acceptance will only become **effective if it is received first** (basically the mailbox rule does not apply and whichever is received first is effective).

   b. **Acceptance dispatched first** is **effective on dispatch** in accordance with the normal rule, thus it doesn't matter if rejection is *received* first. **The acceptance will control unless** the offeror received the rejection first and **detrimentally relied** on it (then offeree can be estopped).

4. **Acceptance varying from offer: The rule** depends on if common law or the UCC applies.

   a. **Common law "mirror image" rule:** An acceptance must be a precise mirror image of the offer. If the response conflicts at all **with the terms** of the offer, or adds new terms, the purported acceptance is a **rejection and counteroffer.**

   ★ b. **UCC:** Any "expression of acceptance" or "written confirmation" will act as an **acceptance even if terms are "additional to or different from"** those contained in the offer, **unless**

acceptance is expressly made conditional on assent to additional or different terms. The outcome here depends on if the terms are additional or conflicting to those in the offer.

Example: Distributor and Retailer negotiated a contract that stated that any order for windows placed by Retailer would be binding on Distributor, "only when expressly accepted by the Distributor." For the next two years, Retailer forwarded orders to Distributor, and Distributor always filled the orders. In the third year, Distributor accused Retailer of overcharging customers for installation. Retailer responded that Distributor had no control over installation prices. Distributor refused to fill the next order from Retailer. Retailer cannot sue for breach because Distributor did not accept since the contract stated Distributor had to expressly accept to be bound. (The course of dealing is irrelevant since the contract was clear about what constituted acceptance, though it provides a nice decoy answer.)

1. **Additional terms in the acceptance:** The **"battle of the forms"** rule determines the outcome and depends on whether one or both parties are merchants.
   a. **If one party or more is not a merchant,** any additional term is a **proposal** and will not become a part of the contract unless the other party assents.
   b. **If both parties are merchants,** the additional term **automatically becomes a part of the contract *unless***:
      i. **Offer expressly limits acceptance to its terms.**

      ii. **Material alteration** with added term (the term results in an unreasonable surprise or hardship).

      Example: Wholesaler received a purchase order form from Retailer for an order of 1000 widgets. Both parties are merchants with respect to widgets. Wholesaler mailed to Retailer its own form accepting the order with an additional printed clause that provided for a maximum liability of $100 for any breach of contract by Wholesaler. Wholesaler's response is an acceptance. The additional term limiting liability to $100 will not be included in the contract because it materially alters the contract.

      iii. **Objection:** If the offeror objects to the additional term within a **reasonable time**.

MATERIAL ALTERATION EXAMPLES

YES a Material Alteration	NOT a Material Alteration	Courts split on YES/NO
Clause requiring a guaranty of 90/100% deliveries (i.e., catching fish), where the usage of trade allows more leeway	Clause on seller's exemption due to supervening causes beyond his control	Forum selection clauses
Clause requiring complaints be made in a time materially shorter than is customary	Clause fixing reasonable times for complaints within customary limits	Arbitration clauses
Clause reserving to the seller the power to cancel upon the buyer's failure to meet any invoice when due	Interest clauses on overdue invoices	Limitations on remedies
Liability limitation	Attorney fees	
Disclaimer of warranties*		

*In UCC examples this is a material alteration, but courts are split in reality

MBE tip: When the MBE question tests the areas where courts are split, the calls will often be phrased in way to ask you what the best argument is for one of the parties (e.g., a best argument answer might state that the arbitration clause did not materially alter the contract—as a best argument for seller who wants to have it *included* in the contract). Similarly, some answer choices will tell you that the contract is formed but the court must decide whether the additional term should be excluded as a material alteration. This way you aren't required to analyze whether or not the term is a material alteration or not since both sides usually have good arguments (the court will do that for you in the answer choice).

MBE tip: Where there is an attempt to add a term that is a material alteration, the failure to add that term does not affect the validity of the contract. The original contract still exists with the original terms, but the new term will not become part of the contract.

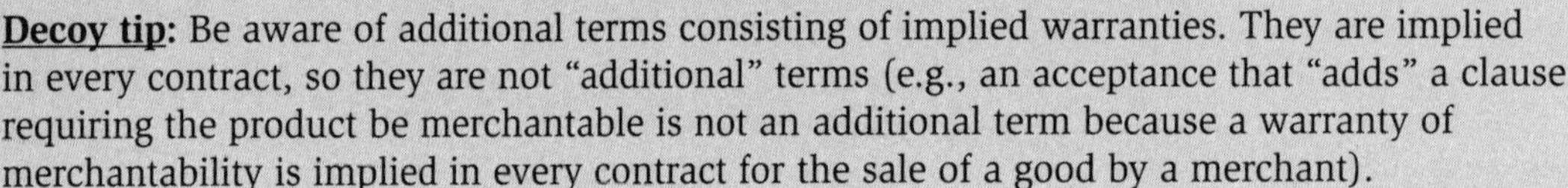

Decoy tip: Be aware of additional terms consisting of implied warranties. They are implied in every contract, so they are not "additional" terms (e.g., an acceptance that "adds" a clause requiring the product be merchantable is not an additional term because a warranty of merchantability is implied in every contract for the sale of a good by a merchant).

2. **Different terms** are treated in three ways depending on the jurisdiction: [This rule is rarely MBE tested.]
   a. **Knock-out rule (majority rule):** Conflicting terms cancel each other out and **neither term enters the contract.** The contract then consists of the agreed-to terms, and the court will supply missing terms if needed.
      i. **UCC:** The contract then consists of the agreed-to terms and **UCC gap fillers** will supply the missing terms as follows:
         a. **Price** is the **"reasonable price"** at the time of delivery.
         b. **Place of delivery:** Buyer **picks up the goods** from Seller.
         c. **Time for shipment** is a **"reasonable time."**
         d. **Time for payment:** Payment is **due upon receipt** of goods.

b. **Treat as additional terms (minority rule):** Apply the test above in additional terms.

c. **Fall out rule (another minority rule): The offeror's terms control.**

d. **Common law:** The contract consists of the agreed-to terms and the court may supply missing terms on a "reasonable basis" if necessary. The courts can apply the UCC rules through analogy.

5. **Acceptance by shipping goods:** Unless the offer specifies otherwise, **an offer to buy goods may be accepted by shipping** the goods (e.g., a "purchase order" sent to the seller and the seller fulfills the order). The offer is accepted by promptly shipping **conforming or nonconforming** goods.

   a. **Shipping conforming goods is an acceptance.**

   b. **Shipping nonconforming goods:** The effect of shipping nonconforming goods depends upon whether the seller acknowledges the nonconformity of the shipment.

      1. **Shipment without acknowledging nonconformity:** The offer has been **accepted and breached** simultaneously.

      2. **Shipment with acknowledging nonconformity** (accommodation shipment): This is an "accommodation" to the buyer and **will not serve as an acceptance.** Rather, the seller is making a **counteroffer** that the buyer is then free to accept or reject.

      Example: In response to an order for 5000 blue widgets, Seller sends 5000 red widgets and states, "Temporarily out of blue. In case red will help, am shipping 5000 red at the same price. Hope you can use them." This shipment will not constitute acceptance (as a result there is no breach here), but rather a counteroffer has been created so Buyer now has the power to accept this new offer or reject it.

      > **MBE tip:** A seller can also accept by *promising* to ship goods (rather than just shipping them). If this is the case, then a contract exists at the time of the promise and *before* shipping the goods. In this situation, shipping nonconforming goods would result in breach (the buyer can still reject or accept the goods but can also sue for damages).

      3. **Payment:** A buyer **who accepts** conforming or nonconforming **goods** becomes **obligated to pay** the seller the contract price for the goods, less any damages for losses resulting from nonconforming shipments.

      > **MBE tip:** Nonconforming goods are not only the wrong type of good, but also includes an insufficient quantity from goods being destroyed in transit.

6. **Right to inspect goods:** When goods are **delivered**, the buyer has **a right to inspect** them at any reasonable place and time and in any reasonable manner ***before*** **payment or acceptance.**

   a. **Exception—C.O.D.:** The buyer does **not have the right to inspect** the goods before payment **if the contract provides for delivery "C.O.D."** or like terms. (C.O.D. means "**C**ash **O**n **D**elivery or **C**ash **O**n **D**emand" where payment is made on delivery rather than in advance.)

   b. **Payment before inspection:** When the contract **requires payment before inspection,** nonconformity of goods does not excuse the buyer from making payment **unless the nonconformity is apparent** without an inspection.

1. **Payment is not acceptance:** When the **contract requires payment before inspection,** the payment **does not constitute acceptance** of the goods **or impair** the buyer's right to any of their **remedies.**

Example: Buyer purchased 100 bolts of standard blue wool, No. 1 quality, from Seller. The contract provided that Buyer would make payment prior to inspection. The 100 bolts were shipped, and Buyer paid Seller. Upon inspection Buyer discovered that the wool was No. 2 quality. Buyer tendered back the wool to Seller and demanded return of his payment. Seller refused on the ground the two wools were the same quality. Since the contract required payment before inspection, payment did not constitute acceptance (so Buyer can seek applicable remedies).

Decoy tip: Once a valid contract has been formed, a request for a confirming memo or a request for signature does not affect its validity (e.g., if part of the contract states that the parties agree "to memorialize the contract," and they later do not do so or fail to sign it as agreed, this will not make the contract invalid if formation requirements have already been met).

E. **Consideration** is a **bargained-for exchange of legal detriment** and can be a promise **to do an act, or forbearance** from doing an act one is otherwise entitled to do.

Decoy tip: The reason or motive for bargaining is irrelevant and not part of the analysis. Answers that attempt to find no consideration based on an improper motive or selfish reasons of a party are always wrong answers.

MBE tip: A benefit alone does not equate to consideration. There must be some "bargained for" exchange.

1. **Benefit for a third party:** Consideration can be bargained for the benefit of a third person (i.e., a third-party intended beneficiary).

   Example: Son negligently drove his father's car and crashed into a woman. The father, erroneously thinking he was liable because he owned the car said to the woman that he would pay for any losses she incurred. The father promised a physician he would pay him to take care of the woman and that he would pay the bill. The physician promised to take care of the woman. The physician's promise with the father is adequate consideration even though it was for the benefit of a third person.

2. **Illusory promise:** An illusory promise is one **not supported by consideration** and is thus not enforceable. The promisor appears to promise something, but in fact **does not commit** to do anything at all.

   Example: A shovel manufacturer received an order for the purchase of 500 snow shovels from a wholesaler to be delivered between September 15 and October 15. On the order, typed conspicuously across the front of the order form was: "The wholesaler reserves the right to cancel this order at any time prior to September 1." The manufacturer accepted the order. Even though there is an offer and acceptance, no contract was formed because there is no consideration. The promise is illusory since the wholesaler can cancel the order; the wholesaler did not commit to anything at all. (Note: once the manufacturer ships the shovels there is consideration because the time the wholesaler had to cancel would have passed.)

   a. **Conditional promise:** Where a promisor's obligation is **conditioned upon the occurrence of an event** that is **outside of the promisor's control,** the mere fact that the obligation is subject to a condition **does not render the promise illusory.**

Example: A buyer contracted with a shareholder, who owned all of XYZ's outstanding stock, to purchase all of her stock. Part of the contract stated that the commitment to buy was conditioned on obtaining approval of the contract from the parent company. This condition does not make the contract illusory because the buyer does not control that condition being met or the actions of the parent company in approving the purchase.

b. **Requirements and output contracts are not illusory,** though they can appear illusory. The **implied obligation of good faith** requires both parties to use their best efforts to supply the goods and promote the sale.

   1. **Requirements contracts:** In requirements contracts, the parties agree that the seller will be the **exclusive source of all of the buyer's requirements** for a particular item for a specified period of time.

      Example: County agrees to purchase from a tire salesman, all of the tires required for the county's vehicles for the next year.

   2. **Output contracts:** In an output contract, the buyer agrees to buy **all of the seller's output** of a particular item for a specified period of time.

      Example: Buyer agrees to purchase for the next year the entirety of Seller's baked buns.

Decoy tip: Many requirements and output contracts questions involve the parties promising to buy/sell goods for a specific period of time (i.e., 2 years) and often result in one party canceling/renouncing the agreement. The correct answer is that the canceling party is in breach because they had a valid contract. Wrong answer choices will argue there was no consideration (when there is pursuant to the rules above).

3. **Inadequate consideration examples:** A court typically will not inquire into the adequacy of consideration, but some types of promises do not provide adequate consideration.

   a. **Gifts:** A promise to make a gift is unenforceable. However, a mixture of a bargain and a gift is acceptable, such as to sell a car at a great discount to a relative.

   b. **Sham or nominal consideration** is insufficient, but it **must be very obvious** because the court is **reluctant to inquire into the adequacy of consideration** ("even a peppercorn will suffice").

      1. **Nominal consideration** is so small there cannot be considered a "bargain" at all.

      2. **Sham consideration**, where the price is recited, but not paid, is insufficient.

         Example (no consideration): Selling a home to a beloved child for $1.00 will likely be an insufficient "bargained-for exchange" to be enforceable because there is not really a bargain as the $1.00 is more likely an effort to make it not appear to be a gift but it is still not a bargained-for-exchange.

         Example (consideration exists): A chef purchased the front portion of the land needed to build a restaurant, but the back portion was subject to a will dispute between a sister and brother, of which the chef was aware. The chef agreed to pay the sister $6000 in exchange for a quitclaim deed. Later the probate court found the sister had no interest in the land. Though the chef walked away with nothing (since the sister did not own the property), there was sufficient consideration for their contract. (Essentially the chef was bargaining for a chance to buy the property cheaply with a risk he may not get it at all if the brother won the dispute.)

   c. **Rewards:** One must be **aware of the reward** offer for it **to provide consideration.**

d. Past consideration: A promise to pay for a **benefit received in the past** will **not provide current consideration** on a new bargain subject to **two exceptions:**

1. **New promise to pay a past debt that is now barred** from collection (i.e., statute of limitations has run) is valid without consideration if it is made in **writing** or **partially performed.**

   Example: Debtor owed Lender $1500. The statute of limitations barred recovery on the claim. Debtor wrote to Lender stating, "I promise to pay $500 if you will extinguish the debt." Lender agreed. Debtor's promise to pay part of the barred antecedent (prior) debt is enforceable without consideration.

2. **New promise to pay for benefits previously received** at the **promisor's request** or in an **emergency** can be binding without consideration.

   Example: A man saved the life of his friend's wife who thereafter changed her will to leave the man $1000. Upon her death, she had no property except real estate held in tenancy by the entirety with her husband. The husband then signed a note to the man stating, "In consideration of saving my wife's life and agreeing to bring no claims against my estate based on her will, I hereby promise to pay [the man] $1000." Upon the husband's death, the executor successfully contested the claim. The claim was not supported by consideration since the man had no duty to save the woman's life and it was a promise to pay for benefits previously received that the husband (the promisor) did not request. (The result would be different if the husband asked the man to save his wife.)

Decoy tip: Don't be tricked by quotes using the language "in consideration of . . . ." Just because they use the term "in consideration of" in their promise, does not mean there was consideration. Also, note how MBE questions will add in language from inapplicable exceptions they are not testing to distract you. In the above example, they add the line about not bringing claims against the estate, but that is not at issue since there was no dispute here that they were trying to settle.

e. Preexisting duty rule: The preexisting duty rule provides that a **promise to do something that one is already legally obligated to do** or to refrain from doing something one is already legally required to refrain from doing will **not provide consideration** for a new bargain because there is no legal detriment, **subject to the following exceptions:**

1. **Duty** is **owed to a third party.**

   Example (no third-party duty owed so no consideration): A car dealer owed a bank $10,000, due on June 1. The car dealer subsequently sold a car to the buyer for $10,000 payable at $1000 a month beginning June 1. The car dealer asked the bank whether the bank would accept payments of $1000 per month for 10 months beginning June 1 in payment of the debt. The bank agreed, but when the buyer tendered the first payment to the bank, the bank refused to accept it and said it would only accept payment from the dealer. On June 2, the bank demanded that the dealer pay the full amount. The bank can seek full payment from the dealer because there was no new consideration for the agreement and the dealer already had a preexisting duty to pay the bank. (Note: if the dealer actually *assigned its right to payment* from the buyer to the bank there would be a third party involved and the bank would now benefit from being able to sue another party (the buyer) in addition to the dealer which would meet the exception here.)

2. **Substituted performance**, such as by an executory **accord** where the parties agree that the **new contract will replace the old contract** (usually this arises in conjunction with settling a claim for a new lower amount as discussed below).

3. **Additional duties**, even if a very minor change.

4. **Settlement or release of claim in dispute:** A **promise to settle a claim** (often by paying less money than the original contract called for) may be consideration to support a return promise so long as there is a **good faith dispute** over the validity of the claim.

   a. **Partial payment in satisfaction of a debt in dispute:** Where a party cashes a check marked **"in full settlement"** or similar language signifying the amount is being paid in full (construed as a proposed settlement of the disputed debt), this resolves the **good faith dispute** on the debt *if* the statement is **conspicuous.**

   Example (partial payment satisfied): A contractor painted an owner's house under a contract for $2000. The owner, contending in good faith the porch was not properly painted refused to pay anything. On June 15, the contractor mailed a letter stating he needed money and the $2000. On June 18, the owner replied that he would settle for $1800. The contractor did not reply but the owner mailed a check for $1800 marked "payment in full on the painting contract dated June 18." Because he was badly in need of money, the contractor cashed the check without objection. If the contractor sues for the additional $200, he will not succeed because he cashed the check without objection and the new promise was sufficient consideration to release a claim in dispute and was made in good faith. (The fact about him badly needing money is a decoy.)

   Example (partial payment not satisfied): A testator, whose nephew was his only heir died leaving a will that gave his entire estate to charity. The nephew, knowing full well that the testator was of sound mind, filed a suit contesting the will. The testator's executor offered the nephew $5000 to settle the suit and the nephew agreed. This agreement to settle is not supported by consideration because the settlement was not based on a good faith dispute.

> **MBE tip:** Often, consideration to settle or release a claim in dispute also gives rise to an accord and satisfaction (see sec. VII.F.). Be aware that both issues are easily tested with the same fact pattern (e.g., in the above fact pattern, the newly agreed amount of $1800 was also an offer of an accord and satisfaction).

4. Contract modification rules **for consideration** differ in common law and UCC.

a. Common law: A modification **benefitting solely one party** is insufficient consideration, though even a **very minor detriment,** or the imposition of a small and disproportionate **additional duty will count as sufficient** consideration.

Example (consideration): Contractor and Owner contract for the building of a home for $100,000. Contractor is losing money on the job and asks Owner to renegotiate. The parties agree that Contractor will receive $15,000 in exchange for using a higher quality roofing material than specified in the contract. This slight modification is sufficient to find consideration for the modification.

Example (no consideration): Landowner and Contractor entered into a written contract where Contractor agreed to build a building and pave an adjacent sidewalk for $200,000. Later, Landowner entered into an oral modification that Contractor no longer had to pave the sidewalk. Contractor completed the building. After discussions with the landscaper, Landowner decided Contractor should pave the sidewalk. Contractor refused. Contractor is in breach because the oral modification was not supported by consideration so his duty to pave the sidewalk was not discharged.

1. **Except** where **unanticipated circumstances** make the modification **fair and equitable** (such as impracticability).

   Example: Two parties have a construction contract, but neither party knew the land where they planned to build a new apartment building was unstable, which greatly increases the cost to perform. Modification is fair.

b. **UCC: Consideration is not required** for a contract modification.

1. Oral modifications without consideration are acceptable, but if a contract contains a no oral modification clause, it is binding.

> **Examples of promises binding without consideration:**
> - Promises to pay past debts and obligations, such as those discharged by bankruptcy or past the statute of limitations.
> - Promises to pay for benefits received at promisor's request or in an emergency.
> - Modification of UCC contracts.
> - Guaranty to pay the debt of another. (They must state the consideration to be paid, though it need not actually be paid.)
> - Promissory estoppel (below).

F. **Promissory estoppel:** A promise that **foreseeably** (to the promisor) **induces reliance** (the promisor **intends** that the promisee rely), and is **actually relied** upon, may be enforceable **to prevent injustice,** even without consideration.

Example: An insurance company manager, aged 60, with no plans for early retirement, had worked for his company for 20 years. The company's president wrote to the manager that if he should decide to retire, the company would pay him a $2000 per month lifetime pension in recognition of his past work. Shortly thereafter, the manager retired and bought a $30,000 recreational vehicle for his planned retirement travels. After receiving the promised $2000 monthly pension for 6 months, the manager received a letter that the company would cease the pension due to budget constraints. The manager could sue for breach of contract because while the consideration was inadequate since it was for his past service, his decision to retire early and buy the recreational vehicle was in reliance on the president's promise.

1. **Substitute for consideration:** Promissory estoppel serves as a substitute for consideration.
2. **Recovery limited to reliance damages:** The plaintiff will not get the benefit of the bargain, but rather will be put in the position he would have been in if the promise was never made to prevent injustice.

> **MBE tip:** If a contract is lacking consideration, consider if promissory estoppel could make the promise enforceable. The recovery is higher with a valid contract (which would be the best choice for the highest recovery, but promissory estoppel is a good alternative where consideration is lacking).
>
> 
>
> **Decoy tip:** Avoid answers that use promissory estoppel when there was valid consideration. If valid consideration exists, then promissory estoppel will be the decoy answer. So always first analyze whether there is consideration and only look for promissory estoppel as a last resort.

III. DEFENSES TO CONTRACT FORMATION

- **Void contracts** are those that cannot be enforced by either party (as if no contract was ever formed).
- **Voidable contracts** are valid contracts but only one party is bound by the contract and the unbound party can cancel the contract.

A. The **Statute of Frauds (SOF)** provides that certain types of contracts are unenforceable unless they are in writing.

1. **Five categories** of contracts "fall within" the SOF.

a. **Marriage:** A contract made **upon consideration of marriage,** such as a promise to do or not do something if people marry (i.e., a prenuptial agreement).

Example: A father promises a man he will buy him a new yacht if he agrees to marry his daughter. This promise would need to be in writing.

b. **Real property:** A promise creating an interest in land.

Examples: The sale of a house, a mortgage, easements, or leases of at least one-year duration, etc. need to be in writing.

 c. Promise to pay the **Debt of another** (suretyship).

Example: A mom promised her daughter that she would pay her tuition, room, and board if she would go to law school. The daughter's uncle, who was present at the time, said if the mom didn't pay it, he would. The mom paid the expenses for the first year and then died. The uncle's promise to the daughter falls within the suretyship provision of the SOF and would need to be in writing to be enforceable.

d. **One-year:** A contract **incapable** of being **fully performed within one year** of the making. Time starts to run the day after the contract is made, not how long it takes to perform under the contract. Performance must be literally impossible to perform in one year.

Example: On Jan. 1, 2020, Actor contracts with Broadway to perform in a new musical for 2 years. It is impossible for Actor to perform within one year of the execution of the contract since the performance date lasts for 2 years after contracting. Therefore, the contract must satisfy the Statute of Frauds and be in writing.

 e. **Sale of Goods of $500 or more.**

Memorization tip: Use **Mr. Dog** to memorize the five categories of contracts to which the SOF applies: Marriage, Real Property, Debt of another, One-year, Goods.

MBE tip: Remember that a violation of the SOF does not affect the contract's validity, just its enforceability.

2. **SOF Exceptions** apply to each of the five categories of contracts covered by the SOF and an oral contract would be enforceable if:

a. **Marriage—Promise to marry: Contract** for the marriage itself consisting of **mutual promises to marry.**

Example: Mary promises to marry Mark. Mark promises to marry Mary.

b. **Real estate — Part performance:** Applies to an interest in **real estate** where the **conveyance** has been made, or **performed in part** (payment, improvements, or possession — think PIP). Most jurisdictions require two out of the three PIP to establish part performance. (These performance exceptions are covered thoroughly in Real Property sec. I.B.1.b.*2*.)

c. **Debt of another — Main purpose:** To pay the debt of another where the "main purpose" of the agreement is the **promisor's own economic interest** (maker's benefit) or an indemnity contract.

Example: Seller orally agreed to sell his land to Buyer for $50,000. Buyer orally agreed to pay $25,000 of the purchase price to a creditor of Seller in satisfaction of a debt that Seller said he had promised to pay the creditor. In an action filed by the creditor, the SOF would not apply here since the surety promise was made to the maker/principal (Seller) and not to the obligee (creditor) and was for Seller's benefit (payment on Seller's loan). (Note: while an interest in land is also in this question, that is not being tested and is a decoy because the contract at issue is not for the sale of an interest in land, but rather for the promise to repay Seller's $25,000 debt owed to the creditor.)

d. **One year — Full performance:** The contract can't be performed in **one year, but full performance has occurred.** If only part performance has occurred, restitution may still be available.

e. **Sale of goods $500 or more where:**

1. Goods are **Accepted or Paid for.**

2. **Admission** in a pleading or court testimony.

3. **Specially Manufactured goods** are not suitable for sale to others.

> **Memorization tip:** Following Mr. Dog for the categories that raise the SOF, continue with **Mr. Dog Can Pay Money For A Puppy And Some Milkbones** to memorize all exceptions (Can-contract for marriage itself; Pay-part performance PIP for Real Property; Money-main purpose or maker's benefit for debt; For-full performance for one-year rule; A-accepted goods; Puppy-paid for goods; And-admission for goods; Some Milkbones for specially manufactured goods).

3. **SOF writing requirement:** There must be one or more writings that combined include the **essential terms** of the contract (including the subject matter; and quantity for goods) and is **signed by the party to be charged.**

a. **Delivery:** The writing **need not be addressed to or sent to the other party.**

b. **Timing:** The writing **need not be made at the time** the promise is made.

Example: In financial straits, a nephew orally asked his uncle for a $4000 loan. The uncle replied that he would lend the nephew money if the nephew's mother guaranteed the loan. The mother agreed and wrote her son a note the next day: "Son, I was happy to do you a favor by promising your uncle I would repay your $4000 loan if you don't. /s/ Mother." Neither the son nor the mother repaid the loan. The mother raised the SOF as a defense. Her defense will not succeed because she created a writing with essential terms and she signed it (the fact that it was not addressed or sent to the uncle and that it was drafted after the agreement was made are all irrelevant decoys).

c. **Exception to the writing requirement:** The **merchant's confirming memo** allows a writing to be enforced (but only for the quantity stated in the memo) against **both parties** (signer and recipient) where it is:

1. **Between two merchants.**
2. **One party receives signed confirmation** (can be letterhead, email, fax, etc.) within a "reasonable" time and has reason to know its contents.
3. **No objection** by the recipient within **ten days** of receipt.

   Example: A ski-shop operator placed a phone order for 12 pairs of vortex-lined gloves at $600 per dozen. The glove manufacturer faxed the ski-shop operator a signed memo, "Confirming our agreement today for your purchase of a dozen pairs of vortex-lined ski gloves for $600, the shipment will be delivered in 30 days." The ski-shop operator received and read the message within minutes, but changed her mind 3 weeks later. The SOF will not be a defense for the ski-shop operator who did not sign because the fax was sufficient to satisfy the SOF as a merchant's confirmatory memo.

d. **Exception to the writing requirement: Judicial admissions** in pleadings or testimony that there was an agreement will allow the agreement to be enforced without a writing.

e. **Exception to the writing requirement:** A **promissory estoppel** theory where a party **detrimentally relied** on the agreement. (This allows a plaintiff to recover only to the extent necessary **to prevent injustice.**)

   Example: Restaurant hires Chef to open its new restaurant in a different state and orally promises a 5-year contract. In reliance on the agreement, Chef quits his current job and sells his home. If Restaurant breaches the agreement, a court could apply a promissory estoppel theory to prevent injustice, even though the contract fails to satisfy the Statute of Frauds.

STATUTE OF FRAUDS CHEAT SHEET

Statute of Frauds Approach

1. Does the contract (or modification) fall within the SOF-writing requirement? (**MR. DOG**)
2. Do any exceptions apply that take the contract out of the SOF (so no writing is required)? (**MR. DOG C**an **P**ay **M**oney **F**or **A P**uppy **A**nd **S**ome **M**ilkbones)
3. If no exceptions, is there a writing?
4. Does the writing satisfy the SOF? (Writing requirements are all met.)
5. If not, do any writing requirement exceptions apply?

SOF Applies to Contracts:	Exception (No writing required)
Made upon consideration of **M**arriage ⟶	**C**ontract for the marriage itself
Interest in **R**eal property ⟶	**P**art performance (payment, improve, possess)
Pay the **D**ebt of another ⟶	**M**aker's benefit
Can't be performed in **O**ne year ⟶	**F**ull performance
Sale of **G**oods of $500 or more ⟶	**A**ccepted or **P**aid for goods/**A**dmission/ **S**pecially **M**anufactured goods

Memorization tip: MR. DOG **C**an **P**ay **M**oney **F**or **A P**uppy **A**nd **S**ome **M**ilkbones

Writing Requirement	Writing Exceptions
Essential terms (i.e., subject matter) Signed by the party to be charged	Merchant's confirmatory memo: ◆ Between merchants ◆ One party received signed confirmation ◆ No objection within 10 days of receipt
Does NOT need to be addressed or sent to the other party	Judicial admission in pleadings or testimony that there was an agreement
Writing NOT needed at the time the promise is made	Promissory estoppel—detrimental reliance

MBE tip: Be aware that contract modifications also need to meet the SOF if the contract as modified is within the SOF.

B. A **misrepresentation** may serve as a contract defense where one party makes a misrepresentation **prior to the other signing** the contract.

1. The **state of mind** of the party making the misrepresentation **need not be intentional** (if it is intentional it is fraudulent misrepresentation, see below); it can be done negligently or even innocently (nonfraudulent misrepresentation).
2. **False statement of material fact:** It must pertain to a material fact to the contract, not an opinion.
3. **Justifiable and actual reliance:** It must be justifiable to rely on the misrepresentation, and the party must in fact rely on the misrepresentation.

C. **Fraud:** The tort of **fraud** (intentional misrepresentation) may serve as a contract defense where one party makes an **intentional misrepresentation prior to** the signing of the contract. Prima facie case:

1. **Misrepresentation of material fact:** The misrepresentation must pertain to a material fact of the contract, not an opinion;

   a. **Nondisclosure:** A person's nondisclosure of a fact known to them is equivalent to an assertion that the fact does not exist **where they know** that **disclosure is necessary** to prevent some previous assertion from being a misrepresentation.

   Example: A woman prepared an accurate statement of her financial condition and submitted it with a loan application to Bank. Shortly thereafter, her financial condition worsened, but she failed to disclose this fact to Bank. Unaware of the woman's changed financial condition, Bank agreed to lend her money. Bank later learned of her true financial condition and refused to honor its promise. Bank could succeed on a misrepresentation claim because the woman had an obligation to correct her previous representations.

2. Made with **knowledge of the statement's falsity** or **reckless disregard** of the truth (scienter);
3. **Intent to induce reliance** so the other party will enter into the contract;
4. **Causation** (actual reliance by plaintiff): The party must in fact rely on the misrepresentation;
5. **Justifiable reliance** by the plaintiff (reliance will be found justifiable unless there is clear evidence to the contrary); and
6. **Pecuniary** (money) **damages** to the plaintiff: Typically, this will be assessed under a "benefit of the bargain" contract damages analysis. A plaintiff will not be able to recover for purely emotional distress in the absence of physical harm. Punitive damages may be available.

   Example: A buyer purchased a used car from a used car dealer. Knowing it to be false, the dealer told the buyer that the car had never been in an accident. He also told him the car gets 25 miles to the gallon, and that the car was a smooth-riding car. In reliance on those statements, the buyer purchased the car. The first two statements are fraudulent statements, but the last statement "smooth-riding car" does not rise to fraud since it is more of an opinion and not a material fact.

> **MBE tip:** Questions that test misrepresentation will often ask whether the wronged party can rescind the transaction (they can) or whether the wrongdoing party will succeed in a breach of contract claim (they will not because of their misrepresentation).

D. A **mistake** is a belief **not in accord with the facts** and can be mutual or unilateral.

1. A **mutual mistake** is one made by both parties to the contract. A contract can be voidable (not enforceable against either party) for mutual mistake if:

   a. **Basic assumption:** The mistake is as to a basic assumption that **existed at the time the contract was formed;** and

   b. **Material effect:** The mistake has a material effect on the deal; and

   c. **Risk:** The adversely affected party **did not assume the risk** of the mistake. **A party bears the risk** of a mistake when:

      1. The **risk is allocated** to them **by agreement** of the parties,

      2. They are **aware,** at the time the contract was made, that **they have only limited knowledge** with respect to the facts but treats their limited knowledge as sufficient, or

      3. The risk is **allocated to them by the court** as reasonable under the circumstances.

      Example (contract voidable): On June 1, a retailer of guns received a signed letter from a gun wholesaler that they had obtained 100 assault rifles for $250 each and could guarantee shipment by August 1. On June 11, the retailer mailed the wholesaler a letter accepting the offer. On June 9, a valid federal statute making the sale of assault rifles punishable as a crime became effective. Neither the retailer nor the wholesaler was aware of this statute until June 15. Their contract is voidable due to mutual mistake.

Example (contract not voidable): A builder contracted with a property owner to design and build a 15-story building. In excavating the foundation, the builder encountered a massive layer of granite at a depth of 15 feet. By reasonable safety criteria, the foundation required a 25-foot excavation. When the contract was made, neither party was aware of the subsurface granite and neither party hired a qualified expert to test for its presence. The builder refused to proceed with the work unless the owner paid an additional $2 million, which was the additional cost to build the foundation. The builder would not succeed on his mutual mistake claim because he assumed the risk of encountering subsurface granite that was unknown to the property owner by failing to investigate the condition of the ground to be excavated.

> **MBE tip:** Look for facts that one of the parties is assuming the risk. It will not be obvious so look to see if they were at least aware they had limited knowledge and that there could be a problem (such as in the example above or where one buys an animal later found to be sterile).

2. A **unilateral mistake** is one made by only one party to the deal. A contract can be voidable by the mistaken party for unilateral mistake if:

   a. **Unconscionable:** The mistaken party can show the **three factors for mutual mistake** *and* that enforcing the contract would be **unconscionable** (see sec. IV.A.); ***or***

   b. **Knowledge:** The other party **knew,** or **should have known** of the mistake, or **caused** the mistake.

   Example: A roofer sent a contractor a bid for a job. The contractor received several other bids that were much higher than roofer's bid. The contractor had reason to suspect that the roofer made a computational error in figuring his bid but entered into an agreement with him to do the roof on an upcoming job anyway. When the roofer discovered his error the contractor refused to renegotiate the deal. The roofer's *best argument* to rescind the contract would be unilateral mistake.

E. **Duress:** If a party's manifestation of assent is **induced by an improper threat** by the other party that leaves the victim **no reasonable alternative,** the contract is voidable by the victim.

   1. **Improper threat:** A threat is improper if **what is threatened is a crime or a tort,** or what is threatened is **criminal prosecution** or the **use of civil process** made in **bad faith.** If the threat is physical the contract is void. Otherwise, the contract is voidable by the party threatened.

   Example: A mechanic agreed in writing to make repairs to a landscaper's truck for $12,000. The mechanic properly made the repairs, but when the landscaper tendered payment, the mechanic refused delivery of the truck unless the landscaper promised to pay an additional $2000. The customary charge for such work was $14,000. Because the landscaper needed the truck immediately to fulfill existing obligations, and no truck rentals were available, he promised in writing to pay the additional $2000. The mechanic will not be able to enforce this additional promise because the landscaper had no reasonable alternative but to yield to the mechanic's improper threat.

F. **Undue influence** is the **unfair persuasion** of a party who is **under the domination** of the person exercising the persuasion or is one who, in view of the **relationship** between them is **susceptible** to undue influence. [This is rarely MBE tested.]

G. **Lack of capacity** to contract because of **minority** or **insanity** (see sec. II.C.5. above).

IV. DEFENSES TO ENFORCEMENT/DUTY TO PERFORM DISCHARGED

A. **Unconscionability:** If the court finds a contract term **so unfavorable** to one party that **no reasonable person would have agreed** to it, the court may **decline to enforce** the contract or any unconscionable part of the contract. Unconscionability is **assessed at the time of contract formation.**

> **MBE tip:** Although this issue is assessed at the time of formation, it is applied as a defense to enforcement because courts may refuse to enforce a contract that is unconscionable. In contrast, the issues above in section III are defenses to formation and can result in the parties acting as though a contract was never formed. With defenses to enforcement, the contract itself is valid, but the courts will not enforce it.

Example: A landowner was land-rich by inheritance but money poor having suffered losses on bad investments. Pressed for cash, he advertised a proposed sale of standing timber on a 2000-acre lot he owned. The only response was an offer by one of the largest logging companies for 70% lower than the prevailing regional price for comparable timber rights. If the man later had investments improve and wished to get out of the timber deal, his *best argument* would be that the contract was unconscionable. (Note: this does not mean he would win, but it is an argument he can make because the contract terms were so unfavorable and unreasonable.)

> **MBE tip:** This is not a heavily tested issue, but when tested it is typically not established (because it usually involves a risk that the person knows about and assumes so it is not unreasonable) or it is used as the answer to a best argument type question since it *may* provide a defense and there are usually facts that can be argued on both sides for this issue that a jury would ultimately decide.

B. **Illegality of contract:** If the **consideration, performance,** or **subject matter** of a contract is **illegal,** then the **contract itself is unenforceable** and the duty to perform is discharged.

Examples: Contracts regarding gambling (where gambling is illegal), lending contracts that violate usury laws, an overly broad non-compete clause, performing services without the proper license, or supervening illegality of the subject matter or conduct.

1. **Exception—policy to benefit contracting party:** Where a contract violates a policy that was **intended for the benefit of a contracting party** seeking relief, the **contract may be enforced** to avoid frustrating the policy behind the statute.

   Example: An insurance company issued a policy to a homeowner. The policy failed to contain certain coverage terms required by state statute. When the homeowner suffered a loss due to theft that was within the policy's terms, the insurance company refused to pay, claiming the contract was unenforceable because it violated the statute. The homeowner will succeed in their action because they belong to the class of persons the statute is intended to protect.

2. **Exception—public policy:** A promise or other term of an **agreement is unenforceable** on grounds of public policy **if legislation provides that it is unenforceable** *or* the **interest in its enforcement** is **clearly outweighed** in the circumstances **by a public policy against the enforcement** of such terms.

   Example: In order to raise revenue, a city requires home-repair contractors performing work within city limits to pay a licensing fee. A contractor who was unaware of this fee requirement agreed to perform home repairs for a city resident. After the contractor completed the work, the resident refused to pay the contractor because he didn't pay the licensing fee. Although the contract violates the law (doesn't include the licensing fee), the court would find that public policy does not bar enforcement of the contract because the purpose of the fee is merely to raise revenue (as opposed to a regulatory purpose; e.g., it would be different if the fee was intended to regulate how contractors perform their services).

C. **Impossibility** occurs when a supervening, unforeseeable event makes performance **impossible** and thus discharges performance. The event must be one that **neither party assumed the risk** of, and performance must be literally impossible.

   Examples: Destruction of the contract subject matter, illegality, death, or the coast guard prohibits a boat from leaving shore due to a heavy storm so the boat cannot charter paid customers.

   1. **Temporary impossibility** will **suspend** contractual duties but not discharge them.

      Example: A logging company that suffered a fire in the forest would not be excused from delivering lumber (the trees will grow back so the delay is temporary).

D. **Impracticability** is when events occur that the parties assumed would not occur and it makes performance **extremely and unreasonably difficult.** The event must concern a **basic assumption** of the contract and the parties must not have **allocated the risk** of that event to the party seeking to use this defense.

   1. **Illness/Injury/Incapacity:** A person unable to perform their duty under a contract renders the performance impracticable and operates as an excuse for nonperformance.

      Example: An engineer entered into a written contract with a landowner to serve as an on-site supervisor for construction of an office building. The next day, the engineer was severely injured in a car accident and rendered physically incapable of performing as the on-site supervisor. His performance is excused due to his injury because performance is impracticable.

> **MBE tip:** Many questions involving incapacity or injury have impracticability as the correct answer for the "best" argument or defense that the incapacitated party could argue to avoid performance on the contract.
>
> 
>
> **Decoy tip:** Financial losses are usually insufficient to establish impracticability, so if money is the only loss suffered due to an unexpected event, impracticability is the wrong answer choice.

E. **Frustration of purpose** occurs when a party's purpose for entering the contract is destroyed by **supervening events.** Both parties **must know the purpose** of the contract, the event must **not be reasonably foreseeable,** and **frustration must be total.**

   Example: Watcher has contracted to rent Owner's apartment at a very high rate for two days because the apartment has a view of the King's scheduled coronation. Both parties know the purpose of the contract, which is subsequently thwarted when the coronation is cancelled. Frustration of purpose is appropriate because the event was unusual, the cancellation was not foreseeable, and Watcher's purpose for the contract was completely frustrated. Watcher will be discharged from the contract.

F. **Condition precedent not met** will **relieve the other party from performing** their obligations under the contract as **their duties are discharged** when the condition precedent is not completed. See sec. V.A. below.

G. **Novation:** Where one party is **substituted** by a new party, **the original party's duties under the contract are discharged.** See sec. VI.D.

H. **Accord and Satisfaction:** When an accord and satisfaction occur, **the original contract promise and duty to perform is discharged** and replaced with a new promise under the accord and the completion of that new promise is the satisfaction. See sec. VII.F.

CONTRACT DEFENSES DECODED

- **Void contracts** are those that cannot be enforced by either party (it is as if no contract was ever formed).
- **Voidable contracts** are valid contracts but only one party is bound by the contract and the unbound party can cancel the contract.

Defenses to Formation & Enforcement	Contract void	Contract voidable	Contract voidable by innocent P	Duty to perform discharged	Other Result
SOF					Contract not binding (can seek restitution)
Misrepresentation			X		
Fraud			X		
Mistake		X			
Duress	X (physical threat)		X*		*Voidable by one threatened
Undue influence			X		
Capacity			X*		*Voidable by incapacitated
Unconscionability					Court may not enforce all/part
Illegality	X				
Impossibility				X	
Impracticability				X	
Frustration of purpose				X	
Condition precedent not met				X	
Novation				X	
Accord & satisfaction				X	

MBE tip: MBE questions may ask a party's best defense to avoid having a contract enforced. While there are traditional defenses to contract formation and enforcement (above), any failure to create a valid contract operates as a defense to avoid the contract (such as no consideration, lack of mutual assent, a condition precedent in the contract was not met thereby excusing the other's performance, etc.).

V. INTERPRETATION OF CONTRACT TERMS AND PERFORMANCE

A. **Conditions:** A condition is an **event that must occur before performance of the other party is due.** If it does not occur, performance of the second party is excused. Conditions can be express or constructive (implied).

> MBE tip: Failure to perform a condition excuses performance, but failure to fulfill a *promise* results in breach and it does not affect the other party's promise to perform. When unclear, courts tend to favor finding promises over conditions.

Example: Buyer and Seller have a contract where Buyer purchases 10,000 tires each month. On the first of each month Buyer must inform Seller of the specific tire sizes and quantity he wants shipped that month (the condition), and then Seller ships the tires one week later in accordance with the specifications. Seller's performance (shipping the 10,000 tires each month) is not due until Buyer meets the condition of informing Seller of the specific tire sizes and quantity to ship.

1. **Express:** An express condition is created by the language of the parties demonstrating the **intent to have a condition** (e.g., "upon condition that," "provided that," or similar language).

   Example: A clause stating, "Buyer's duty to pay under the contract is conditioned upon the carpet stains being entirely removed."

2. **Constructive** (implied): A constructive condition is one **supplied by the court** for fairness. Each party's performance is generally a constructive condition to the subsequent performance required by the other party.

3. **Timing of conditions**

   a. **Concurrent conditions** require that each party's duty to perform is conditioned on the other party's duty to perform (both perform at the same time).

   Example: A and B contract for B to sell A his car for $5000. A must pay B for his car at the same time B delivers the car to A.

   b. **Condition precedent** requires that one party's performance be completed *prior* to the other party's performance.

   Example: A photographer has to take pictures and deliver them to the client before the client must pay. Failure to deliver the pictures would discharge the client's duty to pay.

   c. **Condition subsequent** may excuse a duty to perform *after* a particular event occurs.

   Example: Owner and Buyer contract for Owner to convey land to Buyer and Buyer will pay Owner $1000 per month for 12 months. A provision in the contract states that the obligation to pay the monthly payments will be voided if Owner has not removed the shed from the land within three months of the contract.

4. **Compliance with conditions**

   a. **Express conditions** require **strict compliance,** except where waived or excused, though a waiver can be retracted before reliance. The nonoccurrence of an express condition will discharge the contractual obligation of a party. (Note: if neither party is prepared or able to perform when there are concurrent conditions, then both parties' performances are excused.)

Example: Retailer entered into a contract with Toy Factory that provided Toy Factory had to deliver 1000 mechanical dogs to Retailer no later than November 15 for the Yule shopping season (this is the express condition) and after delivery, Retailer would pay for the dogs. Toy Factory failed to deliver the dogs by November 15 as promised, which gave Retailer the right to terminate the contract and claim damages (since there was not strict compliance).

> **Decoy tip:** While there may also be facts in a question about trade usage (which will provide a decoy answer), evidence of express conditions is given greater weight.

b. **Constructive conditions** only require **substantial compliance.**

   Example: A contractor painted an owner's house under a contract that called for payment of $2000, but didn't specify when payment was due. It is implied that payment is due when the paint job is finished so the painter cannot stop painting after completing 25% and demand payment since 25% completion would not be substantial compliance.

c. **Satisfaction clauses:** When a party's obligation under a contract is subject to a satisfaction condition, generally the party may not avoid liability simply by expressing dissatisfaction with the performance. The dissatisfaction must be expressed either **reasonably** or in **good faith.**

   Example: A homeowner contracted in writing with a kitchen contractor to renovate her kitchen for $25,000, "subject to the homeowner's complete personal satisfaction." The contractor replaced the cabinets, flooring and countertops, and then sought payment. The homeowner only paid the contractor $20,000 and truthfully said that she did not like the finish on the cabinets and therefore was not satisfied. If the contractor sues for the additional $5000 he will not succeed because the homeowner was in good faith not satisfied.

d. **Good faith required:** All contracts have an implied duty of good faith and fair dealing so parties must make good faith efforts to comply with all conditions or they may be in breach for failure to fulfill the condition.

5. **Waiver of conditions:** The party the condition is **intended to benefit** always has the power to waive it. Waiver can occur by:

   a. **Benefit:** Receiving and keeping a benefit, **or**

   b. **Failure to insist on compliance** can operate as a waiver.

      Example: Buyer and Seller have a contract where Buyer purchases 10,000 tires each month for 10 months. The contract requires Buyer to pay for the goods at the time of delivery. However, for the first three months Buyer mails payment to Seller one week after delivery and Seller accepts payment. Seller has likely implicitly waived the condition requiring payment at the time of delivery.

   c. A **waiver can be retracted** unless the other party detrimentally relied.

      Example: If Seller in the above tire example informed Buyer that starting in month 5, they had to pay on delivery as contracted, Buyer would be expected to pay on delivery since Seller can retract its prior waiver.

> **MBE tip:** Some MBE questions use the term "aleatory contract," which is a contract such as insurance policy where the parties do not have to perform until an event occurs (i.e., insurance will not pay until an accident occurs).

B. **Parol Evidence Rule (PER):** The PER limits the extent to which evidence of discussions or writings made **prior to, or contemporaneous with,** the signed written contract can be admitted and **considered as part of the agreement.** The rule depends on whether the writing is a total integration or partial integration.

1. **Partial integration** is one intended to be the **final expression** of the agreement, but ***not* intended to include all details** of the parties' agreement.

   a. **PER is *not*** allowed to **contradict** a term in a partially integrated contract.

   Example: Contract to sell/buy a gray horse. Oral discussions prior to the written agreement are inadmissible to show it should be a brown horse because it is a contradiction to an existing term.

   b. **PER *is*** allowed to **supplement** a term in a partially integrated contract.

   Example: Contract to sell/buy a gray horse. Oral discussions prior to the written agreement are admissible to show the horse was to come with a saddle because it is a supplemental term.

2. **Total integration** is the **final expression** of the agreement, **and** is also **intended to include all details** of the agreement.

   a. **PER is *not*** allowed to **contradict** or **supplement** a term in a totally integrated contract.

3. **PER exceptions:** The PER **will not apply** to bar certain types of evidence.

   a. **Contract formation or enforcement defects are allowed:** The PER does not bar evidence of contract defects (e.g., allegations of fraud, duress, mistake, lack of consideration, illegality, or anything that would make the contract void).

   Example: A seller and a buyer agree to the sale of Greenacre for $5000 and orally marked its bounds as "that line of trees down there, the ditch that intersects them, the fence on the other side, and that street on the fourth side." If the written contract that thereafter followed mistakenly included two acres beyond the fence, the oral discussion as to the bounds would be admissible to show the contract formation mistake that forms the basis for reformation of the contract.

   b. **Conditions precedent to the contract's effectiveness allowed:** The PER does not bar evidence of **conditions precedent** to the contract's effectiveness. This exception applies to a situation where the parties agree that the **contract itself will not take force** until some stated condition is met.

   Example: A written contract is signed between a property owner and an architect for the architect to create a new landscape for the owner's yard. Shortly before the agreement was signed, the parties orally agree that the contract will not be in effect until the owner's spouse approved the design. PER will not bar the introduction of evidence regarding the condition that the spouse first approve the design, because that is a condition precedent to the contract's effectiveness.

   c. **Ambiguous terms allowed:** The **PER does not bar evidence** regarding the interpretation of **ambiguous contract terms.** The UCC provides the following rules to aid in contract interpretation:

      1. **Course of performance** refers to evidence of the conduct of **these parties** regarding the **contract at hand.** (This is the best evidence to use if available.)

      Example: A radio manufacturer and a retailer entered into a final written agreement for the retailer to buy all of its requirements of radios, estimated at 20 units per month, for two years. A dispute later arose at the end of the two-year term when the retailer returned 25 undefective radios for full credit and the manufacturer refused to extend the contract for a second two-year term. The contract was silent as to the return of undefective radios. The retailer seeks to introduce evidence that during the two years of the agreement, they had returned 125 undefective radios for various reasons. The evidence would be admissible as course of performance evidence as to what the parties intended the writing to mean.

2. **Course of dealing** refers to evidence of the conduct of **these parties** regarding **past contracts** between them. (Second best evidence.)

   Example: Seller and Buyer have dealt with each other for five years in hundreds of separate grain contracts. After delivery of the grain, each invoice was silent in regard to any discount but the custom of the grain trade is to allow a 2% discount for payment within 10 days (trade usage). In all of their prior transactions and without objection from Seller, Buyer took 15 days to pay and deducted 5%. Under the present contract, Seller refused to give a discount and Buyer was asked to pay immediately. Evidence of the past discount and time to pay in the previous contracts would be admissible as course of dealing. (Facts about trade usage are decoys.)

3. **Usage of trade** refers to evidence of the meaning **others** in the **same industry and/or locality** would attach to a term. (Least persuasive evidence, so only use as evidence if the previous two are unavailable.)

   Example: A contract calls for a beverage distribution company to distribute Fizzy Cola. The contract said nothing about restrictions on other products the distribution company could distribute. Six months later, the distribution company started distributing Cool Cola. If Fizzy Cola sues the distribution company, evidence that it has been industry practice in the soft-drink industry for distributors to only handle one brand of cola would be admissible as trade usage evidence.

> **MBE tip:** Under the UCC, course of performance, course of dealing, and usage of trade can be used to interpret ambiguous terms even in the absence of the PER. If contract terms are ambiguous, they should always be construed against the party who drafted the contract as they should have known their meaning.

PAROL EVIDENCE CHEAT SHEET

Evidence offered	Evidence allowed	Evidence not allowed
A **contradictory** term in a ***partially integrated*** contract		X
A **supplemental** term in a ***partially integrated*** contract.	X	
A **contradictory** term in a ***totally integrated*** contract.		X
A **supplemental** term in a ***totally integrated*** contract.		X
Terms that go to **contract formation or enforcement defects** (fraud, mistake, duress, consideration, illegality, etc.).	X	
Terms that show a **condition precedent.**	X	
Course of performance for *ambiguous* terms.	X	
Course of dealing for *ambiguous* terms.	X	
Usage of trade for *ambiguous* terms.	X	

MBE tip: Most questions that test the PER ask about the "best" argument a party can make (to either avoid the introduction of the evidence or have it come in). The answer is usually to argue that either the agreement was partially integrated or totally integrated (depending on whether the party wants the extrinsic evidence to come in or not).

Decoy tip: Pay attention to the timing of the other discussions or writings that were separate from the contract as the PER does NOT apply to *subsequent* agreements. Answer choices implicating PER are often wrong when the timing is off.

C. **Risk of loss:** Contracts are often silent as to which party should bear the risk of loss **when goods are damaged or destroyed** *before* the buyer receives them. The following rules determine which party bears the risk when the contract does not contain terms to the contrary.

1. **Goods to be shipped by third-party carrier:** If the contract requires the seller to ship the goods by carrier, the risk of loss depends on whether the contract is a shipment or destination contract.

    a. **Shipment contract (presumed if not stated):** The **risk of loss passes to the buyer** when the **seller delivers** the goods **to the third-party carrier** *and* makes a **reasonable contract for their carriage** (transport) *and* notifies the buyer of shipment. If the **contract does not specify the place of delivery,** it is **presumed to be a shipment contract.** (Just because the contract has the address the goods need to be shipped to does not make it a destination contract.)

Example: A buyer and a seller entered into a contract for the sale of 10,000 novelty bracelets. The contract specified that the seller would ship the bracelets by third-party carrier but did not specify who was to pay the costs of the carriage or the place for tender for the bracelets. The risk of loss would pass to the buyer when the seller delivered the bracelets to a carrier and a proper contract for carriage was made.

b. **Destination contract:** If the contract **requires delivery at a particular location,** it is a destination contract, and the **risk of loss passes to the buyer** when the seller **delivers the goods** at the specified location. Simply noting the buyer's address on the contract is not sufficient to establish a destination contract. The contract itself must contain more language to explicitly indicate that it is a destination contract (i.e., the contract itself states that the goods must be delivered to the buyer at a particular destination as opposed to a contract where the buyer just ordered items online and then later after the contract was formed provided a shipping address).

c. **Goods destroyed before risk of loss passes:** If goods that were **identified when the contract was made** (i.e., a specific antique mirror) are destroyed **without fault** by either party *and* **before risk of loss passes** to the buyer, the **contract is avoided** (as if there were no contract—similar to void in defenses, but the UCC calls it avoided).

Example: Seller and Buyer entered into a contract for the sale of an antique car for $20,000. At the time the car was on display in a museum in a different city and was to be delivered by August 1. On July 15, before the risk of loss had passed to Buyer, the car was destroyed by fire without fault of either party. Subsequent to the contract but before the fire, the car had increased in value to $30,000. Seller sued Buyer for the contract price of $20,000 and Buyer counterclaimed for $30,000. The court will find that the contract is avoided and each party is relieved of its respective obligation to perform.

d. **Terminology** used in contracts:

1. **F.O.B. (free on board)** followed by a location indicates that the **risk of loss passes** to the buyer **at that location** and the **seller needs to give notice to the buyer** that the goods are with the carrier.

a. **Shipment contract:** If the location is the **seller's place** it is a shipment contact. The **risk of loss passes** to the buyer **at that location** (when delivered to a carrier like above).

b. **Destination contract:** If the location is the **buyer's place or another location** (not the seller's business) it is a destination contract. The **risk of loss passes** to the buyer **once the goods are delivered to that location.**

Example: A written contract required Seller to deliver to Buyer 500 chairs at $20 each F.O.B. Seller's place of business. Seller placed the chairs on board a carrier. While in transit the goods were destroyed in a derailment of the carrier's railroad car. Seller can recover the contract price because the risk of loss passed to Buyer when the goods were delivered to the carrier. (Note: if the facts stated "F.O.B. Buyer's place of business," then Seller could not recover the contract price since the risk of loss would not yet have passed to Buyer.)

2. **Goods *not* shipped by third-party carrier** (e.g., goods are delivered by the seller himself or picked up by the buyer, etc.): The **risk of loss** is on the **seller** until the seller satisfies the contractual delivery obligations and the **buyer takes possession** of the goods. If the seller is **not a merchant,** risk of loss passes to the buyer upon tender of delivery. [This is rarely MBE tested.]

RISK OF LOSS CHEAT SHEET		
Facts	**Risk on Seller**	**Risk on Buyer**
Contract to sell a car and Buyer still has to meet Seller to pick up the car. Car is destroyed on the way to meet Buyer. (Goods not shipped by carrier)	X	
Contract to sell goods but delivery details not included. Seller tenders goods to train for delivery to Buyer. Train derails and goods are destroyed. (Shipment contract)		X
Contract to sell goods and contract specifies goods to be delivered at Buyer's place of business. Seller tenders goods to train for delivery to Buyer. Train derails and goods destroyed. (Destination contract)	X	
Antique car named in contract to be delivered in one month. Car is destroyed in an earthquake. (Contract avoided—neither party has risk)		

D. **Contract modification**

1. **Oral contract modifications:** Oral contract modifications are generally allowed.

    a. **Except Statute of Frauds (SOF):** With an oral contract modification, if the **contract as modified** falls within the **SOF,** the **modification must be in writing.** Where the modification must be in writing and isn't, the modification is unenforceable, and **the original contract stands** and is enforceable. However, the ineffective oral modification may operate as a waiver.

2. **Contract modification requirements** differ depending on whether the contract is subject to the common law or the UCC.

    a. **Common law: Mutual assent** and **consideration is required** to modify a common law contract. See sec. II.E.4. for examples.

    b. **UCC: Mutual assent** and **good faith** is required, but **consideration is *not* required** to modify a UCC contract. See sec II.E.4.

    <u>**Example**</u>**:** Manufacturer agreed, in writing, to sell 40,000 pens at $1 each to Retailer, with delivery in two installments. The contract was silent as to the time of payment, but the two parties later orally agreed that the entire purchase price was to be paid on delivery of the second installment. After the first delivery, Manufacturer demanded payment and Retailer refused. Manufacturer would not succeed in an action against Retailer because their modification as to payment was made in good faith and did not require additional consideration under the UCC. (Note: as to the SOF issue with the oral modification, the goods were delivered and accepted so this is an exception for goods with the SOF and a good example of how many rules can be tested with a single fact pattern. The SOF provided a nice decoy answer.)

VI. THIRD-PARTY RIGHTS

THIRD PARTIES CHEAT SHEET

	Party affecting another party's rights or performance	Party performing	Party receiving performance
Third-party beneficiary	Promisee (*promises to benefit another*)	Promisor (PerformOR)	Third-party beneficiary
Assignment-rights	Assignor (*assigns their rights to another*)	Obligor (Obligated to be performOR)	Assignee
Delegation-duties	Delegator (*original party who was supposed to perform*)	Delegatee (takes over duty to perform)	Obligee

MBE tip: To know which rules to apply when third parties are involved in a contract:
- ◆ Third-party beneficiaries are apparent *at the time of* contracting.
- ◆ Assignment and/or delegation occurs *after* contracting.

A. **Third-party beneficiary** contracts are those made for the benefit of a third-party.

1. **Parties to third-party beneficiary:**

   a. The **promisee** is the party in the original contract who intended to confer a benefit on the third party.

   b. The **promisor** is the party in the original contract who must complete the performance to benefit the third party.

   c. The **third-party beneficiary** is the person who benefits from a contract made between two other parties.

2. **Intended beneficiary:** An intended beneficiary is one **intended by the promisee** to benefit from the contract.

   Example: Mother promised her son who had no car that she would "pay anyone from whom you buy a car the full purchase price thereof." The son bought a car from dealership on credit for $8000. At the time, the dealership was unaware of the mother's promise but learned shortly after the sale. The dealership is intended to receive the benefit of the bargain and is a third-party beneficiary who can sue under the contract. (The fact that the dealer found out later is irrelevant because the mother and son intended for the dealer to benefit if the son found a car to buy.)

   a. There are **two types** of intended beneficiaries:

1. **Creditor beneficiary:** This is a third-party beneficiary to whom the promisee intends to benefit because the promisor **owes him money.**

2. **Donee beneficiary:** This is a third-party beneficiary to whom the promisee intends to give a **gift** of performance under the contract.

b. **Vesting of rights:** The promisor and promisee **retain the power to modify the contract or discharge** a duty owed (i.e., rescind the contract) to an intended beneficiary **unless and until the beneficiary's rights vest.** Upon vesting, the contract cannot be modified or a duty discharged. Intended third-party beneficiary **rights can vest** when the third-party beneficiary:

1. **Justifiably relies** *and* **materially changes position** on that reliance; or

2. **Sues to enforce** the contract; or

3. **Manifests assent** at the request of the promisee or promisor.

Example (rights vested): A wealthy widow contracted with a car dealer to buy her son a new Rolls-Royce car worth $200,000 as a wedding gift. The contract stated that the car was "to be delivered to the son as a wedding gift." The widow handed a copy of the contract to her son that same day. In reliance on the prospective gift, the son sold his nearly new expensive sports car to a dealer at a bargain price of $50,000 and informed the widow and car dealer that he had done so. A week later, the widow and the car dealer rescinded their agreement. The son can sue to enforce the contract since his rights vested when he sold his car (justifiable reliance and material change of position).

Example (rights did not vest): A wealthy widow wishing to make a substantial gift to her adult stepson established a savings account for him. She retained possession of it and the stepson was not informed of the account. Thereafter, the widow became disgusted by the stepson's behavior and changed the account so that it was not to go to him. Thereafter the stepson learned of the account and wants the $10,000 in it. While he was an intended beneficiary, the widow abrogated (negated) his rights before they vested because he did not know about the account's existence nor did he rely on it.

3. **Incidental beneficiary:** An incidental beneficiary is one who **indirectly benefits** from the contract, but that result is **not the intent** of the promisee.

Example: Landowner and Developer entered into a contract for Developer to buy 2000 acres with timber and wild game. Developer's plans would flatten the land by cutting down all trees and removing the habitat. Landowner repudiated the contract. The neighbor who was looking forward to the removal of the trees that were obstructing his view sued to enforce the contract. The neighbor would be an incidental beneficiary to the contract because the benefit received by Developer removing all timber is incidental, not for neighbor's benefit and not the point of the underlying contract.

4. **Rights of third-party beneficiary:**

a. **Intended beneficiary v. promisor** (party to perform): An intended beneficiary **can sue the promisor** to enforce the contract, *unless* there is a valid **defense** to the contract (the beneficiary stands in the shoes of the promisee so the promisor can raise any defenses against the third-party beneficiary that they would have had against the promisee).

b. **Intended beneficiary v. promisee** (party who intended to benefit the third-party beneficiary):

1. A **creditor** beneficiary **can sue** the promisee.

2. A **donee** beneficiary **cannot sue** the promisee, *unless* the donee **told them** about the contract and they **detrimentally relied** on it.

c. **Incidental beneficiaries cannot sue** either the promisee or promisor.

d. **Promisee** (party intending to benefit the third-party) **v. promisor** (party to perform): If the promisor fails to perform under the contract, the **promisee can sue the promisor** to enforce the contract.

THIRD-PARTY BENEFICIARY RIGHTS CHEAT SHEET

Plaintiff	Defendant	Can sue	Cannot sue
Intended creditor beneficiary	Promisor/promisee	X	
Intended donee beneficiary	Promisor	X	
Intended donee beneficiary	Promisee		X*
Incidental beneficiary	Promisor/promisee		X
Promisee	Promisor	X	

*Unless detrimental reliance.
Promisor: The party required to perform.
Promisee: The party who intended to benefit the beneficiary.

MBE tip: If you get the parties confused, remember, the promisOR is the performOR.

B. **Assignment:** An assignment is when a party to an existing contract **transfers their rights** under the contract to a **third party**. The **general rule** is that **all rights are assignable,** *unless* the contract contains a **no-assignment clause that specifically states that assignments will be void** (a no-assignment clause alone does not make the assignment invalid without the word "void," or similar language).

1. **Parties to an assignment:**

   a. The **assignor** is the **original party** set to receive performance under the contract who **assigns their rights** to a third party.

   b. The **assignee** is the third party who **receives the rights** from the assignor to receive the performance due under the contract from the obligor.

   c. The **obligor** is the original party to the contract **who will perform** to assignee.

MBE tip: To remember the parties in an assignment, the obligOR is obligated to be a performOR.

Example (assignment): Seller and Buyer have a contract for the purchase of 50 microwaves at $100 per microwave. Seller has Buyer pay directly to Whirlpool the $5000 owed under the contract. This is a contract assignment and Seller (assignor) has transferred their right to receive payment of $5000 under the contract from Buyer (obligor) to Whirlpool (assignee).

Example (no assignment): Builder borrowed $10,000 from Lender to finance a small construction job under a contract with Homeowner. Builder gave Lender a writing that stated, "Any money I receive from Homeowner will be paid immediately to Lender." Builder died after completing the job but before Homeowner paid. Lender demanded that Homeowner pay the $10,000 directly to Lender. Homeowner refused and said he was going to pay Builder's estate. Lender does not have the right to receive the $10,000 from Homeowner because there was no assignment (had Builder wrote that Homeowner was to pay the money *directly* to Lender there would have been an assignment, but Builder promising to pay Lender himself later after Builder pays him is not an assignment).

2. **No consideration** is required.
3. A **gratuitous assignment** (gift) is allowed.
4. The **assignee "stands in the shoes"** of the assignor and takes subject to all defenses, set-offs, and counterclaims the assignor has.

   Example: Seller and Buyer have a contract for the purchase of 50 microwaves at $50 per microwave. Seller (assignor) has Buyer (obligor) pay to Whirlpool (assignee) the $5000 owed under the contract. If Seller fails to supply the microwaves, Buyer can refuse to pay Whirlpool and defend on breach of contract grounds, just as he could against the Seller.

5. **Revocation:** The assignor (original party receiving performance) retains the **power to revoke** the assignment *unless and until* the **assignee obtains performance** from the obligor *or* the assignee has **detrimentally relied** on the assignment.

   Example: A debtor's $1000 contractual obligation to a creditor was due on July 1. On the preceding June 15, the creditor called her niece and said, "As my birthday gift to you, you may collect the $1000 owed to me." The debtor didn't like the niece and refused to pay her and gave the money to the creditor, who accepted it without objection. The creditor accepting the money without objection acted as an effective revocation of the assignment (the assignee niece had not detrimentally relied, so the assignment was revocable).

6. **Exception:** Rights that would **materially change** the **obligor's duty or risk cannot be assigned.**

   Example: A children's book writer has a contract with a publisher to publish the writer's book. The writer assigns the contract to a friend who is a mystery writer. The publisher is not obligated to publish the mystery writer's book. The assignment is ineffective because the publisher's risk and duties with the new writer would be materially changed.

Decoy tip: Even if the contract prohibits assignments (has a no-assignment clause), often the assignment itself will still be enforceable, BUT the party who assigned their rights, against the contract terms, will be in breach. Be careful to distinguish that the assignment may still be valid despite the breach.

Example: In a written contract Seller agreed to deliver to Buyer 500 chairs. The contract provided that neither party will assign the contract. Thereafter, Seller assigned her rights to her friend. Buyer did not pay, and the friend seeks to recover the contract price. Friend is an assignee and can seek to recover the contract price for the chairs. However, Buyer also has the right to sue Seller for breach of contract for violating the no-assignment clause (but this does not mean that the assignment itself was invalid).

C. **Delegation** is when a party to an existing contract **delegates to a third party** the **duties owed** (duties to perform) under the contract. The general rule is that **most duties can be delegated,** *unless* the other party has a **substantial interest** in having the original delegator (person initially required to perform) perform.

1. **Parties to a delegation:**
   a. The **delegator** is the **original party owing performance** who delegates their duty to perform to a third party.
   b. The **delegatee** is **the third party now performing** the performance due under the contract.
   c. The **obligee** is the party receiving performance.

   Example: Owner and Painter have a contract for Painter to paint Owner's house for $5000. Painter (delegator) delegates to another comparable painter (delegatee) the paint job for Owner (obligee). This is a contract delegation since Painter has delegated his *duties* to the other painter to paint the house under the contract. (Note: if the other comparable painter does not paint the house properly, Owner can still sue the original Painter for damages.)

2. **Liability:** The **delegator** (party owing original performance) **remains liable,** absent a novation (see below).
3. **Exception—nondelegable duties: Duties of special skill** or judgment or duties that would **impair** the other party's **reasonable expectations** under the agreement, **cannot be delegated.**

   Example: Contracts to make wine from unique grapes or paint a portrait, may be nondelegable if the party receiving performance would have their expectations impaired or if they have a substantial interest in having the delegator (original performing party) perform personally because there is skill involved.

D. **Novation:** A novation occurs when the obligee (party receiving performance) **expressly agrees to accept** the performance of the delegatee (the new third-party performer) instead of the delegator (the original party owing performance).

   1. **Liability:** A novation **terminates the liability of the delegator.**

DELEGATION/ASSIGNMENT V. NOVATION EXAMPLES

No Novation (Assignment/Delegation only)	Novation
Assignor/Delegator remains liable	**Delegator NOT liable**
Painter contracts to paint Farmer's barn. Painter assigns the contract to a contractor.	Painter contracts to paint Farmer's barn. Painter assigns the contract to a contractor. In writing, Farmer expressly agrees to accept contractor's performance instead of Painter's.
Builder contracts with Owner to install an air conditioning unit. Builder sold his business to Contractor who agreed to install Owner's air conditioning unit.	Builder contracts with Owner to install an air conditioning unit. Builder sold his business to Contractor who agreed to install Owner's air conditioning unit. Owner expressly agreed to substitute Contractor for Builder.

Decoy tip: Novation rarely occurs on MBE questions, so most answer choices that state the original party in an assignment or delegation is not liable are wrong answers. For a novation to occur, the facts have to clearly state that the party expressly agreed to the substitution (which would give the issue away).

VII. BREACH OF CONTRACT ISSUES

A. **Anticipatory repudiation:** An anticipatory repudiation is an **unequivocal** expression by a party, occurring **before the time for performance** is due, that the party **will not perform** under the contract.

Example (anticipatory repudiation): Builder and Landowner signed a contract that Builder would build a house according to Landowner's specifications for $60,000, with work to commence on April 1. On February 1, Builder notified Landowner that he would lose money on the job at that price and would not proceed with the work unless Landowner agreed to pay $90,000. This is an anticipatory repudiation as Builder unequivocally expressed that he would not complete the job before the time for performance was due.

Example (no anticipatory repudiation): Buyer and Seller contracted for Buyer to buy Seller's cattle ranch with the transaction set to close on December 1. On November 1, Buyer told Seller, "I am unhappy with our contract because of the current cattle market, and do not intend to buy your ranch unless I'm legally obligated to do so." This is not an *unequivocal* expression that he will not perform so this is not an anticipatory repudiation.

1. **Non-repudiating party response:** Once a party has anticipatorily repudiated, the non-repudiating party can take four courses of action:

    a. **Sue immediately** for breach even though the time to perform under the contract has not yet passed (but, they **cannot do** this if the only part of the performance left is payment), **or**

    b. **Suspend performance** and wait until performance is due to sue, **or**

    c. **Treat the contract as discharged** and the repudiation as an offer to rescind, **or**

    d. **Urge performance** under the contract and sue later if efforts are futile.

2. **Non-breaching party must** try to **mitigate damages.**

3. **Repudiating party can retract** the repudiation except where the other party:

    a. **Sues for breach,**

    b. Changes position in **reliance** on the repudiation, or

    c. **States the repudiation is** considered **final.**

    Example: Seller and Buyer entered into a contract for Buyer to buy Seller's cattle ranch with a closing date of December 1. Buyer unequivocally repudiated the contract on October 1. On October 15, Seller urged Buyer to change her mind, but Buyer did not respond. On November 30, Seller sold the ranch to another rancher. On December 1, Buyer tried to close by tendering the purchase price. Buyer cannot sue for breach of contract because she did not retract her repudiation before Seller changed his position in reliance on Buyer's repudiation.

4. **Right to demand adequate assurances:** Where the conduct of a party is not unequivocal enough to rise to the level of an anticipatory repudiation, but does cause **reasonable grounds for insecurity** about their forthcoming performance, the insecure party can **demand adequate assurances** of due performance. This must be done in **writing.** The insecure party **may suspend their own performance** until receiving adequate assurances.

    Example: Buyer contracted with Seller to purchase 10,000 bushels of soybeans to be delivered in 90 days. Two days later, they contracted for Buyer to also purchase 10,000 bushels of wheat. Before the time for delivery for the soybeans, Seller notified Buyer that Seller's wheat supplier refused to extend additional credit to Seller and therefore Seller had no wheat available for the Buyer. Due to the lack of credit, Buyer has reasonable grounds for insecurity about the ability of Seller to fulfill the soybean order too (as it might not be able to pay its supplier for that as well) so Buyer can demand adequate assurances that Seller can perform on the soybean contract.

a. **Failure to timely respond:** A **repudiation** of the contract occurs when a party who received a **justified written demand** for adequate assurances **fails to respond** within a **reasonable time,** not to exceed **30 days.**

B. **Material breach under common law:** A contract breach is material where there was **not substantial performance** on the contract. A material breach **will excuse the performance** of the non-breaching party.

1. **Factors to consider** in determining whether the breach was material include:

a. Whether the non-breaching party **received a substantial benefit;**

b. Extent of any **part or full performance** and the **likelihood of completing performance;**

c. **Willfulness of breach:** The more intentional it is, the more likely it's a material breach; and

d. **Hardship to the breaching party.**

Example: Landowner and Builder entered a contract that Builder would erect a boathouse for Landowner. The total price was $10,000 to be paid in three installments. Landowner completed the building one month late and Landowner refused to pay Builder the last installment. Since the one-month delay was not a material breach and Builder did complete the full project, Landowner cannot withhold his entire payment (but he could offset the amount owed with any damages caused by the delay).

2. **Time is *not* of the essence** in a contract **unless specifically agreed to,** and thus a reasonable delay will not amount to a material breach (e.g., having a due date alone does not make time of the essence, *but* having a due date with a promise or performance that must be completed by a date in order to sell the house would be specific enough to make time of the essence **if the parties knew that it must be done by that date and the reason for it**).

3. **Divisible contract:** A divisible contract is one where the parties have divided up their performance into **agreed equivalents,** which means that each corresponding part performance is roughly equal to the corresponding part of compensation. These are similar to installment contracts under the UCC.

Example: Owner agrees to have Builder build him three different structures on three different properties. Each structure is distinct and has its own price. Builder can require payment after each structure is built because the contract is divisible and courts will treat each structure as its own equivalent part.

a. **Breach of a divisible contract:** For purposes of breach, each agreed equivalent **operates as a separate contract.** Thus, a party can recover for substantial performance on one divisible piece, but the other party can counterclaim for breach on the remainder of the contract.

4. **Employment contracts: Permanent employment means "at will"** employment in which either party **can terminate the agreement at any time** without the termination being considered a breach. (Contracts for a set time can be breached resulting in expectation damages to the non-breaching party.)

a. **Exception:** If the termination **violates public policy or a law** (i.e., discrimination), then it can establish a breach.

C. **Material breach under UCC:** The rules for breach are different under the UCC.

1. **Perfect tender:** The "perfect tender" rule applies to contracts for a **single delivery** and provides that if the goods tendered **fail to conform** to the contract in any respect, subject to the seller's right to cure (below), the buyer has three choices:

   a. **Reject the whole** within a **reasonable time** and **seasonably notify** the seller of his rejection, **or**

   b. **Accept the whole, or**

   c. **Accept any commercial unit** (i.e., a "whole" part—a set of 12 mugs if sold in packs of 12; or one machine if sold individually) **and reject the rest.**

   Example: A buyer ordered 500 bushels of No. 1 peaches from the seller. The seller shipped 500 bushels of No. 2 peaches. The error was caused by the negligence of the seller's shipping clerk. Although a contract was formed when the seller shipped the peaches, the buyer may reject the goods if he does so within a reasonable time after delivery. (Note: this is yet another example that illustrates how you need to know multiple issues to answer one question—here you needed to also know that the shipping of nonconforming goods without acknowledgement was an acceptance and breach simultaneously, which gives rise to this perfect tender issue being tested under breach.)

2. **Perfect Tender Exceptions:**

   a. **Installment contracts:** The **"perfect tender" rule does not apply to installment contracts** where the parties have contracted for more than one delivery. The right to reject is determined by **"substantial conformity"** and whether the imperfect tender **substantially affects the contract** (the buyer cannot reject if the seller can cure the tender, but the buyer can deduct damages for losses caused by the nonconformity).

   Example: A mill and a bakery entered into a written contract that obligated the mill to deliver 1000 pounds of flour to the bakery every Monday for 10 weeks. On week 8, the mill delivered 800 pounds of flour on Tuesday and told the bakery that the shortage would be made up on the following delivery. The late delivery and 200-pound shortage *will not significantly disrupt the bakery's operations*. The bakery must accept the 800 pounds because the shortage and timing did not substantially affect the contract. The mill must also notify the bakery it will deduct for losses due to the nonconforming tender.

   b. **Waiver,** which can be express or implied through trade usage or course of dealing.

> **MBE tip:** One way an offer can be accepted is by the shipment of nonconforming goods. When this happens, it is both an acceptance of the offer and a simultaneous breach of the same contract because the goods tendered fail under the "perfect tender" rule.

3. **Seller's right to cure:** The buyer's right to reject nonconforming goods is subject to the seller's right to cure the defect. A seller may cure the defect any time **before performance is due,** with the following provisions:

   a. **Notice:** The seller must give notice to the buyer; **and**

   b. **New tender:** The seller must make a new tender **within the time for performance.** The seller may even make a new tender ***after* the time for performance** *if* the seller has a **reasonable belief the goods would be acceptable** to the buyer or that a financial allowance for the different performance would be acceptable to the buyer.

Example: Buyer ordered 500 two-inch ties to be delivered by July 1. Seller delivered 500 three-inch ties on June 4. Buyer rejected the shipment for nonconforming goods. Seller notified Buyer that they would deliver the proper ties on time. Seller delivered the correct ties on June 30 and Buyer rejected them. Buyer cannot reject the correct ties because Seller had the right to cure and properly did so within the time for performance.

D. **Minor breach:** If a breach is not material, it is a minor breach and the nonbreaching party **may recover damages but must still perform.**

E. **Warranties:** There are several contract warranties that may be violated.

1. **Express:** An express warranty is **made explicitly** from any affirmation of fact or promise (not an opinion) made by the seller to the buyer. These may be made by a merchant or nonmerchant seller.

2. ***Implied* warranty of merchantability** exists in every contract **by a merchant** for the sale of goods and warrants that goods will be **fit for the ordinary purpose** for which such goods are used, and be of fair average quality, adequately contained, packaged, or labeled, conform to promises on the label, etc.

   a. **Disclaimer:** The warranty **can be disclaimed** orally or in writing (i.e., sold "as is") but disclaimers **must mention "merchantability,"** and if it is in writing, it must be **conspicuous.**

3. ***Implied* warranty of fitness for a particular purpose** only applies where the **buyer relies on the seller's judgment** to select appropriate goods for a stated purpose. The seller need not be a merchant.

   a. **Disclaimer:** The warranty can be disclaimed but **only if in writing and conspicuous.** (Unlike the warranty of merchantability, the fitness warranty does not need to utilize any particular language.)

4. ***Implied* covenant of good faith and fair dealing** is inherent in every contract.

   Example: Seller entered into a contract to sell Buyer a house for $150,000. The contract stated that it was conditioned on Buyer's securing bank financing at an interest rate of 7% or below. Buyer did not make an application for bank financing and therefore did not secure any financing and refused to proceed with the purchase. Seller can sue Buyer for breach of contract because he failed to attempt to get financing which is a breach of his implied duty of good faith and fair dealing.

5. **Exclusion of warranty:** An implied warranty can be **excluded or modified** by **course of dealing, course performance, or usage of trade.**

F. **Accord and satisfaction**

1. **Accord:** An accord is an agreement where one party promises to **render substitute performance** and the other party to the existing contract promises to **accept that substitute** in discharge of the existing duty the original party was supposed to perform.

   a. **Discharge timing:** It does **not discharge** the obligation under the original agreement **until the substitute performance has been completed** (a satisfaction of the accord).

   b. **Consideration is required,** but can be (and often is) less than the original contract.

      1. **Payment of a lesser amount** than what is due on a valid claim constitutes **valid consideration** *if* there is a **bona fide dispute** as to the amount owed, and the dispute is made in **good faith.** See Consideration preexisting duty rules for examples of when payment is made.

> **MBE tip:** Most questions that test accord and satisfaction test the consideration aspect so review the examples in sec. I.E.3.e.*4*.

2. **Satisfaction:** A satisfaction is the **performance of the accord,** which then discharges both the original agreement and the accord. If the accord is breached, the other party can sue on the original contract or the accord.

VIII. CONTRACT REMEDIES

A. **Measure of damages**

1. **Common law: Expectation damages** compensate a plaintiff for the **value of the benefit plaintiff expected to receive** from the contract. Expectation damages put the plaintiff in the position he would have been in if the contract was performed. (Also called **compensatory damages.)**

   a. **Real Property:** This would be the **difference between the contract price and the market price.**

      1. **Abatement:** Where the property measures less than the contract indicates, the court can abate the price commensurate with the actual property size.

   b. **Services:** Calculated as the cost of substitute performance.

   c. **Construction contracts:** The amount it would cost to complete the construction, plus damages for the delay.

2. **UCC expectation damages formulas**

   a. **Buyer's UCC damages—Seller has goods and Seller is in breach:**

      1. Damages are the difference between the **contract price and the cover price** (if the buyer covered) OR the **contract price and market price** at the time the buyer learned of the breach.

      2. **In addition,** with either method the buyer can also recover **consequential damages** and **incidental damages** (all compensatory damages)—both discussed below.

   b. **Buyer's UCC damages—Buyer has goods and Seller is in breach:** Typically, the seller has tendered defective goods and the buyer has kept them. Damages are the **difference between perfect goods and the value as tendered.**

   c. **Seller's UCC damages—Seller has goods and Buyer is in breach:**

      1. **If the seller resold the goods:** Damages are the difference between the **contract price and the resale price,** plus any **incidental damages.**

      2. **If the seller did not resell the goods:** Damages are the difference between the **contract price and the market price** (as of the time delivery was to occur).

      3. **Lost volume seller:** A "lost volume" seller is one who has a virtually unlimited supply of goods to sell. A lost volume seller can recover **lost profits** if the seller:

         a. Has a big enough **supply to make both** the contracted sale and the resale,

         b. Would have **likely made both** sales, and

         c. Would have made a **profit on both** sales.

Example: A computer store contracted to sell a customer a computer for $3000. The customer unjustifiably repudiated the contract. Immediately thereafter, the store sold the computer to another buyer who paid the same price. The store has several units it can sell. The store can recover the profit it would have made on the sale to the customer as a lost volume seller.

4. **In addition,** the seller may also recover for **incidental damages, but *not* consequential damages.**

d. **Seller's UCC damages—Buyer has goods and Buyer is in breach:** The measure of damages is the **full contract price.**

3. **Consequential damages** compensate for damages that are a **direct and foreseeable consequence** of the contract nonperformance and are unique to each plaintiff (e.g., lost profits). Consequential damages can be recovered in addition to expectation damages. These damages must be **foreseeable at the time of contracting.**

4. **Incidental damages** are damages for **expenses reasonably incurred** by the buyer or seller as a direct result of the breach. This includes costs such as those incurred while storing the goods, shipping the goods, inspecting them, reselling them, finding an alternative supplier, etc.

5. **Reliance damages** put the plaintiff in the position they would have been in had the **contract never been made.** They are used primarily where there is a contract but the expectation damages are too uncertain to calculate, so reliance damages will compensate for **expenses reasonably incurred** in reliance on the contract less any amount mitigated/recovered (e.g., where lost profits are too speculative or in promissory estoppel situations).

   Example: A developer obtained a bid of $10,000 to tear down her old building and another bid of $90,000 to replace it with a new structure. Having only limited cash available, the developer asked the lender for a $100,000 loan. After reviewing the plans for the project, the lender in a signed writing promised to lend the developer $100,000 secured by a mortgage on the property. The developer promptly accepted the demolition bid and the old building was removed, but the lender thereafter refused to make the loan. Despite diligent efforts, the developer was unable to obtain a loan from any other source. The most likely recovery for the developer would be reliance damages measured by $10,000 to remove the old building, adjusted by the decrease or increase in the market value of the developer's land immediately thereafter.

   a. **Limitation:** Reliance damages may be **limited, as justice requires.**

6. **Liquidated damages** are damages in an amount stipulated to in the contract. They are allowed when actual damages are **difficult to calculate,** and the amount agreed to is a **reasonable approximation** of the anticipated loss from a breach. The clause cannot appear punitive and, if proper, provides the **only measure of damages recoverable** for breach.

   Example: "If Builder fails to complete the construction of Owner's house by Dec. 1, a fine of $100 per day will accrue until such time as the house is completed." This could be a reasonable approximation of the anticipated loss (hotel costs, etc.) and not punitive. However, if the fine was $500 per day and the parties knew that the owner would be gone for the entire month after the time for performance, then it might be unreasonable and more like a penalty.

7. **Nominal damages** are awarded where the plaintiff's rights have been violated but no financial loss has been sustained.

8. **Punitive damages** are **not awarded** for a standard breach of contract.

9. **Potential damage limitation issues:** The concepts below have the potential to limit a damages award. These limitations apply to expectation, consequential, and incidental damages (all discussed above).

   a. **Foreseeability:** Damages must be foreseeable by a **reasonable person at the time of contracting,** or if the damages are unusual, the defendant needs actual notice of their possibility.

   b. **Unavoidable: There is a duty to mitigate losses:** This comes up most frequently in consequential damages for a sales contract where the buyer does not try to "cover" by obtaining goods from an alternate supplier.

   Example: Tutor contracts with Law Student to help him pass the bar exam. Tutor repudiated the contract. Law Student could have hired an equally qualified tutor but failed to do so. If Law Student does not pass the bar, he failed to take reasonable steps to mitigate his damages.

   c. **Certainty:** Damages must be able to be calculated with certainty, and not too speculative (e.g., lost profits for a new business would be difficult to prove with certainty).

> **MBE tip:** If damages are too uncertain, think of reliance damages as an alternative remedy.

   d. **Causation:** Damages must be caused by the breach.

> **Decoy tip:** Always consider these limitations when assessing damages. Often a wrong answer will ignore the facts implicating limitation of damages (e.g., a wrong answer that measures expectation damages but fails to take into account the duty to mitigate damages).

B. **Legal restitutionary remedies**

1. **Restitution Damages** are used to award the **value of the unjust enrichment** that has been **rendered to the other party.**

   a. **Limitation:** An unjust enrichment claim **cannot exceed the contract price** when all of the work has been done and the **only remaining obligation is payment** of the price.

   b. **Quasi-contract** (also referred to as restitution or quantum meruit) is not actually a "contract" at all. Rather, it is a contract implied-in-law **to prevent injustice** where there is **no enforceable contract,** but some **relief is fair** because the **defendant has derived a benefit** and it would be unfair to allow the defendant to keep that benefit without paying money to the plaintiff in restitution.

   Example: A business owner entered into a contract with a painter, by the terms of which the painter was to paint the owner's office for $1000 and was required to do all of the work over the following weekend so as to avoid disruption of the owner's business. The painter commenced work on Saturday morning and had finished half the painting by the time he quit work for the day. That night without the fault of either party, the office building was destroyed by fire. Both parties' contractual duties would be discharged, but the painter can recover in quasi-contract for the benefit conferred (the half paint job).

   1. **Measure of relief:** The measure of relief is often **the value of the benefit conferred.**

   2. Typical situations where **quasi-contract applies** include:

      a. **No attempt to contract,** but defendant derived a benefit, such as an unconscious offeree.

b. **Unenforceable contract,** such as a flaw in the contract making process, but no enforcement unjustly enriches one party.

c. **Plaintiff in material breach** of a valid contract but defendant received a benefit and not allowing recovery unjustly enriches the non-breaching party.

2. **Replevin** applies when the plaintiff wants their **personal property** returned.
3. **Ejectment** applies when the plaintiff wants their **real property** returned.

DAMAGES DECODED

Example to determine damages:
A homeowner and a contractor entered into a contract for the construction of a home for the price of $300,000. The contractor was to earn a profit of $10,000 for the job. After the contractor had spent $45,000 on labor and materials, including $5000 on oak flooring not yet installed, the homeowner informed the contractor that the homeowner had lost his job and could not pay for any services. The homeowner told the contractor to stop working immediately. The reasonable market value of the labor and materials provided by the contractor at that point, including the oak flooring, was $40,000. The contractor used the $5000 worth of oak flooring on another job. The damage computations below are based on this fact pattern.

Type of Damage	Award Computation	As applied
Expectation =	Loss in value (amount received from what was expected) + other loss (consequential & incidental damages) - cost avoided - loss avoided	$300,000 ($0 received yet) + $0 (no other loss) - ($290,000 amount expected to spend - $45,000 already spent so cost avoided on spending the balance of $245,000) - $5000 (used floor on other job) = $300,000 - $245,000 - $5000 = **$50,000**
Reliance	Expenses reasonably incurred - amount recovered	$45,000 (labor and materials) - $5000 (floor used) = **$40,000**
Restitution	Benefit conferred to other party	**$40,000** (reasonable market value)

MBE tip: Some questions will provide a fact pattern and ask you what is the highest amount the plaintiff can receive from the defendant's breach. The answer choices will give you one answer based on expectation damages, one answer based on reliance damages, one answer based on restitution, and one answer based on one of the above that fails to consider a limitation (such as mitigation). Thus, you will need to analyze all the types of damages to determine which one is best because the highest amount is not always expectation damages. These questions will take longer than an average contracts question.

Decoy tip: Always remember to consider the limitations on damages. If you forgot to include the mitigation and didn't deduct the $5000 mitigated on the example above you would have had wrong numbers for two of the damages computations and likely picked the wrong answer. Wrong answer choices often contain numbers that failed to calculate the limitations.

C. **Equitable restitutionary remedies**

1. **Reformation** permits the contract to be **rewritten** to accurately reflect the agreement of the parties where the parties have a **meeting of the minds,** but the **writing is in error,** such as a scrivener's error. [If tested, it is usually tested with mistake or fraud.]

2. **Rescission** permits a party to undo a bargain where there is **no meeting of the minds.** [This is rarely MBE tested, but when it is tested it is usually tested with misrepresentation and fraud.]

3. **Grounds for rescission or reformation:** Allowed where a contract has resulted from fraud, misrepresentation, duress, or mistake.

4. **Defenses:** The equitable defenses of **laches** and **unclean hands** apply (see below).

D. **Specific performance** applies where a party is ordered by the court to render the promised performance under the contract (permanent injunction in contract).

1. **Valid contract** is required with definite and certain terms.

2. **Conditions** imposed on the plaintiff must be satisfied (the plaintiff in good faith satisfied their part for the contract).

3. **Inadequate legal remedy:** Money damages can be inadequate because:

   a. **Certainty:** The monetary value of the damages can't be calculated with certainty.

      1. **Too speculative** and uncertain to calculate.

      2. **Defendant insolvent** so a damages award is worthless.

      3. **Multiplicity of lawsuits:** The breach gives rise to an ongoing problem or multiplicity of lawsuits.

   b. **Property in question is unique.**

      1. **Real property:** Real property is always unique.

      2. **Special personal property:** Where the item is rare or has special personal significance, such as a family bible.

4. **Mutuality of performance:** Both parties must be eligible to have their performance under the contract ordered by the court.

5. **Feasibility of enforcement:** The order must be feasible for the court to enforce.

   a. **Jurisdiction issues:** Present a problem where the actions to be supervised are out of the court's jurisdiction and contempt power.

   b. **Court supervision issues:**

      1. **Multiple series of events** pose greater potential problems.

      2. **Act requiring skill, taste, or judgment.**

      3. **Personal services** will not be subject to specific performance (involuntary servitude concerns).

SPECIFIC PERFORMANCE GRANTED EXAMPLES

- Real property is involved (most MBE questions involve real property when granting specific performance).
- A brother and sister contract to pay $500 a month to help their mother by employing a live-in companion. Brother refuses to pay and the mother refuses to sue him. A court orders him to make the payments because of the difficulty in calculating the damages if the mother does not get the help she needs, and the sister's injury if she is unable to pay in his place, are impossible to ascertain.

Decoy tip: Always look for personal services when a question asks about specific performance. The answers that indicate a party is entitled to relief are decoy answers since specific performance is not awarded in personal services contracts due to the 13th Amendment prohibition against involuntary servitude.

6. **No applicable defenses**
   a. **Traditional equitable remedy defenses**
      1. **Laches** is an **unreasonable delay** that is **prejudicial** to the defendant.
      2. **Unclean hands:** The plaintiff is engaging in **unfair dealing** in the disputed transaction.

   b. **Other contract defenses:** Any failure of the contract operates as a defense that will prevent specific performance including mistake, misrepresentation, failed consideration, lack of capacity, SOF, and sale to a "bona fide purchaser" (one who took for value without notice of the situation that gives rise to the dispute).

Memorization tip: Memorize the specific performance elements with the sentence "**C**hocolate **C**heesecake **I**s **M**y **F**avorite **D**essert." (**C**ontract, **C**onditions, **I**nadequate legal remedy, **M**utuality of performance, **F**easibility of enforcement, and **D**efenses are not applicable.

CONTRACTS CHEAT SHEET

APPLICABLE LAW

UCC	Common law
◆ For sale of goods (special rules if merchants involved) ◇ Goods: movable, tangible property ◇ Merchant: deals in goods of kind; special knowledge/skills	◆ For services, or ◆ Real property

Predominance test (contract (K) contains goods and services)

If **both goods and services** – determine the predominant purpose for the contract as a whole to decide if UCC or common law applies

CONTRACT FORMATION

Offer (Common law)	Offer (UCC)
◆ Intent to be bound (obj. std./reas. person) ◇ No intent if: ◇ Preliminary negotiations ◇ Solicitation of bids ◇ Advertisements (ok if words of commitment & offeree identified) ◇ Rewards/auction bids ok if reas. clear who can accept or win ◆ Definite and certain terms (QTIPS) ◆ Meeting of minds (same subj. belief) ◆ Communicated to offeree	◆ Invite acceptance in any manner ◆ By any reasonable medium ◆ Intent (easier than CL; purchase order ok) ◆ Definite and certain terms ◇ Need subject matter and quantity ◇ Ct. can provide reasonable price and other gap fillers **Types of offers** ◆ Bilateral: promise for promise ◆ Unilateral: promise for performance ◆ Implied-in-fact: inferred from conduct

Termination of offer

Rejection	Counteroffer	Revocation
◆ Express or implied ◆ Can revive later	◆ New offer ◆ More than an inquiry	◆ Direct or indirect ◆ Unambiguous words or conduct ◆ Offeree must be aware

Irrevocable offers

UCC firm offer	Option contract	Death or incapacity
◆ No consideration needed ◆ Made by merchant ◆ Signed writing ◆ Gives assurance will be held open ◆ 3 month max.	◆ Need consideration ◆ Open for stated time period	◆ Minors – under 18 – ok if for necessaries ◆ Insanity – can't understand nature/consequences

Detrimental reliance/Part performance	Lapse of time
◆ Once begun/as justice requires	◆ Reasonable time if none stated

Acceptance	Methods of Acceptance
◆ Manifestation of assent to terms ◆ By words (oral or written) or conduct **Power of Acceptance** ◆ Accept within a reasonable time ◆ Only by offeree (who is aware) ◆ By any reasonable means (objective std.)	Bilateral- accept by promise ◆ Silence not acceptance unless intended or prior dealings, trade practices, etc. Unilateral – accept by performance Implied-in-fact – accept through conduct Ambiguous – promise *or* performance ok

Mailbox Rule	Mailbox Rule Exceptions
◆ Acceptance effective on dispatch (offeree has no control/possession) ◆ If dispatched then effective even if lost	◆ Offer provides otherwise ◆ Option contract (effective upon receipt) ◆ Reject. sent 1st → accept. must be receiv. 1st

Acceptance varies from offer (Common Law)	
◆ Mirror image – no new terms/conflicts	◆ New terms = rejection and counteroffer

Acceptance varies from offer (UCC)		
◆ Expression of acceptance or written confirmation ok ◆ Additional or different terms still acceptance unless ◆ Acceptance expressly made conditional on assent to terms	**Additional terms added** ◆ One party not a merchant ◇ Additional term = proposal ◆ Not part of K unless assent ◆ Both parties are merchants ◆ Add'l term = part of K unless ◇ Offer limits acceptance ◇ Term materially alters K, or ◇ Party objects w/in reas. time	**Different terms added** ◆ Knock-out rule (maj.) ◆ Conflicting terms cancel each other ◆ Ct. uses gap fillers ◆ Treat as add'l terms (minority) ◆ Fall out rule: offeror's terms control (minority)

Acceptance by shipping goods		Right to inspect goods
◆ Ship conforming goods = acceptance	◆ Ship nonconforming goods: ◆ W/o acknowledging = both acceptance & breach ◆ W/acknowledging = counteroffer ◆ Buyer pays if accepts goods	◆ Ok to inspect goods at delivery ◆ Before payment/acceptance ◆ Except – COD contract ◆ If payment req'd before inspect, payment does not = acceptance

Consideration	
◆ Bargained for exchange → ◆ Legal detriment ok ◆ Benefit for 3rd party ok	
◆ No consideration if: → ◆ Illusory promise – no commitment → ◆ Gifts/sham consideration ($ never paid) ◆ Reward if offeree not aware ◆ Past consideration → ◆ Pre-existing duty →	◆ Except consideration ok if: ◆ Conditional promise ◆ Requirement/Output contracts ◆ New promise to pay past debt that is now barred (writing/part partially performed) ◆ Promisor's request or in emergency ◆ Duty owed to 3rd party ◆ Substituted performance (accord/satisf.) ◆ Additional duties ◆ Settlement/release of claim in dispute
Modifications ◆ Common law = need new consideration ◇ Unless unanticipated circumstances/fair ◆ UCC = no new consideration needed	
Promissory Estoppel = substitute if no consideration → limited to reliance damages	

DEFENSES TO CONTRACT FORMATION

Statute of Frauds (SOF)	SOF Exceptions
Contracts that need to be in writing: ◆ Marriage → ◆ Real Property → ◆ Promise to pay the debt of another → ◆ K that can't be performed w/in 1 year → ◆ Sale of goods of $500 or more →	No writing needed if: ◆ Promise to marry each other ◆ Part performance (pay/improve/possess) ◆ Main purpose is maker's benefit ◆ Full performance occurred ◆ Goods accepted or paid or admission or specially manufactured goods
SOF Writing Requirement: ◆ Essential terms (subject matter/quantity) ◆ Signed by party to be charged	Writing requirement exceptions: ◆ Merchant's confirmatory memo ◇ Between 2 merchants ◇ 1 party receives signed confirmation
◆ Need not be addressed/sent to other party ◆ Writing doesn't need to be at time of K	◇ No objection w/in 10 days of receipt ◆ Judicial admission/promissory estoppel

Misrepresentation	Fraud	Mistake	
◆ Need not be intentional ◆ False statement ◆ Of material fact ◆ Justifiable and actual reliance	◆ Misrepresentation ◆ Of material fact ◆ Scienter (knowing) ◆ Intent to induce reliance ◆ Causation ◆ Justifiable reliance ◆ Pecuniary damage	<u>Mutual (both parties)</u> ◆ Basic assumption ◆ Existed at time of K ◆ Material effect ◆ Adversely aff. party didn't assume risk ◆ Assume risk if in K, aware, or by court	<u>Unilateral (1 party)</u> ◆ Unconscionable & ◆ Mutual mistake factors met ◆ Other party knew or should have known

Duress
◆ Assent induced by ◆ Improper threat ◆ No reas. alternat.

Undue Influence		Capacity
◆ Unfair persuasion ◆ Relationship	◆ Domination ◆ Susceptible	◆ Minors ◆ Insanity

DEFENSES TO ENFORCEMENT

Unconscionability	◆ So unfavorable (at time of K formation) ◆ No reasonable person would agree
Illegality	◆ Ok if law to benefit contracting party or public policy allows
Impossibility	◆ Impossible & neither party assumed risk ◆ Temporary impossibility will suspend duty not discharge it
Impracticability	◆ Extremely and unreasonably difficult ◆ Event basic assumption of K & risk not allocated to either party
Frustration of purpose	◆ Both parties know purpose & frustration is total ◆ Supervening events not reasonably foreseeable
Condition precedent not met	◆ Discharges other party's duty to perform
Novation	◆ Original party duties discharged by substituted new party
Accord & Satisfaction	◆ Original K promise & duty to perform discharged ◆ Replaced w/ new promise (accord) and performance (satis.)

INTERPRETATION OF CONTRACT TERMS AND PERFORMANCE

Conditions

- ◆ Event to occur before performance due
- ◆ Express = strict compliance
- ◆ Implied (constructive) = substantial compliance
- ◆ Concurrent = both parties perform at same time
- ◆ Precedent = one party performs before the other
- ◆ Subsequent = performance excused after event
- ◆ Satisfaction clauses = reasonable or good faith
- ◆ Waive by benefit/failure to insist on compliance

Risk of Loss (ROL)

<u>Goods shipped by 3rd party carrier</u>:

- ◆ **Shipment K-** presumed if not stated – ROL passes to buyer when seller delivers to carrier
- ◆ **Destination K** – specifies delivery location – ROL passes when goods delivered at location
- ◆ **Goods destroyed before ROL passes** –as if no K
- ◆ **FOB** = free on board – ROL passes at location

<u>Goods not shipped by 3rd party carrier</u>:

- ◆ ROL on seller until buyer takes possession

Parol Evidence Rule

- ◆ Applies to discussions/writings
- ◆ Prior to/contemporaneous w/ K
- ◆ Partially integrated = not final
  - ◇ Can't contradict
  - ◇ Can supplement
- ◆ Totally integrated = final
  - ◇ Can't contradict/supplement

<u>PER Exceptions</u>

- ◆ Formation/enforcement defects
- ◆ Conditions precedent
- ◆ Ambiguous terms
  - ◇ Course of performance
  - ◇ Course of dealing
  - ◇ Usage of trade

Modification

CL = need new consideration
UCC = need good faith only
SOF = need if modified K w/in it

THIRD-PARTY RIGHTS

3rd Party Beneficiaries	Assignment	Delegation
<u>Intended</u> ◆ Creditor: 3rd party owed $ ◇ Can sue promisor/ee ◆ Donee: 3rd party gets gift ◇ Can't sue promisee ◇ Unless detrimen. reliance ◆ Can modify K unless 3rd party rights vest/reliance <u>Incidental</u> – indirect benefit ◇ Can't sue either party	◆ Transfer rights under K ◆ All rights assignable ◆ Unless no assign. clause ◆ Unless material change to duty or risk ◆ No consideration req'd ◆ Assignee stands in shoes of assignor (same defens.) ◆ Can revoke assignment ◆ Unless detrim. reliance	◆ Delegate duties owed to a 3rd party ◆ Duties delegable ◆ Unless substantial interest in one party performing ◆ Unless duties of special skill/impair reas. expect. ◆ Delegator remains liable unless novation

Novation	
	◆ Express agreement to accept performance from new party ◆ Liability of delegator terminated

BREACH OF CONTRACT ISSUES

Anticipatory Repudiation	Right to Demand Assurances
◆ Unequivocal expression ◆ Before performance due ◆ That party will not perform <u>Non-repudiating party can</u>: ◆ Sue immediately ◆ Suspend performance ◆ Treat K as discharged ◆ Urge performance ◆ Must mitigate damages	◆ Can demand if reasonable grounds for insecurity ◆ Demand in writing (must be justified) ◆ May suspend performance until receive assurances ◆ No response w/in 30 days = repudiation **Material Breach Common Law** ◆ No substantial performance ◆ Look at benefit received/willfulness/hardship ◆ Time not of essence unless specific and known ◆ Divisible K = treat like separate Ks ◆ Employment at will = can terminate at any time

Material Breach UCC	Seller's Right to Cure	Warranties
◆ Perfect tender required ◇ Reject whole ◇ Accept whole ◇ Accept commercial unit ◆ Can waive – dealings, etc.	◆ Before performance due ◆ Buyer gets notice & new tender ◆ Can do *after* time to perform if reasonable belief	◆ Express ◆ Implied ◇ Merchantability ◇ Fit for particul. purpose ◇ Good faith/fair dealing

Accord & Satisfaction	
	◆ Agreement to substitute performance (express promise) ◆ Consideration req'd (can be lesser amt. if bona fide dispute)

CONTRACT REMEDIES

Damage limits	Expectation	Consequential	Reliance
◆ Foreseeable ◆ Unavoidable ◆ Certain ◆ Causation	◆ Put P in position as if K performed ◆ UCC can be lost volume seller	Direct/foreseeable **Incidental** Expenses reasonably incurred	As if K never made **Liquidated** ◆ Diff. to calculate ◆ Reas. approximate
Quasi-K	**Replevin**	**Ejectment**	**Reformation**
◆ Benefit to D ◆ Unjust enrichment	Get personal property back	Get real property back	Rewrite K **Rescission** Undo K

Specific Performance		
◆ Valid K ◆ Conditions met	◆ Inadequate legal remedy ◆ Mutuality of performance	◆ Feasibility (jx/supervision) ◆ No defenses (laches/unclean hands)

CONTRACTS MBE PRACTICE QUESTIONS

These questions are designed to reinforce the skill in how to approach MBE questions. While they will also test your knowledge in the limited areas addressed, you will not master your knowledge by only practicing these questions. To fully master the rules, you need to do practice questions outside of these from your bar company and/or the NCBE.

QUESTION 1

An attorney received a document at his office with an attached note from a client for whom he had just finished drafting a will. The note read as follows: "Do you think this contract of sale for my boat complies with state law? I would have talked to you in person about this, but I'm on my way out of town. I will be back next week."

The attorney reviewed the document and wrote a one-page letter to the client stating that the document complied with state law. The lawyer included a bill for $500, which was a reasonable fee.

The client refused to pay the attorney anything, arguing that she had never agreed to retain the attorney and that she had received nothing of value from the attorney because the sales transaction was never concluded.

Assume that there is no applicable statute or rule governing the formation of attorney-client relationships in the jurisdiction.

If the attorney sues the client for the $500, will the attorney be likely to prevail?

A. No, because even if the parties had an agreement, that agreement was discharged under the doctrine of frustration of purpose.
B. No, because the attorney and the client never agreed on the essential terms of a contract.
C. Yes, because the attorney took action on the client's note to his detriment.
D. Yes, because the client's note and the attorney's performance created an implied- in-fact contract.

QUESTION 2

A buyer sent a signed letter to a seller that stated: "Ship 100 boxes of nails at $3 per box, the price quoted in your circular." The seller mailed the buyer a signed form acknowledgment that agreed to the buyer's terms and stated on the reverse side: "Disputes regarding quality shall be arbitrated." The buyer did not reply to the seller's acknowledgment, and the seller shipped the nails. When the buyer received the nails, it found their quality to be unsatisfactory and sued the seller for breach of warranty. The seller has asked an attorney whether the parties' contract requires arbitration of the buyer's claim.

What is the best advice the attorney can provide?

A. A contract was formed pursuant to conduct when the buyer received the nails, and a court would exclude the arbitration provision from the contract.
B. A contract was formed when the seller mailed its acknowledgment, and the arbitration term became part of the contract.
C. A contract was formed when the seller mailed its acknowledgment, and the court must decide whether the arbitration term should be excluded as a material alteration of the contract.
D. No contract exists, because the arbitration term in the seller's acknowledgment created a counteroffer that the buyer never accepted.

QUESTION 3

A debtor's liquidated and undisputed $1000 debt to a creditor was due on March 1. On March 15, the creditor told the debtor that if the debtor promised to pay the $1000 on or before December 1, then the creditor wouldn't sue to collect the debt. The debtor orally agreed. On April 1, the creditor sued the debtor to collect the debt that had become due on March 1. The debtor moved to dismiss the creditor's complaint.

Should the court grant the debtor's motion?

A. No, because there was no consideration to support the creditor's promise not to sue.
B. No, because there was no consideration to support the debtor's promise to pay $1000 on December 1.
C. Yes, because a promise to allow a debtor to delay payment on a past debt is enforceable without consideration.
D. Yes, because the debtor was bargaining for the creditor's forbearance.

QUESTION 4

On June 1, an appliance manufacturer telephoned a supplier to determine whether the supplier could provide 300 washing machine motors of a particular model by October 1. The supplier offered to do so at a price of $300 per motor (a total price of $90,000). The manufacturer's representative said, "Deal." The next day the manufacturer's representative sent the supplier an unsigned note on company letterhead that stated, "I am happy that you are going to supply us with the motors. I will call you soon to talk about another order." The manufacturer then sent catalogs to its regular customers advertising washing machines that included the specified motors.

The manufacturer did not hear from the supplier until July 1, when the supplier called to say that it would be unable to supply the motors because it was no longer carrying that model. At that time, the manufacturer had received no orders for the machines with the specified motors.

The manufacturer sued the supplier for breach of contract, and the supplier raised the statute of frauds as a defense.

Is the supplier's statute of frauds defense likely to succeed?

A. No, because the manufacturer distributed the catalogs in reliance on the contract, making the contract enforceable under the statute of frauds.
B. No, because the supplier failed to object to the contents of the note sent by the manufacturer.
C. Yes, because the manufacturer's note failed to contain a signature.
D. Yes, because there is no writing that contains the quantity term of the contract.

QUESTION 5

A buyer agreed to purchase a seller's house for $250,000 "on condition that the buyer obtain mortgage financing within 30 days." Thirty days later, the buyer told the seller that the buyer would not purchase the house because the buyer had not obtained mortgage financing. The seller asked the buyer where the buyer had tried to obtain mortgage financing, and the buyer responded, "I was busy and didn't have time to seek mortgage financing."

If the seller sues the buyer for breach of contract, is the court likely to find the buyer in breach?

A. No, because the buyer's performance was subject to a condition that did not occur.
B. No, because the promise was illusory since the buyer was not obligated to do anything.
C. Yes, because a promise was implied that the buyer had to make reasonable efforts to obtain mortgage financing.
D. Yes, because a reasonable interpretation of the agreement is that the buyer had an obligation to purchase the house for $250,000 in 30 days.

QUESTION 6

A contractor agreed to remodel a homeowner's garage for $5000. Just before the parties signed the one-page written contract, the homeowner called to the contractor's attention the fact that the contract did not specify a time of completion. The parties orally agreed but did not specify in the contract that the contractor would complete the work in 60 days, and then they both signed the contract. The contract did not contain a merger clause. The contractor failed to finish the work in 60 days. The homeowner has sued the contractor for breach of contract.

Is the court likely to admit evidence concerning the parties' oral agreement that the work would be completed in 60 days?

A. No, because the court must ascertain the meaning of the agreement from the terms of the written contract.
B. No, because the oral agreement was merely part of the parties' negotiations.
C. Yes, because the contract is ambiguous.
D. Yes, because the time limit is an additional term that does not contradict the partially integrated written contract.

QUESTION 7

Collection of a debtor's $2000 debt to a creditor was barred by the applicable statute of limitations. The debtor sold and delivered his car to a buyer under a written agreement, signed by the buyer, in which the buyer promised to pay the $2000 purchase price to the creditor "in satisfaction of [the debtor's] debt to [the creditor]."

Can the creditor recover the $2000 from the buyer?

A. No, because payment of the $2000 to the creditor would undermine the statutory public policy against enforcement of stale claims.
B. No, because the creditor's rights as an intended beneficiary are subject to any defenses available to the contracting parties between themselves.
C. Yes, because the buyer's promise to pay $2000 to the creditor is enforceable by the creditor regardless of whether the debtor was legally obligated to pay the creditor anything.
D. Yes, because the buyer's promise to pay $2000 to the creditor revived the uncollectible debt.

QUESTION 8

A mill and a bakery entered into a written contract that obligated the mill to deliver to the bakery 1000 pounds of flour every Monday for 26 weeks at a specified price per pound. The mill delivered the proper quantity of flour in a timely manner for the first 15 weeks. However, the 16th delivery was tendered on a Tuesday, and amounted to only 800 pounds. The mill told the bakery that the 200-pound shortage would be made up on the delivery due the following Monday. The late delivery and the 200-pound shortage will not significantly disrupt the bakery's operations.

How may the bakery legally respond to the nonconforming tender?

A. Accept the 800 pounds tendered, but notify the mill that the bakery will cancel the contract if the exact amount is not delivered on the following Monday.
B. Accept the 800 pounds tendered, but notify the mill that the bakery will deduct from the price any damages for losses due to the nonconforming tender.
C. Reject the 800 pounds tendered, but notify the mill that the bakery will accept delivery the following Monday if it is conforming.
D. Reject the 800 pounds tendered, and notify the mill that the bakery is canceling the contract.

QUESTION 9

A builder contracted in writing to construct a small greenhouse on a homeowner's property for $20,000, payable upon completion. After the builder had spent $9000 framing the greenhouse and an additional $1000 for materials not yet incorporated into the greenhouse, the homeowner wrongfully ordered the builder to stop work.

The builder then resold the unused materials that he had already purchased for the greenhouse to another contractor for $1000. At the time the homeowner stopped the work, it would have cost the builder an additional $5000 to complete the project. The partially built greenhouse increased the value of the homeowner's property by $3000.

In a suit by the builder against the homeowner, how much is the builder likely to recover?

A. $3000, the increase in the value of the homeowner's property.
B. $10,000, the total cost expended by the builder at the time of the breach.
C. $14,000, the total cost expended by the builder ($10,000) plus the builder's expected profit ($5000), minus the loss avoided by the resale of the unused materials ($1000).
D. $15,000, the contract price ($20,000) minus the costs saved by the breach ($5000).

QUESTION 10

An employer offered to pay a terminated employee $50,000 to release all claims the employee might have against the employer. The employee orally accepted the offer. The employer then prepared an unsigned release agreement and sent it to the employee for him to sign. The employee carefully prepared, signed, and sent to the employer a substitute release agreement that was identical to the original except that it excluded from the release any age discrimination claims. The employer signed the substitute release without reading it. Shortly thereafter, the employee notified the employer that he intended to sue the employer for age discrimination.

Is the employer likely to prevail in an action seeking reformation of the release to conform to the parties' oral agreement?

A. No, because the employer acted unreasonably by failing to read the substitute release prior to signing it.
B. No, because the parol evidence rule will preclude evidence of the oral agreement.
C. Yes, because the employee's fraudulent behavior induced the employer's unilateral mistake.
D. Yes, because the parties were mutually mistaken regarding the contents of the signed release.

CONTRACTS ANSWER KEY	
Question	**Answer**
1	D
2	C
3	A
4	D
5	C
6	D
7	C
8	B
9	C
10	C

Use this quick answer key to get a general idea of how you did on this set of questions. The answer explanations that follow provide a step-by-step deconstruction of each question.

CONTRACTS MBE ANSWER EXPLANATIONS

START HERE

FACTS **Q1**

An **attorney received a document at his office** with an **attached** note **from a client** for whom he had **just finished drafting a will.** The note read as follows: "Do you think this **contract of sale for my boat complies with state law**? I would have talked to you in person about this, but I'm **on my way out of town**. I will be back next week."

Prior relationship so is this an offer to the attorney to look at the contract?

The **attorney reviewed the document** and **wrote a one-page letter** to the client stating that the **document complied with state law**. The lawyer included a **bill for $500**, which was a reasonable fee.

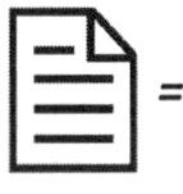 = **Attorney worked on the client's request (but was there an offer to accept)?**

The **client refused to pay** the attorney anything, arguing that she had **never agreed to retain the attorney** and that **she had received nothing of value** from the attorney **because the sales transaction was never concluded.**

IF K created, then irrelevant that sale never went through.

Assume that there is **no applicable statute or rule governing the formation of attorney-client relationships** in the jurisdiction.

This also tells you it is not about PR.

CALL If the **attorney sues the client for the $500**, will the attorney be **likely to prevail**?

Not clear what the issue is, but about a $500 claim (likely contracts since PR not tested on the MBE)

SOLVE

MBE tip:* *STEP 1: Always identify whether the common law or UCC applies as it might affect the applicable rules. *Here, the client asked for services so common law would apply (if there is a K).*

OFFER	TYPES OF OFFER & MANNER OF ACCEPTANCE	ANALYSIS
• Manifestation of intent to enter a bargain (offeree justified in thinking he can assent) • Certain and definite terms (QTIPS) • Communicated to offeree **Next step** →	• Bilateral: promise for promise • Unilateral: promise for performance • Implied-in-fact: inferred from parties' conduct/ circumstances **Apply** →	• Client appeared to intend for lawyer to look at contract by giving it to him w/note • Price likely hourly or similar to what he previously paid for will (& reas. amt. charged here) • Seems performance wanted but at minimum could be implied-in-fact because conduct – prior relationship, asked him if complies with law, said he would be back next week (infer do it by then), and left note with document.

A Yes, **because** at a minimum they had an implied-in-fact contract due to the past relationship and circumstances surrounding the transaction.

→ Now try to find an answer choice that is similar to your answer.

DECODE

~~A.~~ No, because even if the parties had an agreement, that agreement was discharged under the doctrine of frustration of purpose.

Wrong analysis. The purpose of the contract was for the lawyer to give the client advice about whether the contract complied with state law. Whether the sale actually went through was not a basic assumption on which the contract was made (that fact was a decoy).

~~B.~~ No, because the attorney and the client never agreed on the essential terms of a contract.

Wrong analysis. A contract can be created through conduct (implied) rather than on an agreement on the essential terms. And essential terms can be supplied if reasonable under the circumstances when the contract is based on conduct.

~~C.~~ Yes, because the attorney took action on the client's note to his detriment.

This is the correct conclusion but not the best answer. This answer assumes there was no contract ever created so the attorney would need to recover through promissory estoppel (where attorney's recovery would likely be less), but the better answer will find that there was a contract under implied-in-fact conduct and thus the attorney can recover under the actual contract.

D. Yes, because the client's note and the attorney's performance created an implied-in-fact contract.

Yes, this is the best answer choice because the prior relationship, the document with the attached note, timing of when the client would be back, etc. all lead to conduct where it would reasonable to infer a contract.

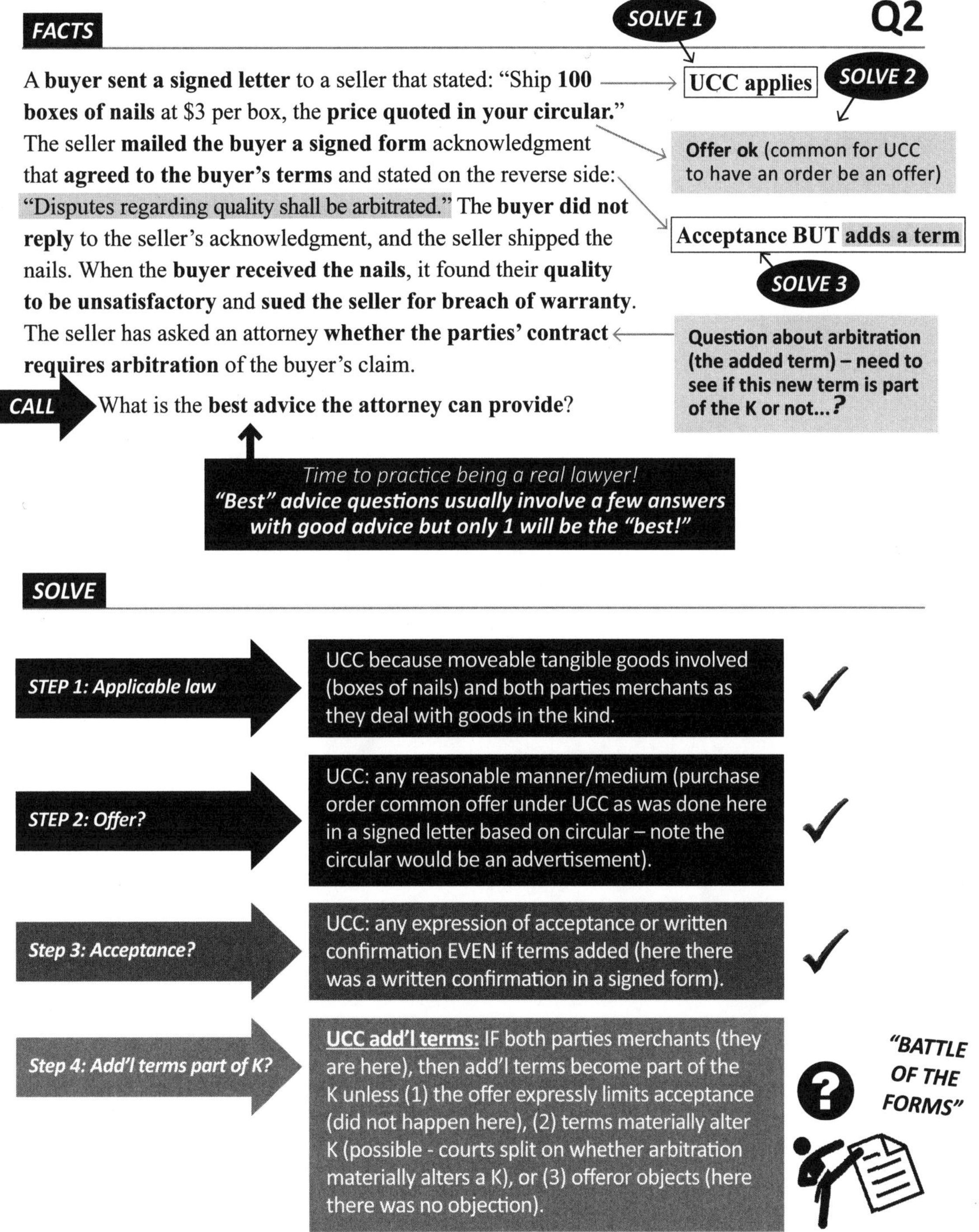

A The attorney could explain that the parties have a valid K, but whether the arbitration clause will be binding (and part of the K) depends on whether it materially alters the K (depends on jx).

Now look for an answer choice that is similar to your answer.

DECODE

~~A.~~ A contract was formed pursuant to conduct when the buyer received the nails, and a court would exclude the arbitration provision from the contract.

Wrong analysis. The contract was formed when the seller sent the acknowledgment form to the buyer which was an expression of acceptance (before delivering the nails). Also, the arbitration clause might not be excluded from the contract if it does not materially alter the contract.

~~B.~~ A contract was formed when the seller mailed its acknowledgment, and the arbitration term became part of the contract.

This is also not the best answer because it is not clear whether the arbitration clause will materially affect the contract (jx are split here so an assumption either way cannot be made certain).

C. **A contract was formed when the seller mailed its acknowledgment, and the court must decide whether the arbitration term should be excluded as a material alteration of the contract.**

YES!!! This answer correctly states when the contract was formed AND it acknowledges that the court may or may not exclude the arbitration term depending on whether it materially alters the contract.

~~D.~~ No contract exists, because the arbitration term in the seller's acknowledgment created a counteroffer that the buyer never accepted.

Wrong analysis. A contract does exist here and the additional term would not create a counteroffer under the UCC (it would under the common law but UCC applies here).

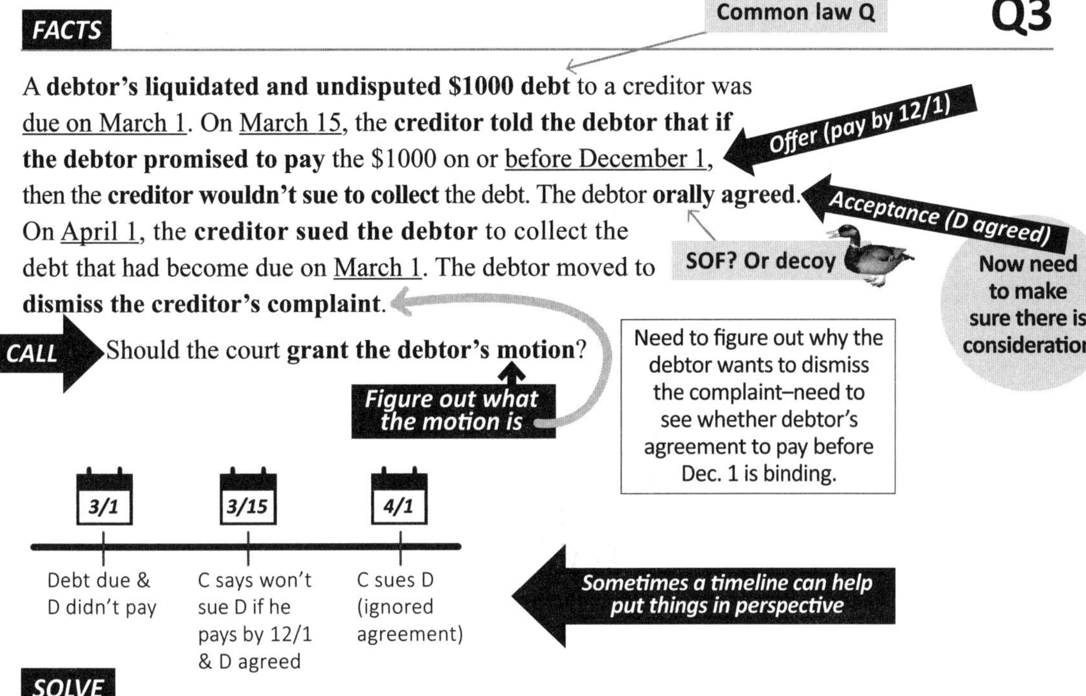

SOLVE

Q **Should the court grant the debtor's motion** (need to see if his agreement with the creditor was a valid contract and binding)?

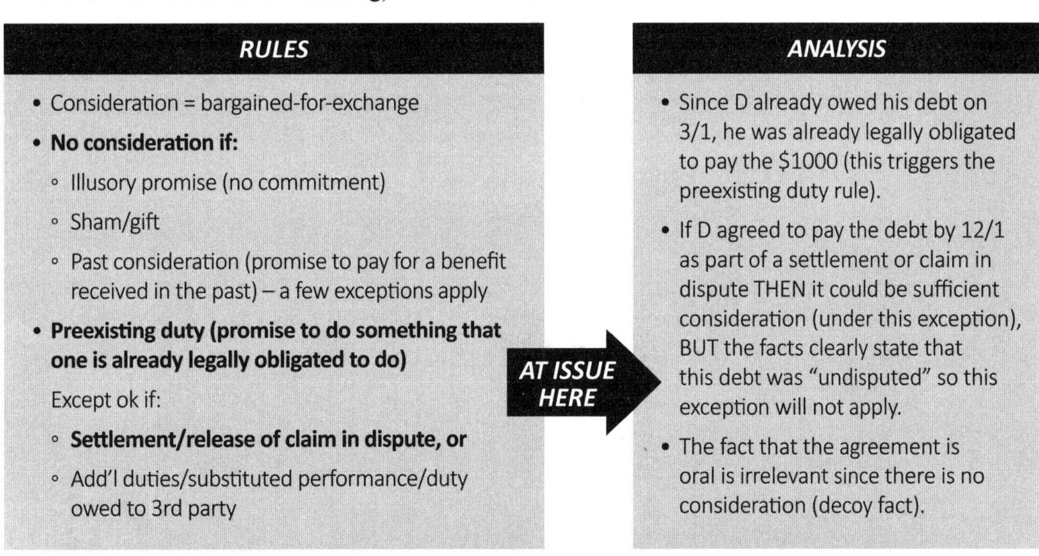

MBE tip: ***If the time to collect the debt is past the statute of limitations (SOL), then there will be a dispute since debtor would no longer owe the $ as the time to sue would have passed. So pay attention to dates and timelines and SOL facts.***

A No, the court should not grant the debtor's motion **because** the new agreement was not supported by consideration (preexisting duty limitation).

Now look for a similar answer choice.

DECODE

A. No, because there was no consideration to support the creditor's promise not to sue.

BINGO!!! Because debtor already owed the money to creditor, the agreement to pay the undisputed and liquidated debt late was not supported by consideration since the debtor had a preexisting duty to pay.

B. No, because there was no consideration to support the debtor's promise to pay $1000 on December 1.

Wrong analysis. This is a very tricky play on words. Here, they have inverted the answer by focusing on which side supported (properly bargained for) the other side's promise. Both the correct answer and this answer use "no consideration to support," and then each answer gives a different party: creditor (correct answer), or debtor (incorrect answer here). The reason the "to support the debtor" is not the correct answer is because the creditor forgoing the ability to sue would have been sufficient consideration "to support the debtor's promise." So this answer focuses on the wrong party not having sufficient consideration, whereas the correct answer "no consideration to support the creditor" is correct because the debtor's preexisting duty did not "support" the creditor's promise. If you are still confused, read this again.

C. Yes, because a promise to allow a debtor to delay payment on a past debt is enforceable without consideration.

Wrong rule. This is allowed if there is a promise to settle or release a claim in dispute, but there is no consideration if the debt is undisputed.

D. Yes, because the debtor was bargaining for the creditor's forbearance.

Wrong analysis of consideration. There must be a bargained for exchange and even if the creditor was willing to delay payment and not sue, the debtor provided no new consideration to support the creditor's forbearance.

FACTS

UCC applies

Q4

On June 1, an appliance **manufacturer telephoned a supplier** to determine **whether the supplier could provide 300 washing machine motors** of a particular model by October 1. The **supplier offered to do so at a price of $300 per motor** (a total price of $90,000). The **manufacturer's representative said, "Deal."** The next day the **manufacturer's** representative **sent the supplier** an **unsigned note on company letterhead** that stated, "I am **happy that you are going to supply us** with the motors. **I will call you** soon to talk about another order." The **manufacturer then sent catalogs** to its regular customers **advertising washing machines that included the specified motors.**

M inquiring at this point

S offered and M accepted

& Consideration = goods for $

SOF pops into my mind right about now!

Reliance? No because no orders

The **manufacturer did not hear from the supplier until** July 1, when the **supplier called to say that it would be unable to supply the motors** because it was no longer carrying that model. At that time, the **manufacturer had received no orders** for the machines with the specified motors.

The manufacturer sued the supplier for **breach of contract**, and the **supplier raised the statute of frauds as a defense.**

Need to determine if SOF is a valid defense now.

CALL Is the supplier's **statute of frauds defense** likely to succeed?

Issue in call – Whoo Whoo!!

SOLVE

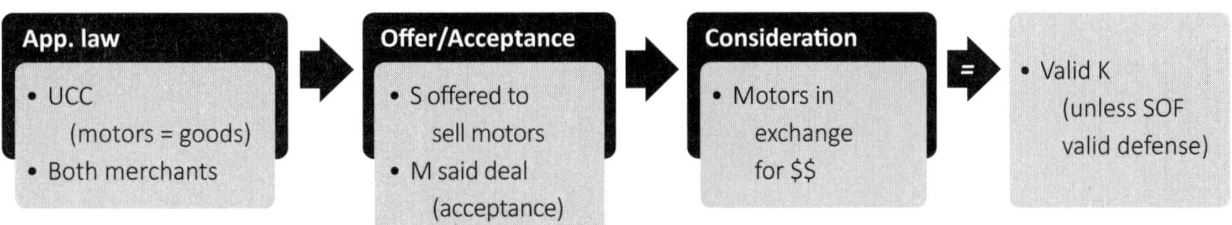

SOF APPLIES TO	WRITING REQUIREMENTS	ANALYSIS
K for the sale of goods $500 or more. **Exceptions:** • Goods accepted or paid for • Admission • Specially manufactured goods	• Essential terms (subject matter & quantity of goods) • Signed by party to be charged **Exceptions:** • Merchant's confirmatory memo ◦ Between merchants ◦ One party receives signed confirmation (w/quantity) ◦ No objection w/in 10 days • Promissory estoppel – detrimentally relied on to prevent injustice	• Here $90,000 in motors so SOF applies to this contract. • Writing on letterhead (ok for signature) BUT did not contain the quantity as it only referred to the motors generally. • No exceptions b/c no quantity still & no customers ordered motors for detrimental reliance.

A Yes, **because** the writing does not contain the quantity as required and no exceptions apply and there was no detrimental reliance since no customers bought the motors after they advertised them.

Now look for a similar answer choice.

DECODE

A. No, because the manufacturer distributed the catalogs in reliance on the contract, making the contract enforceable under the statute of frauds.

Wrong analysis. The reliance must be detrimental reliance and since no customers ordered the motors from the advertising, manufacturer did not suffer any detrimental reliance and it suffered no damages.

B. No, because the supplier failed to object to the contents of the note sent by the manufacturer.

This is not a rule. There was nothing in the contents to object to. There was not a quantity stated to object to and the writing was still insufficient as it did not contain the quantity as required.

C. Yes, because the manufacturer's note failed to contain a signature.

Wrong analysis. The note itself was on company letterhead which is sufficient for a signature under the UCC.

D. Yes, because there is no writing that contains the quantity term of the contract.

Correct. The missing quantity violates the writing requirement under the SOF and no exceptions apply.

FACTS

Q5

A **buyer agreed to purchase a seller's house for $250,000** "on condition that **the buyer obtain mortgage financing within 30 days.**" Thirty days later, the buyer told the seller that the **buyer would not purchase** the house because the **buyer had not obtained mortgage financing**. The seller asked the buyer where the buyer had tried to obtain mortgage financing, and the buyer responded, "I was busy and **didn't have time to seek mortgage financing.**"

Note a condition to the agreement

30 days to fulfill!

Buyer did not fulfill the condition

Time has run out!

CALL If the seller sues the buyer for **breach of contract**, is the court **likely to find the buyer in breach**?

Issue related to whether buyer is in breach, but this could be for a variety of reasons, so we need to read the facts to narrow in on the specific issue related to breach.

***Issue:** Whether buyer's failure to seek mortgage financing was a breach?*

SOLVE

Q If the seller sues the buyer for breach of contract, is the court likely to find the buyer in breach (depends on if buyer not fulfilling the condition to find financing because he didn't have time is a breach)?

VALID CONTRACT?	*CONDITION*	*ANALYSIS*
• Real property so common law applies • Seller and Buyer agree to sell/buy house • Consideration = money in exchange for house • Condition to fulfill – will determine whether the sale actually goes through	• A condition is an **event that must occur before performance of the other party is due.** • **Express condition** – created by clear language with intent to have a condition. • **Condition precedent** requires that one party's performance be completed prior to the other party's performance. • Failure to fulfill the condition will **excuse the other party's performance**. • **Good faith required** in all contracts	• Express condition because says "on condition that" that B must obtain mortgage financing within 30 days. • Condition precedent because required before S will sell house. • B did not obtain financing within 30 days. • B did not act in good faith since his reason for not obtaining financing is because he did not seek any because he didn't have time (after he agreed to do so).

Moral of the story: Don't agree to do something if you don't have time........any guilty parties out there????

A Yes, **because** the buyer had a duty to make an effort to fulfill the condition and seek financing, as every contract has an implied duty of good faith and fair dealing.

Now find an answer choice that is similar.

DECODE

A. No, because the buyer's performance was subject to a condition that did not occur.

Missing a rule here. While the buyer's performance was subject to a condition, he had an implied duty of good faith to make a reasonable effort to fulfill his obligation under the condition and did not do so.

B. No, because the promise was illusory since the buyer was not obligated to do anything.

Wrong analysis. The buyer was obligated to seek financing (at least try) under the implied duty of good faith and fair dealing in every contract and he agreed to do so.

C. Yes, because a promise was implied that the buyer had to make reasonable efforts to obtain mortgage financing.

BINGO!! It is implied under the good faith and fair dealing requirement that one will make reasonable efforts to fulfill contract conditions. Note how the answer hid the ball on the language of the actual duty, but that duty requires that parties try to fulfill conditions.

D. Yes, because a reasonable interpretation of the agreement is that the buyer had an obligation to purchase the house for $250,000 in 30 days.

Wrong analysis of how an express condition works. With an express (precedent) condition, there is no obligation unless and until that condition is met. So buyer did not have an obligation to purchase the house unless he obtained financing within 30 days.

FACTS — Common law

Q6

A **contractor agreed to remodel a homeowner's garage** for $5000. Just <u>before</u> the parties **signed the one-page written contract**, the homeowner called to the contractor's attention the fact that the **contract did not specify a time of completion**. The **parties <u>orally</u> agreed** but **did not specify in the contract** that the contractor would **complete the work in 60 days**, and **then they both signed** the contract. The contract **did not contain a merger <u>clause</u>**. The **contractor failed to finish the work in 60 days**. The homeowner has sued the contractor for breach of contract.

Problem noted about missing date in contract

Oral agreement before K but not in K = PER concern

Clue that the K is not totally integrated (note I can in my head reference the rule as I read the facts to make notes of these facts).

CALL Is the court **likely to admit evidence concerning the parties' oral agreement** that the work would be completed in 60 days?

When dealing with "admitting" evidence of an oral agreement, it is usually a PER issue if the question is about contracts (a quick glance at the facts shows it is about contracts).

<u>MBE tip:</u> While the Q is about the PER, note that if time is of the essence the breach would be material; if not then minor breach.

SOLVE

<u>Rule:</u> *The parol evidence rule (PER) limits the extent to which evidence of discussions or writings made prior to or contemporaneously with, the signed contract can be admitted and considered as part of the K.*

PARTIAL INTEGRATION (not the final agreement & w/o all details) → ***• CANNOT CONTRADICT • CAN SUPPLEMENT***

TOTAL INTEGRATION (final agreement w/ all details) → ***• CANNOT CONTRADICT • CANNOT SUPPLEMENT***

<u>Exceptions:</u>
- Contract formation/enforcement defects
- Condition precedent
- Ambiguous terms

ANALYSIS

- Oral discussions here before the parties signed the contract & not in contract.
- There was not a merger clause which indicates the writing was not intended to be a final expression = K is partially integrated.
- The date for completion does not contradict any terms so it can be used to supplement the existing contract.

A Yes, <u>**because**</u> the contract does not appear to be totally integrated and the date for completion does not contradict any term in the contract; rather it supplements the contract.

Now find an answer choice that is similar.

DECODE

~~A.~~ No, because the court must ascertain the meaning of the agreement from the terms of the written contract.

Wrong analysis for a partially integrated contract. The court can look outside the terms of the written contract in a partially integrated contract to supplement the terms.

~~B.~~ No, because the oral agreement was merely part of the parties' negotiations.

Wrong analysis. The oral agreement was not part of negotiations, but rather was a term they both orally agreed to prior to signing the contract. Therefore, evidence of this agreement is admissible.

~~C.~~ Yes, because the contract is ambiguous.

Wrong analysis. There are no facts to indicate the contract is ambiguous. Rather it is just a missing date/timeline for completion.

D. Yes, because the time limit is an additional term that does not contradict the partially integrated written contract.

Correct. The contract was only partially integrated and the date for completion only supplements (not contradicts) the contract. To answer correctly, you had to start by looking at whether the contract was partially or totally integrated and go from there.

Q7

FACTS

Common law

Collection of a debtor's $2000 debt to a creditor was **barred by the applicable statute of limitations.**
The **debtor** sold and delivered his car to a **buyer** under a **written agreement, signed by the buyer**, in which the **buyer promised to pay the $2000 purchase price to the creditor** "in **satisfaction of [the debtor's] debt** to [the creditor]."

Debt barred by SOL could raise consideration issues (usually ok under exception though so don't focus too much time here).

Make a note of the parties:

1. **DEBTOR** = owes $ to creditor (but SOL passed)
2. **CREDITOR** = Owed $$ by D, but SOL bar
3. **BUYER** = owes D $$ for car, BUT D told B to pay the $$ owed to C & B promised to do so

CALL Can **the creditor recover the $2000** from the buyer?

You see it is about a 3rd party trying to collect a debt.

Issue not clear so read facts

If you aren't sure, go through both quickly in your head but when creditors are involved and trying to get $$ from a 3rd party it is usually a 3rd party beneficiary issue. The answer choices may also limit the issue.

BUT you might also think it is about consideration for a past paid debt since it is past the SOL time.

SOLVE

WHO'S WHO?

Promisee: Party in K who intended to confer a benefit on the 3rd party

Promisor: Party in the K who must complete the performance to benefit the 3rd party

3rd party beneficiary: Person who benefits from the K made between two other parties

- **Intended beneficiary**: One intended by the promisee to benefit from the K
- **Creditor beneficiary**: 3rd party whom the promisee intends to benefit because the promisor owes him $

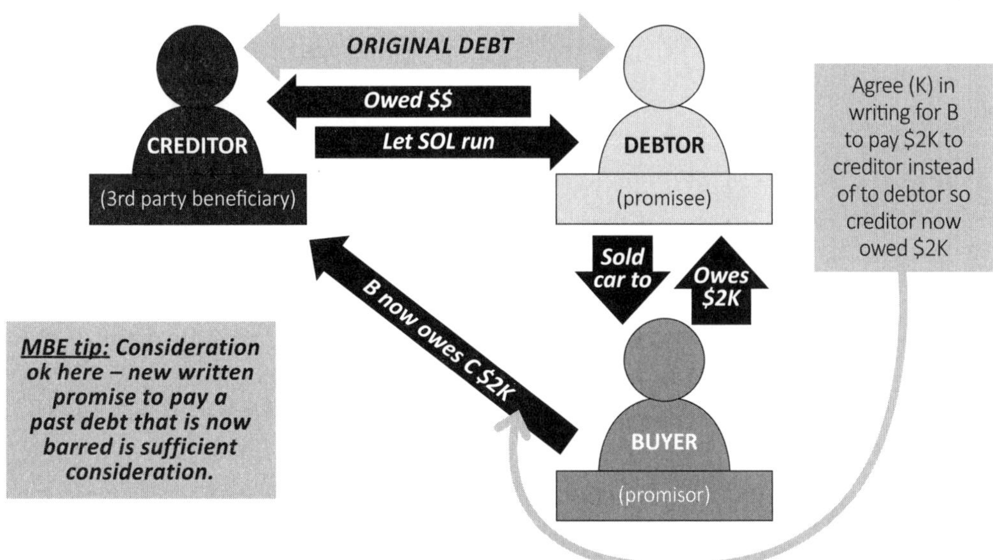

SOLVE (continued)

A Yes, **because** the creditor was a 3rd party intended creditor beneficiary (and the agreement was in writing and a past debt now barred by the SOL provides consideration so there are no applicable defenses).

→ Now look for a similar answer choice.

DECODE

~~A.~~ No, because payment of the $2000 to the creditor would undermine the statutory public policy against enforcement of stale claims.

This is a made-up rule. There is no public policy against having debtors pay off past debts they owe and never paid (public policy wants people to pay off debts they owe; although there is a SOL, that is why there is a consideration exception for agreements to pay off past owed debts beyond the SOL).

~~B.~~ No, because the creditor's rights as an intended beneficiary are subject to any defenses available to the contracting parties between themselves.

Wrong analysis. This assumes there are valid defenses but there are not because here the agreement is in writing and supported by consideration and no other defenses are applicable.

C. Yes, because the buyer's promise to pay $2000 to the creditor is enforceable by the creditor regardless of whether the debtor was legally obligated to pay the creditor anything.

Correct!! The creditor is an intended beneficiary under the agreement between the debtor and the buyer and has nothing to do with the original agreement between debtor and creditor (or the SOL).

~~D.~~ Yes, because the buyer's promise to pay $2000 to the creditor revived the uncollectible debt.

Made-up rule. There is a not a debt "revival" rule (and in fact if the creditor sued the debtor, the debt would still be barred by the SOL). Rather the debt owed is enforceable because buyer agreed to pay creditor the debt (new agreement) and creditor is a 3rd party beneficiary.

Q8

FACTS

UCC

A **mill and a bakery** entered into a **written contract** that obligated the mill to deliver to the bakery **1000 pounds of flour every Monday for 26 weeks** at a specified price per pound. The mill delivered the proper quantity of flour in a **timely** manner for the **first 15 weeks**. However, the **16th delivery** was tendered on a Tuesday, and amounted to only 800 pounds. The mill told the bakery that the **200-pound shortage would be made up** on the delivery due the following Monday. The **late delivery** and the 200-pound **shortage <u>will not significantly disrupt the bakery's operations</u>**.

Installment K

Nonconforming tender

Cure?

KEY fact to this issue!

CALL How may the bakery legally **respond to the nonconforming tender**?

YES!!!
The issue is in the call and we know nonconforming tender implicates UCC and breach. Time to celebrate our knowledge!

SOLVE

UCC PERFECT TENDER RULE		*INSTALLMENT KS*	*ANALYSIS*
• Single delivery must perfectly conform to K • Failure to conform, buyer can: ◦ Reject whole ◦ Accept whole ◦ Accept commercial unit	*EXCEPT* →	• Does NOT apply to installment Ks (more than 1 delivery) • Right to reject determined by substantial conformity – whether imperfect tender **substantially affects the contract** • Buyer cannot reject if seller can cure, but buyer can deduct damages for losses caused by nonconformity	• No perfect tender b/c delivered on Tuesday (not Monday) and only 800 pounds (not 1000) • BUT installment K b/c deliveries for 26 weeks every Monday • The imperfect tender did NOT substantially affect the K b/c late delivery and shortage "will not significantly disrupt the bakery's operation." • Seller can cure by bringing 200 more pounds Monday

A The bakery cannot reject the nonconforming tender **<u>because</u>** it will not substantially affect the K or disrupt the bakery's operation (and the seller can cure Monday). But the bakery can deduct for damages caused by the nonconformity.

→ Now look for a similar answer choice!

DECODE

~~A.~~ Accept the 800 pounds tendered, but notify the mill that the bakery will cancel the contract if the exact amount is not delivered on the following Monday.

Wrong analysis for an installment contract. The buyer cannot cancel the contract because the nonconforming tender did not substantially affect the contract or the bakery's operations and there is no indication that the 200 remaining pounds (if not delivered) would substantially affect the contract.

B. Accept the 800 pounds tendered, but notify the mill that the bakery will deduct from the price any damages for losses due to the nonconforming tender.

Yes! This is exactly what the bakery is permitted to do since the nonconforming tender did not substantially affect the contract. It must accept the 800 pounds, but can deduct any damages.

~~C.~~ Reject the 800 pounds tendered, but notify the mill that the bakery will accept delivery the following Monday if it is conforming.

Wrong analysis for reasons similar to answer choice A. The bakery cannot only accept the delivery Monday if it is conforming. It has to accept the delivery so long as the nonconformity does not substantially affect the contract.

~~D.~~ Reject the 800 pounds tendered, and notify the mill that the bakery is canceling the contract.

Wrong analysis for an installment contract. Bakery cannot reject the nonconforming tender and cancel the contract when the nonconformity does not substantially affect the contract and when seller can cure.

Q9

FACTS

Common law

A **builder contracted** in **writing** to **construct** a small greenhouse on a **homeowner's** property for $20,000, **payable upon completion**. After the builder had spent $9000 framing the greenhouse and an additional $1000 for materials not yet incorporated into the greenhouse, the **homeowner wrongfully ordered the builder to stop work**. The **builder then resold the unused materials** that he had already purchased for the greenhouse to another contractor for $1000. At the time the homeowner stopped the work, it **would have cost the builder an additional $5000 to complete the project**. The partially built greenhouse **increased the value of the homeowner's property by $3000**.

The moment you realize you still need to do math...in law school. Make it easier on yourself and highlight the numbers!

Mitigation ringing a bell??? Smart builder!

Mental note: Benefit to the other party usually goes to restitution.

CALL

In a suit by the builder against the homeowner, **how much is the builder likely to recover**?

Issue = damages ("how much,") so now you need to determine what type of damages are at issue. Read the facts to find out.

***MBE tip:* Expectation damages are the most frequently tested...**

SOLVE

Type	Rule	Application
Expectation Damages	Put P in the position he would have been in had the K been performed = Loss in value + other loss – cost avoided – loss avoided	• Loss in value = $20,000 (K price) • Other loss = $0 • Cost avoided = $5000 (to complete) • Loss avoided = $1000 (resold materials) • Expectation = $20,000 + $0 – $5000 – $1000 = $14,000
Consequential Damages	• Losses that are direct & foreseeable (at time of K formation) such as lost profits • Recovered in addition to expectation damages	No facts to show consequential or incidental damages
Incidental Damages	Expenses reasonably incurred such as expenses incurred when mitigating/reselling products	No facts to show consequential or incidental damages
Reliance Damages	• Put P in the position he would have been in had the K never been made • Usually used when expectation too uncertain	Money spent already that he didn't recover yet = $9000 so this would be the amount to repay P as if the K never happened (but expectation better for P)
Liquidated Damages	Stipulated to in K if difficult to ascertain & reasonable approximation	Not applicable here
Restitution Damages	Measured by the value of the benefit conferred on the other party (can't exceed K price)	Benefit to homeowner is $3000 increase in value to property

Limitations*: *Damages must be certain, foreseeable, mitigated & caused by D's breach.

SOLVE (continued)

A Builder likely to recover expectation damages for $14,000 based on calculations and he did mitigate his damages and they were foreseeable and certain and caused by homeowner's breach. Expectation damages are the best recovery since homeowner wrongfully breached.

→ Now look for a similar answer choice!

DECODE

~~A.~~ $3000, the increase in the value of the homeowner's property.

Wrong measure of damages assessed. These are the restitutionary damages would which be used if there was not a contract (quasi-contract) or if builder (P) breached (they measure the benefit conferred to D), but here homeowner (D) breached by wrongfully ordering the builder to stop work, so the best damages for builder are expectation damages to put him in the position he would have been in had D not breached.

~~B.~~ $10,000, the total cost expended by the builder at the time of the breach.

Wrong measure of damages assessed. These are the reliance damages (put P in the position he would have been in as if the contract was never made) and these don't account for builder's mitigated expenses. This amount represents the amount builder expended so far, but $1000 he was able to recoup by reselling the materials, so his out of pocket reliance expenses are only $9000. And as stated in answer choice A, his best damages would be expectations due to homeowner's willful breach.

C. $14,000, the total cost expended by the builder ($10,000) plus the builder's expected profit ($5000), minus the loss avoided by the resale of the unused materials ($1000).

Yes! This represents builder's expectation damages and takes into account his duty to mitigate his damages. This would put him in the position he would have been in had the contract been completed.

~~D.~~ $15,000, the contract price ($20,000) minus the costs saved by the breach ($5000).

Wrong analysis of expectation damages. This forgets to take into account the limitations to mitigate damages and doesn't account for the $1000 he already recovered by reselling materials.

Q10

FACTS

Common law | Mental note - no writing

An **employer offered** to **pay a terminated employee** $50,000 **to release all claims** the employee might have against the employer. The employee **orally accepted** the offer. The employer then prepared an **unsigned release agreement** and **sent it to the employee** for him to sign. The **employee** *carefully* prepared, **signed, and sent to the employer a substitute release agreement** that was **identical to the original** except that **it excluded from the release any age discrimination claims.** The **employer signed** the substitute release **without reading it.** Shortly thereafter, the **employee** notified the employer that he **intended to sue the employer for age discrimination.**

Facts go to employee altering the K (carefully) so intentionally it appears – look at reasons to reform a K (the issue) to see if this type of behavior fits in.

Didn't read it – see if that matters or if it is a decoy

Reminder that regardless of how misbehaved parties are (some will be snakes), you must always apply the law. These are not real people!

CALL Is the employer likely to prevail in an **action seeking reformation** of the release **to conform to the parties' oral agreement**?

Issue in call – time to do the happy dance!

SOLVE

REFORMATION RULES	*ANALYSIS*	*ORAL AGREEMENT*
• Reformation permits the contract to be rewritten • To accurately reflect the agreement of the parties where the parties have a meeting of the minds • But the writing is in error, such as a scrivener's error, or • **K resulted from fraud, misrepresentation,** duress, or mistake • Defenses: laches & unclean hands	• Employer wants K rewritten to reflect original oral agreement for employee to release ALL claims it might have against the employer. • Meeting of minds was when they orally agreed to release ALL claims for $50,000. • Employee likely committed fraud or misrepresented the new K by carefully changing it to make it look identical when it wasn't. • Employer didn't read it but that doesn't rise to unclean hands (bad faith). ***One more hoop to jump through***	• To show the parties had an agreement that the employee would release ALL claims, the employer will need to introduce the oral agreement, so PER is implicated b/c oral agreement before written K • Here, the "ALL claims" contradicts a term in the new K (employment disputes), but PER exception for formation defects such as fraud & misrepresentation so ok

A Yes, **because** the employee mispresented/committed fraud by carefully changing the employer's agreement, and the PER will not bar the introduction of their oral agreement since it relates to fraud in the formation of the contract.

Now look for a similar answer choice!

DECODE

~~A.~~ No, because the employer acted unreasonably by failing to read the substitute release prior to signing it.

Wrong analysis. While the employer did not read it, his actions were not unreasonable and in bad faith to avoid the court reforming the contract. Since he had no reason to believe the employee would change the entire document carefully making it look identical, his failure to read it was not unreasonable.

~~B.~~ No, because the parol evidence rule will preclude evidence of the oral agreement.

Wrong analysis of the PER. The PER will not preclude evidence if the evidence relates to the contract being formed through fraud or misrepresentation. Note that even though this question tested reformation, you also needed to know and apply the PER as well as be able to recognize fraud or misrepresentation to get to the right answer choice.

C. Yes, because the employee's fraudulent behavior induced the employer's unilateral mistake.

Correct answer. Note the answer choice does not mention reformation due to fraud or misrepresentation nor does it mention the PER. They hide the ball and mention that the employer made a unilateral mistake (which is true but a tricky way to phrase the answer choice given that it was based on reformation through fraud or misrepresentation).

~~D.~~ Yes, because the parties were mutually mistaken regarding the contents of the signed release.

Wrong reason because both parties were not mistaken. The employee knew of the contents since he carefully recreated them. Only the employer was mistaken.

PART 4 CRIMINAL LAW

CRIMINAL LAW MBE TABLE OF CONTENTS

CRIMINAL PROCEDURE TABLE OF CONTENTS

★ Favorite Testing Area

MBE CRIMES AT A GLANCE

12-13 Questions (approx.) **Criminal Law**	**12-13 Questions** (approx.) **Criminal Procedure**

General principles
  Actus Reus
  Mens Reus
Homicide
Theft crimes
Robbery
Burglary
Assault and battery
Rape
Kidnapping
Arson
Inchoate crimes
Defenses
	4th Am.
	  Arrest, Search, & Seizure
	5th Am.
	  Miranda
	  Self-incrimination
	  Double Jeopardy
	  Due Process
	6th Am.
	  Right to Counsel
	  Confrontation Clause
	  Trial issues
	8th Am.
	  Cruel and Unusual Punishment
	Burdens of Proof/Persuasion

SOLVING CRIMES MBE Qs

MBE tip: The MBE instructs to answer questions according to "the generally accepted view" unless otherwise noted. The question may instead provide the statute to apply, in which case you must apply the statute provided verbatim to the facts. Some questions will indicate the jurisdiction uses the common law or the Model Penal Code (MPC) view, so it is important to know the distinctions.

COMMON CRIMES DECOY ANSWERS

- Many questions will ask for the defendant's best defense to the crime. Look for the answer choice most likely to lead to acquittal. Often, D's *best* argument is that D didn't commit the crime in the first place, rather than a traditional "defense." If ranking answers, it is better to argue an element of the crime is unsatisfied (i.e., no mens reus) rather than argue the crime is established, but there is a defense.
- Questions will ask which crime a D committed under the facts. The decoys will be similar crimes (answers will often give you a list of crimes where one element will determine which crime is correct and which crimes are incorrect options).
- When questions provide a statute, you must *only* use that statute to answer the question. A decoy answer will be available that applies the normal standard (i.e., if the facts tell you assault is "maliciously causing another injury," then you use that standard when analyzing the facts, instead of the normal common law specific intent standard for assault).
- Criminal procedure questions will often have a decoy answer that focuses on the wrong person (one who does not have a reasonable expectation of privacy or one trying to assert rights when it was another person's rights that were violated and not their own).

CRIMINAL LAW MBE OUTLINE

I. GENERAL PRINCIPLES

A. **Acts and omissions** (actus reus)

1. **Act:** All crimes require a **voluntary act** by the defendant. Crimes committed unconsciously, by force of police, or with a defense that negates the voluntariness of the act, do not give rise to criminal liability.

   Example (act): A man decided to kill his neighbor. He saw a man who resembled his neighbor, so he pulled out his gun and shot at the man. This constitutes a voluntary act to shoot someone, even if not the intended target (see below for transferred intent).

   Example (no act): Police arrest a man at his house. The man was drunk and in his pajamas at the time of the arrest. The officers hustle the man outside in that condition. The man is later charged for violating a statute that prohibits any person to be in public while intoxicated in indecent clothing. There is no voluntary act here since the man did not voluntarily appear in public while drunk and indecently dressed.

2. **Omission to act:** Failure to act or failing to prevent another from committing a crime is not a crime itself unless there is a **statute** (such as filing a tax return), a **contract** (such as a lifeguard), a **special relationship** (such as a parent with a minor child), or if the **defendant caused the danger** (such as starting a fire).

   a. **Able to perform:** Even if there is a legal duty to act, the defendant must be physically able to perform the act (e.g., one cannot act if they are frozen in shock and unable to move).

3. **Mere presence:** Mere presence, even if accompanied by silent approval and intent, is insufficient to establish actus reus.

   Example: Three men agree to kill a bartender. Another man watching also wants the bartender dead but made no move to help and said nothing when the other men stabbed the bartender. His mere presence and silence does not establish the actus reus to commit murder.

ACTUS REUS	FAILURE TO ACT
Voluntary act required	No duty to warn. Voluntary act not required, except:
Not satisfied when: ◆ D has an involuntary act ◆ D just has guilty thoughts ◆ D is merely present ◆ D omits to act, except IF DUTY →	Duty imposed when: ◆ Statute ◆ Contract ◆ Special relationship ◆ D caused the danger

B. **State of mind** (mens rea) Most crimes require mental intent or a culpable state of mind, the definition of which varies depending on the crime.

1. **General intent:** To merely do the act.

   Example: A student is unprepared for his final exam, so he asks his girlfriend to set off the fire alarm after the test starts. Students were injured in the panic that followed. If charged with *battery* they can be found *guilty* because they intended to pull the fire alarm (to do the act) which is what caused the students to panic and injure themselves running out of the building. (Since one only needs to intend to do the act for general intent (the act of pulling the alarm), they need not have intended the injuries that resulted from the panic.)

2. **Specific intent:** To do the act with a specific intent or objective. Many defenses will serve to negate the specific intent element; such as where one is so intoxicated they are unable to form specific intent.

   Example: A student is unprepared for his final exam, so he asks his girlfriend to set off the fire alarm after the test starts. Students were injured in the panic that followed. If charged with *conspiracy to commit battery* they would be found *not guilty* because there is no proof that both specifically intended for people to be victims of battery. The intent was to avoid taking the exam.

3. **Malice:** This state of mind is used for common law murder and arson. Malice is established by showing the defendant **recklessly disregarded a high risk** that the harmful result would occur. While malice sounds similar to the state of mind for specific intent crimes, malice crimes are **not eligible for the specific intent defenses.**

COMMON LAW CRIMINAL INTENT CHEAT SHEET

General Intent	Specific Intent		Malice
To merely do the act.	To do the act with a specific intent or objective.		Reckless disregard of a high risk of harm.
	Crime	**Intent**	
◆ Battery ◆ Rape ◆ Kidnapping ◆ False Imprisonment ◆ Involuntary manslaughter ◆ Reckless disregard murder	Solicitation	Crime is committed	◆ Arson ◆ Common law murder
	Conspiracy	Crime is committed	
	Attempt	Complete the crime	
	Robbery	Permanently deprive	
	Embezzlement	Defraud	
	Murder-First degree	Kill	
	Assault	Commit battery	
	Vol. manslaughter	Intent to kill-mitigated	
	Burglary	Commit felony therein	
	False pretenses	Defraud	
	Forgery	Defraud	
	Larceny	Permanently deprive	
	Memorization tip: SCARE My FAV BFF Luigi.		

> **<u>MBE tip</u>:** General intent focuses more on the unlawful act, whereas specific intent requires a specific mens rea of the defendant to bring about a particular result; these distinctions matter when determining which defenses negate which crimes (defenses are covered in detail in sec. VI).

4. **Model Penal Code** (MPC) **states of mind:**

   a. **Purposely:** To **consciously do the act.**

   b. **Knowingly: Awareness** of the conduct engaged in or that certain circumstances exist. This is a *subjective standard*. The defendant does not need to know their actions are illegal, just that they knowingly acted in the manner in which they did.

   <u>Example (knowingly)</u>: It is against the law to *knowingly* sell alcohol to a person under 21 years of age. If a clerk *knowingly* sells alcohol to an 18-year-old, but does not know doing so is illegal, they still can be found guilty.

   <u>Example (not knowingly)</u>: A statute defines perjury as *knowingly* making a false statement under oath. When a witness on the stand is asked if he had been convicted of a crime, he said no. In fact, he had been found guilty. But his attorney told him he was only on probation. If the jury believes the witness honestly believed he had not been convicted of a crime, they should find him not guilty of perjury because he *would not have knowingly* made the false statement.

   > **<u>MBE tip</u>:** Questions might provide a statute that modifies the state of mind for a particular crime. If so, use the state of mind in the statute instead of the default state of mind that traditionally corresponds to that crime.

   c. **Recklessly: Conscious disregard** (*subjective standard*) of a **substantial and unjustifiable risk** (*objective standard*) that circumstances exist or a result will follow. A **gross deviation** from the standard of care a reasonable person would use.

   <u>Example</u>: A man is charged with manslaughter after driving over a pedestrian while intoxicated. A statute defines manslaughter as the killing of a human being in a criminally reckless manner. The man will argue he was intoxicated, but the prosecution could argue that by becoming intoxicated, the man *consciously disregarded* the risks that come with driving while intoxicated so he still acted recklessly.

   > **<u>MBE tip</u>:** Be prepared to argue from the defendant's point of view as well as the prosecution's point of view. The calls often ask for the best or strongest argument from either side.

   d. **Negligence: Failure to be aware** (*subjective standard*) of a **substantial and unjustifiable risk** (*objective standard*) that circumstances exist or a result will follow. A **substantial deviation** from the standard of care a reasonable person would use.

      1. **Violation of a statute:** This can include violation of a statute or ordinance (e.g., failure to yield to pedestrians in a cross walk).

   e. **Transferred intent** can apply where a defendant intends to harm one person, but harms another person instead.

Example: Man intends to shoot his neighbor. He sees the neighbor coming home from work and tries to shoot him but misses and shoots a child. Man's intent is transferred from the intended victim (neighbor) to the actual victim (child).

> **MBE tip:** The *best defense* to a charge would be to **negate an element** of the crime, such as the mens rea element by showing the defendant had no control over his actions (i.e., D had a seizure) rather than argue a traditional (affirmative) defense such as intoxication or self-defense.

5. **Exceptions to requiring a mental state:**

   a. **Strict liability:** Offenses imposing **strict liability** do not require a culpable mental state (i.e., statutory rape, selling alcohol to minors, bigamy, etc.).

   Example: A statute provides it is a misdemeanor to sell alcohol to any person under the age of 21. A woman who was only 20 years old but looked older bought a six-pack of beer from clerk. The clerk is guilty of the misdemeanor since it is a strict liability crime (even if the clerk honestly thought she was 21).

   1. **Punishment:** The punishment is usually lighter for a strict liability crime as opposed to a crime where intent needs to be proved.
   2. **Legislative intent:** Since courts disfavor crimes requiring no mens rea, courts look to see if there is legislative intent to dispense with the mens rea requirement.

   > **MBE tip:** If a question asks you which answer choice is likely to be a strict liability offense, look for an answer with a lighter penalty (i.e., a misdemeanor over a felony).

   b. **Vicarious liability:** Some offenses impose **vicarious liability** on a person when they are liable for the actions of another person (i.e., employer/employee). The one held vicariously liable must have had the ability to control the person who physically committed the crime.

   Example: A statute provides it is a misdemeanor to sell alcohol to any person under the age of 21. A woman who was only 20 years old but looked older bought a six-pack of beer from clerk. Store owner can also be held liable for clerk's actions under vicarious liability.

MENS REA		
Common Law	**Model Penal Code**	
General intent: to do the act	**Purposely:** Consciously do act	
Specific intent: to do the act with a specific intent or objective	**Knowingly:** Awareness of → conduct or circumstances	Subjective standard
Malice: reckless disregard of a high risk of harm (negates specific intent defenses)	**Recklessly:** Conscious disregard of → substantial unjustifiable risk →	Subjective standard Objective standard
	Negligence: Failure to be aware of → substantial unjustifiable risk →	Subjective standard Objective standard
	Strict liability: no mental state	
	Vicarious liability: no mental state	

MBE tip: When the question is testing mens rea it can do so by asking whether the defendant is guilty of a particular crime. It is important that you know the rule elements for that crime to determine if the defendant had the requisite mens rea.

Example: A husband decides to kill his wife and asks his friend, a pharmacist, for poison. Suspecting the husband's motive, the pharmacist gave him an antibiotic instead. The husband injected the wife with the antibiotic, and she died from an allergic reaction. If asked about whether the pharmacist can be guilty as an accomplice to various crimes, you need to know the mens rea for accomplice liability (which is intent to aid, abet, or assist). The pharmacist did not intend to aid or abet because she gave the husband antibiotics and didn't know his plan (even if she suspected it). The correct answer would be that the pharmacist is guilty of no crime because she lacked the mens rea to be the husband's accomplice.

C. **Causation:** Some crimes, such as murder, require a showing of causation. [When tested it mostly applies to murder—examples of how it is tested are in the murder section below].

1. **Actual cause (cause in fact):** The defendant must have actually caused the harm to the victim (but-for the defendant's act, victim would not have been harmed).

2. **Proximate cause:** The harm must have been *foreseeable* (natural and probable consequence) at the time of the defendant's act (some causal connection between the defendant's act and the victim's harm that is not too remote).

   a. **Year and a day limit:** If a homicide victim dies a year and a day after defendant's act, defendant will not be the proximate cause of victim's death (modernly this rule is abolished in the majority of jurisdictions).

II. CRIMES AGAINST PROPERTY

A. **Larceny** is the **trespassory taking** and **carrying away** of **personal property of another** with the **intent to permanently deprive** the owner of that property.

Example: D takes neighbor's dog and sells it.

1. **Trespassory taking:** It is important to identify who had **lawful possession** at the time of the taking. If one has lawful possession of the property at the time of the taking, it **can't be a larceny.** Though, **if one only has "custody"** and not possession, there **can be a larceny.**

   a. **Custody** is limited control over property of another (e.g., checking a bag or coat when entering a hotel or restaurant).

   b. **Possession** is the power to exercise control over property.

   c. **Continuing trespass:** The trespass can occur by a continuing trespass such that the **intent to steal arises** not at the time of the taking, but **later while the trespass is still ongoing.**

   Example: A fired worker cleans out her desk and realizes she has some of her employer's possessions, but she takes them home with her intending to sort through them and return the employer's items. Once home, she decides to keep the items. This is a larceny since she formed the intent to steal while the trespass was still continuing.

2. **Carrying away:** The carrying away (asportation) element requires movement **of only a slight distance.**

   Example: A drunk man left a bar to walk home. Another patron who observed the man's condition followed him. The patron saw the man fall to the ground so he reached into his pocket to grab his wallet. When the patron heard police officers approaching he dropped the wallet and ran off. The carrying away was sufficient movement even though he dropped the wallet near the man and did not take it with him.

B. **Larceny by trick** is the same as larceny, except the defendant tricks the other party *to obtain possession* through **fraud or deceit.** [This rule is rarely MBE tested.]

Example: D gets permission to borrow the owner's car for the evening by falsely promising to return it, although he does not intend to do so. Two days later, he changes his mind and returns the car. D can still be charged with larceny by trick since he tricked the owner into giving him the car and did take it.

> **MBE tip:** One can commit larceny if they find lost property (i.e., someone dropped their wallet at a ball game) and then take it if the finder knows who it belongs to and intends to take the property. So beware of the saying "finder's keepers" as that does not always apply!

C. **Embezzlement** is the **fraudulent conversion** of **personal property** of **another** by one who is already in **lawful possession** of that property. Some jurisdictions include real property as well.

Example: P took a diamond ring to a pawnshop and borrowed $20 on it. P had 60 days to pay back the money to get the ring back. 50 days later the shop owner sold the ring thinking P would not come back. Two days later, P came back for the ring. The owner is guilty of embezzlement.

> **MBE tip:** For embezzlement, the embezzler always has lawful possession; whereas for larceny, the person taking the property does not have lawful possession.
>
> **Decoy tip:** When given a choice between embezzlement and larceny, embezzlement is *usually* the wrong answer due to the lawful possession element (but *sometimes* embezzlement is tested outright, so know your rule elements—look for lawful possession facts, such as pawn shops or items given to D as opposed to those stolen by D).

D. **False pretenses** occurs when the defendant **knowingly** makes a **false representation** of a past or present **material fact,** which causes the person to whom it was made to **rely** on the representation and as a result **convey title** to the misrepresenter who **intends to defraud.**

Example: An antique dealer and skilled calligrapher crafted a letter on very old paper. She made it appear to be written by Thomas Jefferson by using a facsimile of his autograph and copying it into the letter. She told collectors that she received it from a foreign collector and could make no promises about its authenticity. A collector paid her $5000 for it. Later it was discovered the letter was not authentic and that the calligrapher had written the letter. She is guilty of false pretenses because she knowingly misrepresented the source of the letter causing the collector to convey title (here it is cash) to her.

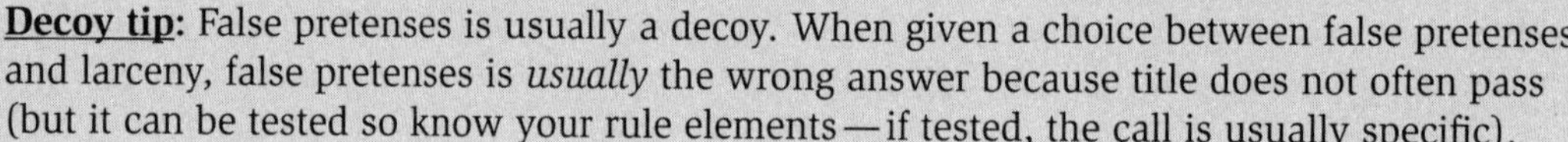

> **MBE tip:** If the victim is tricked into giving up possession, it could be larceny (by trick) as opposed to false pretenses because no title has passed, so look to see if title passes.
>
> **Decoy tip:** False pretenses is usually a decoy. When given a choice between false pretenses and larceny, false pretenses is *usually* the wrong answer because title does not often pass (but it can be tested so know your rule elements—if tested, the call is usually specific).

THEFT CRIME EXAMPLES DECODED			
Facts	**Larceny because**	**NOT Embezzlement because**	**NOT False Pretenses because**
Employee worked as a cashier and one night realized the cash in the drawer didn't match the receipt tapes. He gave everything to the manager who accused him of taking the money. Angry about being wrongfully accused, the cashier went to the back and took the cash from the safe.	Trespassory taking and carrying away with intent to steal	Cashier **did not have lawful possession**	Manager **never conveyed title** to cashier
Employee liked his boss's watch. At a work picnic, Boss took off his watch and left it on a blanket. Employee decided to steal it. After he grabbed it but before he pocketed it, Boss returned and told him he was planning on giving him the watch for his birthday and said he could have it.	Employee picked up the watch, which was sufficient to carry away, and he had the intent to steal	Employee **did not have lawful possession**	Boss **never conveyed title** *before* employee stole it
At a football game, a man saw a wallet fall out of a woman's purse. The man picked up the wallet and found $100 in it. The man put the wallet in his pocket as the woman approached him to ask if he had seen a missing wallet. The man said no and took the wallet.	Trespassory taking and carrying away with intent to steal because he knew the wallet belonged to her	Man **did not have lawful possession**	Woman **never conveyed title** to the man

E. **Robbery** is a **larceny** (elements above) and, in addition, the property has been **taken from the person or presence of the owner** through **force, or by placing the owner in fear** (the force used can be done after stealing the property while trying to flee).

Example: D threatens V with a knife, grabs her purse, and runs off with it.

1. **Third party:** The force or threat can be directed towards a third party.

   Example: Husband and Wife were walking to their car after a movie. D leaped out of a nearby alley with a gun. He pushed Wife against a wall and held the gun to her head, demanding money from Husband. Husband handed over the cash and D ran away. D is guilty of robbery against Husband even though he threatened Wife (the third party).

2. **Larceny is a lesser included offense to robbery,** so a person cannot be charged with both larceny and robbery for the same incident.

MBE tip: Theft crimes questions often ask, "What is the most serious crime D committed?" They will tell you the crimes are listed in descending order of seriousness. With these questions, start with the most serious crime, apply the facts to the elements. If the elements are satisfied, that is the answer. Move on to assess the next answer choice only if the elements are not satisfied.

Decoy tip: In a lesser included offense crime question, the call will ask, "What crime(s) can D be convicted of?" If *both* crimes are listed in each answer choice, the correct answer choice must state "crime 1 *or* crime 2," not "crime 1 *and* crime 2," since D can't be convicted of both crimes when one is a lesser included offense.

F. **Extortion** is a threat of **future harm** to deprive an owner of their property (e.g., blackmailing a person to get something you want). [This rule is rarely MBE tested.]

G. **Theft** is the illegal **taking of another person's property.** Under common law, the general crime of theft was universally applied. Modernly, most jurisdictions use more specific crimes definitions such as larceny, etc. But, you may see the general term "theft" used in MBE questions. [This rule is rarely MBE tested.]

H. **Burglary** at common law is a **breaking** and **entering** of the **dwelling house** of another at **nighttime** with **intent to commit a felony therein. Modernly,** most jurisdictions include **any structure type** and **any time of day.**

MBE tip: Often the felony that D intends to commit is larceny so correct answer choices often state that D can be guilty of both larceny and burglary.

Lesser included offense tip: *Unlike* robbery, **larceny** is **not a lesser included offense** to **burglary.** Robbery includes *every single element* of larceny (and then adds an additional **element**) which is why larceny is a lesser included offense to robbery. However, burglary *does not include every single element* of larceny, so larceny is not a lesser included offense of burglary. A crime is a lesser included offense if *all elements* in the lesser crime are also in the greater crime. See merger chart in sec. IV.D for more examples.

1. **Breaking:** At common law, the "breaking" element of a burglary is only satisfied if the **burglar creates the opening.** Therefore, if an owner leaves the door open, and a burglar uses that opening to enter a home, a breaking does not exist at common law. But, no force or violence is needed to break in (gain entry); the mere opening of a closed but unlocked door, followed by an entry, will suffice.

2. **Entry** can be established when any part of a **person intrudes** into the structure, **even if momentarily.**

   Example: A woman decided to steal her neighbor's necklace when the neighbor was away. She went there one night and opened the bathroom window and started to climb inside. As her leg entered the window, the cat let out a screech so the woman backed out and left. Her leg entering momentarily was sufficient entry.

3. **The intent to commit the felony therein** must occur **at the time of the breaking** and entering. If the intent to commit the felony arises *after* the breaking and entering already occurred, intent will not be satisfied. It is not necessary that the actual felony be carried out, just that the defendant intended to commit one.

> **<u>MBE tip</u>:** Pay special attention to the D's intent—if D didn't gain entry with the intent to commit a felony (such as if D is trying to retrieve something they erroneously thought belonged to them) then there is no intent for burglary. If the call of the question asks for the "best defense," always try to find a defense that negates the intent element.

I. **Receipt of stolen property** is a crime when one **knowingly receives, conceals, or disposes of stolen property** with the **intent to permanently deprive** the owner of their property. [This rule is rarely MBE tested.]

   <u>Example</u>: A new gang member points a gun at a woman and demands she give him her watch. Once he has the watch, he gives it to the gang leader who watched him steal the watch. The gang leader can be charged with receipt of stolen property.

J. **Arson** is the **malicious burning** of the **dwelling of another.** Modernly, most jurisdictions include most structures and burning includes damage caused by explosives too (not just fire). Dwelling refers to **possession** of the premises and not ownership.

   1. **Malice** (mens rea): Arson requires a **mental state of malice,** so even **recklessness** regarding the risk of fire will suffice to establish arson. It is enough that the defendant intentionally took an action that posed a high risk of a burning, even if they did not specifically intend the burning.

      <u>Example</u>: Using a match to read a label on a can in a basement known to be filled with flammable liquid, which causes a fire to erupt, is sufficiently reckless for an arson.

   2. **Houseburning** is the **malicious burning of one's *own* dwelling** if the dwelling is situated near other dwellings to create danger to them. Under this misdemeanor, one can be held liable for burning their own building.

      <u>Example</u>: D decided to burn down his store for insurance proceeds. While looking for an item in the basement, he lit a match to read the label on a can of flammable material. The match burned his finger and in a reflex action he dropped the match. D made no effort to put out the fire and let the building burn down. D is guilty of arson if he could have put out the fire before it spread and didn't do so because he wanted it to burn, even though it was his own dwelling since this is considered houseburning, which is a subset of arson.

K. **Forgery** is the **making of a false writing** or altering of an existing writing that has **apparent legal significance** with the **intent to defraud.** [This rule is rarely MBE tested.]

   1. **Uttering** consists of **offering** as genuine an instrument that may be the subject of forgery and is false, with intent to defraud (essentially this means the passing, selling, or publishing of a known forgery).

> **<u>Decoy tip</u>:** Forgery is often a wrong answer, but you need to understand what it is to rule it out as the correct answer.

III. CRIMES AGAINST THE PERSON

Disturbing content warning: Crimes examples in this outline are based on real MBE questions. Some content may be disturbing, so focus on the law and don't get emotionally distracted by the facts. No actual children, people, or animals were harmed during the making of this book.

A. **Assault** is either (1) an **attempt to commit a battery** (see below) or (2) the intent to place another in **reasonable apprehension** of imminent injury. Assault cannot be established by words alone; some overt gesture or physical act is required.

   1. **Aggravated assault** applies if a **deadly weapon** is used (e.g., waving a gun in a threatening manner). Some jurisdictions also apply aggravated assault if the defendant intended to rape or murder the victim.

   2. **Lesser included offense:** Assault can be a lesser included offense of **robbery** if the "placing another in reasonable apprehension of imminent injury" is done to rob the victim. In that situation, the defendant cannot be convicted of both assault and robbery because the assault is a lesser included offense. See merger chart in sec. IV.D.

B. **Battery** is the **intentional or reckless** causing of a bodily injury or an offensive touching to another.

   1. **Aggravated battery** applies if a **deadly weapon** is used (e.g., waving a gun in a threatening manner and the gun hits the victim in the head). Some jurisdictions also apply aggravated battery when the victim is a child or a police officer.

   2. **General intent:** *Unlike* assault, battery need not be intentional since it can result from criminal negligence/reckless actions.

C. **Mayhem** is the **permanent dismemberment** or disablement of a body part. Modernly it is treated as aggravated battery. [This rule is rarely MBE tested.]

D. **Kidnapping** is the **unlawful confinement** of another, **involving movement** (asportation, though the movement need not be a substantial distance) or **concealment** in a secret place.

   1. **Aggravated kidnapping** applies if done **for ransom,** to **facilitate committing another crime,** or if **children** are taken.

   2. **Consent** to confinement must be freely given by one with capacity. Consent **cannot be obtained by** coercion, threats, or deception. Consent by one with incapacity, illness, or youth is ineffective.

   3. **False imprisonment:** The **unlawful confinement** of another without consent. This is a **lesser included offense** of kidnapping so the defendant can only be convicted of one of these offenses but not both.

MBE tip: Remember that each state has its own laws so a person can be convicted of the same crime in two different states (i.e., if they kidnap someone and cross borders to a different state they could be charged with kidnapping in both states).

E. **Rape** at common law is the unlawful sexual intercourse of a female, not one's wife, without her consent. Modernly rape is gender-neutral and marriage is irrelevant. It is a general intent crime; therefore, mistake regarding consent will not provide a defense. [This rule is rarely MBE tested.]

F. **Homicide** is the unlawful taking of the life of another. The two types of homicide are murder and manslaughter.

1. **Common law murder** is the **unlawful killing** of another person with **malice aforethought.** At common law the required elements are **actus reus** (an act by the defendant), **corpus delecti** (death of victim), **mens rea** (malice aforethought, which can be established four ways as described below), and **causation** (a causal relationship between the defendant's act and the victim's death).

> **MBE tip:** As discussed above in actus reus, D has no affirmative duty to act if someone else is killing another (absent a special relationship or legal duty), there is no duty to warn others about a potential deadly force (i.e., a bomb), and mere presence alone is insufficient to constitute an actus reus for murder.

a. **Malice** is the requisite mental state for murder and can be established by:

> **MBE tip:** Bar exam questions use all of the bolded terms, within each type of malice below, interchangeably. Be familiar with the synonyms.

 *1.* An **intent to kill** (desire to kill or knowledge to a substantial certainty death will occur);

a. Use of a **deadly weapon** or instrument creates the inference of an intent to kill.

 *2.* An **intent to commit serious** (or grievous) **bodily injury.** Here, the defendant does not necessarily intend for the victim to die, but intends serious bodily injury, such as an attack with a baseball bat;

 *3.* A **reckless disregard** to the value of human life (also known as **"depraved heart"** or **reckless indifference** murder); or

4. An **intent to commit a dangerous felony,** known as the **felony murder rule** (FMR).

a. The intent to commit certain dangerous felonies supplies the malice requirement for murder where death is a **natural and probable consequence** (foreseeable) of the defendant's conduct and the death occurs **during the commission** of the felony, even if the death is accidental.

i. **A felon will be liable for a killing committed by his co-felon** when the killing is committed **in furtherance of the felony** and is a **natural and probable result** of the felony.

Example: A and B commit an armed robbery of a bank. The police are in hot pursuit and A drives erratically in an attempt to escape, hitting and killing a pedestrian. The pedestrian's killing was a natural and probable consequence of erratic driving to escape and done during the commission of the felony escape attempt. Both A and B could be charged with felony murder.

ii. **Death of co-felon — Redline view:** The *majority* of courts hold that a defendant is **not liable** for the death of a co-felon when a **non-felon kills the co-felon** during commission of the felony (e.g., a police officer or a victim kills the co-felon).

iii. **Death of bystander:** Jurisdictions are **split** as to whether a defendant is liable for murder when the **non-felon victim, or a police officer, kills a bystander** during the commission of the felony. There are two views:

a. **Agency theory** jurisdictions (majority rule) **No:** Defendant is **not liable** because the non-felon killer of the bystander is not acting as an agent of the felon.

b. **Proximate cause theory** jurisdictions (minority rule) **Yes:** Defendant is **liable** since the felon's actions are the proximate cause of the bystander's death.

> **MBE tip:** Often this issue is tested by questions that ask what D's best argument is to be found NOT guilty. The best answer is usually an option that points out that someone other than D killed the victim (such as a customer or police officer). Remember, unless the question directs otherwise, apply the majority rule when there is a jurisdictional split.

b. The **underlying felony must be independent** of the killing (i.e., felony cannot be aggravated battery).

c. **Inherently dangerous felonies:** The felony murder rule typically applies to the following inherently dangerous felonies: **B**urglary, **A**rson, **R**ape, **R**obbery, or **K**idnapping.

> **Memorization tip:** BARRK
>
> **MBE tip:** Mayhem and sodomy were also included under common law but are rarely tested. Modernly, more felonies are considered inherently dangerous by jurisdiction. A question may provide an additional felony.
>
> 
>
> **Decoy tip:** Felony murder charges may be brought for intentional killings, accidental killings, and for killings by the accused's accomplices. So don't select "no crime" or "no murder" as an answer choice when murder under felony murder can apply.

b. Causation: The defendant's conduct must also be the **cause in fact** (but-for test) and the **proximate cause** (foreseeable) of the death, but need not be the sole cause of the death.

Example (causation): A man had a heart ailment and needed a transplant to survive. Doctors arranged to have the man flown to a hospital for the surgery. His nephew stood to inherit from the man, so he poisoned the man. The poison produced a reaction causing the surgery to be postponed. The next day the man died from a heart attack due to a weakened heart from the poison. The nephew would still be liable for murder as the poison still caused the death and death was a foreseeable result from poisoning a man with a weak heart, even if the poison wasn't the sole cause of death.

Example (no causation): A father began to deprive his son of food during the summer vacation because the child did poorly in school. The son became ill from malnutrition and eventually died. The autopsy disclosed that the child died from cancer and that the malnutrition would have eventually killed the son in a few months. The father did not cause the child's death since cancer was responsible and not the lack of food.

c. Intent can transfer for murder (just as in torts).

2. First-degree murder (statutory murder) can arise two ways:

a. Premeditation and deliberation: First-degree murder applies when the killing was the result of premeditation and deliberation—in other words, where the defendant **had time**

to reflect upon the idea of killing, even if only for a moment, and acted in a **cool and dispassionate** manner.

Example: A woman joins a gang and is ordered to kill a rival gang member as part of the initiation process. She decides she no longer wants to do so, but the gang leader told her he would kill her if she didn't kill the rival gang member. The next day she killed a rival gang member. The woman could be charged with first-degree murder since she acted intentionally with premeditation.

> **Decoy tip:** Duress is not a defense to intentional murder (that is always a wrong answer choice when the murder is intentional), but it can be a defense to a felony if the murder is based on the felony murder rule.

b. **Enumerated inherently dangerous felony** under an application of the **felony murder rule.** See sec. III.F.1.a.*4.c*.

3. **Second-degree murder** (also statutory murder): If the murder does **not rise to the level of first-degree** murder and is **not reduced to manslaughter,** the defendant will be guilty of second-degree murder.
4. **Defenses** may apply to murder. See sec. VI below for defenses.

> **MBE tip:** When the call asks, "What is the *most serious* crime for which D can be convicted?" what they are really asking is what is the *most serious* crime **possible.** If there is a chance D could be guilty of murder (even if facts lean toward manslaughter) the correct answer is murder because it is **possible.**

COMMON LAW MURDER MALICE EXAMPLES

MBE tip: Malice can be established by (1) intent to kill, (2) intent to cause serious bodily injury, (3) reckless disregard, or (4) intent to commit a felony under FMR.

Intent to kill	NO intent to kill*
◆ Husband intends to kill his wife, so he asks his pharmacist friend for poison. His friend gives him an antibiotic instead. Husband injects wife and she dies from an allergic reaction. Husband still had the intent to kill his wife. ◆ A man and woman were business partners. The man had been embezzling money and was afraid the woman would find out during an audit so he hired someone to kill her. She died in a car accident arranged by the killer. The man would be guilty of murder since he had the intent to kill her.	◆ Parents refuse medical treatment for a child with meningitis due to religious beliefs. ◆ Employee of a daycare center did not report bruises on a child. A statute required reporting, but the employee was not aware. The child was beaten to death by her parents two weeks later. *This type of question often asks what is the "best argument" or "best defense" against the murder charge.

Intent to commit serious bodily injury

- ◆ D strikes victim on the head with a glass soft-drink bottle. Victim goes into a coma and later dies.
- ◆ D strikes victim in the face with a baseball bat only intending to injure, but victim dies.
- ◆ D shoots victim in the leg, intending only to injure his leg, but victim dies.
- ◆ A man and his friend were watching football. Mad at a call by the referee, the friend threw a bottle at the TV, breaking the TV. Enraged, the man picked up a nearby hammer and hit the friend on the head killing him.

Reckless disregard (depraved heart) murder

MBE tip: This type of malice is the MOST heavily tested. It is interchangeably called reckless indifference to an unjustifiably high risk to human life, gross recklessness, extreme recklessness, depraved heart recklessness, and depraved heart.

- ◆ D fires a gun into a house that has occupants in it.
- ◆ D drives a car into a crowd to scare people away.
- ◆ D lies to a man (who is known to be violent and jealous), that his wife was having an affair with a bank president, who is heavily guarded. The man goes to the bank with a gun and ends up getting shot by armed guards. D (who lied to the man) has a reckless disregard malice for the life of the man.
- ◆ A marksman went to the country where he previously hunted to try out a new rifle. He noticed new houses and a playground were now present, but went into the woods and posted a paper target to a tree in between himself and the playground. He accidentally shot and killed a kid when he missed the target. The marksman is extremely reckless.
- ◆ D fired shots into the air at work after being fired with the intent to shut down operations. D is extremely reckless.
- ◆ D pointed a loaded gun at someone in a bar to get back an item they took. Someone else throws a beer bottle at the man holding the gun and it hits the gun, which fires and kills another person. The man pointing the gun has a reckless disregard malice for the life of others around him.
- ◆ A woman wants to kill her husband and adds poison to his wine. She changes her mind but leaves the wine out. The maid drinks the wine and dies. The woman is liable for maid's death as she has a reckless disregard for life since others might drink the wine.

Felony Murder Rule

- ◆ While robbing a liquor store, D accidentally drops his gun, which fires and kills a customer (felony = robbery).
- ◆ D deliberately drove his car into a gas pump causing an explosion that burned down the gas station building killing a clerk (felony = arson).
- ◆ D holds a couple at gunpoint in their apartment, ties them up, and steals jewelry and other belongings including the wife's necklace. The husband dies of a heart attack while straining to free himself (felony = burglary and robbery).

 5. **Manslaughter:** In most states there are two types of manslaughter — voluntary and involuntary.

a. **Voluntary manslaughter:** There are two types of voluntary manslaughter—heat of passion and imperfect self-defense.

1. **Heat of passion:** Murder can be reduced to **voluntary manslaughter** if the defendant killed in the heat of passion and the following requirements are met:

   a. **Reasonable provocation:** Defendant acted in response to a provocation that would cause a reasonable person to lose self-control (note: the standard is *not* that a reasonable person would be provoked to kill):

   b. **Acted in heat of passion:** Defendant **was in fact provoked** at the time they acted;

   c. **No cooling off time:** There was **insufficient time for a reasonable person to cool off** between the provocation and the killing; and

   d. **Defendant did not cool off:** The defendant **did not in fact cool off** by the time they killed.

HEAT OF PASSION EXAMPLES

Intent to kill that could be reduced to voluntary manslaughter (heat of passion)**

- D's neighbor stabbed him so D grabbed his own gun and told Neighbor to back off. Neighbor continued to attack D. D shot Neighbor twice. Neighbor fell on the floor. Once Neighbor was on the floor moaning and no longer attacking D, D fired a third shot which killed Neighbor.
- Man came home from work early and found his wife engaged in sexual intercourse with a neighbor. The man grabbed a gun and killed the neighbor. The jury would likely be instructed on both murder and voluntary manslaughter.

** **Call of the question tip:** This type of question often asks you which crimes **D can be convicted** of (murder *or* voluntary manslaughter is the correct answer), or which crimes the **jury should be instructed** on (murder *and* voluntary manslaughter is the correct answer).

2. **Imperfect self-defense:** Murder may also be reduced to **voluntary manslaughter** if the defendant kills under an **unreasonable mistake** about the need for self-defense or the **defendant started the altercation.** [This rule is rarely MBE tested.]

b. **Involuntary manslaughter** can arise two ways:

1. **Gross or criminal negligence:** Involuntary manslaughter arises when a person's behavior is grossly negligent and results in the death of another. Gross negligence is the **disregard of a very substantial danger of serious bodily harm or death.**

   Example: A wife decided to kill her husband so she added cyanide, a deadly poison, to his wine. She changed her mind and hid the glass of wine behind a lamp on the table, planning to leave it for the maid to clean up. The maid found the glass, drank it, and died. The wife could be convicted of involuntary manslaughter based on criminal negligence. (Note: this example was used above as well because the wife could be convicted of either reckless disregard murder or involuntary manslaughter.)

MANSLAUGHTER V. MURDER EXAMPLES

MBE tip: Criminal negligence and reckless disregard (depraved heart) are two points on the same spectrum. Conduct that does not rise to the level of extreme recklessness will likely be criminal negligence.

Criminal Negligence (Involuntary Manslaughter)	Reckless Disregard (Murder)
Failure of a parent to provide medical care for a sick minor child.	Teenagers playing a game of Russian roulette.
Driving while intoxicated.	Driving while intoxicated with prior DUIs.
Bar fight where a person falls and hits their head and dies.	Bar fight where a person pulls out a gun and it accidentally goes off.
Ride operator doesn't properly ensure seatbelt is properly fastened.	Ride operator firing a gun into the air to get the attention of people in line.

2. **Misdemeanor-manslaughter:** Involuntary manslaughter also arises when the defendant commits a **misdemeanor** and a **death occurs accidentally during its commission** or for **felonies that don't rise to the level** of murder under the felony murder rule (FMR).

   a. **Actual and proximate cause** must exist between the illegal act giving rise to the misdemeanor and the resulting death.

   Example: D was driving his car at the legal speed limit. A child ran into the street and was run over and killed before D could prevent it. Unbeknownst to D, his driver's license expired 3 months earlier, and it was a misdemeanor to drive with an expired license. D is not guilty of manslaughter because having an expired driver's license did not cause the death of the child.

   MBE tip: Many manslaughter questions focus on D's best argument for acquittal or D's best defense (put on your defense attorney hat). The correct answer choice often involves showing a lack of causation.

IV. INCHOATE OFFENSES: SOLICITATION, CONSPIRACY, AND ATTEMPT

A. **Solicitation** occurs when one requests or **encourages another to commit a crime** with the intent that the person solicited does commit the crime, regardless of whether they agree to do so.

   a. **No withdrawal: The crime is complete at the time of the request;** thus it is not possible to withdraw.

   Example: A asks B to kill his wife. The solicitation is complete once A has made the request of B, even if he later changes his mind and communicates that to B.

   b. **No agreement required:** The other party **does not need to agree** to complete the crime.

   c. **Merger rule applies: Solicitation merges with the underlying crime.** A defendant cannot be charged with both solicitation and the completed crime. See merger chart in sec. IV.D.

B. **Conspiracy** is an **agreement** between **two or more persons** who **intend to commit** an **unlawful act** or a lawful act by unlawful means.

1. The **agreement can be implied or inferred** and does not require that all persons commit the actual act or be present during the commission of the act.

   a. **Statutory protected class:** When the purpose of a criminal statute is to **protect a type** (or class) **of person** there can be **no conspiracy** between the protected person and the defendant.

   Example: A 21-year-old boyfriend and his 16-year-old girlfriend decide to have sexual intercourse. The girl's mother found out and the boy was charged with statutory rape and conspiracy to commit statutory rape. The age of consent in the jurisdiction is 18. Since the purpose of the statute was to protect the girl, she cannot be a conspirator and the boy cannot be charged with conspiracy.

   b. **Acquittal:** At common law, where **one defendant is acquitted** for conspiracy, the other party (if only two) cannot be charged with conspiracy. However, if **charges are dropped** against one party (i.e., in exchange for testimony), the remaining conspirator can still be charged.

> **Decoy tip:** Even if D has an alibi or was arrested prior to the crime, it will not excuse them from being convicted of conspiracy. Don't be tempted by answer choices that include D's alibi or D's arrest prior to the crime commission as reasons not to be convicted for conspiracy. D could have still agreed to commit the crime without being present during the crime's commission.

2. **Number of parties required:**

   a. **Common law:** Requires a **bilateral agreement** with two or more persons agreeing (also called plurality of agreement) to commit an unlawful act. [This is the default rule unless they tell you otherwise.]

   b. **Modern law/Model Penal Code:** A **unilateral conspiracy** is allowed. The party agreeing to commit the unlawful act can be convicted of conspiracy even if they are the only party with genuine criminal intent, such as when they agree with an undercover police officer.

   c. **Wharton's Rule:** If the crime can only be committed by the actual number of people participating then there is no conspiracy liability.

   Examples: Adultery, incest, bigamy, dueling, etc.

3. **Intent to commit the unlawful act required: Mere knowledge is insufficient** to establish the intent necessary to commit the unlawful act. There is also no legal duty to affirmatively act to prevent another from committing a crime just because the person is present or has mere knowledge.

> **Decoy tip:** MBE questions often raise facts that show D *did not intend* to commit a crime or unlawful act so there is no conspiracy. Wrong answers will find a conspiracy when there isn't one.
>
> **Example:** A, B, and C go to a neighbor's house to take stock certificates from a safe. C believes that the stock certificates actually belong to A and that the neighbor was improperly keeping them from him. C would not be liable for conspiracy, since he did not intend to commit an unlawful act.

4. **Overt act required modernly: At common law,** the conspiracy occurred the moment the agreement was made, but the **majority of jurisdictions (and the MPC) now require an overt act,** which is any act in furtherance of the conspiracy, including mere preparation. The overt act may also be performed by only one conspirator.

CONSPIRACY CHEAT SHEET		
	Common Law	**Model Penal Code**
Agreement	2 + persons (bilateral)	1 person ok (unilateral)
Intent	Crime to succeed	Crime to succeed
Overt Act	None required	Required
MBE tip: Apply the common law rule unless the question directs you to apply the majority, modern, MPC, or unilateral conspiracy.		

5. **Liability for crimes of co-conspirators:** Conspirators are liable for the crimes of co-conspirators if the crimes were committed **in furtherance of the criminal objective** and were **reasonably foreseeable.** This is also known as the *Pinkerton* doctrine. Membership in the conspiracy alone is sufficient to make the defendant liable for reasonably foreseeable crimes.

   Example: A and B operate an illegal brewery. One day B was alone at the brewery and was approached by a buyer. The buyer was in fact an undercover officer who revealed his identify after an illegal sale was made. B grabbed a gun they kept in case of trouble with the law and shot and injured the officer. Both A and B are liable for conspiracy to operate an illegal brewery. A is also liable for B's battery as a co-conspirator (B's battery was in furtherance of the crime to operate an illegal brewery and the battery was foreseeable as they kept the gun in case they had trouble with the law).

6. **Merger rule does not apply:** One **can be charged** with conspiracy and the underlying crime. See merger sec. IV.D.

   > **MBE tip**: The **merger rule does not apply.** Conspiracy is a separate crime, so D can be guilty of both conspiracy to do crime X and crime X.

7. **Defenses**

   a. **Withdrawal:** Once the agreement is made and the conspiracy is formed, one **cannot withdraw** from the conspiracy (because it is already completed), but they **can withdraw for purposes of future crimes** of co-conspirators *if* they **communicate their withdrawal to all co-conspirators** (some jurisdictions allow communications to authorities to serve as withdrawal if timely made) *and* **take an affirmative action** to withdraw.

   Example: A and B agree that A will rob a bank and B will steal a car to use as a getaway. B stole the car and left it at A's house with a note that said he didn't want anything more to do with the robbery scheme. A still robbed the bank. Both A and B can be charged with conspiracy because they agreed to rob a bank. B committed an overt act by stealing the car before B attempted to withdraw, so the withdraw is ineffective.

b. **Factual impossibility** is not a defense to conspiracy.

> MBE tip: Remember that even if one of the conspirators who agreed to commit the crime has a defense (e.g., one party has immunity), it does not negate that there was an agreement for purposes of establishing that element for the *other* party.

★ C. **Attempt** is an **act done with intent to commit a crime** that falls short of completing the crime. It requires the mental state required to complete the underlying crime, and a **substantial step in furtherance** of the intent to commit the crime.

ATTEMPT (INTENT ELEMENT) EXAMPLES	
MBE tip: Most attempt questions focus on D's criminal intent, so first pay attention to whether D intended to commit a crime or not, then look to whether he took a substantial step in furtherance of that intent.	
Intent = attempt	**No intent = no attempt**
◆ Professional poker player cheated a man in a game. The man set out to shoot the player. He got a gun and left for the player's house but was arrested on the way. A statute makes it a crime to "enter the property of another with the intent to commit a crime of violence therein." The man can be charged with attempt to violate the statute because he got a gun and was on his way (showing his intent). ◆ Wife decides to kill Husband so she puts poison in his wine. She gave Husband the wine but he set it down and kissed her so she changed her mind about killing him and hid the glass of wine. She could still be charged with attempted murder (she had the intent to murder).	◆ Man tried to grab his hat that blew off and almost hit Woman but she pushed him away. Man was charged with attempted battery. Man had no intent to commit a criminal battery so there is no attempt of battery. ◆ A statute makes it a crime to sell ammunition to minors. A 16-year-old, who looked 4 to 5 years older entered a store to buy ammunition. The clerk asked her age and she lied and said she was 20. The girl didn't have enough money so she didn't buy the ammunition. Clerk cannot be convicted of attempt to violate the statute because he had no intent to violate it.

1. **Substantial step** is an act beyond mere preparation (unlike overt act used in conspiracy which includes mere preparation). It is usually easy to identify the substantial step, but different jurisdictions use various tests.

SUBSTANTIAL STEP EXAMPLES	
YES substantial step	**NO substantial step**
◆ Attempting to grab a hat (for battery) ◆ Obtaining a weapon and going to a person's house (to commit a statutory crime of wrongfully entering property of another) ◆ Threatening a clerk and going behind a store counter (for robbery) ◆ Lying to a man that his wife was having an affair with V (to cause the man to kill V) ◆ Firing a weapon (for murder) ◆ Putting hand in pocket and threatening to shoot (for robbery)	Drug dealer said to undercover officer he needed to get the drugs, but never did (no attempt to possess cocaine)

2. **Merger rule applies—Attempt merges with the underlying crime:** A defendant cannot be charged with both attempt and the completed crime. But a defendant can be charged only with attempt even if the crime was actually completed. See merger chart in section IV.D.

3. **Factual impossibility is <u>not</u> a defense to attempt:** A defendant can be guilty of an attempted crime where commission of the actual crime is factually impossible. Factual impossibility occurs where, had the facts been as the defendant believed them to be, **there would have been a crime committed,** but since the facts are not as believed, there would be no crime. Therefore, **factual impossibility will not provide a defense to a charge of attempt** for the underlying crime, though it can provide a defense to the underlying crime itself.

   <u>Example</u>: Defendant attempts to poison her boss with a substance believed to be poison, but the substance is actually a laxative. Factual impossibility will not provide an effective defense to the **attempted** murder charge.

4. **Legal impossibility is a defense to attempt:** Legal impossibility (where the defendant believes an act is criminal, but it is not) can provide a successful defense to an attempt charge because even if the facts had been as the defendant believed them to be, **no crime would have been committed.**

   <u>Example</u>: Believing that state law made it a crime to purchase codeine without a prescription, D purchased cough syrup containing codeine without a prescription. Unknown to D, the state law had been repealed and it was now legal to purchase codeine without a prescription. D could not be charged with attempt to purchase codeine because there was no crime D was attempting since his actions were legal despite his mistaken belief.

D. **Merger:** The merger doctrine provides that when two or more crimes merge, the defendant cannot be prosecuted for each crime. Crimes merge when a lesser included offense includes all the same elements as the target crime.

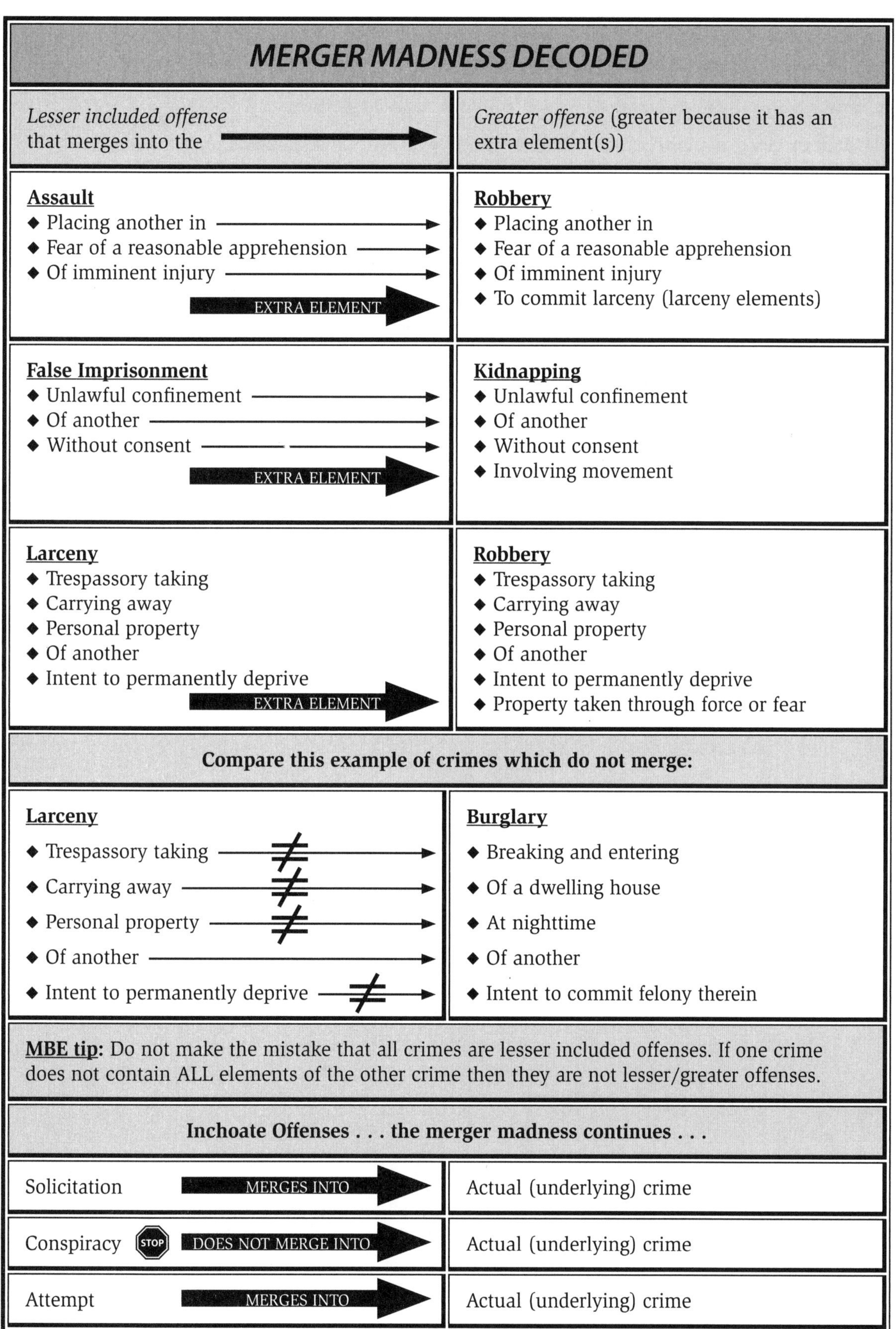

MERGER MADNESS DECODED

Lesser included offense that merges into the →	*Greater offense* (greater because it has an extra element(s))
Assault ◆ Placing another in → ◆ Fear of a reasonable apprehension → ◆ Of imminent injury → EXTRA ELEMENT →	**Robbery** ◆ Placing another in ◆ Fear of a reasonable apprehension ◆ Of imminent injury ◆ To commit larceny (larceny elements)
False Imprisonment ◆ Unlawful confinement → ◆ Of another → ◆ Without consent → EXTRA ELEMENT →	**Kidnapping** ◆ Unlawful confinement ◆ Of another ◆ Without consent ◆ Involving movement
Larceny ◆ Trespassory taking ◆ Carrying away ◆ Personal property ◆ Of another ◆ Intent to permanently deprive EXTRA ELEMENT →	**Robbery** ◆ Trespassory taking ◆ Carrying away ◆ Personal property ◆ Of another ◆ Intent to permanently deprive ◆ Property taken through force or fear

Compare this example of crimes which do not merge:

Larceny	**Burglary**
◆ Trespassory taking ≠→	◆ Breaking and entering
◆ Carrying away ≠→	◆ Of a dwelling house
◆ Personal property ≠→	◆ At nighttime
◆ Of another →	◆ Of another
◆ Intent to permanently deprive ≠→	◆ Intent to commit felony therein

MBE tip: Do not make the mistake that all crimes are lesser included offenses. If one crime does not contain ALL elements of the other crime then they are not lesser/greater offenses.

Inchoate Offenses . . . the merger madness continues . . .

Solicitation	MERGES INTO →	Actual (underlying) crime
Conspiracy	STOP DOES NOT MERGE INTO →	Actual (underlying) crime
Attempt	MERGES INTO →	Actual (underlying) crime

V. ACCOMPLICE LIABILITY

A. **Principal in the first degree:** One who commits the actual crime.

B. **Modern law accomplice:** An accomplice is one who **aids, abets, assists, or encourages** the carrying out of a crime, with a **culpable mental state,** and is **present physically or constructively.**

> <u>MBE tip</u>: When testing accomplice liability, as opposed to conspirator liability, the questions will use language such as "accomplice, accessory, aid, abet, encourage, etc." and there will usually *not* be facts surrounding the actual agreement.

1. **Actus reus:** The **accomplice is liable** for **the crime** he **aided, abetted, assisted,** or **encouraged** if the principal carried out the crime. [This rule is rarely MBE tested.]

   a. **No duty to act:** There is no legal duty to affirmatively act. Even if a person is present or has knowledge, failing to intervene to prevent another from committing a crime does not make one an accomplice, unless there is a special relationship as discussed in sec. I.A.2.

2. **Mental state:** The accomplice must have a **culpable mental state.** The accomplice must **intend to aid, abet, assist, or encourage** the principal to commit the crime **and must intend for the principal to commit the crime.**

   a. **Words may be sufficient** if the accomplice had the culpable mental state and verbally encouraged the principal to commit the crime.

   b. **Mere knowledge or presence at the crime scene is insufficient** to establish the **intent** to aid, abet, assist, or encourage in the crime.

   <u>Example (no intent)</u>: An already married man went through a marriage ceremony with a woman and committed bigamy. The man's friend, who did not know of the man's previous marriage, had encouraged the man to marry the woman and was his best man at the ceremony. Even though the friend encouraged the man and was present, he did not have the intent to aid or encourage bigamy because he was unaware of the man's prior marriage.

   <u>Example (intent):</u> Two bullies hated a bartender and agreed to start a fight with him, and if given the opportunity they would kill him. They met him in the street outside his bar and began to push him around. Two men who also hated the bartender stopped to watch, one gave the bullies a knife and the other yelled "kill him." One of the bullies stabbed and killed him. The man who yelled "kill him" is guilty as an accomplice since he had the intent that the bully kill the bartender and he encouraged him to do by telling him to kill him. The man who provided the knife is also an accomplice.

3. **Additional crimes:** Accomplices are **liable for additional crimes** committed by the principal in the course of committing the intended crime, so long as the crimes were a **natural and probable** (foreseeable) **consequence.**

   <u>Example</u>: A man and woman rob a bank not intending to harm anyone. The man ordered all the persons in the bank to lie on the floor. When some were slow to obey, the woman, not intending to hit anyone, fired 15 rounds into the air. One of those ricocheted off a stone column and killed a customer. The man is guilty of murder as an accomplice. [Note: there are other theories under which the man can be found guilty of murder but here the call focused on accomplice liability.]

4. **Withdrawal:** A withdrawal by an accomplice will only be effective if the defendant has **undone the effects of his assistance or encouragement.** If the accomplice only gave verbal encouragement, then he can verbally withdraw *if* it renders his assistance ineffective. The MPC requires the accomplice to warn law enforcement authorities if they are unable to render their prior assistance ineffective. [This rule is rarely MBE tested.]

C. **Common law—Principal in second degree:** One who **aids, abets, assists, or encourages** and is **present at the scene** of the crime. This is modernly called an accomplice and they are charged with the actual crime.

D. **Common law—Accessory before the fact** is an accomplice who **aids, abets, or encourages the principal** but is **not present** at the scene of the crime. This is modernly called an accomplice and they are charged with the actual crime.

Example: A man asked his girlfriend to lend him something he could use to break into the neighbor's shed to steal a lawn mower. She gave him a crowbar. He went to the neighbor's house with the crowbar but used a bolt cutter instead. The girlfriend can be charged as an accomplice to burglary and larceny in this jurisdiction since she aided the man with the intent of helping him break into a shed (the fact that he used another object for entry is irrelevant).

E. **Accessory after the fact** is an accomplice who knowingly gives assistance to a felon, for the purpose of **helping them avoid apprehension** or punishment following commission of a crime.

Example: A man and woman were engaged to be married. One day the man beat the woman's daughter and was charged with child abuse. The man pleaded with the woman to forgive him and they both left the state with the child, so the prosecution was forced to dismiss the case without testimony from the child. If the jury finds the woman left the state to aid the man in avoiding punishment, she should be convicted as an accessory after the fact to child abuse.

F. **Modern rules:** Modernly **principals, accomplices, and accessories before the fact** are **all guilty of the criminal offense** and are all considered parties to the crime. Modernly, an **accessory after the fact** is only charged with **obstruction of justice,** not the crime.

ACCOMPLICES CHEAT SHEET		
Principal (1st degree)	Does the criminal act	Charged with crime
Modern law accomplice C/L: Principal (2nd degree)	Aids, abets, encourages, and is present at the scene	
Modern law accomplice C/L: Accessory before the fact	Aids, abets, encourages, and is not present at the scene	
Accessory after the fact	Knowingly give assistance to help avoid apprehension	Charged w/obstruction of justice only

MBE tip: Accomplice questions that ask what evidence/arguments are *most useful* (stronger argument) often give you 2-3 answer choices that all look like good arguments (they all show aid, abet, etc.). Look for an answer that shows D had a **personal gain/stake** in the matter since this will be a *stronger argument* to support accomplice liability, even though it is not part of the rule.

Example: A statute provides :"The maintenance of any ongoing enterprise of a betting parlor is a felony." A woman has been renting an office to a man who has been using it as a betting parlor and the woman is aware of this use. If asked what evidence would be *most useful* to the prosecutor to convict the woman as an accomplice, a *good* answer would be that the woman personally placed bets with the man at the office. However, a *more useful answer* (the correct one) is that the woman charges the man considerably more in rent than she charged the prior tenant who used the office for legitimate purposes. This shows she personally benefited by charging more rent, whereas she could lose when she personally places bets (which is why placing bets is the good answer but not the best answer).

VI. DEFENSES

A. **Self-defense:** A person has a **right to self-defense** against unlawful force but must use **reasonable force** in response to their **reasonable belief** such force is necessary; a person may use **deadly force** in defense *only if* they hold a **reasonable belief that they face deadly force** (some jurisdictions include kidnapping and forcible rape as deadly force).

1. **No duty to retreat—majority rule:** The majority of jurisdictions indicate there is **no duty to retreat.**

   Example: D worked in a metal shop and constantly teased a coworker. One day the coworker responded by attacking D with a metal bar. D could have escaped but didn't and suffered a blow to his left arm. With his right arm D struck the coworker in the jaw, killing him. D will not be convicted of any offense since he used reasonable force to defend himself and had no duty to retreat.

   a. **Retreat doctrine—minority rule:** The minority of jurisdictions find there is a duty to retreat **prior to using deadly force, unless** one is in their **own home** *or* **cannot retreat in complete safety.**

2. **Initial aggressor:** The one who initiates a confrontation has **no right to use self-defense** during the confrontation, **unless the victim escalates** a minor altercation (i.e., name calling, teasing, use of nondeadly force such as a slap) into one involving deadly force.

3. **Burden of proof:** Once the prosecution has proved all elements of the underlying crime beyond a reasonable doubt, the defendant bears the burden of proof to prove up a traditional (affirmative) defense like self-defense.

   Example of reasonable force: If the defendant is a martial arts specialist and could have easily disarmed a deadly attack without using deadly force, they will be required to do so.

MBE tip: If the question is testing the minority retreat rule, the facts will tell you the jurisdiction follows the retreat doctrine. Remember, the duty to retreat, if applicable, only applies to the use of deadly force so there is no duty to retreat for use of nondeadly force.

4. **Imperfect self-defense:** Where a person kills in self-defense as a result of an **unreasonable belief that they faced deadly force** against them, murder charges can be reduced to charges of **voluntary manslaughter.**

B. **Defense of others (majority rule):** It is permissible to use **reasonable force to defend another** when one **reasonably believes** that the other person would be justified in using such force and the amount of force used is reasonable.

1. **Minority rule "Stands in shoes"** (also called the alter ego rule): A person may use **reasonable force** to defend another **only if** the person being defended was **justified** in using force for self-defense.

C. **Defense of property** allows an individual to use a **reasonable amount of force,** though **never deadly force,** to protect their real or personal property. [This rule is rarely MBE tested.]

D. **Defense of insanity:** Depending on the jurisdiction, there are various tests for insanity.

1. ***M'Naghten* test:** The defendant must show that they suffered from a **mental disease** causing a **defect in their reasoning powers** that resulted in them not understanding the **nature and quality of their act** or that they **did not know that their act was wrong.**
2. **Irresistible impulse test:** The defendant must show that they were **unable to control their conduct** due to a **mental illness.**
3. ***Durham* test:** The defendant must show that their **conduct** was the **product of a mental illness** (but-for test). (This standard is broader than the other two tests above.)
4. **ALI Model Penal Code:** The defendant must show that they **lacked substantial capacity** to **appreciate the criminality** of their conduct or **conform their conduct to the requirements of the law.**

INSANITY CHEAT SHEET

Test	Rules	Fact triggers
M'Naghten [*most tested]	◆ Doesn't understand nature/quality of act ◆ Doesn't know act wrong	D suffers delusions/hallucinations and acts on them **without understanding or knowing** their actions were wrong.
Irresistible impulse	Unable to control conduct	D knows something is wrong but **cannot control** themselve and feels an **irresistible compulsion** to do the criminal act.
Durham	But for test	D would not have committed the act **but for their mental illness** or psychosis.
MPC [*2nd most tested]	◆ Lacked capacity to appreciate criminality ◆ Can't conform to law	D might know something is illegal and wrong but is **unable to stop themselve and doesn't appreciate what they are doing.**

MBE tip: The questions will often tell you which test to apply or the answer choices will limit the tests in contention.

Decoy tip: If only one or few tests are applicable, eliminate answer choices that include rule language from the other nonapplicable tests.

E. Intoxication

1. **Voluntary, self-induced intoxication** is only a **defense to specific intent crimes** (e.g., first-degree murder, assault, incomplete crimes, specific intent theft/property crimes) such that the intoxication may have prevented the defendant from formulating the requisite specific intent.

   Example (defense): D is charged with assault with intent to kill a victim by shooting him. D claims he was so drunk he did not realize anyone was around when he fired the gun. Assault is a specific intent crime, so D's intoxication did not allow him to form the intent to assault and kill the victim.

   Example (no defense): D is charged with battery. D was under the influence of a performance-enhancing drug at the time of the battery. D knowingly took this drug. Because battery is a general intent crime, D cannot use voluntary intoxication as a defense here.

   a. **Timing:** If defendant formed the intent to commit the crime prior to becoming intoxicated, it will not be a defense.

      Example: A man believed his wife was cheating on him with her trainer so he decided to kill the trainer. He loaded his gun and stopped at a bar on the way to the trainer's house because he was anxious about killing him. He became intoxicated, went to the trainer's house and killed him. Intoxication will not be a defense because the man formed the intent to kill prior to becoming intoxicated.

      > **MBE tip:** On an exam, when a question involves murder and the defendant is voluntarily intoxicated, look for second-degree murder as an option, not first-degree, because intoxication prevents the "cool reflection" and "deliberation" needed for first-degree murder.

2. **Involuntary intoxication** is treated as an illness and may be a defense to all crimes, as it negates the intent to commit the crime when an intoxicating substance is ingested unknowingly or under duress.

   Example: D is charged with battery. D was under the influence of a performance-enhancing drug at the time of the battery. D only took this drug because his coach lied to him and told him it was an aspirin. D could argue the defense of involuntary intoxication since he was tricked into taking the drug, which would provide a defense to battery.

F. **Necessity** may be a defense if the defendant reasonably believed that commission of the crime was **necessary to avoid an imminent and greater injury** to society than that involved in the crime (objective standard used). [This rule is rarely MBE tested.]

G. **Mistake:** There are two types of mistake:

1. A **mistake of fact** may negate a **specific intent crime** (e.g., first-degree murder, incomplete crimes, assault, specific intent theft/property crimes), and may **negate a malice or general intent crime if the mistake was reasonable.** Mistake of fact does not apply to strict liability crimes.

   Example: A man takes a jacket that he thinks is his when it is not. There is no intent to steal property due to his mistake of fact so there is no larceny.

2. A **mistake (ignorance) of law** is generally not a defense.

   Example: A man doesn't know the speed limit was 65 mph, so he drove 75 mph on the freeway. He is still violating the law despite his mistake of law.

a. **Exception:** A mistake of law **may prevent a defendant from having the requisite mental state** for a particular element of the crime.

Example: Larceny requires *knowingly* taking the property of another. If one takes property of another, but mistakenly believes it is their own property, they will not have the requisite mental state for larceny because they did not *knowingly* take another's property even if they knows it is against the law to take someone else's property.

H. **Impossibility**

1. **Factual impossibility** arises when the defendant **makes a mistake such that it would be factually impossible to complete** the crime. This is not usually a valid defense.

   Example: A man intends to shoot his wife, but the gun isn't loaded so when he pulls the trigger no bullets come out. The man is still liable for attempted murder even if it was factually impossible for him to shoot her.

2. **Legal impossibility** arises when the defendant **incorrectly believes that what he is doing is criminal** when it is not. This is a valid defense.

   Example: A woman intends to import foreign whiskey that she thought was illegal, but it wasn't illegal, so no criminal act was committed.

> **MBE tip:** The defense of mistake of fact and factual impossibility are similar concepts and can apply similarly to fact patterns. But they are not tested in a way that requires you to determine which one is more appropriate in a question.

I. **Entrapment** exists where a law enforcement official, or someone cooperating with them**, induces** a person to commit a crime that they **weren't otherwise predisposed to commit.** The majority of states look at the subjective intent of the defendant. [This rule is rarely MBE tested.]

J. **Duress** arises when a third party **threatens or coerces** a defendant, with serious bodily harm or death, to perform an act they ordinarily would not perform. [This rule is rarely MBE tested.]

1. **Exception:** Duress is **not a defense to intentional murder.** But duress can be used as a defense to the underlying felony in felony murder.

> **MBE tip:** Remember that there is no legal duty for a person to stop a crime or warn others about a crime, even if they see another person do something that could endanger others. Questions involving that scenario do not need a valid defense as there was no duty to act to begin with.

DEFENSES CHEAT SHEET		
Crime	**Defenses allowed**	**Defenses not allowed**
General intent Battery Rape Kidnapping False imprisonment Involuntary manslaughter Reckless disregard murder	◆ Involuntary Intoxication ◆ Mistake of fact (if reasonable) ◆ Self-defense (if applicable) ◆ Insanity ◆ Entrapment	◆ Voluntary Intoxication ◆ Mistake of law (unless negates mental state element)
Specific intent Solicitation, Conspiracy, Attempt } Inchoate offenses Robbery Embezzlement Murder—First-degree Assault Voluntary manslaughter Burglary False Pretenses Forgery Larceny	◆ Voluntary Intoxication ◆ Involuntary Intoxication ◆ Mistake of fact ◆ Duress (except 1st degree murder) ◆ Insanity ◆ Self-defense (most tested with murder) ◆ Legal impossibility (most tested with incomplete crimes) ◆ Entrapment	◆ Mistake of law (unless negates mental state element) ◆ Duress for 1st degree murder ◆ Factual impossibility (can still charge with attempt if could not do the actual crime)
Malice intent Arson Common law murder	◆ Involuntary Intoxication ◆ Mistake of fact (if reasonable) ◆ Duress (except for intentional murder) ◆ Insanity ◆ Entrapment	◆ Voluntary Intoxication ◆ Mistake of law (unless negates mental state element) ◆ Duress for intentional murder

CRIMINAL PROCEDURE MBE OUTLINE

I. THE FOURTH AMENDMENT

<table>
<tr><th colspan="4">MBE 4TH AMENDMENT APPROACH</th></tr>
<tr><td colspan="4">Most question calls ask whether a D can suppress evidence.
Ask, WHAT is the underlying issue?</td></tr>
<tr><td colspan="2">ARREST</td><td colspan="2">SEARCH/SEIZURE</td></tr>
<tr><td>No warrant?</td><td>Yes warrant?</td><td colspan="2">1. government Action?
2. Reasonable expectation of privacy?
3. Warrant?</td></tr>
<tr><td rowspan="2">◆ Still need probable cause to arrest
◆ Need a warrant if arrested at home</td><td rowspan="2">◆ Must be valid, or good faith exception</td><td>No warrant?</td><td>Yes warrant?</td></tr>
<tr><td>Need an exception (SPACES)</td><td>◆ Must be valid, or good faith exception</td></tr>
</table>

The Fourth Amendment protects individuals against **unlawful arrests** and against **unreasonable searches and seizures** of property.

A. **Arrest**

1. **Warrant:** An arrest warrant is **generally not required** for an arrest unless a person is arrested in their home.

   a. **Probable cause required for a warrant:** An arrest warrant must be issued based on probable cause, which is a **reasonable belief that the person violated the law** based on the **totality of the circumstances.**

   b. **Warrant required for arrest in home:** An arrest warrant gives police **permission to enter the house to arrest** the person in question, but only if they have a **reasonable belief that the person is home.**

   <u>Example</u>: Police had a valid warrant for a woman's arrest. They learned that a person with her name and description lived at a particular address. They went there and the house appeared to be unoccupied, with the windows and doors boarded up with plywood. The lawn was overgrown and the neighbor said the woman had not been there for several months. Officers went inside anyway and found an illegal shotgun, but the search was not authorized because there was no reasonable belief the woman was home, so entry was not permitted despite having a valid warrant for her arrest. [The legal shotgun is provided as a decoy.]

      1. **Home of third parties:** Police need consent from a third party to enter their home and effect an arrest on someone who is inside their home.

★ 2. **Warrantless arrest:** A warrantless arrest is acceptable (when D is not at home), but it must be **based on probable cause.**

a. **Probable cause** is a **reasonable belief that the person violated the law** based on the **totality of the circumstances.**

Example (probable cause): Police officers were on foot patrol in a neighborhood frequented by drug sellers. When D saw them she turned away and started to walk away quickly. When they asked her to stop, she threw a bag into the bushes and put her arms in the air. The police retrieved the bag, which turned out to be cocaine, and arrested D (probable cause because reasonable suspicion of wrongdoing based on her location being a neighborhood known for drug sales, her trying to avoid the police, and throwing the bag into the bushes).

Example (no probable cause): Police went to D's apartment to search for narcotics based on an anonymous call. When he refused to let them in, they arrested him (an anonymous call alone is not sufficient to show probable cause to arrest someone or search their home).

a. **Indictment:** An indictment by a grand jury will **not be dismissed** because of an **unlawful arrest.**

> **Decoy tip:** Criminal procedure questions often like to focus on grand juries and indictments. Since the rules for grand juries differ from actual criminal trials, the questions often involve unlawful arrests or searches or seizures that are not permissible in a normal trial but would be allowed in a grand jury (rules on these later). Make a note of what type of court you are in to properly apply the rules and avoid a decoy answer that applies to a different court.

B. A **routine stop** by the government is typically permitted. There are several types.

1. **Automobile stop:** The police may randomly stop automobiles if there is a **reasonable suspicion of wrongdoing** based on an **objective standard** (i.e., speeding or driving erratically). All occupants may also be asked to exit the vehicle for any reason.

Example (legal stop): A police officer had a hunch not amounting to probable cause that a man was a drug dealer. While on patrol one day, the officer saw the man and her radar gun clocked him at 68 mph in a 65 mph zone. The officer's usual practice was to not stop a car unless it was going 5 mph or more over the speed limit, but the officer stopped the man anyway. She asked him to step out of the car and saw a clear bag of what appeared to be marijuana on the seat. The man was arrested. The stop itself was fine because it was based on speeding, an objective standard, even if only 3 mph over the limit.

Example (illegal stop): D was driving through an area plagued with recent burglaries. Acting pursuant to a police plan to combat crime by randomly stopping vehicles in the area between 12:00 a.m. and 6:00 a.m., an officer stopped D and saw what appeared to be a gun sticking out from under the seat, ordered D out of the car, and searched the car finding the gun and drugs. This random stop was not permitted as there was no suspicion of wrongdoing and it was not a checkpoint with neutral articulable standards as discussed below.

a. **Dog sniffing at traffic stops:** Absent reasonable suspicion, police cannot extend a traffic stop beyond the time **reasonably required** to conduct a dog sniff of the vehicle.

2. **Checkpoints/roadblocks:** The police may set up fixed checkpoints **to test for compliance with laws relating to driving** or if special law enforcement needs are involved, such as immigration. The stops must be based on some **neutral, articulable standard.**

3. **Stop and frisk** (also called an investigative detention): Police may stop and frisk individuals without arresting them. See sec. I.C.4.f below.

C. **Search and seizure of property:** A **search warrant is required** for government search and seizure of property that is located where one has a **reasonable expectation of privacy.**

1. **Government action required:** The Fourth Amendment search and seizure protections apply only against actions by the government, typically police officers, but will include individuals acting at the direction of the government.

   Example: A woman who is a computer expert wanted to expose persons who traffic in child pornography. She posted sexually-oriented photographs on her website. The picture files contained an embedded program allowing the woman to access the computer of any person who downloaded a picture. D downloaded one of the pictures, which allowed the woman to find a child pornography picture on D's computer. The woman informed the police. The police told her they needed more photos and offered her a reward, so she went back to his computer and found more photos. The first photo found by the woman was private action, but the additional photos were obtained at the direction of the government, so a warrant was required.

2. **Reasonable expectation of privacy (REOP):** The defendant must have a reasonable expectation of privacy in the **property** or **place** being searched or seized to have **standing** for the Fourth Amendment protections to apply. The person must have a **subjective expectation of privacy** that is **objectively reasonable** by a **totality of the circumstances.** [An MBE testing favorite.]

   a. **Homes/private residences:** One always has a reasonable expectation of privacy in their home.

   Example: One has a reasonable expectation of privacy in their **home and its curtilage,** such as a garage, places where one is an overnight guest (e.g., hotels), and in premises owned.

   b. **Public view:** There is **no** reasonable expectation of privacy in **inherently public things.**

   > **MBE tip:** Remember that one **does not have** a reasonable expectation of privacy in *someone else's* property, house, or car. A person would not have a REOP in those places when the police search them, even if they are present in that location at the time.

   c. **Open Fields Doctrine/Fly Overs:** Areas outside the home that are held out to the public **do not have a reasonable expectation of privacy** (e.g., some distant barns, yards visible by plane, discarded trash). Courts will consider the following:

   1. The **proximity** of the area to the house,

   2. Whether the **area is enclosed** by a structure, such as a fence or wall,

   3. The **nature of the use** of the structure or area in question, and

   4. The **steps taken** by the individual to protect privacy in the area.

   d. **Sensory enhancing technology** use will violate a reasonable expectation of privacy, but **technology readily available to the public may be permitted.**

   Examples (not allowed): High-tech items such as heat/thermal imagers and electronic eavesdropping.

   Examples (allowed): Flashlights, binoculars, telescopes, or listening through walls with your ears (all readily available to the public).

   e. **Dog sniffing:** Dogs are permitted to sniff luggage at airports and cars during a legitimate traffic stop. Dogs **cannot extend the stop beyond the time reasonably required** to complete the stop's mission, **unless there is reasonable suspicion of a violation** other than a traffic infraction. Police **cannot use dogs to sniff homes without a warrant** or a warrantless search exception (the dog sniffing itself cannot provide the probable cause).

f. **Commercial premises** in a **closely regulated industry** have a **reduced expectation of privacy.** Where the business owner's privacy interests are weakened and the government interests in regulating these industries are simultaneously heightened, a warrantless inspection may be reasonable.

   1. **Closely regulated industry** is one that has a long tradition of close government supervision (e.g., liquor industry, automobile industry, firearm stores, mine operations, junkyards, etc.).

   2. **Warrantless inspection is reasonable if:** (1) **substantial government interest** in the regulatory scheme pursuant to the inspection, (2) inspection is **necessary** to further the regulatory scheme, and (3) the statute's **inspection program provides an adequate substitute** for a warrant.

      Example: State enacted a statute to regulate vehicle junkyards to deter theft and trafficking of stolen vehicles. The statute requires a junkyard owner to permit law enforcement to take physical inventory during normal business hours. During an inventory, officers discovered 3 stolen vehicles. Junkyard owner is charged with receipt of stolen property. The inspection was allowed since the junkyard is a commercial premises in a highly regulated industry so there was no REOP.

REASONABLE EXPECTATION OF PRIVACY EXAMPLES

MBE tip: Don't get confused; when one has a REOP, it means the police must get a warrant first, which they can easily get if supported by probable cause.

Decoy tip: Don't get confused by an improper arrest or search of one person when the call and facts are asking about the search of another person. Wrong answer choices often focus on the wrong person.

Reasonable Expectation of Privacy	NO Reasonable Expectation of Privacy
◆ Inside one's home that is not visible to the public, or inside hotel rooms ◆ Curtilage ◆ Dorm suite where secret recording microphones were secretly placed ◆ One's backyard and porch which was entered on foot with search dogs ◆ An apparel store fitting room ◆ One's cell site location information ◆ Phone conversation on a public phone in a phone booth (the phone was bugged, which was not ok) ◆ Tracker showing GPS location of car	◆ Trash thrown away in garbage cans set out for collection ◆ Open fields ◆ Account records held by bank ◆ Aerial observation from public airspace (including yards) ◆ In *another person's* home or vehicle ◆ Luggage at an airport ◆ One's voice or handwriting ◆ Odors emanating from one's person ◆ Email communications ◆ Social media ◆ Speaking in public

MBE tip: This area of law is fluid and constantly evolving due to technology. You may encounter old questions with outdated answers and rule explanations.

3. **A warrant is required** for a search and seizure conducted where one has a **reasonable expectation of privacy.** A warrant to search and seize property must be: [This rule is rarely MBE tested.]

   a. **Based on probable cause:** Probable cause is established where it is reasonable that the items to be searched:

      1. Are **connected with criminal activities,** and

      2. **Will be found in the place** to be searched.

      3. If based on **informant information,** sufficiency is determined by the **totality of circumstances,** including:

         a. Whether the informant is a **generally reliable witness,** and

         b. Whether the facts set forth show the **informant's basis of knowledge.** An informant's information will be "stale" when it is too old to have predictive value, usually after a few weeks.

   b. **Issued by a neutral magistrate:** The search warrant is issued based on facts presented to a neutral and detached magistrate.

   c. **Adequate description:** The search warrant must contain a particular description of the **premises to be searched** and the **items to be seized.** The police may only look in places the items in the warrant might plausibly be located and not exceed the scope of the area or items listed in the warrant.

      Example: The police have a warrant to search for a red package inside a house. After they obtain the package, they continue to search the rest of the house and find a machine gun. The additional exploratory search is beyond the scope of the description in the warrant and is not permitted.

   d. **Knock and announce before execution:** To execute the search warrant, the police must knock and announce themselves before entering the premises and wait a reasonable time for an occupant to respond. If there is no response, the police can enter and seize the items described but **may not exceed the scope** of the warrant. [This rule is rarely MBE tested.]

      1. **Exceptions to knock and announce:**

         a. **Exigent circumstances** such that doing so would result in the **destruction of evidence** in the interim wait for a warrant, or when the police are in **hot pursuit** of a suspect.

         b. Knock and announce would create an **unreasonable risk to officers' safety.**

         c. Knocking would be **unreasonable.**

4. **Exceptions to the warrant requirement:** Under certain exceptions, the police may conduct a search or seizure without a valid search warrant.

   a. **Search incident to a lawful arrest** (SILA): When the police are making a lawful arrest, they may search the **area within the arrestee's immediate control** (their wingspan).

      1. **Protective sweep:** Under SILA, police may also conduct a protective sweep of all or part of the premises where an arrest takes place if they have a **reasonable belief** based on specific and articulable facts that other **dangerous individuals may be present.**

      2. **Vehicle:** Under SILA, the police may search the passenger compartment of a car (not the trunk) and its compartments (e.g., glove box, purses, jackets) if it is reasonable to believe that the **arrestee might access the vehicle** at the time of the search *or* the **vehicle contains evidence** of the offense causing the arrest.

> **Decoy tip:** SILA is a wrong answer if the arrestee is in the police car without access to their car and in situations where the police search the car when the arrestee was simply pulled over for a traffic violation.

Example (SILA permitted): Police had probable cause to believe a man committed a series of armed bank robberies with an accomplice. They obtained a valid arrest warrant and went to the man's house. The front door was open and the radio was on but the man didn't answer after they knocked and announced, so they went in and found the man emerging from the basement. They arrested him and went into the basement to look for the accomplice and found cocaine in plain view. This is a lawful protective sweep since the man had a known accomplice.

Example (SILA exceeded): Police were concerned about an increase in drug use in a neighborhood. One night, officers with drug sniffing dogs went to D's house and onto his porch. The dogs acted as if they smelled drugs, so the officers knocked on the door. D let them in and officers immediately arrested him and then searched the house and found marijuana in a linen closet. This search exceeded the scope of SILA because the arrest was not lawful because the dogs cannot be the basis for probable cause for the arrest, thus the search incident to that arrest was unlawful.

> **MBE tip:** If an arrest is unlawful, then any search incident to that arrest is also unlawful because there was no "lawful" arrest.

> **Decoy tip:** SILA is a wrong answer choice if the search occurred ***before*** the arrest so pay attention to the timing of the search and the arrest.

b. **Plain view:** The police may make a warrantless seizure if they see an object or **contraband in plain view,** so long as the police are **lawfully on the premises,** the incriminating character of the object is **immediately apparent,** and the police have **a lawful right to be in the position to obtain the view.**

Example: Police responded to a call that shots were fired at a house. Upon arriving, the police looked through a window and saw a man lying on the floor. They opened the front door and found the man had been shot and was unconscious. Waiting for the ambulance, the police looked around the house to see if anyone else was present. No one else was found, but they did find clear bags that appeared to be cocaine on the table. Police can seize the bags as they were in plain view and the police had a legitimate right to be on the premises due to the emergency call.

> **MBE tip:** The questions that test plain view where the police officer is legitimately on the premises usually involve the owner consenting to the officer's entry, or the police entering the premises due to an emergency. Make sure the officers are lawfully on the premises in order for the plain view exception to apply.

c. **Automobile:** If police have **probable cause** to believe that a vehicle **contains contraband** or evidence of a crime, they may search the **whole automobile** and any **container** therein that might contain the objects for which they are searching. There is no warrantless search allowed for mere traffic tickets.

1. If the driver is arrested, the police may legally **impound the car,** transport it to the station house, and search it there without a warrant.

 Example: Police receive information from an undercover officer that she just saw two men who she described in a blue pick-up truck selling drugs. The police saw a truck and men matching that description and stopped them. They searched the truck and found drugs in a toolbox. The warrantless search is permissible because probable cause existed to search the truck and any container for contraband.

SILA V. AUTOMOBILE WARRANTLESS SEARCH EXCEPTIONS	
SILA (involving a vehicle)	**Automobile (w/probable cause)**
Must be incident to a lawful arrest	No arrest needed
Search extends only to the area within D's immediate control (wingspan) and passenger container of car (not trunk)	Search extends to entire car and any containers within including the trunk
◆ Search must be made at the time D had access to the car, *or* ◆ To uncover evidence of the crime for which D was arrested	◆ D's ability to access the car irrelevant ◆ Officer only needs probable cause to believe car contains contraband or evidence of a crime

d. **Consent:** The police may make a warrantless search if the person voluntarily consents to have their premises, items, or person searched. However, where the consent is limited to a certain area, the police cannot exceed the scope of consent granted without further consent or obtaining a warrant.

 Example: If a person consents to the search of their bedroom, the police may not search the rest of their home without further consent or a warrant.

 1. **Actual or apparent authority:** Only those with actual or apparent authority can consent on defendant's behalf.

  a. **Landlords** do not have actual or apparent authority.

  b. **Parents** generally have authority to consent to the search of a child's room (even an adult child) if the parent has access to the room. *However*, the parent may not provide consent to access locked containers within the room.

  Example (no authority for consent): While D was in jail on a pending charge, his landlord called the police because D had not paid rent and an odor was coming from his apartment. Knowing D was in jail, the police came and entered the apartment with the landlord's consent and found a trunk with the remains of D's former mistress. The landlord's consent to search D's apartment violated D's rights because the landlord had no authority to consent.

  Example (authority for consent): A man and woman planned to rob a bank. They drove to the bank in the man's car. The man entered the bank while the woman remained outside as the lookout. The woman panicked and left. She was pulled over for speeding. Noting her nervous demeanor, the police asked her if they could search the car. She consented. They found heroin in the car. The woman had apparent authority to consent to the search of the car as the driver and sole person in the car, even if she didn't own the car.

e. **Exigent circumstances:** The police may conduct a search or seizure without a warrant if they have **probable cause** *and* it is necessary to:

   1. Prevent imminent **destruction of evidence,** or

   2. Prevent imminent **injury to persons,** or

   3. The police are in **hot pursuit** of a felony suspect and reasonably believe they have a entered a particular premises.

      Example: Police had probable cause to believe that drug dealing was taking place in a hotel room. The hotel manager authorized the officers to enter the room and gave them a key. The officers knocked on the door, announced their presence, and asked to speak with the occupants. The officers then heard yelling and flushing of the toilet. The officers then used the key to enter the room, where they saw the occupants dumping drugs into the toilet. Exigent circumstances existed because the flushing toilet and screaming indicated that the drugs could be flushed and disappear.

f. **Stop and frisk:** A police officer may **stop and frisk** a person if the police have a **reasonable suspicion** (based on the totality of circumstances) of **criminal activity** or involvement that is supported by articulable facts.

   1. **Pat down:** The brief detention may include a **pat-down** search of outer clothing for weapons if the suspect appears dangerous and under the **plain feel doctrine,** they may **seize contraband** discovered if its identity is immediately apparent.

      Example: In a city, numerous armed bank robberies were committed near closing time by a masked man wearing a white hooded sweatshirt and blue sweatpants. Police saw a man matching this description pacing nervously outside a bank just before closing. They stopped the man and frisked his outer layer of clothing for weapons. This frisk is permissible based on reasonable suspicion of criminal activity given the description.

> **Memorization tip:** Use the mnemonic **SPACES** to remember the exceptions for the warrant requirement. (**S**earch incident to a lawful arrest, **P**lain view, **A**utomobile, **C**onsent, **E**xigent circumstances, and **S**top and frisk.)

WARRANTLESS SEARCH EXAMPLES WITH NO EXCEPTION

- Police suspect a woman of dealing in stolen credit cards. An undercover officer goes to her house to pay for usable credit cards. As the woman leaves the room, the officer lifted some papers off a desk and discovered credit cards with different names. The officer seized the cards and arrested the woman. This search was not permitted because there was no warrant and no exception applies.

- Police received information from an undercover officer that two men in a red truck were selling marijuana to kids. The police saw a truck fitting the description, but the passenger was a woman. She got out and went to a bus stop. The police stopped the truck and searched the driver and found drugs. They went to the woman and searched her purse and found drugs. The search of the woman is not permitted because there was no warrant and no exception applies since the woman did not fit the undercover officer's description.

II. FIFTH AMENDMENT

 A. ***Miranda*:** When a suspect is taken into **custody** by the police and is **under interrogation,** their confession will be admissible against them only if they have received the requisite *Miranda* warnings, informing them that they have the **right to remain silent,** that **anything they say can be used against them,** that they have the **right to have an attorney** present, and if they cannot afford an attorney, **one will be appointed** for them.

1. ***Miranda* warnings** apply to **custodial interrogations.**

   a. **Custodial:** A suspect is "in custody" when a **reasonable person would believe that they are not free to leave.** This is a **fact-based inquiry.**

   <u>Example (in custody)</u>: Police go to a man's house to arrest him at 6:00 a.m. and enter the house with guns drawn awaking him. One is not free to leave when guns are drawn on them while they are in bed.

   <u>Example (not in custody)</u>: Police pull over a man for running a red light. The man smells of alcohol, so the officer asks if he had been drinking. General traffic stops without more are not custodial.

   b. **Interrogation** includes words or actions by the police that they should know are **reasonably likely to elicit an incriminating response** from the suspect.

   <u>Example</u>: Police arrive at D's house after receiving a noise complaint and find D's wife dead on the floor. One of the officers asked what happened and D responded that he took care of that witch. This statement did not require *Miranda* warnings because there was no custodial interrogation.

   1. **Suspect must be aware:** A custodial interrogation does not occur when a suspect speaks to an undercover agent or government informant and the **suspect does not know** that they are speaking to a law enforcement officer, even if the suspect is in jail.

   2. **Government words or actions needed:** Merely hoping that D will make incriminating statements is insufficient action to warrant *Miranda* warnings, even if D is in custody.

   <u>Example</u>: Police arrested D pursuant to valid arrest warrant. Hoping D would say something incriminating, police did not give D *Miranda* warnings. Rather they placed her in the police car to drive her to the station. On the way she admitted her part in the crime. At the station, they gave her *Miranda* warnings and afterwards she said she wished to remain silent. D was in custody when she confessed but was not under interrogation; therefore, *Miranda* warnings were not required.

MIRANDA INTERROGATIONS

NOT an interrogation (no *Miranda* required)	IS an interrogation (so *Miranda* required)
◆ Police go to D's house after receiving a noise complaint and find his dead wife. They ask D, "What happened?" D confessed. ◆ A man was a suspect in a robbery. Police asked the man's friend if he would help them. The friend went to the police headquarters and while there, he told them he wanted to get something off of his chest and confessed that he was also involved in the robbery. ◆ Police have a valid search warrant to search for a specific briefcase at a house. They go the house and the suspect had the briefcase in his hands. They placed him in handcuffs. The suspect then stated that they would have never found him with the drugs if it weren't for the snitch Henry (suspect in custody but no interrogation to require *Miranda* warnings).	◆ Police have probable cause to arrest a man, so they enter his house at 6:00 a.m. and wake him up. Startled, the man asks what is going on. An officer replies and asks the man if he committed a particular robbery. The man said that he had. This is an interrogation because the officer elicited incriminating information without giving *Miranda* warnings.

MBE tip: The circumstances drive the analysis. A specific leading question is more likely to trigger *Miranda*, as opposed to a more general question or a D who spontaneously blurts out information.

Decoy tip: *Miranda*, the right against self-incrimination, and due process (voluntary confessions) are all related concepts. If *Miranda* warnings are not warranted (i.e., no custodial interrogation), then a correct answer will implicate an admissible confession if it was voluntarily made (see sec. II.D.) and a decoy will implicate *Miranda* or the right against self-incrimination being violated when they were not.

2. **Public safety exception:** *Miranda* warnings **do not apply** to questioning that is reasonably prompted by a concern for public safety. [This exception is rarely MBE tested.]

3. **Re-*Mirandize*:** Once the suspect has unambiguously invoked their rights under *Miranda*, the **police cannot re-*Mirandize* the suspect** in an attempt to get the suspect to speak, unless there has been a sufficient break in custody (14 days is deemed sufficient). [This rule is rarely MBE tested.]

4. **Waiver of *Miranda*:** A suspect may waive their *Miranda* rights, expressly or impliedly, but such a waiver is admissible only if it is **voluntarily, knowingly,** and **intelligently** made. Mere silence is insufficient to demonstrate a waiver.

MBE tip: Even if *Miranda* warnings are appropriately given, a defendant's incriminating statement might still be suppressed if the *arrest* was illegal.

B. **Fifth Amendment right to counsel under *Miranda*:** When the accused **unambiguously** indicates that they wish to speak to counsel, the police are required to **cease all questioning** until the suspect has consulted a lawyer, and the **lawyer must be present** while any **further questioning** occurs.

Example: Police suspect a high school student of committing a burglary. Officers arrest the student, bring him to the police station, and give him *Miranda* warnings. The student asks to see a lawyer. The police then call the student's parents and place the student in a room with his parents and secretly record the student's conversation with his parents. The student confesses the burglary to his parents. The recording violated *Miranda* as police attempted to elicit incriminating statements *after* the student asked for a lawyer. *However*, if the suspect said, "*Maybe* I should talk to a lawyer," that request would not be unambiguous enough to invoke the right to counsel.

1. **Not offense specific:** *Unlike* the Sixth Amendment right to counsel (see below), a detainee's rights under *Miranda* are not offense specific. If a detainee requests to speak with an attorney, the police cannot ask them any questions about *any* crime.

C. **Right against self-incrimination:** This right protects a criminal defendant from compulsion **to give testimony or communicative evidence** (not real physical evidence) that could expose them to criminal liability.

1. **Does not apply to one's voice or likeness:** Forcing one to record their **voice or speak words** in a line up is **not testimony or communicative evidence.**

   Example: During a lineup, D was required to say the phrase, "Give me all of your money," for a teller from a bank robbery to potentially identify the voice of the robber. The right against self-incrimination is not violated.

2. **Immunity:** The best way to avoid self-incrimination is for the prosecution to offer the witness **use and derivative use immunity** so that anything they say cannot be used against them and any evidence derived from what they say also cannot be used against them (use immunity *alone* is insufficient).

   Example: A woman was subpoenaed to appear before a grand jury. Afraid she might incriminate herself, she did not want to answer a question about her whereabouts on a specific night when a murder occurred. The prosecutor believed the woman's nephew committed the murder and the nephew claimed he was with the woman. They believe his alibi is false, but need to know where the woman was to show the nephew wasn't with her. In order to compel her to answer the question, the prosecutor needs to provide her with use AND derivative use immunity, otherwise she can claim the right against self-incrimination to avoid answering the question.

3. The Fifth Amendment privilege against self-incrimination **does not apply to corporations.**

4. **Silence cannot be used against a defendant** to imply a particular meaning.

D. **Due process** is applicable to the states through the **Fourteenth Amendment,** and requires that:

1. **Confessions must be made voluntarily,** without police coercion, in light of the totality of the circumstances, with the court considering the susceptibility of the suspect and the environment and methods used.

   Example: A man was a suspect in a homicide committed during a robbery of a liquor store. A barber was the friend of the suspect. The police called the barber and asked him to help locate the suspect. The barber agreed and met the officers at the police station. After a discussion about the suspect, the barber said he wanted to get something "off his chest" and told the officers he was in on the robbery, but the suspect shot the store owner. Officers then gave the man his *Miranda* warnings. His confession is admissible as it was voluntary.

   a. **Nongovernmental coercion allowed:** A confession obtained by nongovernmental coercion is admissible.

b. **Confession by mentally ill person is allowed:** A confession made by a person suffering from mental illness is admissible.

Example: A man entered the police station and announced that he wanted to confess a murder. The police advised the man of his *Miranda* rights and the man signed a waiver. The man described the murder in detail and pinpointed the location where the victim was located. Later, a court-appointed psychiatrist determined the man was suffering from a serious mental illness that interfered with his ability to make rational choices and that his psychosis induced his confession. The confession is still admissible as it was made voluntarily.

c. **Police coercion totally inadmissible:** Where a confession is the result of police coercion, the prosecution **cannot use it during its case-in-chief *or* to impeach the defendant.** This rule is in contrast to a confession obtained in violation of *Miranda*, where a confession obtained in violation of *Miranda* is still admissible for impeachment purposes.

2. **Identifications (due process):** A defendant's due process rights are violated if an identification of the defendant based on the totality of the circumstances is **unnecessarily suggestive** and so conducive to mistaken identification that it is **unfair** to the defendant.

a. **An improper out-of-court identification** procedure may require suppression of in-court testimony if the out-of-court identification produces a **substantial likelihood of irreparable misidentification.**

Example: A store owner's jewelry store was robbed. Police showed him D's photograph. The owner asked the police if they believed the man in the photo was the robber. The police said yes and afterwards the owner stated that the man in the photograph was the one who robbed her. Here, one photo coupled with the police comment was sufficiently suggestive and violated D's due process rights.

b. **Eyewitness reliability:** Even if an out-of-court identification procedure is unnecessarily suggestive, suppression of in-court testimony is **not required if the eyewitness's identification is shown to be reliable** under a multi-factor inquiry. [This rule is rarely MBE tested.]

c. **Testimony with immunity:** Testimony obtained by a promise of immunity is considered coerced and involuntary (so immunized testimony cannot be used for impeachment).

d. **In-court identification:** The prosecution is allowed to have a defendant give demonstrative evidence if it is relevant and material to a proper in-court identification.

Example: D was charged with murder. Several witnesses testified the crime was committed by a person of D's description who walked with a severe limp. D in fact walks with a severe limp. The prosecution is allowed to order D to give a demonstration of how they walk.

3. **Failure to disclose exculpatory evidence (*Brady* doctrine):** Failure to disclose evidence favorable to the defense (including impeachment information),whether willfully or inadvertently, that would have created a reasonable probability of a **different outcome** had it been disclosed earlier is a **violation of due process** (and enables a defendant to a new trial—see Civil Procedure outline for new trial rules).

a. **Grand juries do not apply *Brady*:** The *Brady* doctrine does not apply to grand juries and the prosecutor has no legal obligation to present evidence exculpating the defendant to the grand jury.

4. **Plea bargains allowed:** A defendant can settle by plea bargain to receive a conviction on a less serious charge or a lighter sentence if they are **competent, understand the charge,** and

understand the consequences of the plea (e.g., maximum penalty, rights being waived, D knows they have the right not to plea). Contract law principles govern.

a. **Voluntarily and intelligently:** Plea bargains must be made voluntarily and intelligently, in open court, and on record (this is because a plea bargain is both a confession and a waiver of various constitutional rights.)

b. **No right to a plea bargain:** The prosecutor has **no obligation to agree to a plea** and the **judge can refuse** to accept the guilty plea if they think the defendant didn't commit the crime.

c. **A defendant's plea made in response to the prosecution's threat** to bring more serious charges **does not violate the defendant's Due Process** rights when the prosecution has probable cause to believe that the defendant committed the crimes.

E. **Double jeopardy:** This protects an individual from being **tried for the same offense twice** (or punished twice) after jeopardy attaches.

1. **Offenses are considered separate offenses** if conviction for one requires proof of at least **one additional element** not included in the first offense.

a. Double jeopardy **prohibits a subsequent trial on lesser included offenses** even if they arose from the same transaction.

Example: Once tried for robbery, D cannot later be tried for larceny for the same transaction. *However*, D could later be tried for murder from the same transaction, because it is a separate offense.

b. Double jeopardy **prohibits a subsequent trial on a greater offense** if D was already tried for the lesser included offense. *However*, a state may continue to prosecute a greater offense despite D's guilty plea to a lesser included offense arising from the same transaction if the greater offense was charged before the plea was entered.

Example: After D is convicted of larceny, double jeopardy prohibits a subsequent trial on robbery arising from the same incident.

2. **Attaches to criminal trials and acquittals** (includes punishment).

3. **When jeopardy attaches:**

a. **Jury trial:** When the **jury has been empaneled and sworn in.**

b. **Bench trial:** When the **first witness has been sworn in.**

4. **Exceptions: Jeopardy does not attach to the following:**

a. Cases ending in **mistrial where there is a manifest necessity** to abort the original trial (i.e., judge dies or a key witness is ill),

Example: Four hours into D's assault trial, the lawyers gathered in the judge's chambers to discuss an evidentiary issue. While there, the judge received a phone call that his mother died. The judge declared a mistrial, excused the jury, and rushed home. A second trial would violate double jeopardy because there was no manifest necessity for a mistrial.

b. Hung jury (they cannot agree),

c. Defendant **breaches a plea** bargain,

d. There is **legislative intent** to allow both charges,

e. **Appeals based on trial errors** such as the admission of hearsay, improper jury instructions, or weight of evidence issues.

   1. **Except:** When the **defendant is successful based on insufficiency of the evidence,** double jeopardy does apply.

f. **Preliminary hearings, grand juries,** and civil proceedings (except juvenile proceedings),

g. **Dual sovereign** doctrine provides that a conviction or acquittal by one jurisdiction **does not bar a prosecution in another jurisdiction,** even on a charge stemming from the same events. This includes two different states and two different courts (state and federal).

   Example: D is a loan shark for the mob. D can be tried in a state court for loan sharking and violation of state usury laws. D can also be tried in a federal court for a RICO charge and tax evasion on the same loan sharking activities.

> **Decoy tip:** Pay close attention to the **type of court hearing** involved in the fact pattern. Jeopardy does not apply to preliminary hearings or grand juries, but the decoy answers will indicate jeopardy attaches to those.

F. **Grand juries:** Grand juries act independently of the judge and prosecuting attorney; their goal is often to act as an **investigative body** to determine whether the defendant should be **indicted** for a crime (though this formal charging process is not required, or used in all states, and has not been incorporated into the Fourteenth Amendment).

1. **Special grand jury rules** apply, and essentially "anything goes" including:

   a. Grand juries are conducted in **secret.**

   b. **Inadmissible evidence is allowed,** or what will be inadmissible evidence at trial.

      1. **Hearsay rules** do not apply.

      2. The **exclusionary rule** does not apply.

> **MBE tip:** A defendant can't object, either initially or at trial to an indictment from a grand jury proceeding on the grounds inadmissible evidence was relied upon.

   c. **Witnesses** have:

      1. **No right to counsel** in a grand jury room, but a witness can consult her attorney outside the grand jury room.

      2. **No right to *Miranda* warnings** for statements made in the grand jury room.

   d. **Defendant has no right to:**

      1. Be present in the grand jury room.

      2. Confront witnesses in the grand jury room.

      3. Introduce evidence in the grand jury room.

   e. **Double jeopardy does not apply to grand juries** (e.g., if one grand jury refuses to return an indictment, it does not prevent another grand jury from doing so; it also does not prevent a criminal trial being brought forward).

Decoy tip: Pay attention to what court you are in because grand jury proceedings have special "anything goes" rules. These special rules implicate the rights listed above which are often decoy answers.

III. SIXTH AMENDMENT

A. **Right to effective counsel:** A suspect against whom formal criminal proceedings **have been commenced** has a right to effective counsel at **all critical stages** of a prosecution, including any **post-charge lineup or show-up and at sentencing.** This right **does not apply to** photo identifications, or when police take physical evidence such as handwriting samples or fingerprints.

Example: D was indicted and arrested for bank robbery. D had an initial appearance before a magistrate judge in which he was notified of the charges and told counsel would be appointed for him the next day. Police then required D to participate in a lineup. A witness identified D at the lineup. The Sixth Amendment right to counsel was violated for the lineup, but not for the initial appearance when D was notified of the charges.

1. **Offense specific:** This right is offense specific, so the **defendant must invoke** his right to counsel for **each offense charged.** Note: this rule is *unlike* the Fifth Amendment right to counsel in sec. II.B.
2. **Standard of effectiveness:** To establish ineffective assistance of counsel, the defendant must prove that counsel's performance was deficient in that counsel **did not act as a reasonably competent attorney** would have acted, and that this deficiency was prejudicial such that, but for the deficiency, the **result would have been different.** (This is a high standard to prove.)
3. **Attorney substitution:** A court will **allow** the defendant to substitute their attorney **if the interests of justice so require,** taking into account any conflicts, the interests of the defendant and the court, and the timeliness of the request.
4. **Waiver/self-representation allowed:** The defendant is permitted to **knowingly** and **intelligently waive their right to counsel** and represent themself.

   Example: D was charged with armed robbery. D had only an eighth grade education and no legal knowledge. D told the judge he was unhappy with his public defender and the judge refused to appoint D another lawyer telling D his only option was to represent himself. D agreed to represent himself. D was convicted after not raising any objections during the trial. The waiver of counsel is not valid here because D did not knowingly and intelligently waive his right to counsel with his education level.

5. **Exception:** Right to counsel **does not apply to grand jury witnesses** inside the grand jury room.

   Example: A federal grand jury was investigating drug trafficking. It subpoenaed a witness to testify. The witness asked that his counsel be allowed to advise him inside the grand jury room but the prosecutor refused to allow the attorney inside. The witness then testified and ended up making self-incriminating statements. The witness was subsequently indicted for drug crimes. His right to counsel was not violated because there is no right to counsel for a witness inside a grand jury room.

> **MBE tip:** The Sixth Amendment right to counsel only applies when custody is imposed (i.e., the defendant can be sentenced to incarceration). If the defendant only faces a fine (i.e., a speeding ticket), then the Sixth Amendment right to counsel does not apply.

B. **Right to confront adverse witnesses:** The Sixth Amendment allows a defendant in a criminal prosecution the right to confront adverse witnesses.

1. **Compel testimony:** The right to confront includes **issuing subpoenas to compel testimony** of an adverse or hostile witness, as well as to **cross-examine** hostile witnesses, and to be **physically present during the testimony** unless public policy prohibits the presence (e.g., protecting child witnesses).

2. **Testimonial statements:** The prosecution may not admit testimonial statements by a third person against the defendant unless the **declarant is available for cross-examination either** at the time the statement was made or during trial. [This rule is rarely MBE tested.]

   a. **Statements are nontestimonial** when made in **conditions that don't suggest it will be used in a future proceeding** (e.g., business records, statements by a co-conspirator during the conspiracy, statements made to police during an ongoing emergency).

   b. **Statements are testimonial** when the circumstances indicate that there is no on-going emergency, and that the primary purpose of the interrogation is to **establish or prove past events potentially relevant to later criminal prosecution** (e.g., police interrogations, preliminary hearings).

3. **Joint co-defendants** can raise "right to confront" issues.

   a. **Confession of one co-defendant:** Where two defendants are **jointly tried** and one of them confesses, the right to confront adverse witnesses **prohibits use of that statement** against the other defendant unless the statement can be **redacted or** the co-defendant who made the statement takes the stand and subjects themself to **cross-examination.**

   Example: A man and woman were charged with murder. Each confessed to the police implicating the other person. The woman later retracted her statement claiming it was coerced. They were tried together. The prosecutor offered both confessions into evidence. Both confessions were found to be voluntary. The woman testified at trial and the man did not. The man's confession is *not* admissible against the woman unless he testified at trial and the woman can confront him.

   b. **Severance of joint trial:** Where co-defendants are charged for the same crime, courts prefer joint trials for judicial economy, but will sever the co-defendants if a joint trial would result in **substantial prejudice** to one of the defendants.

   c. **Limiting jury instructions:** Instructing the jury to consider adverse testimony against only one defendant **is insufficient to overcome a defendant's right to confront** their accuser.

   Example: Two defendants were tried together for bank robbery. The prosecutor sought to introduce testimony from the first defendant's prison cellmate that the first defendant told him both defendants robbed the bank. The prosecutor asked the court to instruct the jury that the testimony could only be used against the first defendant. This limiting instruction is insufficient to avoid the risk that the jury will consider the incriminating statement against the second defendant.

C. **Right to a jury trial:** The Sixth Amendment, applicable to the states through the Fourteenth Amendment, guarantees **criminal defendants** the right to a jury trial for **serious offenses** that have a potential imprisonment of **greater than 6 months,** regardless of the actual penalty imposed.

1. **Judge involvement:** The judge cannot direct a jury to enter a particular verdict. Even if the defense attorney does not object prior to the jury verdict, the judge's direction to the jury to enter a particular verdict violates the defendant's right to a jury trial.
2. **Waiver permitted:** The defendant may **voluntarily, knowingly,** and **intelligently** waive their right to a jury trial.
3. **Number of jurors required:** Juries must consist of **at least 6 persons** and can consist of 12 persons.
4. **Unanimity:** Federal and state **criminal trials** require a **unanimous verdict.**

> MBE tip: This unanimity rule was changed in a 2020 Supreme Court case, so some old bar questions might have the wrong rule if they are not yet updated to the new rule. Follow the newer rule.

5. **Impartial jurors:** A jury must be impartial, consisting of a fair cross-section of a community. [This is rarely MBE tested.]
   a. A **jury does not consist of a fair cross-section of a community if** the defendant can prove that:
      1. The group alleged to be **excluded** is a **distinctive group** in the community,
      2. The representation of this group in venires (jury pools) from which juries are selected is **not fair** and reasonable **in relation to the number of such persons in the community,** and
      3. This **underrepresentation** is due to **systematic exclusion** of the group in the jury-selection process.
6. **Voir dire** is the process through which potential jurors are questioned to select a jury. During voir dire **each side** (not party) has:
   a. **Unlimited strikes for cause** (bias, prejudice, related to a party, etc.), and
   b. **Limited peremptory strikes** (the number varies by jurisdiction) that may be used for **any reason,** so long as the reason is **gender and race neutral** (some courts have expanded this to include sexual orientation neutral).

> MBE tip: When tested, this rule is often classified as a Civil Procedure question.

7. **Discrimination not permitted:** The Equal Protection Clause of the Fourteenth Amendment prevents the state or any state actor, including the court, from intentionally discriminating against a distinctive group in selection of the jury pool.
8. **Defendant's presence:** Defendant is entitled to be present during jury selection since it is a critical stage of prosecution.

D. **The right to a speedy trial:** The Sixth Amendment right to a speedy trial is guaranteed to defendants in both federal and state courts. It commences when the defendant has been arrested or charged.

1. **Factor test:** Whether the right to a speedy trial is violated is viewed on a **case-by-case basis** with the court balancing the **following factors:**
   a. The **length** of the delay (period commences at time of arrest or charge),
   b. The **reason** for the delay,
   c. The **prejudice** to the defendant as a result of the delay, and
   d. The **time and manner** in which the defendant asserted their right.
2. **Attorney delay:** Delays attributed to the defendant's attorney, even if state appointed, is **attributed to the defendant** and not the state (so the defendant's right to a speedy trial is not violated if the defendant's attorney delays).

> MBE tip: The remedy for a violation of the right to a speedy trial is a dismissal with prejudice (so the defendant cannot be retried).

E. **The right to a public trial:** The Sixth Amendment guarantees a criminal defendant the right to a public trial. The defendant **may waive this right** and request a closed proceeding. [This rule is rarely MBE tested.]

1. **Rights of press/public:** Members of the press and public also have a Sixth Amendment right to be present at all criminal trials, unless the court finds an overriding interest that requires a closed trial.

F. **Right to a preliminary hearing:** A defendant who pleads not guilty has a right to a preliminary hearing if probable cause has not been established unless they waive such right. The rules for preliminary hearings vary among jurisdictions. [This rule is rarely MBE tested.]

IV. THE EXCLUSIONARY RULE AND GOOD FAITH WARRANT EXCEPTION

A. **The exclusionary rule** is a judge-made rule (not statutory) that **prohibits the prosecution from introducing evidence** obtained in violation of a defendant's Fourth, Fifth, or Sixth Amendment rights.

> Decoy tip: The exclusionary rule only applies to evidence obtained in violation of D's rights. If D's rights were not violated, then the exclusionary rule does not apply, so the evidence will be admitted (e.g., if D voluntarily made a statement, excluding it under the exclusionary rule is not the correct answer because there was no violation).

1. **Standing required:** The defendant must have standing to assert the exclusionary rule, such that the evidence wrongfully obtained must have been in violation of the **defendant's *own* constitutional rights** and not a third person.

> MBE tip: Just as in search and seizure situations, standing often prevents a party from using the exclusionary rule to exclude evidence if the evidence pertains to the violation of another person's rights (i.e., a friend's car or home).

2. **"Fruit of the poisonous tree":** Evidence wrongfully obtained is **inadmissible** as the "fruit of the poisonous tree"—in other words, **all evidence that is found as a result of the original**

wrongfully obtained evidence is also tainted and deemed unlawfully obtained and is equally unusable, subject to the following **exceptions:** [These rules are rarely MBE tested.]

a. **Independent source:** The evidence obtained could have been obtained from an independent source separate from the illegal source; or

b. **Inevitable discovery:** The evidence obtained would inevitably have been discovered by other police techniques, had it not first been obtained through illegal discovery; or

c. **Purged taint:** There are a sufficient number of **additional factors that intervened between the original illegality and the final discovery** that the link is too tenuous, such that the intervening factors have purged the taint of the illegal discovery.

Example: If the original illegally obtained evidence leads the police to focus on a particular suspect, who is then fully investigated and arrested, the arrest will not be tainted by the original illegality.

3. **Allowed for impeachment:** Illegally obtained evidence **may still be used to impeach** the defendant but not any witnesses.

4. **The exclusionary rule does not apply to civil proceedings** (i.e., wrongful death actions), **grand juries, parole proceedings,** or violations of the "knock and announce" rule.

Example: Federal agents had a hunch that a man was engaged in illegal gambling activities, so they decided to enter his house when he was not home to see what they could find. They found names of people who the man paid and interviewed those people. From those people they found more incriminating information. The agents testified to all of these findings before a grand jury, which later indicted the man. The testimony is not excluded because the exclusionary rule does not apply to grand jury proceedings.

> **MBE tip:** Pay close attention to what hearing is at issue because often the questions are lengthy when the only fact you need to know to answer the question is that the evidence was presented in a grand jury proceeding.

5. **State constitutional rights:** A state **can grant broader rights** under its own constitution than those granted by the federal U.S. Constitution (so something that is not excluded under the exclusionary rule can still be excluded under a state constitution).

Example: After a liquor store was robbed, the police received an anonymous call naming a store employee as the robber. Believing their actions were constitutional, the police talked one of the employee's neighbors into going to the employee's home with a hidden tape recorder to ask him about the crime. The employee admitted to the neighbor he robbed the store and was charged in state court. The State Supreme Court held that the conduct of the police in directing the making of the recording violated the employee's rights under the *state* constitution. Thus, the recording would be excluded under state constitutional rules, even though it would be admitted in federal court under the U.S. Constitution since it does not violate the Fourth Amendment as recordings with defendants and government informants are allowed.

B. **The good faith warrant exception:** Where an officer acts in **reasonable reliance** on a facially valid search warrant issued by a proper magistrate and the warrant is **ultimately found to be unsupported by probable cause,** the exclusionary rule will not apply and the evidence will not be barred. [This exception is rarely MBE tested.]

Example: The police conduct a search subject to a warrant that appears valid but is later found to be the result of inadequate probable cause. The evidence will not be barred under the good faith exception if the officer has a good faith, objectively reasonable belief that the warrant was valid.

1. **Exceptions:** The good faith warrant exception does not apply (and thus the evidence will be excluded under the exclusionary rule) where:
   a. **The affiant knew** the information they were providing in the affidavit was **false,** or they would have known except for their reckless disregard of the truth, or
   b. **There was a lack of probable cause** such that the magistrate's reliance on the affidavit was unreasonable, or
   c. The warrant was **defective on its face.**

V. EIGHTH AMENDMENT

A. **Bail:** The Eighth Amendment requires that though bail is not required, **bail shall not be excessive or unduly high** based on several factors, including the following: [This rule is rarely MBE tested.]

   1. The **seriousness** of the offense (e.g., defendant's dangerousness),
   2. The **weight of the evidence** against the defendant (e.g., flight risk),
   3. The defendant's **financial abilities,** and
   4. The defendant's **character.**

B. **Cruel and unusual punishment:** The Eighth Amendment prohibits cruel and unusual punishment by preventing the penalty imposed on the defendant from being **grossly disproportionate** to the seriousness of the crime.

   1. **A defendant cannot be sentenced to death** if:
      a. At least one juror finds the defendant is **mentally retarded,** or
      b. The defendant was a **minor** at the time of the crime.
   2. A **minor cannot be sentenced** to a mandatory life without parole sentence, nor can a minor be sentenced to a non-mandatory life without parole sentence for nonhomicide crimes.

      Example: A 14-year-old was tried as an adult for armed robbery and was convicted. No one had been harmed in the robbery but due to his lengthy juvenile criminal history which included violent offenses, he was sentenced to life in prison without the possibility of parole. This sentence violates the Eighth Amendment ban on cruel and unusual punishment.
   3. **Victim impact statements** during the penalty phase do not violate a defendant's Eighth Amendment right against cruel and unusual punishment.
   4. **Mitigating circumstances:** When considering the death penalty, the jury **must consider** mitigating circumstances, such as the defendant's age, capacity, previous criminal liability, duress, other defendants' involvement, and any other factors that mitigate against imposition of a death sentence.
   5. **Capital punishment trials:** A majority of states require a different jury to decide defendant's sentence than the jury that decided defendant's guilt.

VI. BURDENS OF PROOF AND PERSUASION

A. **Presumption:** All defendants are **presumed innocent** until proven guilty.

Burdens

1. **Prosecution burdens:** The Due Process Clause requires in all criminal cases that the **state prove every element** of a case **beyond a reasonable doubt** (the prosecution must **produce** evidence and **persuade**—convince—the jury that there is no other reasonable explanation that can come from the evidence presented at trial).

   Example: A state statute provided that "the burden of proof as to a defense claimed by the defendant shall rest on the defendant." The same state defines rape as, "Sexual penetration inflicted on an unconsenting person by means of force. Consent is a complete defense to rape." When instructing the jury on the issue of consent, the judge needs to explain that the burden of proving the victim did not consent, by proof beyond a reasonable doubt, rests on the prosecution because consent is an element of the crime.

> Decoy tip: Questions will try to trick you and give you statutes that place a burden on D (i.e., for a defense, such as the example above) but often you don't get to the defense because the element at issue in the defense is also an element of the actual crime, so the burden will always be on the prosecution to prove every element (all elements) even if an element is also an element in a defense.

   a. **Directed verdict:** A judge can order a directed verdict **for the defendant** if the judge believes that the jury could not possibly find that the state met its burden of proof as to the guilt of the defendant.

   b. **Alibi:** An alibi is not a traditional defense but rather **negates an essential element of a crime** (the defendant's actual commission thereof). A defendant will not have the burden to prove an alibi because the **prosecution has to prove the defendant committed the act** (if a defendant has an alibi then this negates an element the prosecution is required to prove).

   c. **Increased penalty:** Any fact that increases the penalty beyond the maximum set by statutory guidelines must be proved to the jury beyond a reasonable doubt.

2. **Defendant's burden:** Once the prosecution proves every element beyond a reasonable doubt, the **defendant can offer an affirmative defense** (e.g., self-defense, insanity, etc.).

   a. **If D presents evidence that negates an element** of the crime, such as an alibi, that shows D did not commit the actus reus, then this will also help a jury to find D not guilty, but the burden was not on D to do this. Rather, this shows that the prosecution failed to prove all elements beyond a reasonable doubt (either way—D negates an element or has a defense—the result is the same in that D will be found **not guilty**).

      Example: D is charged with murder and is claiming he acted in self-defense. The trial court instructed the jury that D had the burden of proving by a preponderance of the evidence that he acted in self-defense. This instruction does not violate Due Process because D can bear the burden to prove a defense.

VII. APPEAL

A. **No right to appeal:** The Constitution does not guarantee an individual the right to appeal, but many jurisdictions provide for appeals.

   1. **Right to Counsel:** In jurisdictions that do provide an opportunity to appeal, indigents must be given counsel at state expense during a **first appeal** granted to all defendants as a matter **of right.**

B. **Harmless error standard:** Many jurisdictions uphold a conviction if the conviction would have resulted despite the admission of improperly obtained evidence.

C. When determining the **sufficiency of the evidence to sustain a charge,** the appellate court considers the evidence in **light most favorable to the state.**

> **MBE tip:** These rules are rarely MBE tested and when they are tested they are often classified as Civil Procedure questions and test the standard of review.

CRIMINAL LAW CHEAT SHEET

MENS REA (INTENT)

Voluntary act
- Not unconscious
- No police force

General: Do the act
Specific: Act with specific intent/ objective
Malice: Reckless disregard of high risk

Strict liability
No mental state

Transfer. intent
D intends to harm one person but harms another

Omission to act
- Not a crime unless:
  - Statute
  - Contract
  - Special relation.
  - D caused danger
- D **physically able** to perform
- Mere **presence** not enough

Model Penal Code
- Purposely: consciously do the act
- Knowingly: awareness (subjective std.)
- Recklessly: conscious disregard of risk
- Negligence: failure to be aware of risk

Vicarious liability
One is liable for another's action

CAUSATION

Actual cause
But-for test

Proximate cause
Foreseeability test

CRIMES INTENTS

General Intent
- Battery
- Rape
- Kidnapping
- False Imprisonment
- Involuntary mansl.
- Reckless disregard murder

Specific Intent
- Solicitation
- Conspiracy
- Attempt
- Robbery
- Embezzlement
- Murder-Fir. Deg.
- Assault
- Vol. mans. (intent to kill mitig.)
- Burglary
- False Pretenses
- Forgery
- Larceny

Memorization tip: SCARE My FAV BFF Luigi

Malice intent
- Arson
- Common law murder

CRIMES AGAINST PROPERTY

Larceny
- Trespassory taking
  - *No lawful possession*
- Carrying away
- Of personal property of another
- Intent to steal

Embezzlement
- Fraudulent conversion
- *D has lawful possession*
- Of personal property of another

False Pretenses
- D knowingly makes
- A false representation
- Of material fact
- Cause to rely &
- *Convey title*

Larceny by trick
Larceny, with possession obtained by fraud or deceit

Extortion
- Threat of future harm to
- Deprive one of property

Theft
- Illegal taking of
- Another's property

Robbery
- Larceny, and
- Property taken from person or their presence
- Through force or fear
- Larceny is a lesser-included offense

Burglary
- Breaking and entering of
- Another's dwelling house
- At nighttime
- Intent to commit felony
  - At time of break/enter
- Modern: any structure or time ok

Receipt of stolen prop.
- One knowingly
- Receives, conceals, or disposes
- Stolen property
- With intent to permanently deprive

Arson
- Malicious burning (modern explosives too)
- Another's dwelling (modern most structures)
  - *Houseburning* includes one's own dwelling

Forgery
- Making of false writing or
- Altering of existing writing
- Apparent legal significance
- Intend to defraud

CRIMES AGAINST THE PERSON

Assault

- Attempt to commit battery, or
- Intent to place another in reasonable apprehension of imminent injury
- Aggravated if deadly weapon/rape
- Lesser included offense to robbery

Mayhem

- Permanent body dismemberment or disablement
- Modernly aggravated battery

Battery

- Intentional or reckless
- Causing of
- Injury or offensive touching of another
- Aggrav. if deadly weapon/child/police

Rape (modern)

- Unlawful sexual intercourse
- Without consent

Kidnapping

- Unlawful confinement
- Move or conceal in secret
- False imprison. = lesser included offense

Common law murder

Malice types:

- Intent to kill
  - ◇ Presumed if deadly weapon used
- Intent to inflict serious bodily injury
- Reckless disregard - depraved heart
- Felony murder rule (burglary, arson, rape, robbery, kidnapping - BARRK)

Felony Murder (special rules)

- Natural and probable consequence
- Occurs during commission of felony
- Felony independent from killing
- D not liable if non-felon kills co-felon (majority – Redline view)
- Jurisdiction split if victim kills a bystander
  - ◇ Agency theory (majority) = D not liable
  - ◇ Proximate cause theory = D is liable

Causation	Transfer. intent	1st degree murder	2nd degree murder
Also need for murder	Also applies to murder	◆ Premeditated & ◆ Deliberate, or ◆ Felony murder rule	All other murders: ◆ Not 1st degree and ◆ Not manslaughter

Voluntary Manslaughter

1st degree murder reduced if:

Heat of passion killing	Imperfect self-defense
◆ D reasonably provoked ◆ Acted in heat of passion ◆ No cooling off time ◆ D did not cool off	◆ Unreasonable mistake, or ◆ D started altercation

Involuntary Manslaughter

Gross or criminal negligence

Disregard of substantial danger of serious bodily harm or death

Misdemeanor manslaughter

- D commits misdemeanor, or
- Death accidentally occurs

INCHOATE CRIMES

Solicitation

- Request or encourage
- Another to commit a crime
- Intent they do so
- Withdrawal not a defense

Conspiracy

- Agreement between
- Two or more people
- Intent to commit an unlawful act
- Maj. requires overt act

- Modern/MPC allow unilateral conspiracy
- No withdrawal
- No factual impossibility

Attempt

- Intent to commit crime
- Substantial step taken

Co-conspirator liability (for other crimes)

- Foreseeable and
- In furtherance of objective

Merger

No merger

- Conspiracy (can be charged with actual crime too)

Yes merger

- Solicitation
- Attempt
- Lesser-included offenses into greater offenses

ACCOMPLICE LIABILITY

Charged w/ Crime		
Principal in 1st degree Does the actual crime	**C/L Principal in 2nd degree (modern accomplice)** ◆ Aids, abets, encourages ◆ Present at the scene ◆ Mere presence not enough	◆ **C/L Accessory before the fact (modern accomplice)** ◆ Aids, abets, encourages ◆ Not present at the scene ◆ Mere knowledge not enough
Not Charged w/ Crime	**Additional crimes**	**Withdrawal**
Accessory after the Fact ◆ Helps accomplice avoid ◆ Apprehension or punishment ◆ Obstruction of justice charge	◆ Other accomplice liable if ◆ Natural and probable consequence (foreseeable)	◆ Only if prior assistance rendered ineffective ◆ MPC need to warn law enforcement

DEFENSES

Self Defense	Defense of Others	Defense of Property
◆ Reasonable force ◆ Reasonable belief ◆ Majority: no duty to retreat	◆ Reasonable force ◆ Reasonable belief ◆ Minority: stand in shoes	◆ Reasonable force ◆ Never deadly force
Insanity (4 possible tests varies by jurisdiction)		**Intoxication**
M'Naghten: ◆ D can't understand nature/ quality, or ◆ D doesn't know wrong	***Durham*:** ◆ Conduct product of mental illness (but-for test)	**Voluntary** ◆ Self-induced ◆ Defense to specific intent crimes
Irresistible impulse: ◆ D unable to control conduct	**Model Penal Code** ◆ D lacked capacity to ◆ Appreciate criminality, or ◆ Conform conduct	**Involuntary** ◆ Ingest unknowingly or under duress ◆ Treated as illness ◆ Defense to all crimes
Mistake		**Entrapment**
Of fact ◆ Negates specific intent crime ◆ Negates malice/general intent crime if mistake reasonable	**Of law** ◆ Generally not a defense ◆ Unless negates an element of a crime	◆ Law enforcement induces ◆ D to commit a crime ◆ D wasn't predisposed to commit
Impossibility		**Necessity**
Factual (no defense) ◆ D makes a mistake ◆ Impossible to do crime	**Legal (valid defense)** ◆ D thinks act is criminal but it isn't	◆ Reasonable belief ◆ Crime necessary to avoid ◆ Imminent/greater society injury
Duress		
◆ Third party threatens or coerces D ◆ To perform an act they otherwise wouldn't	◆ With serious bodily harm or death ◆ Not a defense to murder	

CRIMINAL PROCEDURE CHEAT SHEET

FOURTH AMENDMENT

Arrest

- No warrant required
- Unless at home
- Can enter D's house with warrant
- Need consent to enter 3rd party house

Warrantless arrest

- Probable cause required
  - Reasonable belief law violated
- Indictment not dismissed for unlawful arrest

Routine stops

Automobile
- Reasonable suspicion of wrongdoing
- Objective standard
- Cannot extend to dog sniff w/o reasonable suspicion

Checkpoints/Roadblocks
- Test compliance with driving laws
- Neutral, articulable standards

Stop and frisk
- See search exceptions

Search and Seizure

- Gov. action required
- Warrant required if:
- D has reason. expectation of privacy (REOP)
  - D's subjective expec.
  - Objectively reason.
  - Totality of circumst.

No REOP
- Public view
- Open fields/fly overs
- Sensory enhanc. tech.
- Dog sniffing unless reas. suspicion/airport

Low REOP
- Commercial premises

Search Warrants

- Based on prob. cause
- Item connected to crim. act.
- Found in place named
- Neutral magistrate issued
- Particular description
- Knock and announce
- If informant – totality of circum. (reliable/knowledge)

Warrantless Exceptions (memorization tip: SPACES)

SILA

- During a lawful arrest
- Can search D's wingspan
- Protective sweep ok if
  - Reas. belief that other
  - Danger. indiv. present

Vehicle
- Can search passenger car/ containers (no trunk) if:
- Arrestee can access it or
- For evidence of offense

Automobile

- Probable cause that
- Vehicle has contraband or
- Evidence of a crime
- Can search whole car & trunk/any container therein
- Can impound car and search later

Stop and Frisk

- Reasonable suspicion
- Of criminal activity
- Can pat-down for weapons
- Plain feel
- Can seize contraband if identity apparent

Plain View

- Lawfully on the premises
- Incriminating character apparent
- Lawful access to view object

Consent

- Voluntary
- Police cannot extend scope of area
- Apparent authority ok

Exigent Circumstances

- Probable cause
- Necessary to prevent:
  - Destruction of evid.
  - Injury to persons
  - Hot pursuit of suspect

FIFTH AMENDMENT		
Miranda	**Waiver of *Miranda***	***Miranda* Rt. to Counsel**
◆ <u>Custody</u>: not free to leave ◆ <u>Interrogation</u>: likely to elicit incriminating response ◆ Suspect aware its police ◆ Gov't words or actions needed	◆ Must be voluntary ◆ Knowingly and intelligently ◆ Silence insufficient	◆ Unambiguous request ◆ Police must cease questions ◆ Until lawyer present ◆ Not offense specific
◆ Can't <u>re-*Mirandize*</u> unless break (14 days)		

Right against self-incrimination	
◆ Protects D from giving ◆ Testimony or communicative evidence (not physical) ◆ No voice or likeness ◆ That exposes D to criminal liability	◆ Not for corporations ◆ Only use and derivative use immunity will protect D ◆ Silence not self-incriminating

Double Jeopardy		
◆ Cannot be tried for same offense twice ◇ Different elements ◇ No subsequent trials on lesser/greater offenses ◆ Applies to state & federal	**<u>Attaches when</u>** ◆ Jury trial (jury empaneled and sworn in), or ◆ Bench trial (first witness sworn in) ◆ Attaches to criminal trials and acquittals (& punishments)	**<u>Does not apply to</u>:** ◆ Preliminary hearings ◆ Grand juries ◆ Civil Proceedings (except juvenile) ◆ Dual sovereigns ◆ Legisl. intent/pleas ◆ Mistrial if necessity

Confessions	Identifications	
◆ Must be voluntary ◆ Ok if mentally ill ◆ Can't even use to impeach if coerced	◆ Can't be unnecessarily suggestive ◆ Based on totality of circumst. ◆ In-court ID ◇ Demonstrative evidence ok	◆ Out-of-court ID not ok if ◇ Substantial likelihood of irreparable misidentification ◇ OK if eyewitness reliable ◆ Coerced if w/immunity

Brady **rule (must disclose evidence)**	**Plea Bargains**
◆ Disclose evidence favorable to D, or ◆ D can get new trial ◆ If different outcome probable ◆ No obligation to present to grand jury	◆ D competent ◆ Understands charge & consequences ◆ Made voluntary & intelligently ◆ Judge can refuse to accept

Grand Juries	
◆ Act independent of judge as an investigative body for indictment	
◆ Hearsay rules don't apply ◆ Exclusionary rule doesn't apply ◆ Double jeopardy doesn't apply ◆ D can't introduce evidence	◆ No *Miranda* warnings needed for witness ◆ No right to counsel for witness inside room ◆ D can't present or confront witnesses ◆ Not incorporated into 14th Amendment

SIXTH AMENDMENT

Right to Counsel

- At all critical stages
  - Post-charge
  - Lineup/show-up
- Not for photo IDs, fingerprints, physical evid.
- Offense specific
- Ineffective assistance
  - Not reason. competent
  - Result would be differ.
- Substitute attorney
  - If justice requires
- Waive if knowingly & intelligently

Right to Confront

- Compel testimony
- Cross-examine
- Adverse/hostile witness
- For testimonial stmts.
  - To interrogate
  - NOT emergency stmt.
- Joint co-defendants
  - Must redact or cross-examine other D
  - Sever if substantial prejudice
- Can't overcome D's rt. by limiting jury instructions

Right to Jury Trial

- For serious offenses
  - Prison > 6 mo.
- Judge can't direct verdict
- D can waive if voluntary, knowingly & intelligent
- 6 jurors min. (up to 12)
- Unanimous verdict req'd
- Impartial jury-fair repres.
- Voir dire (for each side)
  - Unlimited for cause
  - Limited peremptory
  - Gender and race neutral
- D entitled to be present

Right to Speedy Trial

- Case-by-case evaluation
  - Length of delay
  - Reason for delay
  - Prejudice to D
  - Time/manner D asserted
- D's attorney delay attributed to D not state

Right to Public Trial

- D can waive and request closed
- Press/public also have a right to access trial
- If overriding interest then court can close trial

Rt. to Preliminary Hearing

- For D who pleads not guilty
- If probable cause not yet established
- D can waive

Exclusionary Rule

- No evidence that violates D's 4th, 5th, 6th Am. rights
- D needs standing – only their rights not 3rd parties
- Fruit of poisonous tree
  - Evid. stemming from violation excluded too

<u>Exceptions</u>

- Independent source
- Inevitable discovery
- Purged the taint
- Allowed to impeach

<u>Does not apply to</u>

- Civil proceedings
- Grand juries
- Parole proceedings
- Knock & announce rule

State constitutional rights can be **broader** than federal U.S. Constitutional rights

Good faith warrant exception

- Invalid warrant (no prob. cause)
- Officer reasonably relied on it
- Exclusionary rule doesn't apply
- Evidence not barred

- Exceptions
  - Affiant knew info provided was false
  - No probable cause for magistrate to rely on
  - Warrant was defective on its face

EIGHTH AMENDMENT	
Bail	**Cruel and Unusual Punishment**
◆ Not excessive/unduly high ◆ Courts consider ◇ Seriousness of offense ◇ Weight of evidence ◇ D's financial abilities ◇ D's character	◆ Penalty cannot be grossly disproportionate ◆ No death if mentally retarded or a minor ◆ No life w/o parole for minors w/nonhomicide crimes ◆ Victim impact statements ok ◆ If death, jury must consider mitigating circumstances ◇ D's age, capacity, duress, other Ds, etc.
APPEAL	**BURDENS OF PROOF AND PERSUASION**
◆ **No right to appeal** but many jurisdictions allow it ◆ If allowed, indigents have a right to counsel-1st appeal ◆ Many jx uphold conviction if **harmless error** ◆ Appellate ct. considers sufficiency of the evidence in light **most favorable to the state**	◆ All Ds presumed innocent until proven guilty ◆ Judge can enter a directed verdict for D **Prosecution burden** ◆ Prove all elements of a crime ◆ Beyond a reasonable doubt ◆ Alibi negates an element of the crime so burden on P to prove element, not D to prove alibi **Defendant burden** ◆ After P proves all elements ◆ D can offer affirmative defense

CRIMES MBE PRACTICE QUESTIONS

These questions are designed to reinforce the skill in how to approach MBE questions. While they will also test your knowledge in the limited areas addressed, you will not master your knowledge by only practicing these questions. To fully master the rules, you need to do practice questions outside of these from your bar company and/or the NCBE.

QUESTION 1

A man was paroled after serving five years in prison for forgery. Three weeks later, he found a handgun in a high school parking lot. Fearing that students from the school might find the gun and get into trouble using it, the man put it in the trunk of his car. The man drove off, was lawfully stopped by a police officer for speeding, and allowed the of officer to search his car and the trunk. During the search, the officer discovered the gun.

The man was charged under a federal statute prohibiting the knowing possession of a firearm by a convicted felon.

Which of the following additional facts, if established, would be most helpful to the man's defense?

A. He did not intend to use the gun for an unlawful purpose.
B. He did not know about the federal statute.
C. He was driving to the police station to give the gun to the authorities when the officer stopped his car.
D. His previous conviction did not involve the use of a gun or other weapon.

QUESTION 2

In a crowded football stadium, a man saw a wallet fall out of a spectator's purse. The man picked up the wallet and found that it contained $100 in cash. Thinking that he could use the money and seeing no one watching, the man put the wallet in the pocket of his coat. Just then, the spectator approached the man and asked if he had seen a missing wallet. The man said no and went home with the wallet.

Of what crime, if any, is the man guilty?

A. Embezzlement.
B. False pretenses.
C. Larceny.
D. No crime.

QUESTION 3

A man who believed that his wife was cheating on him with her gym trainer decided to kill the trainer. He loaded his handgun and set off for the trainer's house. Because he was anxious about committing the crime, the man first stopped at a bar, drank eight shots of hard liquor, and became intoxicated. He then left the bar and went to the trainer's house. When the trainer answered the door, the man shot and killed him. The man then passed out on the trainer's porch.

The man has been charged with murder in a jurisdiction that follows the common law.

Can the man raise an intoxication defense?

A. No, because drinking at the bar was the proximate cause of the killing.
B. No, because the man intended to commit the murder and drank to strengthen his nerve.
C. Yes, because drinking at the bar was a foreseeable intervening cause of the killing.
D. Yes, because the man's intoxication negated the specific intent required for murder.

QUESTION 4

A wife decided to kill her husband because she was tired of his infidelity. She managed to obtain some cyanide, a deadly poison. One evening, she poured wine laced with the cyanide into a glass, handed it to her husband, and proposed a loving toast. The husband was so pleased with the toast that he set the glass of wine down on a table, grabbed his wife, and kissed her passionately. After the kiss, the wife changed her mind about killing the husband. She hid the glass of wine behind a lamp on the table, planning to leave it for the maid to clean up. The husband did not drink the wine.

The maid found the glass of wine while cleaning the next day. Rather than throw the wine away, the maid drank it. Shortly thereafter, she fell into a coma and died from cyanide poisoning.

In a common law jurisdiction, of what crime(s), if any, could the wife be found guilty?

A. Attempted murder of the husband and murder or manslaughter of the maid.
B. Only attempted murder of the husband.
C. Only murder or manslaughter of the maid.
D. No crime.

QUESTION 5

A man decided to steal a valuable coin collection from a collector's house while the collector was away. Knowing that the house had an alarm system, the man contacted the pool cleaner who worked at the house twice a week. The man offered the pool cleaner part of the proceeds from selling the coin collection if she would disarm the alarm and leave a side door unlocked so that the man could enter the house. The pool cleaner pretended to agree but then contacted the police, who immediately arrested the man.

In a jurisdiction that follows the common law and has adopted the bilateral requirement for conspiracy, what crime has the man committed?

A. Attempted burglary.
B. Attempted larceny.
C. Conspiracy.
D. Solicitation

QUESTION 6

Without a warrant, police officers searched the garbage cans in the alley behind a man's house and discovered chemicals used to make methamphetamine, as well as cooking utensils and containers with the man's fingerprints on them. The alley was a public thoroughfare maintained by the city, and the garbage was picked up once a week by a private sanitation company. The items were found inside the garbage cans in plastic bags that had been tied closed and further secured with tape. The man was charged in federal court with the manufacture of methamphetamine.

Did the search of the garbage cans violate the Fourth Amendment?

A. No, because the man had no reasonable expectation of privacy in garbage left in the alley.
B. No, because the probative value of the evidence outweighs the man's modest privacy claims in his garbage.
C. Yes, because the alley was within the curtilage of the man's home and entry without a warrant was unconstitutional.
D. Yes, because there is a reasonable expectation of privacy in one's secured garbage containers.

QUESTION 7

Police officers had probable cause to believe that a man had committed a series of armed bank robberies with an accomplice. The officers obtained a valid arrest warrant for the man and went to his house to arrest him. The officers found the front door ajar and could hear a radio playing inside. They knocked on the door, identified themselves as police officers, and stated that they had a warrant. Getting no response, the officers entered the house. After the officers called the man's name several times and again identified themselves as police officers, the man emerged from the basement and was arrested. The officers went into the basement to look for the accomplice. They opened a closet door and found cocaine in plain view. They did not find the accomplice.

The man was indicted for cocaine possession. He has moved to suppress the cocaine as evidence on the ground that it was obtained in violation of the Fourth Amendment.

Should the court grant the motion to suppress?

A. No, because the officers discovered the cocaine during a lawful protective sweep of the house looking for the man's accomplice.
B. No, because the search was incident to the man's arrest.
C. Yes, because the officers did not have a search warrant.
D. Yes, because the officers did not have probable cause to believe that cocaine would be in the closet.

QUESTION 8

A police officer stopped a driver who had run a red light. Upon approaching the car, the officer noticed a strong odor of alcohol and immediately asked whether the driver had been drinking. The driver admitted having had several alcoholic drinks that evening.

The driver, charged with driving while intoxicated, moved to suppress the officer's testimony regarding the driver's statement about his drinking. The driver argued that the officer had elicited the statement without providing the requisite Miranda warnings. The prosecutor has responded that the statement should be allowed in the prosecution's case-in-chief or, at a minimum, should be allowed as impeachment in the event the driver testifies and denies drinking.

How should the court rule regarding the driver's statement admitting his drinking?

A. The statement should be allowed, because although the driver was in custody, the officer's spontaneous utterance upon smelling alcohol did not rise to the level of interrogation.
B. The statement should be allowed, because the driver was not in custody for *Miranda* purposes when the admission was made.
C. The statement should be suppressed both in the prosecution's case-in-chief and as impeachment evidence, even if the driver testifies.
D. The statement should be suppressed in the prosecution's case-in-chief, but it may be used as impeachment evidence if the driver testifies.

QUESTION 9

A defendant was indicted and arrested for bank robbery. The defendant had an initial appearance before a magistrate judge in which he was notified of the charges and told that counsel would be appointed for him the next day. The police then required the defendant to participate with other prisoners in a lineup in which each person had to wear a white T-shirt and say, "Put your hands in the air." At the lineup, witnesses to the bank robbery identified the defendant as the bank robber. The next day, the defendant was arraigned on the charges.

The defendant argues that his Sixth Amendment right to counsel was violated when he was denied counsel at two critical stages of the proceeding: his initial appearance in court before the magistrate judge and the lineup identification.

Was the defendant's Sixth Amendment right to counsel violated?

A. No.
B. Yes, based only on the denial of counsel at the initial appearance.
C. Yes, based only on the denial of counsel at the lineup.
D. Yes, based on the denial of counsel at both stages of the proceeding.

QUESTION 10

A defendant was charged with attempted murder. At the preliminary hearing, the presiding judge heard the testimony of four prosecution witnesses and found that the prosecution had failed to establish probable cause that the defendant had committed any offense. Accordingly, he dismissed the charge. The prosecutor then called the same four witnesses before a grand jury. The grand jury indicted the same defendant for attempted murder.

The defendant has moved to quash the indictment on the ground of double jeopardy.

How should the court proceed?

A. Grant the motion, because the dismissal of the first charge on the merits, whether correct or incorrect, bars any further prosecution.
B. Grant the motion, unless the prosecution has evidence that was not presented in the first case.
C. Deny the motion, because the defendant has not yet been in jeopardy of conviction on the attempted murder charge.
D. Deny the motion, because the protection of the double jeopardy clause does not come into play until there has been a conviction or an acquittal.

CRIMES ANSWER KEY	
Question	**Answer**
1	C
2	C
3	B
4	A
5	D
6	A
7	A
8	B
9	C
10	C

Use this quick answer key to get a general idea of how you did on this set of questions. The answer explanations that follow provide a step-by-step deconstruction of each question.

CRIMES ANSWER EXPLANATIONS

START HERE **FACTS** **Q1**

Likely still on parole

A **man was paroled** after serving five years in prison for forgery. **Three weeks later, he found a handgun** in a high school parking lot. **Fearing that students** from the school **might find** the gun and get into trouble using it, the **man put it in the trunk of his car**. The man drove off, was **lawfully stopped** by a police officer for speeding, **and allowed the officer to search** his car and the trunk. During the search, the officer discovered the gun.

The man was charged under a federal statute prohibiting the ***knowing*** **possession of a firearm by a convicted felon.**

Reason (intent) man took the gun

Facts show no 4th Am. issue at play – stop lawful as was search (consent)

Law violated – when the crime is not a traditional crime you've studied, the question will likely focus on the actus reus or mens rea (note the "knowing" and run through each element)

CALL **Which of the following additional facts**, if established, would be **most helpful** to the **man's defense**?

You have to read the answer choices first to see what "additional facts" they provide. Also note that "most helpful" indicates more than one answer will be helpful, but only one will be the "most helpful." AND you know you are looking for facts to support the man's "defense."

SOLVE

Decoding a statute: Go through each element to see if all elements are met. Then, look for any defenses/deficiencies that would help the man's defense.

STATUTE ELEMENTS	ANALYSIS
KNOWINGLY: (intent/subjective standard) – awareness of conduct engaged in or that certain circumstances exist	The man was aware he had a gun in the trunk b/c he put it there (note that the reason he did it is not relevant to his knowledge that he did it).
POSSESSION: Essentially D has the item	The man had possession of the gun in his trunk.
FIREARM: Item at issue	The gun is a firearm.
CONVICTED FELON: D's status	The man was a convicted felon b/c of forgery and was on parole as he was released 3 weeks earlier.
DEFENSES: Self-defense/defense of others/ mistake of law/necessity/etc. or look for facts to show elements not met	Need to look at answer choices and try to find one that would show one of these defenses might be met or show an element is not met.

SOLVE (continued)

A Did not intend unlawful purpose	B Did know about law	C (PICK ME!) Going to police to turn it over	D Previous conviction different
R: Knowing = aware of conduct **R: Possession - not** knowing an unlawful purpose **A: Man knew he possessed** the gun (knowing he would not use it for an unlawful purpose is the wrong mens rea/intent b/c it is **knowing possession**).	**R: Mistake (ignorance) of law** is NOT a defense. **A:** Not knowing something is against the law is not a defense so this is not a helpful defense.	**R: Necessity** – D **reasonably believed** that commission of the crime was necessary **to avoid an imminent/ greater injury to society.** **A:** D committed the crime b/c reas. belief he was protecting high school kids, so he drove to the police station to give them the gun.	**R: Knowing** **R: Possession** **R: Firearm** **R: By convicted Felon** **A:** Statute does not differentiate between different types of felons/prior convictions so not a good argument.

 The most helpful additional fact would be that the man was going to the police to turn over the gun which would go toward a necessity defense since he could have reasonably believed that he was protecting the high school kids.

DECODE

~~A.~~ He did not intend to use the gun for an unlawful purpose.

Wrong analysis of the mens rea (intent) element. He must have knowing "possession" not knowing not use the firearm for an unlawful purpose. The intent needs to focus on the possession not the unlawfulness (or not) of the act.

~~B.~~ He did not know about the federal statute.

Incorrect rule analysis. Mistake (ignorance) of law is not a defense. Though this answer does not use that language to clearly identify the defense they are testing, not knowing about the statute is not knowing (mistake of) the law and not a defense.

C. He was driving to the police station to give the gun to the authorities when the officer stopped his car.

This is the most helpful additional fact because this could be used to show he was acting out of necessity to protect the high school kids from an imminent or greater injury since they could find the gun and harm themselves or others.

~~D.~~ His previous conviction did not involve the use of a gun or other weapon.

Incorrect analysis of an element. The statute only requires the defendant to be a convicted felon. It does not distinguish between different types of felons or prior convictions.

Q2

FACTS

In a crowded football stadium, a **man saw a wallet fall out of a spectator's purse**. The man **picked up the wallet** and found that it contained **$100 in cash**. Thinking **that he could use the money** and **seeing no one watching**, the man **put the wallet in the pocket of his coat**. Just then, the **spectator approached the man** and asked if he had seen a missing wallet. The **man said no** and **went home with the wallet**.

Not his wallet

Took the wallet

Carried away wallet

Say what? It's not always finders keepers??? But I don't have my own socks...

CALL Of **what crime**, if any, is the man guilty?

Subject clear (yay!) so now you need to look at the answer choices to see what possible crimes are options and then go through them

SOLVE

MBE tip: *Quickly list the elements (using abbreviations) for each crime and go through each.*

CRIMES	ANALYSIS
Embezzlement	
Fraudulent conversion	☑ Fraudulently stole (converted)
Personal property of another	☑ A spectator's wallet
Already has lawful possession	☒ Was NOT already in lawful possession
False Pretenses	
Knowingly (awareness)	☑ Knew he picked up wallet/saw it fall
Makes a false representation	☑ Told spectator he hadn't seen it when he had it
Past or present material fact	☑ Material fact – location of wallet
Other person relies/conveys title	☒ Spectator did NOT convey title
Larceny	
Trespassory taking	☑ Took wallet/wanted $/intended to keep & did
Carrying away	☑ Put wallet in pocket & took it home
Personal property of another	☑ A spectator's wallet
Intent to permanently deprive	☑ Lied to spectator and took wallet home to keep

A The man would be guilty of larceny **because** he took and carried away the spectator's wallet with the intent to keep it and not return it.

Now look for a similar answer choice.

DECODE

~~A.~~ Embezzlement.

A required element is missing. The man was not in lawful possession of the wallet to begin with so he can not be guilty of embezzlement.

~~B.~~ False pretenses.

A required element is missing. The spectator did not convey title to the man for her wallet, so he is not guilty of false pretenses.

C. Larceny.

Correct!! All elements are met as the man took (trespassory taking) the spectator's wallet (personal property of another), put it in his pocket and took it home (carrying away), with the intent to keep the wallet and not return it (intent to permanently deprive).

~~D.~~ No crime.

Wrong answer because the man is guilty of larceny.

FACTS **Q3**

A man who **believed that his wife was cheating** on him with her gym trainer **decided to kill the trainer**. He **loaded his handgun** and set off for the trainer's house. Because **he was anxious** about committing the crime, the man **first stopped at a bar**, drank eight shots of hard liquor, and **became intoxicated**. He then left the bar and **went to the trainer's house**. When the trainer answered the door, the man shot and killed him. The man **then passed out** on the trainer's porch.

Need to figure out why these facts about him wanting to kill the trainer matter.

He was voluntarily intoxicated so the key is to figure out if this will provide a defense or not

The man has been charged with **murder** in a jurisdiction that follows the **common law**.

CALL Can the man raise an **intoxication defense**?

Issue clear in call. Yay!! Rare for criminal law questions!

SOLVE

	VOLUNTARY	INTOXICATION	DEFENSE
	• Self-induced intoxication • Defense only to specific intent crimes	• Prevents D from formulating the required intent	• If D formed the intent prior to becoming intoxicated then it will not be a defense
ANALYSIS	☑ The man voluntarily went to a bar and drank 8 shots of hard alcohol	☑ Murder w/intent to kill is a specific intent crime	☒ D was not prevented from formulating intent b/c drunk since he already formed the intent before and that is why he went to drink first because he was anxious

A No, **because** the man formed the specific intent to commit murder before becoming intoxicated so becoming intoxicated did not prevent him from formulating the specific intent to kill.

Now look for a similar answer choice.

DECODE

~~A.~~ No, because drinking at the bar was the proximate cause of the killing.

Wrong reasoning. Being intoxicated does not make it foreseeable that someone will kill another person. He already wanted to kill the trainer before going to the bar because he thought he was having an affair with his wife. Also, causation is irrelevant to whether an intoxication defense is valid.

B. No, because the man intended to commit the murder and drank to strengthen his nerve.

Correct. The man formulated the intent to kill the trainer before going to the bar so drinking did not prevent him from formulating an intent to kill because it already existed, and he only went to the bar because he was anxious from forming the intent to kill.

~~C.~~ Yes, because drinking at the bar was a foreseeable intervening cause of the killing.

Wrong reasoning. Drinking was voluntary so it was not an intervening cause as he knew he was drinking. Also, he already formed the intent to kill before drinking and causation does not have any affect on an intoxication defense.

~~D.~~ Yes, because the man's intoxication negated the specific intent required for murder.

Wrong analysis. The intent was formed before he became intoxicated so the intoxication could not have prevented him from forming the intent that was already formed.

FACTS **Q4**

Intent to murder?

A **wife decided to kill her husband** because she was tired of his infidelity. She managed to **obtain some cyanide**, a deadly poison. One evening, she **poured wine laced with the cyanide** into a glass, **handed it to her husband**, and proposed a loving toast. The husband was so pleased with the toast that he set the glass of wine down on a table, grabbed his wife, and kissed her passionately. After the kiss, **the wife changed her mind** about killing the husband. She **hid the glass of wine** behind a lamp on the table, **planning to leave it for the maid to clean up**. The **husband did not drink** the wine.

What do these facts prove? Substantial step for attempt?

Withdrawal? Is that even possible?

So no murder of husband

The **maid found the glass** of wine while cleaning the next day. Rather than throw the wine away, the **maid drank it**. Shortly thereafter, she **fell into a coma and died** from cyanide poisoning.

Dead person = consider murder and manslaughter (both options in answers)

CALL In a **common law jurisdiction**, of **what crime(s)**, if any, could the wife be found guilty?

No MPC

Need to evaluate answer choices to see options and go through each

SOLVE

	MURDER	*ATTEMPT*	*MANSLAUGHTER*
	Unlawful killing of another w/**malice**	• Act done with intent to commit a crime • Actual crime not committed	**Voluntary** • Heat of passion • Imperfect self-defense
	• Intent to kill • Intent – Serious bodily injury • Reckless disregard • Felony murder rule	• Requires a **substantial step** in furtherance of the intent	**Involuntary** • Gross/criminal negligence • Misdemeanor-manslaughter
ANALYSIS	**Maid**: killed unlawfully • No intent to kill/serious bodily injury • No felony for FMR • Reckless disregard possible b/c left glass of wine with cyanide out & anyone who drank it could die	**Husband:** • Wife wanted to kill husband (intent) • Did not kill him b/c husband set down glass before drinking it (doesn't matter that she later changed her mind) • Substantial step = gave him the wine glass to drink	**Maid:** • No provocation to kill the maid and no imperfect self-defense • No misdemeanor • Could be gross negligence to leave out a deadly glass of wine as anyone could drink it which shows a disregard to the danger of harm or death

SOLVE *(continued)*

A The wife could be guilty of murder (reckless disregard) or manslaughter (gross negligence) of the maid (not both but one or the other) **because** she left out the wine glass with deadly cyanide for anyone to drink, and attempted murder of the husband because she intended to kill him and took a substantial step.

Now look for a similar answer choice.

DECODE

A. Attempted murder of the husband and murder or manslaughter of the maid.

Correct! Since the wife took a substantial step by giving the husband the wine with cyanide with the intent to kill him, she could be guilty of attempted murder. And she left out a glass of cyanide wine for anyone to drink knowing the maid would be coming, which shows a reckless disregard for human life (murder) or gross negligence (manslaughter).

(B.) Only attempted murder of the husband.

Incomplete answer because the wife's actions also give rise to murder or manslaughter of the maid since the wife left out poisoned wine knowing the maid would come and it is deadly (reckless disregard or gross negligence).

(C.) Only murder or manslaughter of the maid.

Incomplete answer because she intended to kill the husband and took a substantial step by giving him a glass of wine with cyanide in it. The fact that she changed her mind later is a decoy because she already completed the substantial step and he could have died had he drank the wine.

(D.) No crime.

Wrong because her actions give rise to both attempted murder of the husband and possibly murder or manslaughter of the maid.

Q5

FACTS

A man decided to **steal a valuable coin collection** from a collector's house **while the collector was away**. Knowing that the house had an **alarm system**, the **man contacted the pool cleaner** who worked at the house twice a week. The man **offered the pool cleaner part of the proceeds** from selling the coin collection **if she would disarm the alarm** and leave a side **door unlocked** so that the man could enter the house. The pool cleaner **pretended to agree** but then contacted the police, who immediately arrested the man.

Intent to commit a crime (burglary/larceny)?

Solicitation? Accomplice? How far do his actions go? Why or why not?

Key words here - no agreement for conspiracy (bilateral jx so need both parties to agree)

CALL In a jurisdiction that follows the **common law** and has adopted the **bilateral requirement for conspiracy, what crime** has the man committed?

No MPC and need to look at the answer choices to see the possible crimes

SOLVE

	ATTEMPT	CONSPIRACY	SOLICITATION
	• Intent to commit crime • Substantial step in furtherance of crime (beyond mere preparation)	• Agreement between • 2 or more people • To commit an unlawful act • No overt act & no unilateral conspiracy (b/c common law)	• Request or encourage • Another person • To commit a crime • Intent that person does it • Complete at time of request
ANALYSIS	• Man had intent to steal coins (larceny) or burglary since he would break/enter to commit larceny • But no substantial step since arrested before he could do anything (asking for help only mere preparation)	• No agreement with 2 people because pool cleaner pretended and reported him to the police so she never agreed to commit the unlawful act	• Man requested pool cleaner to help him steal the coins by leaving door unlocked and alarm off • Intended for her to help commit larceny/burglary

A Man never completed a substantial step toward either larceny or burglary for attempt. The pool cleaner did not agree with the man to commit the crime so no conspiracy. But the man is guilty of solicitation **<u>because</u>** he asked the pool cleaner to help him commit the crime.

Now look for a similar answer choice.

DECODE

Ⓐ Attempted burglary.

Wrong analysis. There is no attempt because there was no substantial step to commit a burglary since the only thing the man did was ask the pool cleaner for help which was mere preparation.

Ⓑ Attempted larceny.

Wrong analysis. There is no attempt because there was no substantial step to commit a larceny since the only thing the man did was ask the pool cleaner for help which was mere preparation.

Ⓒ Conspiracy.

Wrong analysis. There was no agreement for conspiracy since the pool cleaner only pretended to agree and the common law adopts a bilateral agreement requiring two people to agree to commit the unlawful act.

D. Solicitation.

BINGO! The man requested the pool cleaner to help him steal the coins (larceny) or possibly burglary if he would break and enter to steal them, so the man would be guilty of solicitation.

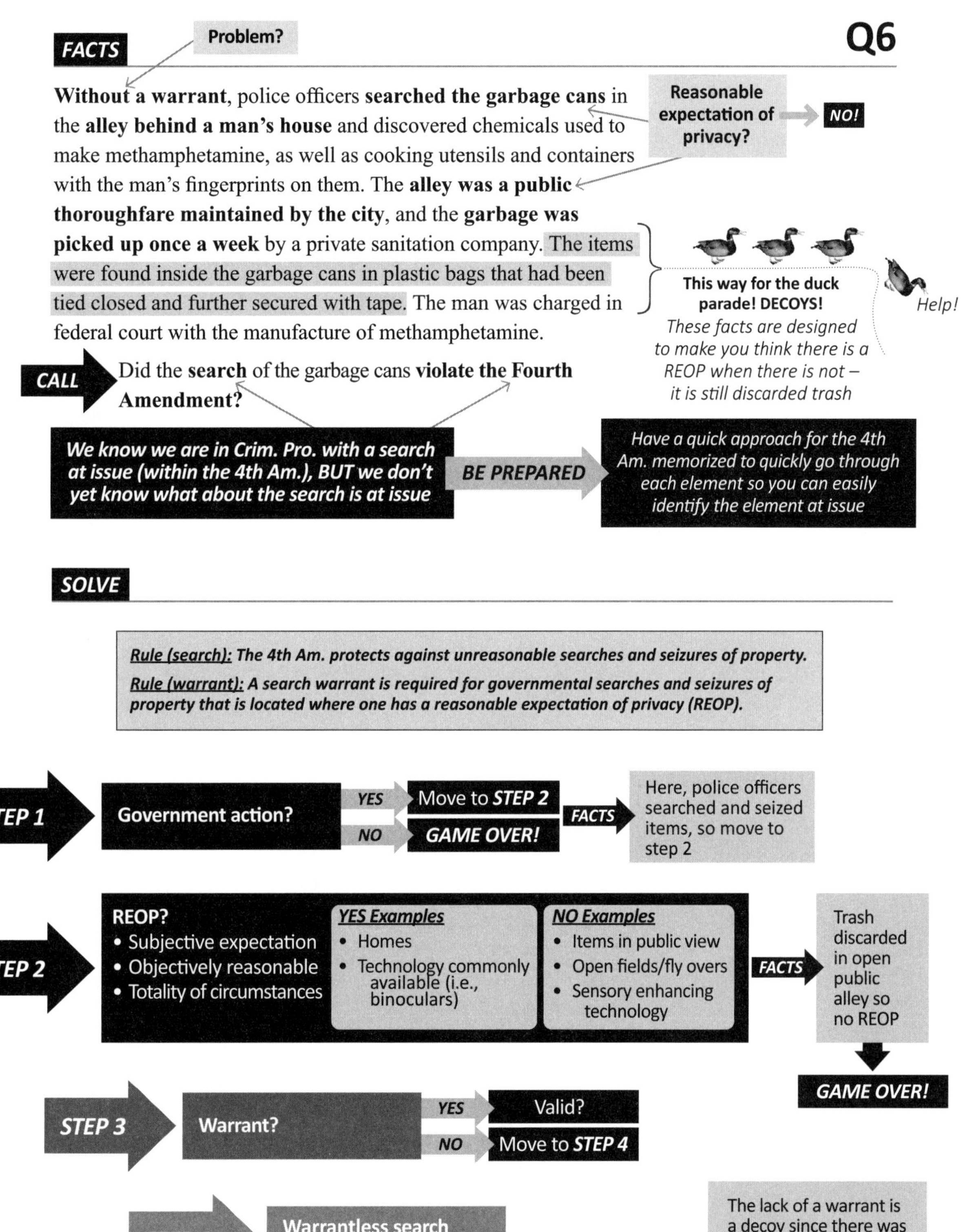
FACTS
Problem?
Q6
Without a warrant, police officers searched the garbage cans in the alley behind a man's house and discovered chemicals used to make methamphetamine, as well as cooking utensils and containers with the man's fingerprints on them. The alley was a public thoroughfare maintained by the city, and the garbage was picked up once a week by a private sanitation company. The items were found inside the garbage cans in plastic bags that had been tied closed and further secured with tape. The man was charged in federal court with the manufacture of methamphetamine.
Reasonable expectation of privacy?
NO!
This way for the duck parade! DECOYS!
These facts are designed to make you think there is a REOP when there is not – it is still discarded trash
Help!
CALL
Did the search of the garbage cans violate the Fourth Amendment?
We know we are in Crim. Pro. with a search at issue (within the 4th Am.), BUT we don't yet know what about the search is at issue
BE PREPARED
Have a quick approach for the 4th Am. memorized to quickly go through each element so you can easily identify the element at issue
SOLVE
Rule (search): The 4th Am. protects against unreasonable searches and seizures of property.
Rule (warrant): A search warrant is required for governmental searches and seizures of property that is located where one has a reasonable expectation of privacy (REOP).
STEP 1
Government action?
YES
Move to STEP 2
NO
GAME OVER!
FACTS
Here, police officers searched and seized items, so move to step 2
STEP 2
REOP?
• Subjective expectation
• Objectively reasonable
• Totality of circumstances
YES Examples
• Homes
• Technology commonly available (i.e., binoculars)
NO Examples
• Items in public view
• Open fields/fly overs
• Sensory enhancing technology
FACTS
Trash discarded in open public alley so no REOP
GAME OVER!
STEP 3
Warrant?
YES
Valid?
NO
Move to STEP 4
STEP 4
Warrantless search exception?
The lack of a warrant is a decoy since there was no REOP. No need to analyze steps 3 and 4.

SOLVE (continued)

A No, **because** the man did not have a reasonable expectation of privacy in the discarded garbage cans outside of his house in the alley. The fact that he tied the bags up and taped them is not relevant because he still discarded them to where the public had access to them.

Now look for a similar answer choice.

DECODE

A. No, because the man had no reasonable expectation of privacy in garbage left in the alley.

Correct. The man discarded his trash into the trashcans outside of his house in the public alley where the sanitation company would pick them up once a week. Tying and taping the bags does not prevent them from being discarded in public where anyone could access the trash so the man had no reasonable expectation of privacy in his discarded trash.

B. No, because the probative value of the evidence outweighs the man's modest privacy claims in his garbage.

Wrong rule. The 4th Amendment does not require an analysis of legal relevance to determine if a search was valid or not.

C. Yes, because the alley was within the curtilage of the man's home and entry without a warrant was unconstitutional.

Wrong analysis. The trash cans were not within the curtilage of the man's home because they were discarded in an alley that was in a public thoroughfare maintained by the city and the trash was left out so anyone could rummage through it until the sanitation company picked it up once a week.

D. Yes, because there is a reasonable expectation of privacy in one's secured garbage containers.

Wrong analysis. The garbage containers were not secured because they were in public. This answer is the decoy answer because it makes it appear as though tying and taping trash bags suddenly makes them secure and private, which is not the standard. Even if they were "secured" the reasonable expectation of privacy is based on an objectively reasonable expectation under the circumstances and reasonable people don't expect privacy in their discarded trash left for the sanitation company to pick up.

FACTS

Q7

Gov. action

Police officers had **probable cause** to believe that **a man** had **committed** a series of armed **bank robberies with an accomplice.**

Think about why it would matter if he had an accomplice

The officers obtained a **valid arrest warrant** for the man and went to his house to arrest him. The officers found the **front door ajar** and could hear a **radio playing inside**. They **knocked** on the door, **identified themselves** as police officers, and stated that they had a warrant. Getting **no response**, the **officers entered the house**. After the officers **called the man's name several times** and **again identified themselves** as police officers, the **man emerged from the basement and was arrested**. The **officers went into the basement to look for the accomplice**. They **opened a closet door and found cocaine in plain view**. They did not find the accomplice.

Take note – arrest NOT a search warrant

Knock & announce ok

This is the issue...is this ok? Why?

The man was indicted for cocaine possession. He has **moved to suppress the cocaine** as evidence on the ground that it was obtained in **violation of the Fourth Amendment**.

Read the preceding sentence as there is usually a clue in there as to what is being suppressed

CALL Should the court grant the **motion to suppress**?

Motion to suppress usually means 4th Am. violation

SOLVE

Should the court grant the **motion to suppress** (4th Am. search/seizure of cocaine)?

Rule (for arrest): ***A warrant is required to arrest a person in their home and it gives police permission to enter the house to arrest the person if they have a reasonable belief the person is home. Police should knock & announce their presence.***

Rule (for search): ***A search warrant is required for governmental searches and seizures of property that is located where one has a reasonable expectation of privacy (REOP), unless an exception applies.***

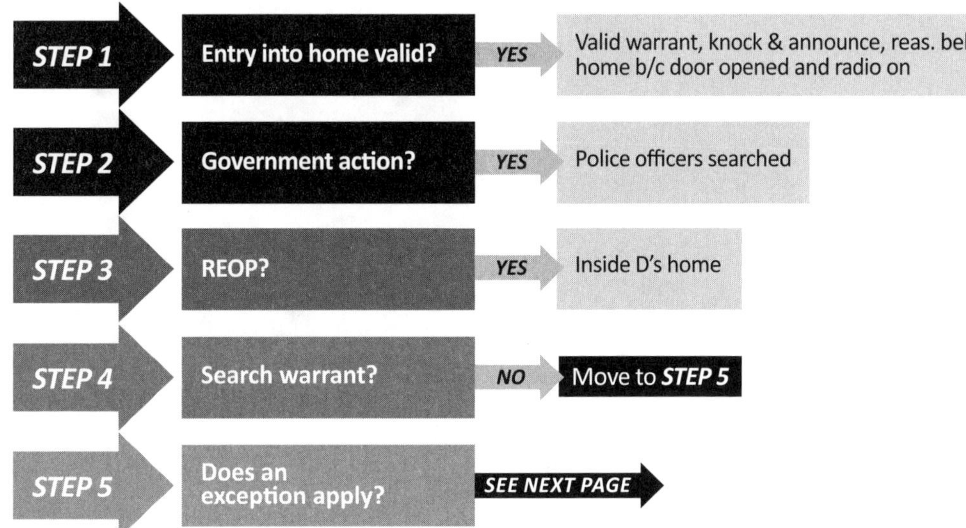

SOLVE *(continued)*

DOES AN EXCEPTION APPLY?	ANALYSIS
• **SILA** – can search wingspan when making a lawful arrest & can do a **protective sweep** of premises if reasonable belief other dangerous individuals present	• **SILA** – closet beyond wingspan when arrested already, but police knew D had an accomplice and they could have reasonably believed the accomplice was with him, so they were entitled to search the premises looking for the accomplice in places big enough for a person to hide in (such as the closet here)
• **Plain view** – ok if legitimately on premises & have a lawful right to be in the position to view	• **Plain view** - police were legitimately on the premises b/c arrest warrant and valid protective sweep so cocaine in plain view
• Automobile • Consent • Exigent circumstances • Stop and frisk	• Other exceptions– N/A

A No, **because** the police were legitimately on the premises to make an arrest with an arrest warrant and the cocaine was in plain view while they were performing a valid protective sweep to look for the man's accomplice.

→ Now look for a similar answer choice.

DECODE

A. No, because the officers discovered the cocaine during a lawful protective sweep of the house looking for the man's accomplice.

BINGO! The police were rightfully on the premises with a valid arrest warrant for the man who was believed to have had an accomplice. Under the SILA exception to a warrantless search, they were permitted to search the premises in a protective sweep to look for the accomplice and the cocaine was in plain view while doing the sweep. Note that they left out the words SILA and plain view to somewhat hide the ball.

B. No, because the search was incident to the man's arrest.

This is not the best answer (this is the second best answer). The reason they were able to find the cocaine in plain view is because they were doing a protective sweep. The arrest itself only gives them the ability to search the wingspan of the defendant. The area outside the place where defendant is arrested must meet the requirements for a lawful protective sweep or it cannot be searched with an arrest warrant.

C. Yes, because the officers did not have a search warrant.

Incomplete rule. This does not account for the warrantless exceptions that apply such as SILA with a protective sweep and the plain view exception.

D. Yes, because the officers did not have probable cause to believe that cocaine would be in the closet.

Wrong rule. Probable cause is not needed under a valid protective sweep if the officers reasonably believe other dangerous individuals may be present.

FACTS

Q8

A **police officer stopped a driver** who had **run a red light**. Upon approaching the car, the **officer noticed a strong odor of alcohol** and immediately **asked whether the driver had been drinking**. The **driver admitted having had several alcoholic drinks** that evening.

Legitimate stop

Admission/confession

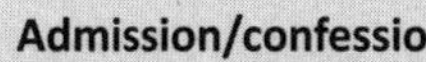

The **driver, charged with driving while intoxicated**, moved to **suppress the officer's testimony regarding the driver's statement** about his drinking. The driver argued that the officer had elicited the statement without providing the requisite Miranda warnings. The **prosecutor has responded** that the statement should be **allowed in the prosecution's case-in-chief** or, at a minimum, should be allowed **as impeachment** in the event the driver testifies and denies drinking.

Motion to suppress statement – likely crimes

Issue!

Evidence crossover? More like a decoy to get you to go down the evidence path when testing Crimes

CALL How should the court rule regarding the **driver's statement admitting his drinking**?

Issue not clear – could be crimes or evidence – need to read facts

SOLVE

MIRANDA RULES	*FACTS/ANALYSIS*
Miranda warnings (right to remain silent, anything you can say can be used against you, right to have an attorney present) are required if: • Suspect is in **custody** (not free to leave), and	• Suspect pulled over for running a red light but not in custody at the time of the question because suspect not arrested or anything yet
• Suspect **interrogated** (words or actions by the police that are reasonably likely to lead to an incriminating response)	• Interrogation irrelevant because no custody so no need to analyze interrogation

***MBE tip:** Note that the facts tell you Miranda is the issue and nowhere in your Miranda rules is anything about impeachment. Keep this mind when you look at the answer choices.*

A The court should rule that the driver's statement is admissible **because** there was no Miranda violation since the driver was not in custody at the time of the statement so Miranda warnings were not required.

Now look for a similar answer choice.

DECODE

(A) The statement should be allowed, because although the driver was in custody, the officer's spontaneous utterance upon smelling alcohol did not rise to the level of interrogation.

Wrong analysis. The driver was not in custody yet as traffic stops are temporary and brief (unless arrested which then would become custodial).

B. The statement should be allowed, because the driver was not in custody for Miranda purposes when the admission was made.

Correct! The driver was temporarily pulled over (until arrested which had not occurred yet) so he was not in custody for Miranda purposes.

(C) The statement should be suppressed both in the prosecution's case-in-chief and as impeachment evidence, even if the driver testifies.

Wrong issue. The issue is Miranda, but even if it was testing evidence too, the fact that Miranda was not violated would allow the evidence in for both substantive and impeachment purposes.

(D) The statement should be suppressed in the prosecution's case-in-chief, but it may be used as impeachment evidence if the driver testifies.

Wrong issue. The issue is Miranda, but even if it was testing evidence too, the fact that Miranda was not violated would allow the evidence in for both substantive and impeachment purposes, not just the latter.

Need to know when right to counsel attaches. Yet?

FACTS **Q9**

A defendant was **indicted and arrested** for bank robbery. The defendant had **an initial appearance** before a magistrate judge in which **he was notified of the charges** and **told that counsel would be appointed for him the next day**. The police then required the defendant to participate with other prisoners in **a lineup** in which each person had to wear a white T-shirt and say, "Put your hands in the air." At the lineup, witnesses to the bank robbery identified the defendant as the bank robber. **The next day, the defendant was arraigned** on the charges.

Alleged violation 1

Alleged violation 2

Decoy to make you think formal commencement not started yet

The defendant argues that his **Sixth Amendment right to counsel was violated** when he was **denied counsel at two critical stages** of the proceeding: his **initial appearance** in court before the magistrate judge **and the lineup** identification.

2 alleged violations

What arguments can I make to get out of here?!

CALL Was the defendant's **Sixth Amendment right to counsel** violated?

Issue in the call. Yay!!

SOLVE

RIGHT TO COUNSEL RULE	*INITIAL APPEARANCE*	*LINEUP*
• After formal proceedings commenced • At all critical stages • Offense specific	• D indicted & arrested, BUT didn't know charges yet b/c was being notified at the initial appearance so no formal proceedings yet • Initial appearance not a critical stage yet since D doesn't even know what charges were being brought until that initial appearance	• D indicted, arrested, and had initial appearance (formal proceedings commenced then); ok if before arraignment because D knew what he was being charged with and had an initial appearance • Lineup is a critical stage as one can be identified and has a right to have an attorney present

A Yes for the lineup **<u>because</u>** that was after formal commencements began and was a critical stage, but not for the initial appearance since that is when defendant found out about the charges so the formal commencement started after that appearance.

Now look for similar answer choices.

DECODE

Ⓐ No.

Wrong analysis. Defendant's Sixth Amendment right to counsel was violated since the lineup was after formal proceedings commenced and the lineup was a critical stage of the prosecution. Note that this question was atypical with one no answer and three yes answers. Do not let this fool you. Treat it the same as any other question that has two of each.

Ⓑ Yes, based only on the denial of counsel at the initial appearance.

Wrong analysis. The defendant did not have the right to counsel at the initial appearance since formal proceedings had not yet commenced because he didn't even know what charges were being brought against him yet (which was the purpose of the initial appearance).

C. Yes, based only on the denial of counsel at the lineup.

Correct. The formal proceedings commenced after the initial appearance, so at the lineup defendant had a right to counsel because it was a critical stage of the prosecution.

Ⓓ Yes, based on the denial of counsel at both stages of the proceeding.

Wrong analysis. The initial appearance was before formal proceedings commenced since they commenced at the initial appearance so the right to counsel attached after that appearance.

Q10

FACTS

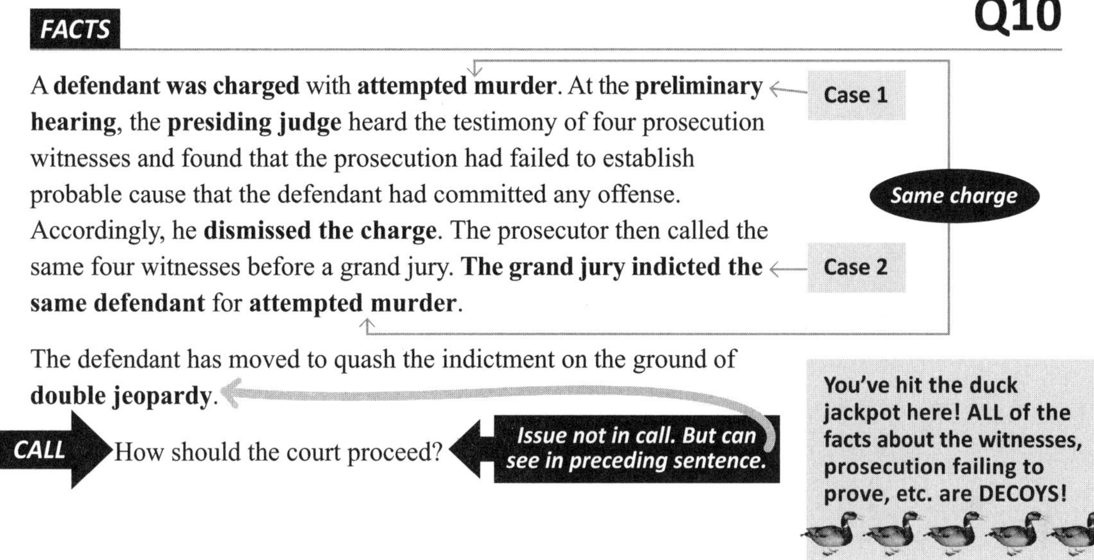

SOLVE

How should the court proceed (on double jeopardy argument)?

Rule: ***Double jeopardy (DJ) protects an individual from being tried for the same offense twice after jeopardy attaches.***

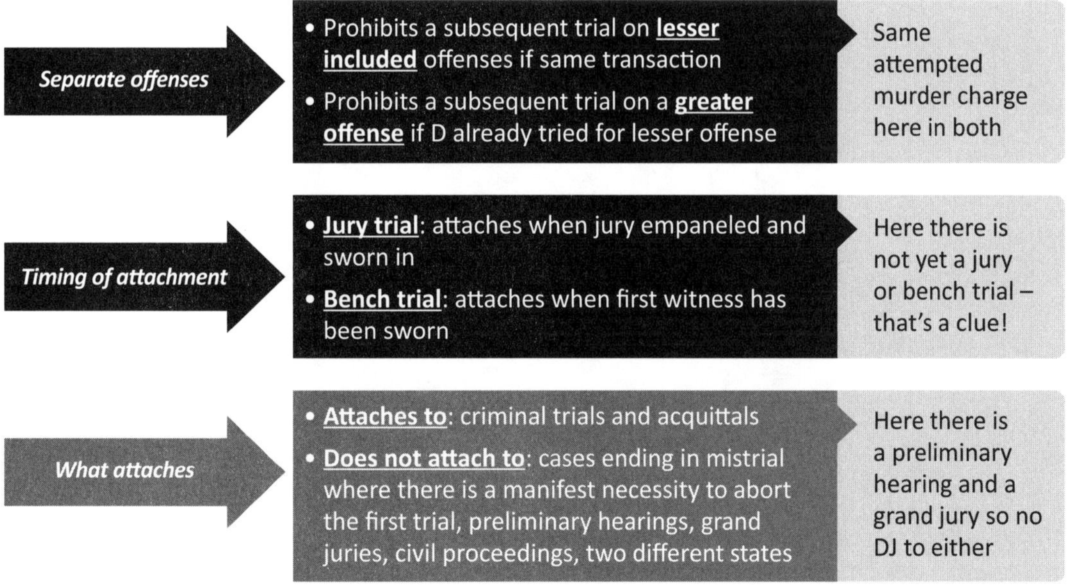

A The court should deny the motion **because** double jeopardy did not attach since double jeopardy does not attach to preliminary hearings or grand juries.

Now look for a similar answer choice.

DECODE

~~A.~~ Grant the motion, because the dismissal of the first charge on the merits, whether correct or incorrect, bars any further prosecution.

Incorrect rule. Double jeopardy does not attach to preliminary hearings which is what the first charge was.

~~B.~~ Grant the motion, unless the prosecution has evidence that was not presented in the first case.

No such rule. The rule does not consider whether evidence was or was not presented and here double jeopardy did not attach because there was a preliminary hearing and a grand jury.

C. Deny the motion, because the defendant has not yet been in jeopardy of conviction on the attempted murder charge.

YES!!! Because neither the preliminary hearing nor the grand jury proceeding give rise to double jeopardy. Note that the answer choice does not explain why and use those names – they hide the ball!

~~D.~~ Deny the motion, because the protection of the double jeopardy clause does not come into play until there has been a conviction or an acquittal.

Incorrect rule. Double jeopardy attaches when the jury is sworn in for a jury trial or when the first witness is sworn in for a bench trial and has nothing to do with whether there is a conviction or acquittal.

PART 5 EVIDENCE

EVIDENCE TABLE OF CONTENTS

★ Favorite testing area

EVIDENCE MBE OUTLINE

MBE EVIDENCE AT A GLANCE

Applicable Law: The Federal Rules of Evidence (FRE) apply to most proceedings, except for a few, such as grand jury proceedings (but FRE regarding privileges do generally apply there). The MBE tests the federal rules, which are the FRE and where there is no FRE on point, the federal common law. You do not need to know the rules by FRE number.

8-9 Questions	6-7 Questions	6-7 Questions	4-5 Questions
Relevance Character Expert opinion Authentication	Impeachment Personal knowledge Refresh recollection Lay opinion Judicial notice Role of judge/jury	Hearsay Hearsay exceptions	Privileges Policy exclusions Best evidence rule

<u>MBE tip</u>: Evidence questions tend to be short, and you will most often be asked to identify the **basis on which the evidence is admissible** or not admissible. Always ask, "**Why** is the evidence being offered; for what **purpose**?" This will help lead you to the correct **rule** to apply (e.g., to impeach and/or for its substance). Also pay attention to the **proceedings** themselves since this can have an impact on the appropriate rule to apply (civil or criminal; Plaintiff's or Defendant's witness; on direct or cross examination). Solve the questions **methodically** and **sequentially**.

COMMON EVIDENCE DECOY ANSWERS

<u>Decoy tip</u>: You need to know the rules very well because the distinctions between rules can be subtle and a rule that almost (but not quite) works will always be a decoy answer choice. Read carefully, because another favorite decoy is to misstate the rules.

Wrong answer	**Why it is** (probably) **wrong**
Inadmissible because it is **self-serving.**	There is no such rule.
Inadmissible because the **conviction was not the result of a trial.**	There is no such rule.
Admissible as **res gestae.**	The FRE has abolished this rule.
Admissible to establish **criminal propensity**.	Evidence is (almost) never admissible to establish criminal propensity, with a narrow exception for sex crime propensity.
Inadmissible because (the evidence) was not **corroborated.**	Evidence must be corroborated only in the limited situation where a statement against interest is offered in a criminal case.
Inadmissible because of the **Dead Man's statute.** This is a real rule, which prevents a person from testifying in their own interest and against the interest of a dead person about the statements made by that dead person. It is almost always a decoy.	Only ½ of the states use a Dead Man's statute, so it is not a federal rule or even a majority rule. The Q would have to tell you it was enacted to test it, but they typically do not.

I. PRELIMINARY EVIDENTIARY CONCEPTS

A. **Direct or circumstantial:** Evidence can be direct or circumstantial.

1. **Direct evidence** is identical to the factual proposition it is intended to prove, requires no inferences be made and can automatically resolve an issue, if believed (e.g., "I saw D stab V.").
2. **Circumstantial evidence** indirectly proves the factual proposition it is intended to prove and only resolves an issue if additional **inferences** are used (e.g., "I saw D holding a bloody knife and standing near V's dead body.").

B. **Form of evidence:** Evidence can come in **several forms.**

1. **Testimonial evidence** is when a **witness** makes an assertion in court.
2. **Real evidence** is the actual physical **thing** involved in the case (e.g., gun).
3. **Documentary evidence** is in the form of a writing (e.g. a contract).
4. **Demonstrative evidence** is a tangible item that is prepared to **illustrate a concept** (e.g., map of an accident scene).

II. RELEVANCE

Only relevant evidence may be admitted.

A. **Logical relevance:** All evidence must be logically relevant.

1. **Evidence is relevant** if it has **any tendency to make a fact more or less probable** than it would be without the evidence and the fact is of consequence in determining the action (i.e., material). (FRE 401)

LOGICAL RELEVANCE EXAMPLES

RELEVANT	NOT RELEVANT
◆ Car accident, allegedly caused by faulty car part. D asserts driver was intoxicated. (Intoxication evidence may be prejudicial to the victim, but is circumstantially relevant to show alternate causation for the accident.) ◆ VP sued to return $230k of embezzled funds. VP earned $75k/year. P calls Banker to testify VP deposited $250k in 2 years. (Circumstantial evidence ok.) ◆ D is charged with arson. P introduces the house and contents are fully insured. (Motive.) ◆ D charged with battery and is arrested with a knife. Coroner says the knife is similar to V's wound, but many knives could have caused the wound. (Weak evidence, but *any* tendency/more or less probable is the standard, so it goes to the jury.)	◆ P is injured in accident caused by a faulty car part. The part's authenticity is in dispute. P wants to introduce a judgment from another P on similar facts in another case to prove authenticity. (Facts unrelated, so *no* tendency.) ◆ Slip and fall shortly after floor is waxed. In the preceding week, 1000 people used the hallway without slipping. (Too remote in time to fall.)

B. **Legal relevance discretionary exclusion:** A **balancing test** is used to determine legal relevance. The court **may exclude** relevant evidence if its **probative value is substantially outweighed by a danger of unfair prejudice**, confusing the issues, misleading the jury, undue delay, wasting time, or needlessly presenting cumulative evidence. (FRE 403)

LEGAL RELEVANCE EXAMPLES

FACTS	ANALYSIS
D arrested for robbery. At time of arrest, D is holding illegal drugs.	Inadmissible; too unfairly prejudicial since this could taint the jury's view of D such that they think D is likely to be a criminal.
D arrested for DUI. Videotape from booking shows him unsteady with slurred speech.	Admissible, to show intoxication
P is injured in accident and submits photo showing his bloodied head protruding through the windshield at a grotesque angle.	Admissible, to show extent of P's injury

Decoy tip: When evidence is relevant and admissible (the evidence is both logically and legally relevant), there is usually a decoy answer indicating the evidence is unfairly prejudicial. In legal relevance, the concern is only **unfair** prejudice, since all evidence against a party is potentially prejudicial/harmful.

III. PUBLIC POLICY EXCLUSIONS

Otherwise-relevant evidence can be excluded for public policy reasons. This is because for the greater good of society, we want to encourage certain types of responsible behaviors. [Both the rules and their exceptions are frequently MBE tested.]

A. **Subsequent remedial measures:** (FRE 407)

1. **General rule:** Evidence of **safety measures**, or repairs performed **after** an accident, are **not admissible to prove culpable conduct**, negligence, a defect in a product or its design, or a need for a warning or instruction.

   Example: After a car accident caused by a patron of a bar, the bar subsequently instituted a four drink per night minimum.

   Example: After a speeding employee causes a car accident, the company installed speed regulators on its company trucks.

2. **Exception:** Evidence of subsequent remedial measures **is admissible to establish** (list is not exclusive):

   a. **Ownership or control:** The ownership or control of an instrumentality, such as a vehicle or property.

Example: A patron slips on a hallway located between two businesses. Evidence that one of the two businesses replaced the flooring the next week is admissible to establish that business had ownership/control of the hallway.

b. **Precaution not feasible:** To **rebut** a claim that precautionary measures were not feasible.

Example: Consumer is injured operating a slicing machine alleging negligent product design. Evidence that the machine was subsequently redesigned is admissible to rebut a claim by the manufacturer that a safer design was not feasible.

c. **Impeachment,** where the party made a conflicting statement.

B. **Liability insurance:** (FRE 411)

1. **General rule:** Evidence that a person has, or does not have, liability insurance is **not admissible to prove culpable conduct**, such as negligence or the defendant's ability to pay a judgment.

Example: A small plane crashes causing injuries to a person on the ground. Evidence that the owner had liability insurance is inadmissible.

2. **Exception:** Evidence of liability insurance **is admissible to establish** (list is not exclusive):

a. **Ownership or control:** Showing ownership or control of an instrumentality is allowed.

Example: A small plane crashes causing injuries to a person on the ground. The defendant claims he does not own plane. Evidence that the defendant bought an insurance policy for the plane is admissible to establish he owned the plane.

b. **Impeachment,** such as to prove a witness's bias.

Example: If a witness testifies that the plaintiff has minimal injuries from an accident, that witness can be impeached with evidence of bias that the witness is an employee of the insurance carrier and thus has a vested interest in diminishing the extent of the plaintiff's injuries.

c. **Collateral admissions:** A **statement of fault made in conjunction** with a statement regarding the possession of liability insurance is **admissible.** The statements can be **bifurcated** (split), so the admission of fault is admissible, while the statement regarding possessing insurance is inadmissible.

Example: After a car accident, one party states, "It's all my fault. Don't worry; I have good insurance." The statement "It's all my fault," is admissible as a collateral party admission, while the statement, "I have good insurance," is inadmissible under the liability insurance policy exclusion.

 C. **Offers to pay medical expenses:** (FRE 409)

1. **General rule: Offers to pay medical**, hospital, or similar expenses resulting from an injury are **not admissible to prove liability** for that injury.

Example: After a car accident, one party states, "I'll pay your medical expenses." This statement is inadmissible to prove liability for the injury because it is an offer to pay medical expenses resulting from an injury.

a. **Offer to pay medical expenses/settlement offer hybrid**: Where an offer to pay medical bills is also phrased as an offer to settle, **use the more restrictive rule for settlements/** offers in compromise below since that rule precludes the admission of any collateral statements.

Example: If a party made the statements, "I'll pay your medical expenses *if* you agree to drop the case," the entire statement would be deemed an offer of settlement and thus is inadmissible.

2. **Exception: Collateral admissions of fact** made during an offer to pay medical expenses **are admissible.**

   Example: After a car accident, one party states, "I'll pay your medical expenses. It's the least I can do since I wasn't paying attention." The first statement is inadmissible as an offer to pay medical expenses resulting from an injury. The second statement is admissible as a collateral admission of fact made during an offer to pay medical expenses.

D. **Offers of settlement (compromise):** Where one party offers money **in exchange** for settlement of a claim (a *quid pro quo* arrangement). (FRE 408)

1. **General rule: Offers to compromise to settle a *disputed* claim** are **not admissible** to **prove or disprove the validity or amount** of the disputed claim or to **impeach** by a prior inconsistent statement or a contradiction.

   Example: After a car accident, in response to Plaintiff's claim, Defendant says, "Your claim seems high, but since it was somewhat my fault, I'll split it with you." This statement is inadmissible since it is an offer to compromise to settle a disputed claim.

> **Decoy tip:** To have a disputed claim, a party need not have already filed suit, but there must be an indication a party will make a claim, so watch out for facts where a party blurts out a settlement offer at the scene before there is a dispute.
>
> **Example:** *Immediately* after a car accident, one party blurts out, "I'd like to give you $500 because I feel so bad about this." This statement is admissible because it does not qualify as a settlement offer (which would be inadmissible) since there was no "claim" pending (disputed as to validity or amount) at the time of the statement since it was said immediately after the accident.

a. **Collateral admissions made during settlement negotiations are <u>not</u> admissible.** This is an important distinction from the liability insurance and offer to pay medical expenses rules above. Collateral admissions are treated like the settlement offer itself and are also inadmissible for public policy reasons.

   Example: After a car accident, one party states, "I'll pay you $1000 to settle. It's the least I can do since I wasn't paying attention." The entire statement is inadmissible. This result is in contrast to the rule for offers to pay medical expenses above.

b. **Exceptions:** Settlement negotiation information may be permitted for purposes such as to prove bias, to negate a contention of undue delay, or to prove obstruction of justice. [This exception is rarely MBE tested]

E. **Offers to plead guilty:** [This rule is rarely MBE tested.] (FRE 410)

1. **General rule:** An **offer to plead** guilty to a crime, a no lo contendere plea, withdrawn guilty pleas, and **statements made during plea negotiations are not admissible** in any proceeding to prove a criminal defendant is guilty, or has a consciousness of guilt, or in a civil case on the same subject.

   a. **Except:** In a criminal proceeding for **perjury** if the defendant made the statement under oath, or in the interest of fairness, if another statement was made in the same negotiations and the statements should be considered together.

POLICY EXCLUSIONS CHEAT SHEET

Decoy tip: Know these rules and exceptions well. Look carefully at the language used to determine which rule applies to the facts. Since this evidence may be admitted for one purpose, but not another, it is important to determine the **purpose** for the evidence. Most decoy answers are crafted from the inapplicable rules and exceptions that apply to the other policy exclusions.

<table>
<tr><th></th><th>SRM</th><th>Insurance</th><th>Medical</th><th>Settlement</th></tr>
<tr><td>Not admissible for:</td><td>◆ Culpable conduct
◆ Negligence
◆ Product or design defect</td><td>Culpable conduct</td><td>Liability</td><td>◆ Claim's validity
◆ Claim's amount
◆ Impeach (Prior Inconsistent Stmt)</td></tr>
<tr><td rowspan="2">Admissible for:</td><td rowspan="2">◆ Ownership & Control
◆ Precaution not feasible
◆ Impeach</td><td rowspan="2">◆ Ownership & Control
◆ Impeach</td><td>All other purposes</td><td>Any other purpose, but disputed claims only</td></tr>
<tr><td colspan="2">◆ If an offer to pay medical bills is also an offer to settle, use the more restrictive settlement rule.</td></tr>
<tr><td>Collateral Admissions</td><td>Allowed</td><td>Allowed</td><td>Allowed</td><td><u>Not</u> allowed</td></tr>
</table>

IV. JUDICIAL NOTICE

A. **Judicial notice** is the process of **establishing facts as true** without presenting evidence. There are three types of judicial notice, but the MBE focuses on adjudicative facts, which are facts of the case at hand. (FRE 201) The court can take judicial notice of facts **not subject to reasonable dispute** because they are either:

1. **Generally known** in the community, which is the trial court's territorial jurisdiction, but does not include facts personally known to the judge; or
2. Capable of **accurate and ready determination** by a source whose accuracy cannot be reasonably questioned.

JUDICIAL NOTICE EXAMPLES

Judicial Notice	No Judicial Notice
◆ Certified copy of judgment of conviction (self-authenticating) ◆ The birthdate of a historical figure ◆ Records of a state or local codified ordinance ◆ That a particular date fell on a Tuesday ◆ That a street in town runs east-west	◆ Court's telephone call to court clerk to prove previous conviction (accuracy can be questioned) ◆ The birthdate of a party to the suit (not generally known) ◆ That a particular day was sunny based on the judge's recollection (facts known personally to the judge)

B. **Instructions and judicial discretion:** A party **must request judicial notice** to **compel** judicial notice of any fact that meets the requirements. If *not* requested by a party, the **court has discretion** to take judicial notice on its own. Judicial notice can occur at any time, even on appeal. As a result, the jury will be instructed:

1. **Civil case:** The jury **must accept** conclusively the judicially noticed fact as established.
2. **Criminal case:** The jury **may** (but is **not required** to) **accept** conclusively the judicially noticed fact.

V. DOCUMENTARY EVIDENCE

Documentary evidence is evidence presented in the form of a writing.

A. **Authentication:** All evidence, other than testimony, **must be authenticated** as genuine in order to be admitted. Authentication is proof that the item **is what the proponent claims** it is. (FRE 901-903)

1. **Methods of authentication:**

a. **Writings and recordings (sound or video)** can be authenticated by admissions, eyewitness testimony, voice identification, handwriting verifications (expert or non-expert with personal knowledge, or trier of fact with sample comparisons), circumstantial evidence (e.g., postmark, address), etc.

1. **Handwriting** can be authenticated by:

a. A **handwriting expert**;

b. A non-expert **layperson *already* familiar** with the person's handwriting**.** The non-expert may not purposely become familiar with the handwriting in question for the purpose of testifying.

c. **Handwriting exemplars shown to the jury** for their own assessment and comparison.

2. **Voice** can be authenticated by a layperson that has heard the voice in question **at any time**. The witness need not have been familiar with the person's voice prior to the trial (in contrast to the rule for a layperson authenticating handwriting).

3. **Outgoing phone call** authentication: Authenticated by testimony that a witness called a number assigned to a particular person, and the person who talked on the other end was in fact the person the caller was trying to reach (by self-identification, voice familiarity, etc.) or the conversation related to the business of a dialed business number.

4. **Reply letter doctrine** allows authentication of a letter written in response to another communication. Evidence that the inquiry letter was sent is sufficient to authenticate the response.

5. **Ancient documents** can be authenticated by evidence that the document is in a **condition to be free from suspicion** of inauthenticity, was **found in a place** such a writing would be kept, and was prepared before Jan. 1, 1998.

b. **Self-authenticating documents:** Certain documents are self-authenticating and do not need a sponsoring witness, such as **certified copies** of **public records** (e.g., deeds, death certificate), **official publications**, **newspapers** and periodicals, and **trade inscriptions** and labels that would be affixed in the course of business (e.g., a can of Coke is produced by the Coca Cola Company).

c. **Real evidence:** Physical evidence can be authenticated by **distinctive characteristics** (e.g., a gun identifiable by serial number), **chain of custody,** or personal knowledge.

   Example: When approached by police a suspect drops a plastic bag and runs. After apprehending the suspect, the police return to pick up the bag a few minutes later. This is sufficient to establish the plastic bag is the one the suspect dropped based on the personal knowledge of the police officer.

d. **Demonstrative evidence** must be a **fair and accurate representation,** which illustrates a matter of concern (e.g., photographs, crime scene diagrams, models, maps, summaries, etc.).

B. **Best evidence rule** (BER) is also called the original document rule: To prove the **contents** of a writing (including photos, X-rays, and recordings), the **original writing must be produced. Machine duplicate copies** (not handwritten) **are also allowed** *unless* the authenticity of the original is disputed. (Essentially, this means the original is preferred.) (FRE 1001-1003)

1. If the **original or a photocopy is unavailable without fault of the proponent: Other evidence of the contents may be admitted** at the judge's discretion, such as through oral testimony or handwritten notes. (FRE 1004)

   Example: A plaintiff sues a defendant for a libelous letter, which cannot now be found. If the judge finds the letter is unavailable through no fault of the plaintiff, she may allow testimony on the contents of the letter.

   a. **Non-production of documents is *excused*** when the originals have been lost or destroyed through no fault of the proponent, the original is not obtainable, or the original is in the opponent's possession and the opponent won't produce the document. (FRE 1004)

2. **Best evidence rule does not apply** when the **witness can testify from personal knowledge** about the fact to be proved and that personal knowledge **exists independent of the writing** (e.g. the witness did not learn the fact from the writing), where the writing is **collateral** (minor), or for **public records**. [The witness's ability to testify from personal knowledge is the point most frequently tested on the MBE.] (FRE 1007)

   Example: An undercover officer is prepared to testify about what the defendant said in a conversation pursuant to a drug selling conspiracy. Even if the conversation was secretly recorded, the BER does not apply because the officer can **testify from memory based on their personal knowledge** of being a participant in the conversation. Proving the details of the conversation by producing the audiotape is not required. *In contrast,* if the officer did not participate in the conversation and only learned of its contents through listening to the audiotape, the BER would apply and the audiotape would need to be produced.

   Example: In explanation for why the witness knows a conversation with the defendant occurred on a certain day, the witness explains the defendant mentioned in the conversation that his daughter's wedding announcement was published in the paper that same day. The reference to the newspaper article is a **collateral matter** and the BER does not apply.

3. **Completeness rule**: When a party introduces **part of a writing** or recorded statement at trial, the other party may require the introduction of any other part to establish the full context. (FRE 1006)

4. **Absence of an entry:** Records can also be admitted to show the absence of an entry to prove the nonoccurrence of an event.

Decoy tip: BER is frequently thrown in as a decoy when a MBE Q is testing a completely different concept, such as any fact pattern containing a written document (e.g. business or public record hearsay exceptions, past recorded recollection, present recollection refreshed, learned treatise, etc.). However, the rule itself is also tested, and when it is, it often does not apply. Remember, BER only applies when a party is **trying to prove the *contents*** of a writing. When a witness testifies **from personal knowledge to facts that are also memorialized in a writing**, the fact that a writing or recording also exists, and even would be more persuasive evidence on the point in question, does not mean the writing/recording must be produced and thus, BER will not apply.

C. **Summaries of voluminous writings:** If original documents are so voluminous that they can't be conveniently introduced into evidence, a summary, such as a chart, may be introduced through a **sponsoring witness**. The originals must be made available for examination or copy at a reasonable time and place. (FRE 1006)

   Example: A graph summarizing a 15-year log on the water levels of a riverbank would be the appropriate subject of a summary.

VI. WITNESS EXAMINATION

A. **Flow and scope of examination**

   1. **Direct examination** is the questioning of a witness by the party that called that witness.

      a. A **trial judge may call witnesses** and ask questions of any witness.

   2. **Cross-examination** is conducted by the opposing party and is limited to the **subject matter of the direct examination** and **witness credibility**. The court has discretion to allow cross-examination that exceeds the scope of direct [but this is rarely the case in MBE questions]. (FRE 611)

   3. **Re-direct examination** is limited to the **subject matter of the cross-examination.**

   4. **Re-cross examination** is limited to the **subject matter of the re-direct examination.**

B. **Competence to testify:** Whenever a witness is testifying from the stand, the witness's competence to testify is potentially at issue. A witness must testify from **personal knowledge**, have the capacity to **recollect** and **communicate**, and must understand the mandate to **testify truthfully**.

   1. **Personal knowledge:** A witness must have **personal knowledge** (also called **first-hand knowledge**) of the matter about which the witness is to testify. (FRE 602)

   2. **Truthful testimony**: A witness must understand and declare an **oath** that the witness will **testify truthfully**. (FRE 603)

   3. **A witness must testify to facts rather than opinions**, subject to the following **exception:**

      a. **Lay opinions are allowed** if rationally based on the witness's perception; are helpful to the trier of fact; and are not based on scientific, technical, or other specialized knowledge. (FRE 701) See sec. VI.F. for lay opinion rules.

   4. **Everyone is presumed competent to testify, unless shown otherwise.** (FRE 601) There are no general rules making certain witnesses incompetent to testify, such as young children, who

will be found competent based on their intelligence and ability to understand the importance of telling the truth.

a. **Except judges and jurors** in the case at issue **may not testify**.

1. **Judge:** A judge presiding at a trial may not testify as a witness in that trial. (FRE 605)

2. **Jurors may not testify** about a verdict, deliberations, or their mental processes in reaching a verdict. (FRE 606)

   Examples: A juror would not be permitted to testify if the juror misunderstood the judge's instructions, or the juror was feeling ill and wanted to get home quickly, or that the juror relied on testimony the judge had stricken, etc.

3. **Exception—verdict inquiry: Jurors may testify for the limited purpose** of identifying whether improper outside influence was brought to bear on any juror, improper extraneous prejudicial information that was brought to the jury's attention, or whether there is an error on the verdict form. (FRE 606)

   Example: If a juror learned from the court clerk that the defendant had been accused of fraud in several lawsuits, the juror would be permitted to testify to that extraneous prejudicial information that was brought to his attention by the court clerk.

> **MBE tip:** Competence to testify may be tested in combination with rules regarding the **judge's role** in first determining evidence **admissibility**.
>
> **Example:** An informant testifies he bought cocaine (lay opinion) from the defendant. This will be admissible testimony *if* the judge determines the informant has sufficient knowledge and experience to identify cocaine.
>
> 
>
> **Decoy tip:** The best evidence rule is a common decoy answer when a witness *testifies about business events* that are also recorded in writing. So long as the witness is testifying from memory as to the witness's personal knowledge, they need not present the corresponding documents under the best evidence rule.

C. **Exclusion of witnesses:** At the request of a party, the judge shall order other witnesses excluded from the courtroom while another witness is testifying so a witness cannot hear other witnesses' testimony. This can happen at the trial **judge's own discretion** or is **mandatory at the request of either party** to the trial. [This rule is rarely MBE tested] (FRE 615)

1. **Exceptions:** This rule does not apply to a **party** to the suit, a person whose presence is **essential**, or one **statutorily authorized** to be present.

D. **Objections to the form of the question** (or answer). Evidence will not be excluded unless there is a timely, **specific objection** (which the judge sustains) since the judge may exercise reasonable control over witness examination. (FRE 611)

1. **Leading question:** The question itself is phrased to suggest the answer the questioner desires (e.g., "Isn't it true the traffic light was red when the collision occurred?").

   a. **Direct examination:** Leading questions are generally **not permitted** on direct examination. However, they may be allowed at the **judge's discretion** to question **children**, a **"hostile" witness**, an adverse party, or to elicit **preliminary background information** that is not in dispute.

   b. **Cross examination:** Leading questions typically are permitted on cross-examination of lay or expert witnesses.

2. **Other common objections** [These rules are rarely MBE tested.]
   a. **Non-responsive:** The witness's answer is unresponsive to the question.
   b. **Compound question:** Two questions are contained in one question.
   c. **Narrative:** Questions calling for a narrative response are phrased too broadly.
   d. **Misleading question** is meant to trick the person being questioned.
   e. **Assumes facts not in evidence,** when those facts are subject to dispute.
   f. **Argumentative:** The question is unnecessarily combative or tries to get the witness to agree with the questioner's interpretation of evidence.

E. **Present recollection refreshed** is a technique that allows **any item** (photo, report, handwritten notes, etc.) to be used to **refresh a witness's memory** when the witness's recollection is currently uncertain. Once shown the item, the witness must then **testify only from their refreshed memory**. (FRE 612)

<u>Example</u>: A witness testified that four people attended a meeting, but cannot remember all of their names. The witness may consult handwritten notes, and then testify to the names from their refreshed memory.

1. **Memory stimulus is not evidence:** The item used to refresh memory is not considered evidence and may even be otherwise inadmissible evidence. The memory stimulus can be used to refresh the witness's memory **before** testifying, **or while** testifying in court.
2. **Adversary's right to inspect and admit into evidence:** When the item used to refresh the witness's recollection is presented ***while*** **testifying**, the ***adversary*** has a right to inspect the item, cross-examine, and admit pertinent portions into evidence. When the item has been used ***before*** **testifying**, the right is at the court's discretion. The **proponent cannot admit** the item into evidence **unless it is otherwise admissible**. (FRE 612)

<u>MBE tip</u>: Present recollection refreshed is often confused with the hearsay exception **past recorded recollection**. With present recollection refreshed the item shown to the witness is a memory stimulus, which then allows the witness to *testify entirely from memory*. **Past recorded recollection** (see sec. XI.E.1) applies when the document consulted *does not actually refresh* the witness's memory, so *if* it otherwise qualifies, the document itself is read into the record as a hearsay exception.

<u>Decoy tip</u>: Anything can be used to refresh the witness's recollection and it need not be admissible, so hearsay and various hearsay exceptions (e.g. business record, past recorded recollection) are frequent decoy answers.

F. **Opinion testimony** (FRE 701)

1. **Lay opinions** are not legal conclusions, but opinions.

   <u>Examples</u>: **Authentication** of familiar handwriting or voices; describing a person's appearance or demeanor (worried, scared, insane, drunk etc.); estimations, such as driving speed, property value etc.

   a. Lay opinions are admissible if they are:
      1. Rationally based on the **witness's perceptions,**
      2. **Helpful to the trier of fact,** and

3. **Not based** on scientific, technical, or **specialized knowledge.**

> **MBE tip:** Handwriting authentication is the lay opinion most frequently tested.

★ 2. **Expert opinion** (FRE 702-703)

a. **Expert opinions are admissible** subject to the following requirements:

1. The witness is **qualified as an expert** by knowledge, skill, experience, training, or education.

   a. A party may challenge the witness's qualifications since it is relevant to the weight given the expert's opinion.

   Example: It is permissible to ask an expert chemist if they failed two chemistry classes.

2. **Specialized knowledge** will **assist the trier of fact** in understanding the evidence or determining a fact. Typically, this is information laypersons do not ordinarily evaluate (e.g., county coroner, doctor, chemist, accident investigator).

3. The testimony is **based on sufficient facts** or data. This information can be learned before or at the trial. The expert's opinion may be based on:

   a. **Firsthand knowledge**;

   b. **Observation of prior witnesses** or other evidence at the trial; or

   c. A **hypothetical question** posed by counsel, though it must include all significant facts at issue.

4. The testimony must be the product of **reliable principles** and methods (*Daubert* standard) and to determine reliability the followings factors may assist the trier of fact: (1) whether the expert's theory is **peer reviewed and published** in scientific journals, (2) whether the theory is **tested** and subject to retesting, (3) the **known or expected rate of error**, (4) the existence and maintenance of **standards and controls used**, and (5) whether it is subject to a **reasonable level of acceptance** in the scientific community.

5. The witness must have **applied the principles reliably** to the facts of the case.

b. **Ultimate issue rule**: An expert may have an opinion on an **ultimate issue** in a case, **except** not on the requisite mental state of a criminal defendant. (FRE 704)

c. **Cross examination of expert**: Expert credibility can be challenged based on (1) the adequacy of the expert's general knowledge in the field of expertise and (2) the basis of the facts underlying the expert's testimony.

EXPERT OPINION EXAMPLES

<u>MBE tip</u>: **Learned treatises** can be used to cross-examine experts, and also may be admitted under the learned treatise hearsay exception (see XI.E.4) so these topics can cross over.

<u>Decoy tip</u>: The facts the expert relied on need not be in evidence or even admissible. The *basis* for an expert's opinion need not be disclosed during direct examination *before* the expert can give an opinion. Both of these scenarios provide decoy answers.

ADMISSIBLE	NOT ADMISSIBLE
◆ A psychologist in a **negligence** case can testify that at the time of the car accident the mental state of the driver was unbalanced, but not self-injurious. ◆ A product safety expert can testify that an allegedly defective lawn mower blade could not fly off in the manner claimed by the plaintiff, even though it is an opinion on causation. (The ultimate issue of causation is ok in a civil case.) ◆ DEA agent can testify on common drug slang and code words. ◆ County coroner can testify that the victim died of poisoning (though the tissue sample slides are not offered in evidence). ◆ A doctor listening in court to plaintiff's testimony about her injuries can testify about the permanence of the injuries.	◆ A psychologist in a **murder** trial cannot testify that at the time of the killing the defendant was in fear for her life. (A **criminal's mental state** is an **ultimate issue,** and not a permissible subject for an expert opinion.)

G. **Confrontation Clause of the Sixth Amendment** protects a criminal defendant's **right to confront and cross-examine witnesses against** that criminal defendant. Thus, **testimonial statements will not be admitted** against an accused unless the declarant is available for cross-examination by the accused. This frequently arises with co-conspirator statements. A statement will <u>not</u> be admitted if:

1. The statement is offered against a **criminal defendant,**
2. The declarant is **unavailable** for cross-examination,
3. The accused had **no opportunity to cross-examine,** and
4. The **statement was testimonial** in nature. Testimonial statements typically are made during non-emergency situations where the primary purpose of the interrogation is to establish or prove past events potentially relevant to later criminal prosecution (e.g., **police interrogations, preliminary hearings,** and **grand jury proceedings**).

    a. **Non-testimonial statements can be admitted** without triggering the protections of the Confrontation Clause. These are statements made in **conditions that don't suggest it will be used in a future proceeding**. Non-testimonial statements include **business records** (e.g., a computer printout of bank deposits), **statements by a co-conspirator *during* the conspiracy**, statements made to police in an ongoing emergency, excited utterances, present sense impressions, state of mind statements, dying declarations, etc.

> <u>MBE tip</u>: Confrontation Clause issues are often tested and classified as Criminal Procedure issues, but since the right to cross-examine one's accusers also invokes a witness on the stand, these rules are included in both subject matter outlines.

VII. PRIVILEGES

A. A **privilege** provides testimonial protection for certain relationships, allowing one claiming the privilege to refuse to disclose, or prohibit others from disclosing, specified confidential information. Once asserted, neither the judge nor counsel for the parties may comment on the privilege.

1. **Federal privilege rules** apply in **federal court** for criminal, federal question, or federal law cases. The FRE provides that the **federal common law applies** to privileges, unless otherwise provided by the U.S. Constitution, federal statutes, or the Supreme Court. (FRE 501)
2. **State privilege rules** apply in **federal court diversity jurisdiction** (following the state whose substantive law applies), or in state court.
3. **Effect of privilege:** Invoking a privilege makes the person **unavailable for hearsay purposes.**
4. **Waiver:** Privileges can be waived by failure to claim or voluntary disclosure of confidential information.

B. **Types of privileges** (The privileges are listed in descending order of MBE testing frequency.)

1. **Attorney-client:** A **client has a right** not to disclose, and may prevent the client's attorney from disclosing, any **communication,** intended to be **confidential**, between the **attorney and the client** made to obtain advice in a **legal consultation.**

   a. **Client:** A client can be an **individual** or a **corporation.** The privilege also applies to **employees/agents/accountants** if **authorized** by the corporation to make the communication to the lawyer.

   b. **Confidential communications:** The privilege applies only to **communications** that are ***intended* to be confidential.**

      1. **Waiver:** The presence of a **third party** may serve to waive the privilege where it defeats the confidentiality requirement.

      Example (not waived): A client may have an agent or confidential secretary present, or use a third party as a translator and still retain the privilege.

      Example (waived): If a client brings a friend to an attorney meeting for moral support, or voluntarily discloses the confidential information to a third party, the privilege will not apply because confidentiality has been breached.

      2. **Does not apply to physical evidence** turned over to the lawyer, only to communications, so the presentation of physical evidence (e.g., a gun) is not privileged. Nor does it apply to physical observations the lawyer makes that a third party could also make (e.g., a dye pack from a bank heist that has stained the client's face).

      3. **Only applies to communications.** The **existence of lawyer-client relationship** and client's identity are *not* privileged, just communications.

      Example: Attorney billing records are not privileged.

   c. **Legal consultation:** The communication must be made for the **purpose of facilitating legal services**, though a fee need not be paid. The privilege extends to communications to the attorney's employees.

   Example: A report prepared by a company's general manager at the request of the company attorney in response to litigation is privileged.

d. **Duration: Privilege lasts after death,** with the exception of a will contest, where the privilege will not apply.

e. **Holder: Client is the only holder** of the privilege, but the lawyer may assert it on the client's behalf.

f. **Exceptions:** The privilege does not apply if:

   1. **Crime or fraud:** The communication was used in **furtherance** of something the client should have known was a future **crime *or* fraud**. The **lawyer need not know** of the illegal purpose for this exception to apply.

      Example: A defendant is on trial for obstructing justice by concealing subpoenaed records. If the defendant seeks a lawyer's advice on how to transfer the records in question to an out-of-country safe deposit box, the communication is not privileged, whether the lawyer knew of the illegal purpose for the question or not.

   2. **Dispute with lawyer:** The communication relates to a dispute between the lawyer and client regarding services.

   3. **Two or more parties consult** on a matter of common interest and **one party** offers the communication **against the other**, such as when two former co-clients become adverse parties.

      Example: An employee has an accident while driving the company truck and jointly consults an attorney with the company owner. If the owner later files a cross-claim against the employee, the communications made by both during their joint consultation are not privileged as to actions against each other, though both retain the privilege as to third parties.

MBE tip: Know the nuances of this straightforward rule and its exceptions well and you should get the attorney-client privilege questions right.

Decoy tip: You may see decoy answers that concern the attorney's right to protect **work product,** which are documents prepared by an attorney for the attorney's own use in managing the case (e.g., a list of potential trial witnesses). The attorney-client privilege **does not cover attorney work product**, but work product is **not subject to discovery** unless there is a showing of necessity. See the Civil Procedure chapter for the complete work product rules.

Example: An attorney sued a client for non-payment of his fee. The client subpoenas the attorney time records of other clients to show the attorney was overbilling. The billing records are not privileged, nor are they attorney work product.

2. **Marital privileges:** There are **two types** of marital privileges, both of which exist because of our societal interest in preserving marital harmony.

   a. **Adverse testimony privilege** (also called **adverse spousal privilege** or **spousal immunity):** One spouse **cannot be compelled** to testify against the other spouse in a **criminal case**, though the witness spouse may opt to testify.

      1. **Duration:** The privilege can only be **claimed *during* the marriage,** but covers information **learned *before* or *during*** the marriage.

      2. **Criminal** proceedings only.

3. **Holder: Only the witness spouse** holds the privilege, so the witness spouse may testify or not as they wish.

b. **Marital confidential communications privilege:** One spouse **may not disclose** the confidential communications of the other spouse **made *during* the marriage**.

1. **Communications** include both **words and acts** (nonverbal conduct) intended to communicate (e.g., a nod). It **does not include acts observed** during the marriage that were **not intended to convey a meaning** to the spouse (e.g., observing a spouse commit a crime).
2. **Duration:** The **privilege survives the termination of the marriage**. The communication must be **made *during* the marriage**, but the privilege applies even ***after* divorce**.
3. Applies in **civil or criminal court**.
4. **Holder: Both spouses** may assert the privilege not to disclose and one spouse **may prevent the other spouse** from disclosing.

   Example: If Husband told Wife about a criminal scheme, Husband can prevent Wife from testifying to the confidential communication.

c. Marital privileges **exceptions:** Neither marital privilege applies to:

1. Actions **between the spouses,**
2. When one spouse is charged with a **crime against the other spouse** or the children of either spouse,
3. Communications made to **plan or facilitate a joint crime or fraud,** or
4. **Waiver-disclosure by one spouse:** When a spouse discloses a confidential communication to a third party, the **disclosing spouse will lose the privilege**, but the **non-disclosing spouse still retains** the privilege.

MARITAL PRIVILEGES CHEAT SHEET

Decoy tip: Know the differences between these rules. Decoy answers are crafted from the rules for the other inapplicable privilege, with focus on what the privilege includes, if it survives the marriage, and most commonly, who is the holder.

	Adverse Testimony	Confidential Communications
What it protects	No testifying against spouse	Communications including acts (but not observations)
Period of coverage	Info learned *before* marriage and *during* marriage	Made *during* marriage
Case type	Criminal only	Civil and criminal
Holder	Witness spouse only	Both spouses
Duration	Only *during* marriage	Survives end of marriage
Exceptions	◆ Suit between spouses ◆ Crimes by one spouse against other spouse/kids ◆ Plan or facilitate a joint crime or fraud ◆ Waiver, but disclosure waives for disclosing spouse *only*	

3. **Self-incrimination:** The **Fifth Amendment** provides the broad protection that no person shall be **compelled** to be a **witness** against themself.

   a. **Person must assert the privilege.**

      1. **A person must assert that their *own* privilege is violated.** One cannot keep a statement out by asserting that *another person's right* against self-incrimination is being violated.

      2. **Corporations** or other business associations **do not have this privilege.**

   b. **Only** applies to **testimonial or communicative statements** and **does not apply to furnishing physical samples or identification procedures** (e.g., hair samples, blood samples, fingerprints, voice samples, appearance in lineups).

   c. **Standard:** A person may invoke if there is a **reasonable possibility** the person may incriminate themself. A mere possibility of prosecution is sufficient to invoke the privilege.

   d. **The privilege applies to *any* proceeding,** such as a police investigation, civil proceedings, another person's criminal trial, pre-trial procedures, grand jury investigations, etc.

      Example: A woman was injured as a passenger in a car accident. On cross-examination, if the witness is asked if she was under the influence of illegal drugs at the time of the accident, she may invoke the privilege against self-incrimination and refuse to testify.

   e. **Exception: A grant of immunity invalidates the privilege.** The privilege against self-incrimination may not be asserted if the witness is granted immunity for the statements, or fruits of the statements, in a domestic prosecution. The exception applies to both types of immunity:

      1. **Transactional immunity:** Broader immunity that protects the witness from prosecution for the **entire criminal transaction** about which they testify.

      2. **Use immunity:** Protects the witness from the **direct or indirect use** of testimony in a subsequent prosecution. While transactional immunity provides more protection, **use immunity is sufficient to nullify the witness's right against self-incrimination** and compel the witness's testimony.

         Example: A grant of use immunity to a businessman for his grand jury testimony regarding the bribery of government officials is sufficient to prevent him from claiming the privilege against self-incrimination.

> **MBE tip:** While immunity can arise in an evidence question, particularly as a counterpoint to the right against self-incrimination, this topic is more accurately categorized as criminal procedure and is covered more thoroughly in the Criminal Procedure chapter.

4. **Physician-patient privilege:** The federal courts **do not recognize** a physician-patient privilege, but it can come up in federal court with diversity jurisdiction. **Most state jurisdictions** have a physician-patient privilege, though it is a statutory privilege and not applicable under federal common law.

   a. Where permitted, it applies to **confidential communications** between a patient and the patient's doctor made in the **course of treatment** and **necessary for treatment.**

      1. If a client's **attorney has requested the medical evaluation** for their case, the exam is **not for treatment,** so the physician-patient privilege will not apply, but the **attorney-client privilege will apply.**

b. **Holder:** The patient, or a lawyer on the patient's behalf, holds the privilege.

5. **Psychotherapist-patient/**social worker-client: The U.S. Supreme Court recognizes this federal privilege, so it is more widely accepted than the physician-patient privilege above. It operates similar to attorney-client privilege.

   a. **Psychotherapist-patient privilege** applies to **confidential communications** made to facilitate therapy or **obtain treatment**. Psychiatrist-patient privilege operates similar to the attorney-client privilege.

   Example: A patient at a mental hospital told a nurse she wanted to kill the President. This is not privileged since it was not made for the purpose of treatment.

   b. **Holder:** The patient, or a lawyer on her behalf, holds the privilege.

6. **Other privileges** [These rules are rarely MBE tested.]

   a. **Clergy-penitent**: Protects confidential disclosures made to a spiritual advisor. The penitent holds the privilege, but the advisor must assert the privilege on the penitent's behalf.

   b. **Governmental**, such as protecting the identity of an informant in criminal cases or other official information. This applies to all government levels.

VIII. CHARACTER EVIDENCE

Character evidence is used to prove a person's character traits. (FRE 404, 405)

Which type of character evidence, if any, can be admitted is determined by:
◆ The **purpose** of the character evidence (to prove up a trait or to impeach a witness);
◆ The **form** the character evidence takes (reputation, opinion, specific acts), and
◆ Whether the case is **civil or criminal**.

A. **Preliminary character evidence matters:** There are special rules that apply regarding the form of evidence permitted when introducing of character evidence. [Note: These form of evidence rules are shaded throughout for easy identification.]

1. **Form of evidence.** There are three forms of evidence used for proving character, including one's character for truthfulness: (FRE 608)

   a. **Reputation:** Testimony regarding one's reputation in the **community** for a particular character trait.

   b. **Opinion:** Testimony regarding the witness's opinion of the person in question's particular character trait.

   c. **Specific acts** (also called specific instances of conduct) engaged in by the person in question, which the witness testifies to in court.

2. **General rule:** When character evidence is admissible, it may be proved by **reputation and opinion** evidence. On **cross-examination, reputation and opinion** evidence is permitted, and the court may allow inquiry into **specific acts**. (FRE 405)

   a. **Direct examination: Reputation and opinion** testimony regarding **character is allowed,** but **no specific acts** inquiry into any specific acts that led to the witness's opinion or the person's reputation is permitted.

      1. **Exception:** In the rare situation where a person's character trait is an **essential element** of a charge, claim or defense, the trait may also be proved with **specific acts** evidence (e.g., convicted felon in possession of a firearm; defamation).

b. **Cross-examination: Specific acts** that are **probative of character** typically may be raised *only* on **cross-examination** of a witness. **Reputation and opinion** evidence is also permitted.

1. **Good faith required:** The questioner must have a good faith belief that the specific act **occurred.**

2. **No extrinsic evidence** is allowed. **Extrinsic evidence** is introducing evidence **other than through the witness on the stand**, such as proving up a specific act through another witness or introducing a document. The result of this rule is that if the witness denies knowledge of the specific act, the questioner is stuck with the answer received from the witness and **additional evidence cannot be introduced** to prove the specific bad act did occur.

B. Civil court character evidence

1. **General rule:** Character evidence is generally **not admissible to prove conduct in conformity** with that character trait on a particular occasion. (FRE 404(a))

   Example: In a car accident case, testimony that the defendant's reputation in the community is that he is a "lead foot" (fast driver) is inadmissible to show he acted negligently in this car accident.

2. **Exceptions:** Where character evidence will be admitted in a civil case, **all three forms of** evidence (**reputation, opinion, and specific acts**) are generally allowed. (FRE 405(b))

   a. **Character directly "at issue" exception:** Character evidence is admissible where character is **"at issue" and is an essential element** of the cause of action or defense (e.g., character is directly at issue in cases of defamation, wrongful death, negligent hiring or entrustment, etc.).

   Examples: A person's character is directly at issue for a damages determination in their defamation case because if the *person defamed* already had a reputation for poor character, they would sustain less damage from defamation than a person who previously had an excellent reputation for good character. In negligent hiring or entrustment, the character of *the person hired or entrusted* is at issue in making a determination that the hiring or entrusting was unreasonable (e.g., loaning a car to a known careless driver is not reasonable).

   b. **Character for truthfulness** is at issue whenever a witness takes the stand to testify. (Subject to the impeachment rules in sec. IX.B.1.)

> MBE tip: The overlap between character evidence and impeachment can be confusing. This is the place where they merge. To keep it straight, determine the **purpose** for the character evidence. If it is to prove that a ***witness* is *untruthful*, use the impeachment rules** (see sec. IX.B.1); if it is for ***any other purpose***, use the **character evidence rules**.

   c. **Propensity—sex crimes: Prior sexual assault/child molestations** (specific acts) by a defendant **are admissible** to show "propensity" to commit the act on any relevant issue in both criminal and civil sexual assault or molestation proceedings.

3. **Rape shield provision in civil court:** Rape and sexual assault cases have special rules, known as "rape shield" provisions, which generally **disallow** evidence of a rape or sexual assault **victim's past sexual conduct.** (FRE 412) [This rule is rarely MBE tested.]

   a. **Exceptions:**

   1. **Reputation, opinion, and specific acts** evidence are only admissible if the **probative value substantially outweighs the danger of unfair prejudice**. (A higher standard than the typical FRE 403 balancing test.)

2. **Plaintiff must put plaintiff's own reputation at issue** for **reputation** evidence to be admitted.

C. **Criminal court character evidence: Character evidence is generally inadmissible.** As a baseline, the probative value is substantially outweighed by the danger of unfair prejudice. Where character evidence is allowed, the character trait must always be **relevant** to the case, but the rules for admission differ depending on whose character it is—the criminal defendant or the victim.

1. **Criminal defendant's character:** A criminal defendant's character is **generally not admissible** to prove conduct in conformity with the character trait on a particular occasion. This is because we don't want a criminal defendant convicted because they are seen as a bad person. (FRE 404)

   a. **Defendant's good character:** A **criminal defendant** can **"open the door"** to evidence of a **specific character trait pertinent to the charge** faced to help prove **innocence**. When a defendant asserts self-defense, the defendant puts their own character for peacefulness at issue.

   Example (allowed): If a man is charged with armed robbery or another violent crime, a relevant specific good character trait pertinent to the charge is the man's character for peacefulness.

   Example (not allowed): If a man is charged with armed robbery or another violent crime, the trait that he is friendly is not admissible since it is not pertinent to the charge. Similarly, unless the defendant is being charged with a crime of dishonesty, the defendant's good character for truthfulness is not admissible unless the defendant puts his credibility in issue by taking the stand.

   1. **Direct examination—form of evidence:** If a criminal defendant wants to provide evidence of their own good character, only **reputation** and **opinion** evidence are allowed to show character; **no specific acts** evidence is allowed.

   a. **Exception**: In the very rare situation where a **character trait is an essential element** of the crime/defense all three forms of evidence (**reputation/opinion/specific acts**) are allowed, such as in a case of entrapment where the prosecution could rebut by showing the defendant was predisposed to commit the crime.

   2. **Rebuttal/Cross-examination**: To **rebut** the defendant's good character evidence the prosecution may bring in its own witness to contradict the defendant's assessment of defendant's own character through **reputation or opinion** evidence. Additionally, through **cross-examination**, the prosecution can inquire into the basis for the witness's opinion or reputation evidence by asking about **specific acts**, if asked in good faith but **no extrinsic evidence** is allowed.

   Example: D is charged with assault with a deadly weapon. During direct testimony, D's attorney questions a witness about the peaceable character of D. On cross-examination, the prosecutor asks the witness if he is aware that last year D punched his son's teacher in the face (specific bad act). If the witness denies knowledge of the incident, the prosecutor is stuck with the witness's answer. Testimony from the teacher or a police report about the incident are extrinsic evidence and thus would not be admissible to refute the witness's testimony.

   b. **Criminal defendant exceptions** to general rule:

   1. **Victim's character "opens the door":** Where the ***defendant*** **offers** evidence of the **victim's character,** prosecution can offer evidence that the **defendant has the same character trait** (e.g., if the defendant claims the *victim* has a violent character, the prosecution can offer evidence (through **reputation and opinion**) about the *defendant's* violent character).

Example: In a murder case, the defendant offers testimony the victim has a violent nature. In rebuttal, the prosecution can offer evidence (by reputation and opinion evidence only) that the defendant also has a violent character.

2. **Propensity—sex crimes: Prosecution can be the first to offer** character **"propensity"** evidence (specific acts) in **sexual assault or child molestation** cases to show the defendant had the propensity to commit the act. Thus, evidence of a defendant's prior sexual assaults and molestation are admissible on any relevant issue in both criminal and civil sexual assault or molestation proceedings.

c. **Character for truthfulness.** A **defendant testifying on the stand** always puts their own **credibility** and **character for truthfulness** at issue, but not their general character. (Subject to the impeachment rules in sec. IX.B.1.)

2. **Victim's character**

a. **Victim's bad character: Only the defendant can "open the door"** to evidence of a ***victim's* pertinent specific character trait** relevant to proving innocence (subject to rape shield provisions below). Typically, this will be a showing that the victim was violent or the first aggressor. On direct only, **reputation and opinion** evidence is allowed. On **cross-examination, specific acts** may be asked about if done in good faith, but **no extrinsic evidence** is permitted.

1. **Result: defendant's same character trait is admissible.** Once the defendant "opens the door," the prosecutor may bring evidence that the ***defendant* has the same bad character trait.**

Example: D is charged with assault with a deadly weapon against Victim. D's attorney introduces evidence that Victim was the initial aggressor and has a violent nature. Since D "opened the door" to the character trait of Victim's "violent nature," the prosecutor is permitted to present evidence of D's violent nature.

b. **Homicide case with a self-defense claim:** In a homicide case in which the defendant pleads self-defense, if the **defendant** offers evidence that the **victim** was the **first aggressor**, this alone will **"open the door"** to the victim's character and the prosecution may offer evidence of the **victim's good character for peacefulness**. (FRE 404)

1. **Form of evidence:** Evidence of the victim's good character for peacefulness can only be by **reputation and opinion** evidence, **no specific acts** evidence is allowed.

c. **Rape shield provision in criminal court:** "Rape shield" provisions generally disallow evidence of a rape or sexual assault victim's past sexual conduct to show the victim engaged in other sexual behavior or to show an alleged sexual predisposition. Criminal court rape shield provisions are more protective of the victim than those used in civil court. (FRE 412)

1. **Reputation and opinion** evidence are **always inadmissible**.

2. **Specific acts** are *only* admissible to prove a **third party** is the source of semen, injury, or other physical evidence; **prior acts** of consensual intercourse **with the defendant**; or as required by the Constitution.

★ D. **"Other purpose" for character evidence allowed** (civil and criminal): While character evidence of other crimes, wrongs, or specific **bad acts are not generally admissible to show conduct in conformity** with the character trait, such **specific acts** evidence **may be admissible for some other purpose,** such as to show (list is *not* exclusive): (FRE 404)

1. **Intent** to commit the act. Where intent is a part of a crime, such as forgery, evidence that the defendant committed similar prior wrongful acts could be admitted to negate a claim of good faith.
2. **Preparation** to commit the act. Evidence of preparatory steps taken to commit the act can be admissible, such as an arsonist purchasing gasoline.
3. **Identity** of the perpetrator, including M.O. (modus operandi). Prior acts can be used to establish that the defendant engaged in a pattern of behavior so specific that it leads to revealing their identity.

   Example: A clerk was held up by a man holding an unusual revolver with a red painted barrel. A witness testifies that one week after this robbery, the defendant robbed him while holding an unusual revolver with a red painted barrel. The evidence is admissible to show identity of the perpetrator.
4. **Knowledge** of some fact or event.

   Example: D is charged with smuggling drugs in a secret compartment in her platform shoes, and a witness testifies that she saw D put the drugs in the compartment when D had done so previously. This is admissible to prove D *knew* the shoes had a secret compartment for drugs, not that she smuggled drugs previously.
5. **Absence** of mistake or accident. Evidence that the defendant engaged in similar misconduct in the past would negate any possibility of a mistake or accident.

   Example: D shot his father and claims it was an accident, but a witness testifies that on two prior occasions he had intervened to stop D from beating his father. This is admissible to show absence of accident.
6. **Motive** to commit the crime. The defendant's alleged commission of a prior crime that in some way facilitates the commission of the crime of which the defendant is presently accused points to a motive to engage in the later crime.

   Example: In an arson case, evidence establishes that D purchased two insurance policies from two different companies on the same property that burned. This evidence is admissible to establish D's motive to commit the arson.
7. **Opportunity** to commit the act.
8. **Plan** or scheme. Evidence of a common plan or scheme can be shown by specific acts undertaken to further the plan or scheme.

   Example: A man is on trial for arson and he threatened to kill his wife if she testifies for the prosecution. This evidence can be offered as proof of his plan and the consciousness of guilt since he is undertaking to further the plan or scheme by stopping evidence against him.

Memorization tip: **I PIK A MOP**

MBE tip: A question testing if character evidence can come in for "other purposes," may also have the defendant make a denial of some key fact first, and then be coupled with a question asking if the evidence can come in **substantively** (for the "other purpose") and to **impeach**. For example, in the absence of mistake example above, if the defendant first denied ever being violent with his father, the witness's testimony could be admitted both to impeach and to prove the absence of mistake.

Decoy tip: When evidence can come in for some "other purpose," decoy answer choices typically will include that the evidence is too prejudicial under the legal relevance balancing test, and/or state that the evidence can come in to show the character trait demonstrated (e.g., that the defendant is violent or has a propensity to commit crime) and/or that the evidence is improper character evidence.

CHARACTER & IMPEACHMENT OVERLAP DECODED

Character rules can overlap with impeachment rules when a **witness is on the stand** because that witness's character trait for truthfulness is at issue in an impeachment inquiry. If the **purpose** of the character evidence is to prove a **witness is untruthful**, use the **impeachment** rules. If the character evidence is for **any other purpose**, use the **character** evidence rules. Both rules are combined on this chart; the complete impeachment rules immediately follow in the outline. See sec. IX.B.1.

CHARACTER RULES

Civil Court	Civil & Criminal	Criminal Court
Gen. Rule: No Except: ◆ If "at issue" ◆ Reputation ◆ Opinion ◆ Specific acts ok	Gen Rule: No Except: **ok for "other purposes"** ◆ Specific acts ok ◆ **Intent** to commit act ◆ **Preparation** to commit act ◆ **Identity** of perpetrator (MO) ◆ **Knowledge** of fact/event ◆ **Absence** of mistake/accident ◆ **Motive** to commit crime ◆ **Opportunity** to commit act ◆ **Plan** or scheme **[I PIK A MOP]** **Civil & Criminal Exception** ◆ Propensity sex crimes ◆ Rape shield provisions apply	**Defendant's Character** Gen. Rule: No Except: ◆ If D "opens door" to own ◆ D offers V's character, then D for same trait ◆ D testifies: truthfulness @ issue **Victim's Character** ◆ Only D can "open door" ◆ Homicide w/ self-defense claim "open's door" to V's peaceful character Direct: Rep/Op Cross ex: Specific acts ◆ Good faith Q ◆ No extrinsic evidence

IMPEACHMENT RULES: CHARACTER TRAIT FOR TRUTHFULNESS

Reputation/Opinion	Specific Acts	Criminal Conviction	Admiss?
◆ Allowed ◆ Except: Evidence of "good character" for truthfulness only *after* attacked	◆ Allowed on **cross-examination** ◆ **Good faith** Q ◆ **No extrinsic evidence** to prove up	◆ Crime of dishonesty ◆ Felony conviction* ◆ Misdemeanor conviction ◆ Over 10 years old	Yes Yes* No No**
		*Judge's discretion, different test for criminal D and other witness **Ok if probative substantially outweighs prejudicial effect	

E. **Habit and custom** is a **regular response to a repeated situation** and is **admissible** to show **conduct in conformity** with that regular response on a particular occasion. Habit evidence may be admitted without corroboration and without an eyewitness. (FRE 406)

1. **Applies to persons and businesses.**

   a. **Habit—personal habit:** Evidence of a **person's habit** is admissible to show the person **acted in accordance** with the habit on a particular occasion (e.g., driver who *always* fastens their seatbelt before driving).

   b. **Custom—business practices custom:** The **routine practice** of an organization is admissible to show the **practice was followed** by the business or organization on a particular occasion (e.g., a company's routine practice is to send cost overrun notices to clients; outgoing mail placed in the outbox is collected and placed in a U.S. mail deposit box daily).

2. **Three factors** are considered to determine if a behavior is habit or custom evidence:

   a. The more **specific** the behavior, the more likely it's habit (e.g., a person always "drives under the speed limit" is a specific behavior; in contrast, the description that a person is a "careful driver" is too general to rise to the level of habit and is character evidence).

   b. The more **regular** the behavior, the more likely it's habit.

   c. The more **unreflective or semi-automatic,** the more likely it's habit.

3. **Is the evidence habit or character?** Behaviors that are not sufficiently specific, regular, or unreflective to be habit or custom evidence will be considered character evidence and subject to character evidence rules. See sec. IX above).

> MBE tip: Look for language describing habits, such as "always, invariably, customarily or habitually." In contrast, descriptions such as "generally" or "often" or that one has a "tendency" do not describe behavior with enough frequency or specificity to establish a habit.
>
> 
>
> Decoy tip: Decoy answers often involve corroboration and personal knowledge. Habit evidence need not be corroborated to be admissible, so an answer choice stating corroboration is required will be wrong. The witness need not have personal knowledge of what happened in the *instance in question* to testify to habit or routine business practices.

IX. IMPEACHMENT

Statements admitted into evidence are subject to impeachment. Statements can be admitted through (1) a witness testifying on the stand or (2) the statement of an out-of-court hearsay declarant, which is deemed admissible. For purposes of this section, the term "witness" applies equally to both.

A. **Impeachment:** Testifying always puts a **witness's credibility** in issue. A witness's credibility may be impeached by **cross-examination** (e.g., questions posed to the witness that may discredit the witness), or when allowed and with the proper foundation, by **extrinsic evidence** (e.g., questioning other witnesses or introducing documents to establish the impeaching facts). Either party may impeach a witness, so a party can impeach their own witness, even on direct examination. (FRE 607) There are several ways to attack a witness's credibility.

<u>MBE tip</u>: There are many small important details in impeachment analysis, and sequencing is important because certain types of evidence are only allowed on cross-examination. It is especially important to go slowly and pay attention to the following considerations:

(1) Where you are in the proceedings (e.g., direct, cross, re-direct, re-cross)?

(2) Whose witness is being questioned (P or D)?

(3) What form of evidence is being used (opinion/reputation or specific acts)?

(4) Is the case criminal or civil?

<u>Decoy tip</u>: Evidence that is admissible to impeach, may or may not also be admitted substantively (for its truth) subject to hearsay rules. Be aware that you may need to analyze a statement for impeachment and its substantive admissibility. This concept is a frequent source of decoy answers.

B. Five methods to impeach a witness:

1. **Impeaching a witness's *character for truthfulness.*** This can be shown by **reputation** and **opinion**, past **specific bad acts,** and/or **past crimes**.

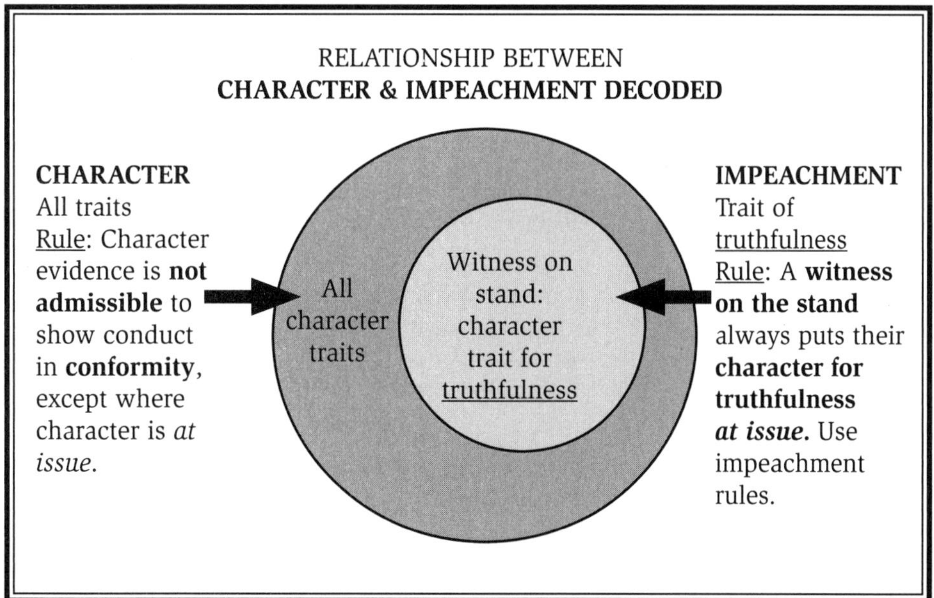

<u>MBE tip</u>: The relationship between character and impeachment can be confusing. Impeaching a witness's character for truthfulness is a subset of character, subject to special rules. Ask: **What is the purpose for the evidence?** If the evidence about character is **coming in to impeach** (e.g. the witness is lying), **apply impeachment rules**; if it is coming in for **any other reason** (e.g. character in issue as an element of cause of action or defense, or a criminal defendant raises the defendant's own character or that of the victim), **apply character rules.**

a. **Preliminary character evidence matters:** There are special rules that apply to the introduction of character evidence, which includes evidence regarding the character trait for truthfulness as arises in impeachment.

> The "form of evidence" rules here are the same as were in the character evidence section. They have been reproduced here for convenient reference.

1. **Form of evidence** definitions.

   a. **Reputation:** Testimony regarding one's reputation in the **community** for **truthfulness**.

   b. **Opinion:** Testimony regarding the witness's opinion of the person in question's **truthfulness.**

   c. **Specific acts** (also called specific instances of conduct) engaged in by the person in question, which the witness testifies to in court.

   d. **Extrinsic evidence is other than through the witness on the stand**, such as proving up a specific act through another witness or introducing a document. The result of this rule is that if the witness denies knowledge of the specific act, the questioner is stuck with the answer received from the witness and **additional evidence cannot be introduced** to prove the specific bad act did occur.

      i. **Exception:** for proving a criminal conviction (see sec. d below).

b. **Character for truthfulness on direct examination: Reputation and opinion** testimony regarding **truthfulness is allowed** on direct, but **no specific acts** evidence.

Example: A bystander testifies about a car accident he witnessed in an auto negligence case. A subsequent witness is permitted to testify that the bystander has a bad reputation for truthfulness and is known as a liar in the community to impeach the bystander.

1. **Except:** Reputation and opinion of **good character for truthfulness** is permissible ***only after*** the witness's truthfulness has been attacked (otherwise it is impermissible bolstering).

 c. **Character for truthfulness on cross-examination: Specific bad acts** that are **probative of truthfulness** may be raised *only* on **cross-examination,** must be asked in **good faith,** and **no extrinsic evidence** is allowed. Admissibility is subject to the court's discretion under legal relevance (FRE 403, 608). [This rule is frequently MBE tested.]

Examples (allowed): Specific bad acts that could be raised on cross-examination are falsifying a transcript, filing a false insurance claim, perpetuating a hoax on the police, filing false expense vouchers at work, filing a false affidavit to avoid paying sales tax, an expert witness providing false testimony in his own divorce case, etc.

Example (not allowed): It is not permissible to ask about the witness's prior multiple car accidents since they are not prior bad acts probative of *truthfulness.*

Example: D is charged with mail fraud, but does not testify in his own defense. A witness testifies that D has a good reputation in the community for honesty (essential element to the crime so in issue). On cross-examination, it is proper to ask the witness if she was aware that D had been previously arrested for embezzlement, a specific bad act, to impeach the witness. This is allowed because the cross-examiner has the right to test the credibility of the witness's knowledge and the quality of the community assessing D's reputation. If the witness did know of the arrest, a negative inference could be raised about the values of the community. If she did not know of the arrest, it would indicate she was not very knowledgeable about D's reputation. Further, it is not permissible to prove the arrest with extrinsic evidence, such as calling D's former boss as a subsequent witness to testify about the arrest because that is extrinsic evidence.

> **Decoy tip:** It is important to remember that the rules pertaining to the **form of evidence** (reputation/opinion/specific bad acts) **only apply** when a witness is being **impeached** regarding their **character for truthfulness**. These limitations on the admissibility of evidence **do not apply when a witness is impeached by other methods** (e.g., a prior inconsistent statement, bias or direct contradiction) and decoy answers frequently will misstate these rules.

d. **Impeaching character for truthfulness with criminal conviction.** Sometimes a witness can be impeached by proof of a prior criminal conviction. Since the purpose is impeachment, the prior conviction is admitted to show the **witness is inclined to lie.** A prior conviction can be established by questioning the witness, or through extrinsic evidence by introducing a record of the conviction, subject to the rules below. (FRE 609)

1. **Crime of dishonesty (crimen falsi):** All convictions for crimes (felonies and misdemeanors) involving **dishonesty or a false statement are admissible** and the **judge may not exclude** under the legal relevance balancing test, unless the conviction is more than 10 years old (e.g., forgery, perjury, embezzlement, false pretenses, tax fraud, etc.). However, property crimes (e.g., burglary, robbery and larceny) are not considered crimes of dishonesty.

> **MBE tip:** If the MBE question does not indicate if a prior conviction was a felony or misdemeanor, it is probably a crime of dishonesty. The felony/misdemeanor distinction is irrelevant for a crime of dishonesty.

2. **Felony conviction: A felony conviction** for a crime *not* involving dishonesty **may be admitted at the judge's discretion.** A felony is a crime punishable by death or a jail term of more than one year. A **balancing test** is used to determine admissibility, depending on the witness's status, with a criminal defendant getting more protection than other witnesses. (FRE 609)

   a. **Witness is the criminal defendant:** The conviction is admissible only if the **probative value outweighs its prejudicial effect** to the defendant. This test provides more protection to a criminal defendant than a regular witness.

   b. **Other witness:** The conviction is admissible in a civil or criminal case unless the **probative value is substantially outweighed by the danger of unfair prejudice** (standard FRE 403 legal relevance balancing test).

3. **Misdemeanor convictions** for crimes that are not crimes of dishonesty are **not admissible to impeach**.

4. **Old convictions** may not be used if **more than 10 years** have elapsed from the **conviction**, or the **release from prison** for the conviction, whichever is later, unless specific facts make the probative value of the conviction substantially outweigh the prejudicial effect and the adverse party is given advanced written notice. Old convictions are much harder to get admitted than newer convictions.

5. **Other convictions:** Pardoned offenses based on innocence and juvenile offenses may not be used to impeach, except in limited circumstances not MBE tested.

2. **Prior inconsistent statement (PIS):** A witness may be impeached by showing that on a prior occasion the witness made a statement inconsistent with the witness's current testimony. The inconsistent statement may be proved by cross-examination or through extrinsic evidence. If the hearsay rules allow, a PIS can also be admitted substantively for its truth.

   a. **Intrinsic evidence** can be used to impeach, by asking the witness on the stand about the PIS.

   b. **Extrinsic evidence may be used** to prove the PIS, but ***only if*** the witness who made the PIS is given an opportunity at some point to **explain or deny** the PIS, and the adverse party is at some point given an opportunity to **interrogate** the impeaching witness, though the opportunity *need not take place prior* to the introduction of the extrinsic evidence. (FRE 613)

> **MBE tip:** These requirements only apply to impeach a "live" witness and do not apply when the inconsistent statement is a party admission or against a hearsay declarant.

Example (allowed for impeachment and substantively): A plaintiff has sued a defendant for negligence stemming from a car accident. A witness testifies at trial that the defendant ran the red light. On cross-examination, the defendant asks the witness about a statement he made in a deposition claiming that the light was yellow. Since the statement was made under oath and subject to cross-examination, the PIS can be admitted both to impeach the witness and substantively for its truth.

Example (allowed for impeachment only): Same facts as above but if the prior statement had not taken place under oath, it would only be admitted here for impeachment purposes since the witness was not a party to this suit, thus it is not a party admission.

PRIOR INCONSISTENT STATEMENTS (PIS) DECODED

MBE tip: Consider if the PIS can come in **substantively** (for the truth of the matter contained in the statement), in addition to being admitted for **impeachment** purposes. The hearsay rules most commonly implicated are party admission and PIS hearsay exception, though there could be others.

PIS—IMPEACHMENT	ADMIT SUBSTANTIVELY
The PIS can only be used for **impeachment** purposes, not for its substance, unless a hearsay rule allows it to be admitted for its truth. If so, the judge will provide a limiting instruction.	**PIS Hearsay:** If the PIS is **given under oath** and subject to cross-exam, the PIS can **also be used substantively** (for its truth) pursuant to the hearsay exception for PIS. **Party Admission** can always be admitted for its substance (for its truth).

Decoy tip: Most of the decoy answers involve whether the PIS can also come in substantively.

3. **Bias:** A witness may be impeached by establishing the witness has an **interest in the outcome of the case**, is biased, self-interested, or has a **motive to lie** (e.g., a witness has been offered a plea deal). This rule is liberally construed. Frequently, this is established with evidence the witness has a personal or business relationship with a party (e.g., a cousin, a friend, a partner in a gambling operation, an employee of the plaintiff, etc.).

   a. **Extrinsic evidence is allowed** with a proper foundation so long as the witness is given an opportunity to **explain or deny**.

      Example: A man is prosecuted for sexually abusing his daughter. Evidence that he had punished her for violating the house rules immediately before she accused him of abuse is admissible to show the accuser had a motive to lie.

> **Decoy tip:** Among others, decoy answer choices will state that the bias evidence is impermissible specific acts character evidence (which is permitted to prove bias), and/ or that the inquiry is "outside the scope of direct examination."

4. **Sensory or mental defect:** A witness may be impeached, by extrinsic evidence or on cross-examination, by showing that their capacity to observe or remember is impaired (e.g., an ear witness with poor hearing, or a witness under the influence of alcohol or drugs).

5. **Contradiction of a witness's testimony.** Extrinsic evidence (e.g. a second witness or document) may contradict the testimony of a prior witness to impeach that witness, so long as the fact testified to is **material** and significant to **credibility**. [This rule is rarely MBE tested.]

   Example: A defendant charged with drug possession testifies he has never possessed or used drugs. In rebuttal, the prosecution can impeach by contradiction by having a police officer testify that she saw the defendant buy cocaine from a street dealer three years earlier. This is a direct contradiction and is permitted. The witness is not being impeached about his character for truthfulness. Since the specific acts evidence is a direct contradiction, it is admissible to impeach.

   a. **Contradiction can't concern a collateral matter**. A collateral matter would be when the contradiction is on a fact not material to the case, so while it contradicts the witness, it is not important to the matter at hand. [This is most frequently how this rule is MBE tested.]

      Example: A bystander to a car accident testifies to the facts of the accident. The bystander witness further testifies the defendant was wearing a green sweater on the day of the accident. The defense would not be allowed to call a second witness to testify that the defendant wore a blue sweater because the color of the sweater is a collateral matter.

C. **Rehabilitating impeached witnesses**. A lawyer may offer rebuttal evidence supporting a witness's credibility **only after it has been attacked**. The rehabilitation can be in the form of redirect examination or extrinsic evidence (e.g., another witness).

1. **Must meet the attack:** The rehabilitating evidence must **support the witness's credibility in the same respect as the attack** (e.g., if a witness's truthfulness is attacked, the rehabilitation must also be about the trait of truthfulness).

   Example (allowed): If a witness's testimony is attacked because he made a prior inconsistent statement, introducing evidence of a prior consistent statement by the witness would be an appropriate way to meet the attack and rehabilitate the witness.

   Example (not allowed): If a witness's testimony is attacked because he made a prior inconsistent statement, introducing evidence that he is not biased would not be appropriate because the witness was not attacked for being biased.

2. **Good character for truthfulness:** A witness's good character for truthfulness can be established by calling **additional witnesses** to testify to their **opinion or the reputation of the impeached witness** regarding their **good character** for **truthfulness** *after* evidence of the impeached witness's character for untruthfulness has been shown.
3. A **prior consistent statement (PCS)** can be used to rebut an express or implied charge of recent fabrication, improper influence, or that the witness's testimony was the product of improper motive. To be admissible, the prior consistent statement in question **must have been made *before* the motive to fabricate arose.**
   a. **Admissible to impeach and substantively** (for the truth of the matter contained in the statement): In contrast to the rule for PIS above, a **PCS need not have been made under oath to be admissible substantively**. See hearsay rule in sec. X.B.2.

D. **Bolstering the witness's credibility is not allowed.** A lawyer may not offer evidence supporting a witness's credibility until *after* it has been attacked. As with much of the rules about impeachment, the sequencing of evidence is important.

<table>
<tr><th colspan="4">IMPEACHMENT CHEAT SHEET</th></tr>
<tr><th colspan="4">Character for TRUTHFULNESS</th></tr>
<tr><th>Reputation/Opinion</th><th>Specific Bad Acts</th><th colspan="2">Criminal Convictions</th></tr>
<tr><td rowspan="2">◆ Allowed
◆ <u>Except</u>: Evidence of "good character" for truthfulness only after attacked</td><td rowspan="2">◆ Allowed on cross-examination
◆ Good faith Q
◆ No extrinsic evidence to prove up</td><td>◆ Crime of dishonesty
◆ Felony conviction*
◆ Misdemeanor conviction
◆ Over 10 years old</td><td>Yes
Yes*
No
No**</td></tr>
<tr><td colspan="2">*Judge's discretion, different test for criminal D and other witness
**Ok if probative substantially outweighs prejudicial effect</td></tr>
<tr><td>PIS</td><td colspan="3">◆ Cross examination, or
◆ Extrinsic evidence allowed, if opportunity to explain/deny
◆ Can also come in substantively if hearsay rules allow</td></tr>
<tr><td>Bias</td><td colspan="3">◆ Interest in the outcome
◆ Extrinsic evidence allowed if opportunity to explain/deny</td></tr>
<tr><td>Sensory or Mental defect</td><td colspan="3">◆ Capacity to observe/remember</td></tr>
<tr><td>Contradiction</td><td colspan="3">◆ Must be material and regarding credibility
◆ Not regarding a collateral matter</td></tr>
<tr><td>Rehabilitation</td><td colspan="3">◆ Must meet the attack
◆ Good character for truthfulness
◆ PCS (made before motive to lie arose)</td></tr>
<tr><td>Bolstering</td><td colspan="3">◆ No evidence in support until witness's credibility is attacked</td></tr>
</table>

X. HEARSAY

A. **Hearsay** is an **out-of-court statement** offered for the **truth of the matter** asserted. (FRE 801) **Hearsay is inadmissible unless an exclusion or exception** applies. (FRE 802) However, even if a hearsay exception applies, the evidence may be inadmissible for other reasons (e.g., an offer to settle which is barred for public policy reasons).

1. **"Out of court"** means that the declarant made the statement at some time and place other than while testifying at the current trial or hearing.

   Example: An accident bystander cannot testify that a passenger from one of the vehicles said, "We should have had our lights on," because it is hearsay, not within any exception. The statement itself was made out of court at the scene of the accident, even though the witness is currently testifying in court.

   a. **Witness repeats own statement:** Hearsay includes a declarant repeating their own prior out-of-court statement, a statement made at a deposition, or a statement made in the judge's chambers during the present trial.

2. The **statement** can be oral or written, or even nonverbal conduct if it is **intended as a communicative assertion** (e.g., a shake of the head or pointing). Silence can be treated as a statement *if* it is intended to make an assertion. However, an animal cannot make an assertion (e.g., an alert by a drug sniffing dog). The declarant must be a person.

3. **Truth of the matter:** The statement must be offered for the truth of matter asserted in the statement.

B. **Nonhearsay purpose:** An out of court statement **may be nonhearsay** (by definition) when it is **not being offered for the *truth*** of the matter asserted, but is **being offered to establish that it was *said*** for some other reason, such as in the following situations where evidence is offered to show:

1. **Effect on listener or reader**, such that the listener or reader **heard or read a statement** and was thus **put on notice** of some information, **obtained certain knowledge**, had a certain emotion, or behaved reasonably or unreasonably.

   Example: A consumer sues a microwave manufacturer for burn injuries. The consumer offers three letters the manufacturer received prior to the sale of this microwave in which customers complained of similar injuries. The letters are hearsay as to the assertions contained in the letters, but admissible to establish the manufacturer was **put on notice** of a potential danger. Note: since the evidence is admissible for a limited purpose, the court will issue a limiting instruction.

2. **Declarant's state of mind**. These are statements **made by the *declarant*** that demonstrate the declarant's *own* **state of mind**. Such statements are admitted not to prove their truth, but that the **declarant believed the facts to be true.** This typically arises when the information provides a motive or explanation for a subsequent act.

   a. **Knowledge** of facts

   Example: Before crashing and sustaining serious injury a snowboarder said, "This run is for experts." The statement is not admissible to establish that the run was actually for experts, but it is admissible to establish that the declarant *thought* it was and proceeded anyways.

   b. **Insanity or mental state,** such as feeling fear (e.g., declarant stating, "I'm Abraham Lincoln" is offered not to prove its truth, but that the declarant is insane).

3. **Words of independent legal significance** (also known as verbal acts or legally operative statements/acts): A statement that itself has legal significance such as words of transaction (e.g., words establishing a contract, deed or will), or tortious words (e.g., defamation) or words that establish a crime (e.g., solicitation or conspiracy).

<u>Example</u>: A husband and wife are in a car accident and a will dispute arises over who died first. A witness testifies that she heard a woman's voice from the wreckage say, "I'm dying," is not hearsay and is admissible not for its truth (that she was dying) but to prove the woman was alive to make the statement.

4. **Reputation:** A statement about a person's reputation may not be offered for its truth, but it can be offered to show that was the **state of the person's reputation**, even if false.

   <u>Example</u>: After being defamed, P had a reputation for being a crook, which would not be offered for its truth (that P is a crook), but that it is P's reputation.

5. **Impeachment:** The statement is not coming in for its truth, but to establish a **discrepancy** between the two statements.

> <u>MBE tip</u>: Before considering hearsay exceptions, always first consider whether the evidence is being offered for its truth. Often it is not, and that is the answer to the question.

C. **Multiple hearsay** (also called hearsay within hearsay or double hearsay) occurs where an out-of-court statement quotes or paraphrases another out-of-court statement. **Each level/layer of hearsay must fall within an exception** or exclusion to be admissible.

   <u>Example</u>: A police report containing a quote from an accident witness is multiple hearsay, with the inner layer being the witness statement, and the outer layer being the report itself.

> <u>MBE tip</u>: Multiple hearsay problems are often found in business records or public records. The outer layer of hearsay is the record itself; the inner layer of hearsay can occur where the record contains information provided by another person. Party admissions often provide the inner layer of hearsay.

D. **Hearsay policy:** The following policies behind the hearsay rule and hearsay exceptions can provide guidance and may be helpful to consider when making a difficult determination.

   1. **Hearsay rule purpose:** The purpose of the hearsay rule is that some communications are suspect because of the **danger of misinterpretation** without the speaker present to clarify. The hearsay dangers are ambiguity, insincerity, incorrect memory, and inaccurate perception.

   2. **Hearsay exception purpose:** The purpose of the hearsay exceptions is that where circumstances provide an **aura of authenticity** to a statement, it should be admissible.

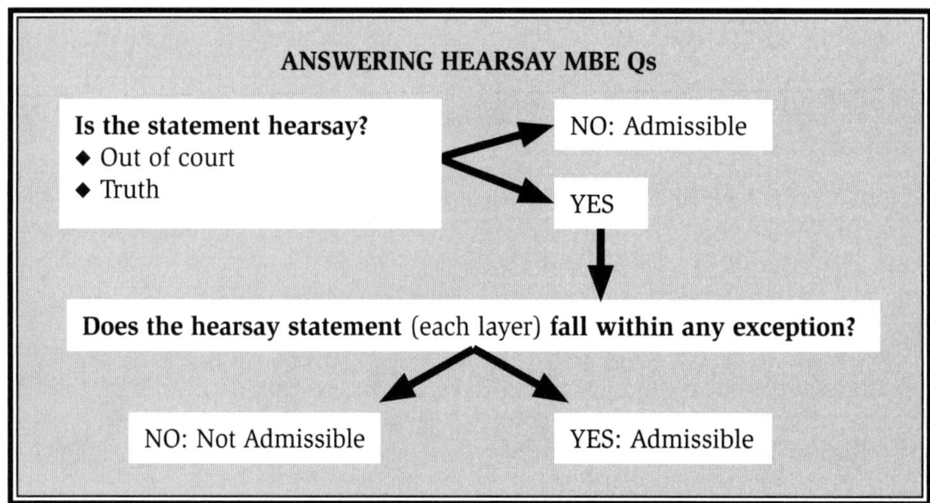

XI. HEARSAY EXCLUSIONS AND EXCEPTIONS

HEARSAY CHEAT SHEET				
Nonhearsay Purpose: (Not offered for the truth)		◆ Effect on listener/reader ◆ Declarant's state of mind ◆ Words of independent legal significance ◆ Reputation ◆ Impeachment		
Exclusions		**Exceptions**		
Admissions	**Prior Stmt.** Avail. Witness	**Spontaneous**	**Unavailable** Declarant	**Documents**
◆ Party ◆ Adoptive ◆ Vicarious ◆ Conspirator	◆ PIS (under oath) ◆ PCS (ok not under oath) ◆ PID	◆ Medical diagnosis or treatment ◆ Then-exist. SOM ◆ Present Sense Impression ◆ Excited Utterance	◆ Former Test. ◆ Dying Decl. ◆ Stmt. Against Interest ◆ Forfeiture	◆ P. Recorded Rec. ◆ Biz Record ◆ Public Record ◆ Learned Treatise ◆ Family History

A. **Admissions** are **excluded** from the hearsay rule and will be admitted. While admissions otherwise meet the definition of hearsay, they are deemed not hearsay by the FRE and are thus **excluded from the hearsay rules**. (FRE 801)

1. **Party admission** (also known as admission by a party opponent, statement by opposing party, statement by a party-opponent): A party admission is **any statement** made by a party, and it may be **offered against** the party. The statement need not be against the declarant's interest, but it must be offered against them. Thus, a party aligned with the declarant cannot offer the statement into evidence. All statements made in pleadings are party admissions. "Statement" includes conduct intended to communicate, such as a nod.

   Examples: An anonymous letter admitting tax liability sent to the IRS and determined to be in the defendant's handwriting is a party admission. Defendant pleads guilty to drunk driving after causing a car accident. That DUI conviction can be used as a party admission in a subsequent *civil* suit stemming from the car accident since the guilty plea is a party admission. A party's signed and sworn answers to interrogatories is a party admission.

> **MBE tip:** The examiners may try to hide the ball and not use the word "admission" anywhere in the question or answer choices.
>
> **MBE tip:** An admission that is otherwise admissible, may still be excluded for policy reasons (e.g., when it is a part of a settlement offer). See sec. III.
>
> 
>
> **Decoy tip:** A party admission that is also a prior inconsistent statement will be admissible both to impeach and substantively. A decoy answer will frequently state the statement can only be admitted to impeach.

2. **Adoptive admission:** An adoptive admission occurs when a statement is made by another, and the adopting party **knows of its content** and voluntarily **manifests belief in the truth** of the statement by words or action. Always analyze the statement in consideration of the surrounding circumstances.

   Example: In response to an interrogatory asking for the total annual insulation sales in an antitrust suit, the defendant refers the plaintiff to a trade journal that contains the data, which is then the defendant's adoptive admission of the information in that journal.

   a. **Silent adoptive admission:** An adoptive admission can be made by silence if a **reasonable person would have spoken up**, but this is always subject to one's Fifth Amendment right to remain silent.

SILENT ADOPTIVE ADMISSION EXAMPLES

MBE tip: Look for such statements between "partners in crime."

FACTS	ANALYSIS
A drug seller introduced the defendant to an undercover drug officer as "my partner in this" and the defendant shook hands with the undercover officer but said nothing.	This is an adoptive admission by the defendant because his silence and shaking hands indicates agreement with the statement, since a reasonable person would protest if they weren't partners in an illegal drug scheme.
The police were questioning two drug dealers at the police station and one of them said, "We sold the drugs. What else is there to say," just as the police started giving the *Miranda* warning.	This is not an adoptive admission by silence because the non-speaking partner has a Fifth Amendment right to remain silent and has no duty to respond.
A bartender observed a lot of money in a bar patron's wallet and said, "You must have robbed a bank," and the bar patron said nothing.	This is not a silent adoptive admission because the bar patron had no reason to respond to the bartender's statement.

3. **Vicarious admission (representative):** A vicarious or representative admission can arise two ways.

   a. **Explicit authorization:** A statement made by an authorized spokesperson of the party on that matter.

   Example: Company is involved in litigation regarding a defective product and authorizes S to speak on their behalf. As an explicitly authorized spokesperson, any statement made by S will be attributed to Company.

   b. **Employee or agent:** A statement made by an agent/employee of the party concerning a transaction within the **scope of the agent/employee relationship** and made **during the existence** of the relationship.

   Example: An employee driving a company truck hits a cyclist and says, "I'm sorry for what I did." This admission will be imputed to the employer because it was made in the course and scope of the employee relationship and during the existence of the relationship.

> **<u>MBE tip</u>:** The MBE answer choice may simply call it an admission (of the party opponent,) without reference to the agency relationship.

4. **Co-conspirator admissions** are statements made **during the course** of the conspiracy and **in furtherance** of the conspiracy objectives. [This rule is rarely MBE tested, except occasionally it comes up in the context of the Confrontation Clause. See sec. VI.G.]

B. **Prior statements of *available* declarant witnesses** are **not hearsay** by definition and are **excluded from the hearsay rules**, though the statements would otherwise meet the definition of hearsay. There are three types of prior statements: inconsistent, consistent, and identification. (FRE 801(d)) Prior statements meeting the requirements outlined below will be admissible as **substantive evidence** (this means for the truth of the matter asserted in the statement), unless excluded for some other reason.

1. **Prior inconsistent statement (PIS):** A witness's prior inconsistent statement may be admissible for both its substantive truth and to impeach.
   a. **Substantively admissible:** A PIS is substantively admissible for its truth, if:
      1. **Oath:** The PIS was **made under oath** as part of a **formal proceeding**, such as a hearing or deposition or grand jury proceeding.
      2. **Cross-examination:** The declarant is **subject to cross-examination** concerning the PIS in the **current proceeding**.
   b. **Impeachment only PIS:** If the PIS does not meet the requirements outlined above and cannot be admitted substantively, it can still be admitted for impeachment purposes, subject to a **limiting instruction**.

> **<u>MBE tip</u>:** A PIS will always come up in the context of witness **impeachment.** If the PIS was not made under oath, it will be admitted for impeachment purposes only. If the PIS was made under oath, it will also be admitted **substantively**. [This topic is heavily MBE tested.] See sec. IX.B.2.

2. **Prior consistent statement (PCS):** A PCS is only admissible **substantively** if offered to **rebut a charge** of recent fabrication, or improper motive in testifying, or to **rehabilitate** a witness when attacked on other grounds. To be admissible, the prior consistent statement in question must have been made *before* the motive to fabricate arose. See sec. IX.C.3. It need not be made under oath.

3. **Prior identification (PID)** of a person as someone the declarant perceived earlier. A PID is **substantively admissible** if the **declarant testifies** at trial and is **subject to cross-examination.**

   <u>Example</u>: A bank teller previously identified the robber from a group of photos. The defendant robber has since grown a beard and the teller cannot presently identify him in court. The teller can be shown the group of photos and testify to her prior identification.

   a. **No current memory** of the facts surrounding the prior identification is required.

> **<u>Decoy tip</u>:** PID decoy answers often include the right to confrontation and past recorded recollection. Know those rules well so you know when they do and do not apply.

C. Spontaneous hearsay exceptions: The following four types of statements are exceptions to the hearsay rule and are thus admissible for the substantive truth of the matter asserted in the statement. The **declarant need not be unavailable** for these hearsay exceptions to apply.

1. **Medical diagnosis or treatment statements:** A statement made for the **purpose** of medical diagnosis or treatment is admissible. This includes describing medical history, past or present symptoms, pain or sensations, and the cause of a current condition if reasonably related to diagnosis or treatment. (FRE 803(4))

   a. Statement may be made by a **third person** if made to help obtain treatment (e.g., the victim is unconscious).

   b. Statement may include the **cause** of the condition, so long as it is reasonably pertinent to diagnosis and treatment, but **not statements of fault.**

MEDICAL DIAGNOSIS & TREATMENT EXAMPLES	
FACTS	**ANALYSIS**
A plaintiff's statement to her doctor that prior to the car accident in question she had no pain or limitation of movement.	Admissible, because a statement of past medical history is reasonably related to current medical treatment.
A plaintiff's statement to an X-ray technician that he fell off a 15-foot ladder and injured his back.	Admissible, because the cause of the injury is reasonably related to obtaining medical diagnosis or treatment.
A plaintiff's statement to his doctor, "The car that ran the stop sign hit me."	Not admissible, because while the cause of injury is important to obtaining diagnosis and treatment, who was at fault in the car accident is not. In contrast, the statement, "I was hit by a car" is admissible.

2. **Statement of then-existing** (present) **mental, emotional, or physical condition** (also called present or then-existing state of mind) is admissible to show the condition or state of mind. This exception is used when the ***declarant's* state of mind is at issue,** but it **may not describe a *past* state of mind.** (FRE 803(3))

   a. **Applies to statements of intent, plan, motive,** design, mental feeling, pain, and bodily health.

      1. **Intent:** A statement of declarant's then-existing **mental condition to show an intent** to do something in the future is circumstantial evidence the declarant carried out the intended act. [This is the most frequent use of this exception on the MBE.]

      Example: The defendant's statement to a friend, "I am leaving later today to visit relatives in a distant state," is admissible under the present state of mind exception to show the declarant subsequently carried out his intended act and went to visit his relatives in a distant state (and thus, was not in town when an event occurred).

      2. **Physical condition:** A statement of declarant's ***current*** **physical condition** is admissible.

Example: A defendant's statement, "I have a headache," is admissible as a statement of then-existing physical condition.

a. In comparison, the **medical diagnosis and treatment hearsay exception** above can include **past** symptoms and injury causation if reasonably necessary to obtain diagnosis and treatment (but not fault).

b. Does not apply to a statement of memory or belief to prove the fact remembered or believed about *past* actions or events.

Examples: "In retrospect, I was at fault for the accident." This is a statement of belief as to past actions and would not be admissible as a statement of then-existing state of mind (though this would qualify as a hearsay exception for statement against interest if the witness was unavailable). The statement, "I believe my husband poisoned me," would not be admissible to prove the husband poisoned his wife since it is a statement of memory or belief. It is also not a then-existing state of mind.

1. **Exception: past statements regarding wills are admissible.**

Example: The statement, "Last week I changed my will to disinherit my ungrateful son," would be admissible under the exception, which allows a statement of memory or belief regarding a will.

> **Decoy tip:** Pay attention to whose state of mind is at issue. The declarant must be making a statement of their *own* state of mind for this exception to apply.

3. **Present sense impression (PSI):** A statement is admissible if describing or **explaining an event** or condition and **made while declarant was perceiving** the event or condition or *immediately* thereafter. (FRE 803(1)) The statement must:

a. Describe or explain an event.

Example: While observing a car speeding by, the declarant says to his friend, "If the driver keeps up that rate of speed he'll surely crash." This description of an event (the car driving by) will qualify as a PSI.

1. The event need not be startling, in contrast to an excited utterance (immediately below).

b. Made while declarant perceives the event. Statement must be contemporaneous, with virtually no passage of time between the declarant perceiving the event and the statement.

Example: While observing a drunk bar patron, if a person turns and says to his friend, "Look at that drunk," the statement was made while perceiving the event and will qualify as a PSI.

Example: A woman observes a smash and grab robbery through her window. *As the robbery transpires*, she calls police and relays the getaway car license number. A properly authenticated tape recording of the police call will be admitted as a PSI because she was describing an event while perceiving it. Since the description does not indicate she is under stress (though you might imagine she is) this is more properly classified as a PSI than an excited utterance.

4. **Excited utterance:** A statement is admissible if it relates to a **startling event** or condition and was **made while the declarant was still under the stress** of excitement caused by the event or condition. (FRE 803(2)) The statement must:

a. Relate to the startling event or condition (e.g., a car accident).

b. Be made while under the stress of excitement caused by the event or condition. Look for statements made "immediately" after the starling event or occurring shortly after. Look for words demonstrating excitement or words describing stress (e.g., the declarant was agitated or yelled or the use of exclamation points in the fact pattern).

Example: A defendant is charged with murder. A neighbor testifies that the night of the murder, he heard the defendant's wife scream, "You killed him! You killed him!" This is an excited utterance by the wife.

> **MBE tip:** Descriptions that the declarant "shouted" or "yelled" or "exclaimed" indicate excitement. Exclamation marks are always a reliable tip-off that the statement is an excited utterance!!!

D. **Declarant *unavailable* hearsay exceptions.** The following statements are exceptions to the hearsay rule and are thus admissible for the substantive truth of the matter asserted in the statement, but **only if the declarant's unavailability is also established** since it is an element of each of these hearsay exceptions.

1. **Witness is unavailable:** The witness must be deemed unavailable and that every reasonable effort was made to procure the witness's attendance. If the witness is unavailable as a result of the proponent's wrongdoing, the declarant will not be considered "unavailable." (FRE 804(a)(1-5)) Witness unavailability can be established in one of the following ways:

   a. **Privileged** from testifying. See sec. VII.

   b. **Death or illness** prevents the witness from testifying.

   c. **Reasonable means can't procure the witness**, such as the witness is beyond the reach of the court's subpoena power.

   d. **Witness refuses to testify** despite a court order.

   e. **Witness testifies of an inability to remember.**

2. **Four hearsay exceptions requiring witness unavailability:**

   a. **Former testimony:** Former **sworn testimony** is admissible where the witness is now **unavailable** to testify and the **party *against whom*** the testimony is now offered had, during the **earlier sworn hearing or deposition**, an **opportunity to examine** that person and had a ***similar motive*** **to develop the testimony**. Typically, this includes the opportunity for the one against whom the testimony is being offered to cross-examine the witness at the earlier proceeding. (FRE 804(b)(1))

      1. **Criminal case limitation:** In a criminal case, the **accused or their attorney** must have had the **opportunity to cross-examine** the declarant. The concern here is that the person against whom the testimony is now offered had a full opportunity to cross-examine and develop the testimony.

      2. **Civil cases only:** It is sufficient that a **predecessor in interest** was present in an earlier proceeding to develop testimony of the now unavailable witness.

      3. **Grand jury testimony will not qualify** as former testimony because there is no opportunity to cross examine the witnesses.

> **MBE tip:** Prior testimony given at a previous hearing, such as a preliminary hearing, or bankruptcy hearing will qualify.
>
> 
>
> **Decoy tip:** In contrast, testimony from a previous grand jury proceeding will not qualify because there is no opportunity to cross-examine and develop the testimony.

b. **Dying declaration** is admissible when a statement is made by a declarant while **believing their own death was imminent**, concerning the cause or **circumstances of their impending death,** and the declarant is currently **unavailable** to testify. (FRE 804(b)(2))

1. Applies to **civil** and **criminal** ***homicide*** cases **only**. Thus, it does not apply to non-homicide criminal cases.

2. **Must believe death is imminent** at the time the statement is made, though the declarant **need not actually die.**

3. **Must be concerning the cause or circumstances of impending death,** not a "get it off my chest" deathbed confession.

4. Declarant **need only be unavailable, but not actually be dead.** If the declarant is dead, it is not necessary that the declarant died from the situation causing them to make the dying declaration.

Decoy tip: Excited utterance is frequently used as a decoy answer to a dying declaration.

c. **Statement against interest** (also known as a declaration against interest): A statement against interest is admissible if declarant is now **unavailable**, and **at the time** the statement was made, it was against the **declarant's proprietary** or **pecuniary interest** (financial), or exposes the declarant to **civil or criminal liability,** or had a great tendency to **invalidate a claim** of declarant against another. These are statements **so contrary to the declarant's interest** that it is unlikely the statement would have been made unless **believed to be true**. (FRE 804(b)(3))

Example: A hospital patient burned in a fire says to a nurse before dying, "I was paid to set the fire." This is a statement against interest since it is so contrary to his interest it is hard to believe he would say it unless it was true. Note that even though it was said to a nurse, it is not a statement for the purpose of medical diagnosis or treatment since it does not pertain to the injury.

1. **Criminal case: Corroborating evidence** must support the statement if offered in a criminal case and the statement exposes the declarant to criminal liability.

2. The **Confrontation Clause** may keep the statement out of evidence when the prosecution tries to introduce a third-party statement against the accused, unless the declarant takes the stand in the current proceeding. See sec. VI.G.

d. **Forfeiture by wrongdoing:** A hearsay exception will apply where a party has engaged in **witness tampering** intended to make the witness unavailable (e.g., where a potential witness is threatened with death if they testify). If that witness has previously made a statement, such as to the police or in a grand jury proceeding, that statement which would otherwise be excluded as hearsay, will be admitted subject to this exception. (FRE 804(b)(6)) [This rule is rarely MBE tested.]

E. **Document hearsay exceptions**. There are special hearsay exceptions where a document is the hearsay being admitted. All document hearsay exceptions need a **sponsoring witness** to establish the elements are satisfied. If admitted, the document must also be authenticated.

1. **Past recorded recollection:** If a witness **cannot testify from memory** about an event, a party may introduce a **written record** of an event. (FRE 803(5))

a. **Requirements** must be satisfied by a **sponsoring witness:**

1. **First-hand knowledge** of events by the sponsoring witness.

2. Events were **fresh in the memory** when record was made or adopted by the witness.
3. Witness now has **impaired recollection** and can't testify from memory.
4. Record was **accurate when written,** but the sponsoring witness need not be the person who actually made the record itself.

b. **Document will be read to jury:** The writing itself is not admissible evidence, but its contents will be read to the jury. The proponent may never offer the record into evidence. However, the ***adverse party*** only **may offer the document as an exhibit**, and then that evidence can come in substantively (for its truth), and to impeach.

> **MBE tip: Past recorded recollection** applies when the document consulted to refresh memory *does not actually refresh* the witness's memory, so if it otherwise qualifies, the document is then read into the record. Because of the strict requirements, this exception is typically not satisfied since often one of the requirements will not be met. In contrast, **present recollection refreshed** (see sec. VI.E.) allows an item to be shown to the witness as a memory stimulus, which then allows the witness to testify entirely from memory.
>
> **Decoy tip:** Past recorded recollection is hard to satisfy and is frequently used as a decoy answer.

★ 2. **Business record** is admissible where a **sponsoring witness** establishes the record was kept in the course of **regularly conducted business activity.** The method and circumstances of the record should indicate trustworthiness. A sponsoring witness will be needed to ensure the requirements are satisfied, and then the **record itself is admitted**. (FRE 803(6))

a. **Business activity** includes events, conditions, opinion, or diagnosis. "Business" includes institution, association, profession, non-profits, and occupations of every kind.

b. **Regular practice** to keep such a record is required (e.g., memorandum, report, data compilation). Special occasion notes and those made in anticipation of litigation likely will not qualify.

Example (allowed): A **hospital record** detailing information such as the patient's vital signs is admissible as a business record since this is the type of activity recorded during the regular course of hospital business.

Example (not allowed): A letter from a treating physician **drafted for the purpose of litigation** would not be admissible since it was not prepared in the ordinary course of business activity, but for the special occasion of litigation.

1. A police report may qualify as a business record in a civil case, but it is not allowed to be admitted in a **criminal case**.
2. **The absence of a record** of a matter that would ordinarily be noted in the business record can also be admitted to prove the **nonoccurrence** of the event. (FRE 803(7))

c. **Personal knowledge:** The record is made by a person with personal knowledge of the information contained in the record. Requires:

1. **Firsthand knowledge** by the ***original*** **supplier** of information. The person making the record itself need not personally have firsthand knowledge, so long as one with firsthand information transmits it to the recorder of the information.
2. **Business duty to report:** The record must be **made by one with a business duty to report** (e.g., witnesses to accidents quoted in police reports or consumer complaints do not have a business duty to report).

d. **Timeliness:** Made at or near the time of the matter referenced.

3. **Public records and reports** are admissible, typically through a sponsoring witness, if within one of the following categories: (FRE 803(8))

   a. **Agency's record of its own activities** (e.g., car registration).

      1. **The absence of a record** of a matter that would ordinarily be noted in the public record can also be admitted. The custodian of records must testify to a diligent search and failure to find the record. (FRE 803(10))

         Examples: (1) A defendant's alibi is that he could not commit the crime because he was in jail. However, there is no record the defendant had been incarcerated. (2) A defendant claims he is a licensed real estate agent, but the State Board of Realtors has no record the defendant was licensed.

      2. **Judgments and prior convictions:** Certified copies of judgments are admissible in both civil and criminal cases to prove the judgment has been entered. In federal court, a judgment of conviction is admissible to prove any fact essential to the judgment. The judgment must be certified by the appropriate public custodian.

   b. **Matters observed in the line of duty** and under a **duty to report** and the report is made **at or near the time** of the event. One reporting the facts must have firsthand knowledge and a duty to report.

   c. **Investigative reports** with factual findings resulting from investigations.

   d. **Criminal case limitation:** The prosecution cannot use police observations or investigations *against* a criminal defendant.

      NOTE: if this addition causes a spacing/page numbering issue, it is fine to take the example above (Example: A fire department inspection record) and move it to the last sentence of the section immediately above it as (e.g., a fire department inspection report).

      Example: A fire department inspection record.

4. **Learned treatises** are admissible when called to the attention of an **expert witness** and established as **reliable authority** by witness testimony, admission, or judicial notice. These can be used with **expert witnesses** on direct (to establish the basis of the expert's opinion) or on cross-examination. (FRE 803(18)) The statements are **read** into evidence and **not admitted as exhibits**. This exception covers a broad scope of materials, including:

   a. **Published treatises,** periodicals, or pamphlets on a subject of history, medicine, or other science or art.

   b. **Standards and manuals** published by government agencies and industry organizations.

   c. **Commercial publications** relied on by business people in certain occupations, such as market quotations, tabulations, lists, and other public compilations.

   > **MBE tip:** Experts may reference a learned treatise in giving their **expert opinion** and/or they can be used to cross-examine an expert, so these topics can cross over.

5. **Statement of personal or family history** (record): Statements of fact concerning family history (births, marriages, adoptions, etc.), such as information recorded in a family bible. (FRE 803(13))

> **Decoy tip:** Decoy answers for all document hearsay exceptions frequently include the best evidence rule and authentication, among other rules.

F. **Residual "catch-all" hearsay exception:** Statements may be admissible if **trustworthy**, regarding a **material fact**, are **more probative** on the point than other evidence, the **interests of justice** are served, and **notice** is given to the opposing side. (FRE 807) [This rule is rarely MBE tested.]

FAVORITE HEARSAY DECOYS DECODED

Decoy tip: Decoy answers will primarily consist of inapplicable hearsay exceptions. Be sure to know the differences between the rules listed below.

ANSWER	FAVORITE DECOY	OTHER DECOYS
Admission	Statement against interest	Excited utterance, State of mind, PIS, Former testimony, *Settlement (policy exclusion)
Excited utterance	Dying declaration	
PSI	State of mind	PID, PCS, Excited utterance, Admission
Medical diagnosis & treatment	State of mind	Business record
PID	BER, Public record	Past recollection recorded, *Right of confrontation
PIS	*Admit for substance and/or impeachment	Former testimony
Past recorded recollection	BER	Authentication
Public record	BER	Authentication
Business record	BER	Authentication

XII. PROCEDURAL ISSUES

A. **Burdens of proof:** There are two different burdens of proof.

1. **Burden of production:** Where a party has the burden of production, that party must come forward and **produce evidence to establish that fact** or issue.

2. **Burden of persuasion:** The produced **evidence must be sufficient** to establish the fact or issue.

   a. **Civil case:** The burden typically rests with the **plaintiff** and usually must be established to a **preponderance of the evidence** standard (which states the fact is more probably true than not true).

1. **Clear and convincing proof** (a high probability the fact in question exists) is used in some civil cases.

b. **Criminal case:** The burden of persuasion rests with the **prosecution** and must be proven **beyond a reasonable doubt.**

B. **Presumptions** require that the jury draw certain inferences from a set of facts.

1. **Civil case**: A civil case presumption operates to **shift the burden** of **producing evidence** (not persuasion) to the opposing party.

a. **Rebuttable presumptions** include those such as that mail properly stamped and addressed was properly delivered, legitimacy, sanity, that a death is not suicide, death from seven years' absence, etc. The presumption is not conclusive, but it may be rebutted by the opposing party.

<u>Example</u>: If a party relies on the presumption that a recipient received a properly addressed, stamped and mailed letter, the burden shifts and the opposing party must produce evidence to rebut the presumption. The intended recipient could rebut the presumption by testifying she never received the letter.

b. **Choice of law:** Substantive state law controls regarding presumption rules in civil diversity actions in federal court.

2. **Criminal case:** Presumptions in criminal cases are permissible inferences. The burden of production and persuasion is always on the prosecution to prove every element of a crime beyond a reasonable doubt. There cannot be a mandatory presumption imposed on an element of a crime.

<u>Example</u>: It is improper to have a *mandatory* presumption that a person missing seven years is presumed dead in a murder prosecution because death is an element of the charged crime.

<u>Example</u>: It is improper to have a *mandatory* presumption that a person with a blood alcohol level over .10 is intoxicated in a DUI case since intoxication is an element of the DUI crime.

C. **Judge and jury allocations**

1. The **judge** decides issues of **law.** A judge is not bound by the rules of evidence in making preliminary determinations, except the law of privileges. Consequently, the judge may consider inadmissible testimony in ruling on preliminary questions, such as evidence admissibility or an expert witness's qualifications.

a. **Admissibility:** The judge must make a preliminary determination of admissibility (e.g., the judge will decide if a business record was one kept in the regular course of business).

1. **Inadmissible evidence is allowed.** The **judge** may *consider* inadmissible evidence in making a determination of admissibility.

<u>Example</u>: In a murder case, the prosecution seeks to introduce a note from the victim identifying his killer. The judge may consider an affidavit from the victim's doctor stating the victim knew he was dying at the time he wrote the note (which would be hearsay) in making a determination on the admissibility of the victim's note.

2. **Confessions:** A hearing on the determinations on the admissibility of a confession must be conducted outside the presence of the jury. (FRE 104(c))

b. **Witness qualifications** are determinations for the judge.

Example: Whether a witness's qualifications are sufficient such that the witness qualifies as an expert witness is a determination for the judge.

c. **Irrelevant evidence:** A judge **may admit** irrelevant evidence if it is curative and rebuts previously admitted irrelevant evidence and is not prejudicial.

2. The **jury** typically decides issues of **fact**, including witness credibility.

D. **Limited admissibility:** Evidence may be **admissible for one purpose, but not for another** purpose. The judge may provide a **limiting instruction** and instruct the jury that evidence may only be considered for a particular purpose, and not for any other purpose.

EVIDENCE CHEAT SHEET

RELEVANCE

Logical

Any tendency to make fact more/less probable

Legal

Can exclude if: Prob. value subst. o/w by danger prej. etc.

JUDICIAL NOTICE

- Generally known in community
- Capable of accurate, ready determination

Civil: Jury *must* accept
Criminal: Jury *may* accept

PROCEDURAL ISSUES

Burden of Proof

Civil: Preponderance
Crim: Beyond a reas. doubt

Presumptions

Civil: Shifts to opponent
Crim: None on element

POLICY EXCLUSIONS

	Sub. Remedial Meas.	Insurance	Medical	Settlement
Not Admissible for:	◆ Culpable conduct ◆ Negligence ◆ Product defect	◆ Culpable conduct	Liability	◆ Claim validity ◆ Claim amount ◆ Impeach PIS
Admissible for:	◆ Ownership & control ◆ Rebut "unfeasibility" ◆ Impeachment	◆ Ownership & control ◆ Impeachment	All other purposes	Any other purpose, but *disputed* claims
Collateral Admission	Allowed	Allowed	Allowed	**Not** Allowed

PRIVILEGES (Fed. common law)

Attorney Client

- Intend confidential
- Legal consultation
- Extends after death
- Holder: Client

Except:

- Crime facilitation
- Dispute w/ lawyer
- 2 or more & against same

Self Incrimination

- Person's own violation
- Testimonial stmt. *only*
- Reasonable possibility can assert qualifies

Immunity

Can't assert 5th Am. if:

- Transactional (broader)
- Derivative use (5th)

Physician-Patient

No fed priv., but most states

Psychiatrist-Patient

All states

- Confidential communication
- Course & purpose of treatment
- Holder: Patient

MARITAL PRIVILEGES

Adverse Testimony

- No testifying v. spouse
- Info before & during
- Criminal only
- During marriage
- Holder: Witness spouse

Marital Confidential Communications

- Communication/acts
- Made during marriage
- Civil & criminal
- Survives end of marriage
- Holder: both spouses

Exceptions for **both** marital privileges:

- Suits between spouses
- Crimes by one spouse against other spouse or kids
- Plan or facilitate joint crime or fraud
- Waiver, but for disclosing spouse only

DOCUMENTARY EV.

Authentication

- Need sponsoring witness
- Writings/recording
- Handwriting—lay ok
- Voice—lay ok any time
- Phone call: outgoing
- Reply letter doctrine
- Ancient documents

Self-authenticating Doc.

[No witness needed]
Ex: Certified copy public records, newspaper etc.

Best Evidence Rule

- Sponsoring witness
- Contents of writing
- Original/copy
- Excused if no fault
- Can testify w/out doc if personal knowledge

Summary of Voluminous Writings

- Need sponsoring witness

CHARACTER

Civil Court	Civil & Criminal	Criminal Court
Gen. Rule: No Except: ◆ If "at issue" ◆ Propensity sex crimes ◆ Rape shield provisions apply *[Reputation Opinion Specific acts]*	Gen. Rule: No Except: ok for "other purposes" *[Specific acts ok]* ◆ **Intent** to commit act ◆ **Preparation** to commit act ◆ **Identity** of perpetrator (MO) ◆ **Knowledge** of fact/event ◆ **Absence** of mistake/ accident ◆ **Motive** to commit crime ◆ **Opportunity** to commit act ◆ **Plan** or scheme **[I PIK A MOP]**	**D's Character:** Gen. Rule—No; Except: ◆ If D "opens door" to own ◆ D offers V char., then D same trait ◆ Propensity sex crimes ◆ D testifies: truthfulness at issue **V's Character:** Gen. Rule—No; Except: ◆ Only D can "open door" ◆ Homicide w/ self-defense "opens door" to V's peaceful character ◆ Rape shield provisions apply

Criminal Court - Form of Evidence
Direct: *Reputation & Opinion* Cross Ex: *Specific acts w/ good faith Q, but no extrinsic evidence*

WITNESSES

Competence	Lay opinion
◆ Personal knowledge ◆ Oath	◆ No spec. knowledge ◆ Helpful trier of fact

Expert opinion
◆ Qualified as expert ◆ Specialized knowledge ◆ Based on sufficient facts ◆ Reliable principles & apply

Present recollection refreshed
◆ Refresh memory w/item ◆ Testify from refreshed memory ◆ At trial-adversary can inspect/admit ◆ Before trial-inspect/admit judge's discr.

Confrontation Clause
◆ No testimonial statements v crim. D ◆ Against criminal defendant ◆ If declarant is unavailable for cross-ex ◆ Accused had no opportunity to cross-ex

HABIT
◆ Personal habit (specific/regular) ◆ Business practices custom/routine

REHABILITATION
◆ Must meet the attack ◆ Good character truthfulness ◆ Prior Consistent Statement (made before motive to lie arose)

IMPEACHMENT

Character for truthfulness
Direct: *Reputation & Opinion* Cross Ex: *Specific acts w/ good faith Q, but no extrinsic evidence*

Character truth: w/ criminal conviction
◆ Crime dishonesty admissible ◆ Felony: judge discretion (Crim. D or W) ◆ No misdemeanor or crimes over 10 years ◆ *Extrinsic evidence allowed*

Prior Inconsistent Statement
◆ Cross examination, or ◆ *Extrinsic evidence* ok if explain/deny [Can come in substantively too if hearsay exception or admission]

Bias
◆ Interest in outcome ◆ *Extrinsic evidence* ok

Sensory or mental defect
◆ Capacity observe/remember

Contradict- another witness
◆ Must be material & regarding credibility ◆ Not a collateral matter ◆ **No bolstering**

HEARSAY

◆ Out of court statement	◆ Truth of matter asserted	◆ Not admissible unless...
NONHEARSAY PURP.	**ADMISSIONS-excluded**	**PRIOR STMTS-excluded**
Not that it's true, But that is was said	**Party** ◆ Any statement ◆ Offered against	**Prior Inconsistent Stmt.** ◆ Under oath ◆ Subject to cross-ex now ◆ Comes up w/impeachment
Effect on listener/reader ◆ Put on notice, or ◆ Has certain knowledge	**Adoptive** ◆ Knows contents of stmt. ◆ Manifest belief in truth ◆ Silence- RP, but 5th Am.	
Declarant's state of mind ◆ Declarant believed true ◆ Knowledge of facts ◆ Insanity/mental state	**Vicarious** ◆ Explicit authorize, or ◆ Employee/agent scope ◆ During relationship	**Prior Consistent Statement** ◆ Oath not required ◆ Rebut/rehabilitate ◆ Said *before* motive to lie
Independent legal signif. ◆ Words of contract-offer ◆ Words of tort-defame ◆ Words of crime-threats		
Reputation ◆ State of, even if false	**Co-conspirator** ◆ During scope ◆ In furtherance of conspiracy	**Prior Identification** ◆ Testify at trial ◆ Subject to cross-exam
Impeachment ◆ Discrepancy between two		

HEARSAY EXCEPTIONS

Spontaneous	**+ Unavailable Declarant**	**Docs + Sponsoring witness**
Medical diagnosis/treatmt ◆ Made for purpose dx/tx ◆ 3P ok ◆ Cause ok, but not fault	**Unavailable because:** ◆ Privilege ◆ Death/illness/memory ◆ Can't get reasonably ◆ Witness won't testify	**Past rec. recollection** ◆ Firsthand knowledge ◆ Fresh/acc. when made ◆ Impaired recollection now ◆ Read or adverse can offer
Then existing SOM ◆ Present (then existing) ◆ Mental, emotional, physical condition ◆ Stmt. of intent ok, but ◆ Memory/belief not ok	**Former Testimony** ◆ Sworn testimony ◆ Opp. to examine ◆ Same motive to develop Crim-D or attorney Civil-Predecessor in int.	**Business record** ◆ Business activity ◆ Regular practice ◆ First hand knowledge rec. ◆ Biz duty to report- not crim ◆ Timely made
Present Sense Impress. ◆ Explain event/condition ◆ Made while perceiving	**Dying declaration** ◆ Believe death imminent ◆ Re: cause of death ◆ Cr. homicide /civil *only* ◆ Need not be dead	**Public record** ◆ Agency own activity, or ◆ Matters in line of duty ◇ duty to report/timely ◇ Criminal case limitation
Excited Utterance!!! ◆ Relates to startling event ◆ While still under stress	**Statement v. interest** ◆ At time made against ◇ Proprietary/pecuniary ◇ Or civil/crim. liability ◇ Crim-corroborate reqt.	**Learned treatise** ◆ Expert witness ◆ Reliable authority ◆ Read to jury only
Residual catch all ◆ Interest justice/notice	**Forfeiture by wrong** ◆ Witness tampering	**Personal family history** ◆ Facts: birth, death etc.

EVIDENCE MBE PRACTICE QUESTIONS

These questions are designed to reinforce the skill in how to approach MBE questions. While they will also test your knowledge in the limited areas addressed, you will not master your knowledge by only practicing these questions. To fully master the rules, you need to do practice questions outside of these from your bar company and/or the NCBE.

QUESTION 1

A plaintiff sued a defendant, alleging that she was seriously injured when the defendant ran a red light and struck her while she was walking in a crosswalk. During the defendant's case, a witness testified that the plaintiff had told him that she was "barely touched" by the defendant's car.

On cross-examination, should the court allow the plaintiff to elicit from the witness the fact that he is an adjuster for the defendant's insurance company?

A. No, because testimony about liability insurance is barred by the rules of evidence.
B. No, because the reference to insurance raises a collateral issue.
C. Yes, for both substantive and impeachment purposes.
D. Yes, for impeachment purposes only.

QUESTION 2

A plaintiff has sued a defendant for personal injuries the plaintiff suffered when she was bitten as she was trying to feed a rat that was part of the defendant's caged-rat experiment at a science fair. At trial, the plaintiff offers evidence that immediately after the incident the defendant said to her, "I'd like to give you this $100 bill, because I feel so bad about this."

Is the defendant's statement admissible?

A. No, because it is not relevant to the issue of liability.
B. No, because it was an offer of compromise.
C. Yes, as a present sense impression.
D. Yes, as the statement of a party-opponent.

QUESTION 3

A plaintiff sued a utility company that owns a reservoir that is open to the public for recreation pursuant to a license from a federal agency. The plaintiff was severely injured in the reservoir when he dove from a boat into what he thought was deep water and hit an unmarked submerged island. The plaintiff alleges that the company was negligent in failing to mark the submerged island. At trial, the plaintiff has called an engineer and qualified him as an expert in managing reservoirs.

Which of the following opinions by the plaintiff's expert is the court most likely to admit?

A. "The accident probably occurred in the manner shown by this computer-animated film I made."
B. "The company could have marked the island in a day and at a cost of $300."
C. "The company was required by federal law to mark the island."
D. "The plaintiff was not contributorily negligent."

QUESTION 4

A defendant has been charged with making a false statement to a federally insured financial institution to secure a loan. At trial, the prosecutor calls the defendant's wife as a willing witness to testify that the defendant told her in confidence that he had misrepresented his assets on the loan application.

The defendant objects to his wife's testimony.

Should the testimony be admitted?

A. No, because even though the wife is a willing witness, the defendant has the right to exclude confidential marital communications in federal court.
B. No, but only if the law of the state where the defendant and his wife reside recognizes a privilege for confidential marital communications.
C. Yes, because in federal court the right not to testify belongs to the testifying spouse, and she is a willing witness.
D. Yes, because while the adverse testimonial privilege is recognized in federal court, the marital communications privilege is not.

QUESTION 5

A defendant has been charged with selling cocaine to a police informant. At trial, the alleged cocaine no longer exists, and the only evidence that the substance sold was cocaine is the informant's testimony that it tasted like cocaine and gave her a cocaine-like sensation. The informant has no formal training in identifying controlled substances.

Should the court admit the informant's opinion testimony that the substance was cocaine?

A. No, because identification of a controlled substance requires an expert with formal training.
B. No, because, without a quantity of the controlled substance for testing, opinion testimony is insufficient to make a prima facie case against the defendant.
C. Yes, if the court determines that the informant has sufficient knowledge and experience to identify cocaine.
D. Yes, provided there is evidence sufficient to support a jury finding that the informant has sufficient knowledge and experience to identify cocaine.

QUESTION 6

A defendant who is an accountant has been charged with fraud for allegedly helping a client file false income tax returns by shifting substantial medical expenses from one year to another. The defendant has pleaded not guilty, claiming that he made an honest mistake as to the date the expenses were paid. At trial, the prosecutor offers evidence of the defendant's involvement in an earlier scheme to help a different client falsify tax returns in the same way.

Is the evidence of the defendant's involvement in the earlier scheme admissible?

A. No, because it is impermissible character evidence.
B. No, because it is not relevant to the issues in this case.
C. Yes, to show absence of mistake.
D. Yes, to show the defendant's propensity to commit the crime.

QUESTION 7

A defendant is charged with mail fraud. At trial, the defendant has not taken the witness stand, but he has called a witness who has testified that the defendant has a reputation for honesty. On cross-examination, the prosecutor seeks to ask the witness, "Didn't you hear that two years ago the defendant was arrested for embezzlement?"

Should the court permit the question?

A. No, because the defendant has not testified and therefore has not put his character at issue.
B. No, because the incident was an arrest, not a conviction.
C. Yes, because it seeks to impeach the credibility of the witness.
D. Yes, because the earlier arrest for a crime of dishonesty makes the defendant's guilt of the mail fraud more likely.

QUESTION 8

A plaintiff sued an industrial facility in her neighborhood for injuries to her health caused by air pollution. At trial, the plaintiff was asked questions on direct examination about the days on which she had observed large amounts of dust in the air and how long the condition had lasted. She testified that she could not remember the specific times, but that she maintained a diary in which she had accurately recorded this information on a daily basis. When her attorney sought to refresh her recollection with her diary, she still could not remember. The plaintiff's attorney seeks to have the information in the diary admitted at trial.

Is the information admissible?

A. No, because reviewing it did not refresh the plaintiff's recollection.
B. No, unless it is offered by the defendant.
C. Yes, and the plaintiff should be allowed the option of reading it into evidence or having the diary received as an exhibit.
D. Yes, and the plaintiff should be allowed to read the diary into evidence.

QUESTION 9

A plaintiff has sued a defendant, alleging that she was run over by a speeding car driven by the defendant. The plaintiff was unconscious after her injury and, accompanied by her husband, was brought to the hospital in an ambulance. At trial, the plaintiff calls an emergency room physician to testify that when the physician asked the plaintiff's husband if he knew what had happened, the husband, who was upset, replied, "I saw my wife get run over two hours ago by a driver who went right through the intersection without looking."

Is the physician's testimony about the husband's statement admissible?

A. No, because it relates an opinion.
B. No, because it is hearsay not within any exception.
C. Yes, as a statement made for purposes of diagnosis or treatment.
D. Yes, as an excited utterance.

QUESTION 10

The plaintiff, who is the executor of her late husband's estate, has sued the defendant for shooting the husband from ambush. The plaintiff offers to testify that the day before her husband was killed, he described to her a chance meeting with the defendant on the street in which the defendant said, "I'm going to blow your head off one of these days."

Is the witness's testimony concerning her husband's statement admissible?

A. Admissible, to show the defendant's state of mind.
B. Admissible, because the defendant's statement is that of a party-opponent.
C. Inadmissible, because it is improper evidence of a prior bad act.
D. Inadmissible, because it is hearsay not within any exception.

EVIDENCE ANSWER KEY

Question	Answer
1	D
2	D
3	B
4	A
5	C
6	C
7	C
8	D
9	B
10	D

Use this quick answer key to get a general idea of how you did on this set of questions. The answer explanations that follow provide a step-by-step deconstruction of each question.

EVIDENCE MBE ANSWER EXPLANATIONS

START HERE

Q1

FACTS

CIVIL

Evidence Qs tend to be short and have fewer decoys.

A plaintiff sued a defendant, alleging that she was seriously **injured when the defendant ran a red light** and struck her while she was walking in a crosswalk. **During the defendant's** case, **a witness testified** that the **plaintiff had told him that she was "barely touched"** by the defendant's car.

CALL On **cross-examination**, should the court allow the plaintiff to elicit from the witness the fact that he is an **adjuster for the defendant's insurance company**?

Get in the habit: notice the stage of proceedings & if the case is in civil or criminal court in evidence Qs.

employee

EVIDENCE Q & the insurance reference may implicate the policy exclusion rule

SOLVE

R **Insurance - Policy exclusion**

- **Not admissible** to show culpable conduct
- **Admissible** to show:
  - Ownership & control
  - **Impeachment (bias)**

Hint: what is the **purpose** of the evidence?

- Not admissible to show D has insurance (& may be careless or have deep pockets)
- Admissible to show witness has a **motive to lie (impeach by bias)** since the testimony benefits his employer (insurance company would pay less on the claim, which may make him look good to employer.)

A The court can allow the testimony only for purpose of impeachment **because** witness may be biased.

Now look for a similar answer choice.

DECODE

This is a typical Evidence Q answer pattern with 2 "not admissible" options and 2 "admissible" options.

(A) No, because testimony about liability insurance is barred by the rules of evidence.

Inapplicable rule. This is the general rule, however the exception for impeachment applies here.

(B) No, because the reference to insurance raises a collateral issue.

Incorrect analysis. That the witness is employed by the defendant's insurance company is a legitimate ground for impeachment for bias and is not a collateral matter.

(C) Yes, for both substantive and impeachment purposes.

Incorrect analysis. The evidence is not admissible substantively because the general rule prohibits it, but it is admissible to impeach on the basis of bias.

D. Yes, for impeachment purposes only.

*Correct. That the witness is employed by the defendant's insurance company is a legitimate ground for impeachment for **bias** since the witness is not disinterested and may be motivated to lie to gain favor from his employer.*

FACTS **Q2**

CIVIL

A plaintiff has sued a defendant for **personal injuries** the plaintiff suffered when she was **bitten** as she was trying to feed a rat that was part of the defendant's caged-rat experiment at a science fair. At trial, the **plaintiff offers evidence** that **immediately after** the incident the **defendant said** to her, **"I'd like to give you this $100 bill, because I feel so bad about this."**

CALL Is the defendant's statement admissible? **EVIDENCE Q**

Settlement offer? *Hearsay?*

SOLVE

HEARSAY & EXCEPTION *Testing 2 rules*

Hearsay • Out-of-court statement • Truth of matter asserted	**Hearsay** • At science fair • That D felt bad (responsible for rat bite)
Hearsay exception? • Party admission	**Hearsay exception?** • D is a party & statement is being offered against • The statement is admissible as a party admission

SETTLEMENT OFFER

Not admissible: • Liability • Claim validity/amount • Impeach • Disputed claims only	• Claim is not yet in dispute because D made the statement "immediately" after the incident. • The statement will **not be excluded** since the settlement/compromise offer policy exclusion does not apply.

A The statement is admissible **because** it is a party admission and not excluded.

DECODE Now look for a similar answer choice.

~~A.~~ No, because it is not relevant to the issue of liability.

Wrong analysis. Defendant's statement that he felt bad has a tendency to show he is liable for the rat-biting incident.

~~B.~~ No, because it was an offer of compromise.

Wrong analysis. This is not a settlement offer because there was no disputed claim at the time of the statement. (If you hadn't issue spotted this up front, you would do the full analysis as you consider this answer choice.)

~~C.~~ Yes, as a present sense impression.

Wrong analysis. This is not a statement describing an event as it is perceived or immediately after, so this is not a present sense impression.

D. Yes, as the statement of a party-opponent.

Correct. The defendant's statement is one by a party opponent (also called a party admission) and is admissible.

Be familiar with common synonyms, like this one.

FACTS

Q3

CIVIL

Not all Qs can be solved without looking at the choices

A **plaintiff sued** a utility company that owns a **reservoir that is open to the public** for recreation pursuant to a license from a federal agency. The plaintiff was severely **injured** in the reservoir when he dove from a boat into what he thought was deep water and **hit an unmarked submerged island.** The plaintiff alleges that the company was **negligent in failing to mark the submerged island.** At trial, the **plaintiff has called** an **engineer** and **qualified him as an expert** in managing reservoirs.

Expert opinion & qualified

CALL Which of the following opinions by the plaintiff's expert is the court most **likely to admit?** **EVIDENCE Q**

A. "The accident probably occurred in the manner shown by this computer-animated film I made."
B. "The company could have marked the island in a day and at a cost of $300."
C. "The company was required by federal law to mark the island."
D. "The plaintiff was not contributorily negligent."

SOLVE

EXPERT OPINION

- Specialized knowledge to assist the trier of fact
- ✓ Qualified as an expert
- Sufficient facts or data. May be based on:
  - Firsthand knowledge
  - Observation witnesses/evidence at trial
  - Hypothetical Q
- Reliable principles and methods
  - Peer reviewed/published
  - Tested/subject to retesting
  - Low error rate &
  - Reasonable level of acceptance
- Applied the principles reliably

OPTIONS	ANALYSIS
A. Computer animated film	• This is demonstrative evidence that is not clearly based on sufficient facts or data or reliable principles.
B. Marked island in a day/$300	• Seems based on firsthand expert knowledge & the type of info an expert in the field would reliably know.
C. Required to mark by fed. law	• This is a legal conclusion about the content of the federal law.
D. P not contributorily negligent	• This is a legal conclusion and a matter for the trier of fact to determine.

DECODE

~~A.~~ "The accident probably occurred in the manner shown by this computer-animated film I made."

Wrong rule. This is demonstrative evidence, not as clearly an expert opinion. This is the second best answer, but is not clearly as factually based or reliable as choice B.

B. "The company could have marked the island in a day and at a cost of $300."

Correct. This is the best option. By process of elimination it is the only option containing the appropriate content of an expert opinion (an opinion on how long marking the island would take and the cost to do so).

~~C.~~ "The company was required by federal law to mark the island."

Wrong rule. This calls for a legal conclusion, which is not the proper basis for an expert opinion.

~~D.~~ "The plaintiff was not contributorily negligent."

Wrong rule. This calls for a legal conclusion, which is not the proper basis for an expert opinion.

FACTS **Q4**

CRIMINAL

A **defendant** has been **charged** with making a **false statement** to a federally insured financial institution **to secure a loan**. At trial, **the prosecutor calls** the **defendant's wife as a willing witness** to testify that the **defendant told her in confidence** that he had misrepresented his assets on the loan application.

The defendant objects to his **wife's testimony**. 

Confidential communication
Adverse testimony (always analyze both)

CALL Should the testimony be admitted?

EVIDENCE Q and probably about marital privileges

SOLVE

Confidential Communication

- ✓ Communications only/ intended confidential
- ✓ Made **during** marriage
- ✓ Any case
- **Both spouses hold** → ***D holds, can prevent W testimony***
- Survives marriage

Except:

- Suit between spouses
- Crimes v. spouse/children
- Comm. plan/commit crime
- Disclosure to 3P waives for disclosing spouse ONLY

N/A

Privilege applies

The marital privileges will provide decoys for each other.

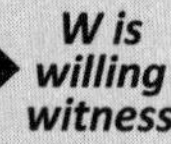

Adverse Testimony

- ✓ No testifying against spouse
- ✓ Includes info learned before marriage
- ✓ Criminal case only
- **Witness spouse only holds** → ***W is willing witness***
- Only testify during marriage

Privilege does not apply

A The testimony should not be admitted **because** the D can prevent the testimony as a confidential marital communication.

Now look for a similar answer choice.

DECODE

A. No, because even though the wife is a willing witness, the defendant has the right to exclude confidential marital communications in federal court.

Correct. This question is testing the difference between the two marital privileges in terms of who holds the privilege.

B. No, but only if the law of the state where the defendant and his wife reside recognizes a privilege for confidential marital communications.

Incorrect rule. Federal common law recognizes the marital privileges.

C. Yes, because in federal court the right not to testify belongs to the testifying spouse, and she is a willing witness.

Wrong rule. While this is a correct statement of law for the adverse testimony privilege, both spouses hold the confidential communications privilege, and the defendant can assert it to prevent wife's testimony.

D. Yes, because while the adverse testimonial privilege is recognized in federal court, the marital communications privilege is not.

Incorrect rule. Federal common law recognizes both marital privileges.

Q5

FACTS

CRIMINAL

A **defendant** has been **charged** with selling cocaine to a police informant. At trial, the alleged cocaine no longer exists, and the only evidence that the substance sold was cocaine is the **informant's testimony that it tasted like cocaine and gave her a cocaine-like sensation.** The informant has **no formal training** in identifying controlled substances.

CALL Should the court admit the informant's **opinion testimony** that the substance was cocaine?

Lay opinion

EVIDENCE Q and testing lay or expert opinion

SOLVE

RULE	ANALYSIS
Lay opinion admissible if:	
• Based on witness's perceptions,	• Witness testified she tasted substance, so based on her perceptions
• Is helpful to the trier of fact, &	• Helpful to know if substance was cocaine since D is charged with selling cocaine & there is no other evidence
• Not based on scientific, technical or specialized knowledge.	• Based on personal experience of witness using cocaine

A The court should admit the testimony **because** it is a proper lay opinion.

Now look for a similar answer choice.

DECODE

You may need to analyze a rule you didn't anticipate to eliminate wrong answer choices.

Testing a 2nd rule

Ⓐ No, because identification of a controlled substance requires an expert with formal training.

Not a correct rule statement. There is no such requirement.

Ⓑ No, because, without a quantity of the controlled substance for testing, opinion testimony is insufficient to make a prima facie case against the defendant.

Not a correct rule statement. There is no such rule requiring a quantity of the substance.

C. Yes, if the court determines that the informant has sufficient knowledge and experience to identify cocaine.

Correct. The court determines admissibility of evidence.

Ⓓ Yes, provided there is evidence sufficient to support **a jury finding** that the informant has sufficient knowledge and experience to identify cocaine.

Wrong rule. The jury would not make a determination of the informant's qualification to provide a lay opinion, that is a determination of admissibility reserved for the judge.

Rule: A judge decides issues of law, including admissibility of evidence.

Analysis: A jury would not be making a finding regarding the admissibility of evidence (here the witness's basis for her opinion).

FACTS **Q6**

CRIMINAL

A **defendant** who is an **accountant** has been charged with **fraud** for allegedly helping a client **file false income tax returns** by **shifting substantial medical expenses from one year to another.** The defendant has pleaded **not guilty**, claiming that he made an **honest mistake** as to the date the expenses were paid. At trial, the **prosecutor offers evidence** of the defendant's involvement in an **earlier scheme to help a different client falsify tax returns in the same way.**

Character-Specific act

CALL Is the evidence of the defendant's involvement in the earlier scheme admissible? **EVIDENCE Q**

SOLVE

Character evidence:
Not admissible to show conduct in conformity
Except it is admissible **substantively** (to prove conformity) if:

- Character at issue (COA/Defense)
- Char. for truthfulness (Impeachment)
- Propensity (sex crimes)
- **OTHER PURPOSE**

I PIK A MOP

- Intent
- Preparation
- Identity of perpetrator
- Knowledge (fact or event)
- **Absence of mistake**/accident
- Motive
- Opportunity
- Plan or scheme

ANALYSIS
D claims honest mistake, but
..."help a **different client** falsify tax returns in the **same way**"
= absence of mistake

A The evidence is admissible to show D did not make a mistake **because** D did this before.

Now look for a similar answer choice.

DECODE

A. No, because it is impermissible character evidence.
Inapplicable rule. This is the general rule, but an exception applies here.

B. No, because it is not relevant to the issues in this case.
Wrong analysis. Defendant's prior similar act has a tendency to show he also committed the fraud here.

C. Yes, to show absence of mistake.
*Correct. The **rule exception**, that character evidence is admissible to prove absence of mistake, is admissible here since the prior conduct was so similar to the conduct here and the D is claiming he made a honest mistake.*

D. Yes, to show the defendant's propensity to commit the crime.
Inapplicable rule. Propensity evidence is typically excluded under the general rule. Propensity evidence is admissible for the narrow exception to show a D's propensity to commit sex crimes, which is inapplicable here.

Q7

FACTS

CRIMINAL

A defendant is charged with **mail fraud**. At trial, the **defendant has not taken the witness stand**, but he has called a **witness who has testified that the defendant has a reputation for honesty**. On **cross-examination**, the prosecutor seeks to ask the witness, "Didn't you hear that **two years ago the defendant was arrested for embezzlement**?"

Specific act

CALL Should the court permit the question? **EVIDENCE Q**

SOLVE

Is impeachment or character evidence at issue?

To determine which rules to use, ask:
Why is evidence (D arrested for embezzlement) being offered?
To **impeach witness** or show **D's bad character?**
Who is the prosecutor attacking? W or D? Here, Q on **cross-ex**, and attacking **W's credibility** by showing W is not knowledgeable about D's reputation or the questionable nature of the community itself that assesses D's reputation.
Rule Impeach: Specific acts can be asked about w/ good faith, but no extrinsic evidence allowed.

A The court should permit the Q **because** it tends to impeach the witness' credibility.

Now look for a similar answer choice.

DECODE

Ⓐ No, because the defendant has not testified and therefore has not put his character at issue.

Incorrect analysis. The witness's credibility is at issue.

Character is a frequent decoy for impeachment & visa versa.

Ⓑ No, because the incident was an arrest, not a conviction.

Incorrect rule. To test the witness's knowledge of the defendant's reputation, it is not necessary there be a conviction. Even an arrest for embezzlement would likely have a negative effect on defendant's reputation.

C. Yes, because it seeks to impeach the credibility of the witness.

Correct. Since the witness has testified about the defendant's reputation for honesty, the prosecution may inquire about the adequacy of her knowledge and the nature of the community itself in which defendant has that reputation.

Ⓓ Yes, because the earlier arrest for a crime of dishonesty makes the defendant's guilt of the mail fraud more likely.

Incorrect rule. Bad acts are not admissible to show criminal propensity.

FACTS **Q8**

CIVIL

A **plaintiff** sued an industrial facility in her neighborhood for injuries to her health caused by air pollution. At trial, the plaintiff was asked questions on **direct examination** about the days on which she had observed large amounts of dust in the air and how long the condition had lasted. She testified that she **could not remember** the specific times, but that she **maintained a diary** in which she had **accurately recorded this information on a daily basis.** When her attorney sought to refresh her recollection with her diary, **she still could not remember.** The plaintiff's attorney seeks to **have the information in the diary admitted** at trial.

Present recollection refreshed
Past recorded recollection
(Always analyze both. They will be decoys for each other.)

CALL Is the information admissible? **EVIDENCE Q**

SOLVE

Present Recollection Refreshed	*Analysis*
• Any item can be shown witness	• Diary
• To refresh W's recollection • W testifies from currently refreshed memory ◦ The item used to refresh is NOT evidence ◦ Adversary has right to inspect	• W cannot testify from refreshed memory
	Not a Present Recoll. Refreshed
Past Recorded Recollection	***Analysis***
Hearsay Exception: **A written record may be read to jury if:**	
• Firsthand knowledge by sponsoring W	• **W on stand** who made diary ✓
• Events fresh in memory when record made	• Recorded on **daily basis** ✓
• W now has impaired recollection	• W **cannot testify** from refreshed memory ✓
• Record was accurate when written *Can be read to the jury or opposing party can offer as exhibit	• Recorded **accurately** at time ✓ Now look for a similar answer choice.

DECODE **A** The diary may be read into evidence as a Past Recorded Recollection.

~~A.~~ No, because reviewing it did not refresh the plaintiff's recollection.

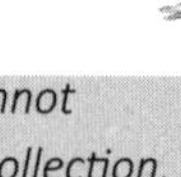

Wrong rule. While the witness's memory is not refreshed, and the information cannot come in as a present recollection refreshed, it is admissible as a past recorded recollection.

~~B.~~ No, unless it is offered by the defendant.

Inaccurate analysis. While only the opposing party can offer the diary as an exhibit, the plaintiff's attorney can have the diary information admitted by having the witness read the diary to the jury.

~~C.~~ Yes, and the plaintiff should be allowed the option of reading it into evidence or having the diary received as an exhibit.

Incorrect. The plaintiff may only have the witness read the diary to the jury (though the opposing party may admit the diary as an exhibit).

D. Yes, and the plaintiff should be allowed to read the diary into evidence.

Correct. Notice they are hiding the ball by not mentioning "past recorded recollection" by name. You must know the sub-rule about how the evidence is admitted (and which party is introducing the evidence) to get this question right.

FACTS **Q9**

CIVIL

A **plaintiff has sued a defendant**, alleging that she was **run over** by a speeding car driven by the defendant. The plaintiff was **unconscious** after her injury and, **accompanied by her husband, was brought to the hospital** in an ambulance.

At trial, the **plaintiff calls** an emergency room **physician to testify** that when the physician asked the plaintiff's husband if he knew what had happened, the husband, who was upset, replied, **"I saw my wife get run over two hours ago by a driver who went right through the intersection without looking."** Hearsay

CALL Is the physician's testimony about the husband's statement admissible? **EVIDENCE Q**

SOLVE

Physician

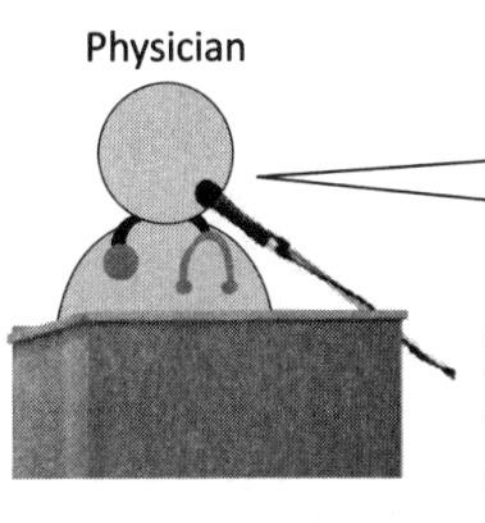

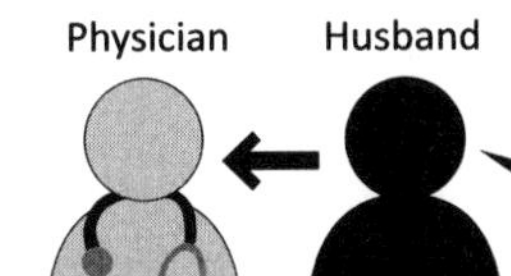

I saw my wife get run over two hours ago by a driver who went right through the intersection without looking.

Hearsay
- Out-of-court statement
- Truth of matter asserted

- Said by H at hospital
- That driver was at fault for accident

Hearsay rule: Exclude unless a hearsay exception applies.

Hearsay Exception?

Consider all likely exceptions triggered by the facts. An accident is classic excited utterance & a hospital setting is classic medical diagnosis & treatment.

RULES	*ANALYSIS*
Med. Diagnosis/Treatment • May include cause if reasonably pertinent to dx/tx (but not fault)	• Statement of fault, not for purpose of procuring medical care/treatment. • NO
Excited Utterance • Relate to startling event • While still under stress	• Startling event, but • 2 hours later, not still under stress of observing accident. • NO

 The physician's testimony is not admissible **because** it is hearsay without any exception.

Now look for a similar answer choice.

DECODE

~~A.~~ No, because it relates an opinion.

Wrong rule. The testimony does not relate to the physician's opinion, rather the physician is repeating the husband's statement, which raises hearsay.

B. No, because it is hearsay not within any exception.

Correct. No hearsay exceptions allow the admission of the statement.

~~C.~~ Yes, as a statement made for purposes of diagnosis or treatment.

Wrong analysis. The statement was not made for the purpose of obtaining medical treatment, but was a statement indicating who was at fault for the accident, which is not allowed.

~~D.~~ Yes, as an excited utterance.

Wrong analysis. The husband was not under the immediate stress of the startling event since he made the statement 2 hours after the accident.

FACTS **Q10**

CIVIL

The plaintiff, who is the **executor of her late husband's estate**, has sued the defendant for **shooting the husband** from ambush. The plaintiff offers **to testify** that the day before her husband was killed, **he described** to her a chance meeting with the defendant on the street in which **the defendant said**, **"I'm going to blow your head off one of these days."**

CALL Is the witness's testimony concerning her husband's statement **admissible**? **EVIDENCE Q**

Inner H/S layer | Outer H/S layer

SOLVE

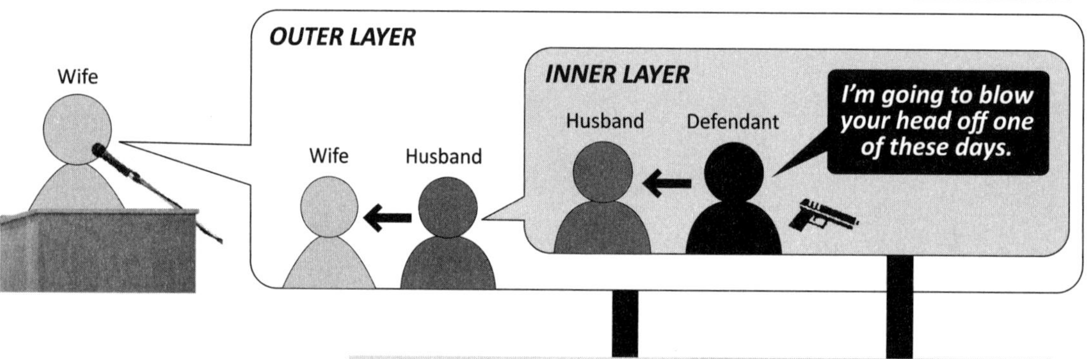

Double Hearsay	Outer statement:	Inner statement:
• Out of court statement • Truth of matter asserted	• Said by H to W • D planned to shoot husband	• Said by D on the street to H • D planned to shoot husband

Rule: Exclude unless a hearsay exception applies for each layer in double hearsay.

You might be thinking of the State of Mind hearsay exception for the outer layer, but there are no facts to indicate the husband's state of mind. Only use the facts provided in the four corners of the question.

Admission: *Party opponent*

A The witnesses testimony is not admissible **because** it is hearsay without any exception.

Now look for a similar answer choice.

DECODE

(A.) Admissible, to show the defendant's state of mind.

Incorrect rule and analysis. The statement does not show D's state of mind. Had the Husband's statement to his wife indicated his own state of mind (that H is scared), it may have been admissible under the state of mind exception, but there are no facts showing Husband's state of mind here.

(B.) Admissible, because the defendant's statement is that of a party-opponent.

Incomplete analysis. This allows the inner layer statement, but no exception allows the outer layer statement.

(C.) Inadmissible because it is improper evidence of a prior bad act.

Incorrect analysis. This is evidence of a statement by D, not an act.

D. Inadmissible, because it is hearsay not within any exception.

Correct. If one layer of hearsay is excluded, the whole statement is excluded in double hearsay situations.

PART 6 REAL PROPERTY

REAL PROPERTY TABLE OF CONTENTS

Note: See Torts chapter for nuisance rules.

★ Favorite testing area

REAL PROPERTY MBE OUTLINE

MBE REAL PROPERTY AT A GLANCE

5 Questions	5 Qs	5 Questions	5 Questions	5 Questions
Present estates Future interests RAP JT and TIC LLT	Restrictive covenants Easements Profits License Fixtures Zoning	Real estate contract Marketable title Equitable conversion Options Right of 1st refusal Merger rule	Mortgage type Title/lien theory Transfers Discharge Pre-foreclosure Foreclosure	Adverse possession Transfer by deed Transfer by will Recording acts Title insurance

MBE tip: A vast amount of material is eligible for testing and unlike the other subjects, there are not as many "clear favorite" testing areas, so the questions are dispersed over many topics. Additionally, the fact descriptions in questions and the rules themselves are long and cumbersome. For these reasons, the real property chapter and MBE questions run longer than other subjects. Expect to average 2.4 minutes per real property question; you will make the time up on other subjects.

Decoy tip: Adding decoy ducks (irrelevant facts) to the fact pattern is the favorite decoy used in real property (e.g., a question may add a recording act statute or rule against perpetuities language to take up space and distract when it is irrelevant to solving the question posed).

MBE REAL PROPERTY QUESTIONS DECODED

Real property facts: The NCBE (drafters of the MBE questions) is headquartered in Wisconsin. Many questions are set in rural areas (e.g., there are a lot of farm questions) and colder climates (e.g., lack of heat is uninhabitable). This is particularly noticeable in real property and contracts questions. If you come from an urban area or warmer climate you may be unfamiliar with the terms or context for some questions (e.g., typical storm windows are removable inserts, so they are not fixtures). Many people from warm climates do not know this (or maybe it was just us).

Rule splits by jurisdiction: Many real property rules vary by jurisdiction. We have noted where the MBE applies a default rule. If no default rule is noted, the question itself should provide the statute/rule to use, or phrase the call of the question to ask, "If X wins, it will be because..." with the answer choice supplying the rule that *must* be in place in that jurisdiction to reach the indicated result.

"No applicable statute" means apply the default rule: Many of the rules tested have jurisdictional splits where one is the default rule. (The default rule could be the common law rule or majority rule. Where there is a default rule we could identify, we have so noted in this outline.) The question may state, "No applicable statute applies." This means there is no statute in the jurisdiction that *modifies* the default rule (e.g., in a will distribution question, "no applicable statute applies," means the common law lapse rule applies—which is the default rule—and that an anti-lapse statute is not in effect).

GLOSSARY OF FREQUENT REAL PROPERTY TERMS

MBE tip: One reason real property is challenging is because many of the terms are unfamiliar and their meanings are not intuitive.

Ademption Adeemed	When specific property devised under a will is no longer a part of the estate at the time of testator's death.
Alienable	Property is fully transferable to another owner by descent (intestacy), devise (will), and inter vivos gift or sale.
Convey	Transfer property ownership, through sale or gift.
Defeasible	Potentially subject to termination (because of a limitation, condition or restriction).
Descendible	Capable of being inherited.
Devise Devisee Devisor	To convey real property through a will. One who is to receive real property conveyed through a will. One who conveys real property through a will.
Divest	To take property away from an earlier property owner.
Donee	The recipient of a gift.
Earnest money	Money paid as partial payment of the purchase price to bind a sales contract. Also called a down payment.
Grantee	The person receiving the interest in property.
Grantor	The person giving the interest in property.
Incorporeal	Rights that can't be seen or touched, such as an easement.
Indenture	A legal agreement or contract.
Ingress/egress	A right to go to and from.
Inter vivos	Between living persons, typically a gift of property.
Intestate/intestacy	To die without a will.
Legatee	The person inheriting.
Marketable title	Title free from reasonable doubt about seller's ability to convey.
Mortgagee	The one who holds the mortgage, usually a bank.
Mortgagor	The person who borrows money by mortgaging their property.
Privity	A recognized relationship existing between parties.
Plat	A piece of land, a plot.
Residuary legatee	One entitled to the residue of an estate (left over assets) after payment of debts and distribution of specific gifts.
Testate Testator	To die testate is when one leaves a legally valid will at death. A deceased person who left a legally valid will.
Settlor	One who creates a trust of property.
Surety	One who takes responsibility for another's payment of debt.
Vendor	One who provides products or services.

I. LAND ACQUISITION

Many real property issues concern the acquisition of real property or an interest in real property. Typically, property is acquired through an inter vivos (between living people) transfer, such as a land sale contract or grant of a deed. Property can also be acquired through a devise in a will. A less common method of acquisition is adverse possession.

A. **Adverse possession** allows one who has **wrongfully entered a property to obtain** that land when there has been **actual exclusive possession, which is open and notorious,** and the possession is **hostile continuously** for the **statutory period.**

1. **Requirements**

a. **Actual possession:** The claimant must have **actual and exclusive use** of the property; which means actual **physical possession or occupancy** of the premises.

1. **Exclusive use:** The **true owner must be excluded** from (not sharing) the premises and the property may not be open to the public.

2. **Partial possession:** A **reasonable percentage of the property must be actually used**. A claimant may only claim possession of the portion of the property actually used (e.g., if a claimant occupies 1 acre of a 200-acre parcel, they may only claim adverse possession of the 1 acre).

a. **Except: Constructive possession of part** will allow possession of the whole property where there is a **reasonable proportion** possessed compared to the whole property and the possessor has **color of title** to the whole property. Color of title means a document seems to provide valid title, but for non-obvious reasons it does not. [This nuance is rarely MBE tested.]

3. **Possession through a tenant is acceptable:** The claimant need not physically possess the premises themself, and possession through **leasing the property to a tenant** will satisfy the actual possession element.

4. **Two adverse possessors:** Two adverse possessors can work together to obtain title, which will be as tenants in common, but in a conflict between two potential adverse possessors, the first possessor has priority.

Example (actual possession): Owner was unclear of the boundary between his property and Neighbor. Owner planted a row of trees and erected a fence between the two properties, which was actually 10 feet onto Neighbor's land. Assuming the statutory period is met, this is sufficient to establish Owner's actual possession of the 10-foot strip of land.

Example (no actual possession): Owner owns vacant land. Neighbor and others occasionally hunt rabbits on Owner's vacant land. This is insufficient for Neighbor to establish possession of Owner's land because the use is infrequent and not exclusive of other hunters.

b. **Open and notorious and visible possession:** The claimant must possess and use the property in a way that a **typical owner** of similar property would use the property. The use must be sufficiently open to **put the true owner on notice** of the trespass by the adverse possessor, though the owner need not have actual knowledge.

Example (open and notorious possession): A farmer entered his neighbor's vacant land, used it to tend his cattle, and even constructed a dam across a waterway, which remained in place for the statutory period. This is sufficient to establish the open and notorious element.

Example (no open and notorious possession): If the farmer had not built the dam, it would be harder to establish the use was open and notorious because tending cattle alone is less likely to put the true owner on notice.

c. **Hostile possession:** Possession of the land must be **without the owner's permission.** This does not mean that the possession must be done in a hostile manner. A possession that starts permissive can become hostile if the owner withdraws consent.

   1. **Boundary disputes:** The majority view is that the adverse possessor **need not know they are on another's land**, which can arise in boundary disputes. Where one property owner occupies land, mistakenly thinking it is their own, but it actually belongs to the adjacent property owner, this possession will be deemed hostile since the entry is not with the true owner's permission.

      a. **Boundary line agreements:** Where neighbors are unsure about the boundary line, most courts will fix the boundary to an agreed line if there was uncertainty and the agreed line was used for a long time.

   2. **Ouster** occurs when a **co-tenant claims an exclusive right** to possession and **refuses occupancy** to his co-tenant. **Ouster is required to find hostile possession against a co-tenant** since all co-tenants have equal right to possession of the property.

> **MBE tip:** Be alert for a convoluted fact pattern that is employed to hide that the possession was permissive, and not hostile/adverse.

d. **Continuous use** without interruption for the given **statutory period**.

   1. **Statutory period:** At common law it is 20 years; it varies among the states but on the MBE they are typically 10 or 15 years.

   Example (not continuous use): A person had possession for 12 of the 10 years required under the statute, but in the 5th year he lived in Europe for the year. The clock started again after his return, thus he has only had continuous possession for 7 years.

      a. **Statute does not begin to run against a disabled owner**, *but only if* the owner is **disabled *on the day*** when the adverse possession **began.** A disability (mental incompetence, status as a minor, military service, or incarceration) occurring *during* the statutory period will not toll the statute from running.

      b. **Statute does not run against a future interest holder:** Since a future interest holder does not yet have a right to possession, the statutory period cannot start against their interest until it becomes possessory (e.g., the statute will only start against the remainder holder of a life estate when the life tenant dies and their interest becomes possessory).

   2. **Continuous possession:** The owner **may not reenter** to regain possession during the statutory time. If they do, the adverse possessor's statutory time period for possession starts over.

   3. **Seasonal use** of a property may still satisfy the continuous possession element if this is the way a **typical owner of similar property** would use the land. The intermittent activities must be of the sort only done by true owners.

   Example: Erecting a small cabin to use during hunting season may be typical seasonal use, but simply using the property to hunt would not be since non-owners would do the same.

   4. **Tacking: One adverse possessor may tack their time with the time of another adverse possessor** to meet the required statutory period for adverse possession if the two adverse possessors are in **privity** (e.g., an adverse possessor leasing the premises to another and acting as landlord is in privity with that tenant).

2. **Effect of adverse possession on title:**

   a. **Not marketable title:** One who takes as an adverse possessor obtains actual title to the property, but it is **not marketable title** for purposes of a **sale** of the property. However, the title can be perfected and made marketable by means of a **judicial action to quiet title.** Title cannot be recorded until such time.

   b. **New transfer must satisfy the statute of frauds (SOF):** Consequently, any attempt to transfer title to another, including back to the original owner, must meet the SOF. The property can also be conveyed by deed.

   Example: A man was record owner of a farm that he had never occupied. A woman met the requirements of adverse possession to the farm. The woman then orally told the man she was wrong to take his farm and waived her claim to the farm. Subsequently, she executed a deed conveying the farm to her son. The deed to the son is valid. The oral waiver to the man has no effect because it does not satisfy the statute of frauds.

3. **Exception—government land** cannot be adversely possessed.

> **MBE tip:** If a statute of limitations is provided in the question, you can safely guess adverse possession (or an easement by prescription) is being tested. Such a statute will typically read, "The period of time to acquire title by adverse possession in the jurisdiction is X years."

B. **Land sale contract:** Most conveyances of real property are by contract.

1. **Contract law governs** a contract for the sale of an interest in land. Common law rules apply.

   a. **Contracting process:** A typical sale of land has a written contract, an escrow period (during which the deed is held by a third party until the purchase price is paid), a closing of escrow (the deed and money are exchanged), and the conveyance by deed.

      1. **Merger doctrine:** The contract for a conveyance of an interest in real estate typically **governs the agreement until the time of closing,** at which time the **deed** becomes the operative document governing the land transfer under the **merger doctrine.**

★ b. **Statute of frauds (SOF) applies to** a **contract** regarding the sale or conveyance of an interest in land, which includes **liens, leases, easements, and restriction on land use (restrictive covenants/equitable servitudes).**

      1. **SOF requirements:** All **essential terms** and in **writing**:

         a. Name the **parties** (buyer and seller);

         b. **Land description** sufficient to identify the land; and

         c. State some **consideration** (purchase **price** and manner of payment typically).

         d. **Signed by the party to be bound** (this is interpreted liberally and can include a printed name on an email).

         Example: An unmarried couple owned a home as tenants in common. They orally agreed that if one of them died, the other would acquire the decedent's interest in the home. This agreement violates the SOF.

      2. **Part performance exception to the SOF** (thus allowing an oral contract) applies where a buyer has **performed in reliance** on an **unambiguous oral contract,** and the performance **clearly indicates a contract existed.** Most courts require **two** of the following:

a. **Possession** of the land by the buyer.

b. Substantial **improvements** made to the premises by buyer.

c. **Payment** of all or part or the **purchase price** by buyer.

Example (satisfied): Landlord (L) and Tenant (T) orally agreed T could buy the rental property by making the monthly mortgage payment, which was the same amount as her rent. In addition, T agreed to pay $25,000 up front, all taxes, insurance, and maintenance costs. At the end of 6 years, T would own the property. T made all agreed payments and made structural improvements, which raised the property value by 50%. T's part performance of possession, improvements, and payments (in excess of rental value) is sufficient to overcome the lack of SOF writing.

> **Memorization tip:** Use PIP to remember the part performance exception.

3. **Full performance will satisfy the SOF.** Where a seller actually **makes a conveyance** (by signing over the deed) in reliance on an oral agreement (e.g., the buyer's promise of payment in exchange), the contract will be taken out of the SOF and deemed valid.

4. **Detrimental reliance exception** (minority rule) to SOF is permitted in some states.

c. Time of performance:

1. **Presumption** is that **time is not of the essence,** unless specifically contracted. Closing within a **reasonable time** (1-2 months) is acceptable.

2. **Time of the essence clauses are enforceable** in real property contracts, but ***only if* expressly specified** in the contract. If so, a party's failure to tender timely performance is considered a material breach and the breaching party may not enforce the contract.

Example (time is of the essence): Seller contracted to sell a home to Buyer, with marketable title due on a specified date and "time is of the essence." At the specified date, the title showed a woman owned a 1/8 interest in the home. Seller told Buyer the woman was his daughter and she would gladly deed over her share in 2 weeks upon her return from a trip. Seller was in breach because title was not marketable at the closing date and time was of the essence.

Example (time is not of the essence): Seller contracts to sell a home to Buyer, with closing to occur on May 1 at 10 a.m. A week before closing, the title search revealed there was an undisclosed easement on the property. Seller need only close within a "reasonable time" after the scheduled closing date. If Seller can make title marketable by eliminating the easement within a reasonable amount of time, Seller is not in breach.

> **MBE tip:** "Time is of the essence" is often tested in conjunction with the rule that marketable title is due at closing, as shown in the examples above. When a time is of the essence clause is present in MBE questions, they are usually express and enforceable.

d. Conflicts of law: Real property is subject to the **law of the jurisdiction in which the property sits.**

★ **2. Marketable title:** There is an implied promise (also called a warranty) in every land sale contract that the seller covenants to transfer **marketable title**, which is **title free from**

reasonable doubt about the seller's ability to convey what they purports to convey (the full interest of the property) by the **closing date** (but not before) such that the buyer can resell the property in the future and is not subject to an **unreasonable risk of litigation**.

a. **Marketable title is for buyer's benefit**. The purpose of the rule is to protect a *buyer* from immediately entering into a dispute over whether the title is good. Thus, the *seller* cannot refuse to perform on the contract because of marketable title issues.

   1. **Remedy for breach:** If title is unmarketable, the *buyer* may rescind and sue for damages, or sue for specific performance with price abatement.

b. **Merger doctrine: The deed controls upon closing**. Once the deed takes effect, the **sales contract merges into the deed** and the deed controls the transaction. Absent fraud, the parties **cannot sue regarding title issues on the underlying contract**. Any obligation imposed in the contract is deemed discharged at closing unless the obligation is repeated in the deed, though seller may be liable under any warranties provided in the deed (depending on the type of deed provided). See types of deeds and covenants of title in sec. I.C.4 below.

> **MBE tip**: Careful reading is key! Be alert for a tricky question that asks about the success of a *breach of contract* action on unmarketable title grounds when the contract has already closed. After closing, a suit regarding title deficiencies must be brought on an action under the *deed* (e.g. for breach of warranty).

c. **Chain of title defects** can make title unmarketable.

   1. **Future interest holder** who is unborn/unascertained.

   2. **Adverse possessor** (without a judicial action to quiet title) who is not the record owner of the property has unmarketable title. [Use this as the default rule on the MBE, though modern decisions are contrary.]

   Example: Seller contracted to sell a home to Buyer. A title search reveals the record owner is not Seller, but rather Seller has valid adverse possession of the home. Buyer will not be required to perform under the contract since title is not marketable (unless Seller can quiet title prior to closing).

d. **Encumbrances render title unmarketable.** An encumbrance is any right or interest that exists in someone other than the owner of real property that restricts or impairs the transfer of the property or lowers its value.

   1. **Mortgage/liens are encumbrances**, but if the **funds from the closing** are sufficient to **pay off the mortgage** or lien, **title is marketable.**

      a. **Mortgage:** Typically, this occurs when there are sufficient funds to pay the mortgage or lien off with the sale proceeds at the closing.

      Example (mortgage): Seller contracted to sell a home for $300,000, with closing in 60 days. There was an unsatisfied $50,000 mortgage. Since there are sufficient funds to pay the mortgage off from the sale proceeds, title is marketable.

      b. **Installment contract:** In an installment contract, though the period between contracting and closing may last many years, the rule remains the same. See sec. I.H.1.c.

      Example (installment contract): Seller contracted to sell land to Buyer through an installment purchase of 300 installments. After making 10 payments, Buyer was concerned to discover there was an outstanding mortgage for approximately 25% of the purchase price. However, title was still marketable because Seller has until all payments have been made to deliver marketable title in an installment contract.

2. **Use restrictions on property**, such as **easements, restrictive covenants** or **purchase options, are encumbrances** that render title unmarketable because they make the property less valuable.

   a. **Except—beneficial, visible,** or **known easements:** Most jurisdictions find a **beneficial easement** (e.g., utility that provides a benefit by servicing the property) or one that is **visible** (provides inquiry notice, such as train tracks) or **known to the buyer** (disclosed) will not constitute an encumbrance on the property.

   Example (use restriction): A 10-lot subdivision was subject to building restrictions for "all lots on said map." The (corresponding 10-lot) subdivision map filed by the developer included an undesignated (unnumbered) parcel amongst the 10 numbered lots (the map filed had 10 numbered lots, but one unnumbered lot). Since it is unclear if the unnumbered lot is subject to the use restrictions, the unnumbered lot does not have marketable title.

3. **Existing zoning *violations*** typically are treated as an **encumbrance** making title unmarketable. However, simply having **zoning restrictions imposed** on the property is **not an encumbrance**.

   Example (zoning encumbrance): Seller contracted to sell a home to Buyer. The zoning ordinance required an 8.5-foot sideline setback (meaning the home could *not be closer* than 8.5 feet to the side lot line). During escrow, a survey determined a portion of the house was 8.4 feet from the sideline. Title is unmarketable because of the existing zoning violation.

4. **Significant encroachments** render title unmarketable. However, it will not be considered an encumbrance where there is a slight encroachment (a few inches and not disruptive to use), or one where the encroached upon owner has indicated they will not sue.

e. **Timing: Title must be marketable upon closing,** thus a seller may use the escrow period to remove any encumbrance.

f. **Waiver:** The **buyer can waive** any defect in marketable title in the sales contract and agree to purchase the property with the limitation.

MARKETABLE TITLE CHEAT SHEET

- For Buyer's benefit, so *Seller* can't use marketable title issues to get out of the deal
- Merger rule: Deed controls after closing, so no suits on contract basis *after* closing
- Buyer can waive defect in marketable title

Marketable	Unmarketable
Mortgage/lien—satisfied by closing	Mortgage/lien—not satisfied by closing
Zoning restrictions	Existing violations of zoning ordinances
◆ Easement that is beneficial, visible, or known ◆ Slight encroachment	◆ Easement (undisclosed) ◆ Restrictive covenant (undisclosed) ◆ Significant encroachment
	◆ Adverse possession (unless quiet title) ◆ Future interest holder (unascertained)

Decoy tip: A **quitclaim deed** must still provide marketable title. Look for a decoy answer that states that since the buyer agreed to accept a quitclaim deed, the buyer can't dispute the marketability of the title (because they can).

3. **Real estate brokers and agents** typically are used to facilitate the sale and execute documents. The broker representing the seller is the listing agent.

   a. **Duties:** Both brokers and agents owe a **fiduciary duty to the seller**, and a **duty to disclose** *known* material information to the **buyer**.

   b. **Compensation:** Brokers/agents earn a **commission** on the sale. Typically, the seller's agent earns the commission and the buyer's agent receives a portion of the seller's commission for bringing in the buyer.

   c. **Exclusive right-to-sell listing agreement:** A broker can enter into an agreement to use their **"best efforts"** to sell the property for an exclusive period of time, such as for three months. If the property is sold during the exclusive period, the **listing agent will earn a commission**, regardless of who locates a buyer. The date of the sales agreement will control whether the buyer was obtained during the exclusive time period, not the date of closing.

      Example: If the seller located their own buyer during the time of an exclusive right-to-sell listing agreement, the broker would still earn his commission.

      1. **Best efforts** by the broker include expending time, effort, and/or money on marketing efforts.

   d. **Exclusive agency agreements** prevent the seller from **listing** the home for sale with more than one agency simultaneously.

4. **Title insurance** typically is obtained during escrow. It ensures that good title exists and will defend record title if litigated. A title insurance policy can be an **owner's policy,** which protects *only* the policy owner (which could be the property owner or mortgage holder) or a **lender's policy,** which will follow with any mortgage assignment to a new lender.

   Example: Ten years ago Seller sold land to Buyer. Buyer purchased a title insurance policy, running to (protecting) Buyer and Buyer's mortgage holder. After paying off the mortgage, Buyer sold the land to Investor. Investor then gave the land to Donee with a quitclaim deed. Subsequently, Donee discovered an outstanding mortgage on the land that predated all of the conveyances. Donee sued Buyer for the cost of the outstanding mortgage. Buyer can recover from the title insurance company even though Buyer no longer owns the land. *In contrast,* if Donee directly sued the title insurance company Donee would not have won since Donee was not a named insured.

5. **Liability for property defects**

   a. **New builder construction** of a home extends to the buyer an **implied warranty of habitability, fitness** or **quality**, and that the home is fit for human habitation. This warranty is limited to new home construction.

      1. **Subsequent purchasers of new construction:** Courts are split on whether this warranty of quality extends from the builder to subsequent purchasers of the new home construction.

      2. **No implied warranty of quality, fitness, or habitability on *resale* homes** (any home sale other than new builder construction). A contract for the **resale** of a home **does not include** any implied warranties.

      Example: A builder of a new house sold it to a buyer. The buyer resold the house to a woman. Four months later the woman discovered latent defects that caused the basement to take on water in heavy rains. *If* the woman is successful against the builder, it will be because they were in a jurisdiction where the implied warranty of habitability is enforceable by a subsequent purchaser. (There is no implied warranty on a resale home otherwise.)

b. **Seller may not misrepresent and *may* have a duty to disclose.** A seller may not make **materially false statements** (fraud), **actively misrepresent** the property, or **actively conceal** a defect (e.g., paint over a water damaged wall to conceal there is a leak). Modernly, many states impose an implied promise to **disclose known latent** (hidden) **defects** to a buyer that would not be obvious (though there is no such requirement at common law).

Examples (latent defect): A seller has a duty to disclose the interior of a wall is rotted, if known, since an inspection would not reveal that latent defect. A seller has a duty to disclose that sewage seeps into the basement when the toilets are flushed since that latent defect would not be obvious to a buyer, unless someone flushed during an inspection.

Example (misrepresentation): The city informed a warehouse owner that after 90 days he could no longer use the warehouse loading docks because the trucks blocked the street. The warehouse owner quickly sold the building. Failure to inform the buyer about the upcoming loading dock prohibition is a misrepresentation (by omission).

1. **Exception—parties can agree** that defects that would otherwise make title unmarketable (e.g., existing zoning violations) are acceptable.

2. **Exception—property sold "as is"** *may* be sufficient to put a buyer on notice that there may be defects in the property other than those that are open and obvious so long as the disclaimer is sufficiently clear and specific. However, even selling a property "as is" will not overcome a seller's fraud, concealment of a defect, or failure to disclose known defects. The more specific the disclaimer is, the more likely it will be upheld.

Example: A woman inherited a home she had never visited from a distant relative. A neighbor of the home offered to buy it. The woman agreed, so long as it was sold "as is." Though a termite infestation was discovered after the sale, the "as is" disclaimer holds up since the woman made no active misrepresentations and had never even been to the house.

Decoy tip: "Breach of the covenant of warranty" or some reference to a "warranty deed" are common decoy answers in a question testing disclosures. Remember, a warranty deed warrants the condition of the *title*, not the physical condition of the property. The physical condition of resale property can raise a disclosure issue. If it is new construction, it can raise a *warranty of fitness or quality* issue.

Decoy tip: "Caveat emptor," translates to, "let the buyer beware," and puts the responsibility for the property condition on the buyer. This is not the rule, but it is a frequent decoy answer.

6. **Equitable conversion** covers the executory period (time between contracting and closing) and provides that once the contract is signed, property ownership equitably "converts" and the new **buyer is deemed the owner**, even though the seller retains legal title until closing.

a. **Risk of loss equitable conversion (majority rule):** If the property is damaged or destroyed (through no fault of either party) prior to closing, the **risk of loss** is **imposed on the buyer** of the property. Thus, the buyer would have to cover any losses in addition to paying the purchase price to the seller. The courts will give the purchaser the benefit of the seller's insurance, if any, to avoid unjustly enriching the seller (who would otherwise be entitled to the insurance proceeds and purchase price).

Example: Seller contracts to sell his apartment building to Buyer. The day before Buyer takes possession a fire destroys the building. There is no insurance. The risk of loss will fall on Buyer, entitling Seller to specific performance even though the building is destroyed.

1. **Exceptions:** The doctrine is subject to the following exceptions and the **seller bears the loss** where:

   a. Loss results from their **own negligence**, and

   b. At the time of loss, the **title was unmarketable**.

2. **Risk of loss—Uniform Vendor and Purchaser Act (minority rule):** The equitable conversion doctrine is not universally applied, and some states have adopted the Uniform Vendor and Purchaser Act that places the risk of loss on the **one in possession**, which is typically the seller during escrow.

> **MBE tip:** The MBE questions frequently will include the language "there is no applicable statute" to indicate the default *majority rule* applies.

b. **Death of seller or buyer does not terminate the contract.** Equitable conversion doctrine also applies when a party to the contract dies before escrow has closed. The contract remains in force.

1. **Seller dies: The sale proceeds are personal property.** In the absence of a specific devise of that property to a specific person in a will, the proceeds are paid to the inheritor of the seller's personal property, not the inheritor of real property.

   Example: Seller contracts to sell a home to Buyer. Seller dies before the closing. Seller's will gives his personal property to a friend and his real property to his sister. At the close, the friend is entitled to the proceeds as the inheritor of Seller's personal property.

2. **Buyer dies:** The **buyer's estate is required to pay** the purchase price for the real property **from the personal property** of the estate since it equitably owns the property. However, the property then goes to the person inheriting the decedent buyer's real estate.

   Example: Seller contracts to sell a home to Buyer. Buyer dies before the closing. Buyer's heirs will pay the purchase price out of the estate's personal property.

> **MBE tip:** Equitable conversion is a testing favorite—likely because the risk of loss rules feel illogical in a modern era, and the rules regarding the death of a buyer or seller during escrow are not intuitive.

7. **Remedy for breach of land sale contract:** The non-breaching party to a land sale contract can sue for **damages** or **specific performance**. The buyer may also forfeit any deposit as a form of liquidated damages. Specific performance is usually the preferred remedy because land is unique, and the court can enforce the terms of the contract.

   a. **Damages:** Typically, damages are calculated as the **difference between the market price and the contract price**, plus incidental costs.

   b. **Specific performance** is a permanent injunction in contract where the court orders the defendant to perform on the contract as promised. Both **the buyer and the seller** can bring suit for specific performance. The following requirements must be met:

   1. **Contract is valid.** (However, even in the absence of a SOF writing, a party can get specific performance with part performance on an oral contract.)

2. **Contract conditions** imposed on the plaintiff are satisfied. (This means the person asking for specific performance is ready and able to perform.)
3. **Inadequate legal remedy:** Money damages are inadequate to compensate because **real property is unique**.
4. **Mutuality of performance:** Both parties to the contract must be eligible to have their performance under the contract ordered by the court.
5. **Feasibility of enforcement:** The injunction cannot be too difficult for the court to enforce. (Typically not an issue for a property transaction.)
6. **No defenses,** such as laches, unclean hands, or any defenses to the underlying contract (e.g., lack of consideration, SOF, sale to a bona fide purchaser, etc.).

> **Memorization tip:** Use **Chocolate Cheesecake Is My Favorite Dessert** to memorize the six elements of specific performance: valid **C**ontract, contract **C**onditions satisfied, **I**nadequate legal remedy, **M**utuality of performance, **F**easibility of enforcement, and no **D**efenses.
>
> **MBE tip:** A question call that asks if a party can obtain specific performance is frequently used as a mechanism to ask about the validity of the underlying land sale contract (e.g., if the SOF is satisfied).

c. **Deposit** (also called "earnest money") **forfeiture:** A deposit is money paid by the buyer as security and applied to the purchase price, but it is forfeited to the seller as damages in the event the buyer breaches. The deposit must be a **reasonable estimate** of the seller's damages if the buyer breaches; typically **10%** of the purchase price is reasonable. If the deposit amount is so large it operates as a penalty, it will not be enforced. The deposit effectively functions like a **liquidated damages clause**.

Example: Buyer agreed to buy a home for $100,000 and paid a $5000 deposit. During escrow, Buyer's job was transferred and he notified Seller that he could not close. Seller waited until the contract closing date and sold the home to a cash buyer for $98,000, closing quickly. Despite actual losses of only $2000, Seller was entitled to keep the full $5000 deposit.

 C. **Conveyance** (transfer of ownership) **by deed:** A deed is a document that **serves to pass legal title** from the grantor (one giving the interest) to the grantee (one receiving the interest) when it is (1) **lawfully executed,** and (2) **properly delivered**.

Example: A conveyance can be by sale or inter vivos (during lifetime) gift. A gift of land can also be made by will, but the transfer is not effective until death.

1. **Lawful execution of deed requirements:** Much like a land sale contract, a deed must meet the following formalities in order to be lawfully executed or it is void (with the big difference being that **consideration is not required** for a deed):

a. **Identification of the parties,** especially the grantee. The grantee must be identifiable and living (e.g., a deed to a dead person or a corporation that is not yet formed is void).

Example: A grant to "the leaders of all the Protestant churches in York County" is too broad and vague to adequately identify the grantee, rendering the deed invalid.

b. **In writing and signed by the grantor**, which is witnessed or notarized. The grantee need not sign. The **statute of frauds applies** since a deed conveys an interest in land.

c. **Words of intent** to transfer ownership (word **"grant"** is sufficient). You may also see the words "present intent" or "actual intent."

d. **No consideration is required** (the transfer may be an inter vivos gift). The deed remains valid even if consideration is recited in the deed and not paid.

e. **Adequate land description:** The land description in a deed need only be **specific enough to identify and locate the property**. It need not be exact and can contain minor discrepancies (e.g., a description that lists the property address and indicates the property is one acre, when it is actually 7/8 acre is sufficient).

   1. **Metes and bounds:** The description may use "metes and bounds," which is a surveyor's description of a parcel using carefully measured distances, but metes and bounds are not required. However, if present, a metes and bounds description will control, even if contradicted by other descriptive language in the deed.

   2. An **insufficient land description** will render the deed **void for vagueness**.

   Examples: A land description reads, "All that part of my farm, being a square with 200-foot sides, the southeast corner of which is in the north line of my neighbor." This description is insufficiently vague because it would be impossible to locate the property. A land description of "my house on Elm Street," would be inadequate if the grantor owned two houses on Elm Street.

 2. **Proper delivery and acceptance of deed** is required for the deed to have effect.

a. **Delivery requirements**

   1. **Intent of present transfer:** Words or conduct indicating the grantor's **intent to make a *present* transfer** of the deed. Intent to make a future transfer is insufficient (e.g., an intent to gift land and for title to pass in five years is insufficient). **Parol evidence**, which is evidence outside the deed itself, **is allowed** to prove the grantor's intent.

      a. **Present intent presumption:** Though neither is required to establish effective delivery, the following acts create a strong presumption of present intent to transfer:

         i. **Recording** the deed. (Though recording is not dispositive or even necessary to a determination of deed delivery.)

         ii. Grantor **physically delivering the deed** to the grantee. (Though there is no requirement the grantee have possession of the deed.)

      b. **Third party delivery—Grantor must relinquish control:** Delivery can be accomplished through a third-party intermediary, such as a lawyer or trusted agent so long as the grantor **intends that title passes immediately**, even though the right of possession may be postponed. Grantor must relinquish control and **may not retain a right to revoke**. Title passes automatically and relates back to the date of delivery to the third party. This may be called a **death escrow**.

      Example (intent of present transfer): Landowner handed a deed of property to Friend, and stated, "This is yours, but please do not record it until after I am dead." This statement, along with delivery to Friend, sufficiently demonstrates grantor's intent to make a present transfer. The request to delay recording is irrelevant since delivery is present.

      Example (no intent of present transfer): A man decided to give his farm to his nephew. The man gave the deed to his lawyer with the instructions to deliver the deed to his nephew upon his death. He also told the attorney to return the deed if asked. This does not demonstrate intent to make a present transfer since the deed would be returned at the man's request and was never out of the man's control.

2. **Acceptance of the deed** by the grantee must also occur. Acceptance is **presumed** for a beneficial conveyance. If the grantee explicitly rejects the deed, delivery is defeated.

b. **Upon proper delivery, title passes *immediately*** to the grantee, thus it is **not revocable**.

Example: Landowner handed a deed of property to Friend, and stated, "This is yours, but please do not record it until after I am dead." The next day, Landowner asks Friend to return the deed because he wants to handle the transfer in his will instead. Friend tells Landowner he will destroy the deed, but he doesn't. Landowner never made a will and dies intestate. Title passed at the delivery of the deed to Friend and the subsequent actions had no legal effect. The request to delay recording is irrelevant.

Decoy tip: Once the requirements for a valid deed delivery are met, it is done and can't be undone. The parties would need a new valid conveyance to reconvey the property back to the original owner. Actions such as handing the deed back or tearing the deed up to destroy it will not undo the effective delivery and conveyance.

3. **Defective deeds**

a. **Void deed** is a forged deed, or one issued to a dead grantee or non-formed corporation. A void deed will be **set aside *even if* it has subsequently transferred to a BFP** (bona fide purchaser, one who takes for value and without notice,) so a **BFP is not protected** where the deed is void.

bold BFP is not protected

b. **Voidable deed** is where the deed was executed by one without capacity, such as a minor, or through fraud, including fraud against a grantor's creditors. A voidable deed **will be set aside, *unless* the property has subsequently transferred to a BFP**, so the recording statutes **protect a BFP** of a voidable deed.

c. **Recording a defective deed does not make it valid.**

4. **Types of deeds and covenants of title**

a. **Quitclaim deed:** A quitclaim deed conveys **whatever interest the grantor actually has** in the property but contains **no covenants/warranties of title** (promises about what that interest is). However, a quitclaim must still provide marketable title for the land sale contract. See sec. I.B.2.

b. **General warranty deed:** Warrants against all **defects in title** and contains **six covenants for title.** Three of the covenants are present and three are future covenants. This is also called simply a warranty deed.

1. **Present covenants** are **breached at the time of the sale** (when the deed is delivered), if breached at all, and **cannot be enforced by a subsequent grantee** in most states.

a. **Seisin:** Grantor warrants they **own what they purport to own** and have conveyed.

b. **Right to convey:** Grantor warrants they have the **power and authority to make the conveyance.**

c. **Against encumbrances:** Grantor warrants there are **no mortgages, liens, easements, or other use restrictions** on the land that diminish the owner's property rights. (e.g., a right of way deed to build and maintain an underground oil drilling pipeline). Most jurisdictions find this covenant would be breached even if the purchaser had notice of the encumbrance.

2. **Future covenants** run with the land, are continuous, and are **breached**, if ever, **at the time the grantee is disturbed in possession**. Future covenants **can be enforced by subsequent grantees.**

   a. **Warranty of title:** Grantor promises to **defend** should there be any **lawful (meritorious) claims of title** asserted by others.

   Example: Landowner conveyed property to Teacher. Neighbor asserted a claim of title to the property and brought suit against Teacher. Landowner refused to defend the claim and Teacher successfully defended the action (thus, it was not meritorious because Neighbor lost). Teacher will not prevail in a suit against Landowner to recover her expenses in defending the suit since Neighbor's claim of title was not meritorious and the covenants do not provide defense of *invalid* claims.

   b. **Quiet enjoyment:** Grantor promises grantee will not be disturbed in possession by any third parties' **lawful (meritorious) claims of title.**

   c. **Further assurances:** Grantor will do whatever **future acts** are **reasonably necessary** to perfect title.

> **Decoy tip:** The type of deed used to make a conveyance is often referenced in an MBE question, and the type of deed may provide a decoy answer, but the deed features are not frequently tested outright.

c. **Statutory special warranty deed:** Some states enforce promises by statute where the grantor promises (on their own behalf only) that grantor hasn't conveyed the property to others and that the estate is free from encumbrances. [This rule is rarely MBE tested.]

> **MBE tip:** Note the word "covenant" used here in a deed context (meaning promise) is also used in other real property contexts, such as a "covenant" that runs with the land in the land use rules.

5. **Estoppel by deed** (also called after-acquired title): If one purports to convey an interest in realty that **they do not own at the time**, but they **subsequently obtain title to the property**, they cannot deny the validity of that conveyance. The property title will ***automatically*** **pass to the grantee** once the grantor acquires title.

   a. **Only applies to transfer by warranty deed,** which warrants the quality of title. Estoppel by deed does not apply to a transfer by quitclaim deed.

   b. **Only applies against the original grantor:** Most courts hold that estoppel by deed will not be applied against a *subsequent* BFP (see sec. I.G.3. below) of the same property. Even if the original grantor records the deed, it will not put a BFP on notice because such recording will appear outside the chain of title.

   Example: Mother told Son he would inherit a tract of land. Son then purported to convey the land by warranty deed to Friend, who paid value. Friend failed to conduct a title search, but he recorded his interest. Subsequently, Mother died and Son inherited the property. Son now wants to keep the property but estoppel by deed will prevent this and Friend will own the property. *In contrast,* if instead Mother had subsequently sold the property to a BFP, that BFP would own the property. Friend's earlier recorded interest would not provide notice since it did not come from the true owner, Mother, and would appear outside the chain of title. However, Friend could sue Son for breach of the warranty deed.

> **<u>Decoy tip</u>:** A decoy answer choice will indicate the original grantee's failure to have properly conducted a title search at the time of the transfer prevents them from taking the property, however, there is no such requirement and failure to conduct a title search will not prevent application of estoppel by deed.

6. **Damages for breach of covenant(s):** If there are title issues, then damages awarded are the lesser of the purchase price or the cost to defend or perfect title; if there are encumbrances, then damages awarded are the lesser of the difference between the amount paid and the value of the land with the encumbrance, or the cost of removing the encumbrance.

7. **Defenses** to breaches of covenants can include **unclean hands**, **laches**, and **waiver** (similar to land sale contract defenses).

D. **Devise by will:** Property may be conveyed by will. A will is a document prepared by a person (the testator) during their lifetime that specifies who will inherit and own his property upon his death. Wills only "speak" at death, so a **disposition in a will has no legal effect** and can be revoked or modified at any time **until the death of the testator.**

> **<u>MBE tip</u>:** On the MBE, most wills provide that one person will inherit a specific piece of property, while another person will inherit the residue of the estate (residuary legatee), which consists of all property that is *not* designated to go to a specific person. This is a frequent set up for a future interests and/or rule against perpetuities question.

1. **Ademption:** The common law rule of ademption occurs where a testator has devised a **specific property to a specific party** under testator's will, but that specific property is **no longer a part of the estate** at the time of testator's death. The gift is "adeemed," in other words **fails**, and the legatee gets nothing. (MBE default rule.) Many states have statutes limiting the ademption rule.

   <u>Example</u>: Woman devised her farm to Nephew and the estate residue to Niece. Twelve years after executing her will, she sold the farm and bought a house in the city. There is no applicable statute. Upon Woman's death, Niece inherits the city house because Niece inherits the estate residue as the residuary legatee, which includes the house. The gift of the farm to Nephew is adeemed (fails).

2. **Exoneration:** The common law rule of exoneration provides that when a person receives a bequest of specific property, and that **property is subject to a lien** or mortgage, the **encumbrance will be paid off** with the estate's personal property, and the recipient receives the property "free and clear" of the mortgage, unless the testator indicated a contrary intent. (MBE default rule.) Most states alter the common law exoneration doctrine and provide the property passes to the recipient "subject to" the mortgage.

3. **Lapse and anti-lapse:** The common law doctrine of **lapse** provides that if a beneficiary named in a will **predeceases the testator, the bequest fails.** (MBE default rule.) Most states have **anti-lapse** statutes that allow the predeceased beneficiary's heirs to take, especially if they are kin to the testator.

   <u>Example</u>: A man died and his will devised his home to Friend and the estate residue to Charity. Friend predeceases Man, but is survived by a wife and a disabled child. There is credible evidence Man wanted Friend to own the home so he could care for his wife and child there. There is no applicable statute. Upon Man's death, Charity inherits the home as the residuary legatee since the gift to Friend lapsed and there is no anti-lapse statute provided (this is what the language "no applicable statute" means, so you use the default rule). The information about the wife and disabled child was included to emotionally distract you.

> **Decoy tip:** A sympathetic person will often be the loser in an MBE questions. It is a favorite bar examiner technique intended to distract you from mechanically applying the law to the facts. Remember, these aren't real people.

4. **Power of appointment** is the right to designate the new owner of property.

   Example: A man leaves a woman property for life and then gives her the right to select one of her children as the new owner of the property after her death—the woman has the power of appointment and her children are the objects of the power.

   a. **Failure to appoint:** If the person with the power of appointment does not appoint a new owner as instructed, the property reverts back to the donor's estate and goes into the donor's residuary estate.

> **MBE tip:** If the MBE question states, "There is no applicable statute," use the general default rules for ademption, exoneration, and lapse.
>
> **Decoy tip:** A will speaks at death. A will has no effect prior to the testator's death. Be alert for decoy answers that would be correct if the will took effect upon drafting, but are wrong because it doesn't.

E. **Conveyance by trust:** Property can be conveyed by trust.

1. **Private trusts** involve property being managed by one person for the benefit of another (the beneficiary). The rule against perpetuities (**RAP) applies** to private trusts. A valid trust must have:

   a. **Intent:** The settlor (one who creates a trust of property) must manifest an **intent to create the trust**.

      1. **Precatory language**, such as "I wish" or "I hope," **is inadequate** to establish intent to create a trust.

   b. **Property (res):** Trust must have **identifiable property** (the res). The property cannot be an expectancy under a will or illusory.

   c. **Purpose:** The trust must have a **purpose** that is not illegal or against public policy.

   d. **Beneficiary:** The property is managed for the benefit of the beneficiary. The beneficiary must be ascertainable, unless it is a charitable trust or the selection of the beneficiary is left to the discretion of the trustee.

   e. **A trustee** is the person with the power to manage the trust. The trustee need not be named.

2. **Charitable:** A charitable trust is one that is for **charitable purposes and benefits society. RAP does not apply** to charitable trusts.

   a. **Cy pres doctrine:** When a charitable objective becomes impossible or impracticable to fulfill, courts often apply the cy pres doctrine and **substitute another similar charitable objective** that is as near as possible to the settlor's (person creating the trust's) intent.

   b. **Resulting trust:** If the cy pres doctrine cannot be used to fulfill the settlor's intent, the courts will apply a resulting trust to manage the property that was intended for the charitable trust,

3. **Lapse/anti-lapse rules** apply to trusts as they do in wills. See sec. I.D.3.
4. **Power of appointment** rules apply to trusts as they do in wills. See sec. I.D.4.

> **MBE tip:** Trusts are often tested in the context of future interests and RAP.

F. **Dedication**: Land can be **transferred to a public entity** by dedication. A public dedication of land is established with **intent to dedicate** and **acceptance**:

1. **Intent to dedicate** the land for public must be expressed (offer). Intent to dedicate can be established by submission of a building plan (plat), statement (written or oral), or by opening the land to public use.
2. **Acceptance** of the dedication. The public entity typically will accept by approving the building plan, but may also accept by resolution, assumption of property maintenance, or by making improvements to the land.

   Example: A builder prepares a development plan for a large subdivision, including public streets. The plan was approved by a government agency and recorded. This constitutes a public dedication of the streets on the plan because the plan demonstrates the builder's intent and the recording indicates acceptance.

G. **Recording acts** allow a grantee to record their interest to **provide notice** to everyone that they are the owner of the property (or hold an interest, such as a mortgage). Recording protects their interest by preventing a **subsequent grantee** to divest (take the property away from) an earlier grantee. Recording acts typically **protect subsequent BFPs**. (BFP rules immediately below in sec. I.G.3.)

> **Recording act context:** The recording acts come into play in these situations:
>
> (1) The recording acts provide a method for determining which of two innocent grantees should prevail-when an unscrupulous owner has conveyed the same property (by gift or sale) to more than one person when both are claiming the property.
>
> (2) The recording acts create a system for providing notice for the purpose of encumbrances on property such as mortgage or easements.
>
> (3) The recording acts determine priority of funds disbursement in foreclosure.
>
> **MBE tip:** When approaching recording acts, always first determine if the subsequent grantee is a BFP since that drives the whole analysis.
>
> 
>
> **Decoy tip:** In recording act questions, watch out for decoy duck facts. The questions typically provide a lot of extra facts that are irrelevant to solving the question posed, such as recording by the *other* party, possession when it isn't relevant for determining inquiry notice, or the type of deed used in the transaction.

1. **Common law rule** of **"first in time, first in right"** applies unless application of the recording act allows a *subsequent purchaser* to divest (take the property from) an earlier grantee.

   Example: Man conveyed land by quitclaim deed as a gift to Cousin, who did not record the deed or take possession. Six months later, Man (still in possession) conveyed the land by quitclaim deed as a gift to Friend. Friend is not a BFP because the deed was a gift (i.e., not a purchaser for value). Since Friend is not a BFP, the recording acts do not apply and the common law rule applies. Cousin takes because he was first in time. (The extraneous information about recording and possession are decoy ducks and are not relevant to solving the problem since the subsequent grantee did not take for value.)

2. Three types of recording acts.

a. **Pure notice statutes** (also called notice statutes):

The last BFP wins, so a **subsequent BFP prevails** over an earlier grantee that didn't record.

<u>Example</u>: On Jan. 10, Bank gave Man a $50,000 mortgage on his home. The mortgage was recorded on Jan. 18. On Jan 11, Man sold the home to Buyer. Neither party (Bank nor Buyer) knew of the other transaction. Buyer recorded her deed on Jan. 23. The recording act provides, "No conveyance or mortgage of real property shall be good against subsequent purchasers for value and without notice unless the same be recorded according to law." Buyer will prevail because Buyer was a BFP, and had no notice of the Bank mortgage *at the time* she took her interest. (Bank can sue Man personally.)

b. **Race-notice statutes:** A **subsequent BFP who records <u>first</u>** (wins the race) prevails over an earlier grantee who did not record first.

<u>Example</u>: On Jan. 10, Bank gave Man a $50,000 mortgage on his home. The mortgage was recorded on Jan. 18. On Jan 11, Man sold the home to Buyer. Neither party (Bank nor Buyer) knew of the other transaction. Buyer recorded her deed on Jan. 23. The recording act provides, "No unrecorded conveyance or mortgage of real property shall be good against subsequent purchasers for value and without notice, who shall <u>first</u> record." Bank will prevail because though Buyer was a BFP, she did not win the race to record first.

c. **Pure race statutes:** The first to record wins. This statute rewards the winner of the race to the recorder's office, regardless of if they are a BFP or have notice of the earlier interest. [This rule is rarely MBE tested.]

RECORDING ACTS DECODED

<u>MBE tip</u>: If the word "first" is in the statute, it is probably a **race-notice** recording act. If not, it is probably a **pure notice** recording act.

Type	Language Example	Who wins?
Pure Notice ¾ on MBE	"No conveyance or mortgage of real property shall be good against subsequent purchasers **for value and without notice** unless the same be **recorded** according to law."	Subsequent BFP
Race-Notice ¼ on MBE	"No unrecorded conveyance or mortgage of real property shall be good against subsequent purchasers **for value and without notice**, who shall **<u>FIRST</u> record.**"	Subsequent BFP *who records first* (wins race)

<u>Decoy tip</u>: The wrong decoy answer is often a correct analysis of the *other* recording act, so understand the differing language to identify each act.

3. Bona fide purchasers: A **BFP takes for value *<u>and</u>* without notice** of the prior interest. BFPs are protected by pure notice and race-notice recording acts.

a. **Take for value: Purchasers and mortgagees** take "for value" because they paid money for the property through a purchase price or by providing a loan secured by the property. The court won't look into the adequacy of the consideration; so long as it is more than nominal. **Gift recipients, heirs** (through intestacy), and **devisees** (through wills) **do not take "for value"** so they are **not BFPs.**

   1. **Exception—judgment leins: Judgment lien creditors are *not* protected** in the majority of jurisdictions, in contrast to mortgage lenders and other creditors. A judgment lien creditor occurs when a plaintiff who has obtained a money judgment in court files a judgment lien against the defendant's property.

      Example: A typical statute will state, "Any judgment properly filed shall, for ten years from the filing, be a lien on the real property then owned or subsequently acquired by any person against whom the judgment is rendered." This statute **does not allow protection under the recording act**; it simply **allows judgment liens to be filed**. Unless the statute in the question *specifically* indicates that judgment creditors are protected by the recording act, assume they are not.

   2. **Exception—void deeds: Void deeds** are not protected (e.g., a forged deed, or one issued to a dead grantee or non-formed corporation).

      Example: A woman owned several lots in a subdivision. She obtained a mortgage for $10,000 each on lots 1-5. After paying off the mortgage on lot 2, she altered the release to include lot 5 and recorded it. She then sold lot 5 to an innocent purchaser. The bank brought an action against the woman and the purchaser to set aside the sale. The forged deed (the release) was invalid, so the innocent purchaser is not protected and the bank will prevail. (The purchaser can sue the woman for breach of warranty.)

   3. **Exception—Shelter rule:** The **shelter rule allows anyone who took their interest from a BFP**, including donees/heirs/devisees, to **"stand in the shoes" of the BFP** and prevail in an action in which the transferor-BFP would have prevailed. This rule applies **even if the transferee,** or a subsequent transferee, **had actual knowledge** of the prior unrecorded interest.

      Example: Man conveyed land to Woman by warranty deed. Woman was a BFP, but she did not record or take possession. Man subsequently sold the same property to Neighbor, a BFP, by quitclaim deed. Neighbor recorded the deed and took possession. Neighbor subsequently sold the property to Friend, who knew about the earlier conveyance to Woman. Friend did not record, but took possession. Between Woman and Friend, Friend prevails because he bought the property from a BFP, Neighbor. Neighbor would prevail over Woman since he was a subsequent BFP and recorded his interest. The Shelter rule allows Friend to stand in the shoes of Neighbor and assert a claim for superior title even though Friend had actual knowledge of Woman's prior interest. (The facts about the type of deed, quitclaim or warranty, are irrelevant decoy ducks.)

b. **Without notice of the prior interest.** Notice can be provided three ways: **actual, inquiry,** or **record** (constructive) notice.

   1. **Actual notice** occurs when, prior to the time of closing, the buyer has **actual subjective knowledge** from any source of a prior, unrecorded interest.

   2. **Inquiry notice** occurs where the purchaser of a property (or mortgagee) is in possession of facts, or could make an inspection of the property, which would lead a **reasonable person to make further inquiry** as to ownership (e.g., **possession** of the premises by one who is not the record owner is common, or visible evidence of the existence of an easement such as a driveway to a neighbor's property). A mortgagee has the same

responsibility to make further inquiry as a human purchaser. **Notice is imputed** whether the purchaser makes the inquiry or not.

Example: Man owned a farm, which he conveyed to Son as a gift. Son did not record the quitclaim deed, but he took possession and began farming. Man subsequently sold the property by warranty deed to Doctor, who promptly recorded the deed and began removing timber from the land. The recording act provides, "No conveyance or mortgage of real property shall be good against subsequent purchasers for value and without notice unless the same be recorded according to law." Son will prevail. Though Doctor took for value, Son's *possession* of the farm put Doctor on inquiry notice, so he is not a BFP protected by the recording act. (Like most real property MBEs, there are a lot of decoy ducks here. The extraneous information about the types of deeds is irrelevant (i.e. ignore the quacking ducks). That there is a notice recording act is irrelevant since Doctor does not qualify as a BFP. It is also irrelevant that Son took by gift (thus not a BFP) since he is not the subsequent purchaser trying to utilize the recording act).

> **MBE tip:** Be alert for inquiry notice when there are facts in the question regarding who is in possession of the property. Possession by someone other than the record owner provides inquiry notice.

3. **Record** (constructive) **notice** occurs when the prior interest was **properly recorded within the chain of title,** such that one doing a title search of the indexes would find it. **Notice is imputed** whether the purchaser performs the title search or not.

   a. **Title search:** Depending on the jurisdiction, title search is done by grantor-grantee index or tract index: [Aside from a basic understanding, these rules are rarely MBE tested.]

      i. **Grantor-grantee index:** This index tracks property by the name of the grantor and grantee. One purchasing a property would look up the seller under the *grantee* index to ensure good title. Then they look up the seller in the *grantor* index to ensure no prior conveyances. Next, they go through the same process for all previous transactions.

      ii **Tract index:** One searches by the property, and all recorded interests are visible.

   b. **Exception—wild deeds: "wild deeds" do not provide constructive notice.** A wild deed is one that is recorded, but outside the chain of title, thus a BFP wouldn't be able to find it.

      Example: Owner sells his lot to Doctor. Doctor does not record. Doctor then sells the lot to Surgeon, and Surgeon records in the grantor-grantee index. If Owner subsequently sells the same lot to Architect, Architect does not have constructive notice of Surgeon's interest because Surgeon's recording is a "wild deed" and will not show up in the chain of title since Surgeon took her interest from Doctor, who did not record.

> **Memorization tip:** Remember **AIR** for the types of notice: **A**ctual, **I**nquiry, and **R**ecord.

4. **Exception—Shelter rule:** The Shelter rule may allow protection under the recording acts for one who takes from a BFP but has notice of a prior interest. See sec. I.G.3.a.*3* above.

4. Recording acts apply to every instrument by which an **interest in land** can be created, modified or recorded, including **deeds,** conveyances, **mortgages**, judgment-creditor liens (though they aren't protected in the majority of jurisdictions), life estates, restrictive covenants, easements, etc.

MBE tip: Recording act MBE Qs can be complicated and the sequence of events matters. Diagram out the parties and timeline to keep it straight.

Decoy tip: Extraneous facts are common decoys in recording act MBEs.
- **First grantee's BFP status is irrelevant.** The person first in time need not take for value (gifts are o.k.) and has the superior claim (because first in time) *unless* a ***subsequent*** **BFP** can use the recording act to take the property away.
- The text of the jurisdiction's recording act is often included in MBE Qs, but **the type of recording act is irrelevant unless the subsequent purchaser is a BFP** who qualifies to use the recording act to take the property away.
- Whether a deed is quitclaim or warranty is irrelevant to a recording act inquiry.

H. **Security interests in land:** Real property is often encumbered by a mortgage or other security interest. Security interests can be used to **finance** the initial purchase of property or to **borrow** money, using property already owned. A loan is **secured** when the property is collateral for the loan, which means the property is pledged as security to ensure repayment, and it will be forfeited in case of default. [Much of the mortgage rules are frequently MBE tested.]

1. **Types of security interests:** Security interests typically must satisfy the SOF. [Mortgage is the most frequently tested security interest on the MBE.]

MORTGAGES & FORECLOSURE DECODED

MBE tip: Mortgages and foreclosure are favorite MBE testing areas. This preview is intended to give you an idea of how mortgages/foreclosure works generally and to provide context for the rules that follow. Let's picture what's happening with an example:

Purchase: Buyer wants to buy a home, but does not have enough cash to buy it outright. Typically, if the person has a down payment (historically 10-20% of the purchase price) and good credit (a history of paying their bills responsibly), a bank lends them the remainder of the purchase price and the home is collateral for the loan. This means if the person doesn't make the mortgage payments (defaults on the loan), the bank can foreclose through the courts and take over ownership of the home. A typical home loan is repaid over 30 years and the interest rate (which is how the bank makes money on the transaction) varies depending on the economy and the type of loan. [For our example, Buyer's house costs $500,000 at purchase.] The loan used to *originally buy* a house gets special treatment and is aptly called a *purchase* money mortgage (PMM). [Here, Buyer had $100,000 cash for the down payment and has a purchase money mortgage for $400,000.]

Mortgages: Over time, property values usually increase and the home's market value exceeds the original purchase price, this is called the home's "equity." [Here, property values have gone up and Buyer's home market value raises to $650,000, which provides $150,000 in equity that lenders would be willing to loan against.] A homeowner can subsequently take out another loan(s), and use the property as collateral, meaning if the loan is defaulted on, that lender(s) also has the right to foreclose on the property. [Here, Buyer takes out a second loan with Lender for $40,000 to remodel the kitchen, so now Buyer has his original mortgage of $400,000 and a new second mortgage for $40,000. Both are tied to a house that is worth $650,000.] (People who inherit or are gifted property can similarly take out mortgages, but they would not have a PMM.)

Foreclosure: For foreclosure, mortgagees/creditors are given priority for repayment based on the date filed/recorded. PMM takes priority over all claims and a senior (earlier) creditor gets paid in full before a junior (subsequent) creditor receives anything. If Buyer stops paying *all* mortgages, all lenders will want to foreclose, but even if they didn't, all junior mortgagees would be joined in the action and a judge will order a foreclosure sale of the property. The proceeds from the sale will be distributed to the lenders in descending order of priority. [Here, Buyer loses their job and stops making payments on all mortgages. PMM institutes foreclosure proceedings, joining Lender. During the foreclosure sale, the house sells for $600,000. The first thing to be paid out of the $600,000 is $400,000 to PMM. Then, the second mortgage with Lender for $40,000 would be paid in full. The remainder of $160,000 would go back to the mortgagor, Buyer. *If home values had decreased instead,* and the house only sold for $425,000 at the foreclosure sale, PMM would be paid in full for $400,000 and Lender's junior interest mortgage for $40,000 would be paid the remaining sale proceeds of $25,000.]

Deficiency: A lender can get a deficiency judgment for the shortfall if the proceeds from a foreclosure sale are insufficient to cover the amount owed. A lender can sue the mortgagor *personally* for the deficiency after a judicial foreclosure sale, though some jurisdictions will not allow a deficiency against a PMM. [Here, if the house sold at foreclosure for $425,000, Lender only receives $25,000 on a $40,000 debt, leaving $15,000 unpaid. Lender could seek a deficiency judgment against Buyer for $15,000.]

a. **Mortgage:** A mortgage is a financing arrangement that **conveys a security interest in land** where the parties intend the land be collateral for the repayment of a monetary obligation the borrower owes the lender (creditor). The buyer and/or borrower is the **mortgagor**. The lender is the **mortgagee**.

  1. A mortgage consists of two documents:

    a. A **promissory note**, which is the **personal promise** from the purchaser to repay the loan and makes the borrower **personally liable** for loan repayment that is the basis of a **deficiency judgment**. [When MBE questions refer to a "note," they mean the promissory note.]

      i. A promissory note without a mortgage attached is an unsecured loan.

    b. The **mortgage** itself (which secures the note to the property as collateral for the mortgage holder).

  2. **Future advance mortgage:** A type of financing device where a clause is included that provides for the availability of funds in the future, which are used as needed (e.g., home equity loan, construction loan) and not fully disbursed at the loan closing.

  3. **Mortgage can secure the debt of another:** A person can grant a mortgage on their own property to secure the debt of another person (who made an *unsecured* personal promise to repay).

  Example: A sister takes out a loan for $20,000 and her brother secures that loan by putting the mortgage for that loan on his home. The brother's loan on his home is an acceptable form of security for his *sister's* loan.

b. **Deed of trust** is an arrangement similar to a mortgage, except the debtor is the trustor and the deed of trust is given to a third-party trustee. The lender is the beneficiary.

> Decoy tip: Deeds of trust are rarely MBE tested, but be careful because a "deed of trust" is a **financing arrangement** and not the same thing as a regular "deed" that conveys title.

c. **Installment land contract:** In this financing arrangement a buyer makes a down payment on property and pays off the balance to the **vendor** in installments. This is different than a mortgage because the **buyer does not receive the deed until the land is fully paid off.**

  1. **Forfeiture for default:** If the borrower defaults on payments, the property is forfeited back to the vendor (lender), who can keep all installment payments, which is a harsh result. Modernly, if the buyer has paid a substantial portion of the purchase price, regular foreclosure proceedings will be used.

d. **Equitable mortgage** (also called absolute deed) is created when an **absolute deed** to the property **is handed over to the lender as security** for a loan, and the lender promises (which may be oral or in writing) to **reconvey** the deed back to the borrower **once the loan is paid off**. Though the lender holds the actual deed, this is really a disguised mortgage and is treated like a mortgage. An equitable mortgage may not satisfy the SOF and will still be enforced.

Example: The owner of a home needed money. Lender agreed to loan Owner $60,000, but only if Owner conveyed the home to Lender outright by warranty deed. Lender *orally promised* to reconvey the home back to Owner once the loan was paid in full. This is an equitable mortgage. If Owner defaults on the loan, Lender can foreclose like a normal mortgage.

e. **Equitable vendor's lien** results by implication (rather than agreement) in the unpaid amount when a portion of the purchase price for a property is unpaid after the seller transfers title to the buyer.

Example: A buyer buys a home for $100,000 and pays the seller $95,000. The seller has an equitable vendor's lien for the unpaid $5000.

MORTGAGES SYNONYMS CHEAT SHEET	
Owes money	**Money is owed to**
Mortgagor Homeowner, Buyer Borrower	Mortgagee Bank, Lender Lienholder, Vendor
MBE tip: These terms are often used interchangeably.	
MBE tip: Remember, the MortgaGOR is the homeowNOR, if you tend to get the parties mixed up.	

2. **Mortgages: Rights of the mortgagor** (borrower)

   a. **Possession and title:** Mortgagor (borrower) has the right to possession of the property and title, unless a foreclosure occurs.

   b. **Transfer the property:** Mortgagor can transfer the property to another by gift, devise, or sale. Usually when a property has a mortgage, the mortgage is paid in full by the sale proceeds (the property is redeemed of the mortgage), but the property can also be sold without paying off the mortgage.

   c. **Sale** (or gift) **of mortgaged property:** The new owner will make the mortgage payments, but whether the new owner also has personal liability for the loan depends on if they take the property "subject to" the mortgage or they "assume" the mortgage. The distinction impacts deficiency judgments in foreclosure [which are heavily MBE tested].

      1. **Sale "subject to" the mortgage":** The buyer is **not *personally* liable** for paying the unpaid mortgage debt. If the buyer fails to make the mortgage payments, the property can be foreclosed, but the buyer won't be personally liable for any deficiency.

      2. **Assumption of mortgage:** The buyer agrees to be ***personally* liable** to the original mortgagor, and the mortgagee for repayment of the loan, including any deficiency in the event of foreclosure.

         a. **Acceptance of deed with an assumption clause** included (e.g., the buyer "assumes" the mortgage) constitutes an assumption, even if the buyer doesn't sign the deed.

         Example: Woman conveyed property to Friend "subject to an existing mortgage to the bank, which grantee assumes and agrees to pay." This language alone is sufficient to find Friend assumed the mortgage and has personal liability to the lender.

         b. **Suretyship:** When a grantee assumes the mortgage, the **original mortgagor is still secondarily liable** to the lender as surety (one taking responsibility the debt is repaid), absent a release of liability from the lender.

c. **Release of liability—original borrower:** The original mortgagor **remains personally liable** (because of the signed note providing personal liability for repayment) unless the lender provides a **release of liability**.

Example: Man borrowed money from Lender and mortgaged land he owned to secure repayment of the loan. Before the loan was paid off, Man conveyed the land to Investor, who expressly assumed the loan (which did not have a due-on-sale clause.) Investor defaulted on two payments and Lender notified Man and Investor of its intention to accelerate the loan (as allowed in the terms) if the default was not cured within 60 days. Neither paid, so Lender initiated foreclosure proceedings and the sale resulted in a deficiency. Even after Investor's mortgage assumption, Man remains liable as a surety (absent a release from the lender), so Lender can sue Man only for the deficiency *if* Investor is insolvent.

3. **Mortgages: Rights of the mortgagee (lender)**

   a. **Payment:** Mortgagee (lender) has right to payment on the loan. A failure to pay allows the mortgagee to foreclose on the property. See sec. I.H.6 below.

   b. **Enforce contract provisions** present in the mortgage agreement:

      1. **Acceleration clauses** require the mortgagor to **pay the loan off *in full* immediately** under stated conditions, such as missing payments.

      2. **Prepayment penalty clauses** and their associated fees are enforceable, though some states may not allow prepayment penalties.

      3. **Due on sale clauses** require a property owner who transfers ownership of the property (usually by the sale of the property to a new owner) **to pay the entire loan balance to the mortgagee in full**. This means the loan cannot be "assumed" and transferred to a new owner.

Decoy tip: A frequent decoy answer choice states that a due on sale clause is an unreasonable restraint on alienation, but they are reasonable and enforceable.

   c. **Transfer by mortgagee:** The mortgagee can transfer the loan to another mortgagee (lender), but the note and mortgage must pass to the same entity for the transfer to be deemed complete.

   d. **Recording:** Mortgagees can record their interest, which provides **notice** of the mortgage to potential buyers or other lenders for determining priority amongst lenders in the event of foreclosure.

   e. **Foreclosure in the event of default** since the mortgagee has a **lien on the property**, and the property is collateral for the loan. See sec. I.H.6. below.

4. **Mortgagee in possession** (MIP): All jurisdictions allow the mortgagee to take possession of the premises (to mitigate losses) **after default**, but **before foreclosure**, if the defaulting mortgagor **consents** or **abandons** the property. A mortgagee *may* also have the right to take possession, depending on the jurisdiction:

   a. **Lien Theory** (majority rule): The mortgagee holds a security interest only, so they **may not take possession** *before* foreclosure. [This is the default rule on the MBE unless instructed otherwise.]

   b. **Title Theory** (minority rule): The mortgagee **may take possession** *before* foreclosure **because** the mortgagee actually holds title until the loan has been paid or foreclosed.

1. **MIP duties** are similar to an actual owner. The MIP must maintain the property in reasonable condition and has the same tort liability as the actual owner. The MIP must credit any net rents received or profits earned against the mortgage debt.

c. **Intermediate theory:** Upon default, legal title shifts to the mortgagee, and they **may demand** possession. This rule is used in a few states and functions similar to title theory jurisdictions for MIP. [This rule is rarely MBE tested.]

<u>**Example**</u>: Owner of an orchard had a mortgage with Lender. Halfway through the growing season, Owner got sick and abandoned the orchard. Lender took over the harvesting operation, with the net proceeds being applied to payment of the mortgage debt. A business invitee was injured. In this jurisdiction, the *owner* of the premises would be liable for the business invitee's injury. Lender, as MIP, would be responsible for the injury in a title theory state (or intermediate theory) because the Lender is the titled owner.

5. **Discharge of the mortgage:**

a. **Paying the mortgage in full** discharges the mortgage and releases the mortgagor from liability.

b. **Deed of release:** Alternatively, the mortgagee may accept the deed (the mortgagor hands over the property—also called a **deed of release**) **in lieu of the mortgagee taking a foreclosure action,** which also serves to release the mortgagor's obligation on the mortgage. A deed of release transaction must be **reasonable and fair** under the circumstances. Mortgagor cannot be forced to release the deed through duress, undue influence, or unconscionable bargaining.

<u>**Example**</u>: Builder sold Buyer a new house. Buyer paid 10% and financed the rest with a PMM to Builder. A year later, Buyer missed several payments and was unable to pay anymore. Property values declined substantially that year. Builder suggested that Buyer deed the house back to him to settle all claims and avoid other costs and disadvantages with foreclosure. Buyer agreed. Builder now owns the house in fee simple (so the mortgage was discharged and Buyer is released from the mortgage obligations) because the transaction was reasonable and fair under the circumstances.

 6. **Foreclosure** is a process by which the **mortgagee may reach the land** in satisfaction of the debt if the mortgagor is in default on the loan.

a. **Procedure:** All states allow a judicial **sale**, where the property is sold at **auction** to satisfy the debt. Lenders may bid at the sale.

1. **Parties:** All **junior interests (mortgagees** and creditors) **must be joined** in the foreclosure action (they are necessary parties). After foreclosure, their interest is destroyed and will no longer attach to the property. However, failure to join preserves their interest, meaning their interest stays attached to the property and the foreclosure buyer takes the property "subject to" the non-joined junior mortgage/lien. (Though the buyer is not *personally* responsible to pay, nonpayment risks the property being foreclosed again.)

b. **Redemption:** When the entire mortgage is **paid off**, the property is "redeemed" from the mortgage. This can arise in foreclosure.

1. **Equitable redemption** allows the mortgagor, after going into default but ***before* the foreclosure sale**, the **right** to redeem the mortgage (pay off the amount due to the mortgagee) and pull the property out of foreclosure.

a. **Acceleration clause** will require the mortgagor to **pay in full** the entire mortgage in the event of default.

b. **Right to redeem cannot be waived in the mortgage itself.** This is known as "clogging the equity of redemption" and is not allowed.

2. **Statutory redemption:** Some states allow **statutory redemption,** which allows the mortgagor a **fixed period of time *after* foreclosure** (usually 6 months to 1 year) to redeem (pay off) the amount due on the mortgage.

Example: Man owned a home with a mortgage through Bank. Man defaulted and Bank foreclosed. Bank bought the property at a proper judicial foreclosure sale. Shortly after, Man inherited money and wished to repurchase the home. *If* the man prevails to recover the property, it will be because the jurisdiction allows a statutory right of redemption (which is not the rule in all jurisdictions).

3. **No partial redemption. *Entire* mortgage must be paid.** A fractional owner (e.g., a joint tenant) cannot pay off only their own fractional portion of the mortgage and have that portion be redeemed.

Example: A brother and sister own a property as joint tenants. Their joint mortgage went into foreclosure. The sister paid off her half of the mortgage in full. The mortgage is not redeemed because the brother's half of the mortgage is still unpaid.

c. Priority: After the land is sold at a foreclosure sale, the **proceeds** will be used to **satisfy the debt(s)** secured by the property based on priority of the interest holder. Priority is primarily determined by **chronology** based on the time of recording, with a few exceptions.

1. **Order of payment from foreclosure proceeds** with proceeds distributed in descending order or priority, with **each mortgagee/ lienholder satisfied in *full*** before a lower priority creditor takes anything:

a. Fees from **attorneys/trustees;**

b. Purchase money mortgage; **(PMM) or secured senior interests;**

c. **Secured junior interests;**

d. **Unsecured interests;**

e. **Any surplus balance to mortgagor.**

2. **Purchase money mortgage (PMM)** is a mortgage given to secure a loan that enables the debtor to **originally purchase** the property. A third-party lender can hold a PMM or the vendor (seller) can hold a PMM for a portion of the purchase price unpaid at closing. A **PMM receives priority** over non-PMM mortgages and preexisting judgment creditors. A PMM is paid first, even if it is not recorded. [This rule is heavily MBE tested.]

Example: To buy a new home, Buyer had 5% in cash for a down payment, borrowed 80% of the purchase price from Bank, and Seller personally financed 15%. Buyer gave Seller a promissory note for the 15% loan, but did not execute a mortgage on that loan. Bank knew of the loan and promissory note to Seller. Buyer executed a mortgage with Bank. If Buyer defaults, Bank has priority. Though both loans were made at the same time, Bank has a purchase money mortgage, which takes priority over this unsecured loan with Seller.

Example: Man has an outstanding judgment lien for $10,000. Two years later Man bought a home, borrowing $180,000 from Bank. The bank loan was secured by a mortgage. Immediately after closing, the judgment was recorded first, and the mortgage recorded second. In a foreclosure proceeding, despite recording second, the mortgage gets first priority because it is a PMM (and secured).

a. **Deficiency judgment for PMM:** Some jurisdictions do not allow a deficiency judgment for a PMM against the debtor if the funds from foreclosure are insufficient to cover the outstanding balance.

b. **Two PMM** (one vendor and one third party): Where both the vendor (seller) and third party (bank) have PMM, the **vendor PMM takes priority.**

c. **Two third party PMM:** Chronological order determines priority.

3. **Secured debts** are those where the property is pledged as collateral for repayment (e.g. mortgage). Unsecured debts/interests are those where the property is not pledged as collateral.

a. **Future advances clause mortgages** (also known as lines of credit) date back to the recording date of the original mortgage for purposes of foreclosure priority, even though the funds are distributed later, effectively allowing the mortgagee to gain priority over other lenders.

b. **Changes in priority:**

i. **Loan modification** (an agreement to change the terms of an existing loan) does not change priority of the original loan *if* the modification does not make the loan more burdensome (e.g., a reduction in the interest rate or payment amount would not be more burdensome). *However*, if the modification makes the loan more burdensome (e.g., increase in the interest rate) then the mortgage date would switch to the date of the modification and the senior mortgage could lose priority to a junior mortgage.

ii. **Subordination agreement:** A mortgagee may agree to subordinate their mortgage to a junior mortgagee so they have a lower priority in foreclosure than they would otherwise enjoy.

4. **Judgment lien** is unsecured and the lien priority is measured from the date the lien is **filed**, not when the debt accrued.

Example: A man owned a house and incurred $10,000 in credit card debt, but failed to pay. A statute in the jurisdiction provides, "Any judgment properly filed shall, for 10 years from filing, be a lien on the real property then owned or subsequently acquired by any person against whom the judgment is rendered." The creditor could place a lien on the man's property, and the date for priority would be the date the lien was filed, not the date the debt was incurred.

> **MBE tip:** The text of the statute that permits a judgment lien in the jurisdiction is often included in an MBE question, as in the example above. When you see a statute like this, it is a tip off that a judgment lien issue is involved.

a. **Execute the judgment**: A **creditor** may obtain a writ of execution to force a property sale, which is **similar to a foreclosure action**.

b. **Joint tenancy severance:** Once a judgment is **executed**, the joint tenancy is severed. Filing the judgment alone does not sever a joint tenancy.

Example: A mother died testate and devised her farm to her son and daughter as joint tenants with right of survivorship. The son defaulted on a personal loan and his creditor obtained a judgment for $10,000 against him, and promptly filed the judgment. A statute provides, "Any judgment properly filed shall, for 10 years from filing, be a lien on the real property then owned by any person against whom judgment is rendered." Later the son died. The creditor cannot enforce its judgment against the farm because filing the judgment without an execution did not sever the joint tenancy and now the daughter owns the entire farm through the right of survivorship.

5. **No foreclosure is binding on a senior interest holder.** Thus, if a *junior* mortgagee (one lower in priority) forecloses, the foreclosure will not terminate any interests that are *senior* (higher in priority) to the mortgage being foreclosed.

   Example: A mortgagor has a 1st, 2nd and 3rd mortgage and stops paying on only the 2nd, so the 2nd starts a foreclosure proceeding, joining 1 and 3. As a senior mortgagee, the 1st can opt to get dismissed. Thus, at the foreclosure sale, the new owner will take the property subject to the 1st mortgage (they will need to continue making the 1st mortgage payments or risk foreclosure, so the property will sell for a lower price because the 1st mortgage is still attached to the property). The funds from the sale will be distributed to satisfy the 2nd, then to the 3rd and then the owner (if anything is left) with the 1st mortgage transferring to the new owner.

d. **Deficiency:** When the proceeds from a foreclosure sale are **insufficient to cover the amount owed**, a lender can get a **deficiency judgment** for the **shortfall**, though some states limit recovery to the difference between the debt and the fair market value when the fair market value is higher than the foreclosure price.

1. **Personal liability:** A lender can only sue the original mortgagor **personally** for the deficiency when there was a **judicial foreclosure.**

2. **Subsequent purchaser liability:** A subsequent purchaser must have **"assumed" the mortgage** to have **personal liability**. If a subsequent purchaser took the home "subject to" the mortgage, the subsequent purchaser does not have personal liability for any deficiency.

3. **Anti-deficiency statutes** limit a lender to receiving **no more than the value owed on the loan.** Once *all* debts have been paid in full with the proceeds of the foreclosure sale, any excess is returned to the mortgagor. [Use this rule on the MBE unless told otherwise.]

> **MBE tip:** The default rule is that deficiency judgments are allowed and an anti-deficiency statute is in place. The question may state, "There are no special statutes in the jurisdiction regarding deficiency…" to indicate the default rules apply.

4. **Surplus:** Once all debts have been paid in full, any surplus is returned to the mortgagor.

   Example: Man had a mortgage with Bank on a building. Man conveyed the building to Woman, who took subject to the mortgage, but did not record. After several years, Woman defaulted and Bank foreclosed. The building sold for less than the outstanding mortgage balance at the foreclosure sale. Bank can collect the deficiency from Man (he remains personally liable) but not from Woman, since she did not assume the mortgage. (The failure to record is irrelevant.)

e. **Marshaling:** In a foreclosure, when a mortgagee has extended a loan on several parcels, the holder of a junior interest may ask the court to marshal the assets. This means the foreclosing mortgagee must first foreclose on parcels without junior interests.

> **Decoy tip:** Marshaling is most often used as a decoy answer.

II. ESTATES IN LAND

Estates in land are **possessory interests in land**. They can be presently possessory, or the interest may become possessory in the future (future interests).

A. **Present possessory estates** are also known as freehold estates.

1. **Fee simple absolute (FSA)** conveys absolute ownership of potentially infinite duration. It is the most unrestricted and longest estate (e.g., "to A" or "to A and his heirs").

   a. **Fully alienable** and the holder may pass by will (devise), intestacy (descent), and is transferable inter vivos.

Decoy tip: The language to create a fee simple absolute, "To A and his heirs," means that A gets a fee simple absolute and the "heirs" get nothing. The language "heirs and assigns," is used traditionally to indicate the interest is fully devisable, descendible, transferable inter vivos, etc.

2. **Defeasible fees: A fee simple defeasible** has the *potential* to run indefinitely, however, the property is subject to a limitation and can terminate upon the happening of a stated limiting event.

   There are three types [though MBEs may simply refer to these more generally as a "defeasible fee" rather than by their names]:

   a. **Fee simple determinable (FSD)** is a fee simple estate that upon the happening of a stated event ***automatically*** terminates and the property reverts back to ***grantor*** (identified as O).

      1. **Possibility of reverter** is the future interest the **grantor retains**.

      2. **Fully alienable:** In most jurisdictions the holder may pass by will (devise), intestacy (descent), and is transferable inter vivos.

      3. **Created by words of duration** such as "so long as," "during," "while," "until," or "unless."

      Example: Grantor conveys a tract of land to his church by deed, which states, "to church, so long as the premises are used for church purposes." Though not stated, the grantor (O) has a possibility of reverter.

   b. **Fee simple subject to condition subsequent (FSSCS)** has the potential to terminate an estate at the occurrence of a stated event and property reverts back to the grantor, but the termination is ***not automatic.***

      1. **Right of reentry** is the future interest the **grantor retains**, but it is not automatic and must be exercised to have effect.

      2. **Alienability:** In most jurisdictions the holder may pass by will (devise) and intestacy (descent), but it is **not** transferable inter vivos.

      3. **Created by words that carve out a right of reentry** in the grantor and includes conditional language such as "but if," "provided that," or "upon the condition that" to identify the conditional event.

      4. **Must be affirmatively exercised** (e.g., bringing an action to recover possession) since it is not automatic.

Example: O grants "To A, provided that A uses the property as an art gallery." Should A stop using the property for an art gallery, O has a right to re-enter, but until he does, the property remains with A.

c. **Fee simple subject to an executory interest (FSSEI)** is a fee simple estate that upon the happening of a stated event ***automatically*** terminates and the estate then *passes to a **third person*** rather than reverting to the grantor.

   1. **Executory interest** is the future interest the **third party holds.**

   2. **Fully alienable:** In most jurisdictions the holder may pass by will (devise), intestacy (descent), and is transferable inter vivos.

   3. **Created by words of duration** such as "so long as," "during," "while," "until," or "unless" similar to a fee simple determinable. It can also be **created by words that carve out a right of reentry** and includes conditional language such as "but if," "provided that," or "upon the condition that" to identify the conditional event similar to a fee simple subject to a condition subsequent. However, in both cases, the **future interest goes to a third party**, not back to the grantor.

   4. **RAP** (rule against perpetuities) **applies** to executory interests.

   Example: "To A, but if A dies without children surviving him, then to B." Here, the stated event is that A dies without having any children survive him. If that happens, the estate automatically passes to B (the holder of the executory interest). RAP applies to executory interests, but this interest does not violate the RAP because we will know at A's death if he has any surviving children.

d. **Contrast defeasible fees with mere contract conditions** or obligations:

   Example (contract condition only): Grantor conveys a tract of land by deed, which states, "to buyer, subject to the understanding that within one year from the date of the instrument, said grantee shall construct and thereafter maintain and operate on said premises a public health center." This is merely a contractual obligation (a condition). To qualify as a defeasible fee the language must be specific, such as "to buyer so long as the premises are used..." **When the language is not sufficiently specific** (like the language "subject to the understanding" used here), **courts will favor a fee simple absolute over a defeasible fee** as courts disfavor restraints on alienation.

   Example (no contract condition): Grantor conveys a tract of land by deed, which states, "to church for purpose of erecting a church building thereon." This language is too vague and does not provide a condition on the use of the land and the church holds in fee simple.

e. **Rights and obligations:** The owner of a defeasible fee has the same rights and obligations as that of a fee simple absolute owner, unless the grant or devise itself limits their use.

   Example: A defeasible fee holder has exclusive use and possession of the land, including the right to remove minerals or resources.

3. **Fee tail** allows an owner of land to ensure that the property remains within the family (e.g., to "heirs of the body"). It lasts only as long as there are lineal blood descendants of the grantee. Modernly, it is virtually abolished. [This rule is rarely MBE tested.]

4. **Life estate** is a possessory interest that only lasts for the lifetime of a named person. It is generally neither devisable (will) nor descendible (intestacy) because it only lasts for the life of the named person.

   a. **Future interest:** At the end of the life estate holder's lifetime, it can revert to the grantor, or go to a third party.

1. **Reversion** is the future interest if retained by the **grantor** (e.g., "to A for life"). Though not stated, this leaves the grantor with a reversion.
2. **Remainder** is the future interest if held by a **third party** (the remainderman) (e.g., "to A for life, then to B").

b. Regular life estate: A regular life estate lasts for the lifetime of the named person (the measuring life).

<u>**Example**</u>: "To any wife who survives me with the remainder to such of my children as are living at her death." Note: the words "life estate" aren't used, but the reference to a remainder provides the clue it is a life estate.

c. Life estate pur autre vie is a life estate for the lifetime of an identified third party, who is the measuring life (not the possessing life tenant).

<u>**Example**</u>: "To A for the life of B."

1. **Lapse**: If the measuring life ends before the gift takes effect, the interest to the life estate holder **lapses** (i.e., is extinguished) before taking effect, and the future interest holder will take.

   <u>**Example:**</u> Testator's will devises a life estate pur autre vie, "To A for the life of B." If measuring life B dies before Testator, the interest lapses.

d. Life estate defeasible: A life estate may be defeasible like a fee simple such that the life estate ends before the life tenant dies if the limiting event occurs.

<u>**Example**</u>: A landowner died, devising his land "to wife for life or until remarriage, then to my daughter." Wife has a determinable life estate, which can be cut short by her own remarriage. Daughter has a vested remainder (on the life estate) and a simultaneous executory interest (on the event of wife's remarriage, which would cut short wife's life estate).

 **e. Rights and duties of a life tenant**

1. **Right to convey:** A life estate holder may convey (lease, sell or mortgage) their interest, but not for an estate greater than what is held, so for a time no longer than the lifetime of the measuring life.
2. **Right to all ordinary uses and profits from the land**, including the right to possession, the ability to lease out the premises and collect rents.
   a. **Exception: No natural resource depletion (exploitation) allowed** (it is considered voluntary waste, see below). Unlike the holder of a fee, a life estate holder **may not remove minerals** and other resources that deplete the land, with the exception they may continue to mine an already open mine (called the "open mines" doctrine).
3. **Duty to pay expenses** [MBE favorite testing area.]
   a. **Expenses a life tenant must pay** (called carrying costs):
      i. **Current operating expenses**, which includes maintenance-type repairs and taxes.
      ii. **Interest on a mortgage:** When there is a mortgage on the property, the life estate holder is responsible for the interest payments, while the remainderman is solely liable for the principal.

      <u>**Example**</u>: Owner conveyed home to Wife, for life, remainder to Daughter. The home mortgage is $20,000, with monthly payments comprised on principal and interest. Wife must pay the portion of the monthly mortgage payment

that represents interest (while Daughter is responsible for paying the mortgage principal part of the loan).

b. **Limitation on out-of-pocket expenses:** A life tenant must only pay the expenses above *to the extent* the life tenant either **received income generated from the property** (e.g., rents), ***or*** to the extent of the **property's fair rental value *if*** the life tenant **occupies** the property. Thus, there is **no personal liability** beyond the net financial benefits received (e.g., if the land is vacant, the future interest holder must pay all expenses).

c. **Consequence for failure to pay:** Failure to pay is considered committing **permissive waste**. If the mortgage is not paid, foreclosure is possible. If the remainderman pays the life tenant's expenses to avoid foreclosure, they can obtain a judgment against the life tenant for reimbursement.

4. **Duty not to commit waste:** A tenant (including a life tenant) has duty to avoid committing waste. The tenant cannot impair the value of the property or damage leased premises without repair. Reasonable wear and tear is acceptable. There are three types of waste:

a. **Voluntary (or affirmative) waste** occurs when a tenant engages in conduct, intentionally or negligently, that causes a **decrease in the value** of the premises. This includes a prohibition on exploiting minerals (e.g., removing gravel is waste).

i. **Exception: Exploitation of minerals, oil, and timber** is permitted if such use was authorized by the grantor, was in effect at the time the tenancy began ("open mines" doctrine), or is necessary to maintain the property.

b. **Permissive waste** occurs when the tenant **neglects** the property or fails to reasonably protect it, and it falls into disrepair.

c. **Ameliorative waste** occurs when a tenant makes **substantial alterations** to the property **that *improves* the value** of the premises. The tenant must restore the premises to the original condition.

i. **A life tenant may demolish** and rebuild a better building on the property when a **substantial and permanent neighborhood change** makes it **necessary** to continue **reasonable use** of the property, so long as the property value is not diminished.

Example (not necessary): Replacing a one-story mansion with a 13-story apartment building is not necessary to continue reasonable use of the property, even if the mansion was expensive to maintain. If the tenant made this change, the tenant would be required to restore the premises to the original condition.

5. **Duty not to remove fixtures.** Fixtures rules also apply to life tenants. See sec. V.

LIFE TENANTS CHEAT SHEET	
Life Tenant (LT) Rights & Duties	**Remainderman (R) Rights & Duties**
◆ Right to convey ◆ Right to ordinary use and profit Except: No resource depletion	◆ Right to convey
Source of funds: ◆ Only from net benefit (net rental benefit if leasing premises, or fair rental value if occupying) ◆ No personal liability for shortfall **Duty to pay**: ◆ Current operating expenses-repairs & taxes ◆ Mortgage *interest*	**Source of funds**:: ◆ R also has no personal liability to pay, but if the taxes or mortgage are unpaid, R stands to lose the property through foreclosure. **Duty to pay**: ◆ Operating expenses in excess of life tenant share ◆ Mortgage *principal*
◆ Duty: not to commit waste	
◆ Duty: not to remove fixtures	
MBE tip: It is sufficient to understand that mortgage expenses are shared between the life tenant and remainderman. You won't be asked to make calculations.	

B. **Future interests** follow a presently possessory estate on the same property and offer the potential for a future interest in that estate. Future interests can follow the present possessory interests of a life estate or the defeasible fess of a fee simple defeasible (FSD, FSSCS, FSSEI).

> **MBE tip:** Some future interests are subject to the rule against perpetuities (RAP), which is covered in detail in sec. II.D.

1. **Future interest retained by transferor** (grantor, also called "O" in examples).

   a. **Possibility of reverter** follows a fee simple determinable and is held by the grantor. See sec. II.A.2.a. above.

   Example: A man conveyed a tract of land, "to the school district, so long as used for school purposes." This is a fee simple determinable. Should the school district stop using the property for school purposes, the land will *automatically* revert back to the man. The possibility of reverter is inheritable, so if the man was no longer living at the time the property was no longer used for school purposes, it would pass through his will, or if he had no will, to his heirs through intestacy. (The man could have also conveyed the possibility of reverter inter vivos.)

   b. **Right of reentry** follows a fee simple subject to a condition subsequent and is held by the **grantor**. See sec. II.A.2.b. above.

   c. **Reversion**, is held by the **grantor,** and is created when the holder of an estate transfers to another something *less than* the entire estate, such as a **life estate** or a lease for term of years, and retains a future interest for themself (e.g., O grants "To A for life" and the interest left after A's death is the reversion in grantor). See sec. II.A.4. above.

      1. **Reversions are completely alienable** and may pass by will (devise), intestacy (descent), and is transferable intervivos.

2. **Remainder** follows a **life estate** and is held by a **third party** (not the grantor). It is **expressly created in the same instrument** that creates the possessory interest and only becomes possessory upon the expiration of a prior possessory estate of known fixed duration (e.g., O grants "To A for life, then to B." B has a remainder interest that becomes possessory at A's death.). Remainders can be vested or contingent.

   a. **Fully alienable:** In most jurisdictions the holder of a remainder may pass by will (devise), intestacy (descent), and it is transferable inter vivos.

   b. **Vested remainder** is one created in a born, ascertained person, and that is not subject to a condition precedent, which means no condition must be met before the interest becomes possessory (e.g., O grants "To A for life, then to B." B's remainder is vested).

      1. **Rule against perpetuities (RAP) does not apply** to fully vested remainders. (But see vested remainders subject to open, below.)

   c. **Vested remainder subject to open (class gifts)**—also called vested subject to partial divestment or partial defeasance. The remainder is vested in one or more ascertainable people, but with the possibility that more people will be added to the class.

> <u>MBE tip</u>: The MBE questions and bar prep companies often use different language for the same concept. So if you see vested remainder subject to open, or vested remainder subject to partial divestment, or vested remainder subject to partial defeasance—they all mean the same thing (in fact the word "defeasance" implies open).

   <u>Example</u>: A testator devised his farm to, "my son for life, then to my son's children and their heirs and assigns." (Analyze future interests questions clause by clause.) The son has a life estate. The son has two adult children. The remainder to the son's children is a vested remainder subject to open (partial divestment/defeasance) because the son could have more children enter the class and the two existing children would have to share the farm with them. At the son's death, the class would close since he could not have any more children to enter the class.

      1. **RAP applies to vested remainder subject to open** (unlike other vested remainders).

         a. **Class gift transfer limitations:** If the **RAP voids a transfer to any member** of the class, then the **entire gift fails** and the transfer is void as to all class members, even members whose interests already vested.

         b. **Except: Rule of convenience** will **allow the gift to stand** as to any member of the class who is alive at the time the gift is created and could thus call for a distribution of their share.

> <u>MBE tip</u>: If a class can obtain new members after the testator's death, RAP may be violated (because it is possible the new member's interest may not vest within 21 years of the measuring life's death).

      2. **Title is not marketable** where there are outstanding interests in unborn children.

   d. **Contingent remainder** is one created in an **unborn or unascertained** person, or one that is **subject to a condition precedent,** or both.

      1. **RAP applies** to contingent remainders.

      2. **Unborn:** A remainder is created in the "Children of A," but A has no children at the time of the conveyance.

Example: A man wants to give his ranch to his descendants. He has one son and one grandchild, who is childless. The grandchild wants to be skipped in the disposition. The man conveys the ranch "to son for life, remainder to grandchild's children in fee simple." This is a contingent remainder, with the grant to the grandchild's children (who do not yet exist) contingent on being born.

3. **Unascertained:** A remainder is created in "A's oldest surviving child," which cannot be determined until A's death.

   a. **Time to vest:** Once A dies, the interest will vest since A's oldest surviving child can then be determined.

4. **Subject to a condition precedent:** Some condition or event must occur before the remainder can become possessory.

   Example: A remainder is created in "B, if B has married at the time of A's (the life tenant) death." A has a life estate, B has a contingent remainder, and O retains a reversion which will take effect if B has not married by A's death.

5. **Destructibility of contingent remainders:** At common law, unless a contingent remainder vests *before* the termination of the preceding estate, it is destroyed. **Modernly,** the **rule is mostly abolished**, so the remainderman's interest would be converted to a springing executory interest. See II.B.3.b. below.

e. **Alternative contingent remainder** occurs where both contingent parties have the capacity to take over and it pivots on the same condition (e.g., "to A for life, then to B and his heirs if B marries C, otherwise to D").

3. **Executory interest** is an interest in favor of a future grantee and follows a fee simple subject to an executory interest. See sec. II.A.2.c. There are two types:

   a. **Shifting executory interest** cuts short the interest of the prior interest holder and is created in the same conveyance. It **shifts from one interest holder to another interest holder.**

   Example: O, who owns Blackacre, conveys "to A and her heirs, but if the premises are ever used for a purpose other than a church, then to B and his heirs." This is a fee simple subject to an executory interest, and is a shifting executory interest in fee simple in B. If A or her heirs fail to use the property for a church, Blackacre will shift over to B.

   b. **Springing executory interest** springs from the **grantor's possession** and becomes possessory in another at some point in the future. It **springs from the grantor to another** interest holder. It can happen two ways: (1) It can spring from the **owner's interest** to become possessory in another interest holder, or (2) It follows a **gap in possession** in which the owner has a reversion.

   Example (spring from grantor to another): A man conveys a farm to, "my son, his heirs and assigns, upon the condition precedent that he earn a college degree by the time he reaches the age of 30." The father has a fee simple subject to an executory interest and the son has a springing executory interest because it divests (cuts short) the estate of the father.

   Example (gap in possession): O conveys his house "To A for life, and five years after A's death to B." A has a life estate, O has a reversion (for the gap), and B has a springing executory interest.

> **MBE tip:** Don't forget about the RAP with executory interests. About 75% of executory interest questions violate the RAP (typically because there was no time limit imposed on the vesting of the executory interest.)

FUTURE INTERESTS DECODED

It's all about decoding the language...

Present Possessory Estate	**Language used to create** (... is the stated event)	**Future Interest** Devisable (will), descendible (intestacy) & transfer inter vivos	**FI** in O	**FI** in 3rd party
Fee simple absolute	"To A" "To A and his heirs"			
Fee simple determinable	Durational language "To A so long as..." "To A during..." "To A while..."	Possibility of reverter (*automatic forfeiture)	X	
Fee simple subject to a condition subsequent	"To A upon condition ..." "To A provided that..." "To A, but if..." And, right of reentry language	Right of reentry (* not automatic, must exercise or it's waived) (Not transferable inter vivos)	X	
Fee simple subject to an executory interest	"To A so long as X. If not, to B" "To A, but if X occurs, to B"	Executory Interest RAP (***shifting*** 3P (A) to 3P (B)) Upon event, A's interest is cut short & interest shifts from 3P interest holder (A) to 3P (B)		X
RAP applies	"To A when and if A marries B"	Executory Interest RAP (***springing*** out of O to 3P) Upon event, 3P takes from O		X
	"To A for life, & X years after A dies, to B"	Executory Interest RAP (***springing from gap*** in possession) O has reversion interest during gap & B has executory interest	X	X
Life estate	"To A for life"	Reversion	X	
Life estate defeasible RAP may apply	"To A for life, then to C" "To A for life, then to B & heirs, but if...then to B immediately"	Remainder can be ◆ Vested: born, ascertained, or ◆ Vested subject to open RAP ◆ Contingent RAP: unborn, unascertained or subj. to condition precedent		X
Life estate pur autre vie	"To A for the life of B"	Reversion	X	
Life estate pur autre vie defeasible	"To A for the life of B, then to C"	Remainder (see above)		X

MBE tip: To solve future interest problems, analyze them sequentially, clause by clause. If you are struggling with classifying future interests, remember a third-party transferee can only obtain two types of future interests: (1) a remainder (at the natural end of a life estate), or (2) an executory interest, which does not occur at the natural termination of the preceding estate—rather, it cuts short, or divests the preceding estate.

Decoy tip: If a decedent has a valid will, it doesn't matter who their surviving heirs are at the time of death. The devisees specified under the will take, not the heirs.

C. **Potential restraints on alienation**

1. **Absolute restraints on alienation are void**, such as a condition that a property may never be sold, or not be sold for a lengthy time period, such as 10 years (e.g., "to A, but A may never convey to a third party").

   Example: A woman acquired land by a deed "to [the woman], her heirs and assigns, provided, however, that said grantee may not transfer any interest in the land for 10 years from the date of this instrument." This restraint on alienation is void.

2. **Options and right of first refusal**

   a. A **purchase option** gives the holder a right to purchase specific property for a set period of time at a stated price. Typically, the landowner retains the payments for the purchase option whether the holder purchases the property or not. It can also be attached to a lease. Requirements:

      1. **SOF** requires **a writing** (because it is an interest in land).

      2. **Land description** sufficient to identify the land.

      3. **Terms** for exercising the purchase option, including the **time period** the option is available and the **price**.

      4. **RAP does not apply** to purchase options as part of a lease (but it does apply to options "in gross," below).

      Example: Tenant is leasing Blackacre. In exchange for $5000, Tenant (the option holder) has the right to purchase Blackacre for $100,000 and the option is open for 3 months.

   b. **Option in gross** means the holder of the **purchase option** (a right to purchase specific property for a set period of time at a stated price) does not have any other interest in the land that is the subject of the option.

      Example: Owner of a farm has a cousin who has always loved her farm. In a duly executed instrument, Owner grants Cousin the right, upon Owner's death, to purchase the farm from her estate at market value, if exercised within 120 days of her death. Cousin has an option in gross because Cousin has no other interest in the land.

      1. **RAP applies to options in gross.**

      Example (No RAP violation): Owner of a farm has a cousin who has always loved her farm. In a duly executed instrument, Owner grants Cousin the right, upon Owner's death, to purchase the farm from her estate at market value, if exercised within 120 days of her death. Cousin's option in gross does not violate the RAP because within 120 days of the death of the life in being (Owner) we will know if Cousin will exercise her option.

      Example (RAP violation): Holder has an option to purchase a particular piece of land with the option period (the period during which Holder may purchase the land) set to begin when the city acquires rights-of-way to build a proposed highway. Holder assigned his rights to purchase the land to Assignee. This violates the RAP because the option could conceivably be exercised by Assignee more than 21 years after the death of the life in being (Holder) at the creation of the option. This could happen if more than 21 years after Holder's death the city finally obtained the rights-of-way to build the highway, triggering the option to purchase the land.

   c. **Right of first refusal:** Allows the holder the opportunity to acquire property prior to its sale (transfer) to another. They are allowed if reasonable.

      1. **RAP may apply:** Rights of first refusal are **presumed to be personal** to the holder and **not assignable** and thus, usually the RAP does not apply. But if there is no time limit and it is assignable, then it can violate the RAP.

D. Rule against perpetuities (RAP):

The rule against perpetuities provides that "no interest is good unless it must vest, if at all, not later than 21 years after some life in being at the creation of the interest." The idea of RAP is that we want certainty in land ownership, so we don't want people to hold future interests allowing them to reach out and divest someone of their property too far into the future.

> MBE tip: Though the majority of states have adopted the **Uniform Statutory RAP** (which uses a "wait and see" approach and adds a 90-year period,) and some states have repealed the RAP all together, the MBE default rule is the common law RAP.

1. **RAP only applies to** (the top three are the most commonly MBE tested):
   a. **Contingent remainders.** See sec. II.B.2.d.
   b. **Vested remainder subject to open—class gifts.** See sec. II.B.2.c.*1*.
   c. **Executory interests.** See sec. II.B.3.
   d. **Purchase options "in gross"** (of land, not connected with a lease) that extend indefinitely into the future. Applies only in some jurisdictions. See sec. II.C.2.b.).

      Example: "The premises shall be solely used for residential purposes, and if not, the landowner, his heirs and assigns, shall have a right to repurchase the premises for $1,000." Since the triggering event could happen indefinitely in the future, this violates the RAP.
   e. **Right of first refusal** to purchase or re-purchase land that extends indefinitely into the future. Applies only in some jurisdictions. See sec. II.C.2.c.

      Example: "In the event the larger tract of land I own is ever for sale, I will notify grantee in writing, and the grantee shall have the right to purchase the larger tract at fair market value." Since the triggering even could happen indefinitely in the future, this violates the RAP.
   f. **Powers of appointment** that extend indefinitely into the future. See sec. I.D.4., I.E.4.
   g. **Private trusts,** which includes people who will be born in several generations. See sec. I.E.1.
2. **Measuring life:** The measuring life (or life in being) is typically one or more persons who are identifiable and in existence at the time the conveyance is created. These are the people mentioned in the conveyance.
3. **Triggering event** is the event by which an interest must vest or fail.
4. **Analyze all the possibilities** of what could possibly happen if the triggering event is postponed 21 years (plus gestation) after the measuring lives in being are dead and assess each clause. A RAP violation exists for any event that can take place indefinitely in the future (beyond the 21 years after the death of a measuring life). Consider all the possible scenarios, including the following:
   a. **Fertile octogenarian:** There is a conclusive presumption that a person of any age or physical condition is capable of having children.
   b. **Unborn widow:** Since it cannot be determined who someone's widow (or widower) is until that person's death, gifts to a widow's *children* can (but do not necessarily) violate RAP. It is triggered when testator devises consecutive life estates, first to the child, then to the child's spouse (the potential unborn widow).

5. **RAP violations are stricken:** Strike out an interest that violates RAP. With that provision removed, **reclassify what remains of the interest.**

RAP DECODED

Five-steps to analyze RAP:

1. **Classify the future interests—RAP only applies to:**
   - ◇ Executory interests
   - ◇ Contingent remainders
   - ◇ Class gifts (vested remainder subject to open)
   - ◇ Purchase options "in gross"
   - ◇ Right of first refusal to purchase or re-purchase land (sometimes)
   - ◇ Powers of appointment
2. Identify the **measuring life in being**.
3. Identify the **triggering event** (by when an interest must vest or fail).
4. **Analyze the possibilities** (postpone the triggering event 21 years after the lives in being are dead and assess each clause).
5. **Strike** any interest violating RAP. Remove that provision. **Reclassify the interest.**

Example (violates RAP): A man conveys a farm "to my daughter, her heirs and assigns, so long as the premises are used for residential purposes, then to her son and his heirs and assigns." (1) The daughter has a fee simple subject to an executory interest and her son has an executory interest, so RAP applies. (2) The daughter is a measuring life. (3) Using the premises for nonresidential purposes is the triggering event. (4) It is possible for the premises to be used for nonresidential purposes indefinitely into the future, so that clause violates the RAP. (5) To reclassify, the executory interest is stricken, "my daughter her heirs and assigns, so long as the premises are used for residential purposes, ~~then to her son and his heirs and assigns~~." Leaving the daughter with a fee simple determinable, and the grantor with a possibility of reverter.

Example (does not violate RAP): A man conveys his house "to my niece and her heirs and assigns in fee simple until my niece's daughter marries, and then to my niece's daughter and her heirs and assigns in fee simple." (1) The niece has a FSSEI (may be called a defeasible fee) and the niece's daughter has an executory interest, so RAP applies. (2) The niece's daughter is a measuring life. (3) The niece's daughter's marriage is the triggering event. (4) It will be known during the life of the niece's daughter if she has married or not, so it does not violate the RAP.

MBE tip: Study smart! Don't be overly worried about mastering the challenging future interest' rules. On the exam, there are only at most 6 questions combined covering all of the topics included in estates in land, joint ownership, and landlord/ tenant. You can get half of the RAP questions correct just by knowing to which interests RAP applies.

Decoy tip: RAP is analyzed at the time the interest is created. Ignore facts about what actually happened subsequently, since they are included to provide decoy answers.

Decoy tip: RAP does not apply to vested remainders, reversions, possibility of reverter, right of reentry, and **charity-to-charity** conveyances.

III. JOINT OWNERSHIP (CONCURRENT ESTATES)

An estate in land can be held jointly. There are three types of joint property ownership:

A. **Joint tenancy (JT) is when two or more people hold a single, unified interest** in a property with a right **to survivorship.**

1. **Joint tenancy key features:**

   a. **Automatic right to survivorship:** At the death of one joint tenant, the surviving joint tenant *automatically* becomes the owner of the deceased joint tenant's interest. The heirs and devisees of the deceased joint tenant take nothing since that interest is extinguished at death. However, if the joint tenants die simultaneously, the right of survivorship is irrelevant.

   b. **Equal right to possession of the whole:** Each joint tenant has an equal right to possess and occupy the entire premises.

   c. **Equal shares:** Each joint tenant must own the property in equal shares with the other joint tenants (e.g., two parties each with a half interest, three parties each with a one-third interest, etc.).

   d. **Severance:** One joint tenant may take actions that unilaterally sever the joint tenancy, resulting in a tenancy in common. See sec. III.A.3. below.

2. **Creation of a joint tenancy:** A joint tenancy requires the **four unities** at the time of creation *and* an **express right of survivorship**.

   a. **Time:** Interest created at the same time in a single instrument.

   b. **Title:** Parties take the same title as joint tenants.

   c. **Interest:** Identical equal interests.

   d. **Possession:** Equal right to possession of the premises.

   e. **Express right of survivorship** included. In the absence of this, a tenancy in common will be presumed.

   Example: Husband and Wife buy a home, taking title as "join tenants with the right of survivorship." They took at the same time (at purchase), titled as joint tenants, in equal interest (50/50), with equal right to possession and an express right of survivorship. This is a proper joint tenancy.

3. **Severance of a joint tenancy by unilateral action of one JT:** Unilateral action by one joint tenant ***may* sever the joint tenancy**. Once severed, the right of survivorship is extinguished and the owners hold the property as **tenants in common.**

   a. **Conveyance severs a JT:** A conveyance (sale or inter vivos transfer) made by one joint tenant will sever a joint tenancy immediately.

      1. **Severance with two joint tenants:** The remaining joint tenant will hold the property with the new owner as tenants in common.

      Example: Woman conveyed her farm to Friend and Neighbor as joint tenants with the right of survivorship. Friend conveyed her interest to Boyfriend. The inter vivos conveyance of Friend severs the joint tenancy and Neighbor holds the farm as tenants in common with Boyfriend.

      Example: Man and Friend owned a lot as joint tenants with the right of survivorship. Man conveyed his interest to Wife. Wife immediately re-conveyed the interest back to

Man. Man was subsequently killed in a car accident and his will devised his interest in the lot to Wife. Friend claims she is the sole owner. However, Man severed the joint tenancy the moment he conveyed his interest to Wife. That Wife conveyed it right back to Man does not restore the joint tenancy because the four unities of title were destroyed. Man and Friend thereafter held the property as tenants in common, so upon Man's death, Wife would take his half share through his will.

2. **Severance with three or more joint tenants:** The new owner will take their portion as a tenant in common to the remaining joint tenants, but the remaining joint tenants will continue to have a joint tenancy with each other *only*.

   Example: Three joint tenants, A, B and C, each have a one-third interest. A sells his interest to D. D holds a one-third interest as a tenant in common to B and C. B and C continue to have a joint tenancy with each other only, and retain the right of survivorship, but only to each other.

b. **Contract to convey made by one joint tenant severs JT:** A valid contract to convey a property will sever a joint tenancy, even though title has not yet transferred, in most jurisdictions.

c. **Mortgage *may* sever depending on jurisdiction:** One **joint tenant may not encumber the interest of the other joint tenant.** Whether a severance occurs when one joint tenant obtains a mortgage is dependent on whether the jurisdiction adopts the lien theory or title theory approach.

1. **Lien theory** (majority rule) **does not sever:** Execution of a **mortgage by one JT** on their share is considered a **lien** on title and **does <u>not</u> sever the joint tenancy**. Lien theory means just what it says; a lien is just a lien.

   a. **Foreclosure of one JT's mortgage will sever the JT** and the joint tenant remaining would hold the property as tenants in common with the mortgagee or foreclosure sale buyer.

   b. **Death of JT with mortgage does not sever the JT**. The interest to which the mortgage is attached vanishes at death (because of automatic survivorship) and the mortgagee or judgment lien holder has no interest in the property.

2. **Title theory** (minority rule) **severs:** The execution of a **mortgage by one JT** on their share is considered a **transfer of title** and **severs the joint tenancy** as to their share only and they will hold their share as a tenant in common.

   <u>Example</u>: Man and Woman owned a home as joint tenants with the right of survivorship in a title theory jurisdiction. Man executed a mortgage, but he died before it was paid off. Man died intestate, leaving one son as his heir. Since it is a title theory state, severance of the joint tenancy occurred when Man obtained the mortgage. Man and Woman then owned the property as tenants in common, and only Man's share was subject to his mortgage. Upon Man's death, his son inherits his share, subject to the mortgage, and holds as tenants in common with Woman, whose share is not subject to the mortgage.

   a. **Foreclosure:** Upon foreclosure of a mortgage obtained by one tenant, the non-mortgaging tenant would retain their share and hold the property as tenants in common with the foreclosing mortgagee (or the foreclosure sale buyer).

> **<u>MBE tip</u>:** The facts should identify whether the jurisdiction follows the title or lien theory. But sometimes they will just tell you whether you are in a majority or minority jurisdiction so know which is which. Also, when they tell you it is a nice issue spotting tip!

d. **Lease may sever depending on jurisdiction:** The courts are split as to whether issuing a lease by one joint tenant severs a joint tenancy.

e. **Judgment lien does not sever JT** (majority rule): A lien placed on a joint tenant's property to satisfy a judgment **will not sever the joint tenancy**. Thus, when the joint tenant with the lien against them dies, their interest evaporates and the judgment lien holder can no longer attach the property.

Example: A brother and sister owned a home as joint tenants. The brother injured a third party and that person obtained and filed a judgment against the brother for $10,000. The brother then died, at which point the sister has 100% interest in the home and it is *not* subject to the lien because the brother's interest, which the lien was attached to, evaporated at his death.

1. **Foreclosure (judgment sale) will sever:** But, if the judgment lien against one joint tenant is enforced by foreclosure on the property (a judgment sale), the joint tenancy will be severed and the judgment sale buyer will own the interest of the one joint tenant against whom they got the lien. Thus, the property will be owned half to the judgment sale buyer and half to the other original joint tenant, as tenants in common.

f. **Will execution does not sever a JT:** Any attempt to devise a JT interest by will is **void** because the decedent's interest in a joint tenancy is **extinguished at death** since their interest automatically transfers to the surviving joint tenant. Signing a will does not operate as a severance and a testamentary disposition has no effect.

g. **Partition action will sever.** See sec. III.D.5 below.

JOINT TENANCY SEVERANCE CHEAT SHEET

MBE tip: It is helpful to chart out each party's interest as events occur. Most joint tenant questions concern the nuanced severance rules and the interests remaining after severance.

MBE tip: One JT cannot bind the other, so any action taken unilaterally by one JT applies to their *own* interest only.

Unilateral action taken by one JT	Does it sever the JT?		
	Y	N	Other Info
Present conveyance	X		
Contract to convey property	X		In most Jx
Mortgage in LIEN theory jx (Majority)		X	
Foreclosure of the mortgage in LIEN theory jx	X		
Mortgage in TITLE theory jx (Minority)	X		
Lease			Depends on jx
Judgment lien		X	
Foreclosure on judgment lien (judgment sale)	X		
Will execution (because will speaks at death)		X	
Partition action	X		

B. **Tenancy in common (TIC)** is a concurrent estate where two or more own a property with no right of survivorship. At common law, a joint tenancy was presumed, but modernly a tenancy in common is presumed and the default.

1. **No right of survivorship** for TIC.
2. **Equal right to possession of the whole property:** Each TIC has a joint right to physical **possession** of the whole property.
3. **Nonequal shares acceptable:** TIC may hold different proportionate interests (e.g., A owns one-third interest and B owns two-third interest).
4. TIC **may sell, will, or gift their interest.** The new grantee will step in the shoes of the grantor and own as a tenant in common with the remaining TIC(s).

C. **Tenancy by the entirety** is similar to a joint tenancy, and requires the same four unities (time, title, interest, possession) but can only exist between **spouses** and in some jurisdictions same-sex partners. [This rule is rarely MBE tested.]

1. **Right of survivorship** operates the same as in a joint tenancy.
2. **Neither tenant can unilaterally convey** their share or encumber the entire property or **break the right of survivorship**.
3. **Limits on severance:** A tenancy by the entirety may *only* be **severed by divorce** (leaving a TIC), **death** (surviving spouse takes the full interest), **mutual agreement**, or by a **joint creditor** of both spouses.

D. **Co-tenancy general rules:** These rules apply to all forms of co-tenancy and are frequently MBE tested.

1. **Possession and use of the property: Each co-tenant has the right to possess and occupy the whole** property, but no co-tenant has the right to exclusively possess any part of the property. An absent owner has the same rights as a possessing owner.
   a. **Lease of *own* share allowed:** A co-tenant can even **lease** their interest, however any tenant would have a concurrent right to possession with any other co-tenants.
2. **Rents, profits, and losses:** In most jurisdictions, there is **no duty to account for profits and losses for co-tenant's *own* use,** absent an ouster of the other tenant. Since both parties are equally entitled to possession, a co-tenant in possession has no duty to account to another co-tenant for the:
   a. **Rental value of their *own* occupancy** of the premises, or
   b. **Profits** retained from their ***own use*** of the land.
      1. **Exception: Must share rents collected from third parties** and **exploitation profits.** Exploitations of the land are those that reduce the value of the land itself, such as mining.
   c. **Losses:** A co-tenant is **solely responsible for their own losses** from their use of the property and may not seek contribution from co-tenants.
3. **No right to bind co-tenant:** One co-tenant cannot bind the other tenant, such as by the sale of the property, obtaining a mortgage, granting an easement, settling a boundary dispute, etc. Such actions are effective only against the granting **co-tenant's undivided interest**, and not against the share of the other co-tenant.
4. **Ouster:** If a co-tenant has **refused occupancy** (possession) to their co-tenant and claims an exclusive right to possession, this constitutes an ouster of the co-tenant.

a. The ousting co-tenant must **make an accounting** to their ousted co-tenant for the **fair rental value** of the premises for their own occupancy.

b. An ousted co-tenant may also bring an action to regain possession.

c. **Adverse possession:** The ousting tenant may be able to use the ouster as the basis for an adverse possession claim to the co-tenant's share.

Example: Brother and Sister inherited a home as tenants in common. Brother lived in the home for 30 years, paying all taxes and insurance and maintenance costs. He paid no rent to Sister. There is a 20-year adverse possession statute in the jurisdiction. In an action by Brother to quiet title, he will lose. Brother has not done anything sufficient to constitute ouster of Sister, and her failure to take possession the property in no way diminishes her full ownership rights.

5. **Partition (remedy)** occurs when, through voluntary agreement or judicial action in the best interest of all parties, the **property is divided**. One party can force a partition, even when the other is opposed. Partition terminates the co-tenancy and divides the common property. Partition is not available to a tenancy by the entirety.

a. **Partition in kind** is a physical division of the common property, and this is preferred, so long as it is fair and equitable.

b. **Partition by sale** is allowed when a fair and equitable physical division of the property is impossible. The co-tenants will split the sale proceeds.

Example: A rectangular 3-acre piece of land has 150 feet of frontage onto a public street. The zoning ordinance requires that to build on a lot, there must be a minimum 2-acre lot and 100 feet of street frontage. Brother and Sister own as TIC with Brother holding a one-third interest and Sister holding a two-third interest. Sister wants to partition and proposes she receive a 2-acre lot with 100 feet of frontage. However, this would not be fair and equitable since the brother could not build on his share, so the land will be portioned by sale and the proceeds split proportionately.

6. **Accounting action: A co-tenant can seek contribution** (reimbursement) for payments made and received on behalf of the jointly owned property.

a. **Taxes and mortgage:** Co-tenants have a duty to pay their proportionate share of "carrying costs," such as taxes and mortgage payments.

1. **Right to contribution:** A co-tenant not in sole possession may seek contribution for payments in excess of their pro rata share. The majority view is that contribution can be compelled. The co-tenant may also deduct these payments from rents received or seek reimbursement "off the top" if the property is sold.

b. **Repairs:** A co-tenant has a duty to pay their proportionate share of the cost of necessary repairs.

1. **Right to contribution:** A co-tenant not in sole possession may seek contribution for payments in excess of their pro rata share, and some jurisdictions will compel contribution.

c. **Improvements:** Co-tenants have **no duty to improve** the property and thus have **no right to reimbursement** for improvements. Only in a partition action can the cost for improvements be recouped.

d. **Profits** from **rents received from third parties** and profits from **land depletion** (this is removing natural resources from land, such as mining) must be shared with co-tenants.

7. **Duty of fair dealing** exists between all co-tenants.

Decoy tip: In questions with disputes among co-tenants, there will often be an adverse possession statute included as a decoy. A co-tenant opting not to be in possession does not impact their ownership rights or allow their co-tenant to take the whole interest through adverse possession, absent an ouster.

IV. LANDLORD AND TENANT

A. **Types of tenancies:** A tenancy is created when an owner of land conveys to another a lesser interest in a property. In addition to the life estate (covered in section II.A.4.) there are several types of tenancies.

1. **Tenancy for years** (also called lease for years and term of years) refers to a lease for a **fixed period of time**, such as one day, two months, five years, etc.

   a. **SOF requires a writing** for terms greater than one year.

   b. **Automatically terminates** on the time period end date, so no notice is required to terminate.

2. **Periodic tenancy:** Automatically continues indefinitely from one period to the next, unless one of the parties terminates the lease by giving notice of termination (e.g., leases running month-to-month, year-to-year, etc.).

   a. Can be **created by implication** if the lease includes a start date, but there is no stated end date.

   b. **Written notice is required to terminate** a periodic tenancy since the tenancy is **automatically renewed** in the absence of a termination notice. At common law, notice must match the length of the lease time period, except modernly, one-month notice is sufficient for a lease of one year or longer.

3. **Tenancy at will:** A tenancy for no fixed period of time, created by express agreement, and can be **terminated at any time** by the landlord or tenant effective immediately.

4. **Tenancy at sufferance** is when a tenant wrongfully holds over past the expiration of a valid lease. The landlord can evict the tenant as a trespasser or bind the tenant to a new periodic tenancy (holdover tenancy).

5. **Holdover tenant** is one whose lease has terminated, but who remains in possession and tenders rent, which the landlord accepts. A holdover tenant is **deemed to have a periodic tenancy** with the **same terms** as the previous lease. In a **commercial** tenancy longer than one year, a **one-year** periodic tenancy results. In a **residential** tenancy, a **month-to-month** periodic tenancy (or week-to-week for a previous weekly rental) results.

   a. **If landlord accepts rent**, acceptance to a new term is implied.

   b. **If landlord gives notice of increased rent** *before* the previous term expires, the new periodic tenancy will be at the increased rent, even if the tenant objects.

B. **Landlord duties:**

1. **Deliver possession of the premises:** Tenant has a right to possession once the lease commences. The majority rule is the landlord must put the tenant in actual possession. In

minority rule jurisdictions, the landlord must only provide the legal right to possession and the tenant would have to bring eviction proceedings against a holdover tenant. [On the MBE, use the majority rule unless told otherwise.]

2. **Condition of rental premises:** A landlord must comply with the following:

   a. **Modern view:** The landlord must maintain all common areas, **fix latent defects** of which the landlord has knowledge, and **make repairs that landlord has undertaken** in a **non-negligent** manner. Any residential lease provision placing the duty to repair on the tenant is void.

   b. **Covenant of quiet enjoyment** is implied in **every** lease. The landlord warrants that they, or anyone acting on landlord's behalf, will **not interfere with the tenant's use and enjoyment of the premises**. (This may include acts of other tenants, but it does not include the acts of strangers.)

      1. **Constructive eviction** occurs when the premises are in such disrepair they are virtually uninhabitable. It is treated as an eviction. Requires:

         a. **The premises are virtually uninhabitable** for their intended use because of a **substantial interference** with the property use and enjoyment **caused by** the landlord or persons acting for landlord.

         <u>Examples</u>: Toilets that are non-functional, no heat in winter, etc.

         b. **Notice** to the landlord by the tenant of the need for repair,

         c. The landlord **fails to meaningfully respond;** and this

         d. Causes the tenant to **actually move out** within a **reasonable time**.

      2. **Actual eviction:** Tenant is excluded from the entire property and is relieved of responsibility to pay rent.

      3. **Partial actual eviction:** Landlord makes it physically impossible for the tenant to occupy **some portion** of the premises. Tenant may **withhold the entire rent** and does not have to move out.

      <u>Example</u>: Tenant leases a home and attached garage, but finds the garage is padlocked and unusable.

   c. **Implied warranty of habitability** applies to **residential leases *only*** and requires that the premises be fit for human habitation, such that no basic necessities are missing (e.g., running water). This obligates a landlord to make necessary repairs. Where premises are not habitable, the tenant has the option to:

      1. **Terminate the lease and move out;** or

      2. **Make repairs and deduct** the cost from the rent; or

      3. **Pay reduced rent,** remain on the premises, and sue for damages.

   d. **No retaliatory eviction** in many jurisdictions. A landlord may not retaliate against a tenant asserting their right to adequate housing. A tenant has a right to report housing, building code, and local housing code violations.

      1. **Presumption of retaliation** (e.g., eviction, termination or non-renewal of a lease, rent increase or diminishment services) **when occurring shortly after** a tenant has asserted their rights, though a landlord can rebut with proof of a non-retaliatory motive.

      2. **Punitive damages** available.

Example: Tenant organized a tenants' association and demanded certain repairs and improvements of the rental property. In response, Landlord raised her rent, which previously had been the same as the other tenants. When she complained, Landlord gave proper notice that her lease was terminated. Tenant asserts the termination was in retaliation, which is barred in most jurisdictions. Landlord would need to rebut with proof of a non-retaliatory motive.

3. **Comply with Fair Housing rules**

   a. **Fair Housing Act (FHA): Discrimination** based on **race, national origin, religion, sex** (gender), **disability and familial status is prohibited** in the **sale, rental, or financing** of housing, **subject to several exceptions**:

      1. **Mrs. Murphy exemption** provides that owner-occupied dwellings with no more than four units are exempt from the FHA.

      2. **Religious organizations** and **private clubs** which limits housing occupancy to members is exempt from the FHA.

      3. **Single family homes** sold or rented without a broker are exempt from the FHA, unless the owner owns more than three houses.

      4. **Senior housing.** However, **families** with children under 18 may be discriminated against in designated senior citizen communities.

   b. **No discriminatory advertising.** Advertisements may not state preferences based on the FHA characteristics of race, national origin, religion, sex (gender), disability and familiar status, with **no exception.** Consequently, even housing subject to an exception above may not employ discriminatory advertising.

      1. **All publishers are liable.** Both the **owner and any publisher** of a discriminatory advertisement is liable (e.g., a person placing a discriminatory ad is liable and so is the newspaper that printed a discriminatory ad).

   c. **Disabled tenants** must be permitted to make **reasonable modifications** that may be necessary and housing providers must make **reasonable accommodations.**

C. **Tenant Duties**

1. **Duty to pay rent:** The tenant has the duty to pay rent in the amount agreed to. A tenant may have the following **defenses** available for the non-payment of rent (see sec. IV.B. for landlord duties):

   a. **Failure of landlord to deliver possession** of the premises.

   b. Breach of the **covenant of quiet enjoyment.**

   c. **Constructive eviction.**

   d. **Destruction of the premises** through no fault of the landlord, or the tenant. Modernly, many states allow the tenant to terminate the lease.

   e. **Potential contract defenses**, such as frustration of purpose.

   f. **Surrender of the premises** by the tenant, which the landlord accepts.

   g. **Re-letting of the property after an abandonment** done on behalf of the tenant. If the new tenant's rent is less, the old tenant will owe the difference, so long as they were properly notified.

2. **Security deposit:** Most leases require the payment of a security deposit to secure payment of rent and good condition of the premises upon return. Landlord must return to tenant upon lease termination the deposit, less any damages.

3. **Avoid committing waste:** A tenant (including a life tenant under a life estate) has duty to avoid committing waste. See above section III.A.4.e.*4.* to review these rules as they apply to tenants in the same way as life tenants.

4. **Surrender premises** at the end of the lease.

5. **Not breach the lease and/or abandon the property** without justification.

   a. **Breach — Eviction:** A landlord may typically terminate a lease for a material breach. A landlord must evict through the courts or continue the rental relationship, give notice, and sue for damages.

   b. **Abandonment:** If a tenant abandons the premises the landlord at their option may (options may vary by jurisdiction):

      1. **Accept the surrender** of premises and terminate the lease;

      2. **Re-let** on behalf of the tenant (tenant must be **notified**). **Modernly**, many courts impose a **duty to mitigate** requiring the landlord to re-let the premises with the breaching tenant responsible for any shortfall.

      3. **Leave the premises vacant and sue for rent** as it becomes due. This common law approach is the minority view currently.

D. Tort liability of landlord and tenant

1. **Landlord:** At common law a landlord has no general duty to make the premises safe for a tenant or the tenant's guests. Modernly, landlords have a general duty of reasonable care and must do the following:

   a. **Common area: Maintain all common areas** using reasonable care (including using reasonable care to prevent unauthorized access).

   b. **Rental unit: Disclose or fix any latent defects** of which the landlord knows or should know (landlord is responsible if not disclosed).

   c. **Public area: Repair known (or should have known) dangers** where premises will be held **open to the public**.

   d. **Repairs assumed** by the landlord, must be performed with **reasonable care** (non-negligently).

   e. Adhere to any requirements of **building codes.**

2. **Tenant** is treated like an owner for purposes of tort liability to third parties on the property. If the property has a latent defect, the landlord retains liability until the tenant has had a chance to inspect, discover, and correct the defect.

★ **E. Assignments and subleases**

1. **General rule:** An **interest in a lease is transferable** unless the parties agree otherwise. A landlord may prohibit assignments or subleasing or both.

   a. **Strictly and literally construed:** A lease provision against assignments and/or subleases is a type of restraint on alienation and is strictly construed according to its **explicit terms only** (e.g., a lease prohibiting assignments will *only* prohibit assignments and not prohibit a sublease).

   b. **Waiver:** If the lease prohibits assignments and/or subleasing and the landlord gives **permission**, or **knows of the violation and does not object**, the prohibition will be deemed **waived.** However, if the landlord specifically claims it will be "one time only," an acceptance of rent will not serve as a waiver of the lease provision.

Example: Tenant subleases in violation of a no sublease and no-assignments clause in the lease, and Landlord accepts the rent from the sublessee. The sublease prohibition will be deemed waived for future subleases, but not future assignments.

2. **Assignment is the transfer of the entire length of time** remaining on the lease term to another party (the assignee). Essentially, an assignment is a covenant that runs with the land and the assignee is responsible to the landlord for the covenants (terms) in the lease.

   a. **New tenant (assignee) *is* personally liable** to pay rent to the landlord because there is privity of estate (new tenant has the entire interest).

   b. **Old tenant is also liable** to the landlord for the rent, **unless the landlord specifically releases** the old tenant by a **novation** because there is privity of contract (from the lease agreement).

      1. **Novation** is an act that serves to substitute new parties under a contract; here, it would be where the landlord agrees to accept the assignee, in place of the original party to the agreement, thus releasing the original contracting party from liability.

      Example: Tenant leased an apartment for two years. He occupied the apartment for 15 months then had a job transfer. Tenant transferred his "lease rights" for the remaining 9 months of the lease to Friend in an informal writing. Friend paid rent for 4 months, but no rent was paid for the final 5 months. Both Tenant and Friend are each fully liable for the unpaid rent; Tenant under privity of contract (lease agreement), and Friend under privity of estate as an assignee.

3. **Sublease is the transfer of anything less than the entire length of time** remaining on the lease term to another party (the sublessee). A sublease is not a covenant that runs with the land (because there is no privity of estate or contract).

   a. **New tenant *is not* personally liable** to the landlord for the rent because a sublease does not provide privity of estate or privity of contract.

   b. **Old tenant is liable** to the landlord for the rent because there is privity of contract (lease agreement).

4. **Attornment of the lease** occurs when the landlord assigns their rights under the lease to a new property owner.

Decoy tip: Attornment of the lease is sometimes used as a decoy answer.

F. **Condemnation of a leasehold by eminent domain.** See the Constitutional Law outline for complete takings rules.

1. **Total taking**: If the entire leased property is taken by eminent domain, the tenant's liability for rent is extinguished, in the absence of a contrary lease provision.

2. **Temporary or partial taking:** The tenant will receive a **proportionate share** of the condemnation award and must **continue paying rent**. A temporary taking is one for less than the entire length of time left on the lease. A partial taking is one of less than the entire rented premises.

   Example: Landlord leases a 30-acre farm, which includes a home, to Tenant for 10 years. Two years into the lease, the government condemns 20 acres of the farmland and allocated the compensation award to Landlord and Tenant according to their respective interest. The 20 acres embraced all the tillable (farmable) land, leaving the home. This is a partial taking and Tenant must continue paying rent as the lease remains in effect.

V. FIXTURES

A. **Fixtures** are items that were once moveable **chattel** (personal property) but that have become **so attached** to the premises they are **deemed fixtures** and considered part of the real estate and **not removable.**

The following factors are considered to determine if an item is a fixture:

1. **Method of attachment:** The item is **firmly imbedded** in the real estate.
2. **Adaptability:** The item is **peculiarly adapted** or fitted to the real estate.
3. **Removal:** Removing the item would **destroy the chattel or cause substantial damage** to the real estate.
4. **Intention:** For owners who add chattel to their own property, courts look at their objective intention at the time (usually the problem arises when they want to sell the house and take the item with them). But courts will also look at intentions of tenants or landlords who add chattel as well.
5. **Agreement:** For landlords/tenants who add chattels, courts look at whether there was an agreement in the lease regarding who owned the property. Such agreements will be given effect.

Example (fixtures): Electrical wiring, built-in bookcases.

Example (non-fixtures): Freestanding kitchen appliances, storm windows with inserts, which are easily removable.

> **Memorization tip:** Think MARIA to remember the fixtures factors.

B. **Fixture rules apply to:**

1. **Tenant** in a leasehold. The landlord retains the fixture, and the tenant retains personal property. A landlord has no duty to compensate tenant for the value of a fixture.
2. **Life tenants** who hold a life estate. The remainderman retains the fixture, the life tenant retains personal property.
3. **Mortgagee when a property is foreclosed** in disputes between a homeowner or creditor and the mortgagee. The mortgagee retains fixtures, while the homeowner/creditor retains personal property.

Example: Man purchased new windows on credit, granting a security interest in the windows to the vendor. The windows have three inserts: regular windows, storm windows, and screens. They are designed so that each insert is easily removable. Man installed the new windows in his home and stored the old windows in the basement. Man defaulted on his mortgage and the window loan. The mortgagee seeks to enjoin the window vendor from repossessing the window inserts, but mortgagee will be unsuccessful because the inserts are removable and not fixtures.

C. **Trade fixtures are those affixed to the real estate by a commercial tenant** for use in their business. There is a **strong presumption** that **trade fixtures are removable unless removal would cause very substantial damage.** The tenant is responsible for repairing any damage resulting from its removal or pay the cost of restoration.

Examples: Installed counters, display cases, shelving, special lighting, appliances, and an air conditioning system that can be removed without substantial damage are trade fixtures and removable.

VI. LAND USE ISSUES

A. **Easements:** An easement is the **right to use the land of another** for a particular purpose. An easement is an incorporeal (has no material existence) non-possessory interest in land, which means you can use the land but don't own it. [All easement subtopics are heavily MBE tested.]

1. **Easements can be affirmative or negative.**

   a. **Affirmative** easements entitle the holder to do something on another's land (e.g., use a driveway).

   b. **Negative** easements prevent the landowner from doing something on their own land, typically regarding light, air, support or stream of water. These are not common (e.g., Owner cannot develop land in a way that blocks the neighbor's view). [This is the functional equivalent of a restrictive covenant and rarely MBE tested.]

2. **Two types of easements:**

   a. **Appurtenant easement** is an easement that benefits the possessor of a particular parcel of land. There are **two estates** created by an appurtenant easement:

      1. **Dominant estate** is **the benefited parcel**—in other words the holder of the easement. Possessor must be benefited in their *physical use and enjoyment* of the tract of land (it can't just make the land more profitable).

      2. **Servient estate is the burdened parcel**—in other words the parcel providing the benefit to the dominant estate.

   b. **Easement in gross** allows the holder to **special use** of the burdened property, and the right is independent of ownership of another piece of land.

   <u>**Examples**</u>: A particular person has permission to fish in my pond; the utility company has a right-of-way to install and service an underground gas pipeline.

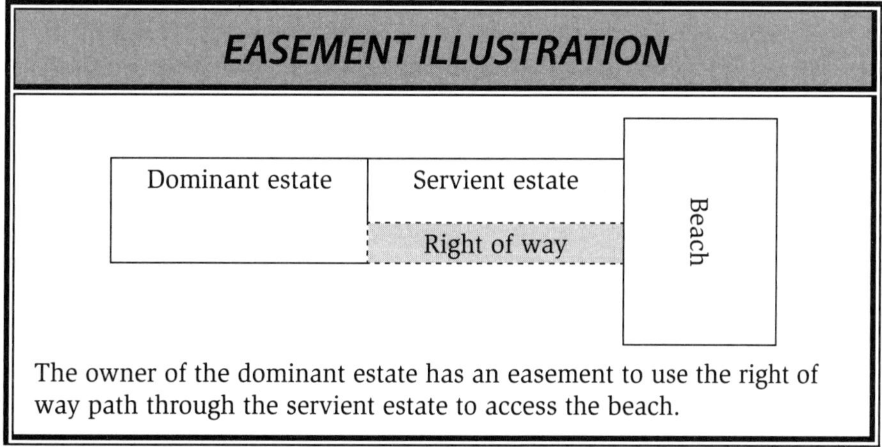

The owner of the dominant estate has an easement to use the right of way path through the servient estate to access the beach.

3. **Creation of easements:** There are five ways to create an easement.

   a. **Express creation** in writing in a deed or will. Must be signed by the servient owner.

      1. The **statute of frauds** writing requirements apply since an easement is an interest in land.

2. **Reservation in grantor** is a type of express easement where the grantor passes title to the land but reserves the right to continue to use the land for some purpose. Typically, this is included in the grant or deed and gives the *grantor only* the right to use the land.
3. **Recording provides notice to purchasers.** An easement typically must be recorded to give future purchasers notice of the encumbrance. However, after being properly recorded the first time, the easement need not be re-identified in later deeds for conveyances of the same property.

b. **Easement by implication (from previous use).** Requirements:

1. Land was **originally one parcel** with **common ownership** by one party,
2. The **land is severed** into more than one parcel,
3. The easement is **reasonably necessary** to the dominant land's use and enjoyment of the property, and

   Example: Another route to the public road exists from the benefitted parcel, but it is much longer and unpaved, making the use of the easement driveway reasonably necessary.
4. The **use of the property existed *prior to* the severance.**

c. **Easement by necessity.** Requirements:

1. Land was **originally one parcel** with **common ownership** by one party **just prior** to when the need for the easement by necessity was created.
2. The **land is severed** into more than one parcel, and that severance deprives one lot of important access (e.g., access to the road or utilities).
3. **Easement is strictly necessary** because there is no other way to access the property for some important function (e.g., landlocked parcel, second floor of a building that needs stair access). If an alternate means of access exists, there is no necessity, even if the alternate way is inconvenient (e.g., another route to the public road exists from the benefitted parcel—even though it is much longer and unpaved, while use of the purported easement driveway is reasonably necessary, it is not *strictly* necessary).

   a. **Necessity must exist at the *time of conveyance*,** not develop later.
4. **Prior use is not required.**

   Example: Man conveyed half of a tract of vacant land to Woman. Man's remaining tract was landlocked, while Woman's parcel fronted the highway. Man died and Cousin inherited the land. Woman refuses to let Cousin cross her land to get to the highway. Another neighbor offered to sell Cousin a right to access the highway for a fair price, but Cousin rejected the offer. Man had an easement by necessity, created at the time of conveyance, which has not terminated, so Cousin has an easement by necessity. It is irrelevant that a neighbor offered to sell highway access.

COMPARE EASEMENT BY IMPLICATION v. NECESSITY

Easement by:	One parcel, then severed	Strict necessity	Reasonably necessary	Prior use
Implication (previous use)	X		X	X
Necessity	X	X		

d. **Easement by prescription** is one obtained using the same principles as adverse possession. Requirements:

   1. **Actual use:** The claimant must have actual use of the property that is adverse to the servient parcel. Unlike adverse possession, it need not be exclusive use (e.g., non-permissive use of neighbor's path to get access to the highway that is used by a neighbor regularly and some occasional hunters).

   2. **Open, notorious, and visible use** of the property.

   3. **Hostile use,** which is without the owner's consent.

   4. **Continuous use** for the given **statutory period**. Tacking is allowed to satisfy the statutory period.

      Example: Man owned a lot, which was in possession of an adverse possessing stranger. Man gave Neighbor permission to use a road across the lot to access Neighbor's property. The stranger quit possession before meeting the adverse possession statutory period. Neighbor continued to use the road regularly for ingress and egress to his property for a total period, from the time he began to use it, sufficient to meet the statutory period for an easement by prescription. Man then blocked the road. However, Neighbor will not obtain an easement by prescription because Man gave Neighbor permission.

> **Decoy tip:** The example above is a classic example of how the examiners provide many extraneous details to distract you from the fact that the property was used with the owner's permission and thus is not hostile.

e. **Easement by estoppel** occurs where the servient parcel allows use of the property such that it is reasonable that the user will substantially change position in reliance on the belief that the permission will not be revoked.

   Example: A man has a landlocked vacant parcel. A neighbor orally tells the man that if the man builds a home on the land, the man may use the neighbor's driveway to access the road. In reliance on the neighbor's promise, the man builds a home on the lot. The man will be able to use the neighbor's driveway to access the road.

4. **Scope of easements**

   a. **Location and relocation of easements:** If the document creating the easement does not specify the location, the grantor (owner of the burdened estate) can pick **any reasonable location**.

      1. **Burdened owner may not obstruct:** Once the location is determined (by agreement or use) the burdened owner may only use the land in a way that does not obstruct or interfere with the rights of the benefitted owner.

         Example: If the burdened owner planted an expensive garden on the land designated for the easement (e.g. a six-foot strip along the north property line for underground pipeline) the easement holder would not be required to repair it if the garden were damaged during routine maintenance because the burdened owner may not obstruct.

      2. **Burdened owner may not relocate** the easement, even if doing so does not burden the benefitted owner.

         Example: A utility company cannot install a second underground pipeline three feet parallel to their original installed pipeline because it exceeds the scope of the right-of-way easement to add a location.

<u>Example</u>: The servient estate holder can't erect a solar panel in the easement location and relocate the easement once the location is established, even if it does not burden the benefitted owner.

b. **Present and future needs:** Courts assume the easement intends to meet both present and future needs of the benefitted parcel due to **normal, foreseeable development** of the dominant estate, so long as it does not impose an unreasonable burden (e.g., an easement may be widened to accommodate wider cars).

   1. **Additional property:** Use **cannot be extended** to benefit an additional property owned by the easement holder.

      <u>Example</u>: Holder has an easement to use a driveway on Neighbor's property to access the road. If Holder buys a second property, which is connected to the benefitted parcel, Holder may not use the easement to benefit the additional property.

c. **Excessive use:** Increased use that unreasonably interferes with the use of the servient estate is not permitted, but it **will not terminate** the easement.

   1. **Remedy** for excessive use or misuse is an **injunction** and/or **damages**.

      <u>Example</u>: A religious group had an easement to use a driveway over the appurtenant owner's land to access the road, which they used for 20 years without incident. They recently built a 200-bed nursing home, which dramatically increased the use of the driveway on Sundays, leading the servient owner to erect a barricade and sue to terminate the easement. The servient owner will not succeed in terminating the easement, though she could get an injunction to limit its use to a reasonable amount.

5. **Maintenance and repair of easements**

   a. The servient **burdened owner is not required** to repair and maintain the easement, but **must allow access** so the dominant benefitted easement holder can maintain and repair the easement land.

   b. The dominant **benefitted owner** has an **implied right to enter the land to make repairs and maintain** the easement.

      1. **Land restoration required:** If the repairs alter or damage the land, the easement holder must restore the condition of the land.

         a. **Exception:** If the burdened owner has unreasonably obstructed the easement (e.g., by planting an elaborate formal garden over the easement land), the easement holder will not have to restore the land to the enhanced condition since the easement access should not have been obstructed.

   c. **Shared use:** If both estates make use of the easement (e.g., a shared driveway), then the court will apportion the repair costs between them based on their use.

6. **Transfer of easements to new owners of the land**

   a. **New owner of servient (burdened) estate: An easement runs (passes) with the land** and transfers to the new owner of the burdened estate (even if the deed does not mention the easement) **except** if the purchaser of the servient estate is a **BFP** (who **took for value** with **no notice**).

      1. **Notice:** An easement **properly recorded in the chain of title provides record notice**, and once recorded the first time, it need not be re-identified in later conveyances to provide notice. A **visible easement provides inquiry notice**.

   b. **New owner of dominant (benefited) estate:** Whether the benefit runs with the land depends on whether the easement is appurtenant or in gross.

1. **Appurtenant easements** are presumed to be perpetual and normally run (pass) automatically with the transfer of the benefited estate to a new owner, and will also transfer to the new owner of the burdened estate, unless the new owner is a BFP.

2. **In gross easements**

a. **Common law** rule is that easements in gross are **not transferable.**

b. **Modernly, commercial** easements in gross are **transferable.**

7. **Termination of easements** (also called extinguish): Easements may terminate in eight ways.

a. **Estoppel:** The burdened owner **materially changes position** in reasonable reliance on the easement holder's assurances that the easement will no longer be enforced.

b. **Necessity:** Easement by necessity ends when the necessity ends (e.g., a new public road provides access to the previously landlocked parcel).

c. **Destruction** of burdened land, so long as it is not willful destruction by the owner.

d. **Condemnation** of the burdened estate by eminent domain.

e. **Release in writing** by the easement holder to the burdened owner.

f. **Abandonment action:** The easement holder **demonstrates a physical manifestation of intent to never use the easement again.** Words alone or mere nonuse will not be sufficient to constitute abandonment (e.g., a railroad had an easement for tracks, but that line closed and the railroad removed the train tracks).

g. **Merger doctrine:** The easement is extinguished when title to both the dominant and servient parcels become vested in same person.

Example: Man owns a parcel that fronts a highway. Woman owns a lot with a home to the south. Five years ago, Man conveyed an easement to Woman providing access to the highway on a path across his parcel; it was recorded. Three years ago, Woman sold her home to Man, but he did not take possession. Two years ago, Man sold the home to Purchaser by warranty deed. When Purchaser began using the path, Man installed a barricade, and Purchaser sued. However, he will lose, because when Man bought Woman's home, the two parcels merged, which extinguished the easement. (The information about Man not taking possession and the warranty deed were irrelevant decoy ducks. The recording didn't help him because of the subsequent merger of the parcels.)

h. **Prescription:** An easement can be terminated by employing the principals of prescription in reverse when there is an adverse, continuous ***interruption* of the use of the easement for the statutory period.**

> **Memorization tip:** Use the mnemonic **END CRAMP** to remember the eight ways an easement can terminate.

> **MBE tip:** A license occurs when a purported easement fails to satisfy the formalities required, such as being in writing.

B. **Restrictive covenants** (also called real covenants) are **written promises** between two parties **about how land is to be used** that meet certain technical requirements, such that the **promises "run with the land,"** meaning they are **binding on future purchasers/holders of the land** (successors in interest). Similar to easements, there is a benefitted (dominant) parcel and a burdened (servient) parcel. The requirements are slightly different depending on whether the benefit or burden of the covenant is running with the land to a new owner. The remedy for breach of a covenant is **money damages**.

> **MBE tip:** The main difference between a restrictive covenant and an equitable servitude is the remedy available. The remedy for a restrictive covenant is money damages, where the remedy for an equitable servitude is an injunction. The MBE questions tend to use the terms "restrictive covenant" and "equitable servitude" interchangeably, so don't get hung up on the distinction on MBEs.

1. **Burden to "run with the land"** (so the covenant (promise) is binding on future purchasers/holders of the land). Requirements:
   a. **Writing** required between the *original* parties/owners who agreed to the covenant, typically this is in the deed.
   b. **Intent** that the promise apply to successors to the property. This is usually easily established by language in the deed that states, "this covenant runs with the land," or referencing that the covenant terms apply to "heirs and assigns."
   c. Must **"touch and concern"** the land. This means the promise **makes the land more useful or valuable.** The promise benefits the dominant (benefitted) parcel by *increasing* the value, use, or enjoyment of the property and/or restricts the use of the burdened parcel in some way, or requires the servient parcel to do something, thus *decreasing* the use or enjoyment.

TOUCH & CONCERN EXAMPLES

Touch & Concern	Does NOT Touch & Concern
◆ Not erect a building on land ◆ Single family dwellings only ◆ Residential purposes only ◆ No mobile homes ◆ No detached storage sheds ◆ Covenant not to compete with a gas station business on premises	◆ Requirement to purchase electricity from a particular company

   d. **Horizontal and vertical privity is required** for the burden to run. Privity refers to the relationship between the parties involved.
      1. **Horizontal privity** refers to the relationship between the **original promising parties** (e.g., the original parties that agreed to the use restriction, such as the developer and purchaser, or an agreement between two neighbors).
      2. **Vertical** (downstream) **privity** refers to the relationship between the holder of the land and a **successor**, such as a buyer. For vertical privity, the successor must **hold the entire interest** that the party making the covenant had (e.g., typically one of the properties will pass to another owner as a grantor/grantee or buyer/seller).

> **MBE tip:** When tested, both vertical and horizontal privity have been present and easy to establish. When the party enforcing the covenant only wants an injunction (instead of damages), privity is not even required. See equitable servitude rule in VI. C. below.

e. **Notice is required** and can be actual, inquiry, or record (constructive) notice. Notice typically is established by the recordation of the deed with the covenant in the chain of title. In the absence of notice, a successor will not be bound. See complete notice rules in sec. I.G.

   Example: Man owned two adjoining parcels. He sold one to a gas station and covenanted that when he sold the other lot, he would impose a restrictive covenant prohibiting that a gas station could be built on the lot. The deed was not recorded. The gas station was constructed and the owner conveyed the property to his nephew. Man then sold his remaining parcel to Businessman, who knew about the gas station restriction, but went through with the deal when there was no such restriction in the deed. Businessman began constructing a gas station and the nephew sued. The covenant burden runs with the land because all elements are satisfied and Businessman was on notice because of his actual knowledge of the restriction, despite the failure to record.

> **MBE tip:** They typically test if the **burden of the covenant runs with the land.** Read carefully, since they don't always use the language "covenant" in the question to tip you off. The question may just describe a "provision" or "term" or "condition" in the deed.

Memorization tip: Use the mnemonic **WITCH VaN** → to remember the requirements for a real covenant **burden** to run. (Picture a spooky van carrying the burden.)	◆ **W**riting ◆ **I**ntent ◆ **T**ouch and **C**oncern ◆ **H**orizontal and **V**ertical privity ◆ **N**otice

2. **Benefit will "run with the land,"** but this is easier to establish than the burden running. The elements are the same as the burden to run (e.g., writing, intent, touch and concern the land), except there is **no horizontal privity or notice requirement.** [This rule is rarely MBE tested.]

3. **Termination or modification of covenants is allowed in the following circumstances:** [These rules are rarely MBE tested.]

   a. **Destruction, release, estoppel, abandonment, merger, condemnation** (as described in easements above, see sec. VI.A.7.), and

   b. **Changed conditions:** Where conditions have changed so significantly that the purpose of the covenant is impossible to accomplish.

 C. **Equitable servitudes** (also called covenants) **are restrictions on how land may be used.** There are two types of equitable servitudes: (1) a standard written equitable servitude and (2) an equitable servitude implied from a common scheme.

1. **Equitable servitudes** (standard written) are very similar to restrictive covenants and will bind successors. Writing and notice are required, but there is **no privity requirement**. The **main difference** from a restrictive covenant is that the remedy for breach of an equitable servitude is an **injunction** in equity.

Example: Two neighbors in a subdivision each agreed in writing not to place storage sheds in their yards, and the deed was recorded. Three years later one of the neighbors gave his home to his daughter. The other neighbor can enjoin the daughter (successor) from placing a storage shed in the yard since there is a writing (deed) and it was recorded (notice).

2. **Servitude implied from a common scheme** (also called an implied reciprocal servitude or reciprocal negative servitude): This is a type of equitable servitude created when the **original owner/developer intended** to develop a **"common plan or scheme"** and bind an entire subdivision and the **purchaser has notice** of the scheme. The remedy for a breach is an **injunction** in equity.

   a. The **common plan or scheme** is typically evidenced by a **developer's building plans** in a **recorded plat or map**, or a general pattern of restrictions, or an oral representation to early buyers (e.g., a new housing development where all homes are one story).

   b. **Notice is required** and can be actual, inquiry, or record (constructive) notice.

      1. **Actual notice.**

      2. **Inquiry notice** is common and can be provided by a **visual inspection of the neighborhood** that gives the appearance of conforming to certain standards.

      3. **Record notice:** If the **recorded plat included the property** and was filed *before* the parcel was purchased, the parcel will be bound, even if the restriction is not mentioned in its own deed.

> **Memorization tip:** Remember **AIR** for the types of notice: **A**ctual, **I**nquiry, and **R**ecord.

   c. **No writing is required.**

   Example: Owner of a 100-acre subdivision recorded a plan for 90 1-acre lots and a 10-acre tract in the center as a future school site. 50 lots were sold and each deed referred to the recorded plan and contained a restriction that mobile homes were not allowed. Owner sold the remaining 40 lots individually and the 10-acre tract to a man intending to erect a restaurant. None of those deeds referred to the plan or the mobile home restriction. The man will be enjoined from building the restaurant because there is an equitable servitude since the plan (for 90 1-acre lots and a 10-acre school site *only*) was recorded in the chain of title of all lots. (Such a scheme will also be enforced without a writing *if* a visual inspection of the subdivision would put one on notice of the restriction. It is unclear a buyer would be on inquiry notice here, but there was record notice.)

3. **Termination or modification** of equitable servitudes is the same as for covenants (see above).

> **MBE tip:** When the MBE uses the word "servitude," they are probably referring to an equitable servitude implied from the common scheme. They tend to call a written equitable servitude a (restrictive) covenant.

D. **Profit** (also called a profit à prendre) entitles its holder the **right to enter** another's land and **remove a natural resource,** such as soil or a product of the land itself. A profit is a non-possessory property right (e.g., mining minerals, drilling for oil, removing timber, hunting, or fishing). It may be appurtenant or in gross and is created and terminated like an easement. [This rule is rarely MBE tested.]

> **Decoy tip:** Profit or profit à prendre is often a decoy answer.

E. **License** is the mere **non-exclusive right to use** the licensor's land for some specific purpose, and it is **revocable at will** by the licensor.

Examples: A license can be something that would be an easement were it in writing, such as the right to use a neighbor's driveway. It can also include the contractual right to use a parking lot or a ticket to attend a sporting event.

1. **Difference from easement: A license may be freely revoked** (unless consideration is provided) and is merely a **privilege** to use land and not an interest in the land.
2. **Irrevocable license** (also called an equitable easement): In most jurisdictions, when a license holder has expended a substantial sum of money or labor in reliance on the license, it makes the license irrevocable under an estoppel theory.
3. A **license coupled with an interest** is not revocable. A license coupled with an interest permits a person who owns personal property that is on the land of another permission to enter the land to retrieve the personal property.
4. **Oral agreements** produce a **license,** not an easement, so a *failed* attempt to create an easement typically will create a license. However, it is possible the oral license creates an easement by estoppel with detrimental reliance. See sec. VI.A.3.e.

Decoy tip: Trespass ab initio occurs when a person enters property with lawful authority (e.g., to make an arrest) but commits an act that abuses their authority. It is a frequent decoy answer.

F. **Water rights:** There are three categories of water rights: [These rules are rarely MBE tested.]

1. **Drainage of surface waters.** Surface water comes from rainfall, seepage, or melting snow.
   a. **Using surface water:** An owner may **use** all he wants.
   b. **Removing surface water**—there are three approaches:
      1. **Common enemy:** Owner may cast water onto neighbor's land.
      2. **Natural flow theory:** Owner has strict liability for interfering with natural flow.
      3. **Reasonable use doctrine** allows owner to act reasonably.
2. **Riparian rights apply to waterfront property** that borders streams, rivers, lakes, and underground watercourses.
   a. **Reasonable use theory (aka "Riparian Rights" theory):** Each riparian (property bordering the waterway) owner may use only as much water as reasonably needed (courts consider the purpose and extent of the use).
   b. **Prior appropriation doctrine:** Used primarily in western states. The water belongs to the state and an owner (need not be riparian) typically must obtain a permit to use the water, and priority of use is determined by permit date or the first party making beneficial use of the water gets priority.
3. **Ground water** is typically called percolating (not in a defined watercourse), which means the water is beneath the surface and withdrawn by well. The common law rule allows absolute use by the landowner, but this approach is only followed in a few states. More states allow the **"reasonable use"** of ground water drawn from property, but it may not be diverted to other properties if it hurts others with rights to use the same water source.

G. **Right to lateral and subjacent support:** Every landowner has a right to receive necessary physical support from **adjacent soil** (lateral support) and **underlying soil** (subjacent support).

1. **Lateral support:** The right to lateral support (side support from an adjacent property) is absolute, but only for land in its natural state.

   a. **Land in natural state:** A landowner is ***strictly liable*** if their excavation causes adjacent land to subside (collapse) while in its natural state.

   b. **Structures on land** (improvements): If the adjacent land has been improved (e.g., buildings), an adjoining landowner **is *strictly liable* for its excavation <u>only if</u>** it is shown that the **land would have collapsed in its natural state**. If the land **would not have collapsed** in its natural state, then the landowner may be still be liable, but through a ***negligence*** action.

   <u>Example</u>: The owner of Lot 1 erects a building, which meets all codes and regulations. The owner of adjacent Lot 2 begins non-negligently to excavate to erect a building, which caused part of Lot 1 to subside. The owner of Lot 1 will be awarded damages only if he can establish that his land would have collapsed without the building on it (in its natural state).

2. **Subjacent support** is the support of **surface land** when something (e.g., minerals) is **extracted from below the surface** by the subjacent (below the surface) landowner. This occurs when one party owns the surface land and another owns the subjacent land. Even when one has the right to remove minerals from the subjacent land, the surface land must be supported and not subside (collapse) whether in its natural state or if there are buildings. Subjacent owners are ***strictly liable*** for failure to support *preexisting* surface structures. A **negligence** standard applies to **structures erected *after*** the subjacent estate existed. [This rule is rarely MBE tested.]

<u>Decoy tip</u>: A landowner does <u>not</u> have a right to sunlight, fresh air, or a view.

H. Zoning

1. **Purpose:** The Tenth Amendment allows states to regulate the use and development of land through zoning for the protection of the health, safety, comfort, morals, and **general welfare of its citizens**.

2. **Standards:** Zoning regulations must be **reasonable, not arbitrary**, and have a **substantial relation** to the public benefits listed above.

3. Types of zoning ordinances:

   a. **Cumulative:** Creates a **hierarchy of uses of land**. Land zoned for a particular use may be used for the **stated purpose or for any higher use** (e.g., a house could be built in an industrial zone, but a factory could not be built in a residential zone).

   b. **Noncumulative:** Land may only be used for the purpose for which it is zoned.

4. **Variance:** A property owner can seek a variance (waiver) from a zoning regulation if they can show **unnecessary hardship** regarding the use of the land due to the unique features of the property or practical difficulty. The harm to the neighboring areas will also be considered.

   <u>Example</u>: Six months ago the city validly revised its zoning and Woman's home was designated as residential use only. The homes on the other side of the street from her home were zoned for residential and light business use. Woman could apply for a variance to operate a court-reporting service from her house.

   a. **Nonconforming use protects preexisting use** when property is rezoned, such that a property use was **previously allowed** under zoning regulations in place at the time the use was established, but that use is no longer permitted under the new zoning laws. That nonconforming use will be **allowed to continue**, and may continue indefinitely, but will not extend to a *different* nonconforming use.

Example: Ten years ago a couple bought a building. They lived on the second floor and operated a shoe store on the ground floor, as was permitted under the zoning regulations. Five years ago, the building was rezoned as residential use only. The couple's daughter inherited the building and will be permitted to continue operating the shoe store as a nonconforming use (but she cannot extend to a different nonconforming business use).

1. **Improvements and rebuilding**: The majority of jurisdictions find that any change or improvement must comply with the new zoning regulation and that if the structure is destroyed, the rebuilt building must comply with the new zoning regulations.
2. **Some statutes will terminate** and use reasonable **amortization** provisions (which provide a time frame for the owners to comply with the new zoning regulations).

5. **Special use permits** may be required for certain unusual types of uses, such as hospitals.
6. **Spot zoning is not allowed.** Spot zoning is rezoning that targets a small number of parcels and is not the same as neighboring parcels. The result is that the rezoned parcel is benefitted, to the detriment of the neighbors (e.g. one parcel is rezoned for commercial use in an otherwise residential neighborhood).

I. **Condominiums and cooperatives** (common interest property ownership): The homeowners and condominium associations typically include restrictive covenants to maintain the community standards. [These rules are rarely MBE tested.]

1. **Condominium:** Each owner owns the interior of their own unit and an undivided interest in the exterior building and common areas.
   a. **Mortgage:** Each owner has their **own mortgage** on their own unit.
   b. **Maintenance:** Each shareholder must contribute proportionately to maintenance fees and operating expenses.
   c. **Homeowners' associations** (also called condominium associations) oversee and manage the property. Each owner is required to be a member of the homeowners' association and pay fees. Typically, there are rules placing restrictions on how an owner can use their property (e.g., no street parking within the complex).
2. **Cooperatives (co-ops):** A corporation holds title to land and buildings and individual apartments are leased to the shareholders of the co-op corporation. The owners of the corporation are also the tenants of the co-op units.
   a. **Mortgage:** The co-op corporation will have **one mortgage for the entire property**, with each tenant responsible for their proportionate share, though not personally liable for the debt. Should the co-op mortgage go into foreclosure, all tenants risk eviction.
   b. **Maintenance:** Each shareholder must contribute proportionately to maintenance fees and operating expenses.

REAL PROPERTY CHEAT SHEET

LAND SALE CONTRACT

SOF

Writing required
- Parties
- Land description
- Consideration
- Sign by party to be bound

SOF Exception

Part performance:
- Possession
- Improvements
- Pay/purchase price

- Time is not of the essence (unless contracted for)

- Liability for defects:
  - **New** builder: implied warranty habitability fitness
  - **All:** Duty to disclose/no active concealment
- Real estate brokers/Title insurance

MARKETABLE TITLE

- At closing
- Chain of title defects
- Encumbrances
  - Mortgages/lien
  - Use restrictions
  - Zoning violations
  - Significant encroach.
- Buyer benefit-can waive

EQUIT. CONVERSION

Before close/Buyer = owner
- Risk of loss on buyer (majority rule)
- Seller/buyer death does not terminate k

MERGER DOCTRINE

Deed controls after close
No suit on contract after

ADVERSE POSSESSION

- Actual & exclusive use
- Open & notorious
- Hostile (no permission)
- Continuous
- Statutory period

*Can quiet title, but not mkt.

REMEDIES

- **Damages**
- **Deposit forfeiture**
- **Specific Performance**
  - Contract is valid
  - Conditions on P satisfied
  - Inadequate legal remedy
  - Mutuality of performance
  - Feasibility of enforcement
  - No Defenses

Memorization tip:
Chocolate Cheesecake Is My Favorite Dessert

CONVEYANCE BY DEED

Lawfully executed
- Identify parties
- Writing signed by grantor
- Words of intent to transfer
- No consideration required
- Adequate land description

Properly delivered
- Intent of *present* transfer
  - Recording — presume
  - Physical delivery — presumed
  - Third party — if control relinquished
- Acceptance (presumed)

General Warranty Deed

Present — If breached, @ time of sale
- Seisin — own as purported
- Right to convey
- Against encumbrances

Future — At any time, Defend *meritorious* claim
- Title
- Quiet enjoyment
- Further assurances

Quit claim deed

- No warranties of title

Estoppel by Deed

- Conveys w/out owning
- Subsequently obtains
- Transfers automatically

Will "speaks at death"

MBE default rules:
- **Ademption** — specific devise fails if not in estate
- **Exoneration** — encumbrance on property paid off
- **Lapse** — Beneficiary Predeceases — gift fails

Trust

- **Private trust**
- **Charitable**
  - **Cy Pres** — substitute charity if possible, resulting trust if not
- **Lapse** (default) — Beneficiary predeceases — gift fails

Dedication

- Intent to dedicate
- Acceptance

Defective Deeds

- Void
- Voidable
- Recording no cure

Powers of Appointment

RECORDING ACTS

◆ Recording provides **notice** ◆ Protects **subsequent** purchasers only	**Common law**: First in time, first in right	**Pure race:** First to record, wins
Pure Notice	"No conveyance or mortgage of real property shall be good against subsequent purchasers **for value and without notice** unless the same be **recorded** according to law."	Subsequent **BFP** wins
Race-Notice	"No unrecorded conveyance or mortgage of real property shall be good against subsequent purchasers **for value and without notice**, who shall **FIRST record**."	Subsequent **BFP *who records first*** (wins race) wins

BONA FIDE PURCHASER

Take for value:	**Without notice**:
◆ Purchasers/mortgagees ◆ Not judgment lien creditors; gift; devisee ◆ Not void deeds ◆ **Shelter rule**—if takes from BFP, can "stand in shoes" even w/ notice	◆ Actual ◆ Inquiry (RP standard) ◆ Record (title search) but no wild deeds Memorization tip: **AIR**

MORTGAGES/SECURITY INTERESTS

TYPES	MORTGAGOR RIGHTS	MORTGAGEE RIGHTS
◆ Mortgage ◆ Deed of trust ◆ Installment land contract ◆ Equitable mortgage ◆ Equitable vendor's lien	◆ Possession & title ◆ Transfer—sale, devise, gift **Sale of mortgaged prop**: ◆ **Subject to**—no personal liability for buyer ◆ **Assume**—buyer has pers. liability, but orig. borrower is surety, absent release	◆ Payment on loan ◆ Enforce contract ◆ Transfer (new lender) ◆ Record (notice)
DISCHARGE		**MIP**
◆ Pay in full ◆ Deed of release (if fair)		Responsible like owner Lien- no poss. before Title- ok poss. before

FORECLOSURE

Process:	REDEMPTION
◆ Judicial foreclosure sale ◆ Must join all junior mortgagees	◆ Mortgage paid off (No partial redemption for JT/TE/TIC) **Equitable:** pay amount owing *before* foreclosure sale **Statutory:** pay amount owing *after* foreclosure sale

PRIORITY	DEFICIENCY
◆ Chronologically- with each creditor paid in full before lower priority creditor takes anything ◆ PMM: mortgage to originally buy property ◆ Secured = property pledged as collateral ◇ Future advances: use original loan date ◆ Judgment lien when filed, not debt accrued ◆ Foreclosure not binding on Sr. mortgagee	If proceeds from foreclosure sale can't cover debts, lender can: ◆ Sue mortgagor personally ◆ Sue subsequent purchaser if "assumed" the mortgage
(1) Fees attorneys/trustees (2) PMM, or Secured Sr. interests (3) Secured Jr. interests (4) Unsecured interests	**ANTIDEFICIENCY** Lender receives no more than amount owed **SURPLUS** Once all debts paid, any balance to mortgagor

ESTATES IN LAND

PRESENT POSSESSORY	FUTURE INTEREST	EXECUTORY INTEREST
◆ Fee simple absolute	◆ None	**RAP applies** **Shifting:** from 3P to 3P Shifts from one interest holder to another **Springing**: from O to 3P ◆ Springs from owner's interest allowing a 3P to become possessory ◆ Follows gap in possess. & O had reversion in gap
Defeasible fees— *May* cut prior interest short: ◆ Fee simple determinable ◆ FS subj. cond. subsequent ◆ FS subj. executory limitation	◆ Poss. of reverter ⇨ O ◆ Right of reentry ⇨ O ◆ Exec. interest ⇨ 3P	
◆ Life Estate ◆ Pur autre vie (life of another) ◆ Life estate defeasible	◆ Reversion ⇨ Grantor/O or ◆ Remainder ⇨ 3P	

REMAINDERS	LIFE TENANT: LT Rights & Duties	LIFE TENANT: Remainderman Duties
Follows life estate & created in same instrument ◆ Vested ◆ Vested subject to open (class gifts) **RAP** ◆ Contingent remainder **RAP** ◇ Unborn/unascertained ◇ Condition precedent ◆ Alternative contingent rem. ◆ Destructibility of cont. rem.	◆ Ordinary use &profit ◇ Except no resource depletion ◆ Pay costs—net rental benefit ◇ Operating expenses: repair/tax ◇ Mortgage *interest* ◇ No personal liability if shortfall ◆ Not commit waste: (Voluntary/ Permissive/Ameliorative) ◆ Not remove fixtures	Pay: ◆ Expenses over net rental benefit ◆ Mortgage *principal*

RAP ANALYSIS	RAP APPLIES TO...
1. Classify the interest—If RAP applies... ⟶ **2.** Identify measuring life **3.** Identify triggering event **4.** Analyze the possibilities—Could the triggering event occur more than 21 years after the death of a measuring life? If yes, RAP is violated, and **5.** ~~Strike~~ any interest violating RAP and reclassify what remains of the interest	◆ Contingent remainders ◆ Vested *subject to open* (class gifts) ◆ Executory interests ◆ Purchase options in gross ◆ Right of first refusal ◆ Power of appointment ◆ Private trusts

RESTRAINT ON ALIENATION

Absolute restraints are void
Purchase option lease—ok
Option in gross—ok, but **RAP**
Right of 1st refusal—ok, but **RAP**

Joint Tenancy Key Features

- ◆ Express rt. survivorship (automatic)
- ◆ = shares
- ◆ = right to possess all
- ◆ 4 unities to create: time/title/ interest/ possession

CONCURRENT ESTATES

Joint T. Severance	Co-T Rules (JT/TIC)
◆ Convey/contract—Yes ◆ Mortgage: ◇ <u>Lien theory</u>—No Unless foreclosure ◇ <u>Title theory</u>—Yes ◆ Partition—Yes ◆ Will—No ◆ Lease—Maybe, by jx ◆ Judgment lien—Yes, but only @ foreclosure	◆ = right to possess all ◆ Own use: no duty to share profit/loss ◆ No right to bind co-T ◆ Ouster (Acctg. reqt.) ◆ Partition (kind/sale) ◆ Accounting: If paid excess share taxes, mortgage, repairs ◆ Duty of fair dealing

LANDLORD & TENANT

Types of Tenancies
- Tenancy for years
- Periodic tenancy
- Tenancy at will
- Sufferance/Holdover T

Tort Liability
Landlord:
- Common: maintain
- Unit: disclose/fix latent defects
- Public: repair known/should know dangers
- Non-negligently repair
- Adhere bldg. codes

Tenant: Like an owner

Landlord Duties
- Deliver possession
- Fix latent defects
- Repair non-negligently
- Cov. Quiet Enjoyment
  - ◇ Constructive eviction:
    - ◇ Notice
    - ◇ Fail to respond
    - ◇ Move out/reas. time
- Implied War. Habitability
  - ◇ T can terminate/move
  - ◇ Make repairs/deduct
  - ◇ Pay less/sue for dmgs
- No retaliatory eviction
- Comply w/ Fair Housing

Tenant Duties
- Pay rent
  - ◇ Defenses to paying rent:
    - ◇ Landlord fail in duties
    - ◇ Destruction premises
    - ◇ Contract defenses
    - ◇ Surrender & LL accept
- Pay security deposit
- Avoid committing waste
- Surrender premises
- Not breach/abandon:
  - ◇ Breach = eviction
  - ◇ Abandon: LL may accept; re-let prefer (mitigate); or sue

ASSIGNMENT & SUBLEASE
- Restrictions are strictly/literally construed
- Waiver if LL knows & no objection

Assignment	Sublease
◆ Entire term ◆ New T personally liable ◆ Old T also liable Except: if novation	◆ Less than entire term ◆ New T not pers. liable ◆ Old T remains liable

FIXTURES
- **M**ethod of attach — firm imbed.
- **A**daptability — peculiarly
- **R**emoval — no damage
- **I**ntent at time
- **A**greement in lease?

Memorization tip: **MARIA**

Fixtures rules apply to:
- Lease tenant
- Life estate holder
- Mortgagee in foreclosure

Trade fixtures: Can remove

WASTE
Tenants & life tenants:
- Voluntary: intentional
- Permissive: neglect
- Ameliorative: improve

CONDEMN LEASE
Total: No pay rent

Temporary/partial: Pay rent, but share in condemnation award

LAND USE

EASEMENT Features
- Affirmative or negative
- Appurtenant: dominant/servient
- In gross (personal)
- Transfers to new owner, except: If servient estate sold to BFP

Creation
- Express
- Implication
- Necessity
- Prescription
- Estoppel

Scope
- Location
- Future needs too
- Right to repair

Termination
- **E**stoppel
- **N**ecessity ends
- **D**estruction
- **C**ondemnation
- **R**elease-writing
- **A**bandon action
- **M**erge 2 parcels
- **P**rescription

Memorization tip: **END CRAMP**

RESTRICT. COVS
Burden run:

Writing
Intent
Touch & **C**oncern
Horz. & **V**ert. Privity
Notice

Memorization tip: **WITCH VaN**

SERV. IMPLIED
- Common plan
- Notice (inquiry)
- No writing

PROFIT
- Remove resource

LICENSE
- Use only — can revoke

WATER RIGHTS
- Surface
- Riparian rights
- Ground water

SUPPORT
- Lateral
- Subjacent

ZONING
- Variance — hardship
- Non-conforming use ok

Condo	Own unit +	Co-op	Co-owns

REAL PROPERTY MBE PRACTICE QUESTIONS

These questions are designed to reinforce the skill in how to approach MBE questions. While they will also test your knowledge in the limited areas addressed, you will not master your knowledge by only practicing these questions. To fully master the rules, you need to do practice questions outside of these from your bar company and/or the NCBE.

QUESTION 1

A seller contracted to sell land to a buyer for $300,000. The contract provided that the closing would be 60 days after the contract was signed and that the seller would convey to the buyer a "marketable title" by a quitclaim deed at closing. The contract contained no other provisions regarding the title to be delivered to the buyer.

A title search revealed that the land was subject to an unsatisfied $50,000 mortgage and a right-of-way easement over a portion of the land. The buyer now claims that the title is unmarketable and has refused to close.

Is the buyer correct?

A. No, because nothing under these facts renders title unmarketable.
B. No, because the buyer agreed to accept a quitclaim deed.
C. Yes, because the right-of-way easement makes the title unmarketable.
D. Yes, because the unsatisfied mortgage makes the title unmarketable.

QUESTION 2

A landlord owned Blackacre in fee simple. Three years ago, the landlord and a tenant agreed to a month-to-month tenancy with the tenant paying the landlord rent each month. After six months of the tenant's occupancy, the landlord suggested to the tenant that she could buy Blackacre for a monthly payment of no more than her rent. The landlord and the tenant orally agreed that the tenant would pay $25,000 in cash, the annual real estate taxes, the annual fire insurance premiums and the costs of maintaining Blackacre, plus the monthly mortgage payments that the landlord owed on Blackacre. They further orally agreed that within six years the tenant could pay whatever mortgage balances were then due and the landlord would give her a warranty deed to the property. The tenant's average monthly payments did turn out to be the same as her monthly rent.

The tenant fully complied with all of the obligations she had undertaken. She made some structural modifications to Blackacre. Blackacre is now worth 50% more than it was when the landlord and the tenant made their oral agreement. The tenant made her financing arrangements and was ready to complete the purchase of Blackacre, but the landlord refused to close. The tenant brought an appropriate action for specific performance against the landlord to enforce the agreement.

Who should prevail?

A. The landlord, because the agreements were oral and violated the statute of frauds.
B. The landlord, subject to the return of the $25,000, because the arrangement was still a tenancy.
C. The tenant, because the doctrine of part performance applies.
D. The tenant, because the statute of frauds does not apply to oral purchase and sale agreements between landlords and tenants in possession.

QUESTION 3

A landowner executed an instrument in the proper form of a deed, purporting to convey his land to a friend. The landowner handed the instrument to the friend, saying, "This is yours, but please do not record it until after I am dead. Otherwise, it will cause me no end of trouble with my relatives." Two days later, the landowner asked the friend to return the deed to him because he had decided that he should devise the land to the friend by will rather than by deed. The friend said that he would destroy the deed and a day or so later falsely told the landowner that the deed had been destroyed. Six months ago, the landowner, who had never executed a will, died intestate, survived by a daughter as his sole heir at law. The day after the landowner's death, the friend recorded the deed from him. As soon as the daughter discovered this recording and the friend's claim to the land, she brought an appropriate action against the friend to quiet title to the land.

For whom should the court hold?

A. The daughter, because the death of the landowner deprived the subsequent recordation of any effect.
B. The daughter, because the friend was dishonest in reporting that he had destroyed the deed.
C. The friend, because the deed was delivered to him.
D. The friend, because the deed was recorded by him.

QUESTION 4

A man conveyed land by quitclaim deed as a gift to his cousin, who did not then record the deed or take possession of the land. Six months later, when the man was still in possession, he conveyed the land by quitclaim deed as a gift to a friend, who knew nothing of the deed to the cousin. The friend did not record his deed. The man then vacated the land, and the friend took possession. The recording act of the jurisdiction provides as follows: "No unrecorded conveyance or mortgage of real property shall be good against subsequent purchasers for value without notice, who shall first record." Recently, the cousin learned about the friend's deed and possession, immediately recorded her deed, and sued the friend for possession and to quiet title. The friend then recorded his deed and raised all available defenses.

For whom is the court likely to decide?

A. For the cousin, because she was first in time and the friend was not a purchaser.
B. For the cousin, because the friend failed to first record.
C. For the friend, because a subsequent good-faith donee has priority over a prior donee who fails to record.
D. For the friend, because he was first in possession.

QUESTION 5

A seller conveyed residential land to a buyer by a warranty deed that contained no exceptions and recited that the full consideration had been paid. To finance the purchase, the buyer borrowed 80% of the necessary funds from a bank. The seller agreed to finance 15% of the purchase price, and the buyer agreed to provide cash for the remaining 5%. At the closing, the buyer signed a promissory note to the seller for 15% of the purchase price but did not execute a mortgage. The bank knew of the loan made by the seller and of the promissory note executed by the buyer to the seller. The buyer also signed a note to the bank, secured by a mortgage, for the 80% advanced by the bank.

The buyer has now defaulted on both loans. There are no applicable statutes.

Which loan has priority?

A. The bank's loan, because the seller can finance a part of the purchase price only by use of an installment land contract.
B. The bank's loan, because it was secured by a purchase-money mortgage.
C. The seller's loan, because a promissory note to a seller has priority over a bank loan for residential property.
D. The seller's loan, because the bank knew that the seller had an equitable vendor's lien.

QUESTION 6

Thirty years ago, a landowner conveyed land by warranty deed to a church (a charity) "so long as the land herein conveyed is used as the site for the principle religious edifice maintained by said church." Twenty years ago, the landowner died intestate, survived by a single heir. One year ago, the church dissolved and its church building situated on the land was demolished. There is no applicable statute. The common law Rule Against Perpetuities is unmodified in the jurisdiction.

In an appropriate action, the landowner's heir and the attorney general, who is the appropriate official to assert public interests in charitable trusts, contest the right to the land.

In such action, who will prevail?

A. The landowner's heir, as successor to the landowner's possibility of reverter.
B. The landowner's heir, because a charity cannot convey assets donated to it.
C. The attorney general, because cy pres should be applied to devote the land to religious purposes to carry out the charitable intent of the landowner.
D. The attorney general, because the landowner's attempt to restrict the church's fee simple violated the Rule Against Perpetuities.

QUESTION 7

A landowner owned in fee simple Lots 1 and 2 in an urban subdivision. The lots were vacant and unproductive. They were held as a speculation that their value would increase. The landowner died and, by his duly probated will, devised the residue of his estate (of which Lots 1 and 2 were part) to his sister for life with remainder in fee simple to his friend. The landowner's executor distributed the estate under appropriate court order and notified the sister that future real estate taxes on Lots 1 and 2 were her responsibility to pay. Except for the statutes relating to probate and those relating to real estate taxes, there is no applicable statute.

The sister failed to pay the real estate taxes due for Lots 1 and 2. To prevent a tax sale of the fee simple, the friend paid the taxes and demanded that the sister reimburse her for same. When the sister refused, the friend brought an appropriate action against the sister to recover the amount paid.

In such action, what should the friend recover?

A. The amount paid, because a life tenant has the duty to pay current charges.
B. The present value of the interest that the amount paid would earn during the sister's lifetime.
C. Nothing, because the sister's sole possession gave the right to decide whether or not taxes should be paid.
D. Nothing, because the sister never received any income from the lots.

QUESTION 8

A landlord leased a building to a tenant for a 10-year term. Two years after the term began, the tenant subleased the building to a sublessee for a 5-year term. Under the terms of the sublease, the sublessee agreed to make monthly rent payments to the tenant. Although the sublessee made timely rent payments to the tenant, the tenant did not forward four of those payments to the landlord. The tenant has left the jurisdiction and cannot be found. The landlord has sued the sublessee for the unpaid rent.

There is no applicable statute.

If the court rules that the sublessee is not liable to the landlord for the unpaid rent, what will be the most likely reason?

A. A sublessee is responsible to the landlord only as a surety for unpaid rent owed by the tenant.
B. The sublease constitutes a novation of the original lease.
C. The sublessee is not in privity of estate or contract with the landlord.
D. The sublessee's rent payments to the tenant fully discharged the sublessee's obligation to pay rent to the landlord.

QUESTION 9

A man owned land along the south side of a highway. To the south of the man's land was a lot owned by a woman who lived on it in a house. Five years ago, the man conveyed a right-of-way easement over his land to the woman because it provided a more direct route between her house and the highway. The easement was evidenced by a clearly marked path. The document granting the easement was promptly recorded. Three years ago, the woman conveyed her house to the man. The man never took actual possession of the house. Two years ago, the man conveyed the house to a purchaser by a warranty deed. Two months after the purchaser moved into the house, a neighbor informed him about the easement. He then began using the path that had been marked on the man's land. When the man noticed the purchaser using the path, he erected a barricade on his land that effectively prevented the purchaser from using the path.

The purchaser has sued the man, claiming that he has an easement over the man's land.

Who is likely to prevail?

A. The man, because the easement was extinguished.
B. The man, because the purchaser did not have actual notice of the easement at the time of acquisition.
C. The purchaser, because he purchased the house by warranty deed.
D. The purchaser, because the easement was of public record when he acquired the house.

QUESTION 10

An owner conveyed Whiteacre "to my daughter, her heirs and assigns, so long as the premises are used for residential purposes, then to my son and his heirs." The common law Rule Against Perpetuities, unmodified by statute, is part of the law of the jurisdiction in which the farm is located.

As a consequence of the conveyance, what is the son's interest in Whiteacre?

A. The son's interest is nothing.
B. The son's interest is a valid executory interest.
C. The son's interest is a possibility of reverter.
D. The son's interest is a right of entry for condition broken.

REAL PROPERTY ANSWER KEY	
Question	**Answer**
1	C
2	C
3	C
4	A
5	B
6	A
7	D
8	C
9	A
10	A

Use this quick answer key to get a general idea of how you did on this set of questions. The answer explanations that follow provide a step-by-step deconstruction of each question.

REAL PROPERTY MBE ANSWER EXPLANATIONS

START HERE

FACTS **Q1**

A seller **contracted** to **sell land** to a **buyer for $300,000**. The contract provided that the **closing would be 60 days** after the contract was signed and that the seller would convey to the buyer a **"marketable title" by a quitclaim deed** at closing. The contract contained no other provisions regarding the title to be delivered to the buyer.

A title search revealed that the land was subject to an **unsatisfied $50,000 mortgage** **and** a **right-of-way easement** over a portion of the land.

The buyer now claims that the **title is unmarketable** and has refused to close.

CLUE: 2 rules are being tested

CALL Is the buyer correct?

> The call didn't identify the subject or rule at issue, but a glance at the **sentence above** provides the clue.
>
> **Real property: marketable title**
>
> Now you can read the facts proactively, looking for those pertinent to marketable title rules. See bolding.

SOLVE

Q **Is the buyer correct** (that title is unmarketable)?

Think of all the marketable title ***rules*** that can apply to solve this problem

- R: **Quitclaim deed** does not affect implied covenant of marketable title.
- R: **Marketable title** measured at closing date.
- R: **Marketable title:** Implied that seller will provide. (Free from reasonable doubt.)

MARKETABLE	UNMARKETABLE
• **Mortgage that can be satisfied at closing**	• Mortgage/lien not satisfied by closing
• Zoning restrictions	• Existing violation zoning ordinance
• Easement that is beneficial, visible or known	• **Easement**/Restrictive covenant (undisclosed)
• Slight encroachment	• Significant encroachment
	• Adv. Possessor/Future interest (unascertainable)

*After analyzing the facts using the rules, **predict the answer.** Answer the call of the question using "because" to identify the specific issue/sub-rule they are testing. (This will help you to tease through the distracting answer choices.)*

A Yes, title is unmarketable **because** of the **easement only** (note, the mortgage is o.k.).

Now look for an answer choice that comports with your analysis.

DECODE

(A) No, because nothing under these facts renders title unmarketable.

Wrong analysis. The easement makes title unmarketable.

(B) No, because the buyer agreed to accept a quitclaim deed.

Wrong rule. A quitclaim deed must still be marketable. Common decoy.

C. Yes, because the right-of-way easement makes the title unmarketable.

*Correct. The general rule applies: **An undisclosed easement renders title unmarketable.** The easement **exception** (where a beneficial, visible, or known easement provides marketable title) **does not apply** because this easement was undisclosed and no facts indicate it was visible or beneficial.*

(D) Yes, because the unsatisfied mortgage makes the title unmarketable.

Wrong analysis. A $50,000 outstanding mortgage can be paid off with the proceeds from a $300,000 sale.

FACTS **Q2**

A landlord owned Blackacre in fee simple. Three years ago, the landlord and a tenant agreed to a **month-to-month tenancy** with the tenant paying the landlord rent each month. After six months of the tenant's occupancy, the landlord suggested to the tenant that she **could buy Blackacre** for a **monthly payment of no more than her rent.** The landlord and the tenant **orally agreed** that the tenant would pay **$25,000 in cash, the annual real estate taxes, the annual fire insurance premiums, and the costs of maintaining Blackacre, plus the monthly mortgage payments** that the landlord owed on Blackacre. They further **orally agreed** that within **six years the tenant could pay whatever mortgage balances** were then due and the landlord would give her a **warranty deed** to the property. The tenant's average monthly payments did turn out to be the same as her monthly rent.

The tenant **fully complied** with all of the obligations she had undertaken. She made some **structural modifications** to Blackacre. Blackacre is now **worth 50% more** than it was when the landlord and the tenant made their oral agreement. The tenant made her financing arrangements and was ready to complete the purchase of Blackacre, but the **landlord refused to close.** The tenant brought an appropriate action for **specific performance** against the landlord to enforce the agreement.

Who should prevail?

One party seeking specific performance is a common mechanism used to ask about REAL PROP contracts.

SOLVE

RULE 1

SPECIFIC PERFORMANCE	**ANALYSIS**
• **Valid <u>C</u>ontract** w/ def. & certain terms	• **Buy Blackacre, but ORAL**
◦ **SOF-** Writing reqt.	• **No writing**
◦ **Except: Part Performance (need 2 of 3)** » **<u>P</u>ossession** » **<u>I</u>mprovements** » **<u>P</u>ay part/all purchase price**	• **T in possession 6 years &** • **Structural modifications &** • **25k, taxes, insurance, maintenance**
• <u>C</u>onditions imposed on P satisfied • <u>I</u>nadequate legal remedy • <u>M</u>utuality of performance • <u>F</u>easibility of enforcement • No <u>D</u>efenses	(All other elements of specific performance are easily met)

RULE 2

A Tenant should prevail **<u>because</u>** she satisfied the **part-performance exception to SOF.**

Now look for a similar answer choice.

DECODE

(A.) The landlord, because the agreements were oral and violated the statute of frauds.

Incomplete analysis. This is the general rule, but it does not apply because the exception is satisfied.

(B.) The landlord, subject to the return of the $25,000, because the arrangement was still a tenancy.

Wrong rule. Since the part-performance SOF exception is satisfied, this is a sale of property, not a mere tenancy.

C. **The tenant, because the doctrine of part performance applies.**

Correct. The rule exception is clearly satisfied since only two of the three part performance PIP factors must be met and here there were facts for all three.

(D.) The tenant, because the statue of frauds does not apply to oral purchase and sale agreements between landlords and tenants in possession.

Not a rule. Tenants often will be a party to an oral land sale contract that may satisfy the SOF part performance exception, as in this question. If there were a rule that limited application of the exception to tenants in possession, you would have heard of it.

Be wary of picking answers with rules you've never heard of; they are often made up.

So, looking for:
- Lawful execution
- Proper delivery

Q3

FACTS

A landowner executed an instrument in the **proper form** of a **deed,** purporting **to convey** his land to a friend. **[☑ lawfully executed]** The landowner **handed** the instrument to the friend **[☑ physical delivery]**, saying, "This is yours, **[☑ words of intent to make present transfer][title has now passed & is not revocable]** but please **do not record it until after** 1
I am dead. Otherwise, it will cause me no end of trouble with my relatives." Two days later, the landowner asked the friend to return the deed to him because he had decided that he should devise the land to the friend by will rather than by deed. **The friend said that he** 2
would destroy the deed and a day or so later falsely told the landowner that the deed had been destroyed. Six months ago, the landowner, who had never executed a will, died intestate, survived by a daughter as his sole heir at law. **The day after the landowner's** 3
death, the friend recorded the deed from him. As soon as the daughter discovered this recording and the friend's claim to the land, she brought an appropriate action against the friend to **quiet title to the land.** ← **REAL PROP Q**

For whom should the court hold?

SOLVE

DEEDS: Must be **1) lawfully executed** & **2) properly delivered**

FORMALITIES (LAWFULLY EXECUTED)	
FACTS	**ANALYSIS**
• "Executed instrument" • "Proper form of deed"	☑ Clearly established in first sentence

DEED DELIVERY	
RULE	**ANALYSIS**
• Intent of present transfer; presumed by:	☑ "This is yours"
◦ Recording ◦ Physical delivery (agent ok)	☑ Physical delivery; handed to friend
• Acceptance	☑ Presumed

RULE: *Title passes **immediately** upon proper delivery and is **not revocable.***

A Court should hold for friend because upon physical delivery, a lawfully executed **deed was properly delivered.**

→ Now look for a similar answer choice.

DECODE

(A.) The daughter, because the death of the landowner deprived the subsequent recordation of any effect.

Not a rule. Don't fall for made up rules. Decoy 1 & 3. 1 3

(B.) The daughter, because the friend was dishonest in reporting that he had destroyed the deed.

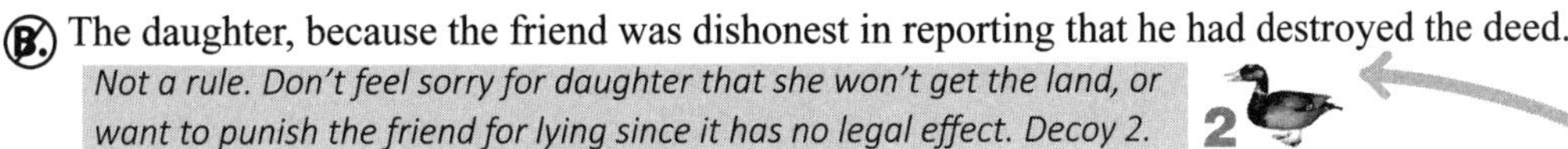

Not a rule. Don't feel sorry for daughter that she won't get the land, or want to punish the friend for lying since it has no legal effect. Decoy 2. 2

C. The friend, because the deed was delivered to him.

*Correct. **Title transfers at proper delivery.***

(D.) The friend, because the deed was recorded by him.

Not a rule. Recording a document does not make it valid if it is not (and here it was not). Decoy 3.

> ***PRO TIP:***
> ***Don't feel sorry for people in MBE Qs, it's a common decoy***

Can be an important fact for inquiry notice

FACTS

Q4

A man conveyed land by **quitclaim deed** as a **gift to his cousin,** who **did not then record** the deed **or take possession** of the land. Six months **later,** when the **man was still in possession,** he conveyed the land by **quitclaim deed** as a gift to a friend, who **knew nothing of the deed to the cousin.** The friend **did not record** his deed. The man then **vacated** the land, and the **friend took possession.**

PRO TIP:
Draw a diagram when facts are confusing

The recording act of the jurisdiction provides as follows: "No unrecorded conveyance or mortgage of real property shall be good against subsequent purchasers for value without notice, who shall **first** record."

Recently, the **cousin learned** about the friend's deed and possession, immediately **recorded** her deed, and sued the friend for possession and to quiet title. The friend then **recorded his deed** and raised all available defenses.

REAL PROP Q

CALL For whom is the court likely to decide?

SOLVE

C/L rule: First in time, first in right protects all 1st grantees (even if not a BFP,) *unless* the recording act allows a 2nd purchaser (BFP) to take the property away from the 1st grantee.

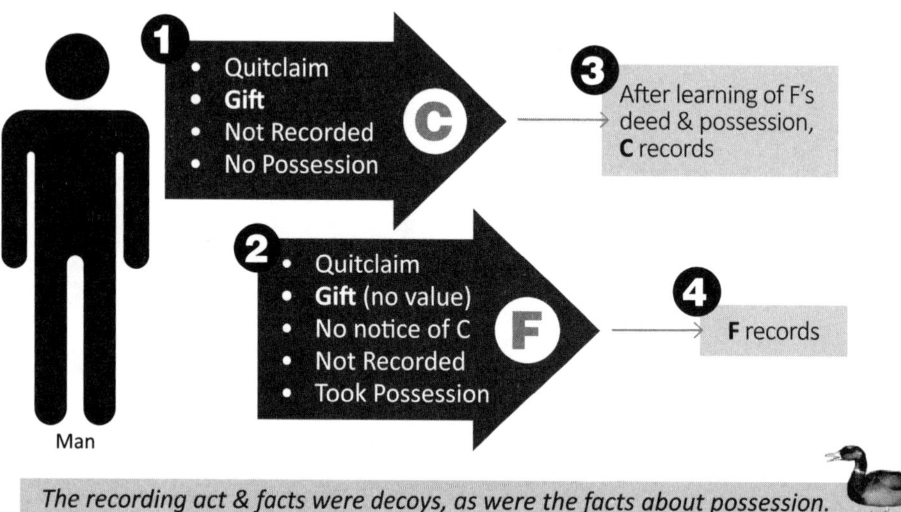

The recording act & facts were decoys, as were the facts about possession.

A The court is likely to decide for C **because** F is not a BFP (gift, so did not take for value), so the common law rule applies.

Now look for a similar answer choice.

DECODE

A. For the cousin, because she was first in time and the friend was not a purchaser.

Correct. The common law "first in time" rule applies.

B. For the cousin, because the friend failed to first record.

Wrong Rule. This rule would apply if F was a BFP, but since F received as a gift, the race-notice recording act rule does not apply and including the recording act was a decoy.

C. For the friend, because a subsequent good-faith donee has priority over a prior donee who fails to record.

Not a rule. They are trying to get you to doubt yourself by making up a rule that sounds like it could be legitimate, but isn't.

D. For the friend, because he was first in possession.

Not a rule. The correct common law rule is first in time, not first in possession. The facts about possession were decoys.

FACTS **KEY FACTS** **Q5**

A seller conveyed residential land to a buyer by a **warranty deed** that contained no exceptions and recited that the **full consideration had been paid.** To finance the purchase, the buyer **borrowed 80% of the necessary funds from a bank.** The **seller agreed to finance 15%** of the purchase price, and the buyer agreed to provide cash for the remaining 5%.

At the closing, the **buyer signed a promissory note** to the seller for 15% of the purchase price but **did not execute a mortgage.** The **bank knew of the loan made by the seller** and of the promissory note executed by the buyer to the seller. The **buyer also signed a note to the bank, secured by a mortgage,** for the 80% advanced by the bank.

The buyer has now defaulted on both loans. There are **no applicable statutes.**

"No applicable statute" means the default rules apply

CALL Which **loan** has priority? **REAL PROP Q**

SOLVE

RULES	ANALYSIS
Promissory note: Loan w/personal promise to repay **Mortgage:** Loan which pledges the land as collateral for repayment **Foreclosure:** A process where the *mortgagee* can reach the land in satisfaction of the loan if *mortgagor* is in default. • **Priority of loans:** In descending order of priority, (usually chronologically) 1. **Purchase Money Mortgage:** Mortgage to originally buy the property 2. **Secured debts** 3. **Judgment liens**	Seller only has a promissory note (even though this was a loan used to originally buy the house, since no mortgage was executed, it is an unsecured loan and *not* a PMM). Bank has a PMM, since the loan was used to originally buy the property.

 The bank mortgage has priority over Seller's loan because it is a PMM.

Now look for a similar answer choice.

DECODE

(A.) The bank's loan, because the seller can finance a part of the purchase price ***only*** by use of an installment land contract.

This is a misstatement of the rule. A property's purchase price can be financed with an installment land contract, a PMM or an equitable vendor's lien.

B. The bank's loan, because it was secured by a purchase-money mortgage.

Correct. A PMM takes first priority in repayment from foreclosure proceeds.

(C.) The seller's loan, because a promissory note to a seller has priority over a bank loan for residential property.

This is not the rule. If this was a rule, you would have learned it. A PMM has priority. The seller could have opted to execute a PMM mortgage here (which as a vendor's PMM would have had priority over a bank PMM), but the seller did not do that here since seller has only a promissory note.

(D.) The seller's loan, because the bank knew that the seller had an equitable vendor's lien.

Incorrect analysis. The seller did not have an equitable vendor's lien (an amount left unpaid to the seller at closing) because "full consideration had been paid." Rather, the seller has an unsecured loan (the promissory note).

Notice how easy it is to find the right answer when you solve the Q first.

FACTS **Q6**

Thirty years ago, a landowner conveyed land by **warranty deed** to a church (a charity) **"so long as** the land herein conveyed is used as the site for the principle religious edifice maintained by said church."

Twenty years ago, the **landowner died** intestate, survived by a **single heir.**

One year ago, the church dissolved and its church building situated on the land was demolished. **There is no applicable statute**. ***The common law Rule Against Perpetuities is unmodified in the jurisdiction.***

This phrasing is used when there are majority/ minority rule splits. "No applicable statute" means the default rule applies

They often put RAP in as a decoy even when it doesn't apply.

In an appropriate action, the landowner's heir and the attorney general, who is the appropriate official to assert public interests in charitable trusts, contest the right to the **land.** ← **REAL PROP Q**

CALL In such action, who will prevail?

***PRO TIP:** If you don't have the rules memorized yet, do Q open book, like here, using the Future Interests Decoded chart from the book.*

SOLVE

Future interest Qs:

1. **Identify the future interest.**
   …to a church (a charity) **"so long as …**the land … is used as the site for the principle religious edifice (building)…"

ANALYSIS:

Present possessory estate: "So long as" is the language used to create a fee simple determinable **(FSD).**

Future interest: Possiblity of reverter (POR) in **Grantor** (O)

- **Automatic forfeiture** at stated event (land not used as a building for church, which happened 1 year ago).
- **Default rules** (apply per "no applicable statute"): Devisable, **descendible (intestacy),** transferable intervivos. (Landowner died intestate, leaving a **single heir as a descendent.)**

2. **Does RAP apply?** No. Classic decoy.
3. **Who owns the property now?**
   Landowner's heir prevails because the land was automatically forfeited once not used for a church building *and* Landowner's POR passed through intestacy to Landowner's single heir since a POR is fully alienable (devisable, descendible, transferable).

FUTURE INTERESTS DECODED
It's all about decoding the language…

Present Possessory Estate	Language used to create (… is the stated event)	Future Interest Devisable (will), descendible (intestacy) & transfer inter vivos	FI in O	FI in 3rd party
Fee simple absolute	"To A" "To A and his heirs"			
Fee simple determinable	Durational language "To A so long as…" "To A during…" "To A while…"	Possibility of reverter (*automatic forfeiture)	X	
Fee simple subject to a condition subsequent	"To A upon condition …" "To A provided that…" "To A, but if…" And, right of re-entry language	Right of re-entry (* not automatic, must exercise or it's waived) (Not transferable inter vivos)	X	
Fee simple subject to an executory interest	"To A so long as X. If not, to B" "To A, but if X occurs, to B"	Executory Interest RAP (*shifting* 3P (A) to 3P (B)) Upon event, A's interest is cut short & interest shifts from 3P interest holder (A) to 3P (B)		X
RAP applies	"To A when and if A marries B"	Executory Interest RAP (*springing* out of O to 3P) Upon event, 3P takes from O		X
	"To A for life, & X years after A dies, to B"	Executory Interest RAP (*springing from gap* in possession) O has reversion interest during gap & B has executory interest	X	X
Life estate	"To A for life"	Reversion	X	
Life estate defeasible RAP may apply	"To A for life, then to C" "To A for life, then to B & heirs, but if…then to B immediately"	Remainder can be • Vested: born, ascertained, or • Vested subject to open RAP • Contingent RAP: unborn, unascertained or subj. to condition precedent		X
Life estate pur autre vie	"To A for the life of B"	Reversion	X	
Life estate pur autre vie defeasible	"To A for the life of B, then to C"	Remainder (see above)		X

MBE tip: To solve future interest problems, analyze them sequentially, clause by clause. If you are struggling with classifying future interests, remember a third party transferee can only obtain two types of future interests: 1.) A remainder (at the natural end of a life estate), or 2.) An executory interest, which does not occur at the natural termination of the preceding estate, rather, it cuts short, or divests the preceding estate.

DECODE

A. The landowner's heir, as successor to the landowner's possibility of reverter.

Correct. Three rules are being tested here: 1) This is a FSD, 2) A POR is automatic, 3) A POR is descendible through intestacy.

~~B.~~ The landowner's heir, because a charity cannot convey assets donated to it.

Misstates facts. The charity did not convey anything, they demolished the building & they can, unless prohibited (as it is here).

~~C.~~ The attorney general, because cy pres should be applied to devote the land to religious purposes to carry out the charitable intent of the landowner.

Classic example of trying to distract you by using an obscure rule.

Rule does not apply here since this is not a trust. Cy Pres applies when a settlor's intent for a charitable trust can't be accomplished and the court substitutes another similar charity to effectuate the settlor's intent.

~~D.~~ The attorney general, because the landowner's attempt to restrict the church's fee simple violated the Rule Against Perpetuities.

Rule does not apply. A fee simple determinable is not subject to RAP.

FACTS

Always an important fact in life estate/remainderman disputes over $

Q7

A landowner owned in fee simple **Lots 1 and 2** in an urban subdivision. The lots were **vacant** and unproductive. They were held as a speculation that their value would increase. The landowner died and, by his duly probated **will,** devised the residue of his estate (of which Lots 1 and 2 were part) **to his sister for life with remainder in fee simple to his friend.** The landowner's executor distributed the estate under appropriate court order, and **notified the sister that future real estate taxes on Lots 1 and 2 were her responsibility to pay.** Except for the statutes relating to probate and those relating to real estate taxes, there is **no applicable statute.** ← Default rules apply

The **sister failed to pay** the real estate taxes due for Lots 1 and 2. To prevent a tax sale of the fee simple, the **friend paid the taxes and demanded that the sister reimburse** her for same. When the sister refused, the friend brought an appropriate action against the sister to recover the amount paid.

In such action, what should the friend recover?

On this Q, you need to read the whole last paragraph to know it is a REAL PROP Q

SOLVE

First, identify the interest:

"…**sister for life** (life estate) with **remainder in fee simple to his friend.**"

RULES

LIFE TENANT (LT) Rights	REMAINDERMAN Rights
Pay <u>**from**</u> **net rental benefits** (if renting or **fair rental value** *if* LT occupies) **No personal liability for shortfall** • Current **operating expenses** (which are repairs & taxes) • **Mortgage** <u>**interest**</u>	Pay **expenses** <u>**exceeding**</u> **LT** net rental benefits (or fair rental value if LT occupies) **No personal liability for shortfall** (but could lose property to foreclosure if left unpaid) • Current **operating expenses** (in excess) (repairs & taxes) • **Mortgage** <u>**principal**</u>
ANALYSIS	
Since the land is vacant, there are **no net rental benefits from which to pay expenses** (taxes). Sister has no personal liability for the shortfall and owes nothing.	Friend must pay all expenses exceeding the LT net rental benefits, which is everything.

The friend will recover nothing <u>**because**</u> the life tenant has no net rental benefits.

→ Now look for a similar answer choice.

DECODE

(A.) The amount paid, because a life tenant has the duty to pay current charges.

Misleading/partial statement of rule. This is true, but the life tenant's duty to pay is only to the extent of the net rental benefit received, and there was none here (which you know because of the key fact that the land is vacant).

(B.) The present value of the interest that the amount paid would earn during the sister's lifetime.

This is not the rule. The sister owes nothing and the friend cannot collect reimbursement from her.

(C.) Nothing, because the sister's sole possession gave the right to decide whether or not taxes should be paid.

Not a true statement of law. While possession is relevant in calculating the net rental benefit (LT is responsible for paying the fair rental value towards "current operating expenses"), possession does not give the LT discretion regarding paying taxes.

D. Nothing, because the sister never received any income from the lots.

Correct. The LT is only responsible up to net rental proceeds, which were zero here.

FACTS — Q8

A landlord **leased** a **building to a tenant** for a **10-year term.** Two years after the term began, the **tenant subleased** the building to a **sublessee for a 5-year** term. Under the terms of the sublease, the **sublessee agreed to make monthly rent payments to the tenant.**

Don't feel sorry for the LL

Although the sublessee made timely rent payments to the tenant, **the tenant did not forward four of those payments to the landlord.** The **tenant** has left the jurisdiction and **cannot be found.** The **landlord has sued the sublessee** for the unpaid rent.

There is no applicable statute. **Default rules apply**

If the court rules that the **sublessee is not liable** to the landlord for the unpaid rent, **what will be the most likely reason?** ← ***REAL PROP Q***

SOLVE

Tenant has LEASE for 10 yrs.

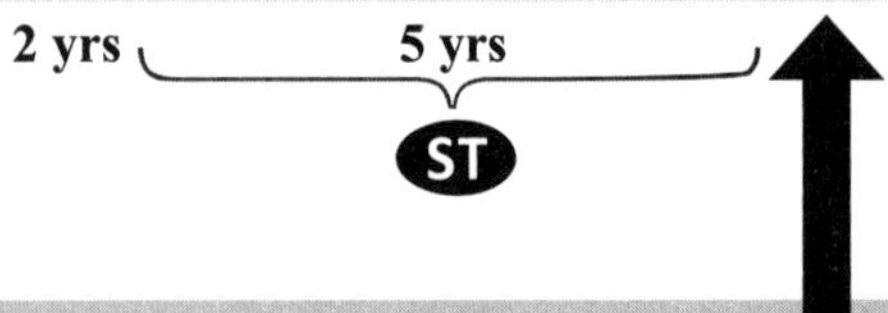

SUBLEASE	*ANALYSIS*
• Transfer by T to ST of **less than his entire interest** (even one day less) • No privity of estate because lease is less than for the full remaining term • No privity of contract between ST & LL • ST does <u>NOT assume personal liability</u> to LL to pay rent because <u>no</u> privity of contract	• 2 yrs. into 10 yr. lease, T transferred 5 yr. sublease to ST • 3 years less than entire interest, so ST has sublease • ST has no privity of estate or privity of contract w/ landlord so the covenant to pay rent will not run with the land

A If sublesee is not liable to landlord it is <u>**because**</u> there is no privity of estate or privity of contract between the sublessee and the landlord.

→ Now look for a similar answer choice.

DECODE

Ⓐ A sublessee is responsible to the landlord only as a surety for unpaid rent owed by the tenant.

Incorrect rule and misstates facts. The sublessee has not agreed to be a surety for the tenant and a suretyship is not implied by a sublease relationship.

Ⓑ The sublease constitutes a novation of the original lease.

Incorrect rule. A sublease is not a novation. A novation requires the landlord to agree to release the tenant from liability and accept the sublessee in the tenant's place, which did not happen here.

C. The sublessee is not in privity of estate or contract with the landlord.

Correct. Since the sublessee is not in privity of estate or contract with the landlord, the covenant to pay rent does not run with the land. This is the most likely reason the sublessee won't be found liable for the unpaid rent.

Ⓓ The sublessee's rent payments to the tenant fully discharged the sublessee's obligation to pay rent to the landlord.

*Misstatement of rule. The sublessee never had an obligation to pay rent directly to the landlord (though an assignee would). The sublessee was obligated to pay rent to the original tenant under the terms of the sublease. This is a tempting option and **very** careful reading is required to discard this answer choice. Classic MBE word play trickery.*

FACTS

Q9

A man owned land along the south side of a highway. **To the south** of the man's land was **a lot owned by a woman** who lived on it in a house.

Five years ago the man conveyed a right-of-way easement over his land to the woman because it provided a **more direct route** between her house and the highway. The easement was evidenced by **a clearly marked path.** The document granting the easement was promptly **recorded.**

Three years ago, the **woman conveyed her house to the man.** The man never took actual possession of the house.

Two years ago, the **man conveyed the house to a purchaser** by a **warranty deed.** Two months after the purchaser moved into the house, a neighbor informed him about the easement. He then began **using the path** that had been marked on the man's land. When the man noticed the purchaser using the path, he **erected a barricade** on his land that effectively prevented the purchaser from using the path.

The purchaser has sued the man, claiming that he has an **easement** over the man's land.

CALL Who is likely to prevail?

Appurtenant

Notice

Express

Merger: terminates easement

Possession irrelevant

REAL PROP Q

Read the Q with easement rules in mind: type, creation, scope, transfer, termination

SOLVE

This was an easy Q to solve as you went through the facts if you started with the call and glanced at the sentence above to identify it was about enforcing an easement.

RULES	ANALYSIS
• Creation- express	• Written in document (the info about the path providing a more direct route is irrelevant). • Recorded: This would normally be important in providing notice to a subsequent purchaser, but it has no legal effect here and is a decoy.
• Transfer: Appurtenant transfers w/ benefitted parcel	• Purchaser bought appurtenant benefitted parcel
• Termination: Merger doctrine • Easement extinguishes when title to both parcels vest in same person	• When the woman conveyed her house to the man 3 years ago, the title to both parcels vested in the man and the easement extinguished (terminates)

A The man is likely to prevail **because** the easement was terminated.

Now look for a similar answer choice.

DECODE

A. The man, because the easement was extinguished.

Correct. The merger rule applies to terminate the easement.

~~B.~~ The man, because the purchaser did not have actual notice of the easement at the time of acquisition.

Incorrect rule and analysis. Actual notice is not required for an appurtenant easement to pass with the benefitted parcel, but the easement terminated here.

~~C.~~ The purchaser, because he purchased the house by warranty deed.

The type of deed is not relevant to the passing of the easement. This is a common decoy fact that is included to provide a decoy answer choice.

~~D.~~ The purchaser, because the easement was of public record when he acquired the house.

This is irrelevant since the easement had terminated by the merger rule once the man owned both parcels.

FACTS

Q10

An owner conveyed Whiteacre **"to my daughter,** ~~her heirs and assigns,~~ **so long as** the premises are used for **residential purposes, then to my son** ~~and his heirs~~." The common law **Rule Against Perpetuities,** unmodified by statute, is part of the law of the jurisdiction in which the farm is located.

This language means the interest is fully alienable. It is easier to work with future interests if you cross it out.

As a consequence of the conveyance, what is the son's interest in Whiteacre? ← **REAL PROP Q**

SOLVE

RAP Approach

1. Classify the interest (to see if RAP applies)
2. Identify measuring life in being
3. Identify triggering event (when an interest must vest or fail)
4. Could triggering event possibly happen 21 years after death of measuring life?
5. Any interest violating RAP is ~~stricken~~, then reclassify the remaining interest

FUTURE INTEREST Qs:

1. **Classify the interest "to my daughter, so long as the premises are used for residential purposes, then to my son."**

ANALYSIS

Present possessory estate: "So long as" is the language used to create a fee simple subject to an executory interest (**FSSEI** in daughter).

Future interest: Executory interest in 3rd Party (son)

RAP Applies

FUTURE INTERESTS DECODED
It's all about decoding the language…

Present Possessory Estate	Language used to create (… is the stated event)	Future Interest Devisable (will), descendible (intestacy) & transfer inter vivos	FI in O	FI in 3rd party
Fee simple absolute	"To A" "To A and his heirs"			
Fee simple determinable	Durational language "To A so long as…" "To A during…" "To A while…"	Possibility of reverter (*automatic forfeiture)	X	
Fee simple subject to a condition subsequent	"To A upon condition …" "To A provided that…" "To A, but if…" And, right of re-entry language	Right of re-entry (* not automatic, must exercise or it's waived) (Not transferable inter vivos)	X	
Fee simple subject to an executory interest	"To A so long as X. If not, to B" "To A, but if X occurs, to B"	Executory Interest RAP (*shifting* 3P (A) to 3P (B)) Upon event, A's interest is cut short & interest shifts from 3P interest holder (A) to 3P (B)		X
RAP applies	"To A when and if A marries B"	Executory Interest RAP (*springing* out of O to 3P) Upon event, 3P takes from O		X
	"To A for life, & X years after A dies, to B"	Executory Interest RAP (*springing from gap* in possession) O has reversion interest during gap & B has executory interest	X	X
Life estate	"To A for life"	Reversion	X	
Life estate defeasible RAP may	"To A for life, then to C" "To A for life, then to B & heirs, but if…then to B immediately"	Remainder can be ▪ Vested: born, ascertained, or ▪ Vested subject to open RAP ▪ Contingent RAP: unborn		X

SOLVE *(continued)*

FUTURE INTEREST Qs:	ANALYSIS
2. ID measuring life	• Daughter or son
3. ID triggering event	• Not residential use
4. Possibly 21 years?	• Yes (could happen indefinitely in future)
5. ~~Strike~~	• **"to my daughter, so long as** the premises are used for residential purposes, ~~then to my son~~."
& Reclassify	• O → Daughter FSD Possibility of reverter (in O)

 The son's interest in Whiteacre fails **<u>because</u>** the interest violates the RAP.

→ Now look for a similar answer choice.

DECODE

A. The son's interest is nothing.

Correct. The interest violates the RAP.

~~B.~~ The son's interest is a valid executory interest.

Wrong analysis. The interest violates the RAP.

~~C.~~ The son's interest is a possibility of reverter.

Wrong rule. This would be the correct future interest if the owner had retained a future interest for himself (and the present possessory estate would be a FSD), but since the future interest was reserved for a third party (son), it is an executory interest (which fails RAP).

~~D.~~ The son's interest is a right of entry for condition broken.

Wrong rule. This identifies the future interest tied to a fee simple subject to a condition subsequent, but that is not the interest described here.

PART 7 TORTS

TORTS TABLE OF CONTENTS

★ Favorite Testing Area

TORTS MBE RULES OUTLINE

MBE TORTS AT A GLANCE

12-13 Questions Negligence	12-13 Questions Other Torts
Duty (failure to act, unforeseeable Ps, 3Ps) Standards of care Claims against owners/occupiers of land Res ipsa loquitur But for and substantial cause causation Multiple causes causation Joint and several liability Proximate cause Superseding cause Negligent infliction of emotional distress Pure economic loss Vicarious liability Independent contractors /nondelegable duties Contributory negligence/Last clear chance Comparative negligence Assumption of risk	Assault Battery False imprisonment Intentional infliction of emotional distress Trespass to land Trespass to chattels/conversion Defenses to intentional torts Strict liability and defenses Strict products liability and defenses Nuisance and defenses Defamation and defenses Privacy torts and defenses Misrepresentation and defenses Int. interf. w/ business relations and defenses

TORTS CALLS OF THE QUESTION DECODED

- Torts questions often have civil procedure question calls, such as asking if the plaintiff's case can withstand a directed verdict (modernly called a judgment as a matter of law), or motion for summary judgment, etc. This is a way of asking whether the underlying cause of action is established.
- If it is unclear what the cause of action is, it is probably negligence.
- The call may ask what is the plaintiff's best theory of recovery or best defense. The best theory of recovery is the easiest one to prove (e.g., strict liability is easier than negligence). Frequently the competing choices will be flawed and ineffective. Negating an element of a tort also provides an effective defense.
- The call may ask if plaintiff "prevails?" A plaintiff prevails if they can recover anything.

MBE tip: "If" is a frequent modifier used in the answer choices when the facts are wobbly and do not indisputably lead to one conclusion. The "if" modifier will add facts that makes the proposition in the answer choice certain.

COMMON TORTS DECOYS

- Don't feel sorry for the people in MBE torts questions. A favorite torts decoy is to make you feel sorry for the good guy or gal, who will often lose if you pick the right answer. Be methodical and remember these are not real people!
- Always completely solve the problem before looking at the answer choices when possible. The wrong answers are often a correct statement of law, so an answer will "look" right, but it isn't the answer to the question asked.
- Focus on the defendant's conduct. Often a wrong answer will "look" correct, but it relates to the actions of a third party, and not the defendant.
- Only answer the question asked in the call.

I. INTENTIONAL TORTS

A. Prima facie case: All intentional torts require an **act** by the defendant, **intent** by the defendant to bring about some physical or mental **effect upon another** person (effect varies by tort), and the effect must have been legally **caused** by defendant's act.

1. Intent (mental state of defendant) is established in one of the following ways:

a. Purpose: The defendant acts with a **purpose** to bring about the effect (required result) through taking **volitional action.**

b. Knowledge to a substantial certainty: The defendant **knows with substantial certainty** that a particular effect (result) will occur.

<u>Example</u>: A bill collector is standing just outside the front door of a debtor and hassling him by shouting through a bullhorn that the debtor is a "deadbeat." The debtor slammed the door shut, which struck the bullhorn jamming the bill collector's face. Though he did not desire it, given the proximity, the debtor knew with substantial certainty the door would hit the bill collector, thus establishing intent for battery.

c. Transferred intent (also called "extended liability")

1. **Transferred intent can apply two ways:** when the defendant had the necessary intent to commit a tort with respect to one person but instead:

a. **Different tort:** Commits a ***different*** **tort** against **that person <u>or</u>** a **different person;** <u>or</u>

<u>Example</u>: A husband and wife trespassed on their neighbor's land. The neighbor approached them with a large guard dog on a leash. The dog rushed the wife. The neighbor only intended to frighten the pair (assault), but the leash broke and the dog bit the wife. The neighbor will be liable for battery because he intended that the dog frighten the wife (assault) and that intent transfers to a different tort (battery). (Notice that while these facts could be focused on the trespass, the call of the question was about the battery by means of the dog.)

b. **Different person:** The ***intended*** **tort** against a **different person.**

<u>Example</u>: Defendant is angry with Friend and wants to punch him in the head. As Defendant throws his punch, Friend bends over and Defendant accidently hits Roommate. Defendant's intent to batter Friend transfers to Roommate.

2. **Exception:** Transferred intent cannot be invoked with the intentional torts of:

a. Conversion; or

b. Intentional infliction of emotional distress (IIED).

d. Reckless disregard standard (of the high probability that emotional distress will occur) can be used to establish the intent element for **intentional tort of infliction of emotional distress *only*.** Reckless disregard is not used to establish intent for any other intentional torts.

e. Children and mentally ill persons are liable for their intentional torts. If a person can formulate tortious intent, youth or mental disability provides no defense.

1. **Children are responsible for their own torts**. Children (as young as four) have been found capable of formulating intent. A **parent is not vicariously responsible** for the intentional torts of their children.

Example: A 6-year old boy had a well-deserved reputation as a bully of younger children. His parents encouraged him to be tough. For no reason, the boy kicked and severely injured a 4-year-old playmate. If the playmate's parents sue the boy for the playmate's injuries, the boy will be liable. (Despite his young age, the boy appears able to form intent based on his well-deserved reputation and that the attack was for no reason. The information about his parents is a decoy.)

2. **Mental disability does not provide a defense to intentional torts,** unless one is so impaired they lack the capacity to formulate intent.

Example: A defendant struck a passerby with a rock, but is mentally ill and did not know he was striking a person. This will provide a defense to a battery on the basis the defendant did not have the intent to contact a person.

2. **Causation** is the effect **legally caused by** the **defendant's act** or some **action that is set in motion** by defendant. Causation can also be satisfied if the defendant's act was a **substantial factor** in bringing about the effect. Causation is usually clear in intentional torts.

Example: A man placed a microphone in the bedroom of his former wife. Her new husband found the microphone and showed it to the wife. The fact that her new husband was the one who showed her the microphone will not relieve the man of liability for intentional infliction of emotional distress since he set the action in motion by placing the microphone.

Decoy tip: In intentional torts questions, decoy answers may state that the conduct of a third party or some instrumentality was the cause of the resulting harm (thus relieving the tortfeasor of responsibility). However, if the defendant set the action in motion, they are responsible.

B. **Battery** is an **intentional** infliction of a **harmful or offensive bodily contact.**

1. **Intent (contact):** The party must **intend the contact,** not the consequence (e.g., the harm). (See full intent rules in sec. I.A.1.) Intent can be satisfied either by:

a. **Purpose** to contact, or

b. **Knowledge with substantial certainty** that contact will occur, or

c. **Transferred intent** from a different tort or person (this occurs most typically where an assault is intended, but a battery actually occurs).

Decoy tip: Intent is often tested with "pranks gone bad" and "practical jokers" where they state the defendant intends no touching, but something goes wrong with the "joke," and the plaintiff is touched. The intent to assault will transfer to the battery, despite the defendant's plan not to touch the other person.

2. **Harmful or offensive:**

a. **Harmful** touching causes **pain or bodily damage;** or

b. **Offensive** touching offends a **reasonable person's sense of dignity.**

Example: Just as a politician was about to be seated at a political dinner, the defendant pulled the chair out from under him, and the politician fell to the floor. Though the politician was not hurt, he was embarrassed in front of the crowd, which would offend a reasonable person's sense of dignity and is sufficiently offensive to constitute a battery.

3. **Contact** to the plaintiff's person.

   a. **Direct:** The contact can be made directly from the defendant's person to the plaintiff's person (e.g., to punch a person in the arm).

   b. **Indirect:** The contact can be made indirectly where the defendant **sets a force in motion** with the purpose or knowledge to a substantial certainty it will lead to contact with the plaintiff's person (e.g., to give cookies with ground up nuts to someone with a severe nut allergy).

   c. **Extension of the body included:** Contact to the plaintiff includes contact with an object **closely identified with the plaintiff's body,** such that the contact with the object has physical impact on the plaintiff (e.g., to grab a tray out of the plaintiff's hands).

   d. **Awareness not required:** The plaintiff need not be aware of the contact at the time (e.g., P does not like D. If D kisses P while P is sleeping, this is a battery even though P was unaware at the time since the contact is offensive to a reasonable person).

C. **Assault** is the **intentional** causing of an **apprehension** of an **imminent** harmful or offensive **contact.**

1. **Intent (apprehension *or* contact):** For an assault, the plaintiff can intend to **cause apprehension of an imminent touching** (anticipation of a battery) <u>or</u> intend to make **contact** (battery). See full intent rules in sec. I.A.1.

   a. **Purpose** to cause apprehension or contact; or

   b. **Knowledge with substantial certainty** that apprehension or contact will occur; or

   c. **Transferred intent** (e.g., where a battery is intended, but the tortfeasor misses and an assault occurs).

2. **Causing reasonable apprehension:** The plaintiff must be put in apprehension of an imminent harmful or offensive touching. Thus, the **plaintiff must be aware** of the threat. The **actual apprehension felt by the plaintiff controls,** rather than the subjective motivation of the perpetrator, though the apprehension **must be reasonable.**

   <u>Example</u>: A host pointed a gun at her guest. The guest knew the gun was unloaded and the ammunition was kept in a locked basement closet, two stories below. The guest was not in reasonable apprehension of an imminent harmful touching.

3. **Imminent:** The defendant must have the **apparent present ability** to carry out the threat. Words alone are insufficient.

   <u>Example</u>: A bank vice president was caught taking kickbacks for approving bad loans. The president fired the vice president and told him, "If you are not out of this bank in ten minutes, I will have the guards physically throw you out." Since the vice president was given ten minutes to leave, there is insufficient apprehension of *imminent* harm.

4. **Harmful or offensive contact**

   a. **Harmful** touching causes **pain or bodily damage;** or

   b. **Offensive** touching offends a **reasonable person's sense of dignity.**

D. **Intentional infliction of emotional distress (IIED)** is the **intentional or reckless** infliction of **severe emotional distress** caused by defendant's **extreme and outrageous** conduct.

1. **Intent (to cause emotional distress)** can be satisfied three ways (see full intent rules in sec. I.A.1.):

   a. **Purpose** to cause emotional distress; or

b. **Knowledge with substantial certainty** that emotional distress will result; or

c. **Reckless disregard** of the high probability that emotional distress will occur.

d. **No transferred intent** is allowed to satisfy the intent element.

> <u>MBE tip</u>: IIED is the only intentional tort where the defendant's mental state can be satisfied by a state of recklessness (rather than intentional conduct).

2. **Severe emotional distress:** The emotional or mental distress suffered by the plaintiff must be severe, though **bodily harm/physical symptom of the distress is *not* required.**

   <u>Examples</u>: Descriptions that the plaintiff was badly frightened, outraged, angered, embarrassed, distressed, or suffered fainting, nightmares, etc. demonstrates severe emotional distress.

3. **Extreme and outrageous** conduct is that **beyond all possible bounds of decency.**

   a. **Public figure—Defamatory speech special rule:** When the plaintiff is a **public figure,** and the conduct at issue is a statement, that **statement must be defamatory** to be considered extreme and outrageous, because of the speaker's First Amendment free speech rights.

> <u>MBE tip</u>: The public figure rule means an analysis of defamation can be tucked inside an IIED analysis.

EXAMPLES OF EXTREME & OUTRAGEOUS CONDUCT

- A man placed a microphone in the bedroom of his former wife.
- A man killed his neighbor's cat with a shotgun in front of the neighbor because he was angry the cat came on his property.
- A bill collector stood at the plaintiff's door and shouted through a bullhorn, in front of the neighbors, that the plaintiff was a "deadbeat."

Threats often give rise to outrageous conduct, such as:

- A bill collector threatens plaintiff that if she doesn't pay, the bill collector will file a criminal complaint of fraud.
- A neighbor threatens plaintiff that if he sold his home to a buyer the neighbor didn't like, plaintiff and his family would have "accidents".
- A developer threatens an elderly landowner that if she doesn't sell to the developer, a state law would allow him to have the home condemned.

4. **Bystander IIED:** Liability can occur where the defendant intentionally or recklessly **directs extreme and outrageous conduct at someone other than the plaintiff** (a third person). The plaintiff can recover for IIED if:

   a. The plaintiff was physically **present** when the injury occurred to the third party, <u>and</u>

   b. **Known by the defendant to be present** (so the plaintiff's emotional distress can be anticipated by the defendant), <u>and</u>

c. The **plaintiff** either:

1. Is a **close relative** of the third person, <u>or</u>

2. **Suffers bodily harm** as a result of the severe emotional distress (e.g., heart attack or stroke).

<u>Example</u>: A mom takes her daughter to the hospital. While mom is out of the room, a doctor molests the child. Two weeks later, the child tells her mom and mom suffers severe emotional distress that causes physical illness. Despite the outrageous misconduct, mom cannot recover under IIED because the outrageous conduct is directed at the child (third person) and mom was not present when it occurred. (Despite the upsetting nature of this question, we've included it here because it is a good example of the extreme lengths undertaken to emotionally distract you on the MBE.)

> **<u>Decoy tip</u>:** The concept of "zone of danger" applies to negligent infliction of emotional distress (NIED), *not* IIED.
>
> **<u>MBE tip</u>:** IIED MBE questions will often not clearly establish the severe emotional distress element. Thus, the correct answer will state that the plaintiff will prevail for IIED *if* she has severe emotional distress, or the plaintiff will *not* prevail *if* she *does not* have severe emotional distress.

E. **False imprisonment** occurs where the defendant **intentionally** causes the plaintiff to be **confined or detained** to a **bounded area** with **no reasonable means of escape**, of which the **plaintiff is either aware or harmed**.

1. **Intent (to confine):** Intent can be satisfied either by (see full intent rules in sec. I.A.1.):

   a. **Purpose** to confine; or

   b. **Knowledge with substantial certainty** confinement will occur.

   c. **Transferred intent** applies.

> **<u>Decoy tip</u>:** Be alert for facts where the defendant is unaware they have confined anyone, thus the confinement is unintentional. (See example below.)

2. **Confined,** restrained, or detained with a physical barrier. The restraint can be obtained through means of duress by the invalid claim of legal authority (e.g. accuse one of theft), and threats of force. However, threats of future injury or events are insufficient. Moral pressure alone is insufficient.

3. **Bounded area:** Confinement must be within a bounded area.

4. **No reasonable means of escape** (e.g., it is unreasonable for the plaintiff not to walk out through an open or unlocked door to escape).

5. **Awareness *or* harm required:** The plaintiff must be aware of the confinement at the time (no harm required), ***or*** if the plaintiff is unaware at the time of confinement, harm to the plaintiff as a result of the confinement is required to recover.

   <u>Example</u>: A car salesman and buyer were looking at cars on the car lot after closing time. A security guard locked the gate to the lot, trapping the salesman and buyer in the lot. They were unable to summon help. The buyer panicked and jumped the fence to escape, breaking his leg. The buyer will not prevail in a false imprisonment action *unless* the security guard knew they were in the lot when he locked the gate. (The information about the broken leg is a decoy duck to distract you that intent is not established under the facts.)

> **MBE tip:** False imprisonment is often tested in conjunction with the defense of legal justification or shopkeeper's privilege. See sec. II.F and II.G. below.

F. **Trespass to land** is the **intentional entry** onto the **land of another**.

1. **Intent (to enter):** The defendant need only **intend to enter the land they actually enter,** and need not intend to enter the *land of another* (trespass) so a mistake as to land ownership (meaning, the defendant thinks they are entering their own land, but is not) will *not* provide a defense. Intent can be satisfied either by:

   a. **Purpose** to voluntarily enter/invade the land; or

   b. **Knowledge with substantial certainty entry will occur** (e.g., a factory that emits chemical particulates into the air can be substantially certain the particulates will enter onto neighboring properties if they have been informed this occurs on windy days).

      1. **Engaging in an abnormally dangerous activity can qualify** to provide the intent to enter (e.g., a blasting operation that launches a projectile onto neighboring land).

      2. **Involuntary entry** will **not** satisfy the intent element (e.g., in an emergency where a car careens out of control onto another's land).

   c. **Mistake** (as to land ownership) **is no defense** to trespass to land.

> **Decoy tip:** If entrant has intent to enter the land, but mistakenly believes it is their own land, or enters land in an emergency, it is still a trespass.

2. **Entry of the land** means a **physical invasion** of the land, but it does not require that the land be harmed by the invasion. Entry includes:

   a. The entry onto another's land **without permission;**

      1. **Particulates** can cause an invasion (e.g., crop dusting).

      2. **Light and sound** is ***not*** an invasion.

   b. **Remaining** on the land without the right to be there; or

   c. **Placing or projecting an object** upon the land without permission.

3. **Land** (real property) **of another,** which includes one in **legal possession** of real property, such as a tenant.

   Example: A landlord who improperly enters a tenant's premises can be liable for trespass because the tenant has the legal right of possession, not the landlord.

4. **No damage** (harm to the property) **is required**. In the absence of actual damages, the plaintiff will be awarded **nominal damages** for the trespass alone. (This is in contrast to the rule for trespass to chattels/conversion.)

   Example: Defendant built a garage that encroached two feet onto his neighbor's property. The neighbor did not realize the encroachment until the property was sold to another. Defendant is liable for trespass whether he knew his building was on the neighbor's property or thought he was building on his own land because he had the intent to enter (build on) that property.

> **<u>MBE tip</u>**: Trespass to land is often tested in conjunction with the defense of private necessity. See sec. II.H.1. below.

G. **Trespass to chattels** is an **intentional interference** with a person's **use** or **possession** of a **chattel**. [This rule is rarely MBE tested.]

1. **Intent (interfere with chattel):** Intent is usually satisfied by the **purpose** to interfere with chattel (take and use the property).
    a. **Mistake** (as to chattel ownership) **is no defense** to trespass to chattels, such as where the defendant mistakenly thinks the chattel is his own, but it is not.
    b. **Transferred intent** applies.
2. **Interference with use or possession:** The chattel owner is precluded from using, enjoying, or possessing their own chattel. Typically, this will be for a temporary time period.
3. **Chattel** of another: A chattel is personal property.
4. **Damages:** There must be **actual harm** to the chattel, or **deprivation of use** of the chattel for a **substantial time**. The measure of damages is the chattel's **loss of value** caused by the loss of use and/or the **cost of repair.**

H. **Conversion** is an **intentional interference** with the plaintiff's **possession or ownership** of property that is so **substantial** that it warrants requiring the defendant to pay the property's full value.

1. **Intent (interfere with chattel):** Intent is usually satisfied by the **purpose** to interfere with the chattel of another (take and use the property). The defendant **need only intend to interfere with the chattel** in the manner done.
    a. **No transferred intent** is allowed to satisfy the intent element.
    b. **Unintentional conduct**: Accidently causing damage to another's chattel is **insufficient.**
    c. **Mistake** (as to chattel ownership) **is no defense** to conversion, such as where the defendant mistakenly thinks they own the chattel, but do not.
2. **Interference with use or possession so substantial** it amounts to an **act of ownership** and warrants the defendant pay the chattel's full value. The key difference between a conversion and a trespass to chattel is the **extent and duration of the interference** and the **degree of resulting harm**.

    <u>Examples</u>: Interference is substantial where one takes possession of a chattel, transfers possession of a chattel to a third person, refuses to return a chattel, or destroys a chattel.
3. **Chattel** of another: A chattel is personal property.
4. **Damages:** The measure of damages is the chattel's **market value at the time of the conversion**, essentially a full value forced sale.

    <u>Example</u>: A woman went into her neighbor's garage and borrowed a chainsaw without permission. While using the saw, it broke. The woman is liable for conversion and must pay the market value of the saw at the time she took it because of the high degree of harm to the saw.

> **<u>Decoy tip</u>:** In intentional tort MBE questions, be alert for decoy answers that reference standards applicable to *negligence* (e.g., defendant was careless; defendant acted as a reasonably prudent person) rather than focusing on a required intentional tort element. Remember, intentional torts require intent; a defendant's carelessness or reasonably prudent behavior is irrelevant to the analysis.

II. DEFENSES TO INTENTIONAL TORTS

MBE tip: When asked for the "best defense" to a cause of action, negating an element of the underlying tort is effective and a better defense to the cause of action than a traditional "defense" because it prevents the underlying tort from ever being established (as opposed to admitting the tort is established, but defending on the basis the defendant has a really good reason for doing it).

MBE tip: Defenses are also called privileges (e.g., the privilege of self defense).

A. **Consent:** Plaintiff consents to defendant's conduct. Consent can be **express or implied.**

1. **Express consent** can occur orally or in writing (typically through signing a waiver).

2. **Implied consent** can occur through custom, conduct, or circumstances measured by an objective reasonable person standard.

   a. **Ordinary touches:** Individuals are **presumed to consent** to ordinary touches that are part of common everyday life given social norms.

   Example: Tapping a bus passenger on the shoulder to get her attention if she left a package on the seat when she got up to leave the bus is an ordinary touch.

   b. **Objective manifestation:** Individuals are **presumed to consent** to touches objectively manifested by their voluntary conduct.

   Example: One playing a game of pick-up basketball impliedly consents to ordinary contact with other players during the course of the game since basketball is a contact sport.

3. **Scope:** Contact may not exceed the scope of the consent given.

   Example: One playing basketball consents to the expected ordinary contact inherent in the sport, but not to an opposing player punching them in the face since that exceeds the scope of contact one expects playing basketball and is a battery.

   Example: Plaintiff consents to allow Dr. A to operate on her left knee. The consent would not apply to Dr. B. If Dr. B operates, it is a battery since it exceeds the scope of consent, even if Dr. B were a superior surgeon.

4. **Consent to crime:** Courts are split if one can consent to a criminal act, but the majority of courts hold that plaintiff's consent is ineffective.

B. **Self-defense:** A person is entitled to use **reasonable force** to prevent any threatened harmful or offensive bodily contact, threatened confinement or imprisonment as **reasonably believed necessary** (objective standard).

1. **Degree of force reasonably necessary:** Defendant may only use the degree of force reasonably necessary **to prevent** the threatened harm.

   a. **Deadly force:** Use of deadly force is **only allowed if** the defendant is in **danger of death or serious bodily harm**. Retreat is not required in most jurisdictions, though some require retreat before use of deadly force unless defending at home.

2. **Injury to third party:** If a person using proper self-defense injures a third party, the **person creating the need for self-defense is liable** for injuries to the third party, not the person self-defending.

3. **Mistake of fact is allowed if the mistake is reasonable.**

   Example: A salesman and a mechanic are identical twins. The salesman threatens another man, telling him that the next time he sees him in the neighborhood, "I'll beat you up." Two days later, the man sees the mechanic coming towards him and as the mechanic reached the man, the mechanic raised his hand. Thinking the mechanic was his twin, the man struck the mechanic in fear. In a battery action, the man can successfully assert a self-defense privilege if it was reasonable to believe the mechanic was going to attack him, which is likely since the men are identical twins. (This example emphasizes the importance of each fact since mistaking identical twins for each other is the picture of a reasonable mistake.)

C. **Defense of others:** A person may use **reasonable force** to defend another person when they **reasonably believe** that the other person could have used force in self-defense. This is the majority rule. [Apply the majority rule unless told otherwise.]

   1. **Degree of force:** The same rules regarding use of force apply as in self-defense.

   2. **Mistake of fact is allowed if reasonable** (majority rule). A reasonable mistake about another's need for self-defense **is allowed** and will not negate the defense.

      Example: A bystander came upon two people fighting. One man was about to kick the other in the head. The bystander pulled out a gun and said, "Stop or I'll shoot." If it was reasonable to believe one man was about to inflict serious bodily harm on the other (and that man was privileged to use self-defense), the bystander will successfully assert a defense of others privilege.

   3. **Stand in shoes—minority rule:** Some jurisdictions use a "stand in shoes" approach, which only allows defense of others if the person being defended was *actually* privileged to use self-defense. Consequently, a mistake of fact (about the other's need for self-defense) is not allowed.

D. **Defense of property (land or personal property).** A person is **privileged** to protect their land from intrusion. A person may use **reasonable force** to defend their real or personal property, but they **may not forcefully expel a trespasser.**

   Example: Surrounding land with an 8-foot fence topped with barbed wire and "no trespassing" signs is privileged. A trespasser injured by the barbed wire assumed the risk of injury since the risk of barbed wire is obvious.

   1. **Warning required before use of force:** Defendant must first make a **verbal demand** that the intruder stop, **unless** it reasonably appears that it would result in imminent violence/harm or be **futile or dangerous**. Once warned, the perpetrator must be given time to comply.

   2. **Use of deadly force is limited:** Defendant may use deadly force to defend land, but ***only if* non-deadly force will not suffice** and the defendant **reasonably believes** that without deadly force, **death or serious bodily harm will result.**

      a. **Indirect mechanical devices:** A property owner may only use a mechanical device (e.g., trap gun) to protect their property **if owner would have been privileged** to use the same degree of force **if present** at the time. It is unlikely to be effective because of the duty to warn first.

         Example: A property owner cannot utilize hidden explosives, which explode when triggered by trespassers on the premises, if he would not have personally been able to detonate explosives if present. Doing so constitutes a battery since the defense of land privilege is ineffective.

E. **Recapture of chattels:** A property owner may use **reasonable force** to regain possession of chattels taken by someone else. [This rule is rarely MBE tested.]

1. **Fresh pursuit:** The property owner must be in fresh pursuit.
2. **Deadly force is not allowed** in the recapture of chattels.
3. **Trespass to retrieve chattel allowed:** One may trespass to retrieve chattel that is located on another's property through no fault of the owner (e.g., the wind blows a tarp onto a neighbor's property).
   a. **Privilege is qualified (incomplete) — must pay for damages.** Should damage to property result from the trespass to retrieve chattel, the defendant must pay for any actual damage to the property.

F. **Shopkeeper's privilege:** Shopkeepers have a privilege to **temporarily** detain individuals whom they **reasonably believe** to be in possession of shoplifted goods.

1. **Temporarily detain:** Temporary detention is allowed for a **reasonable time** to investigate if shoplifting has occurred, typically for 10 to 15 minutes. The police must be called to make any arrest.
2. **Reasonable means** must be used to detain.

G. **Legal justification:** Arrest or detention under a legal authority is allowed when the defendant was **reasonably exercising their legal rights** and duties by restraining the plaintiff (e.g., when police act under a valid arrest warrant). This may provide a defense to false imprisonment.

Example: The police notify local gas stations to be on the lookout for the suspect in a string of gas station armed robberies; a 75-year-old white haired woman driving a vintage tan colored Ford Thunderbird. A woman matching the description arrived at a gas station and the owner falsely told her the car had a mechanical problem as a ruse to detain her for an hour until police arrived, at which point the police determined she was not the wanted woman. If the woman sues for false imprisonment, the owner can successfully defend based on legal justification.

H. **Necessity:** A person may interfere with the real or personal property of another when it is **reasonably** and apparently **necessary to prevent great harm** to third persons or the defendant.

1. **Private necessity** applies when a person acts to prevent greater injury to **the person or their property,** or the person or property of another.
   a. **Privilege is qualified (incomplete) — must pay for damages.** Should damage to property result from the private necessity, the defendant **must pay for any actual damage.**

      Example: Boater is sailing her boat when a freak storm arises, causing very dangerous sailing conditions. Boater docks her boat at a private dock. Boater's trespass will be privileged by necessity, but she has liability for any actual damage done to the dock.

   b. **Property owner has no right to exclude** one trespassing out of private necessity. Should a property owner do so, the owner is liable for any damages to the privileged trespasser.

      Example: An unusually heavy rainstorm caused the highway to flood. A motorist pulled his car up a steep driveway, parked, and walked home. The homeowner rolled the car down the driveway and left it parked on the highway shoulder, where it was engulfed in water. The homeowner is liable for the damage to the motorist's car since the motorist was privileged by necessity to park in the driveway.

      Example: A pilot is forced to make an emergency landing on a field. As he disembarked, two large dogs attacked and bit him. The homeowner had ordered the dogs to attack. In a battery action, the pilot will prevail because his trespass was privileged by necessity.

   c. **Harm must be acute and unforeseeable** (e.g., a hungry person stealing food will not be privileged under necessity).

2. **Public necessity** applies when the threatened harm was to the **community at large** or to many people. Should property be damaged by the public necessity, **no compensation is owed.** [This rule is rarely MBE tested.]

Decoy tip: There is no insanity defense for intentional torts. However, mental illness can operate as a defense if one is so impaired they cannot formulate the requisite intent.

Decoy tip: Contributory or comparative negligence or assumption of risk can never provide a defense to an intentional tort. Pay attention to the cause of action!

INTENTIONAL TORTS DECODED

Tort	Intent to...	Tested with defense of:
Battery	Contact (*not* intend harm)	Consent, Self-defense/Defense of others
Assault	Cause apprehension or contact	
IIED	Cause emotional distress	
False imprisonment	Confine	Shopkeeper's privilege Legal justification
Trespass to land	Enter land*	Necessity Recapture chattel
Trespass to chattel	Interfere with chattel*	
Conversion	Interfere with chattel*	
*Intent to enter/interfere with chattel; need not know it belongs to another.		

III. NEGLIGENCE

MBE tip: 50% of the Torts MBE questions are on negligence.

A. **Prima facie case:** Defendant's conduct imposes an unreasonable risk upon another, which results in injury to that other person. Plaintiff must prove the following elements: **duty, breach, actual cause, proximate cause, and damages**.

Decoy tip: To effectively analyze a negligence MBE question, use the following approach:
- Did the D have a duty?
- If so, what was that duty?
- Did the D breach the duty?

Unlike essays, MBE questions will frequently turn on finding the defendant had no duty or the duty wasn't breached. *Only if* you establish duty and breach should you move on to analyze causation and damages, otherwise it will be easy to get distracted by a wrong answer.

B. Duty of care: A person has a duty to act as a **reasonable person** and use ordinary care. There are two duty considerations: to whom the duty of care is owed and the applicable standard of care.

1. To whom duty of care is owed:

a. Duty owed to foreseeable plaintiffs: A duty is owed to **foreseeable plaintiffs** in the ***zone of danger*** (Majority rule: Cardozo). [Use the majority rule unless otherwise instructed.]

1. **Minority rule:** A **duty is owed to everyone**, including unforeseeable plaintiffs. (Andrews view).

b. Special situations where duty owed:

1. **Danger invites rescue**, so **rescuers are foreseeable plaintiffs**. A rescuer may recover for injuries sustained during the course of a rescue from one who **negligently caused the need for rescue**.

Example: A man was siphoning gas from his neighbor's car when the gas caught fire. A rescuer extinguished the fire and was badly burned in the process. The man is liable for the rescuer's injuries.

a. **Negligent rescue attempt:** A rescuer can recover even if the rescuer's attempt is negligent. However, a rescuer **cannot recover for a reckless/grossly careless rescue** attempt.

b. Subject to the firefighter's rule. See. sec. III.B.2.b.*2.c.*

2. **Prenatal injuries:** [These rules are rarely MBE tested.]

a. A **duty of care is owed to a viable fetus.** A child with pre-natal injuries may have a cause of action for injuries sustained in the womb.

b. **Wrongful birth/pregnancy** suits are **allowed** in many states for a suit **brought by *a child's parents*** to recover damages related to:

i. **Wrongful birth** (misdiagnosis): A baby is born with serious congenital defects and the pregnancy would have been terminated if properly diagnosed. Depending on jurisdiction, parents may be able to recover for their **extraordinary medical expenses and emotional distress.**

Example: Parents had a baby with total deafness caused by a hereditary condition. Their doctor erroneously concluded the baby's hearing was normal. The parents conceived a second child before learning their first child was deaf. The second child was also deaf caused by the same hereditary condition. The parents can sue the doctor for wrongful birth for expenses incurred related to the second child's deafness.

ii. **Wrongful pregnancy** (contraception failure): A negligently and ineffectively performed contraceptive procedure leads to a pregnancy. A mother can recover for pregnancy/birth related medical expenses and pain and suffering, but not expenses to raise the child.

c. **Wrongful life** suits are **not allowed.** A suit **brought by *a child*** to recover damages for having been wrongfully born with misdiagnosed congenital defects or born after an ineffectively performed contraceptive measure is not allowed.

PRENATAL INJURIES DECODED			
Cause of Action	To recover expenses for:	Suit filed by:	
		Parent	Child
Negligence	Injuries sustained in the womb		X
Wrongful birth (Misdiagnosis)	Extraordinary medical expenses, emotional distress	X	
Wrongful pregnancy (Contraception failure)	Pregnancy/birth related medical expenses; pain & suffering	X	
Wrongful life	NOT ALLOWED		X

★ **2. Standard of care**

a. Reasonable person: A person has a duty to act as a **reasonably prudent person under the circumstances**, unless a special duty standard of care applies. See sec. III.B.2.b. below for the special duties of care.

1. **Reasonable person characteristics:** A "reasonable person" determination generally includes consideration of the **circumstances** and a person's **physical characteristics,** but it does **not include mental characteristics.** A few special situations:

a. **Physically disabled person:** Reasonable person with the same physical disability (e.g., visually impaired).

b. **Intellectually disabled person:** A reasonable person of average mental ability.

c. **Intoxicated person:** A reasonable sober person.

d. **Emergency situation:** A reasonable person in an emergency, however, a higher standard applies if the person created the emergency.

Decoy tip: There is no duty to take precautions against events that cannot be foreseen. If the event is unforeseeable, the plaintiff has no duty to act.

b. Special duty rules

1. **Affirmative duties to act:** A person generally has **no duty to take affirmative action** to help another, absent a special relationship (e.g., spouses, parent and child, etc.) **except:**

a. **Parents — Duty to supervise and control:** Parents must exercise reasonable care in the supervision and control of their minor children. Parents are **not vicariously liable,** rather, they are liable for **their own negligence in failing to properly supervise** and control the child. Liability is limited to **foreseeable** actions (e.g., where a child has a known propensity).

Example: An 8-year-old boy rode his bicycle down his driveway and into a busy highway. A car came to a sudden stop, missing the boy, but injuring a car passenger who was not properly restrained. The passenger may recover from the boy's parents if they knew he sometimes rode into the highway (known propensity) and did not take reasonable steps to prevent it. (The unrestrained nature of the passenger is a decoy. He can still recover, though his recovery may be reduced in proportion to his own negligence.)

i. **Exception—Substantial aid:** Parents are **liable** for the torts of their children if they **knowingly provide substantial aid or encouragement** to the child's commission of a tort (e.g., encourage a child to be aggressive and tough).

> **Decoy tip:** Parents are not strictly liable, or vicariously liable, and do not have liability depending on whether their child is old enough to commit a tort or not.

b. **Caretaker institutions:** Courts have tended to recognize that caretaker institutions **have an affirmative duty to protect their patients**, similar to that of parents. This area of law is not settled.

c. **Causing the original harm:** A defendant has an affirmative duty to act when his **conduct placed the plaintiff in danger** (even if not done negligently).

d. **Volunteer rescuer:** Where a defendant voluntarily begins to render assistance to another, the rescuer must proceed with **reasonable care.** Merely stopping at an accident scene may prevent another from stopping to help. Modernly, a promise to assist alone likely creates a reliance interest.

Example: A driver saw an apparently injured man lying in a field near the road on a cold dark night. The driver stopped and determined the man was intoxicated and in danger from exposure to the cold. The man did not help and left. Since the driver did not voluntarily render aid, and *if* the driver did not make the man's situation worse, he is not liable.

2. **Professional malpractice:** Professionals (e.g., lawyers, accountants, contractors, engineers) are required to possess the **knowledge and skill** of a member of their profession or occupation in **good standing in a similar community.**

a. **Medical professionals:** Owe a duty to their patients to use **knowledge and skill** of a member of the profession in **good standing using a national "school of practice" standard** of care.

i. **Duty to disclose:** There is a **duty to disclose all material risks** so patients can make **informed consent** to medical procedures.

a. **Exception:** There is no duty to disclose **common known risks**, or when a patient **waives** the disclosure, or if disclosure would be **detrimental**.

ii. **Duty of care extends to the patient only** (and to the fetus of a pregnant patient).

a. **Exception—credible threats to violence to others:** In the limited situation where a patient threatens to harm another person, the medical professional owes a duty of warning to the other person.

Example: A patient is suicidal, but the doctor makes a misdiagnosis of the situation and the patient subsequently commits suicide. The patient's parent cannot recover for negligent infliction of emotional distress since the parent is owed no duty by the psychiatrist, so the exception does not apply.

> **Decoy tip:** Any breach of the professional standard of care must still be the *cause* of the injury the patient suffered. If the outcome would be the same, causation will fail and so will the negligence action.

b. **Legal malpractice "trial within a trial": Lawyers owe a duty of care to their clients.** To prevail for legal malpractice, the claimant must prove that:

i. The lawyer's lack of action **caused** the loss, **and**

ii. Had the lawyer met the standard of care, the **result would have been different**.

c. **Firefighter's rule:** Firefighters, police officers, and other professional **risk takers** who are injured in the line of duty are **prohibited from suing for negligence** for injuries sustained **stemming from the risks inherent in rescue** they assume with their profession.

Example: Basketball fans get together at Defendant's house to watch the championship game. Defendant asks them to leave when the fans get rowdy. The fans refuse to leave, start to fight, and the police are called. An officer's nose is broken trying to break up the fight. The firefighter's rule will prevent recovery since the negligent conduct (fighting) is what created the need for rescue. Being hit in the face is a risk inherent in the rescue.

Decoy tip: Look for injuries *not* caused by the "risk of rescue," making the firefighter's rule inapplicable (e.g., a firefighter has a car accident on the way to the grocery store to restock the station's food).

3. **Children** are **liable for their own torts** and have a duty to conform to the conduct of a child of like **age, intelligence, and experience**.

a. **Exception—child engaged in adult activity:** Children engaged in a **potentially dangerous activity** normally pursued only by adults are held to an **adult reasonable person standard of care**.

Example: Parents allowed their 14-year-old teen of low intelligence to drive their car. The teen had no license and little experience driving. She tried to do her best, but she hit a pedestrian. If the pedestrian sues the teen, an adult reasonable care standard will be used since driving is an adult activity. (Even though teens may be permitted to drive, it is considered an adult activity. The teen will be liable; the parents' permission and her low intelligence are decoys.)

b. **Parents are not vicariously liable** for the torts of their children, but they can be liable for negligent supervision. See sec. III.B.2.b.*1*.a.

c. A **child's negligence is not imputed to the parent.**

4. **Common carriers** (transporters of passengers) and **innkeepers** must employ a **high degree of care** towards passengers and guests. They must take **reasonable steps to make conditions safe** and conduct operations with **reasonable care** for passengers and guests.

a. **Third-party harm:** Common carriers and innkeepers must use reasonable care to protect customers against **foreseeable harmful/criminal acts of third persons or animals.**

Example: A man on a flight consumed nine alcoholic drinks, served by the flight attendant. The man got agitated and struck a nearby passenger. In a suit against the airline for negligence, the passenger will prevail since the airline must use reasonable care to protect its customers from the foreseeable harmful act of a third person (unruly behavior by a drunk person is foreseeable).

5. **Owners and occupiers of land:** The standard of care owed by a landowner applies equally to a land occupier (e.g., a tenant) and depends on whether the damage occurs outside the premises or on the premises.

   a. **Damage that occurs *outside* the premises:**

      i. **Natural conditions: No duty** exists to protect one **outside** the premises from damage caused by hazardous **natural conditions** originating on the premises (e.g., a stream overflows).

      ii. **Artificial conditions:** A duty exists to use **reasonable care** to prevent one **outside** the premises from damage caused by an unreasonably **dangerous artificial condition.**

      Example: A windstorm blew a slate off the defendant's roof and it hit and injured a pedestrian. The roof is old and had lost tiles in previous windstorms, so the defendant is aware of the unreasonable risk of harm, and it is foreseeable that a loose roof tile could injure a passerby.

   b. **Damage that occurs *on* the premises:** When damage occurs on the premises, the **status of the plaintiff** as a trespasser, invitee, licensee, and/or the status as a landlord or tenant determines the standard of care **owed by the landowner**.

> **MBE tip:** To solve:
>
> (1) Identify the type of land entrant.
>
> (2) Apply the corresponding rule.

i. **Trespassers** are those present on land without consent. There are four types of trespassers:

a. **Undiscovered trespassers:** There is **no duty to make the land safe** or **warn** of dangerous conditions.

Example: A hiker was walking through private property without permission and was struck by a limb that fell from a termite-infested tree. The property owner owed no duty to this undiscovered trespasser and has no liability for his injury.

b. **Invitee** (business guest) **exceeding scope of the invitation:** A landowner has a duty to **refrain from willful and wanton misconduct** (e.g., a store customer who enters an area marked "Employees only" exceeds the scope of the invitation as an invitee).

c. **Known** (discovered or anticipated) **trespasser,** which includes frequent trespassers or where the landowner **should have known** of the trespasser (e.g., a well-worn path provides notice). A landowner has a:

(1) **Duty** to use **reasonable care** to avoid injury to the trespasser; and

(2) **Duty** to **warn** or **make safe** (repair) **known dangers and artificial conditions** that pose a risk of **death or serious bodily harm** that the **trespasser is unlikely to discover**.

d. **Child trespassers** (also called **attractive nuisance** doctrine): A landowner has a **duty** to use ordinary **reasonable care** to avoid **foreseeable injury** to **children** if:

(1) The owner **knew or should have known** that the area is one where **children trespass**;

(2) An **artificial condition** poses an **unreasonable risk** of **serious injury or death**;

(3) The children **do not discover the risk** or realize the danger **due to their youth**; and

(4) The benefit to the owner and **burden** (expense) **of eliminating the danger is slight** compared to the **high risk of harm** (balancing test).

Example: A gravel company has a chute for loading gravel that looks like a slide (artificial condition). After closing, a plywood screen was placed on the chute. Children age 8-10 (too young to realize danger) had been playing on the property after work hours for several months (owner should have known), and they figured out how to use the chute as a slide. A child was badly injured. The company will be liable *if* the burden (cost) to better secure the chute is relatively slight (balancing test).

> **MBE tip:** Be alert for MBE questions where one or more of the elements are not satisfied by the facts. The correct answer will use "if" phrasing to reach a correct result, as in the example above.

 *ii.* **Invitee** is one who enters the land in response to an **invitation** by the owner for a **business purpose** (e.g., a customer and their companions; package delivery person) or members of the public are considered invitees for premises **open to the public** (e.g., stores) The landowner has a:

a. **Duty** to **use reasonable care** to make the property safe; and

b. **Duty** to **warn** or **make safe** (repair) **known hazards** on the premises, **unless the danger is open and obvious** to the invitee; and

c. **Duty** to make a reasonable **inspection to discover hidden hazards**.

d. **Nondelegable duty:** When land or a business is open to the public, the landowner remains **liable** for any work **performed negligently by an independent contractor** (where ordinarily the liability would be delegated to the independent contractor).

Example: An independent contractor regularly maintained the escalator in a store. A shopper was injured when the escalator stopped abruptly, and she fell down the steps. Since work performed by independent contractors in public places are nondelegable duties, the store will be liable if there was negligence in the maintenance or operation of the escalator.

iii. **Licensee** is one who enters the land with the **owner's consent** with no business purpose (i.e., social guests). A landowner has a:

a. **Duty** to use **reasonable care** in conducting its active operations on the property; and

b. **Duty** to ***warn*** of all **known dangerous conditions** that create an unreasonable risk of harm that the **licensee is unlikely to discover**.

Example: A man visiting his son's home tripped over a toy his grandson left on the floor and was injured. He had visited before and was aware his grandson left toys scattered around the house. The son did not warn the man to look out for toys. However, the son had no duty to do so since the man already discovered the scattered toy risk.

Decoy tip: Licensees are social guests and invitees are business guests. Since the legal definitions of the terms "licensee" and "invitee" are the opposite of what they seem to mean, they are frequent decoys (e.g., if you invite friends over, they are *not* an invitee—as you might think—but are licensees).

c. **Landlord-Tenant standards of care:** Landlords (lessor) and tenants (lessee) have the **same duties as outlined above**, and the following additional standards of care (which are also covered in the real property chapter):

i. **Tenant: Duty** to **maintain** the premises.

ii. **Landlord:** A lessor of property has the following duties:

a. **Duty** to **warn** or **make safe** (repair) **existing dangers** of which the landlord **knows or should know** that the **tenant is unlikely to discover.**

b. **Duty** to use **reasonable care** in any **repairs made.**

c. **Duty to** use **reasonable care** to maintain the **common areas**.

LANDOWNER/OCCUPIER DUTIES CHEAT SHEET

DUTY (Damages *outside* property)		
	Natural	No duty
	Artificial	Reasonable care Artificial condition (dangerous)

DUTY (Damages *on* property)	**T**res passer	**I**nvitee exceed scope	**K**nown tres-passer	**C**hild tres-passer	**I**nvitee (bus.) Tenant	**L**icensee (social) **T**enant	**L**and-lord
No Duty	X						
No willful/wanton miscond.		X					X
Reasonable care			X	X	X	X	X
Warn & make safe/repair Known danger/artific. cond. Plaintiff unlikely to discover			X				X
Know/should child trespass Artificial condition (dang.) Not perceive risk bc youth Burden slight v. high risk				X			X
Warn & make safe/repair Known hazards Unless danger open/obvious					X		X
Reas. inspection for hazards					X		X
Nondelegable duty (IC)					X		X
Warn Known hazards Plaintiff unlikely to discover						X	X
Warn: tenants Known/should dangers Tenant unlikely to discover Repairs: use reasonable care							X

Memorization tip: Use this mnemonic to remember all the landowner/occupier duties:

CAN'T KILL IT

Child trespasser, **A**rtificial condition, **N**atural condition, **T**respasser, **K**nown trespasser, **I**nvitee-exceed scope, **L**icensee, **L**andlord, **I**nvitee, **T**enant

6. **Negligence per se doctrine: A violation of a statut**e can be used to **establish the duty and breach** elements of negligence. In the majority rule jurisdictions, the statute violation establishes negligence per se. In a minority rule jurisdiction, the violation provides mere evidence of negligence. [Use the majority rule unless directed otherwise.]

   a. **Negligence per se** is established if the defendant:

      i. **Violates a statute** (civil or criminal) without excuse;

      ii. **Class of person:** Plaintiff is within the class of persons the **statute is designed to protect;** and

      iii. **Type of harm:** Plaintiff suffered the **type of harm the statute is intended to** prevent.

   b. **Rebuttal — violation of a statute may be excused** if:

      i. **Greater risk to comply:** Compliance would create a **greater risk** of harm; or

      Example: One is required to drive on the right side of the road, but a flood washed away the right side of the road.

      ii. **Compliance is beyond defendant's control**, meaning defendant cannot comply.

      Example: A man has a heart attack while driving and runs a stop sign in violation of a statute, hitting a pedestrian. The violation is excused by his medical incapacity to comply.

   c. **Establishes duty and breach only:** Negligence per se establishes the elements of duty and breach in negligence, but plaintiff must still prove **causation and damage**.

   Example: A regulation requires defibrillators at all sports stadiums. A stadium does not have one, and a fan has a heart attack. Though negligence per se is established, if the immediate use of a defibrillator wouldn't save the fan, the negligence cause of action will fail for lack of causation.

   d. **Compliance** with a statute does not itself establish that a defendant used reasonable care (i.e., was *not* negligent).

NEGLIGENCE PER SE EXAMPLES

Statute	Facts	Statute Purpose		NPS?	
		Class Person	Type Harm	Y	N
Do not block crosswalk	Truck blocks crosswalk, pedestrian hit	Pedestrian	Hit by car	X	
Warehouses must have fire sprinklers (criminal statute)	Warehouse did not have sprinkler, fire starts and spreads	Occupants, neighbors	Fire damage	X	
All drivers must have valid driver's license	Unlicensed driver hits pedestrian	Identification of drivers			X
No parking within 10 feet of fire hydrants	Car sideswipes car parked by hydrant	Access for fire trucks			X

C. Breach of duty

1. **Breach** occurs when the defendant acts **unreasonably** and their conduct **fails to conform** to the **applicable standard of care.** Breach is measured at the **time of occurrence**, not with the benefit of hindsight.

   Example (breach): A driver, who was drowsy and inattentive, drove off the road and hit an intoxicated man, who was passed out on the side of the road. The driver breached his duty to drive in a reasonably prudent way.

   Example (no breach): A bright 9-year-old child snuck away from his day care center and was injured when he fell through the ice of a nearby pond. The day care center was well staffed, with a reasonable number of qualified personnel, and the employees were exercising reasonable care to ensure the children did not leave the premises. The day care center did not breach their duty of reasonable care.

   a. **Custom in an industry may provide evidence of an appropriate standard of care,** but failure to meet the custom is not dispositive as to breach.

   b. **Balancing test:** Courts often use a balancing test to determine if the risk is **unreasonable** by balancing the **risk** (foreseeability and severity of harm) against the **burden** to protect foreseeable plaintiffs from injury.

   Example: A trucker was driving down the highway with a full load of beef carcasses hanging freely in his trailer truck. When the trucker changed lanes suddenly, the load shifted and the trailer overturned, causing a driver to hit the overturned trailer and sustain injury. Other truckers had complained that the trailer design was dangerous. A restraining device was available at nominal cost to prevent the load from shifting. The trucker knew about the restraining device, but he had not installed it. In a suit for negligence, the driver will prevail if the use of the restraining device (burden to trucker is nominal cost) would have prevented the trailer from overturning (foreseeability and severity of serious harm).

   c. **Anticipating the misconduct of others** is required in some situations, and the failure to do so can establish a breach of duty.

   1. **Negligence:** One must anticipate the negligence of others.

   2. **Parent:** Has a **duty to supervise** their children, though a parent is not vicariously liable for the torts of their children.

   3. **Crimes/intentional torts of others:** Generally, one may assume a third party will not commit an intentional tort or crime.

   a. **Exception: Innkeepers** and **common carriers** have a **duty to prevent injury to their guests and passengers from third persons,** such as **foreseeable** criminal acts and torts.

   Example: A man rented a car from a rental agency. The car had a hidden bomb, which exploded shortly after he picked up the car, injuring the man. The rental agency had carefully inspected the car to ensure it was in sound operating condition before the rental, but they did not inspect for hidden explosives. Had they done such an inspection they would have found the bomb. There were no prior incidents of bombs hidden in rental cars. The rental agency did not breach their duty since they could not have foreseen the likelihood of someone placing a bomb in the rental car.

> **MBE tip:** Where breach is tested, the correct answer choice may simply state more broadly that negligence is, or is not, established, without mentioning the word "breach" to tip you off that breach is the issue.

2. **Res ipsa loquitur** means "the thing speaks for itself" and can be used to create a permissible **inference of breach** of duty when direct evidence is lacking.

   a. **Application:** Res ipsa loquitur is used in situations where:

      1. **Negligence clearly occurred:** The **accident is a type** that ordinarily **does not occur in the absence of negligence;** and

      2. **Negligence is attributable to the defendant,** which is typically shown where the defendant has **exclusive control** of the instrumentality of injury, so a third party is *not* responsible; and

      3. **Injury is *not* attributable to the plaintiff.**

   b. **Result of res ipsa loquitur:** The plaintiff will have met the burden of production, which **shifts the burden to the defendant to rebut.** In the absence of rebuttal, a **permissible inference of breach** is established.

RES IPSA LOQUITUR EXAMPLES

Facts	Y	N
A pedestrian walking on the highway shoulder is killed when struck by a car that swerved off the highway and onto the shoulder	X	
An airplane, flying in good weather, crashed into a mountain.	X	
A person walking past a 12-story apartment building is struck from above by a flowerpot. (Owner does not have exclusive control.)		X
A person parked her car on a hill. Two minutes later the car rolled down the hill and hit plaintiff. Defendant testifies she turned her wheels in and set the emergency brake. There was evidence that juveniles had been tampering with cars in the neighborhood. (Jury is *not required* to draw inference of breach since Defendant rebutted by showing that the accident could be attributed to the juveniles.)		X

MBE tip: Res ipsa loquitur is often tested using a civil procedure question call, such as if the court should grant the defense's summary judgment motion. If the plaintiff has established res ipsa loquitur, it can withstand such motions.

MBE tip: While res ipsa loquitur establishes an inference of breach (and causation and damages must still be shown), MBE answers tend to state the concept even more broadly as that res ipsa loquitur establishes negligence itself.

Decoy tip: Res ipsa loquitur typically is not mentioned by name in the answer choices. An "inference" of negligence may be used as a synonym. Correct answers may also use language such as "negligence may be inferred," or that a "prima facie case" of negligence is established.

D. Actual cause (cause in fact): The defendant's conduct must be the cause in fact of the plaintiff's injury. Several tests can be used to establish actual cause.

> **MBE tip:** Causation is one of the most difficult MBE testing areas and also one of the most heavily tested. Do extra practice questions on causation, slow down, and take your time.

1. **But-for test:** Generally, **but for** the defendant's act or failure to act, the injury to plaintiff would not have resulted. This test is used most often.

   Example: A driver negligently collided with a pedestrian. But for the driver's negligent driving, the pedestrian would not be injured.

   a. **Concurrent tortfeasors** (each acting independently): Where **more than one act combines** to cause an injury, but **none of the acts independently would cause an injury,** each of the acts is an actual cause of the injury. **But for** each act, the injury would not have occurred.

   Example: Both a shopping center and a railroad negligently failed to maintain their storm drains, which in a heavy rainfall caused a nearby manufacturing plant to flood. Had either drain been maintained properly, the flooding would not have happened. In an action against the railroad, the plaintiff can recover all of his loss since **but for** the railroad's negligence, the flooding would not have occurred. (This also raises the issue of joint and several liability between the tortfeasors. See sec. XII.B.1.)

2. **Substantial factor test:** Where two or more defendants are at fault and their **conduct combines to cause the harm** to the plaintiff, **each is a substantial factor** in causing the injury.

   a. **Concurrent tortfeasors** (acting in concert): Where **more than one act combines** within a common pursuit to cause a single injury, each is a **substantial factor** in causing the injury.

   Example: A man and woman were competing in an illegal drag race. They were driving very carefully, but both were speeding. The woman's tire blew out and she lost control of her car and crashed, injuring a pedestrian. The pedestrian can opt to sue the man (who has better insurance and assets) since he was *acting in concert* in a dangerous activity and his conduct was a **substantial factor** in harming the plaintiff.

   > **MBE tip:** The bar examiners use the language "but for" as a synonym for "actual cause." Consequently, even though the substantial factor test may be more appropriate, a correct answer choice may refer to "but for" causation. They also use the word "causation" to refer to either actual cause or proximate cause.

3. **Alternative causes where only one act at fault:** When **each defendant is engaged in a tortious act** but **only one could have caused the injury** and which is unknown, the plaintiff must show the **harm was caused by one** or more of the defendants, but since the plaintiff cannot reasonably be expected to prove which actor(s) caused the harm, the **burden of proof on causation shifts** to the defendants.

   Example (established): Two hunters negligently fired their guns in the plaintiff's direction, injuring him. The burden of proof on which of the two caused the injury shifts to the defendants.

   Example (not established): A pedestrian was injured when hit by a chair thrown from a hotel window. The pedestrian sued the occupants of all rooms from which the chair could have been thrown. The defendants' motion for directed verdict should be granted since the plaintiff did not establish that each defendant was engaged in tortious conduct.

4. **Joint and several liability** (as relates to causation): Where a **single indivisible injury** results, making it impossible to apportion the damages between the tortfeasors, each is jointly and severally liable for the entire injury. See sec. XII.B.

   Example (indivisible injury): A driver negligently collided with a fire engine that was on the way to fight a fire. As a result, the fire engine was delayed reaching the plaintiff's home, which was 10 blocks away, and the home burned down. But for the driver's negligent driving, the damage to plaintiff's home would have been reduced because the fire engine would have arrived sooner. (As a concurrent tortfeasor, the driver is jointly and severally liable with the one who negligently caused the fire, but can also seek indemnification for the portion of harm *not* caused by the delay.)

5. **Loss of chance of survival:** Some jurisdictions allow recovery for the reduction in the chance for survival where negligent medical care results in a diminished chance of recovery from illness. Essentially, this creates an **exception to requiring establishing cause in fact**. [This rule is rarely tested.]

> **MBE tip:** Concurrent tortfeasor issues are most often tested in combination with third-party joint and several liability, contribution, and indemnification rules. See sec. XII.

 E. **Proximate cause** (also called legal cause).

1. **Reasonable foreseeability test:** Generally, a defendant is liable for all **harmful results** that were **reasonably foreseeable**. The **type of harm** suffered must be reasonably foreseeable as a result of the negligence.

   Example (foreseeable): A pedestrian was hit by a car and injured his knee. Thereafter, his knee would buckle occasionally. Several months later, his knee buckled, causing him to fall down a flight of stairs and injure his shoulder. The pedestrian can recover against the car driver for both the knee and shoulder injury *if* the jury finds falling down the stairs was a normal consequence (foreseeable result) of the original injury.

   Example (unforeseeable): A man negligently caused a fire and his home burned to the ground. As a result, sun streamed into the neighbor's yard, destroying valuable trees that require shade. The type of harm caused (dead trees) by the failure of the burned down home to provide shade to the neighbor is unforeseeable and too remote from the foreseeable risks of causing a fire.

> **MBE tip:** Unforeseeable risks, which are analyzed in causation, and the element of "duty" are linked concepts. If a risk is unforeseeable, a defendant has no duty to avoid that risk, and a correct answer choice may use that language.

   a. **Eggshell-skull plaintiff:** A defendant is liable for **unforeseen physical consequences** (the *extent* of an injury) suffered by the plaintiff, which is caused by a weakness or susceptibility in the plaintiff (e.g., aggravation of a preexisting condition). The defendant **"takes the plaintiff as the defendant finds them."**

      Example: While exiting a negligently maintained elevator, plaintiff fell when it dropped several inches. Plaintiff's fall severely aggravated a preexisting physical disability. Plaintiff can recover for all of her injuries because the type of harm was foreseeable, even if the *extent* of injury was an unforeseen consequence of this fall.

2. **Intervening causes** are responses or reactions that occur **subsequent** to the defendant's negligence.

   a. **Foreseeable:** Defendant is **liable** for **all foreseeable intervening causes.** Negligence of others is foreseeable (e.g., subsequent medical malpractice).

      Example: A driver hit a pedestrian, breaking her leg. While shopping at the market on crutches, the pedestrian non-negligently placed her crutch on a banana peel that had been negligently left on the floor by the store manager. The crutch slipped on the banana peel, causing the pedestrian to fall and break her arm. Had she not been on crutches, she would not have fallen over. The driver is liable for both injuries since it is foreseeable that walking on crutches could make the pedestrian less stable on her feet and vulnerable to falling. (The market is also liable for the arm injury as a concurrent tortfeasor.)

   b. **Unforeseeable:** The defendant generally **is not liable** for **superseding intervening causes** that are not a normal response or **not a reasonably foreseeable reaction** to the situation created by the defendant's conduct; superseding intervening causes often result from an interruption in the chain of causation.

      1. **Criminal acts and intentional torts of others are superseding:** Generally, a tortfeasor is **not liable** for the criminal acts and intentional torts of third parties made possible by his negligence; they are **superseding intervening causes.**

         a. **Exception: If the defendant creates the risk it is *not* superseding.** Where a **defendant should realize a third party will commit a crime** or intentional tort because their **negligence creates the risk**, the defendant is **liable** because the risk is foreseeable and the intervening event will not cut off liability.

            Example: A roofer was hired to repair a roof. The roofer left a 20-foot extension ladder against the side of the house when he was done, intending to retrieve it in the morning. The homeowner was out of town and during the night, a thief used the ladder to gain access through an upstairs window, stealing jewels. The roofer's negligence in leaving the ladder at an unoccupied home created the risk that a person might unlawfully enter, so the criminal conduct of the thief was foreseeable, and not a superseding intervening cause.

      2. **"Acts of God"** that are **not foreseeable** are **intervening superseding causes** that break the chain of causation.

         Example: An ocean liner departed on a voyage knowing the seas would be rough. The ocean liner did not have the type of lifeboats that were statutorily required. A passenger was swept overboard and drowned. Even if they had the proper type of lifeboat, the seas were too rough to launch a rescue. This is an "act of God," and the ocean liner is not liable because the severe storm is an intervening superseding cause.

PROXIMATE CAUSE FOR INTERVENING ACTS

Negligent Act
↓
Intervening Force
↙ ↘

Foreseeable? ↓ **Liable**	**Unforeseeable** (superseding)**?** ↓ **Not Liable**
Ex: ◆ Medical malpractice ◆ Negligence of rescuers ◆ Subsequent accident ◆ Subsequent illness	**Ex:** ◆ Intentional torts ◆ Criminal Acts ◆ Acts of God **Decoy tip:** Intervening causes supersede *only if* they are unforeseeable. Bar examiners like to add facts that make the act foreseeable.

MBE tip: Slow down and read carefully when causation is at issue. Two answers may seem identical, but teasing through the differences will lead you to the correct answer.

Decoy tip: Be alert with question calls about motions for summary judgment. Even with facts that tend to only prove up one side for foreseeability (or any element), a jury should make those determinations of fact and not a judge through summary judgment.

F. **Damages for negligence** [Damages are rarely MBE tested.]

1. **Actual injury required:** Damages require an actual injury to the plaintiff.

   Example: A doctor did not inform a patient about a serious risk associated with a pending surgery. The surgery was a success, but the patient was furious when he found out he had not been properly informed. Since the surgery was successful, the patient has no actual injury.

2. **Types of damages:** Plaintiff may recover damages for direct loss, out-of-pocket economic losses stemming from the injury, pain and suffering, and hedonistic damages (loss of ability to enjoy life).

3. **Establishing damages:** In addition to establishing that the damages/harm are **caused** by the defendant's conduct and that the damages were **foreseeable**, they must be able to be calculated with reasonable **certainty** and **unavoidable**, which requires that the plaintiff **mitigate** their damages (e.g., seek treatment).

4. **Damages** that are **not permitted in negligence:**

   a. **No punitive damages** for ordinary negligence.

      1. **Exception: Punitive damages are available** where the defendant's conduct was **wanton, willful, or reckless**.

   b. **No nominal damages.**

c. **Pure economic loss is not recoverable** without other tangible harm (except where permitted by wrongful death statute). This is because there is no duty to avoid causing pure economic loss, and such a plaintiff may not be foreseeable.

Example: An actress was seriously injured in a car accident caused by Defendant's negligence. Her show was cancelled and the cast and crew were laid off. An actor from the show cannot recover from Defendant for the actor's loss of income caused by harm done to a third party (the actress) because it is a pure economic loss without other harm to the actor.

Decoy tip: When the plaintiff has pure economic loss only, the correct answer will often be phrased that the defendant did not owe a duty to the plaintiff (e.g., there is no general duty to avoid causing pure economic loss).

G. **Negligent infliction of emotional distress (NIED):** There is a duty to avoid causing emotional distress in others. The defendant is liable for NIED when the defendant engages in **negligent conduct** that causes the plaintiff to suffer **serious emotional distress.** [The MBE tests NIED in the context of damages and one's ability to recover for stand-alone emotional distress.]

1. **Stand-alone emotional distress** (no physical impact) recovery is limited in most jurisdictions to the following cases *only:*

a. **Zone of danger and in fear for own safety:** Plaintiff suffers the threat of physical impact (in the zone of danger, but no actual impact) that **directly causes emotional distress.**

1. **Physical symptoms required** in most jurisdictions (e.g., suffering a miscarriage or heart attack).

b. **Bystander recovery- not in zone of danger:** Plaintiff is not in the zone of danger, but contemporaneously **perceives** (see, hear, etc.) bodily **injury** to a **close family member,** resulting in **emotional distress.**

1. **No physical symptoms** are **required** to recover in most jurisdictions.

Example: A bystander witnessed a pedestrian be hit by a car from across the street. The bystander rushed to offer aid and the pedestrian died in her arms. The bystander suffered serious emotional distress but no physical manifestations. The bystander cannot recover because she was not in the zone of danger or a close family member of the pedestrian.

c. **Special cases:** The person affected had a **special relationship** with the tortfeasor and suffers severe **emotional distress. No physical symptoms** are **required** to recover in most jurisdictions.

Examples: Mishandling a dead body, misreporting a death, incorrect terminal medical diagnosis.

Decoy tip: When the facts do not support an NIED claim (because it is not one of the cases above where NIED is allowed), the correct answer will often be phrased that the defendant did not owe a duty to the plaintiff (e.g., there is no general duty to avoid negligently causing emotional distress).

EMOTIONAL DISTRESS CHEAT SHEET

IIED	NIED		
Intentionally	Negligently		
Severe emotional distress (bodily harm/physical symptom not required)	Serious emotional distress (stand-alone) Physical symptoms required? (most jx.)?		
Extreme & outrageous conduct	**Yes**	**No**	**No**
Bystander IIED: ◆ Present, <u>and</u> ◆ Presence known to defendant, <u>and</u> ◆ Third party is relative <u>or</u> P suffers bodily harm from distress	**Zone of danger** ◆ Fear own safety ◆ Physical symptoms required	**Bystander recovery** ◆ Perceive ◆ Family member ◆ Physical symptoms not reqt.	**Special cases:** ◆ Mishandle dead body ◆ Incorrect terminal dx ◆ Physical symptoms not reqt.

IV. DEFENSES TO NEGLIGENCE

A. **Comparative negligence** applies when **plaintiff's own negligence** has also **contributed** to plaintiff's injuries and liability is divided between the plaintiff and defendant **in proportion to their relative degrees of fault.**

1. **Pure comparative negligence** allows recovery in proportion of fault regardless of how negligent the plaintiff was, but the plaintiff's recovery will be reduced by their proportionate negligence. [This is the MBE default rule. Use unless told otherwise.]

   <u>Example</u>: A worker in an elevator got stuck between floors. The worker was in no danger. After 15 minutes of waiting for rescue, the worker became anxious and jumped 12 feet to get out, injuring his back. The worker's recovery will be reduced by his own comparative negligence.

   a. **Plaintiff's share is deducted "off the top."** If there are joint tortfeasors, they are jointly and severally liable for the balance.

      <u>Example</u>: Plaintiff gets into a car accident with D1 and D2. Plaintiff has $100,000 in damages and is found to be 40% at fault. Plaintiff's share of 40% ($40,000) is deducted, and D1 and D2 are each 30% responsible. Plaintiff can recover the entire balance of $60,000 from either D1 or D2, since they are jointly and severally liable.

2. **Partial comparative negligence** (minority jurisdiction) bars the plaintiff's recovery if plaintiff's negligence was more serious than the defendant's (in some states, at least as serious). This typically means that if the plaintiff's negligence was **more than 50%, recovery would be barred.**

B. **Contributory negligence** is where **any negligence** on the part of the plaintiff that contributes proximately to the plaintiff's injuries **completely bars recovery**. This system is abolished in most jurisdictions.

1. **Exception: Last clear chance** doctrine can be used to rebut a contributory negligence defense. The **person with the last clear chance to avoid the accident**, but who fails to do so, **is liable**. (This doctrine mitigates the harsh result of the contributory negligence rule.)

C. **Assumption of the risk:** Plaintiff may be denied recovery if he assumed the risk of any damage caused by defendant's act where:

1. Plaintiff **knew of the risk** (**understood** the risk), and

2. **Voluntarily consented** despite the risk, which requires there must be a reasonable alternative available.

   1. **Waivers of liability** are allowed when an activity poses risks familiar to participants and the risk cannot be entirely eliminated without removing the pleasure of the activity.

   Example: A hot-air balloon company operated near a golf course. A fence surrounded the property with signs warning of the balloon danger. A woman ignored the signs to retrieve her errant golf ball and was injured by a balloon making an emergency landing. She assumed the risk.

D. **No imputed contributory/comparative negligence** generally. The negligence of a child is not imputed to a parent and the negligence of a spouse is not imputed to the other spouse.

E. **Tort immunity:** Municipalities are generally immune from tort liability, except for: (1) torts committed in a propriety capacity, (2) municipality created nuisances, and in some states (3) negligently maintained municipal property, roads, streets, and sewers. [This rule is rarely MBE tested.]

V. STRICT LIABILITY

A. **Animals:**

1. **Trespassing animals:** An owner is **strictly liable** for **reasonably foreseeable damage** done by a **trespass** of their **animals.**

   a. **Exception: Does not apply** to the trespass of **domestic pets** in most jurisdictions.

2. **Wild or abnormally dangerous animals:** An owner is **strictly liable** for harm that results from a wild or abnormally dangerous animal's **dangerous nature** (e.g., lions, tigers, and even cute animals like skunks and koalas, etc.). **Fear** of a wild animal is part of what makes wild animals dangerous.

   a. Strict liability **attaches** even if the animals are released due to a **force of nature** (i.e., flood, earthquake, etc.).

   b. **Trespassers — no strict liability:** A trespasser who is injured by a wild animal will need to prove negligence.

   Example (strict liability): A person owned a large poisonous snake, which was defanged and kept in a cage. A storm damaged the cage and the snake escaped. A volunteer storm clean-up worker came across the snake and tried to run away, but fell and broke his arm.

The owner is strictly liable because fear of attack is a foreseeable reaction to the dangerous nature of a large poisonous snake and the worker didn't know the snake was defanged (that fact is a decoy).

<u>Example (no strict liability)</u>: A lame and blind bear is sitting on the sidewalk and a passerby trips over him. There is no strict liability since the injury is caused by something unrelated to the dangerous nature of the species.

3. **Domestic animals known to be dangerous** or mischievous: An owner is strictly liable for damage caused by domestic animals (e.g., dogs, farm animals, cows, bees, etc.) only if the owner:

   a. **Knew or had reason to know** of that particular animal's...

   b. **Dangerous propensities** for this sort of harm. (For dog bites, this is the one free bite rule.)

   <u>Example</u>: A dog was known to chase cars. One day the dog got out and chased a car, causing the driver to swerve into a pole to avoid hitting the dog. The dog owner is strictly liable because he knew of the dog's dangerous propensity to chase cars.

 B. **Abnormally dangerous** (ultra-hazardous) **activities** are subject to **strict liability** and are those that cannot be performed safely despite using the upmost care. Meaning, the **risk of danger is unreasonably high** when compared to the **social utility of the activity**, even in the absence of negligence and where all proper precautions have been taken.

1. **Abnormally dangerous activities** are those where:

   a. The activity creates an inherent **high degree of risk of serious harm**;

   b. The **risk cannot be eliminated** by the exercise of reasonable care or undertaking proper precautions;

   c. The activity is **not common** in the community;

   d. The **risk of harm outweighs the activity's value** (social utility) to the community (balancing test). [Applying facts to this balancing test and making a judgment call is not how this rule is tested on the MBE.]

2. **Causation:** Operates the same as in negligence. (See sec. III.D. and III.E. above.) Causation will be **limited to the kind of harm that makes the activity abnormally dangerous.**

   <u>Example</u>: A manufacturing plant stores highly volatile explosives. During a heavy windstorm a large tile blew off the roof and crashed through the windshield of a passing car. There is no strict liability because the damage did not result from the abnormally dangerous aspect of the plant.

3. **Damages:** Operates the same as in negligence. See sec. III.F. above.

4. **Independent contractors & nondelegable duties:** Landowners are liable for independent contractors if they are conducting inherently dangerous activities on the property (nondelegable duty). See sec. XII.A.2.a.

<u>Example</u>: A builder hired a contractor to build an in-ground swimming pool on a tract of land. The contractor carried out a blasting operation to excavate the site, which caused cracks to form in a neighbor's home. Despite hiring an independent contractor to conduct the excavation, the builder is strictly liable. The builder had a nondelegable duty of care since using explosives and blasting in a residential area is inherently dangerous.

ABNORMALLY DANGEROUS ACTIVITY EXAMPLES	
Abnormally Dangerous Activity	**NOT**
◆ Explosives: manufacturer/blasting ◆ Dangerous/toxic/hazardous chemicals: manufacture/storage/transportation ◆ Fumigation/crop dusting ◆ Nuclear power plant ◆ Firearms ◆ Demolition	◆ Cutting the roots of a tree back ◆ Airline travel ◆ Making tuna casserole with bad tuna from dented cans ◆ Excavation (not blasting)
MBE tip: Remember strict liability establishes what would be the elements of duty and breach, but you still need to prove causation and damages.	

C. **Defenses to strict liability:**

1. **Assumption of the risk** is a defense to strict liability, where the defendant **knew of risk**, and **voluntarily consented** anyway.

   Example: A copper mining company kept dynamite in a storage facility at the mine, which had state-of-the-art safety standards. Some dynamite exploded for unknown reasons, injuring a state employee who was at the mine to perform a safety audit. The state employee willingly undertook auditing duties in potentially dangerous environments and had assumed the risk. (The facts about the safety standards are decoy ducks.)

2. **Comparative negligence jurisdictions:** Most states **apply comparative negligence principles** to provide a defense for strict liability.

3. **Contributory negligence jurisdictions—no defense:** Contributory negligence does not provide a defense unless the plaintiff knowingly assumes the risk (essentially an assumption of risk defense).

Decoy tip: Strict liability is a frequent decoy answer. Remember, strict liability *only* applies to:
- ◆ Wild animals and domestic animals with a known propensity
- ◆ Abnormally dangerous activities
- ◆ Defective products

VI. PRODUCTS LIABILITY

There are five ways a commercial seller can be liable for injuries caused by a product: strict tort liability, negligence, warranty, misrepresentation, and intent. [The MBE primarily tests harms caused by products using strict products liability and occasionally negligence. They do not seem to test products using intent (which would be similar to a battery), or the warranty rules, which are covered in the Contracts outline sec. VII.E.]

A. Strict products liability: A seller of a product has **strict liability** (liability without fault) for personal injuries caused by a defective product. Plaintiff must prove the following elements: commercial supplier, defective product, actual cause, proximate cause, and damages.

> **Decoy tip:** Suits are not limited to product buyers; anyone can sue. There is no privity requirement for strict products liability. This is a frequent decoy.

1. **Commercial supplier:** A commercial supplier is one who places a product in the **stream of commerce without substantial alteration.**

   a. **Place product in stream of commerce:** A commercial supplier includes all involved in the production and sale of a product, including retailers, wholesalers, component manufacturers, assemblers, and the product manufacturer.

   Example: A man had a car accident caused by the malfunction of his high-beam headlights. The man can sue the manufacturer of the headlight controls, the car manufacturer, and the retailer.

   1. **Not commercial sellers: Occasional sellers** (e.g., yard sale) or **auctioneers** are not commercial sellers for strict products liability.

   b. **Without substantial alteration**, meaning the product has not been altered in a more dangerous way from its intended design.

   Example: A hardware store sells new and reconditioned saws. A customer bought a reconditioned saw. At the customer's request, the storeowner changed out the saw blade with course teeth for a blade with smooth teeth. One week later, the shaft holding the saw blade came loose when a bearing gave way and the shaft and blade flew off the saw, injuring the user. Since the saw had been rebuilt by the storeowner and was substantially altered, the storeowner is strictly liable, but the manufacturer is not. (The facts about the saw blade switch were decoys.)

   c. **No privity required**. The plaintiff need not be the purchaser of the product.

> **Decoy tip:** Medical professionals are not considered commercial suppliers when *using* a product to treat a patient (e.g., inject a patient using a hypodermic needle).

2. **Product is defective:** There are three ways a product can be found defective: manufacturing defect, design defect, and warning defect.

   a. **Manufacturing defect** exists when the product is different and more dangerous than all of the others because it **deviated from the intended design**. In other words, the product was **not manufactured as intended**.

   Example: A single dishwasher has an internal wiring defect, which allowed electricity to be carried into the framework, shocking the consumer.

   b. **Design defect** exists when all products of a line are the same and they all bear a feature whose **design itself is defective** (such as a structural weakness, or lack of a safety feature) and are unreasonably dangerous. Courts use the following two tests to establish a design defect:

   1. **Consumer expectation test:** A product's performance must meet the **minimum safety expectations** of its ordinary users **when used in a reasonably foreseeable** manner.

   Example: An arsonist set a fire using a cigarette lighter, which he then put in his pocket. While standing to admire the fire, the lighter exploded in his pocket, injuring the arsonist. The lighter was defective and the manufacturer is strictly liable. (That the plaintiff was an arsonist is a decoy. He was properly storing the lighter in his pocket when it exploded.)

2. **Risk-utility test** (reasonable alternative design): A product is defective if the **risk of danger inherent in the design outweighs the benefits** of such design and the danger could have been reduced or avoided by the adoption of a **feasible, cost-effective alternative** design. The court will consider the **cost and utility** of an alternative design compared to the current design to determine if it is a reasonable alternative.

   Example (defective): A sports car is very reliable, except it stalls if not extensively warmed up before use. A woman was driving without warming it up first when her car stalled, causing an accident. An alternative design of equal cost (cost effective) was available that eliminated the stalling without impairing engine function (feasible alternative). A trier of fact could find the car had a design defect (and the consumer misuse is foreseeable).

   Example (not defective): A teenager used an educational chemistry set to make a bomb. While making the bomb, the teen carelessly knocked a lit Bunsen burner into a bowl of chemicals, which burst into flames, burning the teen. The product will not be deemed defective *if* it was as safe as possible consistent with its educational purpose and the benefits exceed the risks.

c. **Warning defect** (a type of design defect) exists when the **maker fails to give adequate warnings** as to a **known (or should have been known) danger** in the product or in a particular use of the product at the time that is **not obvious**. Some courts use **risk-utility analysis** when the risk could have been reduced or avoided by reasonable instructions or warnings.

Example (warning defect): While he was removing the restraining wire from a bottle of champagne, the stopper suddenly shot out, injuring the bartender. The bartender sued, contending there was not an adequate warning on the bottle.

Example (no warning defect): A furnace had no warnings or instructions on how it was to be cleaned. A man used a 6-foot ladder to clean the furnace and fell, breaking his arm. There is no warning defect because the danger of falling from a ladder is obvious.

1. **Learned intermediary rule:** A warning for a pharmaceutical of medical device that is provided to the prescribing doctor is sufficient in most jurisdictions.

> **MBE tip:** A warning may trigger a causation issue. If the plaintiff would not have read a warning, the lack of warning did not the cause the injury.

d. **Industry standards:**

1. **Compliance** with industry standards **does not establish that a product is *not* defective.**

2. **Lack of compliance** with industry standards **can establish that a product *is* defective.**

e. **Product misuse** that is reasonably **foreseeable** is **still covered** by strict liability. Product misuse will **only shield** the commercial seller from strict liability **when the misuse is unforeseeable.**

Example: A dandruff shampoo user may foreseeably not heed or read warnings written on the box containing the shampoo bottle and misuse the product by using too much.

3. **Actual cause:** Plaintiff must show that **but for** the defect, they would not have been injured and that the **defect existed at the time it left defendant's control.** See sec. III.D. above.
4. **Proximate cause:** Same analysis as in negligence cases (foreseeability). See sec. III.E. above.
5. **Damages:** Physical injury or property damage must be shown. There is no recovery for purely economic loss. See sec. III.F. above.
6. **Defenses:** The rules below control, unless the question itself provides differently. **If product misuse is unforeseeable**, the misuse may provide a defense, depending on the jurisdiction. See complete defenses rules in sec. IV.
   a. **Assumption of the risk:** For strict products liability, this requires showing the purchaser **discovered the defect** and **unreasonably used the product** despite this.
   b. **Comparative negligence jurisdictions:** Most states **apply comparative negligence principles** to provide a defense for strict liability.
   c. **Contributory negligence jurisdictions—no defense: Contributory negligence does not provide a defense** where the plaintiff simply **fails to discover the defect**. (Though assumption of risk will provide a defense in contributory negligence states.)

      Example: A man became sick after drinking a soda containing a decomposing snail. The snail would have been visible before the man opened the bottle. There is strict liability and any contributory negligence of the man is no defense.
   d. **Disclaimers of liability** are **not effective**.
   e. **Compliance with industry standards is not dispositive** conclusive evidence that a product is *not* defective, so this will not provide an effective defense.

Decoy tip: It is hard to establish a successful defense to strict products liability. Defenses are frequent decoys.

STRICT PRODUCT LIABILITY EXAMPLES

Defective Products	No Strict Products Liability
◆ Tuna fish sold in dented cans which were unfit for consumption. ◆ Stove that tipped over with 25 lbs. of weight hanging on the door. ◆ Bike with faulty brakes. ◆ Blender that shattered when used properly. ◆ Installation and supply of defective airplane engine by aircraft maintenance and repair company. ◆ Sports car designed to exceed 100 mph equipped with tires with a maximum safe speed of 85 mph (with warning contained only in manual). ◆ Metal stamping press without an available safety shield to prevent closing on workers' hands.	◆ Fallen power lines (transmission of electricity is not a "product" until it is metered into a home). ◆ Hypodermic needle *used* by a dentist to inject anesthesia (not a product). ◆ Saw that was disassembled and rebuilt by the retailer (substantial alteration). ◆ Snowblower that was improperly repaired (substantial alteration).

MBE tip: Under any strict liability theory, after establishing the product is defective, plaintiff must still prove actual and proximate cause and damages.

B. Negligence: See sec. III. above.

C. Misrepresentation: See sec. VII below.

<u>MBE tip</u>: **Retailers and wholesalers** are rarely liable under a negligence theory for products liability since they **only have a duty to inspect or warn of known dangers**. A manufacturer is likely to be liable under a negligence theory since the manufacturer is typically responsible for the defectiveness of the product.

<u>Decoy tip</u>: Liability for a defective product is usually based on strict product liability, but pay attention to the call of the question because they occasionally provide a negligence cause of action.

VII. MISREPRESENTATION

A. Fraud: Intentional misrepresentation is common law fraud or **deceit.** One must prove:

1. **Misrepresentation** of a **material fact.** This can be done by words (e.g., lying) or by actions of intentional concealment (e.g., fresh paint on the ceiling to conceal damage left by a leaky roof).
   a. **Not opinions:** False statements of opinion, value, or quality are generally not actionable.

      <u>Example (misrepresentation of material fact)</u>: The seller of a boat told the buyer that the boat was sea worthy and had never sustained significant damage. In fact, the hull had been badly damaged when the boat ran aground and the seller had only performed cosmetic repairs, rather than structural repairs. A statement regarding the hull's integrity would be material to any buyer, and the true hull condition was actively concealed. This is a misrepresentation of material fact.

      <u>Example (not a misrepresentation of material fact)</u>: The seller of a boat told the buyer, "This is the best boat you can find for its size." This statement is an opinion as to quality and not a representation of material fact.
2. Made with **knowledge of statement's falsity** or **reckless disregard** of the truth (scienter),
3. **Intent to induce plaintiff's reliance** on the misrepresentation,
4. **Causation** (actual reliance by plaintiff),
5. **Justifiable reliance** by plaintiff (reliance will be found justifiable unless there is clear evidence to the contrary), and
6. **Pecuniary** (money) **damages** to plaintiff. Typically, this will be assessed under a "benefit of the bargain" contract damages analysis. A plaintiff will not be able to recover for purely emotional distress in the absence of physical harm.

<u>MBE tip</u>: When product liability is in issue, but the product is *not* defective, consider if the manufacturer made an express promise that could be actionable under misrepresentation.

<u>Example</u>: A vaporizer is built as safely as possible (no product defect) and is described as "spillproof" in the booklet that accompanied the vaporizer. A child trips over the vaporizer, and is burned when it tips over, spilling boiling water on the child. This may be actionable as an intentional misrepresentation.

B. **Negligent misrepresentation** [This rule is rarely MBE tested.] The first two elements are different than an intentional misrepresentation.

1. **Misrepresentation** is made in a **business or professional capacity,**
2. **Negligence standard:** Defendant acted with **no reasonable grounds for believing the misrepresentation to be true**, (a lower and easier to meet standard than for intentional misrepresentation),
3. **Intent to induce plaintiff's reliance** on the misrepresentation,
4. **Causation** (actual reliance by plaintiff),
5. **Justifiable reliance** by plaintiff, and
6. **Pecuniary** (money) **damages** to plaintiff. Typically, this will be assessed under a "benefit of the bargain" contract damages analysis. Plaintiff will not be able to recover for purely emotional distress in the absence of physical harm.

   Example (negligent misrepresentation): A job applicant was told the company was worth millions and their portfolio would triple in the next few months. Two days after accepting the job, the company filed for bankruptcy. While this is a negligent misrepresentation, the applicant will only be able to recover upon a showing of actual money damages.

VIII. TORTIOUS INTERFERENCE WITH BUSINESS RELATIONS

A. **Tortious interference with business relations:** Prima facie case requires establishing: [This rule is rarely MBE tested.]

1. **Contractual relationship** or **valid business expectancy** between two parties,
2. A third party **knew or should have known of that relationship** or expectancy,
3. **Intentional interference** by the third party to induce breach or termination of the relationship or expectancy, and
4. **Damages** to the plaintiff.

B. **Defense-Privilege:** The defendant's conduct may be privileged where it is a **proper attempt to obtain business** for itself or protect its own interests (fair competition), particularly if the defendant uses **justifiable and fair methods**.

IX. NUISANCE

A. **Private nuisance** is a **substantial, unreasonable interference** with another person's **use or enjoyment of their own land** or land in which they have an interest.

1. **Substantial interference** is interference that is **offensive, inconvenient**, or **annoying to the average reasonable person** in the community (e.g., sound waves, lights from a stadium, vibrations, etc.).
   a. **Hypersensitivity** by the plaintiff will not meet the test. However, if a **substantial minority** of people in the community share the sensitivity, it will meet the test.

2. **Unreasonable interference:** The interference is unreasonable (**objective standard**) if either:
   a. The **harm to plaintiff outweighs the utility** of defendant's conduct; or
   b. The **harm caused to plaintiff** is greater than plaintiff should be required to bear **without consideration**.
   c. **Test for both:** Consider the **nature, extent, and frequency of harm**, and the **neighborhood**, **land value**, and **alternatives** available for defendant.
      1. **Harm:** The harm can be measured by **personal discomfort** of those on the land, or **threat to the safety** of those on the land, or **tangible harm** to the land itself that diminishes market value.
      2. **Zoning ordinance compliance**, and compliance with **general industry safety standards** are important in making a determination, but not dispositive.

PRIVATE NUISANCE EXAMPLES

MBE tip: To solve a private nuisance question, usually you need only identify that ***if*** the interference is substantial and unreasonable there is a private nuisance, rather than make a judgment call on if a particular interference qualifies as substantial and unreasonable.

(Probable) Private Nuisance	NO (or Probably NOT)
◆ Over 35 years the city limits extended to the lot of a cattle company on a 150-acre tract. They use the best and most sanitary procedures to keep flies and odors down. Nonetheless, nearby residents complain of many flies and obnoxious odors, both of which are substantial health hazards. (Coming to the nuisance and using state of the art procedures are not dispositive.) ◆ A small diner that is open until midnight generates lots of lights, noise, and trash. It is allowed under local zoning (zoning not dispositive). ◆ A school adjacent to a farm built a 5000-seat lighted outdoor stadium. ◆ A landowner built a dam on her property stopping the flow of a stream to her downstream neighbor. ◆ A refinery, which conformed to zoning regulations, emitted fumes that made people at the neighboring properties feel sick (zoning not dispositive). ◆ A dredging company operates a stone-crushing machine that creates continuous and intense noise on the beach near a hotel.	◆ A neighbor's children played boisterously in their pool, disturbing the retired couple next door. (Likely hypersensitivity.) ◆ A manufacturing plant emitted a faint noise. A nearby neighbor who worked the night shift could not sleep because of the noise, but other neighbors did not notice the noise. (Hypersensitivity.) ◆ A woman buys a home for a very good price because it sits across from a fraternity house known for having loud late parties. (While her knowledge of the noise and coming to the nuisance is not a defense, it weighs against her in assessing a nuisance claim.)

Decoy tip: The defendant's compliance with zoning ordinances, or building laws, or general industry standards is not dispositive, but provide frequent decoy answer choices.

B. **Public nuisance** is a **substantial, unreasonable interference** with the health, morals, welfare, safety, or property **rights of the community** (general public). Public authorities typically bring public nuisance cases, but a private person may bring a case if they can establish the following:

1. **Interference:** Courts consider factors establishing harm to the community including the **location of the nuisance**, the **frequency and duration**, the **degree of damage**, and the **social value** of the activity.

2. **Special injury for private party recovery:** A private party must suffer **damage different in kind** than that suffered by the general public, and not merely damage difference in degree to recover for **public** nuisance.

   Example: A shopkeeper clutters and leaves goods on the public sidewalk in front of his store in violation of a local ordinance. If the goods on the sidewalk inconvenience a tenant of the same building, the tenant has suffered the same type of harm suffered as the public. However, if the tenant trips over the goods and falls breaking her arm, she has suffered damage different in kind than that suffered by the general public.

C. **Remedies for nuisance** include **damages** and **injunctive relief** to stop the nuisance.

D. **Defenses for nuisance**

1. **Legislative authority** is persuasive but not dispositive or an absolute defense (e.g., zoning ordinance that permits the conduct in the location).

2. **Coming to the nuisance** is **not a valid defense** to a nuisance action, though the court may consider it when deciding to order an injunction. Coming to the nuisance means the plaintiff moved near the nuisance after it already existed.

   a. **Exception—to harass:** It can provide a defense ***only if*** plaintiff came to the nuisance for the **sole purpose** of bringing a **harassing** lawsuit.

3. **Assumption of the risk** and **comparative negligence** are defenses *if* the plaintiff's case rests on a negligence theory.

> MBE tip: Private nuisance is much more commonly MBE tested than public nuisance.

X. DEFAMATION

A. **Common law defamation** occurs when a **false and defamatory statement of or concerning the plaintiff** is **published** to **another person** causing **damage** to the plaintiff's reputation.

1. **Defamatory statement** is a **false** statement that holds the plaintiff up to **contempt or ridicule.** Slight inaccuracies are acceptable. **Pure opinions or true statements** are *not* defamatory statements. However, an opinion may be actionable if it implies knowledge of specific facts that would be defamatory if stated.

   a. **"Statement" is construed broadly** and includes visual images, satire, etc.

2. **Of or concerning plaintiff:** The plaintiff must be identifiable.

   a. **Group defamation:** When a defamatory statement is made about a group, for an individual plaintiff to recover, the group must be so **small** it can be reasonably understood the plaintiff is a group member.

b. **Corporations** and business entities can be defamed.

c. Defamation only applies to **living persons**.

3. **Publication to a third party:** The publication must be made to a third party who **understands** the statement to effectuate publication.

   Example: A defamatory statement made in Russian would need to be heard by someone who understood Russian.

   a. **Repeaters** of defamatory statements **are publishers** and also liable.

   b. **Overheard statements** qualify as publication if the presence of a third party is foreseeable.

      Example: A defamatory statement made in an office suite.

4. **Standard of fault in publication:** It is the **intent to publish** the statement, not the intent to defame that satisfies this element. The publication can be made:

   a. **Intentionally** (knowledge of falsity), or

   b. **Negligently** (insufficient reasonable care as to falsity).

   c. **Special rules for matters of public concern:** The **constitutional law defamation standard of fault** applies when the defamation is regarding a matter of public concern. See rules at X.B. below.

5. **Causation:** The statement **need not have actually harmed** the plaintiff's reputation, but the plaintiff must show that it **would have had it been believed.**

6. **Damages** depend on the **type of defamation:**

   a. **Libel** is communicated in **writing** or where the statement is **embodied in a physical form.** This includes more permanent communications such as phonograph records, or **radio or TV broadcasts**.

      1. **General damages are presumed** for libel, which will compensate the plaintiff for the presumed injury to her reputation caused by the defamation. The plaintiff does not need to prove special damages.

   b. **Slander** is **spoken** or verbal defamation, which is less permanent than libel. (Note: while communication is verbal, radio and TV broadcasts are libel because they take a more permanent form.)

      1. **Special damages required:** The plaintiff must **prove special damages,** which means the plaintiff has suffered some **pecuniary** (monetary) **loss** as a result of the slander (e.g., loss of a job or inheritance).

      Example: A bill collector went to an alleged debtor's home, and called the man a "deadbeat" through a bullhorn in front of his neighbors. The bill collector was in error and the man did not owe the debt. Since this is slander, in the absence of a showing of special damages, the man will not prevail in his defamation suit.

      2. **Exception: Slander per se damages are presumed** (need not prove special damages). Slander per se identifies the plaintiff as having:

         a. **Business or professional unfitness,**

         b. A **loathsome Disease** (historically a sexually transmitted disease or leprosy),

         c. **Committed a Crime of moral turpitude** (crimes that shock the conscience, which is interpreted broadly to include most crimes), or

Example: A neighbor told a friend that a man set fire to a home. The friend did not believe it and the statement was false. Arson is a crime of moral turpitude, so special damages are not required.

d. Serious **Sexual misconduct**, which historically meant an unchaste woman).

> **Memorization tip:** Use BaD CaSe to remember slander per se cases. **B**usiness; **D**isease; **C**rime; **S**exual misconduct.

★ B. **Constitutional law defamation** requirements must be analyzed if the defamation is a matter of **public concern** because the First Amendment protects freedom of speech. Constitutional defamation requires that the plaintiff prove the **elements of common law defamation** (as noted above) **and** establish **fault** on the part of the defendant. The test to determine fault depends on the status of the plaintiff as a **public figure or private person.**

1. **Public figure** defamation rules apply to two types of plaintiffs: (1) one who has **pervasive fame** or notoriety, or (2) a **"limited purpose" public figure** who has **voluntarily thrust themself** into a **public controversy** for a limited range of issues pertaining to that controversy. Everyone else is a private person.

PUBLIC FIGURE v. PRIVATE PERSON EXAMPLES

Public Figure		Private Person
Pervasive Fame	**Ltd. Purpose**	
◆ Public office candidate ◆ A nationally known amateur basketball star ◆ Governor ◆ Corporation	◆ Community activist prominent in the women's liberation cause	◆ A labor leader's ex-wife. (Public concern: gave sexual favors to help husband while married.) ◆ A "well known" manager of a popular local restaurant. (Public concern: embezzlement caused the restaurant closure.)

a. **Actual malice standard:** When the plaintiff is a **public figure,** actual malice in publication must be proven. Actual malice exists when the defendant made the statement with either:

1. **Knowledge that it was false**, or

2. **Reckless disregard** for its truth, meaning the publisher had **serious doubts** as to whether the statement was true or false.

Example (no actual malice): A newspaper published an editorial that a political candidate was a user of illegal drugs. The editor acted unreasonably (negligence standard) in not investigating the allegation, but honestly believed it to be true. Since a political candidate is a public figure, the actual malice standard applies and is not satisfied given the editor's honest (though mistaken) belief.

> **MBE tip:** Actual malice is rarely tested because the facts would have to be so obvious it would give the issue away.

2. **Private person:** A private person is any person not considered a public figure (see above) and is afforded more protection than a public figure since a private person has less opportunity to set the record straight.

   a. **Negligence standard:** The publisher need only **be negligent regarding the truth or falsity of the statement** if it involves a matter of public concern, and the plaintiff is a private person.

      1. **Only actual injury damages** are recoverable, though these are not necessarily limited to only pecuniary damages. Actual injury includes loss of reputation, mental anguish, etc.

   b. **Damages presumed with actual malice.** While defamation can be established if the publication is negligent (above) and the plaintiff is a private person, if the defendant meets the actual malice standard, damages are presumed, and **punitive damages are allowed.**

C. **Defenses to defamation**

1. **Consent,** which can be express or implied.

   Example: If one alleging defamation asked others to write letters and speak as to particular issues, then any responsive defamatory statements will likely be viewed as invited and thus consensual.

2. **Truth** is a complete defense.

   Example: A man sent a letter to a woman he wanted to date advising her that her fiancé was a cross dresser. She broke off the engagement and her fiancé was humiliated. If the fiancé is actually a cross dresser, the truth is a complete defense to his defamation claim.

3. **Absolute privilege** extends to remarks made during **judicial or legislative proceedings**, by **federal government** and most **state government officials**, and between **spouses**. This privilege exists even if defendant acted with malice.

4. **Qualified** (conditional) **privilege** extends to statements made in a reasonable manner for a proper purpose to:

   a. **Protect the publisher's interests** if the defamation relates directly to those interests (e.g., internal discussions in a company, give and take at a seminar), or

   b. For the **protection of the recipient or a third party** (e.g., a reference for a former employee), or

   c. To act in the **public interest** or report accurately on public proceedings (e.g., report events at open public meeting).

   d. **Actual malice waives privilege**: Qualified privilege can be lost if the defendant abuses it by acting with actual malice or **publishing the statement excessively** when it is not reasonably necessary.

      Example: A nurse worked at a hospital through a referral agency. The hospital asked the referral agency to no longer assign that nurse to the hospital. The referral agency asked why, and the hospital disclosed narcotics had gone missing during her shifts. The statement has qualified privilege.

      Example: At a hearing to grant a liquor license, a person testified that the applicant had underworld connections. As long as the statement was not made with malice (knowledge of falsity or reckless disregard) there is a qualified privilege.

DEFAMATION DECODED

- ◆ Defamatory statement
- ◆ Of or concerning plaintiff
- ◆ Published to third party
- ◆ Fault in publication:

Normal Defamation (no public concern)	Con Law Defamation (public concern)	
	Public Figure	**Private Person**
◆ Intentionally ◆ Negligently	◆ Actual malice required	◆ Negligence standard ok ◇ Actual damages only ◆ *If* actual malice shown: ◇ Damages presumed ◇ Punitive $ allowed

- ◆ Causation
- ◆ Damages
  - ◇ Libel: Damages presumed
  - ◇ Slander: Must establish special damages, *except*
  - ◇ Slander per se: damages are presumed

XI. PRIVACY

A. **Appropriation** (also called right of publicity) is the **unauthorized use** of the **plaintiff's picture or name** for the defendant's **commercial purposes** without knowledge or permission. The celebrity need not be named or pictured, if there is little doubt an ad is intended to depict that certain celebrity.

Examples: Use of a movie star's picture in an ad without consent, imitation of a celebrity's distinctive voice or mannerisms in an ad, etc.

B. **Intrusion upon seclusion** (also called intrusion into private affairs or solitude) is the intrusion into a **private aspect** of the plaintiff's life **in a private place** that is **highly offensive to a reasonable person**.

Examples: A phone tap, secretly taking photos inside someone's home, taking photos of someone sunbathing topless in her enclosed yard, peering over someone's shoulder as they key in their PIN at the ATM or input their email password, etc.

C. **Placing plaintiff in False Light** occurs where: (1) (1) one a**ttributes to plaintiff views** they **do not hold** or actions they do not take; (2) the false light is **objectionable to a reasonable person** under the circumstances; and (3) the publication is **public** (e.g., a biography is published about a famous star that falsely claims she has had much plastic surgery). [This rule is rarely MBE tested.]

D. **Public disclosure of private facts** (also called publicity of private life or invasion of privacy) is the public **disclosure of true facts**, the release of which is **highly offensive** to a reasonable person, and **not of legitimate concern to the public.**

1. **Defense: Newsworthy information (legitimate concern to the public)** disclosure provides a complete defense. Thus, it is harder for public figures and limited public figures to recover under this tort.

   Example (not highly offensive): A newspaper article publishes a story identifying a child with a learning disability by name. While the facts are not a matter of public concern, they are not sufficiently highly offensive to establish the tort.

   Example (not private): A teen was killed in gang violence. Days later, his mother saw a video of herself weeping over his body in the street on a television show about gang violence. The incident was newsworthy and took place on a public street, so mom will not prevail in her tort.

> **MBE tip:** The term "invasion of privacy" may be generally used in an MBE question or answer to refer to any of the four privacy torts.
>
> **Memorization tip:** Use **A FLIP** to remember the types of privacy torts. **A**ppropriation; **F**alse **L**ight; **I**ntrusion on solitude; **P**ublic disclosure of private facts.

XII. THIRD-PARTY ISSUES

A. **Vicarious liability occurs when one person commits a tortious act** against a third party, and **another person is liable** to the third party for the tortious act. Vicarious liability is imposed derivatively **based on a special relationship** between the tortfeasor and the person vicariously liable. One who is vicariously liable **may seek contribution and indemnification** for damages paid to the plaintiff from the tortfeasor more directly responsible for the harm. See sec. XII.B. below.

1. **Respondeat superior:** When an **employee** commits a tort during the **scope of employment**, the employer will be vicariously liable. Similarly, when an **agent** commits a tort during the scope of the agency relationship, the principal is vicariously liable.

   a. **Employee:** An employee is one who works **subject to the close control** of the person who hired them.

   Example (no vicarious liability): A professor at a private university described a psychological experiment in which participants engaged in dangerous behavior. The professor warned her students that they were not to undertake any experiments without first obtaining permission. If the students engage in a similar experiment, the university will not have vicarious liability for any resulting harm because the students were not employees or agents of the university and were not authorized or encouraged to engage in the experiment.

   b. **Scope of employment:** The tort is within the scope of employment if the tortfeasor was acting with the **intent to further the employer's business purpose**.

      1. **Minor deviations are within the scope:** Deviations from employer business that are minor in both time and geographic area are allowed if they are the sort of thing that is foreseeable (e.g., a delivery driver making a personal delivery between employment related deliveries).

      2. **Commuting is not within the scope:** Commuting to and from work typically is not within the scope of employment, **except when an employee is "on call"** and must be ready to go to work when called.

3. **"Frolic of one's own" is not within the scope:** This typically means an employee's commission of an **intentional tort** is not considered within the scope of employment, **except:**

   a. **Nature of job:** Where the conduct contemplated is within the nature of the employment (e.g., a bill collector, a bouncer at a bar) the **employer may be responsible** even if the employee has been instructed not to engage in particular conduct (e.g., instructed not to touch rowdy customers to remove them from a bar, but does).

   b. **Negligent hiring/supervision:** Where the employer **knew of employee's propensity** for that particular type of wrongful conduct (e.g., violence), but failed to act.

   Example (within scope): A pharmacy employee incorrectly filled a man's prescription with higher dosage medicine than prescribed. Shortly after taking the medicine, the man suffered a heart attack, which is a side effect of overdosing on the medicine. The pharmacy is vicariously liable since the employee was performing his job in the scope of employment.

   Example (not within scope): A plumbing company hired a worker to use his own truck to drive between job sites. The worker was paid for driving between the sites, but not for his drive to and from work. The worker's driver's license was suspended for reckless driving, but the plumbing company accepted the worker's word that his license was good. While driving to work, the worker carelessly caused an accident. The plumbing company is not vicariously liable because the worker was not in the scope of employment driving *to* work.

> **Decoy tip:** Watch for torts by non-employees, such as customers, where respondeat superior is an incorrect answer choice.

2. **Independent contractor:** One who hires an independent contractor is generally **not vicariously liable** for the torts of that person, subject to **two exceptions.**

   a. **Independent contractor definition**. Typically, independent contractors:

      1. **Control the details** of their work
      2. Are **not subject to control**.
      3. Have **multiple employers**.

   b. **Nondelegable duties:** A duty is nondelegable when work:

      1. Occurs on **land or premises open to the public** (business invitees). The duty to keep business premises safe is nondelegable.
      2. Involves **inherently dangerous activities,** such that there is a **peculiar risk of physical harm** to others (e.g., blasting, hauling heavy equipment, etc.).

      Example: A hotel carefully selected an independent contractor to build a swimming pool. A guest fell into the excavation site, which the contractor had negligently left unguarded. Since the hotel's duty to make the premises safe for business visitors is nondelegable, they are vicariously liable for the negligence of the independent contractor, despite their own care in hiring.

   c. **Negligent hiring of independent contractor:** One is liable for their **own negligence** in hiring. This is not vicarious liability.

3. **Parents** (and caretakers) **are *not* vicariously liable** for the torts of their children. Though they can be liable for their **own negligence** in failing to properly supervise.

   Example: A grandson was visiting his grandmother at her home where the gun cabinet accidently had been left unlocked a few days earlier. The 8-year-old grandson and his friend removed a rifle from the cabinet and the grandson shot his friend. The grandmother is not vicariously liable, but she may be found negligent for her own breach of the duty of care to properly store the weapon and supervise her grandson.

B. Multiple defendants

1. **Joint and several liability** exists where two or more negligent acts combine to proximately cause an indivisible harm. **Each** party is **liable for the entire harm** and the plaintiff can recover the **entire loss from any defendant**, regardless of each defendant's share of responsibility, **subject to the defendant's ability to seek contribution and indemnity** from other tortfeasors. [This is the default rule on the MBE. Use it unless instructed otherwise.]

   a. **Single indivisible harm:** Where it is **not possible to apportion** the damages between the tortfeasors because there is a single indivisible harm, **each defendant is liable for the entire harm** (e.g., death or a single personal injury or a burned building).

   Example: Two pesticide manufacturers located along a river both discharged pesticides into the river during the same 24 hours. A downstream cattle rancher's cattle were poisoned after drinking from the river. The pesticide manufacturers are jointly and severally liable and the rancher can recover the full amount of damages from either manufacturer because the fault cannot be apportioned between the two.

   b. **Divisible harm:** Where harm is divisible between tortfeasors and it is possible to identify the portion of injury caused by each tortfeasor, the **loss is apportioned to each defendant according to fault** (e.g., one tortfesor broke plaintiff's arm and another broke plaintiff's leg).

   c. **Minority rule—no joint and several liability** (also called pure several liability): In these minority jurisdictions, each defendant is only liable for their own share of the damages, not the entire award.

   d. **Combined with comparative negligence:** A plaintiff's damages are reduced by their own proportionate fault that contributed to the total harm. The plaintiff's share is deducted "off the top."

   > **MBE tip:** Joint and several liability issues cross over with causation.

2. **Contribution:** A tortfeasor required to pay more than their proportionate share of damages may seek partial **reimbursement** from another jointly responsible party. Under comparative negligence, contribution may be sought in an amount **proportionate to fault.**

   Example: Plaintiff has a car accident with Driver1 and Driver2 and suffers $100,000 in damages. Driver1 is 30% at fault, Driver2 is 40% at fault, and Plaintiff is 30% at fault. If Driver1 is required to pay the full $70,000 jointly owed to Plaintiff ($100,000 less Plaintiff's own negligence of $30,000), Driver1 can seek contribution from Driver2 for his 40% share ($40,000).

   a. **Exception: No right to contribution for intentional torts**, even if other tortfeasors are also at fault.

   b. **Exception: The contribution defendant must have liability.**

Example: After a car accident, a wife sues a third party for damages. The third party cannot seek contribution from the wife's husband if he enjoys spousal immunity from suit and thus is not liable.

3. **Indemnity:** One joint tortfeasor can recover from another so the **full amount** of the loss will be paid by the **tortfeasor who was most directly responsible** for causing the harm. Indemnity is **appropriate** where one tortfeasor is only **derivatively liable** for the other tortfeasor's conduct. Indemnity comes up in the following situations:

   a. **Vicarious liability:** One who is vicariously liable can seek indemnity from the tortfeasor (e.g., employer seeking indemnity from an employee; business seeking indemnity from an independent contractor performing a nondelegable duty, etc.).

   b. **Strict products liability:** Each commercial seller in the supply chain is liable for a defective product. Subsequent suppliers (e.g., retail seller) can seek indemnity from those earlier in the supply chain who are directly **responsible for the defect**.

   Example: An engineer designed a game. The engineer entered into a licensing agreement with a toy company to manufacture the game according to the engineer's specifications. A gamer was injured playing the game and recovered against the toy company based on the defective product design. The toy company can seek indemnity against the engineer because his defective design caused the injury.

   c. **Considerable difference in degree of fault:** A negligent tortfeasor can seek indemnity from a jointly liable intentional tortfeasor in some jurisdictions.

   d. Indemnity can be contracted for in an agreement.

C. **Survival and wrongful death** actions are allowed on the MBE unless otherwise indicated. [These rules are rarely tested outright.]

1. **Survival actions** allow one's cause of action to survive the death of one or more of the parties.

   a. **Exception:** These actions **do not include defamation**, **right to privacy**, or **malicious prosecution** (e.g. torts that invade a personal interest).

2. **Wrongful death** acts grant recovery for **pecuniary injury** resulting to the spouse and next of kin for a wrongful death and allows recovery for **loss or support and consortium**.

   a. **Creditors:** The decedent's creditors **have no interest** in the amount recovered under a wrongful death claim.

D. **Tortious interference with family relationships:** A husband or wife may bring an action for interference with consortium (companionship) and services caused by a defendant's intentional or negligent actions **against the other spouse**. A parent can also recover for the **loss of a child's services and consortium**.

TORTS CHEAT SHEET

INTENTIONAL TORTS

Prima Facie Case
- Intent
  - Purpose
  - Knowledge to substantial certainty
  - Transferred intent: tort/ person
- Causation

Battery
- Intent (contact)
- Harmful or offensive
- Contact

Assault
- Intent (apprehen./ contact)
- Cause apprehension
- Imminent
- Harmful or offensive
- Contact

Trespass to Land
- Intent (to enter)
- Entry on land
- Land of another
- No damage required
- Mistake is no defense

Trespass to Chattel
- Intent (interfere w/chattel)
- Interfere w/ use/possession
- Chattel of another
- Damages: actual harm
- Mistake is no defense

Conversion
- Intent (interfere w/chattel)
- Substantial interference
- Chattel of another
- Damages: full value
- Mistake is no defense

False Imprisonment
- Intent (to confine)
- Confine, restrain, detain
- Bounded area
- No reas. means of escape
- Awareness *or* harm reqt.

IIED
- Intent or
  - Reckless disregard
  - No transferred intent
- Severe emotional distress
- Extreme & outrageous

3rd person injured:
  - P present @ scene &
  - Known by D present &
  - P relative *or* bodily harm

Misc. Torts
- Survival action
- Wrongful death
- Tort. interfere family rel.
- Loss of chance of survival

Vicarious Liability
[Negligent hiring, too]

Respondeat superior
- Employee (close control)
- Scope of employment
- Minor deviation ok

Independent contractor
- Nondelegable duty
  - Open to public
  - Inherently dang. activity

INTENTIONAL TORT DEFENSES

Self Defense
- Reasonable force prevent
  - Degree reasonably nec.
  - Deadly only if necessary
- Reasonable mistake ok

Defense of Others
- Reasonable force prevent
  - Degree reasonably nec.
  - Deadly only if necessary
- Reas. belief 3P needs
- Reasonable mistake ok

Necessity
Private:
- Harm acute & unforeseen
- No right to exclude
- Qualified-pay for damage

Public:
- No pay required if damage

Consent
- Express
- Implied
  - Ordinary touches
  - Objective manifestation
- Scope of consent

Legal Justification
- Reasonable

Defense of Property
- Reasonable force
- Warning reqt. before force
- Deadly only if necessary

Recapture of Chattel
- Reasonable force to regain
- Fresh pursuit
- No deadly force
- Trespass ok (pay damages)

Shopkeeper Privilege
- Reasonable belief
- Temporarily detain
- Reasonable means

THIRD-PARTY ISSUES

Joint & Several
- Liable for entire harm
- Can get contrib./indemnity
- Single indivisible = all
- Divisible harm = by fault

Indemnification
- Reimburse full amount
- Other more responsible
  - Vicarious
  - Strict products
  - Big difference in fault

Contribution
- Reimburse portion of fault
- N/A w/ intentional torts

NEGLIGENCE

Duty of care
- ◆ Owed to foreseeable Ps
- ◆ Rescuers are foreseeable
  - ◇ Wrongful birth/preg. ok
  - ◇ Wrongful life not ok

Professionals
- ◆ Knowledge/skill of one in
- ◆ Good standing in comm.

Medical Professionals
- ◆ National std. duty care
- ◆ Duty to disclose risk
- ◆ Duty to patient only

Legal Malpractice
- ◆ Duty of care to clients
- ◆ Lawyer caused loss
- ◆ Different result w/ care

Common Carrier/Innkeep
- ◆ High degree of care
- ◆ Foreseeable crimes of 3P

Breach
- ◆ Fail to meet std. of care
  - ◇ Custom in industry
  - ◇ Balance (risk v burden)

Anticipate misconduct?
- ◆ Negligence-Yes
- ◆ Parent-Yes (supervise)
- ◆ Crimes/Int. torts-No
  - ◇ Except-Yes, common carriers & innkeepers

Res Ipsa Loquitur
- ◆ Permiss. inference breach
  - ◇ Negl. clearly occurred
  - ◇ Negl. attributable to D
  - ◇ Injury *not* attributable P

Damages
- ◆ Actual injury
- ◆ Damages: Causal, certain, foreseeable, unavoidable
- ◆ No punit./nom./pure econ.

Duty—Standard of care
- ◆ Reasonable prudent person

Affirmative duties
- ◆ Parents-supervise/control
- ◆ Caretaker = like parents
- ◆ Cause original harm
- ◆ Voluntarily assist

Firefighter's rule
No negligence suits for risks inherent in rescue

Children
- ◆ Liable for own torts
- ◆ Like age, intelligence, exp.
- ◆ Except: adult activity
- ◆ Parent not vicariously liab.

Negligence per se
- ◆ Violation of statute
- ◆ Class of person to protect
- ◆ Type of harm to prevent
- ◆ Rebut-violation excused if:
  - ◇ Greater risk to comply
  - ◇ D cannot comply
- ◆ Establishes duty/breach

Actual Cause
- ◆ But for test
- ◆ Substantial factor test
- ◆ Concurrent tortfeasors
- ◆ Alternative cause-1 at fault
- ◆ Joint & Several liability

Proximate Cause
- ◆ Reasonable foreseeability
- ◆ Eggshell-skull plaintiff
- ◆ Intervening causes:
  - ◇ Foreseeable = liable
- ◆ Unforeseeable = supersede
  - ◇ Criminal acts/int. torts
    - ◇ Except-D creates risk
  - ◇ Acts of God

NEGLIGENCE DEFENSES
Comparative Negligence
- ◆ Pure: proportionate fault
- ◆ Partial: over 50% barred

Contributory negligence
Bar, but last clear chance

Ass. of risk: know + still do

Owner/Occupier Land
Damage outside land:
- ◆ Natural: no duty
- ◆ Artificial: reas. care

Trespassers
Undiscovered
- ◆ No duty

Invitee exceed scope
- ◆ No willful misconduct

Known/should have
- ◆ Duty: reasonable care
- ◆ Duty warn/make safe
- ◆ Risks of serious harm
- ◆ Tres. unlikely discover

Child trespassers
- ◆ Duty reasonable care if:
- ◆ Knew/should child trespass
- ◆ Art. condition high risk
- ◆ Child not discover risk
- ◆ Balance (burden v risk)

Invitees (Business)
- ◆ Duty reasonable care
- ◆ Duty warn/make safe
- ◆ Known not obvi. hazards
- ◆ Duty inspect hidden hazards
- ◆ Nondelegable duty work by independent contractors

Licensees (Social)
- ◆ Duty reasonable care
- ◆ Duty warn known dangers
- ◆ Licensee unlikely discover

Landlord Tenant
Tenant
- ◆ Duty to maintain premises

Landlord
- ◆ Duty warn/make safe
- ◆ Duty reasonable care in repairs & common areas

NIED
- ◆ Zone of danger- fear
  - ◇ Physical symptom: Yes
- ◆ Witness impact close fam.
  - ◇ Physical symptom-No
- ◆ No symptoms required: corpse/terminal diagnosis

STRICT LIABILITY

Animals

Trespassing animal
- Reas. foreseeable dmg.

Wild animal
Harm from dang. nature
Except: trespassers

Domestic
Knew/should propensity

Products

- Commercial supplier
  - ◇ Stream of commerce
  - ◇ w/out substantial alter.
- Defective product
  - ◇ Manufacturing: deviates
  - ◇ Design
    - ◇ Consumer expectation
    - ◇ Balance (risk v. benefit)
    - ◇ Feasible altern. design
  - ◇ Warning
- (Industry standards)
- (Misuse foreseeable)
- Actual cause
- Proximate cause
- Damages

Abnormally Dang. Activ.

- High risk harm
- Can't eliminate risk w/ due care
- Activity not common
- Balance (risk v. value)
- Nondelegable duty w/ independent contractors

Strict Liability Defenses

Assumption of risk:
- Knew risk & proceeded anyway

Contributory: No defense
Comparative: Provides defense

Fraud

- Misrep of material fact
- Know false/reckless disregard
- Intent to induce P reliance
- Causation
- Justifiable reliance
- Pecuniary damages

Negligent Misrepresent

- Misrep in bus. capacity
- Negligence as to truth
- Intent to induce P reliance
- Causation
- Justifiable reliance
- Pecuniary damages

Tort. Interference Bus.

- Contract relations/expect
- 3Pty knew/should have
- Intentional interference
- Damages
- Defense: Privilege

DEFAMATION

Common Law | Con Law

- Defamatory statement
- Of and concerning P
- Publish to 3P
- Standard of fault

Private Concern:
- Intentionally (know false)
- Negligently (lack care)

Public Concern:
- Pub. figure: actual malice
- Private person: negligence
  - ◇ Only actual damages;
  - ◇ Dmgs. presumed act. mal.

- Causation

Damages Defamation

- Libel: *presumed*
- Slander: Special damages
- Slander per se: *presumed*
  - ◇ Business/profession
  - ◇ Loathsome disease
  - ◇ Crime of moral turpitude
  - ◇ Sexual misconduct

Defenses Defamation

- Consent
- Truth
- Absolute privilege
- Qualified privilege
  - ◇ Act. malice waives priv.

Public Discl. Private Facts

- Disclose true facts
- Highly offensive
- Not legit. public concern

Defense: Newsworthy

NUISANCE

Private:
- Substantial interference
  - ◇ No hypersensitivity
- Unreasonable interference
  - ◇ Harm outweighs utility;
  - ◇ or Harm to P too high

Public:
- Substantial interference (frequent, duration, value)
- To community
- Private party: special harm

PRIVACY TORTS

Appropriation

- P name/likeness
- Commercial purposes

Intrusion Upon Seclusion

- Intrude private aspect life
- Highly offensive to RPP

Placing P in False Light

- Attribute views to P
- Objectionable to RPP
- Publicly

TORTS MBE PRACTICE QUESTIONS

These questions are designed to reinforce the skill in how to approach MBE questions. While they will also test your knowledge in the limited areas addressed, you will not master your knowledge by only practicing these questions. To fully master the rules, you need to do practice questions outside of these from your bar company and/or the NCBE.

QUESTION 1

A man tied his dog to a bike rack in front of a store and left the dog there while he went inside to shop. The dog was usually friendly and placid. A 5-year-old child started to tease the dog by pulling gently on its ears and tail. When the man emerged from the store and saw what the child was doing to the dog, he became extremely upset.

Does the man have a viable claim against the child for trespass to chattels?

A. No, because the child did not injure the dog.
B. No, because the child was too young to form the requisite intent.
C. Yes, because the child touched the dog without the man's consent.
D. Yes, because the child's acts caused the man extreme distress.

QUESTION 2

A security guard, dressed in plain clothes, was working for a discount store when a customer got into a heated argument with a cashier over the store's refund policy. Without identifying himself as a security guard, the security guard suddenly grabbed the customer's arm. The customer attempted to push the security guard away, and the security guard knocked the customer to the floor, causing injuries. The customer sued the discount store for battery on a theory of vicarious liability for the injuries caused by the security guard. The store filed an answer to the customer's complaint, asserting the affirmative defense of contributory negligence. The customer has moved to strike the affirmative defense. Traditional rules of contributory negligence apply.

Should the trial court grant the customer's motion?

A. No, because contributory negligence is an affirmative defense to a cause of action based on vicarious liability.
B. No, because the customer should have known that his argument with the cashier might provoke an action by a security guard.
C. Yes, because contributory negligence is not a defense to battery.
D. Yes, because the customer did not know that he was pushing away someone who was employed as a security guard.

QUESTION 3

While visiting at his son's home, a grandfather tripped on a toy left on the floor by his 4-year-old grandson. The grandfather fell and was severely injured. The grandfather regularly visited his son's home and was aware that the grandson routinely left toys scattered about the house. The son had never warned the grandfather to look out for toys. The grandfather brought an action against his son to recover for his injuries. At trial, after the close of evidence, both the grandfather and the son have moved for judgment as a matter of law as to liability.

The jurisdiction has abolished intra-family immunity and applies the traditional rules of landowner liability.

What action should the court take?

A. Deny both motions and submit the case to the jury based on negligence.
B. Deny both motions and submit the case to the jury based on strict liability.
C. Grant the grandfather's motion, because the son is liable as a matter of law for failing to warn about the risk of toys being left on the floor.
D. Grant the son's motion, because the son had no duty to warn that the grandson might leave toys on the floor.

QUESTION 4

A customer bought a can of corn at a grocery store. While eating the corn later that evening, the customer was injured by a small piece of glass in the corn. The customer sued the canning company that had processed and canned the corn. At trial, the customer presented evidence that neither the customer nor any third party had done anything after the can of corn was opened that would account for the presence of the glass.

Without any other evidence, is the customer likely to prevail?

A. No, because it is possible that someone tampered with the can before the customer bought it.
B. No, because the customer has not shown any direct evidence that the canning company acted negligently.
C. Yes, because a jury may reasonably infer that the canning company acted negligently.
D. Yes, because the grocery store could not have discovered the piece of glass by reasonable inspection.

QUESTION 5

A pedestrian was crossing a street in a crosswalk when a woman walking just ahead of him was hit by a truck. The pedestrian, who had jumped out of the way of the truck, administered CPR to the woman, who was a stranger. The woman bled profusely, and the pedestrian was covered in blood. The woman died in the ambulance on the way to the hospital. The pedestrian became very depressed immediately after the incident and developed physical symptoms as a result of his emotional distress. The pedestrian has brought an action against the driver of the truck for negligent infliction of emotional distress. In her defense, the driver asserts that she should not be held liable, because the pedestrian's emotional distress and resulting physical symptoms are not compensable.

What is the strongest argument that the pedestrian can make in response to the driver's defense?

A. The pedestrian saw the driver hit the woman.
B. The pedestrian was acting as a Good Samaritan.
C. The pedestrian was covered in the woman's blood and developed physical symptoms as a result of his emotional distress.
D. The pedestrian was in the zone of danger.

QUESTION 6

Toxic materials being transported by truck from a manufacturer's plant to a warehouse leaked from the truck onto the street a few miles from the plant. A driver lost control of his car when he hit the puddle of spilled toxic materials on the street, and he was injured when his car hit a stop sign.

In an action for damages by the driver against the manufacturer based on strict liability, is the driver likely to prevail?

A. No, because the driver's loss of control was an intervening cause.
B. No, because the driver's injury did not result from the toxicity of the materials.
C. Yes, because the manufacturer is strictly liable for leaks of its toxic materials.
D. Yes, because the leak occurred near the manufacturer's plant.

QUESTION 7

A construction worker was working at the construction site of a new building. An open elevator, which had been installed in the building by the elevator manufacturer, was used to haul workers and building materials between floors. While the worker was riding the elevator, it stalled between floors due to a manufacturing defect in the elevator. The worker called for assistance and was in no danger, but after waiting 15 minutes for help, he became anxious and jumped 12 feet to get out. He severely injured his back when he landed.

In an action by the worker against the elevator manufacturer to recover for his back injury, is the worker likely to obtain a judgment for 100% of his damages?

A. No, because such risks are inherent in construction work.
B. No, because the worker was not in danger while on the stalled elevator
C. Yes, because the elevator stalled due to a manufacturing defect.
D. Yes, because the worker was falsely imprisoned in the stalled elevator.

QUESTION 8

A man sued his neighbor for defamation based on the following facts:

The neighbor told a friend that the man had set fire to a house in the neighborhood. The friend, who knew the man well, did not believe the neighbor's allegation, which was in fact false. The friend told the man about the neighbor's allegation. The man was very upset by the allegation, but neither the man nor the neighbor nor the friend communicated the allegation to anyone else.

Should the man prevail in his lawsuit?

A. No, because the friend did not believe what the neighbor had said.
B. No, because the man cannot prove that he suffered pecuniary loss.
C. Yes, because the man was very upset at hearing what the neighbor had said.
D. Yes, because the neighbor communicated to the friend the false accusation that the man had committed a serious crime.

QUESTION 9

A manufacturing plant emitted a faint noise even though the owner had installed state-of-the-art sound dampeners. The plant operated only on weekdays and only during daylight hours. A homeowner who lived near the plant worked a night shift and could not sleep when he arrived home because of the noise from the plant. The other residents in the area did not notice the noise.

Does the homeowner have a viable nuisance claim against the owner of the plant?

A. No, because the homeowner is unusually sensitive to noise during the day.
B. No, because the plant operates only during the day.
C. Yes, because the noise is heard beyond the boundaries of the plant.
D. Yes, because the operation of the plant interferes with the homeowner's quiet use and enjoyment of his property.

QUESTION 10

A seller sold his boat to a buyer. During negotiations, the buyer said that he planned to sail the boat on the open seas. The seller told the buyer that the boat was seaworthy and had never sustained any significant damage. In fact, the hull of the boat had been badly damaged when the seller had run the boat aground. The seller had then done a cosmetic repair to the hull rather than a structural repair. The buyer relied on the seller's representations and paid a fair price for a boat in good repair, only to discover after the sale was completed that the hull was in fact badly damaged and in a dangerous condition. The seller has refused to refund any of the buyer's money, and the buyer is contemplating suing the seller.

Under what theory would the buyer be most likely to recover?

A. Fraud.
B. Intentional endangerment.
C. Negligent misrepresentation.
D. Strict products liability.

TORTS ANSWER KEY	
Question	**Answer**
1	A
2	C
3	D
4	C
5	D
6	B
7	B
8	D
9	A
10	A

Use this quick answer key to get a general idea of how you did on this set of questions. The answer explanations that follow provide a step-by-step deconstruction of each question.

TORTS MBE ANSWER EXPLANATIONS

START HERE **FACTS** [Chattel] **Q1**

A man **tied his dog to a bike rack** in front of a store and left the dog there while he went inside to shop. The dog was usually **friendly and placid**. ← [Intent] [Interference]

A **5-year-old child** started to **tease the dog by pulling gently on its ears and tail**. When the man emerged from the store and saw what the child was doing to the dog, he became **extremely upset**.

CALL Does the man have a viable claim against the child for **trespass to chattels**? [Damages?]

TORTS Q

When the rule is in the call, identify the elements first & look for them in the facts →

Intentional
Interfere use/possession
Chattel of another
Damages

SOLVE

 I spy with my little eye 2 ducks in this fact pattern

TRESPASS TO CHATTEL	*ANALYSIS*	
• Intent (to do what you do)	• 5-year-old child intended to pull on dogs ears	CHILDREN CAN FORM INTENT
• Interference with use, enjoyment or possession	• Interfered with dog by disturbing	
• Chattel	• Dogs are (sadly) chattel	
• Damages=actual harm or substantial deprivation of use (loss of value from loss of use or cost of repair)	• No actual harm to chattel shown, or substantial deprivation. Emotional distress is not recoverable in TTC.	NO E.D. IN TTC

A The man does not have a viable claim <u>**because**</u> there was not substantial interference with the chattel.

→ Now look for an answer choice that comports with your analysis.

DECODE

A. No, because the child did not injure the dog.

Correct. To establish damages the man must show actual harm to the chattel or deprivation of its use for substantial time, which are not established here. His own emotional distress in insufficient.

~~B.~~ No, because the child was too young to form the requisite intent.

Incorrect statement of law. Even young children can commit intentional torts if they are able to form the intent required.

~~C.~~ Yes, because the child touched the dog without the man's consent.

Incorrect analysis. To establish the required element of damages, there must be a showing of harm or substantial deprivation of the chattel's use.

~~D.~~ Yes, because the child's acts caused the man extreme distress.

Wrong rule. To recover, there must be a showing of harm or substantial deprivation of the chattel's use. The man's feeling extremely upset is insufficient. The language of emotional distress is utilized to distract.

FACTS

Q2

A **security guard**, dressed in **plain clothes**, was working for a discount store when a **customer got into a heated argument with a cashier** over the store's refund policy. **Without identifying himself** as a security guard, the security guard suddenly **grabbed the customer's arm**. The customer **attempted to push the security guard away**, and the security guard **knocked the customer to the floor, causing injuries**. The customer sued the discount store for **battery** on a theory of **vicarious liability** for the injuries caused by the security guard.

Civ Pro is often used to frame torts Qs

The store filed an **answer** to the customer's complaint, asserting the affirmative defense of **contributory negligence**. The customer has **moved to strike** the affirmative defense. Traditional rules of **contributory negligence** apply.

So contrib. neg. is a total bar to recovery

CALL Should the trial court grant the customer's motion?

*The call didn't identify the subject or rule at issue, but a glance at the **sentence above** provides the clue. **Torts: contributory negligence.** Read the facts proactively.*

SOLVE

Defenses to Intentional Torts

- Consent
- Self-Defense
- Defense of Others
- Defense of Property
- Recapture of Chattels
- Necessity
- Shopkeeper's Privilege
- Legal Justification

What is NOT a Defense to an Intentional Tort? → ***Contributory negligence***

It seems easy with the Q all marked up, but this is a surprisingly easy type of Q to get wrong if you rush or lose focus.

All the facts about the scuffle were decoys

A The court should grant the customer's motion to strike **because** contributory negligence is not a defense to a battery.

Now look for an answer choice that comports with your analysis.

DECODE

MBE TIP: Using a rule that is satisfied but inapplicable is a classic way to distract.

A. No, because contributory negligence is an affirmative defense to a cause of action based on vicarious liability.

Not a rule. If this was a real rule, you would have learned it. Vicarious liability was added to the fact pattern to provide a decoy. Contributory negligence will never work for battery.

B. No, because the customer should have known that his argument with the cashier might provoke an action by a security guard.

Wrong analysis. The security guard was not identifiable as such and contributory negligence is an inapplicable defense to battery.

C. **Yes, because contributory negligence is not a defense to battery.**

Correct.

D. Yes, because the customer did not know that he was pushing away someone who was employed as a security guard.

Wrong analysis. This would go to the merits of a contributory negligence defense, which is inapplicable in a battery case.

Q3

FACTS

While visiting at his **son's home**, a **grandfather tripped on a toy** left on the floor by his 4-year-old grandson. The grandfather fell and was **severely injured**. The grandfather **regularly visited** his son's home and was **aware** that the grandson routinely left **toys scattered** about the house. The **son had never warned** the grandfather to look out for toys.

The grandfather brought an action against his son to recover for his injuries. At trial, after the close of evidence, both the **grandfather and the son have moved** for **judgment as a matter of law** as to liability.

The jurisdiction has **abolished intra-family immunity** and applies the traditional rules of **landowner liability.**

Civ. pro commonly used to set up torts Qs

So you can sue family members

CALL What action should the court take? **TORTS Q, probably negligence**

SOLVE

1 Identify the entrant to find the rule

2 Apply rule to facts

- **Trespassers** w/out consent
- **Invitees** bus. or open to public
- **Licensees** (social) no bus. purpose — Grandpa

RULE	ANALYSIS
• Duty to use **reasonable care** • Duty to **warn** of known dangers **licensee unlikely to discover**	• Toys on floor • No warning • But, grandfather was **aware** of the scattered toys and a regular visitor • No breach

A The court should grant the son's JMOL **because** the son did not breach his duty.

Now look for an answer choice that comports with your analysis.

DECODE

~~A.~~ Deny both motions and submit the case to the jury based on negligence.

Incorrect analysis. A warning was not required since the grandfather knew of the danger of scattered toys on the floor.

~~B.~~ Deny both motions and submit the case to the jury based on strict liability.

Wrong rule. This is a negligence case, there is no strict liability for injuries in homes.

~~C.~~ Grant the grandfather's motion, because the son is liable as a matter of law for failing to warn about the risk of toys being left on the floor.

Incorrect analysis. The son only has a duty to warn of dangers the licensee is unlikely to discover, and the grandfather was aware of the toy danger.

D. Grant the son's motion, because the son had no duty to warn that the grandson might leave toys on the floor.

Correct. Since the danger was one of which the grandfather was aware, the son has no duty to warn.

FACTS

Q4

A **customer bought a can of corn** at a grocery store. While eating the corn later that evening, the customer was **injured by a small piece of glass** in the corn. The customer **sued the canning company** that had processed and canned the corn.

Could be negligence or strict products liability

At trial, the customer presented evidence that **neither the customer nor any third party had done anything after the can of corn was opened that would account for the presence of the glass.**

In torts, if the cause of action isn't clear, it is probably negligence

CALL Without any other evidence, is the customer likely to prevail?

This is the rare Q where it is hard to determine the subject from the call or a quick glance at the paragraph above.

SOLVE

NEGLIGENCE	***ANALYSIS***
Did the D have a duty?	Yes, reasonable corn canning co.
If so, what was that duty?	Reasonable care
Did the D breach the duty?	Glass in corn can, but no facts of breach
Res Ipsa Loquitur? • **Negligence clear** • **Attributable to D** • **Not attributable to P**	 • Glass in corn can is negligent • Canner processed the corn can • P (or others) were not responsible for glass
Causation/Damages	Glass caused injury

Res Ipsa Loquitur creates permissible **inference** of breach (or negligence) and that is the language you will likely see in a res ipsa loquitur answer choice.

A The customer is likely to prevail <u>**because**</u> there is a permissible inference of breach.

Now look for an answer choice that comports with your analysis.

DECODE

(A) No, because it is possible that someone tampered with the can before the customer bought it.

Wrong analysis. A can of corn is sealed at the manufacturer.

(B) No, because the customer has not shown any direct evidence that the canning company acted negligently.

Wrong rule. Direct evidence of breach is not required since res ipsa loquitur creates a permissible inference of breach.

C. Yes, because a jury may reasonably infer that the canning company acted negligently.

Correct. This is the typical phrasing for a correct res ipsa loquitur answer.

(D) Yes, because the grocery store could not have discovered the piece of glass by reasonable inspection.

Wrong analysis. The liability of the canning co. is not based on the grocery store's inability to conduct an inspection. This answer is misstated, but it could provide a distraction if you were looking for an answer based on strict products liability.

FACTS

Q5

A **pedestrian was crossing a street in a crosswalk** when a **woman walking just ahead of him was hit by a truck**. The pedestrian, who had **jumped out of the way** of the truck, **administered CPR** to the woman, who was a **stranger**. The woman **bled** profusely, and the pedestrian was **covered in blood**. The woman **died** in the ambulance on the way to the hospital. The pedestrian became very **depressed** immediately after the incident and developed **physical symptoms** as a result of his **emotional distress**.

Lots of sad facts make me think of decoys; a common ploy in torts Qs.

The pedestrian has brought an action against the driver of the truck for **negligent infliction of emotional distress**. In her **defense**, the driver asserts that she should not be held liable, because the pedestrian's emotional distress and resulting physical symptoms are **not compensable**.

What is the **strongest argument** that the pedestrian can make in response to the driver's defense?

NIED

You can guess this will be a ***TORTS Q*** *(car accident) but, you will need to evaluate each option to pick the strongest argument, rather than solving the Q first.*

SOLVE

	NIED (2 Ways)	ANALYSIS
✓ 1	Zone of danger - in fear (maj. R) → Physical symptoms required (most jx) →	Jumped out of way Physical symptoms, depressed
~~2~~	Witness impact close family member → No physical symptoms required	Witness impact, but stranger

A Pedestrian SAW the driver hit the woman.
Weak. Facts would prove 2nd type of NIED (witness), but W was a stranger.

B The pedestrian was a GOOD SAMARITAN.
Weaker. Not an element of NIED and legally irrelevant.

C Pedestrian was COVERED IN BLOOD & HAS PHYSICAL SYMPTOMS.
Strong. Goes to the physical symptoms most jx's require for a zone of danger NIED claim.

D Pedestrian was in the ZONE OF DANGER.
Strongest. Clearly identifies the 1st type of NIED and zone of danger is required in ***all*** *jx.*

DECODE

~~A.~~ The pedestrian saw the driver hit the woman.

Weak argument. These facts would establish the pedestrian was a witness to the accident, but since the woman is a stranger, he can not recover on this theory of NIED.

~~B.~~ The pedestrian was acting as a Good Samaritan.

Weakest argument. While true, it has no legal significance in an NIED claim.

~~C.~~ The pedestrian was covered in the woman's blood and developed physical symptoms as a result of his emotional distress. 

Strong argument, but not the best. The physical symptoms noted proves up the emotional distress (as required in most jurisdictions), but pedestrian still needs to be in the zone of danger to recover.

D. The pedestrian was in the zone of danger.

Strongest argument. The pedestrian had to jump out of the way to avoid being hit by the truck himself, and was clearly in the zone of danger. Most jurisdictions also require physical symptoms of the emotional distress, though not all jurisdictions require this. This answer best captures the majority rule.

Q6

FACTS

Toxic materials being **transported** by truck from a manufacturer's plant to a warehouse **leaked from the truck onto the street a few miles from the plant**. A **driver lost control** of his car when he **hit the puddle** of spilled toxic materials on the street, and he was injured when his car hit a stop sign.

Classic abnormally dangerous (ultra-hazardous) activity

CALL In an action for damages by the driver against the manufacturer based on **strict liability**, is the driver likely to prevail?

TORTS Q, strict liability

SOLVE

STRICT LIABILITY	***ANALYSIS***
• High degree of harm	• Transporting toxic materials is risky
• Can't eliminate risk with due care	• Can't make toxic chemicals safe
• Activity not common	• Toxic materials not common
• Balance (risk > value to community)	• Risk for toxic chemicals unreasonably high
• <u>Causation:</u> **kind of harm** that makes it **dangerous**	• Slipping on a spilled puddle of liquid in the road is **not the kind of harm** that makes transporting ***toxic*** materials abnormally dangerous.
• Damages	• P injured in car accident

This Q is sneaky. It looks straightforward and checks every box for an abnormally dangerous activity, but fails on causation, which is easy to overlook, and you can predict there will be a decoy answer choice for those that overlook it!

A The driver will not prevail against the manufacturer <u>**because**</u> the harm is not the kind stemming from the dangerousness of the activity.

Now look for an answer choice that comports with your analysis.

DECODE

(A) No, because the driver's loss of control was an intervening cause.

Incorrect analysis. The driver's loss of control is a direct result of the spill, and is reasonably foreseeable (thus, not an intervening cause).

B. No, because the driver's injury did not result from the toxicity of the materials.

Correct. The driver's injury was not a result of the kind of harm that makes toxic materials abnormally dangerous.

(C) Yes, because the manufacturer is strictly liable for leaks of its toxic materials.

Incorrect analysis. The injury still must be caused by the kind of harm that makes the toxic materials dangerous. [This is the decoy answer choice if you forgot that causation must be linked to the dangerousness of the activity.]

(D) Yes, because the leak occurred near the manufacturer's plant.

Misstated rule. Proximity is not an element of strict liability for abnormally dangerous activities. The manufacturer would be responsible regardless of the location of the mishap.

FACTS

Q7

A **construction worker** was working at the construction site of a new building. An **open elevator**, which had been installed in the building by the elevator manufacturer, was used to haul workers and building materials between floors. While the worker was riding the elevator, **it stalled between floors due to a manufacturing defect** in the elevator. The worker called for assistance and was in **no danger**, but after **waiting 15 minutes** for help, he became **anxious** and **jumped 12 feet** to get out. He **severely injured his back** when he landed.

Strict Products ← (it stalled between floors due to a manufacturing defect)

Lots of facts about P's conduct is also a clue the Q is about the defense.

CALL In an action by the worker against the elevator manufacturer to recover for his back injury, is the worker likely to obtain a judgment for **100%** of his damages?

TORTS Q

Defenses

SOLVE

Call of Q & facts lead to defenses but analyze the base COA too since P must prove that 1st to recover at all

RULES	ANALYSIS
Strict products • Coml. supplier • Manufacturing defect • Causation • Damages	• Elevator manufacturer • In facts • Elevator mishap; rescue foreseeable **• Injured back, but 100%?**
Defenses? **• Assumption of risk** • Knew risk/proceed **• Comparative negligence** • Duty • Breach → ***Unreasonable*** • Causation • Damages • No contributory negl.	• **<u>Assumption of risk</u>** • Likely knew risk to jump • **<u>Comparative Negligence</u>** • Reasonable care **• No danger; 15 min.; 12 ft.** • Jump injured back • Reduced comparative to fault

A The worker should **<u>not</u>** recover 100% **<u>because</u>** he was also negligent/assumed the risk.

→ Now look for an answer choice that comports with your analysis.

DECODE

(A) No, because such risks are inherent in construction work.

Incorrect rule statement. There is no such rule.

B. No, because the worker was not in danger while on the stalled elevator. ←

*Correct. Worker was **comparatively negligent** because it was **unreasonable** (breach of duty) to jump 12 feet after only 15 minutes of waiting when he was in no danger.*

(C) Yes, because the elevator stalled due to a <u>manufacturing defect</u>. ←

Incomplete analysis. This captures the general rule, but the worker's recovery would be limited by his own comparative fault.

(D) Yes, because the worker was falsely imprisoned in the stalled elevator.

Wrong rule. This is not an intentional tort.

In torts they hide the ball by using layman's terms, (not the legal terms of a defense) in the *right* answer...

and then putting a key legal term (manufacturing defect) in the *wrong* answer. Sneaky, but a common ploy.

FACTS **Q8**

A man sued his neighbor for **defamation** based on the following facts:

Publication to 3P | Of & concerning P | Defamatory

The **neighbor told a friend** that the **man** had **set fire to a house** in the neighborhood. The **friend**, who knew the man well, **did not believe** the neighbor's allegation, which was in fact **false**. The friend told the man about the neighbor's allegation. The man was **very upset** by the allegation, but **neither** the man nor the neighbor nor the friend **communicated the allegation** to anyone else.

The cause of action is clear, so read the facts with the rule elements in mind

CALL Should the man prevail in his lawsuit?

This is another Q where it is hard to determine the subject from the call or a quick glance at the paragraph above.

SOLVE

DEFAMATION	*ANALYSIS*
• Defamatory statement	• Man set fire to a house (arson)
• Of or concerning P	• Man
• Publish to 3P	• Man's friend is sufficient
• Causation	• Could harm reputation
• Damage P's reputation • **Slander** pecuniary loss **<u>except</u> slander per se** (damages presumed): • Unfit for profession • loathsome disease • **Crime of moral turpitude** • Sex misconduct	• Damages: Pecuniary loss not shown (very upset insufficient) *but* slander per se so not required ARSON

Spoken defamation is slander

Slander usually raises a damages issue

A The man should prevail **<u>because</u>** slander per se does not require a showing of pecuniary loss.

Now look for an answer choice that comports with your analysis.

DECODE

(A) No, because the friend did not believe what the neighbor had said.

Incorrect analysis. The party to whom the statement is published need not believe it is true. This is not a required element of defamation.

(B) No, because the man cannot prove that he suffered pecuniary loss.

Incorrect analysis. Arson is a crime of moral turpitude and is slander per se, which does not require establishing pecuniary loss.

(C) Yes, because the man was very upset at hearing what the neighbor had said.

Incorrect analysis. Being "very upset" would be insufficient to establish pecuniary loss, <u>but</u> pecuniary loss need not be shown for slander per se.

D. Yes, because the neighbor communicated to the friend the false accusation that the man had committed a serious crime.

Correct. This defamatory statement is slander per se since arson is a crime of moral turpitude. A showing of pecuniary harm is not required.

FACTS **Unreasonable interference?** **Q9**

A **manufacturing plant** emitted a **faint noise** even though the owner had installed **state-of-the-art sound dampeners**. The plant operated only on **weekdays** and only during **daylight hours**. A **homeowner** who lived near the plant worked a **night shift and could <u>not sleep</u>** when he arrived home because of the noise from the plant. The **other residents** in the area **did not notice** the noise.

Since you know it is a nuisance case, think of the elements first & read looking for the elements

Not dispositive

Interference/use enjoyment

CALL Does the homeowner have a viable **nuisance** claim against the owner of the plant?

Substantial interference? RP is standard

TORTS Q & nuisance is the cause of action

SOLVE

NUISANCE	***ANALYSIS***

• **Substantial** (Reasonable person objective standard)
• Unreasonable interference (obj. std)
  • Harm to P outweighs utility
  • Harm > should bear w/out $
• Another's use/enjoyment of land
	• Faint noise weekday/ daytime only. **Not substantial** by RP standards since P was **hypersensitive** & other residents did not notice.
	• Not unreasonable
	• Homeowner

Typical torts decoy to provide facts that make you feel sorry for the P (works nights).

PRIVATE OR PUBLIC? Private is more commonly tested, the difference is in the harm

A Homeowner won't prevail in his nuisance action **<u>because</u>** P is hypersensitive and there is no substantial interference to a reasonable person standard.

Now look for an answer choice that comports with your analysis.

DECODE

A. No, because the homeowner is unusually sensitive to noise during the day.

Correct. This is a layman's way to say the objective standard for substantial and unreasonable interference is not satisfied. This nearby homeowner is hypersensitive to noise compared to the other neighbors.

~~B.~~ No, because the plant operates only during the day.

Incorrect analysis. This fact alone would not be dispositive since the noise could constitute a nuisance if the noise was too loud objectively, even though they limited the noise to daytime hours.

~~C.~~ Yes, because the noise is heard beyond the boundaries of the plant.

Incorrect analysis. Producing noise beyond the boundaries of the plant alone is insufficient to constitute a nuisance. The noise must objectively create a substantial and unreasonable interference.

~~D.~~ Yes, because the operation of the plant interferes with the homeowner's quiet use and enjoyment of his property.

Incorrect analysis. Nuisance is judged by an objective standard and the noise must be substantial and unreasonable, which it is not here. This is a tempting answer choice if you feel sorry for the plaintiff who can't sleep.

FACTS

Q10

A **seller sold his boat** to a buyer. During negotiations, the buyer said that he **planned to sail the boat on the open seas**. The seller told the buyer that the boat was **seaworthy** and had **never sustained any significant damage**. In fact, the **hull of the boat had been badly damaged when the seller had run the boat aground**. The seller had then done a **cosmetic repair** to the hull **rather than a structural repair.**

After reading Q it still feels a lot like a contracts Q, but the options are all torts.

The buyer **relied on the seller's representations** and **paid a fair price** for a boat in **good repair**, only to discover after the sale was completed that the hull was in fact badly **damaged and in a dangerous condition**. The seller has refused to refund any of the buyer's money, and the buyer is contemplating suing the seller.

Reliance could implicate fraud, but it's the only clue

CALL Under **what theory** would the buyer be most likely to recover?

This Q is a bit tricky, at first look it appears to be a contracts Q

You will need to look at the answer choices to identify the theories available and analyze each to determine the buyer's best option.

SOLVE

A — *FRAUD (Intentional Misrepresentation)*

✓ • Misrep. material fact	• Seaworthy, no significant damage
• Known false/reckless disregard	• Knew had been run aground, cosmetic repair only
• Intent to induce reliance	• So buyer would buy boat at price for good boat
• Causation	• But for misrep. would not have bought the boat
• Justifiable reliance	• Justifiable because told seller plan to sail on seas
• Pecuniary damages	• Boat is worth less than paid due to condition

B — *INTENTIONAL ENDANGERMENT*

X • Intentional
X • Endanger
• Another

This is not a tort (or bar tested). If there was such a tort, there is no actual endangerment here since the boat never sailed.

SOLVE *(continued)*

STRICT PRODUCTS LIABILITY

X • Commercial seller
X • Defective product
• Causation
• Damages

No facts suggest the seller is a commercial seller and the boat is more damaged than defective

NEGLIGENT MISREPRESENTATION

X • Misrepresentation in **bus.** capacity
• Negligence as to truth
• Other elements of fraud the same

No facts indicate the seller made the misrepresentation in a business capacity and the misrepresentation was intentional here

DECODE

A. Fraud.

Correct. The misrepresentation as to the quality of the boat was made intentionally since the seller actively concealed the hull damage with a cosmetic repair. Buyer told seller he planned to sail on the open seas and was justified to rely on the representation of the boat quality.

~~B.~~ Intentional endangerment. ←

No such tort exists. If it were a tort, it might be similar to battery, but endangerment would be hard to establish since the boat never sailed so no one was actually endangered.

Think twice before picking a rule you've never heard of; it is most likely a wrong answer.

~~C.~~ Negligent misrepresentation.

Wrong analysis. The misrepresentation here was made intentionally and it is unclear if it was in a business capacity. Further, the recovery would be greater for fraud.

~~D.~~ Strict products liability.

Wrong rule. It is not clear that seller is a commercial seller, or that the damaged boat would be considered "defective."

PART 8 GLOSSARY OF ABBREVIATIONS

GLOSSARY OF ABBREVIATIONS	
@	at
3P/3Pty	third party
Acc.	accident or accurate
Acctg.	accounting
Act.	activity or actual
Addl./Add'l	additional
Admiss.	admissible
Aff.	affected
AG	attorney general
Alter.	alteration
Altern.	alternative
Am.	amendment
Amt.	amount
Apprehen.	apprehension
Approx.	approximately
Art.	article or artificial
Ass.	assumption (of risk) or assign
Assn./Assoc.	association
Atty.	attorney

b/c	because
BER	best evidence rule
BFP	bona fide purchaser
Biz/ bus.	business
Bldg.	building
BOP	burden of proof
CE	collateral estoppel
Char	character
Circum./Circumst.	circumstances
Civ	civil
CL; C/L	common law
CNOF	common nucleus of operative fact
COA	cause of action
COD	cash on delivery or cash on demand
Co-D	co-defendants
Comm.	community
Commer.	commercial
Cond.	condition
Consid.	consideration
Cont. rem.	contingent remainder
Co-ops	cooperatives
Co-P	co-plaintiffs
Corp.	corporation
Cov.	covenant
Cr./Crim.	criminal

Cross-ex	cross-examine/cross-examination
Ct.	court
D	defendant
Dang.	dangerous
Danger. indiv.	dangerous individual
D.C.	District of Columbia
DCC	dormant commerce clause
DEA	Drug Enforcement Administration
Decl.	declaration
Detrim./Detrimen.	detrimental
Diff.	difficult
Differ.	different
Disc.	discovery
Discr.	discrimination or discretion
Dist.	district
DJ	double jeopardy
Dmgs.	damages
Doc.	document/documentary
DP	due process
DPC	Due Process Clause
DUI	driving under the influence (of drugs or alcohol)
DV	directed verdict
Dx	diagnosis
Dx/tx	diagnosis/treatment
Dying decl.	dying declaration

Econ.	economic
e.g.	for example
Electronic.	electronically
Enhance.	enhancing
EPC	Equal Protection Clause
Eq./Equit.	equitable/equity
Etc.	and so on
Ev./evid.	evidence
Ex	examine (as in cross-examine) or example
Expec.	expectation
Feas.	feasible
Fed.	federal
FI	future interest
Fir. Deg.	first degree
FMR	felony murder rule
FOB	free on board
Former test.	former testimony
FRCP	Federal Rules of Civil Procedure
FRE	Federal Rules of Evidence
FSA	fee simple absolute
FSD	fee simple determinable
FSSCS	fee simple subject to condition subsequent
FSSEI	fee simple subject to an executory interest
Gov./Govt.	government
GPS	global positioning system

Horz.	horizontal
IC	independent contractor
ID	identification
i.e.	used to refer to explanatory information
IIED	intentional infliction of emotional distress
Imbed.	imbedded
Inc.	incorporated
Incl.	included/ includes
info	information
Inj.	injunction or injury
Instllmnt.	installment
Int.	interest or intentional
Interf.	interference
Int'l	international
Invol.	involuntary
IRS	Internal Revenue Service
Jdg.	judgment
JMOL	judgment as a matter of law
Jr.	junior
JT	joint tenants/joint tenancy
Jx	jurisdiction
K	contract
L/LL	landlord
LAPS	literary, artistic, political, scientific
Legit.	legitimate

Liab.	liability
Licens.	licensee
LLC	limited liability company
LT	life tenant
Ltd.	limited
Maj.	majority
Mansl.	manslaughter
Mat.	material
Max.	maximum
MBE	Multistate Bar Exam
Min.	minority
MIP	mortgagee in possession
Misc.	miscellaneous
Miscond.	misconduct
Mitig.	mitigate/mitigated/mitigation
Mkt.	marketable (as in marketable title)
MO	modus operandi
MPC	Model Penal Code
MSJ	motion for summary judgment
Mtn.	motion
N/A	not applicable
Nat'l	national
NCBE	National Conference of Bar Examiners
Nec.	necessary
NIED	negligent infliction of emotional distress

Nom.	nominal (as in damages)
O	owner/grantor
Obj.	objective
Obvi.	obvious
Occur.	occurrence
ok	okay
Op	opinion
Opp.	opportunity
Orig.	original
o/w	outweighed
P	plaintiff
Particul.	particular
Partn.	partnership
PCS	prior consistent statement
PDP	Procedural Due Process
PER	parol evidence rule
Pers.	Personal/personally
P & I	Privileges & Immunities
PID	prior identification
PIS	prior inconsistent statement
Plead.	pleading
PJ/Pjx	personal jurisdiction
PMM	purchase money mortgage
PPB	principal place of business
P. recorded rec.	past recorded recollection

Prej.	prejudice
Priv.	privilege
Prob.	probative or probable/probably
Prop.	property
PSI	present sense impression
Punit.	punitive damages
Purp.	purpose
Q/Qs	question/questions
QTIPS	quantity, time of performance, identity of parties, price, subject matter
R	remainderman
RAP	rule against perpetuities
Re:	regarding
Reas./reason.	reasonable/reasonably
Rec.	recorded
Reckless dis.	reckless disregard
Receiv.	receive/received
Rehab	rehabilitation
Reject.	rejection
Rel.	relationships
REOP	reasonable expectation of privacy
Rep	reputation
Repres.	representative/representation
Req./req'd/reqt.	required
RICO	Racketeer Influenced and Corrupt Organizations Act